ELIZABETH I

ELIZABETH I

Anne Somerset

Weidenfeld and Nicolson
London

First published in Great Britain in 1991 by
George Weidenfeld and Nicolson Limited
91 Clapham High Street, London SW4 7TA

British Library Cataloguing-in-Publication Data
is available on request.

ISBN 0 297 81178 9

Printed and bound in Great Britain by
Butler & Tanner Ltd, Frome and London

Contents

Author's note

In 1582, Catholic countries throughout Europe adopted the Gregorian calendar, but England continued to use the Julian calendar. This meant that the calendar in England was ten days behind that used in Catholic countries on the continent. When dating events that took place in England, I have continued to use the Julian calendar. However, when dating events which took place on the continent after 1582 I have on occasion used the Gregorian calendar, rather than converting the dates to conform to English usage at that time. Whenever I have done this I follow the date by N.S. in brackets to indicate that the date is in the New Style. Furthermore, although in Tudor England the calendar year was held to start on 25 March, I have taken it to begin on 1 January, in accordance with modern usage.

On the death of King Charles IX of France in 1574, his brother, Henry, Duke of Anjou, succeeded him as Henry III. The latter's younger brother, Francis, Duke of Alençon, thereupon became Duke of Anjou in his turn, but to avoid confusion I have continued to refer to him by his earlier title of Duke of Alençon. In the interests of clarity I have also updated Tudor spelling and punctuation when I thought it necessary.

I should like to thank the following people for the assistance they gave me while I was writing this book: Ms Drusilla Beyfus; Ms Candida Brazil; Sir Raymond Carr; Mr Simon Cobley; Mr John Curtis; Air Commodore J. G. De'ath; Mr Christopher Falkus; Ms Juliet Gardiner; Mr Tom Graves; Judge Bill Gummow; Mr Robin Harcourt-Williams; Ms Judith Jones; Ms Rian King; Ms Hilary Laurie; Mr Douglas Matthews; Mr Raoul Millais; Mr Tobias Rodgers; Lord and Lady Christopher Thynne; Major-General C. Tyler; Ms Margaret D. Young; Mr Ed Victor.

Illustrations

For Matthew, with love

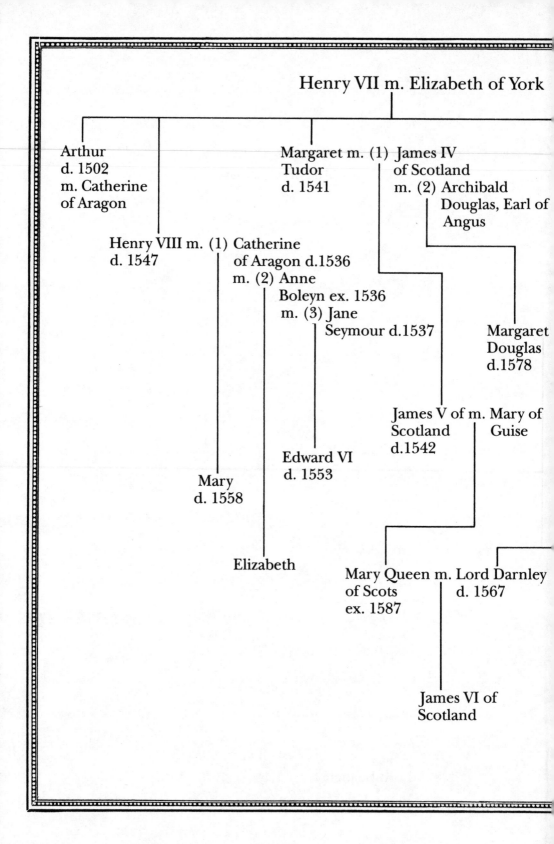

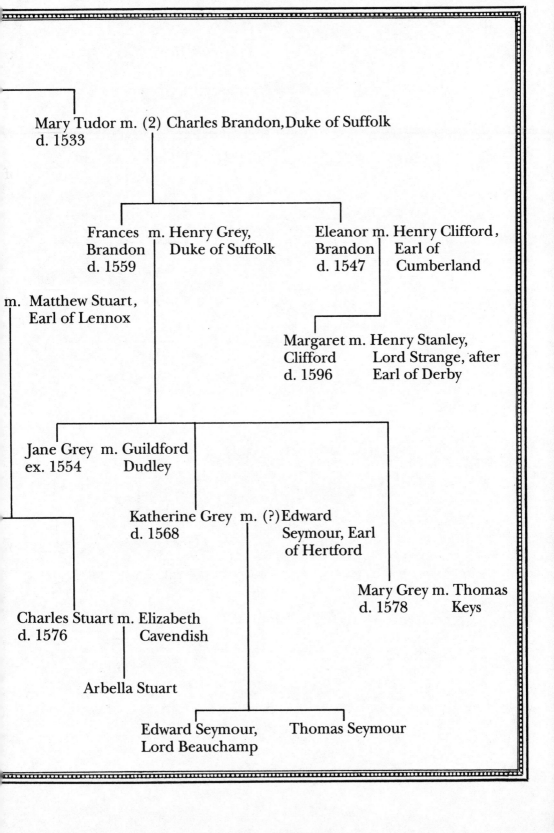

Mary Tudor m. (2) Charles Brandon, Duke of Suffolk
d. 1533

Frances m. Henry Grey,   Eleanor m. Henry Clifford,
Brandon │ Duke of Suffolk   Brandon │ Earl of
d. 1559   d. 1547 │ Cumberland

m. Matthew Stuart,
Earl of Lennox

Margaret m. Henry Stanley,
Clifford   Lord Strange, after
d. 1596   Earl of Derby

Jane Grey m. Guildford
ex. 1554   Dudley

Katherine Grey m. (?)Edward
d. 1568   Seymour, Earl
                 of Hertford

Mary Grey m. Thomas
d. 1578   Keys

Charles Stuart m. Elizabeth
d. 1576   Cavendish

Arbella Stuart

Edward Seymour,   Thomas Seymour
Lord Beauchamp

CHAPTER 1

"As toward a child ... as ever I knew any"

On 9 April 1533, a foreign diplomat named Eustace Chapuys arrived at Greenwich Palace to make a formal protest to Henry VIII about the King's behaviour towards Catherine of Aragon, his Spanish wife of twenty-four years standing. Since 1527, Henry had been seeking to have his marriage to Catherine dissolved, but his wishes had been frustrated by Pope Clement VII's steadfast refusal to grant him a divorce. The Pope's obstinacy on this point was partly the result of pressure from Catherine's nephew, the Holy Roman Emperor Charles V, whose sense of family honour was too strong for him willingly to permit his aunt to be cast aside by Henry. In 1529 Charles had sent Chapuys to England as his ambassador, with instructions to uphold Catherine's interests at all times and to do all that was possible to prevent Henry VIII from discarding her.

For the past four years, Chapuys had carried out this task with commendable resource and tenacity, but this was not a matter on which Henry was prepared to concede defeat. Recently there had been clear indications that the King had found a way of breaking the deadlock that had confronted him in his matrimonial affairs, for on 25 January 1533 Henry had secretly married the woman he now loved, a former maid of honour of Queen Catherine's named Anne Boleyn. As yet Henry had not dared openly to acknowledge this marriage, but in March his legal position had been strengthened by the passage through Parliament of the Act in Restraint of Appeals, which had opened up the way for an authoritative pronouncement within England on the divorce by prohibiting appeals beyond her frontiers to Rome. As Henry's dependence on a favourable ruling at Rome had diminished, so his confidence had increased, and only the day before his meeting with Chapuys he had sent word to Catherine of Aragon "that she need not trouble herself about returning to him, for he had already taken another wife".[1] It was in the light of these developments that Chapuys, as Charles V's representative, had felt it necessary to seek an audience at which he could remonstrate with Henry about Catherine's treatment.

Wasting no time on diplomatic preliminaries, Chapuys reproached Henry for his abuse of Catherine's rights and sternly reminded him that he would have to answer to God for his actions. The King did not flinch. "God and his conscience were perfectly agreed on that point", he told Chapuys, and he added blandly that he wished to secure the succession of his kingdom by having children, "which he had not at present". Chapuys courteously reminded him that, on the contrary, he and Catherine had had a daughter, the Princess Mary, born in 1516, and the ambassador next observed that "it seemed as if nature had decided that the succession to the English throne should be through the female line". Henry was not impressed by a suggestion so patently absurd, and he brushed it aside with the brusque observation "that he knew better than that". True, Salic law (which debarred women from inheriting the crown) did not prevail in England, but there had been no Queen regnant since the brief and troubled rule of Matilda in the twelfth century, and that had hardly constituted a successful experiment. In Henry's view the objections to a female ruler were overwhelming, and Chapuys himself evidently did not think it worthwhile to pursue so flimsy a line of argument.

Instead he told Henry that he could not be sure of having any more children, but at this the King grew positively buoyant. "Am I not a man like others?" he demanded three times of the embarrassed Chapuys, and as the ambassador preserved a diplomatic silence in the face of this insistent enquiry, the King added scornfully, "I need not give proofs to the contrary, or let you into my secrets". Chapuys correctly interpreted this delphic utterance as an intimation that Henry's "beloved lady" was "already in the family way", and as he well knew, it was that fact, above all others, that destroyed the anyway remote possibility that the King might reconsider. Though Chapuys continued doggedly to rehearse the various merits of Queen Catherine's case, Henry was emphatic that "all persuasions and remonstrances are absolutely in vain", and at length the ambassador was obliged to take his leave, his mission having proved utterly futile.[2]

Henry's intransigent attitude was understandable enough. It was now almost seven years since he had first voiced his concern that by marrying his late brother's widow he had unwitttingly transgressed the law of God as laid down in the Book of Leviticus. Catherine's failure to provide him with a male heir, which carried with it such grave implications for the kingdom's future, was, of course, sufficient proof of divine displeasure, but Henry's infatuation for Anne Boleyn had injected yet more urgency into his attempt to remedy the situation. Although English, and of comparatively undistinguished lineage (Anne's mother was a Howard, but her great-grandfather on her father's side was a silk merchant who had made a fortune and married well), Anne's dark hair, "beautiful black eyes" and unpredictable temperament made her seem a far more exotic creature than the homely Queen Catherine, whose limited personal attractions had long since faded. Had the circumstances been less exceptional, Henry would have doubtless been content to have had a brief affair with Anne and then discard her, as he had previously done to her sister, but Anne's initial refusal to become his mistress had happened to coincide with the King's growing awareness that he must remarry in order to beget legitimate male heirs. As a result, desire and dynastic exigency had fused to form for Henry a single, compelling imperative. Since the spring of 1527, his hopes of making Anne his wife had been blighted by the Pope's obstinate refusal to annul his impious union with Catherine but, as the dispute had dragged on, Henry's initially vague threats to reject the authority of Rome had hardened into steadfast determination, and in Thomas Cromwell he had found a minister capable of drafting the necessary legislation and piloting it through Parliament. By the autumn of 1532, Henry felt confident that if the Pope continued to deny him his divorce, he would be able to obtain it on his own terms at home, and it was probably not until then that he and Anne began to cohabit. At the time of their secret wedding in January 1533 Anne was already one month pregnant, and in the ensuing weeks Parliament's action in sweeping away Rome's jurisdiction had left Henry free to order his life as he desired. Knowing this, and convinced too that Anne was bearing the long awaited prince, it was hardly surprising that Henry was in a far from amenable mood when he received Chapuys at Greenwich.

On 11 April, two days after the Chapuys visit, Henry's recently appointed Archbishop of Canterbury, Thomas Cranmer, sought – and speedily obtained – the King's permission to examine his marital situation. The same day Anne appeared at court in royal state for the first time. On 23 May Cranmer formally pronounced Henry's union with Catherine invalid, and retrospectively sanctioned the marriage with Anne. Anne's triumph seemed complete when, on 1 June, she was crowned in a magnificent ceremony at Westminster Abbey.

Preparations for the arrival of Anne's son were equally elaborate. "One of the most magnificent and gorgeous beds that could be thought of" was installed at Greenwich Palace, where the confinement was to take place, and in readiness for the delivery letters were drawn up informing court notables of the arrival of a prince. The King, heartened by assurances from the court physicians and astrologers that the child would be male, made arrangements for a grand tournament to celebrate the birth, and several courtiers sent to Flanders for new horses.[3] As the Queen's pregnancy reached full term, the energies of all at court were absorbed in the happy bustle, but on the afternoon of 7 September 1533, the balloon of confident expectation was rudely burst by the shattering announcement that Anne had given birth to a baby girl.

The King, who had made such heroic efforts to shape his domestic affairs in accordance with the will of God, must have viewed this unlooked-for setback as a joke in extremely poor taste by the Almighty but, outwardly at least, the proprieties were observed. Admittedly, there was no more talk of the jousts and pageants that were to have marked the birth of a prince, but as soon as the news of the Queen's safe delivery was confirmed, a *Te Deum* was "incontinently sung" at St Paul's. It was agreed that the infant should be named Elizabeth after her grandmother, Elizabeth of York, and three days after her birth she was both christened and confirmed in the Friars' church at Greenwich. The ceremony was attended by the Mayor, aldermen and chief citizens of London, the King's Council and the principal nobility (although the King and Queen, in accordance with etiquette, were not present), and the godparents included the Archbishop of Canterbury and the Dowager Duchess of Norfolk. Immediately after the service the child was proclaimed Princess of England, and "then was brought in wafers, comfits and hypocras in such plenty that every man had as much as he would desire".[4] But despite the lavish ceremonial, the informed observer could discern an undercurrent of disappointment, and it proved impossible to disguise the fact that the bad fairy at this particular christening was the baby herself.

For the first three months of her life, Elizabeth stayed at Greenwich with her mother, but in early December it was decreed that the Princess should be moved to Hatfield, "there to remain with such household as the King's highness has established for the same". To the disgust of Chapuys (whose attitude to the new arrival had from the start been one of undisguised hostility), the child was escorted there by a suite of noblemen, and "for the sake of pompous solemnity and the better to impress upon the people the idea of her being the true Princess of Wales", the cavalcade processed through London in state, thus giving the citizens a chance to glimpse the new heiress to the throne. Elizabeth was joined at Hatfield by her elder sister Mary, now stripped of her title of Princess and formally labelled a bastard. When first informed of this alteration in her status the seventeen-year-old Mary had refused to accept it, writing in protest to her father that she did not doubt that he regarded her as his "true daughter, born in matrimony". It was with the specific aim of humbling her rebellious spirit that Henry had sent Mary to Hatfield, where she would have to pay her respects to the child who had supplanted her. As yet, however, Mary remained defiant: when asked on her arrival at Hatfield if she wished to see the Princess, she replied simply "that she knew of no Princess in England but herself". Determined to make her submit, Henry decreed that a variety of humiliations and privations should be inflicted on her by the household at Hatfield, but still Mary could not be induced to acknowledge her sister's title, and would never "pay court to her unless compelled by sheer force".[5] Thus were sown the seeds of bitterness that grew to maturity more than twenty years later.

Despite having an establishment of her own, Elizabeth was not completely cut off from all contact with her parents. Hatfield was only one of several royal residences allocated for her use, and the Queen was a fairly frequent visitor to the various manors where her daughter spent short spells. On occasion, the King himself came to see her – "Her Grace is much in the King's favour, as goodly child should be, God save her", a courtier reported after one such visit – and the child's routine was also interspersed with her own visits to court. She was there, for example, in January 1536, when the King received the glad tidings of Catherine of Aragon's death, and was thus swept up in the impromptu celebrations which the news occasioned. The toddler was taken to church "to the sound of trumpets and with great display", and on her return the King, dressed entirely in yellow, took his daughter fondly in his arms and paraded her before the courtiers.[6]

On such occasions Henry may have been prepared to enter with zest into the role of doting father, but already he valued his daughter more as a diplomatic asset than as a plaything. As early as the spring of 1534 Elizabeth had been displayed "quite naked" to the French ambassadors, and they had evidently approved of what they saw, for in February 1535 negotiations were embarked upon with a view to betrothing her to the King of France's younger son, the Duke of Angoulême. The talks soon ran into difficulties: when the French asked Henry to show goodwill by renouncing the pension that he exacted from them each year, the King "took this ill, saying ... it was a strange recompense when he offered the heiress of a kingdom to a younger son; they ought rather to give him something than ask". The French in turn objected to Henry's demand that the young Duke should be sent to England for his education. The discussions nevertheless continued, and it was only after the proposals had gone "backwards and forwards" for some months that they were finally abandoned.[7] It was a fitting start to a career in which courtship was to play a major part, for these protracted, apparently serious but ultimately fruitless marriage negotiations were remarkably similar to those which Elizabeth herself would conduct when adult.

From Henry's point of view Elizabeth had her uses as a pawn who could be employed to further English diplomacy, but it was not enough. Above all, he still needed a son to rule after him, and Anne had signally failed to present him with one. Only three or four months after the birth of Elizabeth, Anne had again conceived, but in the summer she had lost the child she was carrying. It was only towards the end of 1535 that she again became pregnant, and on 29 January 1536 she miscarried of the son whose survival would have guaranteed her own. On being informed of the catastrophe the King said, with ominous simplicity, "I see that God will not give me male children".[8] In reality, his scanning of the divine will was slightly different, for Henry was rapidly coming to the conclusion that God would deny him a son for as long as he remained the husband of Anne Boleyn.

As a brood mare Anne had failed, and her position was the more perilous in that her emotional hold over the King had long since evaporated. As early as September 1534, she had been distressed by Henry's attentions to one of her unmarried ladies-in-waiting, and when she had attempted to dismiss the girl from her service, the King had merely sent his wife a message to the effect that "she ought to be satisfied with what he had done for her; were he to commence again, he would certainly not do as much". By the early spring of 1536, Henry was in hot pursuit of another of Anne's maids of honour, Jane Seymour, and the young lady herself was assiduous in further eroding the King's feelings for his wife by constantly assuring him "how much his subjects abominate the marriage contracted with the concubine, and that not one considers it legitimate".[9]

A marriage that had become both a dynastic liability and a personal failure was not to be endured. On 24 April 1536, a commission was set up in order to gather information against Anne which could be used to effect her destruction. After they had made preliminary enquiries, a palace musician named Mark Smeaton was taken into custody and interrogated by Thomas Cromwell on 30 April. On 1 May Anne and Henry both attended a tournament at Greenwich, but the King left unexpectedly and rode back to Westminster, "of which sudden departure men marvelled". The following day, a courtier named Henry Norris and Anne's brother, Lord Rochford, were arrested, and before long they were joined in the Tower by Sir Francis Weston, William Brereton, Sir Richard Page and Thomas Wyatt. Meanwhile, on 2 May Anne herself had been conveyed to the Tower, where she awaited trial in moods that ranged between hysterical self-abnegation and frenzied gaiety. No charges were pressed against Page and Wyatt, but the five other men were accused of fornication with the Queen and brought to trial. Only Smeaton pleaded guilty (almost certainly under threat of torture) but they were all convicted and condemned to death. Anne herself was tried on 15 May, and put up a good defence, "excusing herself with her words so clearly as though she had never been faulty", but she was nevertheless found guilty of having taken "divers of the King's daily and familiar servants to be her adulterers and concubines" and sentenced "to be burned or beheaded as shall please the King".[10] In the event the King opted for the more merciful method, even importing a swordsman from Calais to ensure that his wife was despatched with maximum efficiency. On 19 May 1536 Anne Boleyn was decapitated on Tower Green. The following day, Henry was betrothed to Jane Seymour, and ten days after that, the couple were wed.

The extent to which her mother's execution cast a shadow over Elizabeth's later life is incalculable. It is certain that many of the charges preferred against Anne were false, and probable that she was innocent of all of them. The times and places where Anne was meant to have committed adultery were listed in her indictment, and it is possible to prove that on most of the dates mentioned, Anne was nowhere near the supposed scene of the crime. She herself acknowledged that there had been times when she had indulged in flirtatious talk not altogether suited to one of her position, but no evidence survives of more serious misconduct. We do not know, however, whether Elizabeth believed her mother to have been wrongly convicted. As an adult, she owned a ring, made about 1575, which opened to reveal enamel portraits of both herself and her mother, and the fact that she treasured this memento indicates a certain respect for Anne's memory. Furthermore Elizabeth adopted as her own Anne's motto *Semper Eadem* (Always the Same) and her badge of a crowned white falcon perched on a tree stump from which Tudor roses spring. In Elizabeth's case, the image of roses sprouting from a dead stump might even have been intended to serve as a reminder that she was an offshoot of someone whose life had been cut off in its prime. It was also said that the reason she showed consistent favour as Queen to Henry Norris's son, Baron Norris of Rycote, was because she was mindful of the fact that his father had "died in a noble cause and in justification of her mother's innocence". On the other hand, there are only two occasions on which she is recorded as having mentioned her mother by name.[11] When she came to the throne she made no effort to have the verdict against Anne overturned (in contrast to her sister Mary Tudor, for shortly after her accession the latter took steps to declare that Catherine of Aragon's marriage to Henry VIII had been valid), nor is there any indication that her feelings for her father were adversely affected by his treatment of her mother.

This is not unduly surprising when one considers that her personal recollections of the mother who was swept out of her life when she was just over two and a half years old would have been negligible or non-existent, and her image of Anne would have been based on hearsay and whispered scraps of gossip. Inevitably the picture would have been incomplete, for on the whole it seems that during Elizabeth's childhood and adolescence the subject of Anne Boleyn was studiously avoided. A revealing remark made in 1549 by Jane Seymour's brother Thomas shows that, even then, the mere mention of Anne's name could provoke sniggers. When Seymour told one of Elizabeth's servants that he would shortly be leaving for Boulogne (which he, like many of his contemporaries, pronounced 'Boleyn') he added the jocular rider, "No words of Boleyn!" and the tasteless pun gives some indication of the conspiracy of silence that enshrouded Anne's memory. In later years Elizabeth was content that it should remain so. When on the throne it was her frequent boast that she was "the most English woman of the kingdom",[12] but she was not prepared to go beyond this oblique tribute to her mother. There was good reason for her reticence, for she knew that by reviving the controversy concerning Anne's guilt or innocence she would only focus unwelcome attention on the underlying fragility of her own claim to the throne, and Elizabeth was never one to indulge in such misplaced sentimentality.

If the long-term effects on Elizabeth of her mother's execution remain difficult to fathom, at the time it looked as though it had blighted her prospects for ever. For Henry VIII, death had seemed too incomplete a form of severance from his wife, and four days before Anne's execution the Archbishop of Canterbury had annulled her marriage with the King, possibly on the grounds of Henry's previous carnal knowledge of her sister Mary. As a result Elizabeth was automatically bastardized, and though Henry did at least acknowledge her to be his daughter (thus dashing the hopes of Chapuys that she would be deemed to be "begotten by Master Norris"), it was specifically stated in the act of July 1536 regulating the succession that she was "illegitimate ... and utterly foreclosed, excluded and banned to claim, challenge or demand any inheritance as lawful heir ... to [the King] by lineal descent".[13]

On a more mundane level, the repercussions of Anne's fall were felt within Elizabeth's household. Though Chapuys was regretful that Henry had not followed up his execution of the Queen by once again designating Mary his heiress presumptive, by August the ambassador could at least console himself that Mary "was well attended and served even by the little bastard's maids", whereas Elizabeth's domestic arrangements were threatening to degenerate into anarchy. Since birth Elizabeth's upbringing had been supervised by her Lady Mistress, Margaret, Lady Bryan (who had also looked after Mary as a child), but now the poor woman found herself thoroughly flustered by the sudden reversal in the fortunes of her charge. "As my Lady Elizabeth is put from that degree she was in, and what degree she is at now, I know not but by hearsay, I know not how to order her, or myself, or her women or grooms", she wrote plaintively to Cromwell, explaining that as a result of this confusion, discipline within the household had broken down completely. Elizabeth's staff had always been an unruly lot – in 1535 there had been trouble after it was discovered that "several of the Princess's servants kept more servants than were allowed by the standing roll signed by the King" – and now that Lady Bryan's grip was wavering, they were evidently seeking to assert themselves. In particular John Shelton, a cousin of Anne Boleyn who had been appointed Elizabeth's steward, was making a nuisance of himself, insisting that elaborate meals should be set before the little girl every day, so that he and his cronies could later feast on the pickings. "It is not meet for a child of her age to keep such rule", lamented the harassed Lady Bryan. "If she do, I dare not take it upon me to keep her Grace in health, for she will see divers meats, fruits and wines that it will be hard for me to refrain her from". It was hardly surprising that so young a child should be disobedient when exposed to such temptation, and Lady Bryan felt reluctant to punish her as Elizabeth was having problems with her teeth, and was often in considerable pain. The only way to ensure that Elizabeth received a balanced diet would be to arrange for the child to have simple meals sent up to her room, and Lady Bryan begged Cromwell to issue the necessary orders.

To add to Lady Bryan's worries, Elizabeth was woefully short of clothes, having outgrown the gown of orange velvet, the white damask and green satin underskirts, and the purple and crimson satin caps that her mother had fondly ordered her. Now she lacked even nightdresses and underwear, and Lady Bryan implored Cromwell to despatch fresh supplies promptly. Nevertheless, once Elizabeth had been smartened up and order re-established in the nursery, Lady Bryan felt sure that the King would be able to take great pride in his daughter, "for she is as toward a child and as gentle of conditions as ever I knew any in my life, Jesu preserve her Grace!"[14]

The King had a chance to see Elizabeth's progress for himself when she attended the christening of her brother Edward in October 1537, although doubtless Henry's delight at having finally fathered a legitimate son prevented him from paying his daughter much attention. The birth of the Prince had been the signal for an outbreak of national euphoria, and if Henry's own joy was to be somewhat moderated by the death of Jane Seymour twelve days after the event, the loss of a wife was not too high a price to pay for having secured the succession. At the baptism Elizabeth carried the train of the baby's richly embroidered christening gown, although on account of her "tender age", she herself was borne in the arms of Edward's maternal uncle, Viscount Beauchamp.[15] No doubt the four year old was gratified by being allocated this part in the ceremonial, but it must have seemed to all onlookers that from now on, hers was to be no more than a supporting role.

Furthermore, it remained unclear exactly what that role would be, for her uncertain status undermined her chances of marriage with a foreign prince, the normal lot of a princess in the sixteenth century. In 1538, for example, there was talk of plighting Elizabeth with one of Charles V's nephews, but when the subject was broached with the Emperor, he merely "noted the life and death of her mother", which was hardly encouraging. Henry's advisers on his Council ruefully admitted that though "Princes generally conclude amity and things of importance by [marriage] alliances", it was unlikely that either Elizabeth or Mary would procure a good match abroad unless they were "made of some estimation".[16]

The conventional path of advancement seemed effectively blocked but, in one respect at least, Henry VIII saw to it that Elizabeth received a good start in life. In comparison with the ambitious programme of studies that Henry had pursued as a child, his two sisters had received a narrow education, for though they had been taught some French and Latin, the emphasis had been more on non-academic subjects like music and dancing. The next generation of Tudor princesses suffered no such discrimination, for by the time that Mary entered the schoolroom, a change in climate was apparent. Sir Thomas More's daughters had already mastered an impressive curriculum which included classical languages, geometry, theology and astronomy, and though More was aware that erudition in women would be attacked as a novelty, it was his opinion that if a woman had both virtue and learning it would profit her more than "Croesus's wealth joined with the beauty of fair Helen". Catherine of Aragon herself provided an example of a woman who combined learning with high-mindedness, for during her childhood in Spain she had been sufficiently well-educated to draw the tribute from Erasmus that she was "astonishingly well-read, far beyond what would be surprising in a woman, and as admirable for piety as she is for learning".[17] Henry might have preferred it if she had possessed the beauty of Helen as well, but he evidently took a husbandly pride in her accomplishments. As befitted a man who had once remarked that "without knowledge life would not be worth our having", he was also enthusiastic when Catherine commissioned the Spanish humanist, Juan Luis Vives, to draw up a detailed educational programme for her daughter. In time Mary became fluent in French, Spanish and Latin, and her father took great pleasure in her progress. It was therefore a foregone conclusion that Elizabeth would receive similarly advanced tuition, and she would prove a still more talented pupil than her sister.

Elizabeth's education differed from Mary's in that it reflected some of the teachings of the Reformation. All her instructors were to the left-of-centre in religious outlook, and Elizabeth herself was later to tell her sister "that she had never been taught the doctrine of the ancient religion". Like Mary, she was reared on the Bible and the devotional works of St Cyprian and other early Fathers, but she was also familiar with more modern authors, such as the German Protestant, Melanchthon. Whereas the eleven-year-old Mary had demonstrated her linguistic ability by translating into English a Latin prayer of St Thomas Aquinas, Elizabeth at thirteen selected for a similar exercise a work by the Protestant theologian Jean Calvin, named *Institution de la Vie Chrestienne*. As an adult Elizabeth remained acutely conscious of the way her education had shaped her religious outlook.

In a private prayer composed for her own use she went so far as to thank God for having "from my earliest days kept me back from the deep abysses of natural ignorance and damnable superstition, that I might enjoy the great sun of righteousness which brings with its rays life and salvation, while leaving so many kings, princes and princesses in ignorance under the power of Satan".[18]

It remains a mystery exactly when Elizabeth's formal education began. Her earliest lessons were conducted by Katherine (or Kat) Champernowne, a Devonshire gentlewoman who entered Elizabeth's service in 1536. She later forged still closer links with her charge by marrying Anne Boleyn's cousin, John Ashley, another trusted member of the household. Elizabeth herself was later to state that Kat had "taken great labour and pain in bringing me up in learning and honesty", but whether Mistress Champernowne was able to instruct the child in elementary Latin as well as teach her her letters is obscure. Her coaching was certainly of a sufficiently high standard to impress Sir Thomas Wriothesley, who visited Elizabeth when she was six and reported back to court, "If she be no worse educated than she now appeareth to me, she will prove of no less honour to womanhood than shall beseem her father's daughter".[19]

Elizabeth's later education was entrusted to a tightly knit group of scholars from the recently founded St John's College, Cambridge, which had already acquired a reputation for being in the vanguard of the reform movement. Initially, she did not have a tutor of her own, but had to make do with receiving occasional instruction from Dr Richard Cox (who had begun teaching the six-year-old Prince Edward in 1543) and his colleague Sir John Cheke. In 1544, however, she was given as her private tutor William Grindal, a fine Latin scholar, but also accounted "the best Grecian one of them" at St John's. This emphasis on Greek was a new departure: as a boy Henry VIII had never been taught it, while his daughter Mary had acquired no more than a rudimentary knowledge. It was the influence of Sir John Cheke that had led to the language being far more widely studied, and Elizabeth was to attain a much more advanced level than either her father or her sister. Her grasp of Latin was still more assured, for besides being able to read and write it with ease, she spoke it fluently, whereas her oral Greek was only moderate. As for modern languages, French and Italian were "like English" to her, but her knowledge of Spanish was imperfect. She did not begin to learn it until she was in her twenties, and although she had no difficulty understanding it, she was less confident about speaking it herself.[20]

The educational programme was not, of course, designed to train Elizabeth to rule a kingdom. The syllabus did not include an introductory course in the problems of practical politics such as Prince Edward received at the hands of the Clerk of the Council, William Thomas, and Elizabeth herself later remarked that it was only after she became Queen that she "entered . . . first into the school of experience" and devoted herself "to the study of that which was meet for Government". Her classical studies helped train her intellect by making her well-versed in ancient history, philosophy and oratory, while her mastery of so many languages later assisted her conduct of diplomacy by enabling her to converse with foreign ambassadors, but these were incidental benefits of an education which was not intended to qualify her for a career, but aimed simply at making her as learned as possible. From this point of view, however, her schooling was a resounding success. Despite the intensive nature of the timetable, the hours of cramming were for Elizabeth a labour of love, and she never lost the delight in scholarship and study which had been instilled in her as a girl. After five years on the throne she was still in the habit of devoting the period after dinner to re-reading her favourite passages from the classics, and one of her former tutors noted approvingly that there were not six gentlemen at court who bestowed "so many hours, daily, orderly and constantly for the increase of learning and knowledge as doth the Queen's Majesty herself". After receiving bad news from France in 1593, she soothed herself by working on a translation of Boethius's *De Consolatione Philosophiae*, and she also translated extracts from Tacitus, Plutarch and Horace, "for her private exercise". The creative energies which had been released by her education also found an outlet in her artful manipulation of her own tongue. Having been trained to judge a book not solely on content but to appreciate stylistic nuances and elegance of expression, she did not see language simply as a means of communication but as an artistic medium, and it was this that inspired the singular cadences and ornate phraseology of her mature speech.[21]

Preoccupied with her lessons, Elizabeth visited Court only occasionally during these years. In December 1539, when Henry VIII was about to embark on his fourth foray into matrimony, Elizabeth was among the ladies who welcomed his bride Anne of Cleves to England, but she can hardly have had time to become acquainted with her new stepmother before the latter was twitched aside to make way for her nubile maid of honour, Catherine Howard. Catherine was sufficiently fond of Elizabeth to give her some beads and jewellery, "little thing worth",[22] but the discovery that she had been unchaste before her marriage, and possibly an adulteress after it, led to the Queen's execution in February 1542, leaving Elizabeth once again motherless. Some semblance of family life was at least provided by visits to Prince Edward, who was also being brought up away from Court. When apart they corresponded in Latin, exhorting one another to still greater achievements in the classroom, and though one should treat with due scepticism the claims of Protestant hagiographers that their mutual faith brought them closer together, Edward's precocity must have done much to shrink the four-year age gap between them.

In July 1543, apparently unchastened by experiences that might have deterred a lesser man, the King took as his sixth wife Katherine Parr, a wealthy widow in her early thirties. Katherine's formative years had coincided with the first flush of enthusiasm for learning in women, and she herself had been well-educated, providing Elizabeth with an inspiring example at a time when she was about to embark on a new phase in her studies. Having attended the wedding, Elizabeth did not see the new Queen for a whole year, for though she visited court in June 1544 and dined with the King, Katherine was not present on that occasion. The following month, however, Elizabeth was able to display her erudition to her step-mother by penning her a letter in a fine italic hand, lamenting in flawless Italian the fact that "inimical fortune" had once again deprived her of her company. At New Year 1545 Katherine received a further testimonial of her step-daughter's progress in the form of a handwritten volume bound in embroidered canvas and containing a translation of *The Glass or Mirror of the Sinful Soul*, written by the French princess, Margaret of Angoulême. It was an austere work, in which the authoress acknowledged herself to be steeped in sin and wallowed in self-abasement, but Elizabeth knew that its tenor would be acceptable to Queen Katherine, an acknowledged authority on devotional literature who habitually set down in writing her own pious meditations. Elizabeth's only concern was that Katherine would consider her translation from French verse into English prose to be a poor one, and she implored her stepmother to "rub out, polish and mend ... the words (or rather the order of my writing), the which I know in many places to be rude".[23]

Despite her reservations, the gift was evidently a success, for the following New Year Elizabeth felt sufficiently confident to prepare a pair of manuscript books, one to be given to Queen Katherine and the other for presentation to her father. In the latter Elizabeth contrived to pay a graceful tribute to her stepmother's piety, while simultaneously demonstrating to the King how learned she had become, for it contained a selection from Katherine's private prayers, successively translated by Elizabeth into Latin, French and finally Italian. Katherine received Elizabeth's translation of Jean Calvin's *How We ought to Know God*, a controversial choice in view of the fact that less than three years before, the King's organist John Marbeck had been convicted of heresy simply for having copied one of Calvin's letters, but one at which the Queen, who held advanced views in religion, would not have demurred. Katherine could take further pleasure in the fact that the handwriting was more assured than that in the previous year's offering, while the cover design was also more ambitious, consisting of an embroidered monogram in which all the letters in "Henry" and "Katherine" could be discerned. All in all, it was an accomplished production, and Elizabeth herself evidently took pride in her handiwork, for this time no modest disclaimer accompanied the present.[24]

In 1546 it was decided that Elizabeth should be brought to Court, where she could be under the permanent supervision of her stepmother, and Mary and she now headed the list of ladies-in-waiting "accustomed to be lodged within the King's Majesty's house". Her improved domestic situation paralleled the transformation in her political prospects which had occurred in June 1543, when an act of Parliament had reinstated the King's daughters in the succession. This measure stated that if Edward failed to produce a direct heir, the Crown would pass on his death to Mary, and if she in turn left no children to succeed her, Elizabeth would inherit. The wording of the Act gives no clue that the measure represented an astonishing change of heart on the part of the King, merely stating that, as Henry was contemplating going abroad on campaign, he thought it "convenient" to make fresh arrangements for the succession; nor did the King feel it necessary to legitimize his daughters before placing them in line to the throne.[25] He had only been induced to recognize their rights because he had no male relations who could have taken their place, and though this situation had compelled him to accept that they might one day become Queens regnant, he doubtless felt that it was an eventuality that was none the less to be dreaded.

Whatever Henry's reservations, in December 1546 these arrangements were confirmed by his will. In this he also guarded against the remote contingency that all his children would die childless by providing that the succession should then be vested in the descendants of his younger sister Mary, who had had two daughters by her marriage to Charles Brandon, Duke of Suffolk. These dispositions bypassed the senior branch of the family, for Henry had also had an elder sister, Margaret, who had married King James IV of Scotland in 1502. In blood, at least, the claim of her descendants (of whom the most notable was the four-year-old Mary, Queen of Scots) was superior to that of the Suffolk line, but Henry felt no compunction about perverting the laws of genealogy to ensure that all his heirs were of English stock. It was an order of succession of which his subjects heartily approved, and which they would subsequently defend with vigour, frustrating the efforts of both Edward and Mary to bypass Henry's provisions. Only Elizabeth, whose much vaunted filial piety did not extend to endorsing her father's will, could afford to ignore it, and that was only after her long and successful reign had finally destroyed Henry's ability to shape events from beyond the grave.

The King's attention to detail was also evident in his subsidiary bequests. He left both Elizabeth and Mary an income of £3,000 a year until they married, at which time they would receive a final payment of £10,000 "in money, plate, jewels and household stuff". These assignments were far from generous – a near contemporary of Elizabeth's commented, "I have known many a nobleman's daughter left as great a legacy, nay, a larger dower" – and even so were conditional upon the Council approving of their choice of husband. Furthermore, it was expressly stated that if Elizabeth married without conciliar sanction, she was to be struck out of the succession, "as though the said Lady Elizabeth were then dead".[26]

On 28 January 1547 Henry VIII died. The news was broken to the thirteen-year-old Elizabeth at Enfield; after an initial spasm of grief she soon recovered her composure. In a letter which showed a gravity commensurate with his new status, her brother, now King Edward VI, wrote to congratulate her on her fortitude: "There is very little need of my consoling you, most dear sister, because from your learning you know what you ought to do, and from your prudence and piety you perform what your learning causes you to know ... I perceive you think of our father's death with a calm mind".[27]

Her self-possession was understandable enough, for Henry's death can hardly have created a yawning emotional void in her life. Fear and awe were the feelings that the King had principally inspired, and even in a daughter, love would have bordered on presumptousness. When apart from the King, Elizabeth had not even dared to initiate a correspondence with him, and visits to the Court were infrequent and hedged with etiquette. Yet in a sense this did not matter, for even at a distance Henry had succeeded in capturing her imagination. She was thrilled by his power and magnificence, and in an age when fathers were expected to be authoritarian, even tyrannical, she found it gratifying rather than otherwise to have as a father the highest authority in the land. All her life she revered Henry's memory – "She prides herself on her father and glories in him", the Venetian ambassador noted in 1557[28] – and if in the decade after his death she would frequently have cause to remember that she was "but a subject", she never once forgot that she was also "her father's daughter".

CHAPTER 2

"The noblest man unmarried in this land"

I t was the opinion of Elizabeth's governess, Katherine Ashley, that at the time of his death, Henry VIII was on the point of bestowing his younger daughter's hand on one of his subjects. The recipient of this honour, so Mrs Ashley believed, was to have been Thomas Seymour, a brother of the late Queen Jane, who had been appointed Admiral of the Fleet in 1544 and a Privy Councillor five days before the King had died. Whether Mistress Ashley was correct in thinking that Henry had planned to advance him still further is highly unlikely; but as Seymour was an exceptionally attractive bachelor in his late thirties, whose shallow intellect and dangerous streak of instability were hidden beneath a formidable charm, she felt that the idea had much to commend it.

If the match had ever been contemplated, its chances evaporated with the death of Henry VIII, for Seymour found his path to the altar blocked by his elder brother, Edward, Earl of Hertford. The latter was a more austere character than his younger brother, but he was equally ambitious, and unlike Seymour he possessed the abilities and strength of purpose that could bring him real power. Indeed, he gained it only three days after the old King's death, for despite the fact that Henry had provided in his will that during his son's minority England should be governed by the collective rule of the Privy Council, on 31 January Hertford persuaded his fellow councillors to disregard these terms and appoint him Lord Protector and Governor of the young King. A fortnight later the seal was set on his success when he was created Duke of Somerset. His younger brother was simultaneously raised to the peerage as Baron Seymour of Sudeley, and promoted to the position of Lord High Admiral, but Somerset had no intention of allowing him to acquire further responsibility.

It was clear that if Seymour wished to wield greater influence he would have to achieve it indirectly, and accordingly he seriously considered taking one of the late King's daughters for his bride. At this stage it seems that he would have been prepared to become the husband of either Mary or Elizabeth, but despite his admirable flexibility, his plans were not destined to prosper. It is unclear whether Seymour ever formally raised the possibility that he might marry one of the sisters with his brother or the Council, but certainly it became apparent to him that the enterprise would not have their blessing, and for the moment at least, he regretfully abandoned it as too risky. To Kat Ashley, watching impatiently on the sidelines, the Admiral's failure to make a bid for Elizabeth's hand came as a great disappointment. In Henry VIII's day, she had frequently told the Admiral that she believed he and Elizabeth would be well matched, and now she took the opportunity of a chance encounter in St James's Park to reproach Seymour for his failure to propose. Another man might have rebuked Mrs Ashley for her impertinence, but Seymour took it all in good humour, responding jocularly, "Nay, I love not to lose my life for a wife. It has been spoken unto, but it cannot be".[1]

Even Seymour's normally unquenchable optimism had quailed at the thought of marrying the King's sister without conciliar approval, but his nimble brain soon lighted on an excellent alternative. On her father's death Elizabeth had been sent to live with Katherine Parr at her house in Chelsea, and it was to this rich royal widow that Seymour now turned his effervescent attention. The Queen Dowager was overjoyed by his suit, for prior to her marriage with King Henry she had harboured ambitions of becoming Seymour's wife, and had only abandoned the idea when, as she put it, "God withstood my will therein most vehemently" by prompting Henry to take a fancy to her.[2] Now she was determined not to waste this unexpected second opportunity, and in the face of romantic passion her piety and learning counted for nothing. Although she knew that the Council would have expected her to have observed a long period of mourning after her bereavement, Katherine agreed to marry Seymour secretly, possibly in April or early May 1547, and for the next few weeks they stole illicit nights together whenever they could. This unsatisfactory arrangement could hardly be prolonged indefinitely, but Seymour's next step was to take the young King into his confidence and assure himself of his support for the match, thus ensuring that when the marriage finally came to light, serious trouble could not ensue. To a certain extent the plan worked, for although the Protector was "much offended" on learning whom his brother had taken as a wife, he could do nothing about it.

Once his marriage had been acknowledged, Seymour moved in with the Queen Dowager at Chelsea, apparently not a whit dismayed to find himself on such bad terms with his brother. Rumbustious and merry, he soon shattered the cloistered calm of this riverside retreat, and the entire household, from Katherine downwards, was animated by his presence. "His service was ever joyful", one of his employees later recalled, for although Seymour's engaging manner could not take him very far in his dealings with men of equal rank, his inferiors were invariably bowled over by his humour and affability. The Lord Admiral also possessed an ability to communicate with young people which was particularly remarkable in an age when adults were not expected to make an effort to understand them, and as a result Elizabeth too was captivated by his glamour and magnetism. Indeed, she developed something of an adolescent crush on the Admiral, for the more observant members of the household noted that she habitually blushed on hearing his name, and appeared pleased if he was praised in her presence.[3]

This would have been harmless enough if the situation had been handled properly, but irresponsible conduct on the part of those who were old enough to know better only contrived to make it more awkward. With incredible foolishness, Kat Ashley confided to Elizabeth "that if my Lord Admiral might have had his own will", he would have married her "afore the Queen". Seymour's own behaviour was not calculated to make this seem unlikely, for he treated Elizabeth in a boisterous way that was too tinged with sexuality to be dismissed as playfulness pure and simple. He liked to engage the teenage girl in suggestive banter, coming into her bedchamber before she was fully dressed so that he could "bid her good morrow and ask her how she did, and strike her upon the back or on the buttocks familiarly". If he found her still in bed, "he would put open the curtains and . . . make as though he would come at her", forcing Elizabeth to burrow helplessly under the bedclothes. "One morning he strave to have kissed her in her bed", which even Mrs Ashley thought was going too far, and she "bade him go away for shame". Mrs Ashley's presence ensured that these sessions could not get too out of hand, nor was Elizabeth herself an altogether willing victim. She was able to outwit the Lord Admiral by rising earlier than usual, so that when Seymour entered he found her up and dressed, and demurely absorbed in study.[4]

Gradually Mrs Ashley began to have misgivings about these indecorous proceedings. When Seymour took to paying his morning call attired only in a short nightgown, Kat told him outright, "It was an unseemly sight to come so bare-legged to a maiden's chamber", and though the Lord Admiral was plainly irritated by her criticism he dressed more fittingly in future. He refused, however, to discontinue his visits altogether, swearing by "God's precious soul! . . . He meant no evil", and denying that his behaviour might give rise to censorious comment.[5]

By this time Mrs Ashley was sufficiently disturbed to raise the issue with Katherine, but for the moment at least the Queen Dowager saw no need for concern. She promised Kat that in future she would accompany her husband on his forays into Elizabeth's bedchamber, but far from seeking to restrain his conduct, she herself became his accomplice, helping Seymour to tickle Elizabeth as she lay in bed. At Hanworth, another of the Queen's residences, there was a bizarre incident in the garden, when Katherine held Elizabeth fast while Seymour "cut her gown in an hundred pieces".[6]

In time, however, Katherine's attitude underwent a change. By the beginning of 1548, ill health caused by pregnancy not only left her with little enthusiasm for horseplay, but made her disinclined to view it simply as innocent fun, and at Whitsun she concluded that it would be better if Elizabeth left her household altogether. Exactly what precipitated this decision is unclear: in a garrulous moment Kat Ashley told another of Elizabeth's servants, Thomas Parry, that the Queen lost patience with both her husband and Elizabeth after she "came suddenly upon them, where they were all alone, *he having her in his arms*", but when the authorities subsequently questioned Mrs Ashley about these events she appears to have been much less forthcoming. Under interrogation she admitted only that Katherine had claimed that her husband had seen Elizabeth locked in an embrace with a mystery man, but Mrs Ashley said that she had found this impossible to believe. She had deduced from this that Katherine wished to make her suspicious of Elizabeth, so that in future she would supervise the girl more carefully, "and be, as it were, in watch betwixt her and my Lord Admiral".[7]

At any rate, it is clear that, prior to sending Elizabeth to stay with Sir Anthony Denny and his wife at Cheshunt, her stepmother gave her a frank lecture about the vulnerability of one in her position to any sort of scandal, promising to let her know if she heard anything to suggest that Elizabeth's reputation had already been damaged by her incautious behaviour. Upset at her enforced departure, Elizabeth evidently listened in sullen silence, but by the time she arrived at Cheshunt she was able to view the situation in a more mature light. Although it was unfortunate that she should have to suffer when she had done her best to avoid encouraging the Admiral, her feelings for him had never been fully under control, and it was perhaps wisest to remove her altogether from the sphere of temptation. Having come to appreciate that Katherine had her best interests at heart, she wrote to thank her stepmother for her kindness, explaining that "Albeit I answered little, I weighed it more deeper when you said you would warn me of all evils that you should hear of me; for if your Grace had not a good opinion of me, you would not have offered friendship to me that way". As Katherine had acted before relations between them became too fraught, Elizabeth could console herself that she was still on good terms with both the Queen Dowager and Seymour. Furthermore, once free of the Lord Admiral's overwhelming physical presence, her feelings for him could remain affectionate without being overwrought. When Seymour wrote in apology for having failed to perform some errand on her behalf, she replied simply, "I am a friend not won with trifles nor lost with the like".[8] Her tone was still warm, but clearly she had outgrown the giggling intimacy that had characterized their relations in the past.

Elizabeth's removal from her stepmother's establishment left her free to concentrate on her studies, which had recently taken an important new turn. The previous January her tutor, William Grindal, had died suddenly of plague. Among those who wrote to condole with her on her loss was Grindal's own teacher at Cambridge, Roger Ascham, who expressed his conviction that the best way of overcoming her sorrow would be "to bring to maturity that excellent learning of which you have the seeds laid by Grindal". As it turned out, it was he himself who was called upon to perform this task. Initially the Queen Dowager had contemplated hiring a Mr Goldsmith to replace Grindal, but Elizabeth expressed a preference for Ascham, and this, combined with the fact that he had been a pupil of Sir John Cheke and was a friend of the Ashleys, led to his engagement.[9]

It was an excellent choice, for not only was Ascham acknowledged to be "one of the politest Latin writers of that generation", but he was a born teacher who believed passionately that learning should be made as enjoyable as possible. It was his opinion that children responded better to praise than strict discipline, and that it was a mistake to drive them too hard in their studies. One reason why Elizabeth might have favoured his appointment was that some years before he had written to Mrs Ashley, imploring her not to force her pupil to absorb too much at once. He deplored the traditional methods of teaching classical languages, which consisted of little more than "tossing all the rules of grammar". Instead, he sought to bring the subject alive by means of double translation, whereby a passage was first rendered into English and then, after an interval, turned back into Latin or Greek and compared with the original. Already an apt pupil, Elizabeth made great strides under so sympathetic an instructor. Together she and Ascham read "almost the whole of Cicero and a great part of Livy", and her Greek too improved. Every morning she read a few verses from the New Testament in Greek, followed by selections from the tragedies of Sophocles and the orations of Isocrates. Ascham was also renowned for the beauty of his penmanship, and under his guidance Elizabeth's italic handwriting, which had already shown much promise, was brought to perfection. Ascham himself was delighted by the progress of his pupil, whom he claimed possessed a mind "exempt from female weakness, and ... endued with a masculine power of application", and the correspondence he kept up with various foreign scholars abounded with tributes to Elizabeth's industry and intelligence.[10]

There was more to Ascham than his pedagogic skills. It was one of his maxims that "learning should always be mingled with honest mirth and comely exercises", and his best known book, *The Scholemaster*, abounds in metaphors drawn from greyhound racing, horse-riding, archery and cock-fighting, and demonstrates that for Ascham, love of scholarship was merely one of many enthusiasms. With such a tutor there was no fear that Elizabeth would be forced to concentrate exclusively on academic subjects. Riding and hunting were both regular activities, "neither did she neglect music", for though Ascham himself was of the opinion that "much music marreth men's manners", Elizabeth was taught to play on the lute and virginals. She also enjoyed listening to music – her household account books for this period include payments to "Farmor that played on the lute" and "More the harper" – and though there is no record of her receiving dancing lessons, she must have done so, for by the time she ascended the throne she had developed a distinctive style of dancing "in the Italian manner".[11]

If Elizabeth was fortunate in being taught by a man who was at once highly erudite and yet devoid of donnish insularity, the worldly side of Ascham had its drawbacks. After two years as Elizabeth's tutor he left her service, possibly after a quarrel with Thomas Parry, whose position in her household as cofferer gave him overall responsibility for Elizabeth's domestic expenditure. Elizabeth evidently believed Ascham to have been in the wrong, for he sorrowfully admitted that she was "somewhat alien-ated" from him for a time. The estrangement was temporary, for by the autumn of 1555 he was back at court giving Elizabeth Greek lessons, but her faith in his judgment was evidently shaken. When she came to the throne, she made him her Latin Secretary at a pension of £20 a year, and awarded him a prebend, but Ascham had difficulty extracting payment for the latter from the Archbishop of York. In 1566 he despairingly complained to the Earl of Leicester that though Elizabeth's "noble hand and excellent learning in the Greek and Latin tongues" testified to the service he had done her, he feared that if he died, his wife and children would be reduced to beggary. Ascham evidently felt that he had been treated poorly, but Elizabeth's early biographer, William Camden, claimed it was Ascham's addiction to "dicing and cock-fighting" that was primarily responsible for his penury. He died in 1568, and though at the time Elizabeth said "she would have cast £10,000 into the sea rather than lose her Ascham", in the event she did no more than award his widow a modest pension.[12]

In September 1548, Elizabeth's tranquil existence was disrupted by the sad news that Katherine Parr had died shortly after giving birth to a baby girl. The unexpected loss cannot have failed to grieve Elizabeth, but Kat Ashley's distress at the tidings was appreciably lessened by the reflection that the Lord Admiral would soon be looking for a new wife, and Elizabeth was an obvious candidate for his hand. Anxious that Seymour's thoughts should be channelled in the right direction, Mrs Ashley felt it desirable that Elizabeth should send him a timely reminder of her existence in the guise of a letter of condolence, but Elizabeth was too shrewd not to realize that she must be exceptionally guarded in her dealings with him. Although Mrs Ashley insisted that Seymour's bereavement had left him "the heaviest man in the world", and nagged Elizabeth to write to him, the girl was adamant "that she would not, for then she should be thought to woo him".[13]

Mrs Ashley was not so easily deterred, and as time went by her efforts on the Lord Admiral's behalf became more overt. Archly she told Elizabeth, "Your old husband that was appointed unto you at the death of the King now is free again, you may have him if you will". Elizabeth was careful not to encourage such prattle, "and would ever say Nay by her troth". Yet Mrs Ashley was nothing if not persistent: "If all the Council did agree, why not?" she persevered, "For he is the noblest man unmarried in this land". To this Elizabeth reasonably replied, "Though he himself would peradventure have me, yet I think the Council will not consent to it". She pointed out that Mrs Ashley herself had said that Seymour had wanted to marry her before, and as the Council had prevented him from carrying out his intention on that occasion, it was logical to assume that they would do so again. Even this sensible analysis failed to bring Mrs Ashley to her senses. Although in moments of pessimism she agreed that it was unlikely that either Somerset or the Council would permit Elizabeth to marry a subject, she felt sure that if Elizabeth waited until her brother attained his majority he would sanction the match, and "his Grace at full age might do his pleasing".[14]

The fact that the King was only ten years old at the time well illustrates the absurdity of this particular flight of fancy, but now that Mrs Ashley had the bit between her teeth there was no stopping her. Dismissing any suggestion that Seymour's suit might encounter opposition, she did not pause to think of the dangers of inflaming a passion that had scant hope of gratification. Not even the most explicit warnings from her husband, who told her that Seymour's schemes "would sure come to naught ... and forbade her to meddle in anything touching him", could sober her.[15] Elizabeth herself strove gamely to curb Mrs Ashley's fantasies, but even so, she evidently found the subject of the Lord Admiral to be so fascinating that she could not bring herself to forbid Kat to mention him altogether.

Two weeks before Christmas 1548, the situation took a disturbing new turn. Elizabeth was annoyed that Durham Place, which she had understood was to be made available to her as a London residence, had recently been turned into a mint. Accordingly, she sent her cofferer, Thomas Parry, to ask Seymour in London if he could do anything to remedy the situation. A fat, self-important Welshman, Parry was delighted by the welcome he received from the Lord Admiral, who expansively assured him that if Elizabeth needed somewhere to stay in London, he would lend her his own house for as long as she required. Seymour then proceeded to enquire minutely into the details of Elizabeth's financial situation. He asked Parry whether she had yet received her father's bequests to her, where her lands were situated, and offered friendly advice as to how Elizabeth could economize on household expenses – as well he might, for with Parry in charge of her accounts, Elizabeth's affairs were handled highly incompetently.[16] Parry however was too flattered at being taken into the Lord Admiral's confidence to detect any note of criticism, and he obligingly furnished Seymour with as much information as he could.

On his return, Parry hastened to let Elizabeth know of his communications with Seymour, and he noted that she seemed pleased by the Lord Admiral's interest in her. She even coyly enquired of Parry if he knew why Seymour was being so curious about her, and was clearly far from disappointed when Parry answered that he "could not tell, unless he go about to have you also". Parry then went on to ask her outright whether she would marry Seymour if the Council raised no objection, but at this Elizabeth was visibly displeased. Loftily she told him, "When that comes to pass I will do as God shall put in my mind", but despite her haughty manner, a trace of excitement lingered. In some agitation she begged Parry to tell Mrs Ashley of his conversation with Seymour, claiming that she herself wished "to hear no such thing but that Kate Ashley shall know it, she being put by the King's Majesty her father to be her mistress".[17]

Although the late King would hardly have agreed that Mrs Ashley's position entitled her to meddle in concerns of such import, Parry did as he was bid, and early in the New Year he and Kat had a good gossip on the subject of Seymour and Elizabeth. Mrs Ashley was somewhat nettled by Parry's evident belief that he had been the first to guess Seymour's intentions: when the cofferer solemnly informed her that "there is good will between the Lord Admiral and her Grace", she fired back the crushing retort that "She knew it well enough". In her anxiety to let Parry know that she had been in on the secret for much longer than he, she gave him some idea of the indiscretions that had taken place under Katherine Parr's roof, until even she began to fear that she had gone too far, and she made Parry swear that he would never repeat a word of what he had heard. Parry received her revelations with gratifying amazement – "Hath there been such familiarity indeed between them?" he demanded, after Kat had told him how Elizabeth and Seymour were surprised in each other's arms – but when he contended that Seymour would not make a fit husband for Elizabeth, Mrs Ashley sprung promptly to the Lord Admiral's defence. "I would wish her his wife of all men living", she enthused, dismissing the very idea that the marriage would not be permitted with an airy assurance that Seymour "might compass the Council if he would".[18]

In this Mrs Ashley was very far wide of the mark, for Seymour's nemesis was at hand. Marriage with Elizabeth was only one of a number of wild schemes that had been revolving in the Lord Admiral's mind. He was also seeking to prise loose the King from the Duke of Somerset's control. When with Edward, he lost no opportunity to instil in him a fixed dislike of the Protector, constantly denigrating Somerset before him, and exploiting the King's resentment that the Duke kept him short of pocket money by slipping him surreptitious gifts of cash. More sinister still were his attempts to build up a following among the nobility. He assiduously cultivated individual magnates, and urged them to assure themselves of the support of their country neighbours by paying friendly visits to local yeomen and offering them "a flagon or two of wine or a pasty of venison . . . for so you shall cause them to love you". If it came to a showdown between Somerset and him, he was evidently hoping that a large number of men would rally to his cause, and as even Seymour realized that to mount a rebellion required more weighty resources than venison pies and bottles of wine, he applied himself to raising large sums of cash. He abused his position of Lord Admiral by extorting bribes from all ships going to Ireland, and even offered protection to pirates (whom he was in theory supposed to persecute) in return for receiving a portion of their loot. Furthermore, he entered into collusion with William Sharington, a dishonest official at the Bristol mint, instructing him to raise by corrupt means £10,000 which Seymour believed was an amount of money such as "a man might do somewhat withal".[19]

Whether Seymour had either the will or the ability to pull together the numerous strands in his tangled network of conspiracy remains open to question, but it was understandable that when the Council heard of his activities they viewed them in the gravest possible light. They were first alerted to Seymour's wrongdoing in early January 1549 when they stumbled upon evidence of Sharington's frauds, and found that the Lord Admiral was implicated in his crimes. Further enquiries were conducted, and as the case against Seymour was gradually pieced together, Protector Somerset came to the conclusion that his brother had "devised and had almost brought to pass . . . a secret marriage . . . between himself and the L[ady] E[lizabeth], the King's Majesty's sister, in such sort and order as he might easily (and so it appeareth intended) have taken into his hands and order the person of the King's Majesty and of his sister the Lady M[ary], and have disposed of his Majesty's whole Council at his pleasure".[20] Furthermore, the Council suspected that Seymour had been abetted in his marriage plans by Parry, Mrs Ashley, and possibly Elizabeth herself. On 17 January Seymour was sent to the Tower, and four days later the Ashleys and Parry were also arrested at Hatfield and removed to London, leaving Elizabeth to face a searching interrogation at the hands of the Council's agent, Sir Robert Tyrwhit.

It is difficult to imagine a more traumatic experience for a fifteen-year-old girl than to be relentlessly questioned about a compromising episode in her past, in the knowledge that her answers could result in a number of her most trusted associates being tried on a capital charge. But though Elizabeth was naturally upset – Tyrwhit reported with satisfaction that she burst into tears when she learnt that Parry and Mistress Ashley had been sent to the Tower – she did not panic. If Sir Robert had hoped that her distress at her predicament would prompt her to betray her servants, he soon found he was mistaken. Time and again, he expressed his astonishment that Elizabeth should prove so devoted to Mistress Ashley, and though he assured the girl that she would not be held responsible for the misdeeds of her elders, at this stage he could only extract from her the bare admission that she had once sent Parry to confer with Seymour about Durham Place. In some frustration, Sir Robert informed the Lord Protector that though he could "see it in her face that she is guilty", he felt sure she would "abide more storms 'ere she accuse Mistress Ashley".[21]

By the following day, however, Tyrwhit felt that he was starting to make progress. "She hath a very good wit, and nothing is gotten of her but by great policy", he conceded in a letter to Somerset, but he evidently believed that he would be able to handle her. Already by using "gentle persuasion", he had prevailed upon Elizabeth to reveal that when Parry returned from London, he had mentioned the possibility of her marrying Seymour, and Sir Robert hoped that this would be the forerunner of more damaging disclosures.[22]

Before long, however, his confident tone had changed. Far from cracking under pressure, Elizabeth showed unexpected resilience, recovering her composure to such an extent that Tyrwhit could see little prospect of wringing further avowals from her. "I do verily believe that there hath been some secret promise between my Lady, Mistress Ashley and the cofferer never to confess to death", he wrote irritably to the Protector on 28 January. Certainly the letter he enclosed from Elizabeth to Somerset was an indication of the degree to which she had managed to regain the ascendant. In it, Elizabeth repeated the harmless revelations that she had already produced for Tyrwhit's benefit, but far from adopting an apologetic tone, she concluded by registering her lively indignation that Somerset had done nothing to counteract current rumours to the effect that she was in the Tower and with child by the Lord Admiral. "My Lord, these are shameful slanders", she wrote hotly, "For the which, besides the great desire I have to see the King's Majesty, I shall most heartily desire your Lordship that I may come to court after your first determination, that I may shew myself as I am".[23] No wonder Tyrwhit felt dispirited about his chances of beating this cocksure chit into submission.

Her request to visit Court fell on deaf ears, but Elizabeth remained defiant thoughout another whole week of intensive questioning. She refused to make significant alterations in her story, and threatened all those who ventured to criticize Mrs Ashley in her presence that they would "fare the worse for their so saying". If the Council had been obliged to rely solely on her version of events, it is doubtful they would have learnt a great deal more, and Tyrwhit came to the conclusion that it would be more profitable to intensify the pressure on some of the other protagonists in the affair. In particular, he urged the Council to concentrate on Mrs Ashley, for he believed that if she made a full confession that could be laid before Elizabeth, he would then "have good hope to make her cough out the whole".[24]

Initially Mrs Ashley had been confined under quite mild conditions, but in hopes that she would reveal all, she was removed to a grim dungeon, "so cold ... and so dark" that she could neither sleep at night nor see in the daytime. Despite this, she still refused to co-operate, but Thomas Parry, who had doubtless been subjected to similar treatment, was made of frailer stuff. On 4 February, the Council engineered a dramatic confrontation between Mrs Ashley and Parry, at which the latter admitted that he had told his examiners all he knew. "False wretch!" cried Mrs Ashley, for Parry had sworn he "had rather be pulled with horses" than to reveal such secrets, but in the circumstances she too now had no alternative but to make a detailed confession.[25]

The following day, these depositions were rushed to Elizabeth at Hatfield. When she saw their contents, she became "much abashed and half breathless", for the documents made humiliating reading. Here was set down in shameful detail the story of her romps with Seymour, and in her confession Kat Ashley went so far as to admit that she had frequently discussed Seymour with Elizabeth, "and hath wished both openly and privily that they two were married together". In one respect, however, Elizabeth had cause to be grateful, for both Parry and Kat were adamant that it had never crossed their minds that the match could be embarked upon without the approval of the Council. However embarrassing, her servants' confessions contained no really damaging admissions, and though Elizabeth was now obliged to flesh out her originally skeletal evidence with a slightly more frank account of the conversations she had had with Kat about the Lord Admiral, she said nothing that might suggest that Mrs Ashley's behaviour had been criminal as well as foolish. Tyrwhit, for one, remained convinced he had not been given the whole story ("They all sing one song, and so I think they would not do, unless they had set the note before", he grumbled),[26] but mercifully the Council accepted that in essentials at least, they had been told the truth.

Nevertheless, Mrs Ashley's imprudence had been too marked to be overlooked altogether. Elizabeth was informed by the Council that Kat had shown herself to be "far unmeet" to occupy the position of governess, and that accordingly Lady Tyrwhit was to take her place forthwith. The decision was hardly a surprising one, but Elizabeth received it with the liveliest indignation, and far from complying with the Council's hope that she would "accept [Lady Tyrwhit's] service thankfully", she "took the matter so heavily, that she wept all night and loured all the following day". Apparently unchastened by her gruelling experiences, she took the view that she had emerged from the enquiry completely vindicated, and objected to the Protector that the appointment of "such a one" as her governess could only reinforce the false impression that she herself was of a "lewd demeanour".[27] Somerset, however, was more inclined to listen to Tyrwhit, who was adamant that in future Elizabeth would have to be much more closely supervised. Elizabeth's letter of complaint to the Duke accordingly received the most frosty of replies, rebuking her for obstinacy and pertness.

Distressed as she was by the remodelling of her household, such woes paled into insignificance when she learnt the grim news that Seymour's lands were being parcelled out among the courtiers, a certain indication that treason charges were pending. Sure enough, on 24 February the King authorized the instigation of proceedings, and on 5 March 1549 a bill of attainder against Seymour received the royal assent. Fifteen days later, he was beheaded.

Despite the fact that Elizabeth's childhood had taken place against a background of judicial murder and sudden bereavement, Seymour's execution was not an event that she could lightly put behind her. Indeed, when it first appeared that the Lord Admiral was to be tried, she made no secret of her distress at his predicament, and could not "hear him discommended, but she is ready to make answer therein". A few days' reflection nevertheless sufficed to make her realize that as she could do nothing to help Seymour, her energies would be better spent if she did all she could to assist her imprisoned servants. Thus when she again wrote to Somerset on 7 March, two days after Seymour had been condemned, she made no reference to the Lord Admiral's plight, and instead begged that mercy be shown to Mrs Ashley, who was still languishing in the Tower. She no longer attempted to deny that Kat had been irresponsible, stressing that she had no wish to "favour her evil-doings", and that she was only interceding on her behalf out of natural affection for the woman who had brought her up. Her penitent tone had the right effect: Parry and the Ashleys were shortly released, and in due course permitted to resume their positions in Elizabeth's household, Mrs Ashley having sworn that never again would she "speak nor whisper of marriage, no, not to win all the world".[28] Sensibly, therefore, Elizabeth had concentrated on salvaging what she could from the catastrophe, but though she had been realistic enough to resign herself to Seymour's fate, this did not mean that she was indifferent to it. While it would be an exaggeration to say that the Seymour affair permanently stunted Elizabeth's emotional development – her feelings had not been sufficiently deeply engaged for that – the Lord Admiral certainly did not go unmourned.

She gave some indication of her true feelings five years after Seymour's execution, when her sister Mary was on the throne, and she herself was ordered to the Tower on suspicion of treason. Terrified that she would be condemned without having been given a chance to explain herself to the Queen, she wrote to Mary begging her to reconsider. Hoping to move her sister, she told her that she had heard the Duke of Somerset say of his brother's execution that if Seymour had been allowed "to speak with him he had never suffered, but persuasions were made to him so great, that he was brought in belief that he could not live safely if the Admiral lived; and that made him consent to his death".[29] Not only is it clear that Elizabeth believed the Lord Admiral's death to have been unjustified, but it is notable that even when facing the greatest crisis of her life, she found the memory of his fate so poignant that she thought her sister could not fail to be moved by it. As we shall see, the appeal failed, but its significance lay in the fact that it was made in the first place.

In the months following Seymour's execution she could not afford to indulge in unconstructive brooding, for her first priority was to rehabilitate herself in the favour of the King. Anxious not to be branded a shameless hussy, the image she now cultivated was one of modesty and reserve. Her dress was sober to the point of boredom: the Protestant historian, John Foxe, recorded with approval that "she had so little pride of stomach, so little delight in glistering gazes of the world, in gay apparel, rich attire and precious jewels that ... she never looked upon those that her father left her". More importantly, her concern to impress upon the Council that she would undertake nothing without their approval led her to take exaggerated care to keep them informed of her most insignificant activities. In September 1549, for example, Thomas Parry reported to Protector Somerset that the Venetian ambassador had recently visited Elizabeth, and he explained that she had asked him to pass this on as "Her Grace will neither know nor do in matters that either may sound or seem to be of importance without doing of my Lord's Grace to understand thereof". Such precautions had the desired results, for in December 1549 she was invited to spend Christmas at court, where an observer noted that she "was received with great pomp and triumph, and is continually with the King".[30]

In practical terms at least, she had come through a trying time untarnished, and her life now resumed its tranquil course. Her financial affairs, which had been in a precarious state since her father's death, assumed a more healthy aspect when she took over the book-keeping herself, maintaining meticulous records of her expenditure and personally signing each page of the accounts. In part the improvement was due to the fact that in the spring of 1550 she had finally received what was due to her under the terms of Henry VIII's will. As her father had wished, she was granted lands with an aggregate value of just over £3,000 – including, ironically, the former Berkshire estate of "Thomas Seymour, knight, late Lord Seymour of Sudeley, attainted". That summer her settlement was again adjusted when she exchanged a property in Lincolnshire in return for Hatfield, the Hertfordshire manor to which she had become much attached in the intervals that her household had been based there.[31] To help her run these estates she engaged as her surveyor William Cecil, who had recently been appointed the King's Secretary of State. Cecil had already earned Elizabeth's gratitude by acting on her behalf in various minor suits, and though his duties in the government obliged him to delegate to a subordinate much of the day to day business concerning Elizabeth's holdings, his efficient overall supervision of her estates confirmed him in her eyes as a man who combined a shrewd business mind with great administrative skills.

The political upheavals of the reign hardly impinged upon her uneventful life. In October 1549 the Duke of Somerset was ousted from power by his ambitious rival, John Dudley, Earl of Warwick, who assumed the title Duke of Northumberland in October 1551. The Council thought it advisable to send letters to both Mary and Elizabeth explaining why Somerset had forfeited their trust, but Elizabeth can scarcely have imagined that these events held much significance for her. As it turned out, however, Northumberland posed a dangerous threat. He consolidated his position by engineering the execution, in January 1552, of the Duke of Somerset, but he knew that in the final analysis he depended for his power on the King, already in his teens and rapidly becoming a factor in the political equation. Though it seems that Northumberland himself was a man of little faith, he assured himself of the King's support by pushing through a programme of radical religious reform. This policy pleased Edward, a fervent Protestant, but left Northumberland with very little freedom of manoeuvre in the event of his young master's death.

The religious orientation of the regime created no difficulties for Elizabeth – when she paid another visit to Court in early 1551, the Imperial ambassador noted, "She was most honourably received by the Council, who acted thus to show how much glory belongs to her who has embraced the new religion"[32] – but with Mary it was otherwise. She refused to use the new English prayer book which Archbishop Cranmer had produced in 1549, or its revised edition, issued three years later. Despite the Council's pressure on her to conform, she clung stubbornly to her beliefs, hearing mass in secret after royal commissioners were sent to prevent her holding Catholic services for her household. As the man behind this persecution, the outlook for Northumberland was bleak if Mary inherited the throne.

By the spring of 1553 a steady deterioration in Edward's health, due probably to the onset of tuberculosis, made this prospect increasingly likely.

For Edward, who lay in bed bringing up foul-smelling black sputum, the knowledge that Mary would undo all he believed in seemed the harshest aspect of an already harsh fate. As a minor, it was technically treason for fifteen-year-old Edward to tamper with the order of succession laid down by Henry VIII and sanctioned by Parliament, but both he and Northumberland were too desperate to avert Mary's accession to trouble themselves about the legal niceties. In early May there were rumours that Northumberland was intending to obtain a divorce for his eldest son so that the latter could marry Elizabeth, but if the Duke had ever contemplated such a course, uncertainty as to whether Elizabeth would be prepared to connive at his plan to exclude Mary by becoming Queen herself led him to reconsider. It would be more sensible, he decided, to set up as puppet sovereign Edward's first cousin once removed, fifteen-year-old Lady Jane Grey. Her mother, a niece of Henry VIII's, was married to Henry Grey, Duke of Suffolk, and this couple proved more than willing to permit their daughter to become Northumberland's pawn. On 21 May 1553 Jane was married to Northumberland's youngest son, Guildford Dudley. Exactly three weeks later, Edward ordered the Chief Justice to draw up letters patent based on a new "Devise for the Succession" which declared that both Mary and Elizabeth were "illegitimate and not lawfully begotten", and left the crown to "Lady Jane and her heirs male".[33] On 21 June the leading men of the realm endorsed these arrangements, although several of them did so reluctantly.

In his will, Edward had stated blandly that after his death he desired his sisters to "live in quiet order, according to our appointment", apparently assuming that they would not object to being stripped of their birthright. This proved a forlorn hope. Northumberland had hoped to keep from Mary the fact that the succession had been altered, no doubt intending to take her into custody on Edward's death. On 3 July these plans were foiled when "a friend" contacted Mary at Hunsdon, Hertfordshire, and urged her to move somewhere more remote. By the time that Edward died on 8 July, Mary was already safely out of Northumberland's clutches at Kenninghall, Norfolk, an area where she enjoyed much local support. Despite this setback Northumberland pressed on, but he did so in the face of marked public hostility. On 9 July the Bishop of London, Nicholas Ridley, declared in a sermon at St Paul's that both Mary and Elizabeth were bastards, "which the people murmured sore at". By the time that Lady Jane was proclaimed Queen, on 10 July, Mary was already rallying her forces in East Anglia. Elizabeth at Hatfield made no move to counteract the usurper, but her early biographer, William Camden, claimed that she did reject an attempt by Northumberland to bribe her into resigning her title, on the grounds that she would do nothing to prejudice Mary's claim to the throne.[34] On 12 July, Northumberland left London in hopes of crushing Mary's resistance, but in his absence his colleagues on the Council declared for Mary, and by the time the Duke reached Cambridge it was clear his cause was lost. On 19 July he was arrested, and the same day Mary was proclaimed Queen in London.

"What with shouting and crying of the people, and ringing of the bells, there could no one hear almost what was said, besides banqueting and singing in the street for joy", ran one account of the celebrations that greeted Mary's victory.[35] The jubilation had not subsided by 29 July, when Elizabeth came up to town to await her sister's entry into the capital. Amid the general euphoria, however, Elizabeth cannot but have felt some twinges of unease. Even her brother, whose religious outlook she had shared, had ultimately sought to subvert her rights in a way that, if successful, could not have failed to expose her to danger, but with Mary she lacked even that tenuous affinity. In the circumstances, it was logical to assume that trouble loomed ahead.

CHAPTER 3

The second person in the realm

When Elizabeth rode out of London on 31 July in order to meet Mary outside the city's perimeters and escort her into the capital, she faced an uncertain reception. In the years following Anne Boleyn's execution, Mary had treated her little sister kindly, giving her trinkets and doling out small sums of pocket money, but the sisters had never been close in adult life. The Venetian ambassador noted that during the reign of their brother, Mary "had demonstrated by very clear signs" that she did not love Elizabeth, and now she was in a position to make her dislike felt. A small woman with a gruff, manly voice, and eyes "so piercing that they inspire not only respect but fear", Mary made an alarming impression on all who met her. It was true that her disconcerting stare was the product of short-sightedness rather than genuine penetration, but her courage and determination were beyond dispute. For years she had defied her father by insisting that his marriage to her mother had been a true one, and it was only after Catherine of Aragon's death in 1536 that she had been browbeaten into recognizing Henry as Supreme Head of the Church and acknowledging herself to be a bastard. During the reign of her brother Edward her capacity for resistance had once again manifested itself when she had steadfastly refused to accept the legality of the religious reforms enacted in the King's name, and the dispute had not been resolved at the time of Edward's death. In some ways she was painfully insecure, but in matters of faith her trust in her own judgment was absolute. While Edward was on the throne she had once declared, "I am like a little ignorant girl, and I care neither for my goods nor for the world, but only for God's service", and even when she came to power, her political understanding remained limited. Instead it was her conscience that was the lodestar that guided all her actions, and while this sometimes disadvantaged her as a ruler, it made her the most fearsome of adversaries. Elizabeth had youth on her side, and was possessed of a supple intellect that bore no resemblance to Mary's fixed and uncompromising outlook on life, but these were assets that would not necessarily count for much if it came to a contest between them. Elizabeth must therefore have been heartened when Mary gave her the warmest of welcomes: apparently determined to put the past behind her, the Queen greeted her sister effusively, "even to kissing all her ladies", and when Mary entered London in state on 3 August, Elizabeth rode immediately behind her.[1]

Sadly, the reconciliation was no more than a passing phase. Once the euphoria surrounding her accession had died down, Mary's bitterness welled up afresh for the daughter of the woman who had inflicted so much pain on Catherine of Aragon and herself, and her antagonism towards her sister was only sharpened by the fact that Elizabeth had many "characteristics in which she resembled her mother". To make matters worse, Mary did not accept that the blood tie between them entitled Elizabeth to count on her indulgence, preferring to believe that no such bond existed, and that King Henry had not fathered Elizabeth in the first place. To her intimates, Mary was in the habit of remarking that Elizabeth "had the face and countenance of Mark Smeaton, who was a very handsome man". This was unworthy of the Queen, for unbiased observers reported that Elizabeth resembled Henry VIII much more closely than Mary did herself.[2]

Even at the beginning of the reign, when Mary strove to give Elizabeth the benefit of the doubt, her instinctive distrust of her sister was accentuated by outside forces. Lacking experience in government, and uncertain of the reliability of her English ministers, Mary turned for advice to Simon Renard, the ambassador in England of her cousin, the Emperor Charles V. Right from the start, Renard identified Elizabeth as a serious threat. He realized that it would not do to underestimate her, for whereas the Queen was utterly without guile, Elizabeth was both "clever and sly", and moreover endowed with what he picturesquely described as "a spirit full of enchantment". As yet he did not know how best to deal with her, but he wasted no time in pointing out to the Queen that the presence at court of her heiress presumptive was not necessarily conducive to her security, as Elizabeth "might, out of ambition or being persuaded thereto, conceive some dangerous design and put it to execution by means which it would be difficult to prevent". He was pleased by Mary's reaction, for though at times she could be exasperatingly trusting and naïve, as far as Elizabeth was concerned it was not difficult to arouse her suspicions. Having listened to Renard's warnings, she told the ambassador darkly that "the same considerations had occurred to her".[3]

It was religion, above all else, that poisoned the relations between the two sisters and aroused Mary's ire against Elizabeth. Since her girlhood, Mary had cherished a dream of reclaiming England for the Church of

Rome, and though on her accession she announced she had no wish to coerce anyone in religious matters, her declaration stemmed less .from genuine tolerance than from the belief that no one would oppose the restoration of the ancient faith. As yet Henry VIII's laws formalizing the break with Rome remained on the statute book, but freedom of worship was at once restored to all Catholics. At court, six or seven masses were sung daily, sign of a religious revolution that Mary hoped would ultimately prevail throughout the entire kingdom. Yet the Catholic revival did not proceed so smoothly as the Queen wished. In early August a sermon preached by Mary's chaplain provoked a near-riot in London, while the fact that Elizabeth ostentatiously boycotted the services at the chapel royal emphasized that Protestantism in England would not die of its own accord. In the face of this disagreeable discovery, Mary's commitment to toleration evaporated abruptly. This prompted an almost equally swift change of heart on the part of Elizabeth, for though she had taken care to make her opinions known, she was not prepared to die for them.

This is not to say that she gave up her convictions without a struggle, for in early September the Council received "a very rude response" when they summoned her before them to be harangued about her failure to conform. The lecture nevertheless left Elizabeth in no doubt that the Queen was in earnest, and convinced her that she had no alternative but to submit. Accordingly, a few days later she requested the Queen for a private audience, and when admitted to her sister's presence she fell on her knees and tearfully enquired if Mary's attitude towards her was unfavourably coloured by the difference in their religious outlook. She went on to explain that her spiritual waywardness was the result of her defective upbringing, begging Mary to arrange for her to receive instruction, so that she "might know if her conscience would allow her to be persuaded". The Queen complied, and was delighted to find that her efforts were promptly repaid, for after the briefest of intervals Elizabeth felt able to inform her sister that she had seen the error of her ways.[4]

Mary should have guessed that her sister's soul could not be won so easily, and by 8 September, when Elizabeth attended mass for the first time, it seemed that the convert was already on the verge of a relapse. Having failed to be excused on grounds of illness, Elizabeth "complained loudly all the way to church that her stomach ached, wearing a suffering air", and in the ensuing fortnight her religious observances were perfunctory in the extreme. The Queen, who had rewarded her sister for her conversion by showering her with ornaments and jewels (which Elizabeth had pointedly forborne to wear), began to wonder if she had been duped. A woman of patent sincerity herself, it was beyond her comprehension how anyone's behaviour in a matter relating to salvation could be so inconsistent and contrary. In some perplexity, she begged her sister to tell her frankly if her conversion was genuine, but though Elizabeth earnestly insisted that her attachment to Catholicism owed nothing to "fear, hypocrisy or dissimulation", her assurances left Mary unsatisfied.[5] Unable to move against Elizabeth while she maintained her outward obedience, the Queen's frustration at being saddled with an heiress whose principles were so shifting and uncertain grew more acute every day.

Mary's resentment of her sister found oblique expression when the first Parliament of her reign met in October 1553, and addressed itself to dismantling the legal framework of the English Reformation. In addition to repealing the religious enactments of Edward VI's reign, it passed an act invalidating Henry VIII's divorce from Catherine of Aragon, thus tacitly confirming that Elizabeth was a bastard, and casting a question mark over her right to succeed to the throne. Elizabeth retaliated by being yet more irregular in her attendance at mass, but such a move only convinced the Queen that she was justified in seeking to undermine her rights. Far from showing any disposition to be conciliatory, the French ambassador noted that as the autumn progressed, Mary was becoming more authoritative every day.[6]

In part this new assurance derived from her satisfaction at having pledged herself in marriage to Charles V's eldest son, Philip of Spain, ironically one of the most disastrous decisions of her reign. Mary's subjects did not dispute that she urgently required a husband who could provide her with children and help her with the business of ruling (which was assumed to be beyond her feminine capacity), but they had hoped that she would marry within the realm, for a foreign husband could be expected to subordinate the interests of England to those of his own country. In his final will, indeed, Edward VI had adduced his fear that either of his sisters might marry a foreigner as an additional reason for depriving them of the crown, for "the same stranger . . . would rather adhere and practise to have the laws and customs of his . . . own native country . . . to be practised and put in use within this our realm . . . which would then tend to the utter subversion of the commonwealth of this our realm, which God forbid".[7] Though Edward's will had been rejected, in this clause he had spoken for his people but, as was perhaps natural in a Queen who was herself half-Spanish, Mary underestimated her subjects' fierce insularity. Intent on bringing England back into the fold of her mother's Church, she could think of none fitter than her mother's compatriot to assist her in the task. She said as much to Simon Renard when the latter proposed on Philip's behalf, and having thought the offer over for a fortnight, she accepted it on 29 October. As yet the betrothal was not officially announced, but news of Mary's intentions soon leaked out and was received with widespread consternation.

Having committed herself to marriage with the Prince of Spain, Mary received advice from some quarters that the best way to neutralize Elizabeth would be to find her a Catholic husband as well. The obvious bridegroom was Edward Courtenay, a great-grandson of Edward IV whom Henry VIII had imprisoned when but a child after his father had been convicted of treason. Although it soon emerged that Courtenay's years in captivity had left him with "neither spirit nor experience", he was handsome and well-educated, and when the Queen released him from the Tower on her accession there were widespread hopes that she herself would marry him. Mary was too set upon the Spanish match to give this idea the consideration it deserved, but one of Mary's leading advisers, Lord Paget, advocated the alternative arrangement of bestowing Elizabeth upon Courtenay, which he felt would do much to reconcile public opinion to Mary's own marriage to a foreigner. The proposal did not commend itself to Mary, for though she could hardly avoid recognizing Elizabeth as her heiress presumptive if she promoted a union between her and Courtenay, every day she grew more determined to find a way of excluding her sister from the succession. When they met to discuss the issue, the Queen confided to Paget and Renard "that it would burden her conscience too heavily to allow Elizabeth to succeed, for she only went to mass out of hypocrisy, she had not a single servant or maid of honour who was not a heretic, she talked every day with heretics and lent an ear to all their evil designs, and it would be a disgrace to the kingdom to allow a bastard to succeed".[8]

Courtenay himself was in no haste to offer himself as a husband for Elizabeth. As it happened, he was keen to make a royal match, but he considered the Queen to be an infinitely more eligible bride than her sister, and he failed to realize that Mary's marital sights were fixed elsewhere. Anxious to ingratiate himself with the Queen, he told her sycophantically that if she wished to find him a wife, "let it be rather some simple girl than Elizabeth, who was a heretic, too proud, and of too doubtful lineage on her mother's terms". Despite this, Mary told Simon Renard that she would agree to a marriage between Courtenay and Elizabeth if Charles V thought it advisable, but when the problem was referred to the Emperor he counselled against it.[9]

Her future still unresolved, Elizabeth found herself in an anomalous position at Court. At the beginning of the reign she had taken precedence over all other ladies there, but by late November she frequently found her place usurped by her cousin Margaret, Countess of Lennox, whom Mary would have liked to groom as her successor. Even more worrying was the fact that Mary was only too ready to listen to reports that Elizabeth was intriguing against her. When Renard told the Queen that Elizabeth had had secret consultations with the French ambassador, Mary sent the Earl of Arundel and Lord Paget to tell her sister "that her present unwise conduct was known", and to warn her that if she continued to misbehave, "she might have reason to regret it".[10] On this occasion Elizabeth did not have great difficulty convincing them that they had been misinformed, but the incident demonstrated that the Queen was positively eager to believe ill of her sister.

Relations with Mary had become so strained that Elizabeth thought it best to ask her sister's permission to retire to the country, even though she knew that in her absence ill-wishers would not slacken their efforts to poison the Queen's mind against her. In a vain attempt to guard against this, she obtained an audience with Mary before she left court, and at this she once again affirmed her devotion to the Catholic faith and implored her sister to give her an opportunity to defend herself in person if she should hear anything to Elizabeth's discredit. The Queen for her part put on a show of friendliness, and gave her sister a rich coif of sable as a leaving present, but she did so only because Renard had told her that it would be unwise to let Elizabeth depart for the country in a disaffected mood. In private, Mary remained adamant that Elizabeth would "bring about some great evil unless she is dealt with". Her hostility was too deeply ingrained for her to be much impressed when Elizabeth made a further attempt to endear herself to her sister by requesting her to send ornaments for use in her chapel in the country. Mary despatched the required articles, "as it was for God's service", but the days had gone when a glib display of piety could move her.[11]

Meanwhile, opposition to the Spanish match was steadily gathering force. On 16 November, a deputation from the House of Commons issued a formal request to the Queen to marry an Englishman, and Mary's angry rejection of their petition left little room for doubt that her heart was set on Philip. Ten days later a group of conspirators met, and decided that as parliamentary pressure had failed to deter Mary, they would have to resort to force. In the coming weeks it was agreed that on 18 March 1554 the leaders of the rebellion would effect simultaneous uprisings in various parts of the country with the aim of deposing Mary and setting Elizabeth on the throne. Courtenay's disappointment that the Queen had overlooked him in favour of the Prince of Spain led him to support the venture, the plan being that after the rebellion he would marry Elizabeth and rule the country in conjunction with her.

How much Elizabeth knew of these plans is obscure. She was certainly on friendly terms with one of the principal conspirators, Sir William Pickering, and at the end of October she had aroused comment by having a two-hour discussion with him in private. The French ambassador, whose desire to prevent Mary from marrying one of the King of France's most implacable enemies led him into secret talks with the rebels, also recorded that Elizabeth was "*fort familier*" with another of the ringleaders, Sir James Crofts, and the latter even convinced the ambassador that Elizabeth had agreed to move further away from London when the rebellion broke out, so that Mary would be unable to take her hostage. Possibly Crofts was bluffing in order to persuade the ambassador that it would be worthwhile giving the plot his active support, but even if there is no proof that Elizabeth had actually entered into a league with the conspirators, the evidence suggests that she was aware of their intentions. When on the throne, indeed, she effectively admitted as much, for in 1566 she told a parliamentary delegation that her reluctance to name a successor stemmed from her experiences in Mary's reign, which had convinced her that the "second person" in the realm could not avoid becoming the pawn of malcontents and plotters. In that very session, she continued, there were members sitting who had sought to make her a party to their misdeeds. "I had great occasions to hearken to their motions . . . " she noted sarcastically, "Were it not for my honour, their knavery should be known".[12] The implication was that her involvement in these intrigues was both peripheral and unwilling, but she did not pretend that she had managed to remain completely aloof.

Certainly when the rebellion commenced she made no move to assist it, but the possibility remains that if the insurgents had not been forced into premature action they would have succeeded in committing Elizabeth to their cause. The rising had originally been scheduled to take place in mid-March 1554, but by the beginning of the year the Government was already on the conspirators' trail. When the Lord Chancellor questioned Courtenay on 21 January, they panicked, for the young man could not be relied upon to preserve silence under pressure. Accordingly the timetable was hurriedly brought forward. On 22 January, Sir James Crofts rode to Ashridge, where Elizabeth was staying, apparently hoping to persuade her to move to remote Donnington Castle, where the Government would be unable to molest her. His mission was doomed to failure: having suffered from intermittent bad health for the last five years, Elizabeth had recently been assailed by what was probably a form of kidney disease known as nephritis.[13] As a result, she was suffering from pains in her head and arms, and her whole body was swollen, and if she had ever felt any inclination to throw her lot in with rebels, her illness effectively sapped her enthusiasm. The same night Sir James left Ashridge for Wales, while Elizabeth remained on her sickbed.

Despite this the rebellion went ahead, but in Devon and Leicestershire the flame of insurrection was quickly snuffed out. Only in Kent, where Sir Thomas Wyatt raised his standard in revolt on 25 January, did the rising assume a serious aspect. A small band of troops sent by the Government to attack the rebels was scattered at Rochester, leaving Wyatt free to march on London.

On 26 January the Queen had reacted to news of the rebellion by ordering Elizabeth to London, assuring her that she did so only because she thought her at risk while the countryside was in ferment. Yet though the summons was couched in friendly terms, Mary also mentioned that she understood Elizabeth was thinking of moving to Donnington Castle, a well-informed comment that showed that her concern for Elizabeth's safety was not as overriding as she pretended.[14] In the circumstances, Mary's assurances that her sister would "be most heartily welcome" sounded a little thin, and Elizabeth was not eager to put them to the test. Seizing on her genuine ill health as a welcome excuse, she sent word that she was in no condition to travel.

In London Elizabeth's reluctance to come to court was interpreted as a fresh sign of her guilt, and the case against her received further impetus when the French ambassador's postbag was intercepted and its contents were found to include a copy of a letter that Elizabeth had recently sent to the Queen. Exactly how he obtained this has never been established, but to Mary and her advisers it seemed obvious that Elizabeth herself had supplied him with the incriminating document.[15] For the moment, the urgent necessity of suppressing the rebellion occupied their full attention, but on 7 February an attempt by Wyatt to take London ended in ignominious failure, and with his arrest the authorities resumed their enquiries against Elizabeth.

This time there was no possibility that Elizabeth could wriggle out of the summons to London. Three councillors were despatched to Ashridge with instructions to take her away, unless the doctors who accompanied them confirmed that it would be literally fatal for her to move. On 11 February the councillors reported that Elizabeth was certainly unwell but, "all excuses set apart", travel was not out of the question. Despite Elizabeth's objections that she could not make the journey "without peril of life", she was obliged to set out with them the following day, and though her health was indeed so frail that they could only make very slow progress, the party arrived in London on 22 February. Pale and swollen-faced, Elizabeth presented a pitiable sight as she was carried through the city on her litter, but Simon Renard, for one, felt no compassion. On the contrary, he believed that Elizabeth's physical prostration was the product of a guilty conscience, and he even gave credit to a fanciful rumour that she was bearing an illegitimate child. He felt that punishment rather than sympathy was what she deserved, and he was relieved to note that the Government seemed intent on enacting a fearful revenge on the rebels, for all over London decomposing corpses dangled from hastily erected gallows.[16] Furthermore, on 12 February there had occurred the execution of Lady Jane Grey, who had been imprisoned since the beginning of the reign, and whose life had been forfeited because her father had been foolish enough to support Wyatt. It was Renard's fervent hope that Elizabeth would shortly suffer the same fate.

Elizabeth was taken to Whitehall, and for three weeks she remained in virtual isolation while the Council did their best to extract confessions incriminating her from the ringleaders of the rebellion. On 25 February, Sir John Bourne "travailed" with Wyatt "touching the Lady Elizabeth", and when Sir James Crofts was brought up to London from Wales (where he had been arrested in his bed) he too was "marvellously tossed and examined" upon the same subject. Despite the searching nature of these enquiries, nothing conclusive was proved against Elizabeth. It was true that Wyatt admitted that he had sent her a letter begging her to "get as far from the city as she could, the rather for her safety from strangers", and he said that she had sent her servant, Sir William St Loe, to tell him "that she did thank him much for his good will and she would do as she would see cause". Fortunately for Elizabeth, when Sir William St Loe was confronted with this story he was "nothing at all abashed", and "stoutly denied" that there was any truth in it. Another of the conspirators, Lord Russell, confessed to having delivered letters from Wyatt to Elizabeth, but no document was ever uncovered that could have substantiated his evidence. Elizabeth was also lucky in that several of those who might have possessed damaging information against her had fled to France and were never questioned. The Queen was firmly convinced that Elizabeth was guilty – bitterly she told Renard that her sister's character "was just what she had always believed it to be" – but in the absence of concrete proof she was advised by the majority of the Council that it would be inadvisable to try and convict Elizabeth of treason.[17]

This was not the view of Mary's Lord Chancellor, Bishop Stephen Gardiner, a crusty and outspoken prelate whose ultra-conservative views on religion led him to regard Elizabeth with bitter enmity. Even before the rebellion, he had advised Mary to find some excuse to clap Elizabeth in the Tower. Now he would have liked to use this opportunity to rid the realm permanently of the Queen's troublesome sister, for as he told Renard, "he had no hope of seeing the kingdom at peace" for as long as she lived. Elizabeth was fortunate that the Chancellor was hampered from pressing the case against her with full vigour by the fact that he was extremely fond of Courtenay, and he was anxious that the young man should not land in serious trouble as a result of his part in the conspiracy. Though Gardiner had done his best to suppress the evidence against Courtenay, he had been unable to prevent him from being sent to the Tower, and as much remained to link the young man with the plotters, it was difficult for Gardiner to convince his colleagues that Elizabeth should be prosecuted for treason if Courtenay was to be spared. Nevertheless, the Chancellor was at least able to ensure that Elizabeth was imprisoned. A majority of the Council would have preferred it if she had been confined to some nobleman's house in the country, but none of them volunteered to act as her custodian, and as a result Gardiner managed to persuade them that the Tower was the only alternative.[18] Nor was this an insignificant victory, for once Elizabeth was there, Gardiner had hopes that he would be able to uncover more evidence that would establish her guilt beyond doubt.

Elizabeth was informed of the Council's decision on 16 March, and the following morning the Marquis of Winchester and the Earl of Sussex presented themselves at her apartments to escort her to the Tower. During the tense weeks when Mary had been pondering her fate, this was the outcome that Elizabeth had dreaded, and her situation appeared all the more perilous because it was logical to assume that her entrance to the Tower would merely be the preliminary to a formal trial. Desperately she clung to the hope that Mary would relent if she was allowed to see her, and she begged the two peers that she might write her sister a request to that effect. Winchester, who knew well enough that Mary's resolution was inflexible, would have denied her this boon, but Sussex had the foresight to remember that one day his prisoner might be his queen, and was anxious to fall in with her wishes in all but essentials. Accordingly Elizabeth was furnished with pen and paper, and she sat down to compose the letter on which she believed her life depended.

Naturally the letter contained a sweeping affirmation of her innocence, for she swore to the Queen that she had "never practised, counselled, nor consented to anything that might be prejudicial to your person in any way, or dangerous to the state by any means". She also rebutted the specific allegations against her: "As for the traitor Wyatt", she declared, "he might peradventure write me a letter, but on my faith I never received any from him. And as for the copy of my letter sent to the French King, I pray God confound me eternally if ever I sent him word, message, token or letter, by any means. And to this truth I will stand in till my death" She knew however, that these assurances would carry little weight, and that she would never gain her object unless she struck a more personal note. Desperately hoping that her sister's sensitive conscience could not fail to be moved if she conveyed the enormity of condemning her unheard, she reminded Mary of her promise never to punish her "without answer and due proof", and she begged that the Queen would not rely on her councillors to administer justice to her own flesh and blood. "I have heard in my time of many cast away for want of coming to their prince", she urged, citing here the case of Thomas Seymour, whose untimely end might have been avoided if he had been permitted access to his brother. "These persons are not to be compared to your Majesty", she hastily added, "yet I pray God that evil persuasions persuade not one sister against the other, and all for that they have heard false report." Coming to the end of her letter, she saw that she had left more than two thirds of a page blank, an inviting space that her enemies could use to insert a forged admission of guilt.

Determined to leave nothing to chance, she carefully scored across the page.[19]

Without wishing to appear too presumptuous or craven, Elizabeth had sought desperately to kindle in the Queen some spark of sisterly feeling, but this was a futile exercise. Far from being forced to take harsh action by her councillors, it was they who had restrained her, while Elizabeth's moving plea that Mary should refrain from inconsiderately severing the natural tie between them could have little effect on one who refused to accept that Elizabeth was her kindred. When shown the letter, Mary was merely angry that her orders had not been promptly carried out. It had been intended to transport Elizabeth to the Tower by river, and now the tide had turned, making it impossible to employ this mode of transport. As a result Elizabeth had to be kept at Whitehall until the Thames was navigable again, but though she had gained a day's respite, in essence her situation was unchanged.

The next day, 18 March, was Palm Sunday, ironically enough the date originally chosen for the outbreak of rebellion. While the citizens were at church, Elizabeth was conveyed down-river in pouring rain, the sombre weather forming an apt setting for the tragedy she feared was to be enacted. But though disgraced and in danger of her life, she did not give way to abject terror. A lifetime in the public eye had instilled in her the instincts of a performer, and even now, when cast in a role so little to her taste, her dramatic flair did not desert her. Intent on portraying herself as the victim of an injustice, she played out an affecting scene on the very threshold of the Tower. This could not long delay the moment when the doors clanged behind her, but nonetheless had its value as a symbolic protest.

The boat docked at the Tower's Privy Stairs after an unnerving river passage in which they had only narrowly avoided shipwreck when negotiating the rapids under London Bridge. For Elizabeth, however, the journey had come to an end too soon. While Sussex and Winchester clambered ashore, relieved at the prospect of handing their prisoner over to the Lieutenant of the Tower, she remained obstinately on board, balefully surveying the serried ranks of guardsmen who were drawn up for her reception. When she finally agreed to disembark, she paused to proclaim, "Here landeth as true a subject, being prisoner, as ever landed at these stairs", and then, to the consternation of all present, she plonked herself down on the damp flagstones. The Lieutenant of the Tower stepped forward with a tactful plea that she come in out of the rain, only to be told, "It is better sitting here than in a worse place". The exhibition was too much for Elizabeth's gentleman usher, one of the few servants who had been permitted to accompany her from Whitehall, and he broke down in sobs. At this, however, his unpredictable mistress underwent another lightning change of mood. Wishing her sit-down strike to be interpreted as a demonstration against wrongful arrest rather than as a gesture of despair, she told him haughtily that "She knew her truth to be such that no man would have cause to weep for her". Thus, having regained the initiative as far as the difficult circumstances permitted, she swept into the Tower.[20]

The pantomime was not wasted on the onlookers, whose obedience to the Queen had to be balanced against a prudent concern for the future. There were murmurs of assent when Sussex urged those present to handle the captive with restraint, for undue severity might one day have the most unfortunate consequences. As he somewhat superfluously reminded his listeners, Elizabeth "was the King our master's daughter, and therefore let us use such dealing that we may answer it hereafter ... for just dealing is always answerable".[21]

Sussex's caution was shared by many of the Queen's leading advisers, for it soon emerged that as far as Elizabeth was concerned, the appeasers on the Council had gained the upper hand. In the Tower she was again questioned, but Gardiner's hopes of obtaining a conviction were frustrated by his colleagues' evident reluctance to press her too hard. When Mary consulted her judges, they too were emphatic that the evidence against her sister was inadequate to secure a verdict of guilty if she was charged with treason. Renard sorrowfully noted that he believed that even if more evidence did come to light, it would not be acted upon. One reason for this was that Elizabeth had a powerful protector in the shape of her great-uncle, Lord Admiral William Howard, and the Queen could not afford to alienate this influential magnate by taking treason proceedings against her sister. On 11 April 1554, Sir Thomas Wyatt was executed, and Elizabeth's position became still more secure when he declared from the scaffold that she had had no foreknowledge of the rising. It was true that the clergyman who was attending Wyatt on the scaffold made a clumsy attempt to contradict his statement, but the condemned man's last words naturally made a profound impression on the watching crowd.[22]

By mid-April, Elizabeth's terms of confinement in the Tower had become less rigorous, and she was permitted to take exercise under strict supervision in the Tower Garden. Naturally the Queen remained suspicious of her sister: when she heard that a five-year-old child regularly presented Elizabeth with flowers during her morning walks, Mary leapt to the conclusion that Courtenay was using this channel to send her secret messages. At the Queen's insistence, the harmless practice was discontinued. Yet however much Mary might deplore the situation, she had to accept that strong measures against her sister were impossible: execution was plainly out of the question, and though Gardiner was optimistic that Parliament could be prevailed upon to pass an act disinheriting Elizabeth, Mary reluctantly listened to Lord Paget's urgent advice that it would be wiser to dissolve the assembly than to press ahead with such a contentious measure.[23]

In the circumstances it was difficult to justify keeping Elizabeth in prison much longer. Mary still refused to accept that her sister was innocent, but because there was no proof to the contrary she agreed that the plan of placing Elizabeth under house arrest in the country should be revived. As before, no one volunteered to act as Elizabeth's custodian, but this time the Council solved the problem by thrusting the unwelcome responsibility on Sir Henry Bedingfield, a conscientious Norfolk squire whose high sense of duty and utter lack of imagination prevented him from evading the task.

On 5 May 1554, Bedingfield presented himself at the Tower accompanied by a hundred soldiers, and this fresh influx of armed men led Elizabeth to fear the worst. Anxiously she enquired "whether the Lady Jane's scaffold were taken away or no?" and though she was assured there was no cause for alarm, she still could not accept that her life was no longer at risk. Even when she learnt that she was to be removed to Woodstock, in Oxfordshire, where the Queen owned a damp and crumbling manor house, she remained nervous that once away from the capital she would be done away with by stealth.[24] In this, however, she did Bedingfield an injustice, for Sir Henry was no assassin, and his instincts were bureaucratic rather than blood-thirsty. It was not long before Elizabeth's fears for her life were replaced by frustration at being guarded by a man who prided himself on his lack of initiative, and who was not only devoid of charm himself, but impervious to the quality in others.

It soon emerged that Elizabeth's spell in the Tower had done nothing to diminish her popularity with the people, for on 19 May, when she set off for Woodstock in the company of Bedingfield and his men, the citizens of London turned out in force to give her a rousing send-off. From Sir Henry's point of view, this was a bad beginning, and for him at least, the four-day journey proved to be a nightmare. At Richmond Palace, where the party spent the first night, an intruder was discovered skulking in the grounds, and sent to London for questioning. There he managed to convince the Council that he had only wished to present Elizabeth with some apples, but Bedingfield had been right to be suspicious, for in reality the man was an agent of the French ambassador, intent on finding out whether Elizabeth was to be married to an enemy of his country. At least Sir Henry could congratulate himself that the incident had proved the efficiency of his security arrangements, but on subsequent stages of the journey he could not prevent Elizabeth from being showered with attentions which were hardly sinister, but which to him were none the less unwelcome. As the party left Windsor, the Eton boys came running out to catch a glimpse of Elizabeth, and villages all along the route were thronged by countrywomen who pressed forward to throw cakes, wafers and bunches of herbs into Elizabeth's litter. Bedingfield did his best to discourage the popular excitement, imprisoning four men who rang the bells as Elizabeth passed through Aston, but he could hardly punish all the onlookers who cried "God save your Grace!" from the roadside. He noted sourly that even at the gates of Woodstock, a small crowd of well-wishers had gathered to acclaim his charge.[25]

Once installed at Woodstock, Sir Henry was alarmed to discover that the house possessed only three doors that could be locked, for though in general the most unimaginative of men, on this particular assignment he saw conspiracy everywhere. He was even more perturbed when he received a letter from the Queen setting out the terms of his commission. He found from this that he was expected to perform a delicate balancing act, whereby he guarded Elizabeth closely, and yet nevertheless had "regard to use her in such good and honourable sort as may be agreeable to our honour and her estate and degree". Such imprecise directions were anathema to Sir Henry, who liked to operate according to a fixed set of rules, and he made it plain that he considered the guidelines which were supposed to govern his conduct to be woefully inadequate. It was all very well for Mary to state airily that he must prevent Elizabeth from having "conference with any suspected person out of his hearing", but what did she mean by the phrase "suspected person"? If Elizabeth's personal attendants were included in this category, he could not guarantee that he would overhear every word that they exchanged with their mistress. Somewhat wearily, the Council replied on the Queen's behalf that "as for stranger, ye must foresee that no persons suspect have any conference with her at all; and yet to permit such strangers whom ye shall think honest ... to speak with her in your hearing only".[26] Hardly surprisingly, Sir Henry did not feel that this clarified the matter satisfactorily. In his view, the Council were treating the situation altogether too casually, and he was relieved when an incident occurred that prompted them to be more watchful.

One of Bedingfield's many worries was that Elizabeth's cofferer, Thomas Parry, was lurking in the neighbourhood, justifying his sojourn at the Bull at Woodstock on the grounds that, as Elizabeth had to pay for her keep at the Palace, he had to be on hand to supply the necessary funds. When Parry took it upon himself to forward Elizabeth two books from his son-in-law, John Fortescue, Bedingfield seized the offending volumes and sent them up to London for inspection by the Council. Although the Council were unable to find "any matter of suspicion in the said books", they praised Sir Henry's "diligence and circumspection", and agreed that unauthorized actions of this sort indicated that Elizabeth's friends would go to great lengths to communicate with her by stealth. On second thoughts they accepted Sir Henry's recommendation that Elizabeth should be permitted to see no one other than those servants that the Council had sent to look after her at Woodstock.[27]

Right from the start Sir Henry had found Elizabeth an awkward prisoner: she had complained about the four rooms at the Palace allocated for her use, and tried to persuade him that she was allowed to exercise in the park as well as the gardens, expressing herself so tortuously that Bedingfield was often at a loss to know "if her meaning go with her words, whereof God only is judge". Yet try as she might, Elizabeth could not outwit Bedingfield, whose habit of automatically referring all points at issue back to the Council gave him the upper hand in the contest between them. Elizabeth's irritation at being in the grip of this maddening pedant only grew more acute when she learnt that he was doing all in his power to isolate her still further from the outside world. Already chafing under Sir Henry's irksome tutelage, her vexation appreciably increased when one of her favourite servants, Elizabeth Sands, was dismissed on the orders of the Queen, who deemed her to be "a person of evil opinion". Elizabeth was still smarting at her removal when Bedingfield infuriated her again by refusing to supply her with an English Bible, a work that his devout Catholicism caused him to regard with extreme suspicion. He justified his refusal on the grounds that Elizabeth understood Latin so well that he imagined that she would take greater pleasure reading books in that language. With Sir Henry, such ponderous jocularity passed for wit, but he perceived it was a sally that Elizabeth "took not in good part".[28]

Exasperated beyond measure, Elizabeth demanded to write to the Queen. Permission was duly obtained, but in the event the letter only worsened her situation, for it too plainly bore the marks of her resentment. Mary was offended not only that her sister seized the opportunity to reaffirm her innocence, but also that Elizabeth addressed her throughout as "'You', without qualifying her by the title of Highness or Majesty". In her reply, the Queen sharply reiterated her grounds for suspecting Elizabeth, who had been used, she said, with "more clemency and favour ... than in like matters hath been accustomed". She stated that in future she did not wish to be "molested by such her disguise and colourable letters".[29]

The Queen's total repudiation of her appeal came as a blow to Elizabeth, but far worse was the fact that Bedingfield interpreted Mary's ban on further correspondence as applying even to letters to the Council, and refused to let Elizabeth write to them again. Such a prohibition, in Elizabeth's view, was contrary to her rights, but when she passionately objected that this treatment left her "in worse case than the worst prisoner in Newgate", Sir Henry remained as impassive as ever. His unrelenting attitude drove Elizabeth to total despair, and she bitterly concluded that she would have to resign herself to continuing "this life without all hope worldly, wholly resting to the truth of my cause".[30]

Her depression was intensified by the return of the ailment that had troubled her earlier in the year, leaving her face and body swollen and sore. When informed of her condition, the Council refused to authorize a visit from the Queen's physicians, advocating that doctors from Oxford should be consulted instead. Their recommendations were given short shrift by Elizabeth. Haughtily she exclaimed, "I am not minded to make any stranger privy to the estate of my body", and rather than submit to such indignities, she went without treatment until the Council relented and sent two doctors and a surgeon to bleed her.[31]

So the tedious weeks went by. On 7 July the Council lifted Bedingfield's embargo on further letters, but when Elizabeth responded with a request that she might come to court and see her sister, her plea went unanswered. There was nothing for it but to wait, which she did with increasing ill grace: Bedingfield was pained to note that though she regularly took communion according to Catholic rites, she remained obstinately silent in that part of the church service where her chaplain prayed for the Queen. For weeks Sir Henry resisted her entreaties that she might be permitted to submit yet another petition to the Council ("And her Grace sayeth she is sure your Lordships will smile in your sleeves when ye know this my scrupulousness", he reported ruefully), and it was only in mid-September that she was able to send the desired missive. Once again, however, Elizabeth's forceful demand for justice did her little good: a further month elapsed before the Queen herself replied that she found her sister's complaints "somewhat strange", adding coldly that Elizabeth need not worry about being neglected, as "we be not unmindful of her cause".[32]

Despite this cryptic assurance, Mary was in fact too preoccupied to devote much thought to her sister. On 20 July 1554, Philip of Spain had landed in England, and six days later he and the Queen had married in Winchester Cathedral. Subjected to the most appalling emotional deprivation since her teens, Mary was pathetically enamoured of her new husband, and if Philip was less enthusiastic at being tied to a woman nine years his senior, a member of his entourage noted proudly that for the moment he was able "to pass over the fact that she is no good from the point of view of fleshly sensuality".[33] By early November, Mary believed that she was pregnant, and her happiness seemed complete when on 30 November the newly arrived Papal Legate, Cardinal Pole, stood up in Parliament to absolve the nation for its repudiation of Rome. Shriven of its wholesale apostasy, England could once again be restored to the authority of the Pope.

Reunion with Rome nevertheless brought with it a terrible corollary, for Parliament revived the ancient laws authorizing the Church to extirpate heresy by burning offenders at the stake. In February 1555 the holocaust began, and before Mary's death almost three hundred executions had been carried out, sixty of the victims being women. The persecution inspired intense revulsion, not least because the mode of death was so terrible. All too often, a damp or badly constructed faggot pile ensured that the victims were not speedily consumed, and instead literally roasted over a slow fire. Scenes of horror such as the execution of Bishop Hooper, who took nearly three-quarters of an hour to die, pleading with the onlookers to fan the flames so as to put him out of his torment, impressed themselves on the public mind, and with the aid of such skilful propagandists as John Foxe, passed into Protestant folklore. In an age where cruel punishments were relatively commonplace, the physical sufferings of the martyrs cannot wholly account for the sympathy they excited, but many people who would not neccessarily have objected to the burning of a few extremists, were sickened by persecution on such an unprecedented scale. There was indignation too at the way the ecclesiastical authorities conducted the enquiries in the Church courts, delving into the consciences of those who were brought before them, and sifting their opinions on the eucharist and sacraments. If found guilty, the accused (who for the most part were simple men and women from the southern counties) were handed over to the secular arm for punishment, but the role of the clergy in the proceedings was particularly resented, and it was ironic that the campaign against heresy, which was intended to purify and strengthen the Church, fuelled the nation's anti-clerical tendencies.

Abhorrence of the heresy laws was all the greater because of the widespread conviction that it was the influence of the Spaniards at court that accounted for the virulency with which they were enforced, but the English tendency to blame foreigners for all unpleasant occurrences could not prevent the ultimate responsibility being laid at Mary's door. Nor was this unjust, for the stream of directives that emanated from her, urging both civil and ecclesiastical authorities to implement their powers to the full, does much to confirm that it was she who was the driving force behind the persecution. Unable to extend mercy to those whom she believed had contravened God's law, she was convinced that her crusade was necessary for her own salvation. In fact, it only managed to bring her immortality of a different sort in the form of the dreadful nickname "Bloody Mary", and to forge in the nation's consciousness the fearful link between Catholicism and cruelty that was to make "No Popery!" such a potent cry for generations to come.

When it came to dealing with her sister, Mary felt none of the inspired sense of certainty that supported her in the fight against heresy. Gardiner had continued to advocate that Elizabeth be formally declared a bastard, but apart from the difficulties of piloting such an unpopular measure through Parliament, Mary's husband Philip had cogent reasons for opposing the move until Mary had managed to produce an heir. It was possible that neither Mary nor the child she was bearing would survive the delivery, and if Elizabeth had already been declared ineligible for the throne, the French King would certainly press the claim of the youthful Mary Queen of Scots, who had been betrothed to his eldest son at the age of five and sent to live in France. If she inherited the throne, England would become little more than a satellite of France, and Philip could never agree to any action that might bring about a state of affairs so utterly disastrous for Spain.

Another option under consideration was to send Elizabeth abroad, like her fellow suspect in Wyatt's rebellion, Edward Courtenay, who went into voluntary exile in Brussels soon after his release from confinement in 1555. Philip's aunt, Mary of Hungary, offered to accommodate Elizabeth, but the knowledge that it would annoy the English if Elizabeth was forced into exile had made Mary dither. By the spring of 1555 Philip thought it wisest to defer a decision, advocating instead that Elizabeth should be brought to Court to await the Queen's confinement. A macabre logic lay behind this policy, for Philip wished to know that he could count upon Elizabeth's protection if Mary's sudden death left him an unpopular widower in a foreign land.

On 17 April Bedingfield received instructions to bring Elizabeth to Hampton Court, but when Elizabeth arrived at the palace, she soon discovered that her long ordeal was not over. It was three weeks before Mary could bring herself to see the sister whom in her heart she still believed to be guilty, delaying their meeting in the forlorn hope that Elizabeth would break down under the suspense and admit that the Queen's suspicions were justified. Mary even sent Gardiner and three other councillors to tell Elizabeth that, if she confessed, "Her Majesty would be good to her", but having kept silence for so long, it was hardly likely that Elizabeth would now succumb to such blandishments. "Better for me to lie in prison for the truth than to be abroad and suspected of my prince", she told the Chancellor (or at least so John Foxe claimed in what may have been no more than an imaginative reconstruction of these events), utterly unmoved by Gardiner's warning that the Queen would not set her free until she had been more forthcoming. After another week had passed, in which Elizabeth showed no sign of being so obliging as to incriminate herself, Mary had reluctantly to accept defeat. At ten o' clock one evening Elizabeth was suddenly summoned to her sister's presence and conducted by torchlight to the Queen's apartments.[34]

Although Mary had been prevailed upon to relent thus far, the ensuing interview proved that she had not acted in a true spirit of reconciliation. When Elizabeth went down on her knees in humble obeisance, Mary cut short her protestations of loyalty with the bitter observation, "You will not confess your offence but stand stoutly in your truth. I pray God it may so fall out." Elizabeth's grave insistence that, if it happened otherwise, she would not look for mercy only provoked Mary further. In some irritation the Queen sneered that before long Elizabeth would doubtless be complaining that she had been wrongfully punished. She was not mollified when Elizabeth replied that she would not say so to the Queen, as this scarcely amounted to a denial. Sharply Mary demanded whether Elizabeth intended to say so to others, but Elizabeth was not to be drawn, and merely returned a demure negative. She was, she repeated, the Queen's "true subject, not only from the beginning hitherto, but for ever, as long as life lasteth". To Mary such assurances were mere empty verbiage, and she saw no point in prolonging the meaningless exchange. Having brought herself to utter a "few comfortable words" to her sister, she sent Elizabeth back to her apartments.[35]

Even now Elizabeth found that her rehabilitation was far from complete, for during the next few weeks she was obliged to remain in her quarters. There was no official injunction against her receiving visitors, but the majority of courtiers stayed away, for at a time when it appeared that the regime was to be consolidated by the birth of an heir, few risked incurring the Queen's displeasure by friendly attentions to her sister. As the royal pregnancy dragged on, tension mounted, and though on 30 April an unfounded rumour that the Queen had given birth to a son led to spontaneous celebrations in the capital, the truth was that Mary showed no signs of going into labour. Three more months passed, in which the midwives sought to explain the delay on the grounds that Mary must have miscalculated the date of conception, but by the beginning of August the pretence could no longer be sustained. On 3 August the Queen tacitly acknowledged that she had mistaken her condition when she left Hampton Court, where her lying-in was supposed to have taken place, and went to the hunting lodge of Oatlands.

Mary's grief at the débâcle was accentuated by the departure abroad of Philip, who felt that he was now entitled to a respite from a marriage that he had only undertaken out of duty, and which so far had not repaid the sacrifice. Before he left, however, he did his best to lessen the rift between the Queen and her sister, taking the pragmatic view that while Elizabeth was his wife's heiress presumptive, Mary would be unwise to antagonize her gratuitously. As a result Elizabeth began to receive better treatment: on 23 August she was among those who saw Philip embark from Greenwich, and though the Queen had insisted that she travel there by boat so that she could not be cheered on the road out of London, the fact that Elizabeth had been permitted to be present at all was a significant concession. From the continent, Philip maintained his efforts to promote harmony at court. In September the French ambassador noted that Elizabeth evidently still enjoyed "a good share in the favour of the said King", as Philip sent Mary frequent letters urging her to use her sister well. Mary did her best to comply, endeavouring when she saw Elizabeth "to receive her with every sort of graciousness and honour", but her true feelings were too strong to be disguised, and the deception fooled nobody.[36] Despite Philip's efforts, the atmosphere at court remained tense, and the pressure was only alleviated in October, when Elizabeth obtained the Queen's permission to retire to Hatfield with her household.

It was vain to hope that rural seclusion could bring tranquillity, for however much Elizabeth tried to distance herself from the tangled thicket of Marian politics, her position ensured that trouble stuck to her like burrs. By December 1555, another plot was forming, the so-called Dudley conspiracy which like Wyatt's rebellion had as its aim the substitution of Elizabeth for Mary on the throne. As a preliminary to rebellion, it was planned to raise money by robbing the Exchequer, but this operation had not yet been carried out when in early March 1556 one of the conspirators revealed what he knew of the project to Cardinal Pole. Within a fortnight, the majority of his confederates were in the Tower, and though under interrogation none of them said anything to suggest that Elizabeth was personally involved in the plot, the fact that she was the destined beneficiary of the rising led the authorities to mount a search of her London house.

Suspicions mounted when a secret cabinet, said to belong to Kat Ashley, was uncovered and found to contain "several papers, portraits, paintings and other defamatory libels, to the great dishonour and vituperation of the Queen and her husband ... together with all the bishops and ecclesiastics of her kingdom". In early May Mistress Ashley was arrested at Hatfield and taken to the Tower, as was Elizabeth's Italian master, Baptista Castiglione, who had been briefly imprisoned the previous year on suspicion of having circulated subversive literature. Castiglione was adamant that, on the one occasion he had visited London that year, his errand had not been treason but buying lute strings for Elizabeth. Kat Ashley likewise disclaimed all knowledge of the rebels' proceedings. She maintained that she had never been disloyal to Mary, insisting that Elizabeth's "love and truth is such to her Highness ... that if she might prove me corrupt but in thought to her Highness, I am sure she would never see me again".[37] Mary might have had difficulty accepting these assurances at face-value, but even so, Mrs Ashley had regained her freedom by October 1556, though she was not permitted to rejoin Elizabeth at Hatfield.

Another member of Elizabeth's household, Francis Verney, found himself in more serious trouble when he too was arrested in connection with the Dudley conspiracy. In June 1556 he was convicted of treason and sentenced to death, but even he was subsequently pardoned. Furthermore, no attempt was made to link Elizabeth with his delinquencies, for Mary was now too demoralized and unpopular to risk unwarranted action against her sister. Instead, the Queen sent her a diamond ring, declaring that she believed Elizabeth to be "so wise and prudent that she would not wish to undertake anything to the prejudice of her Majesty". She suggested that her sister rejoin her at Court, but knowing that these friendly overtures proceeded less from affection than weakness, Elizabeth unceremoniously rejected the invitation. Mary would have liked to punish her for her insolence by throwing her in the Tower, but her fears that such a move would antagonize the Council and provoke a popular uprising forced her to desist. The only action that she felt able to take was to send to Hatfield Sir Thomas Pope, "a rich and grave gentleman", who was deputed to keep an eye on Elizabeth.[38] Even this, however, was no hardship for Elizabeth, for Sir Thomas was a man of learning and sensitivity who had recently founded Trinity College, Oxford, and a shared interest in scholarship enabled him and his charge to live together without friction in the four months he remained at Hatfield.

It was Sir Thomas who informed Elizabeth at the end of July 1556 of the collapse of yet another rising against Mary, this time led by an adventurer named Cleobury, who had proclaimed Elizabeth "and her beloved bedfellow Courtenay" King and Queen in Essex. Elizabeth was fulsome in her protestations of horror. "It had been my part, above the rest, to bewail such things, though my name had not been in them", she wrote to Mary in righteous indignation, "Yet much it vexed me that the devil oweth me such a hate as to put me in any part of his mischievous instigations."[39] Whether the Queen derived much comfort from this curious screed is open to doubt; perhaps she sourly reflected that Elizabeth had little incentive to dabble in wild intrigues now that her future seemed comparatively secure.

It was the nightmarish prospect of the Francophile Mary Queen of Scots astride the English throne that still deterred Philip from cheating Elizabeth of her inheritance. For a time he hoped to circumvent the problem by persuading his wife to have him crowned, for as an anointed king he felt he would have more chance of forcing through an amendment to his marriage treaty to the effect that he could continue to reign if Mary died childless. Poor Mary would have been only too pleased to have set a date for the coronation, but in view of the fact that the mere rumour that she was contemplating such a step had ensured that the Parliamentary session of November 1555 had been unco-operative and unruly, and had been a contributory factor to the Dudley conspiracy, she felt it to be out of the question.

This being so, Elizabeth's accession appeared more and more of an inevitability, and Philip concluded that it would be statesmanlike to guard against an eventuality that he could not prevent. If Elizabeth could be induced to marry a member of his family or one of their allies, it was less likely that, when on the throne, she would reverse her sister's religious policy or enter into alliance with France, a prospect that Philip particularly dreaded. A number of potential bridegrooms had already been put forward, including Philip's nephew, Archduke Ferdinand, and it had even been suggested that Elizabeth could be betrothed to Philip's eleven-year-old son by his first marriage, Don Carlos. A more practical candidate, however, was Emmanuel Philibert, Duke of Savoy, who had been deprived of his inheritance by the French and looked to the Habsburgs for redress. True, Elizabeth had so far shown little enthusiasm for a union of this sort – the Venetian ambassador heard that when the subject was raised, she "said plainly that she will not marry even were they to give her the King's son, or find any other greater prince" – but pressure had yet to be applied, and there was reason to hope that Elizabeth would not reject outright the match with Emmanuel Philibert. Three years before, Renard had reported that she had sent a cousin on her mother's side to visit the Duke, and he had brought back "a report so favourable that it ... awakened feelings of love and hope in the Lady Elizabeth".[40]

If so, it soon emerged that the feelings had been of very short duration. At the end of November 1556, Elizabeth was summoned to London to see the Queen, who received her "very graciously and familiarly" in the evident hope that her sister would respond by falling in with the plans to wed her to Emmanuel Philibert. Yet when the matter was broached, Elizabeth refused even to consider the proposal, telling the Queen proudly that "the afflictions suffered by her were such that they had ... ridded her of any wish for a husband".[41] Furious at her defiance, on 3 December Mary sent her back to Hatfield in disgrace.

Henceforth, Mary ceased to work for the Savoy match. She had indeed only initially supported the idea out of obedience to her husband, for any plan that entailed recognizing Elizabeth as her successor aroused her instinctive distaste. Having steeled herself to make her sister what she believed to be a very favourable offer, she was outraged at its haughty rejection, and resolved not to do as much again. Instead, she reverted to the hope that Elizabeth could be struck from the succession altogether, a proposal that by now was utterly untenable. Less than a fortnight after Elizabeth had returned to Hatfield, the French ambassador received intelligence that "from one day to another Madame Elizabeth gains new supporters, even among the Lords of the Council, the majority of whom ... today belong to her", but this was a trend that Mary determinedly ignored. Though she accepted that this was not the time to move against Elizabeth, she refused to give up altogether, and even ordered her ministers to search through ancient lawbooks in the pathetic hope that they would uncover a precedent that would enable her to designate the successor of her choice.[42]

Philip was more realistic, but he strove in vain to convince his wife that Elizabeth must be forced to accept Emmanuel Philibert. Even when Philip fulfilled his wife's dearest wish, and returned to England in March 1557, Mary remained obdurate on this point. Philip brought with him his half-sister, the Duchess of Parma, and his cousin, the Duchess of Lorraine, relying on their powers of persuasion not only to make the Queen see reason, but also to overcome Elizabeth's resistance to the match. The French ambassador, who was intent on preventing the Savoy match, was sufficiently alarmed by the arrival of this formidable duo to send the Countess of Northampton on a secret mission to tell Elizabeth what was afoot, and to remind her that it was against her interests to take a husband "so poor and stripped of his wealth". To his relief Elizabeth sent word back that she would rather die than submit, but her resolve was never put to the test, for it soon emerged that the Queen was as anxious as the French ambassador to frustrate Emmanuel Philibert's suit. She refused to summon Elizabeth to Court, or to permit the Duchesses to visit her at Hatfield, and in early May the Duchess of Parma returned irritably to Flanders, having been "very bored" during her stay in England.[43]

To Mary's acute distress, Philip himself left England on 4 July, exasperated by his wife's mulish refusal to defer to his judgment. Determined to overcome the impolitic prejudices that blinded the Queen to her duty, he instructed his confessor, Francisco Bernarda de Fresneda, to remain behind and convince Mary of the necessity of the Savoy match. Fresneda had a hard task, for though he invariably worsted Mary in debate, "he found the Queen obstinately averse to giving Lady Elizabeth any hope of succession, obstinately maintaining that she was neither her sister nor the daughter of ... King Henry, nor would she think of favouring her, as she was born of an infamous woman". To Philip the Queen wrote plaintively that though he had bid her "examine her conscience" whether or not he was in the right, she knew the answer well enough, "for that which my conscience holds it has held this four and twenty years" – or in other words, for Elizabeth's entire lifespan. At length, after days of argument, the Queen agreed to submit to her husband's wishes, but two days later she changed her mind, and from that time forth was implacably opposed to the desired union.[44] Philip's frustration was understandable: however unpalatable, the prospect of the next reign had to be faced, and by preparing for it rationally Mary could have restricted Elizabeth's ability to undo all that she held precious. As it was, Elizabeth's freedom of action was left uncurbed, enabling her to reverse the catastrophic policies of the Marian regime and map out her own triumphant course.

Had Philip been able to concentrate exclusively on the marriage issue during his stay in England, he might have browbeaten Mary into compliance, but his principal energies had been devoted to securing another object. After a brief interlude of uneasy peace, France and Spain had gone to war with each other in November 1556, and it had been Philip's desire to bring England into the war on Spain's side that had prompted him to visit his wife the following spring. Despite the misgivings of the Council, Mary obliged by declaring war in June 1557, but the decision brought her nothing but heartache. Philip rewarded her by leaving the country, never to return, and the war itself merely added military defeat to England's already lengthy list of misfortunes.

In January 1558 Calais, an English possession since the fourteenth century, surrendered to the French, a devastating blow to national morale. The last of England's once extensive holdings abroad, Calais was not only believed to be of great strategic importance, but also prized for providing a base from which English merchants could conduct trading operations on the continent. In fact the expense of maintaining the town and its garrison outweighed its supposed advantages, but the psychological damage caused by its fall was enormous. Mary's famous remark that "when I am dead and opened ye shall find Calais lying in my heart" demonstrates that she herself believed it to be the supreme failure of a reign beset by failure, and Elizabeth too could never resign herself to its loss, for throughout her reign Anglo-French relations were consistently imperilled by her determined efforts to procure the town's restoration. Yet however much she might have shared the general indignation, in one way the fall of Calais was a blessing in disguise, for any event that contributed still further to Mary's unpopularity could not but be to Elizabeth's advantage.

For months after Philip's departure Mary had clung to the pathetic belief that she had managed to conceive during her husband's last visit, but though she only acknowledged that her hopes were illusory at the end of April 1558, this time few others had shared her belief that she was pregnant. In a memorandum drawn up for Philip in March of that year, Simon Renard noted that Elizabeth was now widely "honoured and recognized" as heiress to the throne, and that "the leading men of the realm" would never consent to any attempt to alter her status. He gloomily remarked that though it was probable that when Elizabeth inherited, "religion will be undermined, everything sacred profaned, Catholics ill-treated, churchmen driven out", he saw no remedy unless Elizabeth could be prevailed upon to marry a nominee of Philip's choice. In view of Mary's continued refusal to work for this object, there was little chance of achieving it.[45]

Quite apart from her personal reasons for rejecting Elizabeth as her successor, Mary had always maintained that she could not force her sister to take Emmanuel Philibert as a husband because Parliament would have to be consulted beforehand, and that assembly would certainly oppose Elizabeth's marriage to a foreigner. Philip questioned the accuracy of this statement, and Mary herself was terrified that it would be exposed as false when she learnt that the King of Sweden had sent an emissary to propose to Elizabeth on his son's behalf. Nervously the Queen wrote to find out whether the King's proposal had interested Elizabeth, and she was much relieved when her sister replied that she liked her single status too well to wish to swap it for another. The Queen was content that this should be the last word on the subject. Philip had hoped that her fright over the Swedish proposal would finally induce Mary to promote Emmanuel Philibert's suit, but he was disgusted to find that once her agitation had subsided, she became as stubborn as ever on this point.

Apart from a brief visit to the capital at the end of February 1558, Elizabeth had remained at Hatfield all this time, but despite her seclusion in the country, she was by no means cut off from affairs. In March, Renard noted "frequent communications reach and leave her secretly in regard to the succession". In August Mary was assailed by recurring bouts of fever, and though there were periods in the next few weeks when she rallied, she never fully recovered her health. As it became apparent that the Queen was terminally ill, more and more people established contact with Elizabeth at Hatfield. The Spaniards themselves realized that they must plan for the future by securing Elizabeth's goodwill, and in June the new Spanish ambassador in England, Count Feria, went to see Elizabeth at Hatfield. He was delighted by the reception he received. Elizabeth, he reported, had been "very much pleased by his visit", and he evidently felt it was now possible to look forward to the next reign with greater confidence.[46]

Like the Spaniards, Elizabeth herself was making preparations for her accession, and her arrangements were none the less efficient for being carried out in secret. Although it seemed increasingly unlikely, she could not overlook the possibility that the crown might be wrested from her at the last moment, and throughout the autumn of 1558 she was engaged in consolidating an already strong position. She was in touch with Sir John Thynne, a powerful Wiltshire landowner, whose support would be very useful in the event of an attempt to deprive her of her inheritance. She also accepted undertakings from several captains on garrison duty at Berwick that if the need arose, they would march to Hertfordshire with 10,000 men, "to serve for the maintenance of her royal state, title and dignity".[47] As matters turned out, however, such precautions were unnecessary. On 6 November, when Mary clearly did not have much longer to live, the Privy Council finally prevailed upon her to name her sister as her successor. The following day two of Mary's servants were sent to inform Elizabeth of a decision that all but the Queen had long considered a foregone conclusion.

From the sidelines, Count Feria loudly applauded the move, but to his alarm he found that very few people were prepared to listen. Try as he might, he could not prevent Spanish influence in England from ebbing away as inexorably as the Queen's life. He ruefully admitted that when he solemnly informed the Council that he was now under instruction to serve Elizabeth "on all occasions, and to employ every effort to enable her to ascend the throne", he was received rather like "a man who came with Bulls from a dead Pope". Mindful of the welcome he had received from Elizabeth in June, he hoped that she at least would treat him with greater consideration, but when he paid her another visit on 10 November, he discovered that the knowledge that nothing could now come between her and the throne had given her a disquieting new assurance. She received him politely enough, if "not as joyfully as she did the last time", but he found her more inclined to carp at the treatment she had received from the Queen than to give credit to Philip for the protection he had accorded her. When Feria ventured to suggest that she had her brother-in-law to thank for Mary's ultimate recognition of her as her successor, she contradicted him outright: imperiously she replied that "she owed her crown, not to Philip ... but to the attachment of the people of England".[48]

If she admitted no other mortal claim on her gratitude, she did admit that it was Providence itself that had permitted the will of the people to go unchallenged. In the week that followed Feria's visit, the Queen's condition continued to deteriorate while her country lay in uneasy limbo, nominally under Mary's rule but already committed to Elizabeth. The road to Hatfield was thronged with courtiers eager to pay their respects to the young woman whose accession was clearly imminent, and even Elizabeth, who had been awaiting her sister's demise for so long, was shocked by this premature transfer of allegiance. In the minds of many of her subjects, Mary was already consigned to the past, but if the tie that bound her to her subjects had become well-nigh imperceptible, while life remained it would not be severed. Death alone could free England from its trance, and thus it was that when the news was conveyed to Elizabeth that in the early hours of the morning of 17 November 1558, Mary had finally breathed her last, nothing could rob the moment of its significance. Falling to her knees, she could not immediately master her emotions, in which humility and awe mingled with a rush of exultation. At length, "after a good time of respiration", she turned to the psalms to give vent to her feelings: still kneeling, she quoted in Latin, "This is the doing of the Lord; and it is marvellous in our eyes".[49]

CHAPTER 4

"God hath raised me high"

Between eleven o' clock and twelve noon on 17 November 1558, Elizabeth was formally proclaimed Queen outside the Palace of Westminster, and at various other points around the capital. The Londoners were clearly pleased by the announcement, for they had long since grown weary of Mary's rule. Nevertheless, compared to the wild outpouring of joy that had occurred upon Mary's accession, the celebrations were somewhat muted. Even the most sanguine and loyal of Elizabeth's adherents had to acknowledge that this twenty-five-year-old princess had inherited formidable problems along with her crown, and that her kingdom was weak and divided. One of her subjects later recalled, "Certainly the state of England lay now most afflicted, embroiled on the one side with the Scottish, on the other side with the French war; overcharged with debt . . . the treasure exhausted; Calais . . . lost, to the great dishonour of the English nation; the people distracted with different opinions in religion; the Queen bare of potent friends, and strengthened with no alliance of foreign princes".[1] It was a woman who had landed the country in such a mess, and it was understandable enough that some people were sceptical that a woman would be capable of extricating them from it.

It was hardly reassuring that the Queen was both youthful and a complete novice at the conduct of affairs of state. As Elizabeth herself once remarked, she had been "rather brought up in a school to abide the ferula than traded in a kingdom to support the sceptre", and in recent years her very survival had depended on her maintaining a stance that was rigidly apolitical. It was true that "She had been well instructed by experience and adversity, two excellent teachers",[2] but Mary Tudor had undergone comparable hardships and tribulations prior to her accession, and this had not equipped her to cope with the responsibilities of kingship.

Three days after her sister's death, Elizabeth herself was to declare,

"The burden that has fallen upon me maketh me amazed", but in fact, the composure with which she faced the challenges that awaited her was quite extraordinary. Far from making her uncertain of herself, the vicissitudes she had endured in the past had revealed to her her inner strengths and heightened her self-esteem, for she knew that it was largely owing to her intelligence and willpower that she had emerged unscathed from these ordeals. Merely to have survived was a legitimate cause for congratulation, but the way she had deflected all attempts to blacken her character, or to fetter her future freedom of action, was in many ways a still more remarkable achievement, and one which buoyed her up as she contemplated the uncharted waters ahead. But it was not merely her faith in herself that had been enhanced by her experiences, for she had no doubt that it was God who had placed her where she was, and she was sure that having guided her through the pitfalls and uncertainties of her sister's reign, He would continue to afford her His protection. As she was to state, shortly after her accession, she regarded herself as "God's creature", and though "but one body, naturally considered", she was "by His permission a body politic, to govern".[3]

Because of the certainty that she owed her exaltation to the divine will, Elizabeth was untroubled by feelings of inadequacy on account of her sex. It was an attitude that enabled her to sidestep male prejudice, and was hence an invaluable asset at a time when women were classed as inferior beings who had to be kept in subjugation by their natural masters. Women were commonly stigmatized as being "light of credit, lusty of stomach, unpatient, full of words, apt to lie, flatter and weep, all in extremes, without mean, either loving dearly, or hating deadly, desirous rather to rule than to be ruled, despising naturally that is offered to them". Another authority added to this list by declaring that Nature had made women "weak, frail, impatient, feeble, and foolish; and experience hath declared them to be unconstant, variable, cruel, and lacking the spirit of counsel or regiment". Because of their lamentable tendencies to be "full of tongue and of much babbling", women were urged to keep silent in the presence of men, and to show unfailing obedience to husbands and fathers, and though there were many women who failed to observe these precepts, there were few who dared openly to rebut them.[4]

Elizabeth herself was no feminist, and in many of her utterances she implied that she shared the prejudices of her male subjects with regard to women. Thus in 1563 she acknowledged to Parliament that as "a woman wanting both wit and memory", it would have been "a thing appropriate to my sex" if she had shown "some fear to speak, and bashfulness besides". Nevertheless, on virtually every occasion when she made a reference to what she once termed "my sexly weakness", she balanced this with a reminder of her supreme position within the state. In 1591, for example, she asked King Henry IV of France to forgive her for giving him a lecture when as a woman it would be more fitting for her to listen to others, but then she added the corollary that "my experience in government has made me so stubborn as to believe that I am not ignorant of what becomes a king". This technique reached its apotheosis in the speech which she made to her troops in the Armada year of 1588, when she defiantly affirmed that "the body but of a weak and feeble woman" was joined with "the heart and stomach of a king". She did not try to directly challenge the assumptions that were current about women, but instead she held that, as a sovereign appointed by God, the conventions that governed relations between the sexes were not applicable to her. She genuinely believed that "Princes ... transact business in a certain way, with a princely intelligence, such as private persons cannot imitate", and in her view, the advantages she derived from her sovereign status meant that her gender was not a handicap, but an irrelevance. In a prayer that she composed for inclusion in a book of private devotions she expressed her gratitude and amazement to the Almighty for "making me (though a weak woman) yet thy instrument", but it was clear to her that as He had made an exception of her in this way, He intended her authority to be no less absolute than when He chose male rulers to act as His deputies on earth. She did not risk straining her credibility by asserting in Parliament that she was free of those failings that were regarded as an integral part of the female character, but she stressed that by virtue of "the princely seat and kingly throne wherein God (though unworthy) hath constituted me", her feminine weaknesses were of no account. Towards the end of her reign, she would sum up the position succinctly when she told the Venetian ambassador, "My sex cannot diminish my prestige".[5]

Her confidence that it was Providence that had brought her to the throne gave her an assurance when dealing with people remarkable in one of her years. When Count Feria had visited her in the country, shortly before Mary's death, he had recorded that she struck him as a very clever woman (as well as a very vain one), and he had noticed that even then, Elizabeth "had a certain air of authority about her". This impression was confirmed once she became Queen, for he reported, "She seems to me incomparably more feared than her sister, and gives her orders and has her way as absolutely as her father did". When receiving ambassadors she appeared to be entirely at her ease, and barely three months after her accession a foreign diplomat who came to present his credentials was left dazzled by her poise, and by the way that she addressed him "extempore, with many brilliant, choice and felicitous phrases". But though from the start she had no trace of awkwardness, and could be utterly charming when she chose to be, she likewise had no inhibitions about making her displeasure felt. In March 1559 some of the English commissioners who were engaged in peace talks with the French infuriated Elizabeth because they made no protest when the French commissioners implied that her claim to the throne was unsound. The Queen delivered her servants so harsh a rebuke that it was said that two of them would "carry it to their graves", and one of their colleagues had to beseech her on his knees "to make them men again, who remain so amazed as ... nothing can breed any comfort in them". When the first Parliament of her reign assembled, in January 1559, the Queen was no less assertive, warning a delegation from the House of Commons that she would not tolerate undue presumption from them, it "being unfitting and altogether unmeet for you to require them that may command ... or to draw my love to your liking, or frame my will to your fantasies". Right from the beginning of her reign, it was apparent to Elizabeth's subjects that "none knew better the hardest art of all others, that is, of commanding men".[6]

One reason why the Queen was able to cope so magnificently with her transition to the throne was that, although she had been living a retired existence at Hatfield, she had not been completely cut off from the political scene. In 1566 a Member of Parliament recalled that in the period before her accession, "Few things could be spoken either in the Privy Council or Privy Chamber of the Queen her sister but that they were revealed unto her Majesty". Her contacts within the court had kept her so well informed that when Count Feria saw her shortly before her accession he commented, "It seems to me as though she knows who is who in the realm, at least among those of rank". One of her links to the outside world had been formed by Sir Nicholas Throckmorton, a somewhat controversial figure who had only narrowly escaped being convicted of treason at the time of Wyatt's rebellion. A few days before her accession, Throckmorton had drawn up a secret memorandum for Elizabeth, outlining various steps which it would be desirable for her to take when she came to the throne, and putting forward suggestions as to the men she should select to form a government. Clearly this was not the first time he had addressed her on such matters, for in the memorandum he mentioned that he only ventured to tender her this advice because he had already experienced her "gracious acceptation" of his opinions. Nevertheless, although in the past she had clearly found Throckmorton's communications useful, Elizabeth had no intention of becoming excessively dependent on him. Sir Nicholas was "a man of intelligence, but turbulent", whose religious views were more radical than her own, and whose impetuous nature might prove difficult to curb. Not only did she disregard several of Throckmorton's suggestions about government appointments, but she did not prefer him to very high office in state, awarding him only the secondary position of ambassador to France.[7]

For her chief adviser she preferred to rely on a man whose cautious temperament more exactly accorded with her own. On 20 November, still at Hatfield, she appointed Sir William Cecil her Principal Secretary of State. The son of a minor official at Henry VIII's court, William Cecil had been born in 1520, and brought up on his father's estate at Stamford. He was educated at Stamford Grammar School, and St John's College, Cambridge, and he had then gone to the Inns of Court in London to acquire a grounding in the law. In May 1547 he had entered Protector Somerset's household, and the following year he had been appointed the Duke's private secretary. Although briefly imprisoned in the Tower on Somerset's fall, he was shortly afterwards reinstated in the Council, and in September 1550 the Duke of Northumberland had appointed him Secretary of State. Three years later, he had reluctantly endorsed the project to put Jane Grey on the throne, but when the Council had abandoned Northumberland, Cecil had been among the first to offer fealty to Mary. He had not been punished for his earlier support of Lady Jane, and indeed, it would appear that Mary had contemplated retaining him as her Secretary.[8] Cecil had declined to stay at his post, for his Protestant sympathies were too pronounced for him to be a prominent member of the Marian regime. Nevertheless, his Protestantism was not so fervent that he was prepared to emigrate in order to practise it abroad. Instead he remained in England and quietly conformed, regularly attending mass. He even performed some minor tasks for Queen Mary, travelling to Brussels at her request in order to escort Cardinal Pole to England. The only hint of opposition to Mary's policies came in 1555, when he spoke in Parliament against a bill that proposed to strip the Protestant exiles of their property.

Cecil had had regular dealings with Elizabeth since he became Surveyor of her lands in 1550, and although he had been cautious about seeing her too frequently during Mary's reign, his business connection with her had given him an excuse to maintain discreet contact. Her confidence in him was known to be such that in early November 1558, when Count Feria had returned to England after a brief absence and found that Mary was dying, he was "told for certain that Cecil, who was King Edward's Secretary, will also be Secretary to Madam Elizabeth". Nicholas Throckmorton had also singled out Cecil as the man whom Elizabeth would wish to be her Secretary, and on this point at least, Sir Nicholas's predictions proved correct. The day after Mary's death, Cecil was already at work on the new Queen's behalf, making arrangements to inform various European princes of Mary's demise, and to ensure that Elizabeth's accession went smoothly. When Elizabeth formally appointed him her Secretary of State and a member of her Privy Council she told him, "This judgment I have of you, that you will not be corrupted by any manner of gift, and that you will be faithful to the state, and that without respect of my private will, you will give me that counsel you think best, and if you shall know anything necessary to be declared to me of secrecy, you shall show it to myself only".[9] Cecil did not prove a disappointment to her on any of these counts.

Until the reign of Henry VIII, the Secretaryship had not been regarded as a particularly important post, for the Secretary's duties consisted primarily of drafting the King's private correspondence. Nevertheless Henry's great minister, Thomas Cromwell, recognized the potential of the position, and it was as Secretary that he had master-minded the Henrician revolution in Church and state. Since his occupancy of the post, the Secretary's standing within the administration had been transformed. By the middle of the sixteenth century, the Secretary's duties had come to include drafting all royal correspondence to foreign princes and ambassadors stationed abroad, drawing up the agenda for Council meetings, and relaying the details of what happened at them to the monarch, if the latter had not been present. In the hands of an unusually resourceful or energetic man, the position entailed still more than this, for unlike other officers of state, the Secretary's authority was not circumscribed by the terms of his patent, and hence he could expand or contract his responsibilities as he saw fit. In the words of William Cecil's son, Robert, who became Secretary at the end of Elizabeth's reign, the holder of the office enjoyed "a liberty to negotiate at discretion at home and abroad ... all matters of speech and intelligence".[10] As this definition suggests, the matters that came within the Secretary's province were astonishingly diverse, and included foreign relations, financial affairs, and the state of religion, the Secret Service, and trade and industry.

As Secretary, William Cecil would use his powers to the full, concerning himself with almost every aspect of government. He was endowed with a prodigious memory, and such an astonishing capacity for hard work that after his death a servant of his could testify, "I never saw him half an hour idle four and twenty years together ... He kept himself scarce time for sleep, or meals, or leisure to go to bed."[11] When faced with a complex problem, it was his invariable custom to set down in writing all considerations relating to it, ranging from the most banal statements of fact to highly recondite details, and it was only after he had meticulously examined a question in every one of its facets that he would venture an opinion. He produced memoranda on subjects as far apart as the danger England faced from invasion by foreign powers, to the desirability of making people eat more fish, and in the course of his career there were few matters relating to the welfare of the kingdom that failed to receive his attention.

Together the Queen and Cecil forged a unique partnership. When she had first appointed him, she had made it clear that she wished to hear his opinions even when they conflicted with her own, and for the next forty years she rarely took an important decision without consulting him first. Yet while she had an immense respect for his judgment, she did not defer to it at all times. Cecil himself told his son Robert that on those occasions when he and Elizabeth disagreed, "As long as I may be allowed to give advice, I will not change my opinion by affirming the contrary, for that were to offend God, to whom I am sworn first. But as a servant, I will obey her Majesty's commandment, and no wise contrary the same. Presuming that she being God's minister here, it shall be God's will to have her commandments obeyed".[12] But though in general he was philosophical when she overrode him, there were at least two occasions in the reign when he threatened to resign if Elizabeth did not follow the policy he prescribed, and in both cases the Queen backed down. At other times he brought subtler pressures to bear, such as urging her to summon Parliament at times when he could rely on its members to voice support for policies which the Queen was reluctant to pursue. Such stratagems kept direct confrontations to a minimum, and the only time that their relationship was in serious jeopardy was after the execution of Mary Queen of Scots.

Cecil and his mistress might not invariably have been in agreement, but it was the fact that their thinking coincided on a great many questions, that enabled them to work in harmony for so long. The Queen relied on him as implicitly as she did precisely because their approach to problems was so similar, and for his part Cecil developed an unstinting respect for her intellect. He was fond of saying "There was never so wise a woman born, for all respects, as Queen Elizabeth, for she spake and understood all languages; knew all estates and dispositions of princes. And particularly was so expert in the knowledge of her own realm and estate as no counsellor she had could tell her what she knew not before". Elizabeth in her turn was justly appreciative of Cecil's contribution to her success, paying him the tribute that "No prince in Europe had such a counsellor as she had of him".[13]

Having remained at Hatfield for the first week of her reign, on 23 November the Queen rode into London. For five days she resided quietly at Lord North's city residence, but on 28 November she moved to the Tower, which she had last visited in very different circumstances. As she made her way there, "There was great shooting of guns, the like was never heard before", and "the whole of London turned out" to catch a glimpse of England's new sovereign. The crowds were delighted by what they saw. Although she herself was pleased to think otherwise, Elizabeth had no claims to genuine beauty. Her best assets were her hands, with their elongated and slender fingers, which she drew attention to as often as she could, but her other attributes were less fine. At this stage she was slightly fuller in the face than she became in later years, but "the whole compass of her countenance" was oval, and too long to satisfy the purist. Her most distinctive feature was her nose, which was slightly hooked, and "rising in the middest". Nevertheless, she always knew how to make the most of her attractions, and for her first public appearance of her reign she was dressed strikingly in purple velvet, which contrasted dramatically with her reddish-gold hair. It was not her appearance, however, but her manner, which appealed the most to the spectators, for even this early in her reign she manifested a genius for "stately stooping to the meanest sort". "If ever any person had either the gift or the style to win the hearts of the people, it was this Queen," commented one of her subjects when describing this scene. "All her faculties were in motion, and every motion seemed a well-guided action; her eye was set upon one, her ear listened to another, her judgment ran upon a third, to a fourth she addressed her speech". Although the snobbish Count Feria was shocked that she should act in so ingratiating a fashion before the common people, others were impressed by the way she conveyed her pleasure at their acclamations without any loss of dignity, and certainly the onlookers were thrilled by her performance, and "there-upon redoubled the testimonies of their joy".[14]

After spending a week at the Tower, she took up residence in Somerset House, and then on 23 December she moved again, in order to spend Christmas at the Palace of Westminster. Having previously led such a quiet existence, Elizabeth was clearly delighted that her social life was no longer subject to any restriction, and the Court she kept during these weeks was exceptionally gay. An Italian visitor reported, "They are intent on amusing themselves and on dancing till after midnight", but though he professed himself shocked by such "levities and unusual licentiousness", Elizabeth was not neglecting business. She had to put the finishing touches to her list of household appointments, for on her accession she had unceremoniously dismissed the majority of her late sister's personal attendants. Several of the vacancies were filled by "the old flock of Hatfield", who had stood by her so loyally in the past.[15] Chief of these was Kat Ashley, who now headed the list of the Queen's ladies-in-waiting as Mistress of the Robes. Kat's husband, John, became Master of the Jewel House, and Thomas Parry's stepson, John Fortescue, became Master of the Wardrobe. Several of those who had been arrested at the time of Wyatt's rebellion, and who had maintained under questioning that Elizabeth had not been involved, were now rewarded for their loyalty with offices in the Queen's gift. Sir William St Loe, for example, was given the prestigious post of Captain of the Guard, while Sir James Crofts was made Captain of Berwick, the heavily fortified northern town which would form the first line of defence in the event of an invasion by the Scots. She took this opportunity, too, of conferring favour on her first cousin, Henry Carey, the foul-mouthed but capable son of Anne Boleyn's elder sister, Mary. Ties of kinship meant a great deal to the Queen, and though as yet Carey was not given an official position at court, he was raised to the peerage as Baron Hunsdon, and given a manor in Hertfordshire.

The most pressing necessity of all, however, was for the Queen to select the men who would sit on her Privy Council. In the words of one Member of Parliament, the Council was "the eyes, the ears and the tongue of the Prince and the realm".[16] Its most important function was to advise the sovereign on matters of policy, but it also played a vital administrative role. There was almost no area of English life in which the Council could not intervene, and its influence penetrated even the most remote corners of the country. Every week a stream of directives emanated from it, containing instructions, rebukes and exhortations to royal officials and private citizens, and if the Councillors wished to interview anybody, they were entitled to summon before them whomsoever they chose. Much of their correspondence was directed to the Justices of the Peace, the unpaid local officials who not only acted as magistrates, but who also were charged with the enforcement of many parliamentary statutes. When invasion threatened, or on those occasions when it was necessary to send troops to fight abroad, it was the Council who co-ordinated defence measures, and arranged for the mustering of forces. It was empowered to regulate commerce, intervening on occasion to uphold the monopolies of the large trading companies, or to prohibit the export of grain in times of scarcity. It recommended measures designed to extirpate piracy, disciplined religious dissidents, and acted as arbiter in quarrels between private individuals that were referred to it by interested parties. In short, the Council was the institution which did the most to uphold the authority of the Crown in all parts of the kingdom, and had a key part in both the formulation and execution of royal policy.

Mary's Council had been large and unwieldy, having numbered at one time as many as forty-four members. Elizabeth thought this an inefficient arrangement: on 20 November, most of Mary's Councillors had gone to see her at Hatfield, and the new Queen had made it plain that there would be reductions, telling those present, "I consider a multitude doth make rather discord and confusion than good counsel". In the weeks following her accession, the Council was remodelled, with only ten of her sister's former Councillors retaining their places. Some of these, such as the Earls of Arundel, Derby and Shrewsbury, were kept on solely because it would have been unthinkable for Elizabeth to have removed from the Council such high-ranking aristocrats with their extensive territorial holdings. She had more positive reasons for keeping as Councillors Lord Admiral Clinton, and the Earl of Pembroke, who were both able men who had served on the Council since the reign of Henry VIII. The Queen's great-uncle, Lord William Howard, was retained largely out of gratitude for the loyal way he had stood by Elizabeth when she had been in trouble during the previous reign. Mary's Council had also contained a number of bureaucrats and professional civil servants, and Elizabeth looked on these men as indispensable. The most important was the Marquis of Winchester, who had first been appointed to the Privy Council in 1526. Now believed to be an octogenarian, he had been Lord Treasurer since 1550 and it was out of the question for the Queen to discard a man of his "vast political experience". She had no qualms, however, about dismissing the remainder of his colleagues. Those made redundant were probably relieved that a worse fate had not befallen them, for when Count Feria had arrived in England in early November he had discovered that the majority of Mary's Councillors were "extremely frightened of what Madam Elizabeth will do to them".[17]

Several of the incoming Councillors who replaced the sacked men owed their advancement primarily to the fact that they were Elizabeth's "old and sure servants, who have tarried with her and not shrunk in the last storms". Thomas Parry, who had been in Elizabeth's service since her childhood, came into this category, as did Sir Ambrose Cave, a country neighbour of Cecil's who appears to have formerly occupied the position of Comptroller of Elizabeth's household at Hatfield. Among the other new Councillors, the Marquis of Northampton could claim a tenuous family connection with Eizabeth, for he was Katherine Parr's brother, while a much closer relation was Sir Francis Knollys, whose wife was a sister of the recently ennobled Baron Hunsdon, making Knollys the Queen's first cousin by marriage. Knollys was an ardent Protestant who had fled to Germany during Mary's reign so that he could continue to practise his faith, but he hurried home as soon as he learnt of Elizabeth's accession. He knew he would receive a good welcome from the new Queen: when he and his wife had first set off for the continent, Elizabeth had written to Lady Knollys commiserating with her for having to go on "this pilgrimage", and urging the couple to "relieve your sorrow for your far journey with joy of your short return".[18]

Another strong Protestant was the Earl of Bedford, who had also spent part of Mary's reign in exile. He had fled the country after coming under suspicion of involvement in Wyatt's rebellion, but he had subsequently managed to clear his name, and had been permitted to return. "In person and manners he is a monstrosity", was how one foreign diplomat described him, for he had a grotesquely enlarged head, but however unattractive he was physically, he was known to be "on very good terms" with the Queen.[19] Also in the Council was Cecil's brother-in-law, Sir Nicholas Bacon, a fat and jolly lawyer of great acumen. From having been Master of the Court of Augmentations under Edward VI and Mary, Bacon was promoted to be Lord Keeper of the Great Seal, and since for the time being Elizabeth had decided not to appoint a Lord Chancellor, this made him the highest legal officer in the realm. Bacon carried out all the responsibilities that would have normally devolved on the Chancellor, the most important of which were to preside over the Court of Chancery, and to act as the Queen's spokesman in the House of Lords.

"I mean to direct all my actions by good advice and counsel", Elizabeth had declared shortly after her accession, and in her own eyes at least, she always adhered to this promise. As an old woman of sixty-four, she insisted to a visiting diplomat that "she did nothing without her Council, and that nothing was so dangerous in affairs of state as self-opinion". In 1572, the French ambassador went so far as to say that Elizabeth had so much respect for her Council that she would never do anything that ran contrary to their advice, but this was a complete misreading of the situation. There were instances when representations from the Council induced the Queen to reverse an apparently firm decision, as in 1593, when she had been set on withdrawing troops that had earlier been sent to France, "Yet upon arguments made by her Council to the contrary, she changed her opinion". Nevertheless, she considered herself under no obligation to abide by their recommendations, and there were numerous occasions when her Council begged her in unison to change course, but could not induce her to do so.[20]

Furthermore, the Queen was under no compulsion to consult her Council when formulating policy. During her first year on the throne, she kept the Council "in absolute ignorance" of how her marriage negotiations with the Austrian Archduke Charles were progressing. In 1586, when an English army was fighting the Spaniards in the Netherlands, one of her Councillors reported that Elizabeth "can by no means ... endure that the causes of that country should be subject to any debate in Council, otherwise than as she herself will direct, and therefore men forbear to do that which otherwise they would". If her Councillors sought to make their views known to her by tendering unsolicited advice, the Queen was highly indignant. In 1580, for example, she was displeased when Sir Francis Knollys told her in the strongest possible terms that he was against her taking the French prince, the Duke of Alençon, as her husband. After having been rebuked by Elizabeth, Knollys confided plaintively to a colleague, "I know I am condemned to be too curious, but alas, it is a weighty matter that moveth this curiosity, and this is almost nothing to that which may be said herein".[21]

This was not the first time that Knollys had annoyed the Queen by thrusting unpalatable advice upon her, for two years before this he had clashed with her when he made known to her his disquiet at the way she was handling a wide range of domestic and foreign issues. Elizabeth had not welcomed his criticism, and Knollys knew that in future he would be expected to keep his opinions to himself, but he feared that in doing so he would be shirking his responsibilities. Unhappily, he described his quandary to a friend. "I do know her Majesty is loth to hear me", he admitted, " ... and therefore I am the more silent, although when I may be heard

... rather than my silence should be guilty of her danger, I do utter my unworthy speech unto her Majesty. I do know that it is fit for all men to give place to her Majesty's will and pleasure, and to her affections in all matters that touch not the danger of her estate, but I do know also that if her Majesty do not suppress and subject her own affections unto sound advice of open Council in matters touching the prevention of her danger, that her Majesty will be utterly overthrown".[22]

Knollys's laments were echoed by Sir Francis Walsingham, another zealous Protestant who had been appointed to the Council in 1573. When Elizabeth was refusing to heed the advice of her Council in 1578, Walsingham could only suppose that this was the Almighty's way of manifesting His displeasure with his erring servants, for "when the advice of grave and faithful Councillors cannot prevail with a prince of her Majesty's rare judgment, it is a sign that God hath closed up her heart from seeing and executing that which may be for her safety".[23] Yet the very fact that Elizabeth chose as her Councillors individuals such as Walsingham and Knollys, whose views were by no means a faithful reflection of her own, shows that she regarded independence as an asset in an adviser. She appointed her Councillors safe in the knowledge that they had no means of coercing her to do anything against her will, and in theory they could not even remonstrate with her without her permission, but at times of greatest tension there could be no question of keeping such forthright men totally muzzled. Those who volunteered their opinions uninvited might get shouted at, or even find themselves banned from Court for two or three days, but as severer sanctions were not applied, they not infrequently thought the risk worth taking.

Even while the Queen was still deciding who should serve her in court and Council, arrangements for her coronation had been feverishly set in motion. It was necessary for Elizabeth to emphasize that the validity of her title to the throne was beyond question, for there was a danger that the French might contend that she was illegitimate, and that Mary Queen of Scots, who had married the French King's eldest son in April 1558, was really the rightful Queen of England. On Elizabeth's accession, England remained technically at war with France, and although peace talks had begun, it was possible that the French would elect to break off these negotiations, so that they would be free to uphold Mary Stuart's claim to the throne. Indeed, there were soon indications that this was what they had in mind, for it was revealed that French diplomats in Rome were putting pressure on the Pope to declare Elizabeth a bastard. Fortunately, the Queen could count on her former brother-in-law (who had become King Philip II of Spain in 1556, following the abdication of his father) to block this step, for the two major continental powers were bitter rivals. Having long been locked in conflict as to which of them would gain hegemony over Europe, the Spaniards attached the highest priority to keeping Mary, the Dauphiness of France, off the English throne. Nevertheless, although Elizabeth could expect to receive a measure of protection from Spain, her coronation would be of value in that it would serve as a reaffirmation that her royal title was not spurious. It would invest her occupancy of the throne with a semi-sacred character, and there was a chance that once she had been crowned, the French would have some qualms about advocating the deposition of an anointed Queen. As a result, it was agreed that the service should be held as soon as was feasible, on 15 January 1559, barely two months after Elizabeth's accession. Inevitably this meant that the arrangements were somewhat rushed: at the end of December a visiting Italian reported breathlessly, "They are preparing here for the coronation, and work both day and night, on holidays and weekdays".[24]

Despite this, there was no skimping on the preparations, for no one knew better than Elizabeth "that in pompous ceremonies a secret of government doth much consist, for that the people are both naturally taken and held with exterior shows". To ensure a good supply of finery, in November customs officers had embargoed the sale of any crimson silk that came into the realm, until such time as the Queen had selected what she needed. In all, royal expenditure on cloth of gold and silver, and rich velvets and satins, amounted to nearly £4,000, and the total cost of the festivities, excluding the coronation banquet, was £16,741.[25]

On 12 January 1559, Elizabeth settled herself in the Tower, where it was customary for sovereigns to spend some time prior to their coronation. Two days later, with the cheers of spectators ringing in her ears, she made a triumphal progress through the city to Westminster, wending her way through streets that had been freshly gravelled and hung with banners for the occasion. She was preceded by an impressive horseback procession, with her household officers, the bishops and the peers all forming part of the colourful cavalcade. Then came the Queen, seated on a chariot pulled by "two very handsome mules". A canopy was borne over her head, and she wore a mantle made from twenty-three yards of gold and silver tissue, with fur trimmings. By her side walked the monarch's personal bodyguards, the Gentlemen Pensioners, and her chariot was followed by a troupe of ladies-in-waiting, decked out almost as gorgeously as Elizabeth herself, in crimson velvet, with gold-lined sleeves.

At strategic intervals along the route, figures in costume were grouped on platforms, portraying allegorical scenes, or episodes from the Bible. Each had its own expositor, who stepped forward at the Queen's approach to explain in rhyme the significance of what was represented. Although in theory England was still subject to the authority of the Pope, there was an unmistakably Protestant flavour to some of these tableaux. In one display where children personifying the virtues were shown vanquishing contrary vices, 'Superstition' and 'Ignorance' were trampled underfoot by 'Pure Religion'. At another street corner, "Deborah, the judge and restorer of the house of Israel", was seated in state under an artificial palm tree, and in the recitation that followed she was held up as "a worthy precedent" to Elizabeth, for having freed God's people from the oppression of the Canaanites. So far Elizabeth had given little public indication of where her religious loyalties lay, but on this day at least she was quite content to be cast in the role of deliverer from popish repression. Indeed, she entered into the spirit of it all, and when an English Bible was handed to her by a child representing Truth, "She kissed it; and afterwards applied it to her breast ... promising to be a diligent reader thereof".[26]

Such gestures went down very well with the spectators, and once again it became apparent that Elizabeth had a supreme gift for endearing herself to her people. This was another way in which she differed from Mary Tudor, who had been shy in crowds. During Mary's ceremonial entry into London in August 1553, a group of poor children had made a verse oration to her, but a chronicler disapprovingly reported that Mary "said nothing to them" in reply. In contrast, Elizabeth was in her element when she had a large audience. One observer recounted admiringly how "Her Grace, by holding up her hands and merry countenance to such as stood far off, and most tender and gentle language to those that stood nigh ... did declare herself thankfully to receive her people's goodwill". It seemed that whenever it was called for, she always had some apt rejoinder at the ready. Stopping by one of the pageants in Cheapside, she asked what it signified, and on being told that the central figure in it represented Time, she exclaimed, "Time! and Time hath brought me hither". As she passed the city companies, all arrayed in their livery, "She graced them with many witty formalities of speech", and when the onlookers shouted out prayers for her prosperity, "She thanked them with exceeding liveliness both of countenance and voice, and wished neither prosperity nor safety to her self, which might not be for their common good". She was obviously delighted by the pageants staged for her benefit, entreating the crowd to quieten down so that she could hear the accompanying commentaries, and listening with "a perpetual attentiveness in her face" to each rendition of doggerel verse. The route that the procession took was less than four miles, but the Queen made exceptionally slow progress, for she was constantly halting her chariot so that she could receive nosegays and bunches of herbs that were thrust upon her by her poorer subjects. The spectators were "wonderfully ravished" that she seemed as grateful for these insignificant offerings as she had been for the purse of gold that had been tendered to her, in accordance with tradition, when she had made her entry into the city.[27]

Elizabeth spent the night of 14 January in the Palace of Westminster, and the next day she walked in procession the short distance to Westminster Abbey to be crowned. Seated on a chair of state before the high altar, she listened as she was four times proclaimed Queen, and four times the congregation in unison roared their approval. Having taken her coronation oath, in which she swore to uphold the laws, defend the Church, and to use justice, discretion and mercy in her judgments, she was anointed by the Bishop of Carlisle, and then she withdrew into a curtained pew to don a purple velvet robe and mantle of silk and gold. Then came the climax of the ceremony as, to the sound of trumpets, the ring that bound her symbolically to her people was placed on the fourth finger of her right hand, and she was crowned, first with St Edward's crown, and then with the Imperial crown of England, which weighed over seven pounds. It was too heavy for the Queen to wear for any length of time, and so in turn it too was removed and replaced with a lighter crown, which may have been that which had been made for Anne Boleyn at her coronation in 1533.[28] After the temporal lords and bishops had paid homage to her in succession, mass was celebrated, but in a significant variation of the traditional ritual, the gospel and epistle were read in English as well as Latin. To informed observers, here was another indication that the Queen intended to be the liberator of the Protestant conscience.

The service over, Elizabeth walked from the Abbey to Westminster Hall, her sceptre and orb in her hand, and "with a most smiling countenance for everyone" who lined the carpeted route. In the hall, a great banquet was held to the accompaniment of music, the proceedings being enlivened when the Queen's Champion, Sir Edward Dymoke, rode into the building in full armour and flung down his gauntlet on the floor. He offered to fight any man who questioned Elizabeth's right to the throne, but though naturally no one present took up this challenge, it represented more than a purely symbolic gesture. Even on this day, it could not be forgotten that Elizabeth had enemies on the continent who would have liked to see Mary Stuart enthroned in her place, and no one could rule out the possibility that Elizabeth's Champion would soon be called upon to defend his newly-crowned Queen in earnest.

With the coronation behind her, Elizabeth could devote her full attention to clarifying her country's religious position, a matter which hitherto had been left in abeyance. In theory, at least, Papal jurisdiction was still extant in England, and the Queen had deliberately left it vague as to whether this would continue to be the case. It was therefore not entirely unrealistic for Catholics to hope that the Queen would preserve in its essentials the existing order of religion. Elizabeth had after all conformed during Mary's reign, and even if she had done so involuntarily, she might dread the intellectual ferment that would ensue if the country was subjected to further spiritual upheavals. There were also compelling political reasons that might deter Elizabeth from severing her links with Rome. If she did renounce Catholicism, French attempts to set Mary Stuart on the throne would assume the guise of a holy war, and would be more likely to secure the blessing of the Pope. There was of course still a good chance that Philip II would continue to form a bulwark against French expansionism, but with a man of his piety there could be no certainty that the dictates of dynastic politics would outweigh his abhorrence of heresy. Indeed, far from sheltering Elizabeth from the consequences of her apostasy, he might decide that it fell upon him, as one of the Church's most loyal sons, to chastise her for it.

Undoubtedly a break with Rome could have fearful repercussions, but conversely if Catholicism remained the national religion, this would draw the Queen into a peculiarly humiliating form of servitude. It was obvious that there was little likelihood that the Pope could ever be prevailed upon to recognize that the marriage between Henry VIII and Anne Boleyn had been valid. The best that Elizabeth could hope for from the Papacy would be for Paul IV to issue a dispensation declaring that hers was an exceptional case, and that in these special circumstances it was permissible for a woman who was technically illegitimate to sit on the English throne. Elizabeth would have to acknowledge that the crown was hers not by birthright, but by papal authority alone, an indignity that would be all the more unbearable because of the condemnation it implied of her father. It would be particularly galling for the daughter of the man who had established England as a wholly autonomous sovereign state to be the first English monarch to put herself in a position so uniquely dependent on the Pope.

In the circumstances it was almost a foregone conclusion that the Queen would aim to establish some sort of national Church, independent of the Papacy, but the exact form that this would take was by no means clear. All those who seceded from the Church of Rome were collectively designated 'Protestants', but the term was a loose one, and within the various branches of reformist thought the spectrum of opinion was very diverse. In England since the break with Rome, there had been only gradual changes in doctrine and ritual, for despite having rejected the authority of the Pope, in other respects Henry VIII had advanced very cautiously down the path of reform. During his lifetime, the English Bible was placed in all churches and the weekly lesson was read from it, and the people were taught the creed, the ten commandments and the Lord's Prayer in English. They also were permitted to sing the litany in their own language, but these were the only alterations that Henry could countenance.

Edward VI had taken the Reformation several stages further. Soon after his accession, communion in both kinds had been introduced, according the laity the privilege of partaking of the wine as well as the bread during Holy Communion, a privilege hitherto reserved exclusively for the clergy. This was a fundamental advance, designed to counteract the impression that the priesthood was a superior caste, whose powers of salvation set them apart from the rest of mankind, but it was only the first stage in a major programme of reform. In January 1549 Parliament had passed an Act of Uniformity which had introduced a new liturgy in English, to be used at all church services. The traditional mass was now set aside, superseded by a communion service in which transubstantiation had no place, but the wording still implied that Christ was present in spirit during the administration of the sacraments. Various ceremonies were also retained, such as the wearing of copes, and the invocation of the Holy Ghost on the communion bread and wine. In advanced reforming circles on the continent, such practices were branded as superstitious, and in 1552 a second prayer book had been introduced, purged of these popish remnants. The offensive ceremonies were expunged, and the text of the communion service was altered to imply that it was no more than a commemoration of the Last Supper. Even so, this was far removed from Protestantism in its purest form.

In Mary's reign, fear of persecution had led to an exodus of about eight hundred of her subjects, who were not prepared to imperil their souls by reverting to the Roman usage. The majority of these emigrés had settled in the German or Swiss cities where the intellectual leaders of the Reformation resided, and the exiles spent much of their time there engaged in theological debate. In the course of these discussions, many of them came to see the prayer book of 1552 as an imperfect work, in need of further revision, and at Frankfurt James Whittingham had taken it upon himself to edit it still further. In this new version, clergymen were no longer required to wear surplices while conducting services, and the litany and oral responses were eliminated; but while few of his brethren thought these amendments undesirable in themselves, the more conservative of them thought it improper to adopt on their own initiative any liturgy other than that which had been approved by Parliament in 1552. After bitter dissensions, a splinter group of radicals had left Frankfurt to take up residence at the capital of Calvinism, Geneva, where they would be free to use the prayer book of their choice.

This meant that by the time the exiles returned to England on Mary's death, there was already a substantial number of them who would view the reintroduction of the 1552 prayer book as a retrograde step. The Queen's attitude was very different, for far from desiring any advance on the situation established in 1552, she believed that by that time too much had already been excised from the Book of Common Prayer. She once affirmed that the communion service meant more to her than a mere re-enactment of the Last Supper, and she was also concerned that a liturgy that implied that this was all it signified would be unacceptable to a significant proportion of her subjects. Not only did she personally regard further reform as an uninviting prospect, but she knew that if she was to create a truly national Church, it could not cater exclusively to an earnest minority, but would have to comprehend within it less progressive souls. For this, continuity was essential.

Unlike her father, Elizabeth had no relish for theological arguments, but she always reacted sharply if it was implied that such matters were beyond her. In the Parliament of 1566 she exclaimed crossly, "It is said I am no divine. Indeed, I studied nothing but divinity till I came to the crown". She did her best to suppress debates about religion primarily because she was aiming to achieve a consensus within her Church, and if contentious issues were highlighted, there was less chance of bringing this about. As she remarked to an ambassador from France towards the end of her life, "There was only one Jesus Christ, and one faith, and all the rest they disputed about but trifles";[29] and having succeeded in founding a Church that was sound on fundamentals, she had no intention of seeing its unity endangered by fruitless disputations on insignificant matters of detail.

Because she deplored extremists on both sides of the religious divide, to some observers this denoted a lack of conviction in spiritual matters. In 1565 the Spanish ambassador remarked, "If what some people say is to be believed, she is not comfortable with her Protestants, nor with the doctrines of the other side either ... and gives ground for the assertion that she is an atheist". This was a complete misinterpretation, for although Elizabeth was free of the fanaticism that characterized her age, her faith never wavered. Her piety did not manifest itself in conventional ways, for she only attended chapel once a week and did not much like listening to sermons. She explained this by saying "that she had rather talk with God devoutly by prayer than hear others speak eloquently of God".[30] Throughout her life she also felt no need to avail herself of churchmen who could serve as professional mediators between God and her soul. However, far from denoting a lack of faith, the acknowledgment that one's salvation lay wholly in the hands of the Almighty was one of Protestantism's most fundamental beliefs.

In 1559, the Spanish ambassador reported that the Queen told him that she "differed very little" from Catholics, "as she believed that God was in the sacrament of the eucharist, and only dissented from three or four things in the mass", but while it was true that there was only a limited number of points on which she was at variance with the Catholics, she believed these to be crucial. When dealing with Catholic diplomats, she might choose to emphasize the essential similarity of their outlook, but in doing so she was deliberately tailoring her remarks to suit her audience, and in her communications with Protestant powers, her tone was very different. In a circular letter that the Queen addressed to the Protestant princes of Germany in 1577, it was the breadth of the gulf that separated her from the Catholics that was stressed, rather than the beliefs they shared in common, for Elizabeth urged that all those who "had come out of the darkness and filth of Popery" should band together against their mutual enemy.[31]

Already there had been some modifications in religious observance, and these were harbingers of greater changes to come. Before going to chapel on Christmas day 1558, the Queen had sent word to the officiating divine, Bishop Owen Oglethorp of Carlisle, that during the mass he should not raise high the consecrated elements in a ceremonious manner that implied that a miraculous transformation was taking place. Oglethorp had refused to comply, but when he prepared to celebrate mass in the traditional manner, Elizabeth had risen from her place and stalked out. In the ensuing weeks, more amenable clergymen were called in to conduct the Sunday services.

Outside the Queen's chapel, mass was still conducted as in Mary's reign, but on 28 December a proclamation had been issued, authorizing some changes in the subsidiary parts of the Church service. The gospel, the epistles, the ten commandments and some prayers were once again to be read aloud in English, thus effectively restoring the state of religion to what it had been in Henry VIII's day. Conservatives in religion could draw comfort from the fact that the majority of the Catholic rites and ceremonies remained in use, but the proclamation contained a strong hint that more would soon be done. It stated that the present position would be maintained "until consultation may be had by Parliament, by her Majesty and the three estates of this realm, for the better conciliation and accord of such causes as at this present are moved in matters and ceremonies of religion, the true advancement whereof . . . her Majesty most desireth".[32]

On 25 January 1559, Parliament assembled. As Sir Nicholas Bacon reminded the Lords and Commons in his opening speech, they had been summoned partly for financial reasons. It was customary for the first Parliament of the reign to assign to a new monarch the lifetime right to collect customs duties, but the Crown's urgent need of money meant that these would have to be supplemented with the grant of extraordinary taxation in the shape of a subsidy (a form of income tax) and two fifteenths and tenths, which were levies on moveables. Besides this, there was much important legislation that had to be enacted, and Bacon laid particular emphasis on the pressing necessity for "the well making of laws for the according and uniting of this realm into an uniform order of religion".[33]

The precedent that Parliament should be involved in the enactment of major religious change was now a well-established one, for Henry VIII had seen to it that his break with Rome was enshrined in statute. The keystone of the English Reformation was the 1534 Act of Supremacy, which had recognized Henry as Head of the Church on the grounds that Kings of England had occupied this position since time immemorial, and that it was only recently that the Papacy had usurped this function. This fiction was designed to cover up the innovative nature of Henry's actions but, by the reign of Edward VI, the government no longer thought it necessary to perpetuate such falsehoods, and in the 1549 Act of Uniformity the prayer book was confidently set forth "by authority of Parliament".[34] When Mary came to the throne, it was not possible for unilateral action on the part of the Crown to undo legislation that had received the assent of King, Lords and Commons, and, before Catholicism could be restored, Mary had had to steer laws through Parliament which repealed the enactments of her father and brother. Now the religious pendulum was again moving in a contrary direction, but if the swing was to acquire any momentum, Parliament would have to go with it.

For her present purposes, the Queen did not anticipate serious opposition from the House of Commons. In a bid to secure a co-operative lower chamber, the Marian regime had resorted to sending out circular letters to county sheriffs and mayors of towns at election time, asking them to try and see that "grave men, and of good and honest behaviour and conversation and specially of Catholic religion" were returned as Members of Parliament, but despite these precautions, the last Parliament of the reign had proved sullen and intractable.[35] Now that there was no longer official pressure to exclude those who favoured the new religion, Catholics were completely outnumbered, and those who were returned lacked effective leadership, as the dismissed Marian Councillors did not resume their seats.

The complexion of the House of Lords was very different. In the Commons, the Privy Councillors who were members could be relied upon to help guide through the house legislation which would re-establish Protestantism as the state religion, but their counterparts in the Lords were by no means united in favour of reform. The Earl of Bedford might be an ardent proponent of it, but fellow Councillors, such as the Marquis of Winchester and the Earl of Shrewsbury, were less enthusiastic. These men regarded it as acceptable that the Queen should refuse to recognize papal authority, but they did not want the Church she presided over to be markedly different from the Roman one. Furthermore, the bishops were each entitled to a seat in the upper house, and it was only to be expected that they would oppose an extensive programme of reform. It was fortunate that ten out of twenty-six bishoprics were vacant, for of late there had been a high rate of mortality among the episcopate, and a fever had conveniently carried off Mary's Archbishop of Canterbury, Reginald Pole, less than twenty-four hours after her own death. As the prelates normally constituted about a third of the total membership of the upper house, this reduction in their numbers was a great boon for the government. Nevertheless, when matters of religion were debated, the bishops' expertise in theology gave them an obvious advantage, and might enable them to exert a disproportionate influence over their fellow peers.

On 9 February a bill of Supremacy was introduced into the House of Commons, proposing to sweep away papal authority by establishing Elizabeth as Supreme Head of the Church in England. After the members had had time to familiarize themselves with its contents, the bill was read again on 13 February and debated the following day, and on 15 February it was submitted to the consideration of a Commons committee. In the hands of this committee, it was radically reshaped. On 15 February "a bill for the order of service" had been introduced in the Commons but, though the government had apparently envisaged dealing with this as a separate measure, the committee tacked its provisions on to the Bill of Supremacy and (so it would seem) incorporated some amendments of their own. The bill that emerged from committee to be submitted to the Commons on 21 February was much more extensive than its predecessor. It provided for the reintroduction of the 1552 prayer book, and there were also clauses detailing harsh penalties for non-conformists, which the committee had apparently inserted into the bill on their own initiative. In this form it was again debated, and according to the Spanish ambassador, was by no means universally well-received, but when the House divided it passed without difficulty.

The bill was then sent up to the Lords, but when debated there, it aroused vehement opposition. A committee of the upper house was formed to shear the bill of what the Lords regarded as its most offensive features, and after they had done their work, it reverted to being a much more innocuous measure. It still enabled Elizabeth to take the title of Supreme Head of the Church if she chose, but made no provision for a full religious settlement of the sort that had earlier been proposed. Thus emasculated, the bill was put to the vote in the Lords on 18 March, but even in its present form it proved unacceptable to the bishops, who opposed it to a man. Nevertheless, as most of the temporal lords no longer thought the bill objectionable, it secured a majority.

In the Commons there was indignation at the way the upper house had left their handiwork in tatters, but in view of the fact that Elizabeth had planned to dissolve Parliament before Easter (which fell on 26 March that year), it seemed that both Queen and Commons would have to content themselves with less than what they wanted. There was consolation in the fact that, even as reconstituted by the Lords, the bill of Supremacy retained a section legalizing communion in both kinds, and this at least represented a small advance towards Protestantism. Furthermore, once established as

Supreme Head of the Church, the Queen would be better placed to bring about the settlement she desired, for any bishop who refused to recognize her as such could be deprived and replaced by churchmen who could be relied upon to support any future measures of reform. By 22 March, the bill had again passed the Commons, and only needed royal approval to become law.

The closing ceremony of Parliament, at which the Queen assented to bills she found acceptable and vetoed those she did not favour, was scheduled to be held on 24 March. At the last moment, however, it was postponed, and Parliament was merely adjourned till 3 April. Rather than leave religion in a state of uneasy limbo while the episcopal bench was purged, the Queen had decided to make a second attempt to obtain a proper Church settlement from this Parliament. Her decision may have been influenced by the news which arrived on 19 March that peace with France was imminent, for this lessened the fear that the French might seize upon religion as an excuse to renew hostilities. However, as there was no confirmation that a treaty had been signed until 6 April, the good news from France cannot have been the sole reason for Elizabeth's change of heart.

On 3 April Parliament reassembled, and a week later a new bill of Supremacy was given its first reading in the Commons. It modified the terms of the original bill by declaring the Queen to be Supreme Governor, rather than Supreme Head of the Church, a change of title which it was hoped would allay the scruples of those lords who had been swayed by the arguments of the Archbishop of York, Nicholas Heath, that St Paul's commandment to women to be silent in church meant that it was unfitting for the Queen to set herself up as its head. Even Protestants had expressed some concern about Elizabeth adopting this style, for it was pointed out that Christ was the true head of the Church, and it was improper for a prince to abrogate the title. With characteristic pragmatism, the Queen had been willing to accept a less controversial alternative which in no way undermined her jurisdictional powers. In its new form, the bill encountered few difficulties: it passed rapidly through the Commons, and although the bishops continued to oppose it in the Lords, only one temporal peer voted with them, and the bill therefore secured a comfortable majority in the upper house.

The Act of Supremacy required all clergymen, magistrates and royal officials to take an oath avowing Elizabeth to be Supreme Governor of the Church, but the penalty for refusing to do so was only loss of office. More severe penalties were reserved for those who maliciously affirmed the authority of a foreign prince or prelate, but even so they forfeited no more than their goods and chattels on their first conviction, and it was only at the third offence that their action was construed as treasonous. In addition to the clauses dealing with the Royal Supremacy itself, the bill still contained its section permitting communion in both kinds, and it also repealed the heresy laws which had formed the basis for the Marian persecution. These provisions were an insurance measure, designed to guard against the possibility that the Lords would reject the proposals for a full religious settlement that were yet to come before them. The Queen could now feel confident that, even if the Lords remained recalcitrant, no one could be prosecuted for holding Protestant beliefs.

Meanwhile, on 18 April a bill of Uniformity had been read in the Commons. It prescribed that the 1552 prayer book must be used in all church services, although to make it more acceptable to traditionalists, a few minor modifications were inserted in its text. The most important of these was an alteration in the communion service, whereby a sentence from the 1549 prayer book that implied that Christ was present in spirit, was juxtaposed to the wording settled on in 1552, which did not allow of this interpretation. It was a device typical of the Queen's non-doctrinaire approach. Eighteen months later Elizabeth was to remark to a Scottish diplomat, "In the sacrament of the altar, some thinks [one] thing, some other; whose judgment is best God knows".[36] By adopting this hybrid formula, she sincerely hoped to accommodate all viewpoints.

A similar spirit of moderation was discernible in the sections of the bill dealing with those who disrupted religious uniformity. Clergymen who deviated from the ordained prayer book when conducting services were to be fined one year's salary and imprisoned for six months. Weekly attendance at church was compulsory for laymen, but they did not have to take communion, and the fine for staying away from church was only a shilling a week.

The bill raced through the Commons, but when it went up to the Lords it faced an uncertain fate. The Queen was aided by the fact that Bishops White of Winchester and Watson of Lincoln had been imprisoned in the Tower after expressing themselves intemperately at a disputation between Protestant and Catholic divines that had been held at Westminster during the Easter recess. Two more of their colleagues were absent through illness, and another bishop had returned to his diocese for reasons unknown. All the remaining bishops of course voted against the bill, and they were supported by nine temporal peers, two of them Privy Councillors, but on 29 April the measure nonetheless passed by a majority of three. Elizabeth had triumphed over the forces of reaction.[37]

The Queen prided herself on having established a Church which was at once remarkably broad in its appeal without being in any way inconsistent with the truth. Mass could no longer be legally celebrated, and there was a degree of compulsion in the requirement for regular attendance at church, but so long as her subjects showed outward conformity, there was no effort to delve into their innermost beliefs. By the standards of the day, this was remarkably enlightened. To some eyes, however, the Queen's anxiety to comprehend within her Church those on whom Catholicism had barely relaxed its grip had led her into error. There were complaints that, instead of paring faith down to its essentials, Elizabeth had preserved much that was rotten and corrosive, and in the picturesque phrase of one of her advisers, the more radical of her subjects condemned the state religion as no better than "a cloaked papistry, or mingle mangle".[38]

There was particular indignation over the ceremonial dress that clergymen had to wear in church. The Act of Uniformity had contained a proviso that ministers must conduct services apparelled in the clerical vestments which had been in use in the second year of Edward VI's reign, but as it had also stated that this rule would remain in force until the Queen took "other order" on the matter, it was assumed that she would waive it before long. This proved a misjudgment, for the Queen was to prove implacable in her insistence that vestments must be worn, and when the new prayer book was printed in the summer of 1559, the demand relating to ornaments was reiterated. Opponents of vestments maintained that they were relics of Popery which acted as a snare for the ignorant by encouraging superstition, but the Queen could not accept this. She held that a certain amount of ceremony helped enhance the faith of simple believers, and she furthermore realized that a retention of some ancient usages was essential if those who had felt affection for the Catholic rites were to become acclimatized to her Church.

A radical minority might stigmatize her Church as disastrously flawed, but Elizabeth would never concede that her religious settlement had been in any way inadequate. To her it was immutable, the rock on which true faith could repose, rather than a mere milestone on the way to a more exalted destination. Her Church was founded on statute, which gave it the stability it needed, but once Parliament had performed that service for her, she would not call upon it to deliberate further on matters of religion. She was seriously displeased whenever Members of Parliament sought to amend the Church on their own initiative, for as Sir Nicholas Bacon explained in his dissolution speech, her settlement was intended to endure, and the Queen would have as little patience with those who imperilled it by trying to "go before the law, or beyond the law" as with those who dawdled behind.[39]

With the religious settlement safely through Parliament, the next step was to enforce it. On 23 May 1559 a commission, consisting largely of Privy Councillors, was formed and given powers to administer the oath of Supremacy to the bishops. The Queen admitted that she hoped that some of the more moderate among them, such as Heath of York and Thirlby of Ely, would be prevailed upon to subscribe to it, for she knew that if she had to find an entirely new set of bishops, she could not avoid drawing many of them from the ranks of the exiles, who tended to be too radical for her liking. Once again, however, the bishops disappointed her, for they refused to take the oath. The only exception was Bishop Kitchin of Llandaff, and as he was variously described as "the calamity of his see", and "a greedy old man with but little learning", he was not much of a catch.[40]

Since his brethren had proved less compliant, the Queen had no alternative but to deprive them, and on 30 May Bonner of London was the first to lose his job. His departure afforded Elizabeth no regret, for his prominent role in the Marian persecutions had left her with an abiding disgust for him, but she derived less satisfaction from the removal of the other bishops. Yet although the Queen proceeded against them reluctantly, there were some people who thought the bishops had got off lightly: one returned exile commented angrily that they deserved to be "suspended not only from their office, but from a halter". Doubtless this individual was pleased when Bonner was shut up in the Marshalsea prison the following year, and with the exception of Bishop Poole, all the remaining deprived bishops were either sent to the Tower or the Fleet prison soon afterwards. They had apparently been making trouble by "declaiming and railing" against the religious settlement, but apart from Bonner, they were set free after three years in confinement. Bonner was kept in the Marshalsea till his death in 1569, though Protestant apologists have claimed that his unpopularity in London made this desirable for his own protection, and that he "lived daintily" while in prison.[41]

In August 1559 an ecclesiastical visitation began, covering the entire country. Visitors travelled to every district, bringing with them injunctions that regulated every aspect of clerical procedure and discipline, and requiring all clergymen to attest under oath their support of the religious settlement. Superficially at least, the visitation was a triumph. Of the 8,000 or so clergymen in England, it has been estimated that between two hundred and four hundred were deprived for refusing to take the oath, but the figures are somewhat misleading. As one leading Protestant churchman complained in 1564, some of those who took the oath were "but dissemblers and rank papists" who would not "do anything to commend, beautify or set forward this religion, but mutter against it", thus effectively undermining the Church from within. In 1577 it was further alleged that the returns listing those who had taken the oath contained the names of many who had never done so, and certainly in the North of England, where Catholicism was most entrenched, a large number of clergy evaded having to subscribe simply by not turning up at the sessions at which the oath was to be tendered.[42]

The willingness of the vast majority of the clergy to conform, at least on the surface, meant that not many had to be replaced at parochial level, but the Queen had urgently to address herself to the problem of finding a senior Church hierarchy. She had had no doubts as to the man whom she wished to become Archbishop of Canterbury in the place of the deceased Cardinal Pole. Matthew Parker was the retiring and scholarly son of a Norwich weaver, and the Queen had known him since her infancy, for as a chaplain to Anne Boleyn he had preached before the Princess Elizabeth when she was barely two years old. Since that time he had risen steadily in his profession, and during the reign of Edward VI he had become Vice Chancellor of Cambridge University. In Mary's reign he had been defrocked on the grounds that he was married, but despite the loss of his living, he had not fled abroad, and had spent the reign staying quietly with a friend. As a result he had never been exposed to what Elizabeth regarded as the worst excesses of the continental reform movement, although presumably she found it less gratifying that Parker had employed himself during his enforced retirement composing a treatise in defence of clerical marriage. In her present need of an Archbishop, however, Elizabeth was prepared to overlook this, and the more so because Cecil had long been a "special good friend" to Parker,[43] and believed him to be the best man for the job.

Parker himself was appalled by the prospect of becoming Archbishop of Canterbury. When asked to take the post early in 1559, he said plaintively that he would rather go to prison than accept, and for months he had steadfastly maintained that his "decayed voice and small quality" did not fit him for the task.[44] Elizabeth and Cecil had nevertheless persevered, and in August 1559 Parker had reluctantly given way. Elizabeth had no cause to regret her choice, for Parker was the very embodiment of the moderate spirit of the Anglican religious settlement, and was possessed of just the right combination of tact and firmness needed to maintain discipline in the Church.

Parker's appointment had been a good beginning, but there were twenty-four other bishoprics to fill, and the Queen did not find this easy. It was obvious that if she wanted anything other than an utterly undistinguished episcopate, she must bestow mitres on many of the Marian exiles, for only they had sufficient intellectual and moral conviction to give credibility to her Church. Unfortunately, she did not relish the thought of giving them preferment, knowing that while abroad the exiles had been vouchsafed too dazzling a vision of the truth for them cheerfully to accept her own definition of it. In her present necessity, however, Elizabeth had no alternative, and when she finally brought herself to name her bishops, more than half of them were former exiles. Nevertheless, compared with some of their fellow emigrés, these men were relatively moderate, for the Queen had carefully weeded out all those who had won reputations as firebrands.

Only three of her bishops had spent any part of their time on the continent in Calvin's Geneva, for though in some circles that city was regarded as "the most perfect school of Christ that ever was in earth since the days of the Apostles",[45] Elizabeth did not think its graduates would adapt willingly to her tutelage.

Some of the exiles had qualms about accepting high office in a Church marred by so many obvious imperfections. One of them subsequently recalled how those who were offered preferment on their return "contended long and earnestly" for the abolition of the vestments regulation, but they could not prevail over the Queen, who made it plain that she would withdraw the offer of a bishopric from any man who defied her on this matter. After much soul-searching, the exiles "judged it best ... not to desert our churches for the sake of a few ceremonies, and those not unlawful in themselves, especially since the pure doctrine of the gospels remained in all its integrity and freedom". In September 1559 there was a flurry of consecrations, and during the next eighteen months the remaining vacant sees were so methodically filled that by May 1561 only Oxford and Bristol were left without a bishop.[46]

There were many ways in which her bishops found Elizabeth a difficult mistress, for they were simultaneously expected to be strong-minded enough to assert themselves over their inferiors, while showing themselves totally subservient to the Queen. It was not always possible for them to reconcile these conflicting demands. The Queen kept them up to the mark by bullying them unmercifully, but her rough handling of them often had the effect of lessening their prestige, and this in its turn made it more difficult for them to maintain the order within the Church that she desired. In 1561, after Archbishop Parker had been subjected to an ill-tempered outburst from the Queen, he lamented to Cecil, "It is a wonder to me that her Highness is so incensed by our adversaries that all the world must understand her displeasure against us. Whereby our credits be little, our doings ... shall take less effect among her subjects, to her own disquiet of government. I never heard or read, but that all manner princes ... did evermore cherish their ecclesiastical state ... and we alone of our time openly brought in hatred, shamed and traduced before the malicious and ignorant people, as beasts without knowledge to Godward ... as men ... without discretion or any godly disposition worthy to serve in our state".[47]

One of the major sources of tension between the Queen and her bishops arose from her aversion to married clergy, for the relaxation of the requirement for clerical celibacy was one aspect of Protestantism to which she was never fully reconciled. Clerical marriage had first been legalized in 1549, and had proved so popular that when Mary outlawed it again, four years later, nearly a third of the clergy in London had lost their jobs for having taken a wife. To the annoyance of most churchmen, the 1559 Act of

Uniformity contained no mention of clerical marriage. It soon emerged that Elizabeth was prepared "to wink at it but not stablish it by law", which one indignant clergyman said would serve for "nothing else but to bastard our children". The injunctions published later in the year did something to redress the situation by stating that "the priests and ministers of the Church may lawfully, for the avoiding of fornication have an honest and sober wife", but even so, the Queen begrudged them the privilege, and periodically threatened to withdraw it. In August 1561 Parker (who had a wife himself) confided unhappily to Cecil, "Her Majesty continueth very evil affected to the state of matrimony in the clergy. And if I were not therein very stiff, would utterly and openly condemn and forbid it".[48]

The Queen's prejudice against married clergy expressed itself most strongly when her bishops took wives, for if she had to accept that it was unrealistic to expect all of the clergy to lead celibate lives, she thought it the duty of the senior Church hierarchy to set an example in this respect. From this point of view, her episcopate failed her completely, for of seventy-six bishops appointed during the reign, only eighteen are known to have remained single. Worse still, eleven of them married again after being widowed, a particularly heinous sin in the Queen's eyes.[49] On Elizabeth's instructions, Bishop Cox of Ely was hauled up before the Council and soundly rebuked when at the age of seventy he took a woman many years his junior as his second wife, and the Queen was hardly mollified when he justified his action on the grounds that otherwise he might not have been able to resist the temptations of extramarital sex. Godwin of Bath and Wells also landed in trouble when he remarried late in life, and having extracted a promise from Bishop Fletcher of London that he would remain a widower, the Queen never forgave him when he broke his word and married a saucy young widow.

The temptation for Elizabeth to harry her senior churchmen over their marriages was the greater because so many of her subjects shared her prejudices about clerical celibacy. When summoned before the Council in 1568, Cox of Ely had to admit that by remarrying he had made himself the talk of the town, and exposed himself to much derision and abuse. The widespread distaste evinced by many of the laity for clerical marriage was reflected in rhymes and ballads, such as that which was circulating in Kent in 1576, and which rejoiced in the refrain, "All priests' wives are drabs and quenes". In 1586 Elizabeth Seamer of north Yorkshire was heard to declare, "It was never a good world since ministers must have wives", while six years later, an Essex man expressed himself still more intemperately when he declared, "All priests' wives are whores and their children bastards". A Spaniard once noted that Elizabeth was "very much wedded to the people, and thinks as they do", and certainly there was a sizeable number of her subjects who would not have thought her attitude to clerical marriage in the least eccentric, for their own feelings on the subject were similar to hers.[50]

When her bishops displeased her, Elizabeth could exact financial retribution, for as Supreme Governor of the Church there were various ways in which she was entitled to milk it of its wealth. At the time of the dissolution of the monasteries, the Crown had acquired numerous tithe rights which had formed part of the revenue of monastic estates, but these impropriate tithes were not a very productive asset, because of the difficulties involved in collecting them from the laity. In 1559 the Queen overcame this problem by securing from Parliament the right to force incoming bishops to surrender some of their diocesan lands in return for tithes of a nominally equivalent value. For the bishops, these exchanges were almost invariably bad bargains, to which they did not submit without a struggle. In 1559, the Queen had originally intended to annex almost sixty per cent of episcopal lands, but several of the men who had been offered bishoprics flatly refused to take office on these terms, forcing Elizabeth to moderate her demands. Parker himself, and the Bishops of Ely, London, Hereford and Chichester all succeeded in securing a reduction in the amount of lands to be alienated, but they were able to blackmail the Queen in this way only because of her desperate need for bishops at that time. Subsequent generations of prelates tended to be less successful in resisting her depredations.[51]

As a matter of course, bishops had to pay ten per cent of their annual revenue to the Crown, but when they took over their dioceses, they had to forfeit a whole year's income. By regularly switching her bishops around, Elizabeth could maximize this source of revenue, and though early in the reign she employed this device comparatively rarely, she resorted to it with increasing frequency when money grew short in her later years. It was a liability which pressed heavily on the bishops. In the 1590s, for example, Richard Fletcher was called upon to pay the Crown a total of £3,000 in 'First Fruits' after being moved three times in as many years, and as a result he died in debt to the Queen. His case was not untypical, but in Elizabeth's defence it should be said that she did not exploit the system as ruthlessly as she might have. In 1575 a list was prepared for her advocating the relocation of every single bishop, but the Queen thought this excessive, and did not act on the advice.[52]

Another form of extortion which the Queen practised on her bishops was to exert pressure on them to let their lands to laymen at uneconomic rents, for by this indirect spoliation she could enrich her courtiers at no expense to herself. Thus in 1577, Bishop Cox of Ely was forced to lease his London house to Sir Christopher Hatton at a price below the market rate, and in 1584 Godwin of Bath and Wells was bludgeoned into renting a valuable manor to Sir Walter Ralegh on a ninety-nine-year lease. The bishops protested that such transactions left them stricken with guilt, for in theory they had an obligation to pass on their temporalities intact to their successors, and by denuding their estates of their best assets they laid themselves open to the charge of recklessly impoverishing their sees. In 1594 Bishop Hutton of Durham wailed to Cecil that if he obeyed a royal command to lease one of his episcopal properties to a courtier, "I think verily it would be a mean to bring my hoary hairs with grief into the grave. I did never hurt an ecclesiastical living in my life. I think it not lawful; and I am persuaded in conscience that I ought not to leave any living in worse case to my successor than my predecessor did leave it unto me".[53] Such excuses cut very little ice with the Queen, who reacted with fury when the bishops clung stubbornly to their possessions, and it did not usually take her very long to browbeat them into submission. Hutton himself dared not provoke her with an outright refusal, and prudently sought to deflect the royal wrath by offering some of his personal property in place of the episcopal lands on which Elizabeth had had her eye.

"These be marvellous times", the Archbishop of York lamented in 1588, "The patrimony of the Church is laid open as a prey to all the world". By diminishing the bishops' wealth, the Queen insidiously undermined their standing in the community, and burdened them with financial worries to an extent that distracted them from their real responsibilities. By forcing the bishops to take her courtiers as their tenants, she lessened the prelates' chances of endearing themselves to the gentry in their dioceses by letting their property to them at favourable rates, and the reduction of their incomes also made it more difficult for the bishops to build up local goodwill with lavish displays of hospitality. The Queen was most indignant when, later in the reign, episcopacy itself came under fierce attack, but in some respects she only had herself to blame for the institution's decline. Elizabeth's last Archbishop of Canterbury was even alleged to have warned her, "When they that serve at God's altar shall be exposed to poverty, then religion itself will be exposed to scorn and become contemptible".[54]

There was, however, something to be said for the Queen's rapacity. She did not divert ecclesiastical revenues to her courtiers out of mere caprice, for the monarchy only exerted so strong a hold over the upper strata of the population because of its ability to satisfy their hunger for land or financial privileges. Inevitably the distribution of such favours was a selective process, and only a fortunate few did really well out of it, but so long as all could feel that there was a reasonable chance of participating in the share out, the system was deemed to be working well. However, in view of the limited nature of the Crown's resources, it became increasingly difficult for Elizabeth to maintain the general level of satisfaction, and to keep disillusionment at bay, she had to tap every conceivable source of revenue that might enable her to spread her largesse wider. This was why she thought it legitimate to plunder the bishops' temporalities for, providing she stopped short of beggaring the Church, she could maintain that by engaging in this judicious redistribution of the national wealth she was preserving her kingdom's stability.

The bishops might complain of the way Elizabeth treated Church property, but their own handling of it was none too scrupulous. Although they were supposed to keep their estates in trust for their successors, it was understood that during their tenure of their sees, they and their families were entitled to a competent maintenance, but exactly what was meant by this was never specified. As a result, bishops were exposed to the temptation of squandering diocesan assets in order to enrich their families, and by no means all of them were able to resist it. The son of Bishop Godwin of Bath and Wells claimed that his father had suffered lifelong remorse for having leased Ralegh an estate, but the son did not say whether Godwin felt similar prickings of guilt about having leased him another of the bishopric's properties at a very favourable rate. Matthew Hutton might claim that it was a matter of principle with him to resist the alienation of Church property, but even so, his generosity in granting leases to his children aroused criticism in some circles. In the circumstances it was understandable that the Queen suspected that the bishops resisted her encroachments out of acquisitiveness rather than pious rectitude, and that it was a selfish concern for their family fortunes that counted for their reluctance to deliver up their property to anyone else. As Lord North told Bishop Cox of Ely when the latter was refusing to surrender an estate to him, "Her Highness cannot but think much unkindness that to do the same to other, their wives, children or friends, they make no conscience, [but] when her Majesty requireth any thing for her servants . . . there is such conscience and scrupulosity made, and scripture ready to be alleged".[55]

Elizabeth could congratulate herself on having put an end to the dangerous uncertainty that had prevailed at her accession with regard to religion, and as far as foreign relations were concerned there were also grounds for cautious optimism. On 2 April 1559 the Treaty of Cateau-Cambrésis had been signed with France, and if the terms of the agreement were not all that had been hoped for, to have remained at war would have been immeasurably worse. English commissioners had been trying to reach a settlement with the French since the last weeks of Mary's reign, and immediately prior to her accession, Elizabeth had blustered to Count Feria that "she would have them beheaded if they made peace without Calais". In reality, however, the English were in no position to dictate terms to the French, and for all her talk of chopping off heads, the Queen knew this well enough. Unlike Cecil, who regarded Calais as "more chargeable than worth", the Queen was much pained by the loss of the town, and never ceased to hope that she could one day repossess it, but this was not the moment to stake all on its recapture. It was in fact a legitimate cause of congratulation that her commissioners succeeded in obtaining peace with at least a semblance of honour, for by the terms of the treaty the French agreed that after they had occupied Calais for eight years, they would either return it to the English, or compensate them financially. Unfortunately, few people were under any illusion that the French would abide by these conditions. In London there was such universal scepticism that the French would honour their commitment that Count Feria reported, "The Common people laugh at the idea . . . and are dissatisfied with the agreement made".[56] Nevertheless, the fact that the French tenure of Calais was in theory provisional at least gave the English time to adjust themselves to its loss.

If it was a relief that England and France were no longer at war, there could be no certainty that the peace would endure. Mary Stuart was still waiting in the wings, and it was unclear whether she would content herself with being Elizabeth's understudy, or whether her father-in-law would encourage her to seek a more commanding role. After the French had had time to regroup their forces, there was a real danger that hostilities might break out afresh, and the English were bereft of allies who could help them to fend off such an attack. Conventional wisdom suggested that Elizabeth should do all in her power to bring England out of diplomatic isolation, and if she had wished to secure the friendship of a major continental power, she was in many ways well placed to do so, for any foreign alliance could be sealed with the offer of her hand in marriage. After all, it was obvious that Elizabeth would soon have to find herself a husband, and if she could marry a foreign prince who could take the realm under his protection, this had much to be said for it.

As was inevitable with the accession to the throne of a twenty-five-year-old spinster, the identity of her future husband was viewed as the foremost question of the day. "The more I think about this business", wrote Count Feria four days after Elizabeth became Queen, "the more certain I am that everything depends upon the husband this woman may take". It was assumed to be out of the question that Elizabeth would decide to remain single: she herself wryly remarked, "There is a strong idea in the world that a woman cannot live unless she is married", and no one supposed that she would regard her existence as fulfilled unless she found a man to share it. Shortly after her accession, a German diplomat pronounced confidently, "The Queen is of an age where she should in reason, and as is woman's way, be eager to marry and be provided for . . . For that she should wish to remain a maid and never marry is inconceivable."[57]

The Queen's contemporaries were sure that the instinctive reaction of any woman faced with her responsibilities would be to place herself in the hands of a trustworthy man with whom she could share "the cares, the labours and fatigues of her government". Certainly Mary Tudor had shown herself desperate for a husband's guidance, and the ambassador who had transmitted Philip of Spain's proposal to her had not failed to point out that, if she accepted, she would be "relieved of the pains and travails which were rather men's work than the profession of ladies". Elizabeth clearly was in more urgent need than most of male protection, not least because a husband could give her a direct heir and thus free her of the fear that on her death a disputed succession would give rise to civil war. Apart from this, marriage alone would provide her with the emotional stability that every woman needed (or so it was said), as well as giving her a sexual outlet which was regarded as being essential to feminine well-being. One contemporary authority even averred that women deprived of coitus were not only tormented by "unruly motions of tickling lust", but also suffered from poor complexions and unsteady minds caused by the ascent of "naughty vapour" to the brain. In short, as Cecil was to tell the Queen later in the reign, few people questioned that in marriage lay her "only known and likely surety, at home and abroad".[58]

This assumption was so universal that at first scant attention was paid when Elizabeth voiced misgivings about marriage. At the end of Mary's reign, Elizabeth had received a proposal from the Crown Prince of Sweden, but when Sir Thomas Pope had informed her of the offer, she had firmly rejected it with the words, "I so well like of this estate [spinsterhood], as I persuade unto myself there is not any kind comparable unto it". Sir Thomas did not take this seriously, commenting jovially that he "thought few or none would believe but that her Grace would be right well content to marry so there were some honourable marriage offered her". Much the same attitude prevailed when Elizabeth first ascended the throne. Soon after Parliament assembled in January 1559, the Commons decided to submit a formal request to the Queen asking her to marry as soon as possible, and on 6 February, a delegation from the house presented her with a petition to this effect. Elizabeth told them that while she did not rule out matrimony altogether, she had so far never felt any inclination for it. She cautioned them that it was quite possible that it would "please Almighty God to continue me still in the mind to live out of the state of marriage", and she said that if so, it would cause her little regret, for "in the end this shall be for me sufficient, that a marble stone shall declare that a Queen, having reigned such a time, lived and died a virgin". This answer was reported back to the House of Commons on 10 February, but it does not appear to have caused much of a stir, presumably because few members set any store by what she had said.[59]

Despite the general scepticism, there were many perfectly sound objections that the Queen could allege against marriage. It was true that by marrying a foreign prince she would secure herself a protector, whose mere presence at her side would deter aggressors, but her husband would look to her for reciprocal assistance in the furtherance of his own concerns, and the obligations that she would incur by entering into such a partnership could not be shrugged off lightly. The interests of England would not necessarily be of paramount importance to a member of a European royal family, whose main reason for marrying Elizabeth might rather be that this would leave him well placed to exploit her country for his own ends. Although in some ways a dynastic marriage would make Elizabeth less vulnerable, the enemies of her husband would almost certainly become her enemies too, and the difficulties of remaining detached from continental rivalries once married to a foreigner had been graphically illustrated by the way that Mary Tudor had been sucked into war with France at the behest of her Spanish husband. Whatever safeguards were incorporated into the marriage treaty, a union with a foreign prince would almost inevitably result in some loss of national sovereignty, and in view of the fabled insularity of Elizabeth's subjects, it was unlikely that she would be alone in looking on this as an unwelcome development.

From a political point of view, marriage with a European prince had obvious drawbacks, and there was no guarantee whatever that it would bring personal happiness. Owing to the conventions that governed international relations, it was almost impossible for Elizabeth to assess in advance whether she would find one of her foreign suitors a compatible partner. When dynastic marriages were mooted, it was not customary for either of the principal parties to meet at the outset, and instead proxy courtships were conducted by trusted emissaries. The nearest that bride and groom could come to a physical appraisal of one another was by engaging in a mutual exchange of portraits, and there was no way of telling whether these would be good likenesses. Admittedly, the Queen lived at a time when few individuals had much independence in their choice of marriage partner, which was generally settled for them by parents or guardian, and hence it was arguably unreasonable of her to expect to have her personal preferences taken into account.

Nevertheless, Elizabeth was not the first member of her family to find fault with the way the international marriage market operated. In 1538, when it had been suggested to Henry VIII that he should send an envoy to France to evaluate the charms of various candidates for his hand, the King had burst out, "By God, I trust on no one but myself! The thing touches me too near." Only a year after this, however, Henry had admitted defeat and become betrothed to the Lutheran princess Anne of Cleves without having vetted her personally beforehand. His agent in Germany had given a good account of her attractions, and Henry had also liked the look of the portrait of Anne painted by Hans Holbein, but when he saw her in the flesh he found her utterly repugnant, and complained mournfully that she looked "nothing so well as she was spoken of". Since by that time there could be no question of withdrawing, Henry was left with no alternative but to "put my neck in the yoke" (as he bitterly described it), but the marriage was an utter farce, and after six months of non-consummation it was annulled. The whole thing had clearly made an indelible impression on Elizabeth, and she had been still more deeply affected by the pitiful marriage of her sister to Philip of Spain, whose lack of enthusiasm for his ageing bride had been painfully obvious, despite his manful efforts to conceal it. Utterly determined not to have to undergo a similar experience herself, the Queen gave out that she had "taken a vow to marry no man whom she has not seen, and will not trust portrait painters".[60]

The problem was that few princes would be prepared to present themselves for inspection if there was a good chance that, once Elizabeth had had a look, they would be ignominiously packed off home. Such an ordeal would not only expose the rejected admirer to universal ridicule, but would also bring dishonour on his country. Time and again, ambassadors would tell Elizabeth that it was unrealistic to expect a royal suitor to parade himself before her like a piece of livestock, but the Queen obstinately maintained that she could not ask for anything less.

Since there were so many obstacles in the way of Elizabeth marrying a foreigner, the obvious alternative was for her to take one of her subjects as a husband, and in view of the fact that the English had a reputation for being incorrigible xenophobes, it was not surprising that this was the course that many of her people wished her to adopt. The Queen's old tutor, Roger Ascham, confided to a foreign friend, "We are all of us in favour of one of our own countrymen in preference to a stranger". An Italian living in London likewise formed the impression that "all are agreed in wishing her to take an Englishman". It was in fact not strictly true that opinion on this point was unanimous: to name but three of the leading men at court, William Cecil, the Earl of Sussex and the Duke of Norfolk all thought it would serve the country better if Elizabeth married a foreigner, but they were probably in a minority in taking this view. It would seem that when the House of Commons was drawing up its petition asking Elizabeth to marry, it had been proposed to include in it a request that she choose an Englishman, and although the members ultimately thought the better of it, the indications are that they refrained because they were fearful of being thought presumptuous, and not because the motion commanded insufficient support.[61]

Ostensibly it appeared that it would be an immensely popular move if Elizabeth married within the kingdom, but the Queen herself was sure that public joy at the nuptials would prove short-lived. If she accepted one of her courtiers as a husband, the others would feel aggrieved at having been passed over, and they would also resent the elevation of a former equal to anything approaching kingly eminence. She would henceforth preside over a court seething with jealousy, where angry nobles would blame her husband for the least check in their careers, feeling sure that the latter was promoting at their expense his family and friends, and that Elizabeth's partiality for the upstart had rendered her incapable of according them fair treatment. With the aristocracy united in their hatred of the interloper, bitterness would seep lower down the social hierarchy, until the whole of England was rent by factions and feuding, causing political disintegration. Nor were such fears on the Queen's part by any means fanciful, as the fate that befell Mary Stuart after she married one of her Scots subjects would show.

It was of course arguable that Elizabeth would have a better chance of domestic felicity if she married a man to whom she was attracted, rather than saddling herself with an unknown prince who might well prove uncongenial. On the other hand, the Queen felt strongly that it would demean her if she took a husband who was not of royal blood. Her father, of course, had not been so fastidious, for four of his six wives (including Elizabeth's mother) had been commoners, but in this respect at least, the Queen was more old-fashioned than he had been. Count Feria, who was anxious that Elizabeth should not marry an Englishman, was pleased to see that she was so sensitive on the question of status, and played on her snobbish reservations by telling her that it would be unfortunate if she did less well for herself than her sister, who had hooked a great prince. Delighted by the way that Elizabeth received this remark, Feria noted happily, "I fancy I can get at her through this feeling".[62]

Whether Elizabeth married prince or parvenu, it was obvious that she could not treat her husband as a mere plaything, for he would expect to wield considerable power. In normal circumstances, the rights of husbands over wives were little short of autocratic. "Ye wives, be in subjection to obey your husbands ... for the husband is the head of the woman, as Christ is the head of the Church", ran one admonition in a contemporary sermon, while a treatise published a few years after Elizabeth's death went still further in affirming "though an husband in regard of evil qualities may carry the image of the devil, yet in regard to his place and office he beareth the image of God". As far as property was concerned, the rights of a wife were negligible, for according to a legal handbook of the day, "If before marriage, the woman were possessed of horses ... sheep, corn, wool, money, plate and jewels, all manner of moveable substance is presently by conjunction the husband's to sell, keep or bequeath if he die".[63]

It was true that in the case of a Queen regnant, Parliament was able to make an exception. On Mary Tudor's betrothal, it was established that Philip would be styled King of England and that he should "aid her

Highness, being his wife, in the happy administration of her Grace's realms and dominions", but it was stipulated that he should have no control over the distribution of patronage, and that the sovereignty of the country still resided in Mary. In practice, however, this arrangement had not worked particularly well, not least because Philip had chafed at the limitations on his power. Anxious to be King in more than name, he had pressed Mary to have him formally crowned, and her failure to gratify him on this count had led to marital discord between them. Conversely, although Philip might have felt that it was monstrous that his rights as a husband should be in any way abridged, from the English point of view the safeguards that hedged the marriage treaty did not prove particularly effective. It was explicitly stated in the marriage treaty that "The realm of England, by occasion of this matrimony, shall not directly or indirectly be entangled with the war" then raging on the continent, but this precaution proved of little avail when Philip demanded that his wife declare war on France for his sake.[64]

Acute observers realized that Elizabeth would not relish forfeiting any of her powers to the man she married. Six years after her accession, the Queen confided to the Scots ambassador, Sir James Melville, that she hoped to remain single, whereupon Sir James at once replied, "I know the truth of that Madam, you need not tell it me. Your Majesty thinks if you were married you would be but Queen of England; and now you are both King and Queen". The following year she told the French ambassador that the only way a husband could be of assistance to her was by providing her with an heir, for she did not intend to relinquish control over her wealth and armed forces.[65] As Elizabeth well knew, however, if she did marry, it would prove virtually impossible to preserve her independence in this way. Parliament had done its best to uphold Mary Tudor's status as sole ruler of the country, but her husband had still been able to order her about and, on those occasions when Mary had failed to fall in with his wishes, the resultant unpleasantness had made her profoundly unhappy. Elizabeth found it galling enough that, in the event of her marriage, she would have to apply to Parliament if she wished to prevent her monarchical powers from being encroached upon, but worse still was the fact that there was little guarantee that such legislation would prove of any use.

The Queen thus had ample reason to think it would be a mistake on her part to take a husband. It must be emphasized, however, that her reluctance to marry did not stem solely from the realization that in her own special circumstances it would be advisable to abstain, for her objections to it were more general than this. In 1563, when the pressure on her to marry was intensifying, Elizabeth told Parliament that she thought spinsterhood "best for a private woman", although she qualified this by saying that because of the need for an heir, "I strive with myself to think it not meet for a prince". On another occasion she declared in Parliament, "If I were a milkmaid with a pail on my arm, whereby my private person might be little set by, I would not forsake that poor and single state to match with the greatest monarch". In 1559 she told a German diplomat "that she had found the celibate life so agreeable, and was so accustomed to it, that she would rather go into a nunnery, or for that matter suffer death" than to renounce it against her will, and in a variation on this theme a few years later, she stated she would much prefer to be "beggarwoman and single, far rather than Queen and married".[66] Hence the Queen's aversion to matrimony was at a very fundamental level, and she rejected it not merely because her unique position would make it hard for her to find a husband who could suit her, but because she regarded marriage itself as inherently undesirable.

Since there is evidence which suggests that she had formed this unfavourable view long before she became Queen, political considerations cannot on their own account for her attitude. The Earl of Leicester (who for years was regarded as one of the leading contenders for Elizabeth's hand) once told the French ambassador that he had known Elizabeth since she was a child, and from the age of eight onwards she had always maintained that she would never be married. Evidently she had said much the same to Sir William Pickering, with whom she was on close terms in her early youth, for at the very outset of her reign, he said "he knew she meant to die a maid". In 1559 she herself explained to Parliament that ever since reaching her "years of understanding" she had concluded that spinsterhood would suit her best, and a few months after this she reiterated to the Holy Roman Emperor, Ferdinand I (whose son wished to marry her), that this was "no new or suddenly formed resolution" on her part, but one that she had long cherished.[67]

Exactly what it was that made Elizabeth so sure that marriage was best avoided can never be stated with utter certainty. In the sixteenth century, as now, a high proportion of marriages were unhappy: a homily on marriage, issued in 1562, paints a vivid picture of the disharmony that prevailed in most households, with the comment "How few matrimonies there be without chidings, brawlings, tauntings, resentings, bitter burstings and fightings". Once on the throne, Elizabeth was better placed than most to reflect on the truth of this observation, for at various times she was called upon to act as a sort of marriage guidance counsellor to the nobility. After the Earls of Worcester, Derby and Shrewsbury parted from their wives, the Queen intervened to try and make them take them back again. It is possible, too, that her negative view of marriage had its roots in the conjugal difficulties of her immediate family circle. Not only had Henry VIII divorced two of his wives, but both of his sisters had contracted marriages of uncertain validity, and it was unclear whether the offspring that resulted from these were legitimate. In 1561 Elizabeth told a Scots diplomat that these events made it impossible for her to equate marriage with security, for "some [say] that this marriage was unlawful, some that one was a bastard, some other, to and fro, as they favoured or misliked. So many doubts of marriage was in all hands that I stand aw [i.e. fearful] myself to enter into marriage fearing the controversy".[68]

If Elizabeth admitted to being disenchanted by the high divorce rate in her family, it is surely permissible to speculate that the judicial murders of her mother and stepmother had a more damaging impact on her psyche. As has been said, at the time of Anne Boleyn's execution, she was too young to grasp the implications, but her mother's death and disgrace undoubtedly overshadowed her early years, and though Elizabeth never gave vent to any feelings on the subject, this does not show that she successfully detached herself from the tragedy. The shock of Catherine Howard's execution (when Elizabeth was at the impressionable age of eight) would have been more immediate, for even if Elizabeth had not been especially close to her young stepmother, Catherine's sudden extinction must at the very least have had a powerful effect on her subconscious.[69]

Obviously, the degree to which Elizabeth's early experiences coloured her character remains purely conjectural. One can hypothesize that they left her traumatized and sexually frigid, but empirical evidence for this is wanting, and the most that can be stated with certainty is that Elizabeth did not come from what modern psychologists would describe as a secure home background. Yet the note of hysteria that occasionally crept in to her utterances on marriage makes it hard to maintain that her attitude towards it was at all times that of an eminently well-adjusted woman. It was with an almost perceptible shudder that she told the French ambassador in 1565 that the man she married would be in a good position "to carry out some evil wish, if he had one", and some years later she expressed herself still more forcefully when she burst out that "for her part she hated the idea of marriage every day more, for reasons which she would not divulge to a twin soul, if she had one, much less to a living creature".[70] While it would be a distortion to ascribe Elizabeth's decision to remain single solely to the workings of a crude defensive mechanism which had been triggered by the emotional upheavals of an unusually disturbed childhood, to maintain that these events had no bearing whatever on her outlook as an adult would be equally perverse.

If Elizabeth had longed to have children, then obviously marriage would have appeared more desirable, but it would seem that motherhood held little allure for her. In 1563, when Parliament was urging the Queen to marry, Sir Nicholas Bacon tried to sugar the pill for her by appealing to her maternal instincts. He told Elizabeth, "If your Highness could conceive or imagine the comfort, surety and delight that should happen to yourself by beholding an imp of your own ... it would (I am assured) sufficiently satisfy to amove all manner of lets, impediments and scruples". There is nothing to indicate that such arguments made any impact on the Queen. It is true that the Scots diplomat, Sir James Melville, claimed in his memoirs that when Elizabeth was informed in 1566 that her cousin Mary Stuart had been delivered of a baby boy, she could not hide her jealousy and anguish. According to him, Elizabeth was "in great mirth, dancing after supper" when the news was quietly imparted to her by Cecil, whereupon she sank down disconsolately, "bursting out to some of her ladies that the Queen of Scots was mother of a fair son, while she was but a barren stock". Melville's account, which he wrote in old age, is nevertheless suspect. He did not claim to have been a witness of this affecting little scene, which he maintained had been described to him by friends at court, and no one else has left any record of it. At the time Melville himself was equally circumspect, for when he returned to Scotland, once his mission was completed, he made no mention of the incident to Mary Stuart, merely confining himself to saying that the news of the Prince's arrival was "grateful to her Majesty".[71]

When the Queen herself alluded to the possibility of having children, she gave the impression that she saw little chance of having a loving relationship with them. In 1561 she coldly informed an ambassador from Scotland, "Princes cannot like their children, those that should succeed unto them", and cited many examples from history to prove her point. Two years before this, she spoke in equally pessimistic terms when she pointed out to Parliament that her children would not necessarily prove a blessing to the nation, "For although I be never so careful of your well doings, and mind ever so to be, yet may my issue grow out of kind, and become perhaps ungracious".[72] It was true that when in her mid-forties she was heard to say that she would like to carry on the line of Henry VIII, but this belated declaration, which seems to have taken those who heard it by surprise, can hardly be adduced as evidence of a strong philoprogenitive urge. In general she was remarkably free of such feelings and, as far as one can see, she not only felt that motherhood would afford her little personal satisfaction but she also did not expect that she would be able to take pride in the knowledge that she had perpetuated the dynasty.

It was only as she grew older that Elizabeth began to take pleasure in the company of young children. In 1590, for example, one of Lord Talbot's servants reported to his master, "If I should write how much her Majesty this day did make of the little lady your daughter, with often kissing (which her Majesty seldom useth to any) and then amending her dressing with pins, and still carrying her with her Majesty in her own barge, and so into the privy lodgings and so homeward ... you would scarcely believe me". Seven years later, Sir Robert Sidney was delighted to learn that the Queen was greatly taken with his three young children, and especially with Sidney's daughter Katherine, of whom she said fondly that "she never saw any child come towards her with a better or bolder grace".[73] By this time, of course, there was no longer any question of Elizabeth bearing children herself, but though she had reached an age where she evidently enjoyed acting as a sort of surrogate grandmother to the young, there was nothing wistful in her treatment of them. In her earlier years, she had been less demonstrative towards children (and may even have been somewhat awkward with them, for when the Earl of Essex was presented to her as a little boy, he shrank away in terror), and it is significant that even in 1590, Lord Talbot's servant thought his master would be surprised that the Queen had treated his young daughter so affectionately.

It has to be said that there was no shortage of people who took the view that Elizabeth refrained from marriage not because she did not want children, but because she knew she could not have them. It would seem that inquisitive foreign ambassadors, who wished to find out whether or not the Queen was fertile, were sometimes driven to bribe royal laundrymaids or chamberwomen who could pass on details as to the frequency of Elizabeth's periods, and the information that they gleaned from such sources led some envoys to the tentative conclusion that she was unlikely to conceive. Soon after Elizabeth's accession, Feria wrote home, "If my spies do not lie, which I believe they do not, for a certain reason which they have recently given me, I understand she will not bear children". The following year Feria was replaced as Spanish ambassador by Bishop Alvaro de la Quadra, and he made the same sort of enquiries as his predecessor. As a result he reported in January 1561, "I must not omit to say also that the common opinion, confirmed by certain physicians, is that this woman is unhealthy, and it is believed certain she will not have children". On the other hand, de la Quadra himself clearly did not have implicit faith in his informants, for he felt bound to add that there was also "no lack of people who say she already has some [children], but of this I have seen no trace and do not believe it".[74] The fact that, for years to come, King Philip and his ambassadors continued to work for a marriage between the Queen and Philip's cousin Archduke Charles, shows how little weight they attached to information that had been unearthed in this way.

As the years passed, and Elizabeth turned down all offers for her hand, speculation grew that she did so because she knew that she had some bodily defect which made reproduction impossible. During the 1566 session of Parliament, some members of the Commons were said by the historian William Camden to have "cursed Huic, the Queen's physician, as a dissuader of her marriage, for I know not what womanish impotency". At the end of her reign, Elizabeth's godson, Sir John Harington, alluded to the widespread belief that she was incapable of having sexual relations when he recorded in a tract on the succession, "In mind she hath ever had an aversion and (as many think) in body some indisposition to the act of marriage". After the Queen was dead, the dramatist Ben Jonson confided to a Scots acquaintance that Elizabeth "had a membrana on her, which made her uncapable of man, though for her delight she tried many", but he did not say how he had acquired this intimate knowledge of the Queen's gynaecological history. Of rather more interest is the declaration of the overbearing and shrewish Countess of Shrewsbury to Mary Queen of Scots that Elizabeth was "not like other women", and that this accounted for her failure to marry.[75] Before her marriage to the Earl, Lady Shrewsbury had been one of Elizabeth's ladies-in-waiting and this could arguably have given her opportunities to learn about any irregularities in her mistress's menstrual cycle, and she may possibly have passed on this information to Mary while the latter was in her husband's charge. On the other hand, Mary only put this on record after she and Lady Shrewsbury had fallen out because the Countess had implied that Mary and her husband were having an affair with one another, and the Queen of Scots' aim in recalling these earlier conversations was merely to demonstrate that Lady Shrewsbury was an incorrigible and vicious gossip who was prone to making statements that could in no way be substantiated.

Intriguingly enough, it would seem that the Queen herself had been known to hint that she was barren. In 1566, a nephew of the French ambassador, de la Forêt, had a discussion with one of the Queen's doctors, and in the course of this, the former remarked he did not want Elizabeth to marry a French prince, because in the past she had given out that she understood from her doctors that she was sterile. The physician did not deny that Elizabeth might have made such an assertion, but he insisted that she was talking nonsense, and claimed that she only said such things out of caprice. He added that if the Queen did marry, he would answer for it that she was capable of bearing ten children, and he stressed, "There is not a man in the kingdom who knows her constitution better than I".[76]

If the Queen clearly did not regard the rearing of children as being a great inducement to marry, she also had no reason to fear that she would ever lack companionship if she decided to remain single. She knew that to the end of her days, men and women would vie for her attention, sparing no effort to amuse her or boost her ego, and unlike most old maids, a lonely old age could hold no terrors for her. She was also so absorbed in affairs of state that she scarcely had time to brood on the lack of fulfilment in her private life, and the satisfaction she derived from business obviously acted as a powerful antidote to sexual frustration. She herself hinted at this when she remarked to the Holy Roman Emperor's ambassador, "Love is usually the offspring of leisure, and as I am so beset by duties, I have not been able to think of love". As she once declared, on being pressed to take a husband, "I am married already to the realm of England, when I was crowned with this ring, which I bear continually in token thereof", and the statement should not be dismissed as mere rhetoric.[77]

This is not to say that there was no room in the Queen's life for any form of romance, for she derived immense pleasure from her courtships and flirtations. As a courtier once remarked, Elizabeth was "greedy of marriage proposals", and although she always stopped short of a betrothal, she never wearied of the mating dance. In 1565, her evident delight at being chased by so many men led the Spanish ambassador to comment, "I do not think anything is more enjoyable to this Queen than treating of marriage, although she assures me herself that nothing annoys her more. She is vain, and would like all the world to be running after her, but it will probably end in her remaining as she is".[78] She experienced an unmistakeable frisson of excitement at the start of each new courtship, and took an unfeigned delight in the comedy that unfolded, exulting in the compliments and flattery that accompanied the proposals, and revelling in the confusion of foreign ambassadors, who were baffled by her equivocations and teases. When suitors wooed her in person, she found it still more delicious, but however much she welcomed male attention, she derived much of her enjoyment from the knowledge that she was in control. She regarded each courtship as a duel of wits, conducted within the reassuring framework of courtly convention, and although she greatly relished the flashing interchange of pleasantries and elegant wordplay, she never let down her emotional guard or permitted herself to be possessed by a grand passion.

Elizabeth found it hard to resist being coquettish with her admirers, but this may have had an adverse effect on her reputation, for as the distinguished diplomat Sir Thomas Challoner remarked early in the reign, "a young princess cannot be too wary what countenance of familiar demonstration she maketh". As was perhaps unavoidable for a single woman in her position, there were soon innuendoes that she was rampantly promiscuous, and it was sometimes whispered that she remained unmarried because this made it easier to take a variety of lovers to satisfy her lust. Thus in 1572, a ruffian named Berney was found to be plotting to murder both Cecil and the Queen, and under interrogation he admitted that he had incited a friend to join with him by claiming that Elizabeth was a vile woman, "that desireth nothing but to feed her own lewd fantasy, and to cut off such of her nobility as were not perfumed and courtly-like to please her delicate eye". He had alleged that she only gave advancement to good dancers whom she could use "for her turn", citing Leicester and Hatton as examples, and claimed that these two "had more recourse unto her Majesty than reason would suffer, if she were so virtuous and well inclined" as others claimed. Berney's defamation of the Queen was unusual in that it was avowedly premeditated, for most of the slurs against her came into the category of tavern gossip, purveyed by drunks and ne'er-do-wells. In 1581, for example, one Henry Hawkins was disciplined for saying that the Queen already had five illegitimate children, "and she never went in progress but to be delivered". Seventeen years later, Edward Frances of Dorset found himself in trouble after he tried to persuade Elizabeth Baylie "to lead an incontinent life with him, and upon her refusing said that the best in England had done so, and had three bastards by noblemen of the court, two sons and a daughter, and was herself base born".[79]

Occasionally aspersions were cast on the Queen's character by people who were closer to the court. In September 1572, when the Earl of Southampton was in the Tower on suspicion of involvement in a Catholic conspiracy, Elizabeth Massie deposed that the Earl had told another prisoner that "there was a privy stairs where the Queen and my Lord Leicester did meet, and if they had not used sorcery, there should have been young traitors 'ere now begotten". This may have been pure fabrication on Mistress Massie's part but, even if she reported Southampton aright, it would be wrong to attach much importance to the ramblings of a disaffected peer. According to Mary Stuart, the Countess of Shrewsbury was also guilty of spreading unsavoury tales about Elizabeth, for the Countess allegedly told Mary that Elizabeth had slept with Sir Christopher Hatton, and she went on to say that the Queen behaved so amorously to him in public that Hatton was covered in confusion. Lady Shrewsbury had then compounded this by declaring that Elizabeth had been seen in her chemise, enticing the French Duke of Alençon into her bedchamber, and the Countess had added for good measure that on another occasion the Queen kissed Alençon's friend, Simier, "and took various indecent liberties with him". As has been pointed out, however, Mary only wrote all this down some years after these conversations had taken place, and far from insinuating there was any truth in what she had been told, her aim was to discredit Lady Shrewsbury by exposing her as a pernicious liar.[80]

The tittle-tattle against Elizabeth deserves to be treated with contempt, and on balance the overwhelming probability is that she died a virgin. On practical grounds alone, it is hard to see how it could have been otherwise, for if she had been so lascivious as her enemies liked to think, she would have been continually haunted by the dread of exposure and ruin. In the absence of any efficient methods of contraception, there would have been no way of warding off an unwanted pregnancy, and it would have bordered on insanity for Elizabeth to run such risks. Then again, the Queen was so rarely left unattended that it would have been impossible for covert assignations with lovers to have gone undetected. As she herself observed, "She was always surrounded by her ladies of the bedchamber and maids of honour", and on some nights at least, one of her ladies actually slept in the same room as her. In the circumstances the Queen was entitled to complain that since "my life is in the open, and I have so many witnesses ... I cannot understand how so bad a judgment can have been formed of me".[81]

It is particularly notable that foreign ambassadors consistently dismissed any salacious rumours about the Queen as "but the spawn of envy and malice". As one perceptive foreigner remarked in 1571, ever since her accession, Elizabeth had been watched "with Argus' eyes", and in all that time "there could never be found any manner of suspicion that could once touch her honour". Another witness for the defence was Sir Christopher Hatton, whose name was often put forward as one of the Queen's putative lovers, for Elizabeth's godson, John Harington, thought it worth recording that on one occasion Hatton "did swear voluntarily, deeply and with vehement asseveration that he never had any carnal knowledge of her body".[82]

Virginity in a mature woman is nowadays regarded as a dubious asset, and even in Elizabeth's day it came in for its share of mockery. Shakespeare compared virgins to "one of our French wither'd pears – it looks ill, it eats dryly", and in popular folklore, spinsters were supposed to end up paired with apes in hell. Nevertheless, far from feeling in any way diminished by her lack of sexual experience, Elizabeth gloried in her virginity, which for her represented a triumph of the will over base corporeal desire. It was true that since the Reformation virginity had lost some of its lustre, and in the 1560s the writer Thomas Becon went so far as to say that it was inferior to matrimony, and that the tradition of vowing chastity came from the Pope, rather than from God. Nevertheless, such thinking was by no means universally accepted, and even in advanced Protestant circles, sexual denial was still held up as an ideal. Protestant clergy were no longer required to practise total abstinence, but the requirements on them had been relaxed not because celibacy was regarded as inherently unsatisfactory, but because it was thought unrealistic to expect the entire third estate to live up to such an exacting standard. St Paul had said "it is better to marry than to burn", and there was concern that clergymen who were denied the solace of the marital bed would either be tempted to indulge in fornication, or become sinfully obsessed with sexual fantasies. As keeping a wife was not contrary to the word of God, and did not interfere with priestly functions, it was counterproductive to forbid it, but even apologists for clerical marriage made it clear that celibacy was a far superior way of life. In the words of Bishop John Jewel of Salisbury, "Single life, for many causes, is the best, I grant. Yet it is not best for everybody, but only for him that hath the gift of chastity, and can with quiet mind and upright conscience live single". Those who were naturally predisposed to lead a "sole life" were reverenced as being endowed with a special grace, and

Elizabeth took intense pride at being numbered among this band of elect. In an address to Parliament she made in 1576, she came close to paraphrasing Jewel when she declared that she did not condemn marriage outright, "or judge amiss of such as, forced by necessity cannot dispose themselves to another life; but [I] wish that none were drawn to change but such as cannot keep honest limits".[83] Viewed from this perspective, marriage would amount to an avowal of fleshly weakness, and the Queen was determined never to acknowledge that she was what we would call a victim of her libido. She would have preferred it if those who followed high callings in the land had been capable of exercising similar self-discipline, and this helps to explain her fury when her maids of honour failed to "keep honest limits", and became pregnant out of wedlock, or when her bishops took pretty young wives for the sake of sexual gratification.

Elizabeth's reluctance to marry and beget a direct heir would not have aroused such universal concern if she had been prepared to name an alternative successor, but this she staunchly refused to do. It was true that in January 1559 she had assured Parliament that "the realm shall not remain destitute of an heir", but despite her promise to deal with the question "in convenient time" she had no intention of clarifying the situation. Her own experiences in Mary's reign had left her with the unshakeable conviction that, involuntarily or otherwise, the sovereign's heir presumptive automatically became the fulcrum for treasonous intrigue, and she was determined not to provide plotters with a focus for their energies. Nor were these fears baseless, for many of the difficulties encountered by monarchs of neighbouring countries during Elizabeth's reign were attributable, directly or indirectly, to their heirs. Thus in January 1568, Philip II of Spain had to arrest his eldest son Don Carlos, whom he suspected of plotting against him, and after six months in custody the young man starved himself to death. The year before this, Mary Stuart's Scottish subjects deposed her and set up her fourteen-month-old son as King in her place, and Eric XIV of Sweden lost his throne to his brother, Duke John of Finland, and was subsequently poisoned by him. In France the pattern was similar. There was intense rivalry between Charles IX and his brother, the Duke of Anjou, and when the latter succeeded Charles as King Henry III, he in turn fell out with his younger brother and heir designate, who was at one time imprisoned for his disloyal intrigues.

It was therefore clearly specious to assume that if Elizabeth settled the succession, it would automatically be conducive to stability and good order, and the Queen can be forgiven for believing that the very reverse would turn out to be the case. Yet even if she had accepted that the question of the succession could not be left in abeyance, the way ahead would still not have been clear. There were at least seven individuals whose claim to the throne merited consideration, and in settling on one of them as her heir, the Queen would have drawn on herself the enmity of the others. Each claimant had partisans who would be offended if their candidate was overlooked, and once Elizabeth had indicated a preference, the inevitable debate as to whether she had made the right choice would prove highly disruptive, and intensify resentment and ill-feeling. Far from ensuring that on her death the crown would pass to its rightful possessor in accordance with the law, Elizabeth feared that by settling the succession she would merely precipitate a fearsome struggle for power.

In blood, at least, Mary Stuart had the best claim to be Elizabeth's successor, for she was the grand-daughter of Henry VIII's elder sister Margaret, who had been married to James IV of Scotland in 1502. On the other hand, it could be argued that, as a foreigner, Mary was automatically disqualified, for aliens were debarred from inheriting property in England, and though there was a possibility that the Crown itself was exempt from the rule, the legal position was far from clear. Moreover, by the terms of Henry VIII's will, Margaret Tudor's descendants had been explicitly bypassed in favour of the descendants of Henry's younger sister, Mary, and it was uncertain whether Elizabeth was legally bound to uphold these arrangements. The Queen was anxious to preserve the ambiguity. Unlike her father, she was not opposed in principle to the Stuart claim, and she also had no wish to provoke the Queen of Scots by confirming that she was excluded from the line of succession, but conversely Elizabeth was by no means ready to recognize Mary as her heir. Not only was there confusion as to whether she would be within her rights to do so, but there were obvious reasons why it would be impolitic to lumber herself with a successor who was both a foreigner and a Catholic. So long as Mary believed there was a chance that Elizabeth would bequeath her her crown, she had an incentive to remain on good terms with her, for otherwise she ran the risk of being disinherited. On the other hand, once Elizabeth had named her as her successor, Mary's position as heiress presumptive would be unassailable, and it would be much harder for Elizabeth to exert any form of control over her. From Elizabeth's point of view, therefore, it was essential that the matter remained in suspense.

Mary Stuart was not the only descendant of Queen Margaret of Scotland who could inherit the crown, for after the death of James IV, Margaret had remarried and produced a daughter. This child, also called Margaret, had married the Earl of Lennox in 1544, and they had had two sons. Since Margaret and her sons had been born and brought up in England, they could not be classified as aliens, and in this respect their claim to the throne was arguably superior to that of Mary Queen of Scots. Like Mary, however, Margaret Lennox had been struck out of the line of succession by Henry

VIII's will, and it was also debatable whether or not she was legitimate, for her parents' marriage had been annulled in 1527.

In his will, Henry VIII had laid down that if all his children died childless, the crown was to go to the descendants of his younger sister Mary. Mary had married her brother's jousting companion, Charles Brandon, Duke of Suffolk, and the couple had had two daughters, Frances and Eleanor. The eldest, Frances, had married Henry Grey, Marquis of Dorset, and like so many of Henry VII's descendants, they too had produced only daughters. Of the three Grey girls, Jane, the eldest, had been executed in Mary's reign, but her sisters Katherine and Mary had survived her, and if Henry VIII's wishes had been upheld, Katherine should have been recognized as Elizabeth's heiress presumptive. From early in the reign, however, it was apparent that Katherine was "not regarded or esteemed by the Queen". It was said that Elizabeth "could not well abide the sight of her", and in March 1559 Katherine resentfully confided to the Spanish ambassador that she could tell the Queen did not wish her to succeed.[84] The Queen had no greater liking for Katherine's younger sister Mary, a minute hunchback, whose very existence was easy to overlook. Nevertheless, however preposterous it was to think of such a physical misfit on the throne, Mary Grey's claim could not be altogether discounted.

Perhaps the most serious objection against the Grey girls succeeding was that their father had been convicted of treason during the reign of Mary Tudor, and it could follow from this that his daughters automatically forfeited their right to the throne. In that case they were superseded by Margaret, Lady Strange, the daughter of Eleanor Brandon and hence another of Henry VIII's great-nieces. To confuse matters still further, however, it was arguable that the marriage between the King's sister Mary and Charles Brandon had been illegal, for Brandon was a divorcee, and two of his ex-wives were still alive at the time of his wedding to Mary. If the marriage had been invalid, both of their daughters were bastards, and any descendants from the union were ineligible for the throne. It was indeed a remarkable coincidence that with the exception of Mary Queen of Scots, every surviving descendant of Henry VII was marked to some extent by the stigma of illegitimacy.[85]

Another claimant to the throne was Henry Hastings, seventh Earl of Huntingdon, a descendant of Edward III on both his father and mother's side. He was also the great-great-grandson of Edward IV's younger brother, the Duke of Clarence, but the claim to the throne he derived through him was not as strong as that of anyone who was descended from the union between Henry VII and Elizabeth of York, who had been a daughter of Edward IV. Huntingdon himself was well aware that as far as the succession was concerned, he was "inferior to many others both in degree and princely quality", and he tried to avoid "conceiting any greatness of myself" by maintaining a "continual low sail". Nevertheless, when Elizabeth fell ill with smallpox in 1562, several members of the Council advocated that Huntingdon should succeed her if she died, although undoubtedly their support for him owed more to the fact that Huntingdon was both a man and a strong Protestant, than to the intrinsic merits of his claim.[86]

Collectively the English candidates for the succession were a pretty unimpressive bunch, and when a Scots diplomat commented to Elizabeth in 1561 that, with the exception of Mary Stuart, "none of all the others who had any interest were meet for the crown, or yet worthy of it", Elizabeth did not try to contradict him. Nevertheless, believing as she did that it would be suicidal to take premature action over the succession, she would do nothing to counteract their claims. For the moment the question of who would inherit her throne must be allowed to lie fallow, for she felt it was only by avoiding foolhardy commitments that she would ultimately be able to dispose of the crown to her satisfaction. Understandably, the Queen's subjects saw things rather differently. Elizabeth might think it best to adopt a policy of 'wait and see', but this presupposed that she had a long lifespan before her, and at a time when everyone was "subject every day, yea every hour to God's call", this was by no means certain. If she died unexpectedly and intestate, the nation would be plunged into turmoil, and not unreasonably her subjects thought it her duty to guard against this. As the peers of the realm put it in a petition presented to Elizabeth in 1563, the civil wars of the previous century had branded upon the national consciousness a dread of the "factious, seditious and intestine war that will grow through want of understanding to whom they should yield their allegiances and duties, whereby much innocent blood is like to be shed". It was precisely because of this that Henry VIII had looked on the ordering of the succession as being of paramount importance and, as a member of the House of Commons unkindly reminded Elizabeth in 1566, her father had once declared in Parliament, "If our true heir be not known at the time of our death, see what mischief and trouble shall succeed to you and your children!"[87] Elizabeth might be more concerned about the risks involved in naming a successor, but her people would be unwilling to tolerate prevarication on this issue unless they believed that she intended to deal with the problem by marrying and begetting children. For this reason there could be no question of Elizabeth ruling out all idea of marriage, and as she well understood, it was only by keeping her subjects' eyes fixed on her tricks and acrobatics on the matrimonial high wire that she could stop them worrying about the lack of a safety net in the form of an assured succession.

As was to be expected of a woman whom one of her Councillors was jocularly to describe as "the best marriage in her parish", Elizabeth never lacked for suitors. What was perhaps more surprising was that the first proposal of the reign came from her late sister's widower, Philip II. The fact that he offered her his hand so promptly gave rise to a myth (which Elizabeth did not exactly discourage) that while in England he had nursed a secret passion for his sister-in-law. The legend developed that Philip suffered lifelong remorse at having found it impossible to feel any desire for his wife, "but as for the Lady Elizabeth, he was enamoured with her". In reality, nothing could have been further from the truth. When Philip authorized Count Feria to propose to Elizabeth on his behalf on 10 January 1559, he explained that, as a faithful son of the Church, he thought it incumbent on him "to sacrifice my private inclination" in this way. By marrying Elizabeth he would be in a position to ensure that England remained within the Catholic Church, but he confessed that it was only by bearing in mind this higher purpose that he had been able to resign himself to the prospect. Dejectedly he told Feria, "If it was not to serve God, believe me, I would not have got into this . . . Nothing would make me do this except the clear knowledge that it would gain the kingdom [of England] for his service and faith." He added that with this marriage hanging over him, he felt "like a condemned man awaiting his fate".[88]

Feria did not doubt that when he passed on Philip's proposal to the Queen, she would jump at the match. Four days after Elizabeth's accession he had told Philip that it was a foregone conclusion that if the Queen decided to marry a foreign prince, "she will at once fix her eyes on your Majesty". He deemed it unthinkable that the Queen of a small and impoverished country would turn down a match with a man who was not only the ruler of Spain and the Netherlands, but who possessed in addition a vast empire in the Americas. Philip's control of the Low Countries, which derived from his Burgundian grandfather, was in some ways particularly significant, for about two-thirds of English overseas commerce was transacted through the great entrepôt of Antwerp, and it was obviously desirable to do everything to maintain close links with the country's principal trading partner. As Cecil was to point out in a memorandum composed a few years after Elizabeth's accession, "No prince of England ever remained without good amity with the house of Burgundy", which traditionally had acted as a counterweight to the enmity of France. In view of the fact that at the very outset of the reign the French had been so unfriendly, this was scarcely the moment to try and rearrange the time-honoured alignments. But though Elizabeth was anxious to remain on good terms with Philip, this did not mean that she thought he would make a good choice of husband. Feria would have done well to remember that prior to her accession Elizabeth had told him outright that Mary Tudor "had lost the affection of the people of this realm because she had married a foreigner".[89]

Sometime in early February 1559, Feria proposed on Philip's behalf, but to his surprise Elizabeth did not seem in the least elated, and merely said that she needed to reflect before giving him her answer. His amazement grew over the next few weeks, for whenever he raised the subject afresh, the Queen evinced little interest in Philip's suit. Far from showing herself eager to proceed, she made difficulties about the fact that Philip had previously been married to her sister, which meant that according to the Book of Leviticus, a marriage between them would be within the prohibited degrees. Feria tried to brush this aside, insisting that the Pope could issue a dispensation which would obviate the problem, but Elizabeth would not acknowledge that the Pope was empowered to make pronouncements which contravened the word of God. It was scarcely surprising that she was so punctilious about this point, for if the Papacy had possessed such powers, the marriage between Catherine of Aragon and her father had been a true one, and by deferring to the Pope's authority over this, she would effectively acknowledge that she was a bastard.

Still Feria could not bring himself to believe that Elizabeth would reject so prestigious an alliance, but on 19 March she finally turned down Philip's offer. She had kept her suitor guessing for as long as she dared, for she was in need of Spanish support at the tripartite peace talks that were still being held at Cateau-Cambresis, and obviously this was more likely to be forthcoming while the Spaniards remained under the delusion that she was going to become Philip's wife. By 19 March she had been told that peace was on the verge of being concluded, and it was also impossible for her to keep up the pretence that she was going to remain within the Catholic Church. Almost audibly spluttering with amazement, Feria wrote to Philip that that evening, Elizabeth had told him simply that "she could not marry your Majesty as she was a heretic".[90] For Philip, the news came as a great relief, and he wasted no time sealing the agreement that had been made with France by marrying the French King's daughter. When Elizabeth heard this, she affected to be somewhat wounded that the King had found a replacement for her so hastily, but in reality she thought herself well rid of her brother-in-law's attentions.

Her rejection of Philip did not leave her bereft of suitors from abroad. Philip's uncle was the Habsburg Emperor Ferdinand I, suzerain of the loose confederation of German states known as the Holy Roman Empire, and he had two bachelor sons. Out of avuncular good manners, he had refrained from suggesting that Elizabeth marry one of them until she had made it clear that that she was not interested in Philip, but once his nephew was out of the running he resolved to send an envoy to the Queen, bearing a proposal of marriage from Charles, the younger of the two archdukes.

From the English point of view, the suit of Archduke Charles had much to commend it. Since Charles was a younger son, the Imperial title was not destined for him, and therefore unlike Philip his overseas commitments would be minimal. Not only was there no danger that "his greatness should overrule" England, but because he could be permanently based in the country, he would be more likely to be concerned about its well-being. On the other hand, he was a suitably royal *parti*, and the match would not only bring Elizabeth within the Habsburg family circle, but would also earn her the goodwill of Charles's cousin, Philip II. "He is not a Philip, but better for us than a Philip", one English diplomat opined of Archduke Charles.[91] It was true that Charles was a Catholic, but at this stage it was not envisaged that his religion would seriously complicate matters. The Emperor failed to appreciate the extent of the Queen's commitment to Protestantism, and for their part the English were misled by reports that Charles's attachment to his faith was not very deep.

The Emperor's ambassador, Baron Caspar Breuner, arrived in England in May 1559. On 28 May he had an audience with the Queen, and "breathing a prayer to the Almighty", he put the Archduke's proposal to her. Elizabeth's reaction was non-committal: she warned Breuner that she had never yet felt any inclination to marry, but she did not rule out a change of heart, "for she was but human, and not insensible to human emotions and impulses". Much heartened by his reception, Breuner wrote to Archduke Charles telling him that he would have to wait patiently for Elizabeth's answer. He added that what he had already seen of Elizabeth's palaces and possessions had convinced him that "she is well worth the trouble".[92]

If there was one aspect of the situation that did worry Breuner, it was that the Archduke did not lack rivals, for English suitors were already paying court to Elizabeth. Breuner could draw comfort from the fact that Edward Courtenay, who had been mentioned as a possible husband for Elizabeth in Mary's reign, had died in exile in 1556, but even so, the home team was too well-manned for the ambassador's liking. Perhaps the least serious threat was posed by the twelfth Earl of Arundel, "a flighty man of small ability", who greatly fancied his chances. The Earl was nearly fifty, and had little to recommend him save the antiquity of his title, and never for a second did Elizabeth give his suit serious consideration. His name had been put forward as a suitable consort for her while Mary was still alive, but when Feria had visited Elizabeth in early November 1559, she had laughed with him at the very idea. The Earl himself was blissfully oblivious that Elizabeth looked on him as a figure of fun, and he became puffed up with gallantry and self-importance, reportedly distributing six hundred pounds' worth of jewels to the Queen's ladies in the hope that they would commend him to their mistress. In the summer of 1559 he made a more open bid for favour when he entertained Elizabeth at his house, Nonsuch. The climax of the festivities was a banquet that was followed by a masque "with drums and flutes, and all the music that could be, till midnight". At the Queen's departure, he presented her with an entire cupboard of silver plate, and the general verdict on his hospitality was that, "As for cheer, [the same] has not been seen or heard". Sadly for Arundel, although Elizabeth had greatly enjoyed herself, she still could not take seriously his pursuit of her. Baron Breuner, who had kept Arundel under careful observation for some weeks, gleefully concluded that he had no chance of winning the Queen. In great relief the envoy reported, "He alone entertains this hope, for he is somewhat advanced in years, and also rather silly and loutish, is not well-favoured, nor has a handsome figure".[93]

Breuner might feel able to dismiss Arundel out of hand, but for some months the prospects of Sir William Pickering afforded him a great deal more unease. Pickering was in his early forties, a bachelor "of tall stature . . . handsome and very successful with women", who had been a friend of Elizabeth's for some years. In 1554 he had been implicated in Wyatt's rebellion, and had had to flee abroad, but after a period in exile, he had been absolved of all blame, and he had subsequently represented Mary and Philip on diplomatic missions abroad. While stationed on the continent he had fallen ill, and on Mary's death he was still in no condition to travel, but there was keen speculation that as soon as he came home, Elizabeth and he would be betrothed. It was May 1559 before Pickering was strong enough to return, but excitement mounted when he was at once granted a private audience with the Queen, who stayed closeted with him for several hours. After this promising beginning, Sir William fuelled speculation by leading a princely way of life. He entertained lavishly, though on these occasions he always deserted his guests to dine alone, "with music playing". His grandeur created a great sensation, but he himself cherished no illusions that this was the way to win the Queen, for he admitted frankly that he was sure she would not marry.[94] Despite the great expectations that had been entertained of him, Pickering's star inexorably waned, for his extravagance soon landed him in debt, and his health again went into decline. By the autumn of 1559, he was no longer considered of any account, having been cast into utter oblivion by the rise of Lord Robert Dudley.

Dudley was the younger of the two surviving sons of the late Duke of Northumberland. He was just over two months older than Elizabeth, whom he had known well since childhood. On the death of Edward VI, he had backed his father's attempt to set Jane Grey on the throne, seizing King's Lynn for Northumberland's party and proclaiming Lady Jane Queen in the marketplace there. When the rising had collapsed he had been incarcerated in the Tower and sentenced to death, but though his father and his brother Guildford were both executed, he had been spared. Towards the end of 1554, Lord Robert had been set free, and when war had broken out he had volunteered to serve in France. He acquitted himself well at the victory of San Quentin, and then came back to England, having done much to clear his name of the stain of treason. He had spent most of the remainder of Mary's reign living quietly on his Norfolk estate, but he evidently kept in touch with Elizabeth. Indeed, according to one source, it was at this time that he incurred her lasting gratitude for selling "a good piece of land to aid her",[95] and in his first despatch Feria singled Dudley out as one of the men known to be "on good terms" with her.

No one was surprised when immediately after Elizabeth's accession, Lord Robert was appointed Master of the Horse. In the reign of Edward VI, Dudley had been the King's Master of the Buckhounds, and in every respect he was well-qualified to run the royal stables, which housed about two hundred and seventy-five horses. His responsibilities included the supervision of Elizabeth's stud farms, and the purchase and training of horses which would be used by the Queen, her ladies, her household officials and messengers. As one of the most senior royal officials, the Master of the Horse was automatically allocated lodgings at Court, and the importance of the post was illustrated by the fact that on all ceremonial occasions he rode directly behind the Queen. At first, however, no one imagined that Lord Robert might one day be on more intimate terms with Elizabeth. For one thing, he was not a bachelor, for while still in his teens he had married Amy Robsart, the daughter of a well-to-do Norfolk squire. It has been surmised that their union had initially been a love-match, but if so, the couple had drifted apart over the years, and one contemporary described their relationship as "a carnal marriage, begun for pleasure and ended in lamentation". Like many royal officials, Dudley did not bring his wife to Court, and for the most part Amy lived with relations in the country. Lord Robert visited her from time to time, occasionally bearing little gifts, but though this acquits him of the charge of totally neglecting his wife, his long separations from her clearly did not trouble him.[96]

It was in the spring of 1559 that it began to be suggested that Lord Robert was something more than a trusted royal servant, and that instead he had progressed to being royal favourite. Elizabeth was treating him with such marked affection that it did not escape comment, and since it was rumoured that Dudley's wife was afflicted by a malady in one of her breasts, there was speculation that if Amy "were perchance to die, the Queen might take him for her husband". Elizabeth behaved so demonstratively towards Lord Robert that some observers condemned her conduct as nothing short of immodest, and the shocked Feria reported that it was "even said that her Majesty visits him in his chamber day and night". By June the scandal had attained such proportions that talk of it had reached Emperor Ferdinand in Vienna, and since he had no intention of bestowing his son on a notoriously loose woman, he instructed Breuner to find out if there was any substance in the rumours. Breuner did as he was told, and through a trusted intermediary approached some of the Queen's ladies-in-waiting, and asked them what they thought of Elizabeth's relationship with Dudley. The ladies had to admit that the Queen showed "her liking for him more markedly than is consistent with her reputation and dignity", but to Breuner's relief they were adamant that Elizabeth had "certainly never been forgetful of her honour".[97]

The Queen's ladies might swear that she was not an adulteress, but at least one of them was extremely disturbed by the way she was carrying on, and by August Kat Ashley had decided that matters had reached a stage where it was no longer possible for her to remain silent. One day she flung herself at the Queen's feet and "implored her in God's name, to marry and put an end to these disreputable rumours". Dramatically, she warned Elizabeth that she was running the risk of irreparably sullying her reputation, and she said that by acting in this fashion she would alienate her subjects to such an extent that civil war might well be the outcome. No other person at court would have dared address Elizabeth in this way, but Kat went unrebuked. With great restraint the Queen merely observed that she knew that it was Kat's devotion to her that had made her confront her in this way, but she pointed out that she could not comply with her request to take a husband without delay, for any marriage had to be most carefully weighed. As for her relationship with Dudley, she strenuously defended it, stressing that neither of them was guilty of the least impropriety. Kat's outburst had clearly somewhat shaken Elizabeth, and she had enough of a guilty conscience to feel that she must put it on record that her behaviour had not been remiss, but having done this, she concluded with a sudden flash of defiance. She said challengingly that if she had wished to lead an immoral life, "she did not know of anyone who could forbid her", and the qualifying comment somewhat undermined the effect of her earlier disclaimer.[98]

As Dudley's intimacy with the Queen flourished, so his unpopularity grew, and to the end of his life he remained one of the most cordially detested men in the country. To a certain extent, the dislike he inspired stemmed from envy, pure and simple, and there was also prejudice against him on account of his family history. Not only had the Duke of Northumberland been executed by Mary Tudor, but Lord Robert's grandfather, Edmund Dudley, had been beheaded by the young Henry VIII for offences allegedly committed in Henry VII's reign, and the remarkable sequence of treason convictions that spanned three generations gave rise to sneers that Dudley came of a line that was congenitally disloyal. It was said that Dudley was descended from "a tribe of traitors", and had been "fleshed in conspiracy", and even Elizabeth was not above making jibes about his background, for on one occasion she taunted him that the Dudleys "had been traitors three descents".[99]

Undoubtedly it was somewhat hard that Dudley should be held account-able for the misdeeds of his forbears, but some at least of the hatred he incited was his own fault. His father and grandfather had found it easy to make enemies, but Robert Dudley had what amounted to a genius for it. It was not that Dudley was outwardly unpleasant: indeed the reverse was usually the case, for he rarely permitted himself to be offensive or ill-humoured. Nevertheless, although it was acknowledged that he had the ability "to put all his passions in his pocket",[100] his civility was held to proceed rather from guile than true good nature, and despite his ability to dissemble his malice, his whole being was held to be irradiated with it. His habitual impassivity was taken as a sign of a cold and calculating nature to whom neither individuals nor ideals were of any account, and try as he might to cultivate a more upright image, he could never shake off the unenviable reputation of being an unprincipled opportunist.

The quality that made Dudley particularly feared was his deviousness. When it looked as though the Queen was contemplating marriage with someone other than himself, he was utterly unscrupulous about working against this. Either he would discredit his rival in underhand ways, or he would seek to distract the Queen by interesting her in another candidate for her hand. Alternatively, if she was being pursued by a Catholic, he would oppose the match on religious grounds, concealing his real objections to it under an enlightened mask of concern for the nation's spiritual well-being. More sinister still, however, was the fact that the men who worked with him could never be certain that, even while his demeanour to them was outwardly friendly, he was not denigrating them behind their backs. No one underestimated the damage that could be wreaked in this way, "considering the goodness of her Majesty's nature to be induced to believe whom she favoureth and his subtlety to persuade".[101]

Dudley's notoriety reached its apogee in 1584 when a libel was published against him, portraying him as an evil gangster, who had turned the court into a nest of vice and extortion, and who killed anyone who tried to stand in his way. Poisoning was said to have accounted for most of his victims, and it was alleged that "if it were known how many he hath despatched or assaulted that way it would be marvellous to posterity". This work was Jesuit-inspired, a peculiarly venomous piece of propaganda whose more serious charges were wholly baseless. It stopped short of attacking the Queen herself, but by making out that she permitted such a monster to flourish at her Court, it discredited her by implication, and in intention it was clearly seditious. A colleague of Dudley's labelled it "the most malicious thing that was ever penned sithence the beginning of the world", and the Queen at once outlawed the book, declaring that "none but the devil himself" could believe such malicious and wicked imputations to be true.[102] Nevertheless, it was significant that Dudley, alone of all public figures, was singled out for attack in this way, and while he was in no way deserving of such vicious abuse, the enemies of the regime had chosen shrewdly in targetting him for their onslaught.

Since Dudley had a reputation for being altogether selfish and untrustworthy, it is not surprising that it was widely assumed that he did not really love the Queen, and that he only professed to do so for ulterior motives. William Cecil, for one, privately believed that if Dudley and Elizabeth ever married, Dudley was "like to prove unkind and jealous of the Queen's Majesty", but as this hypothesis was never put to the test, it would be somewhat uncharitable unthinkingly to accept it. Dudley was acknowledged to be unusually "favourable to women", and he clearly derived great pleasure from the company of the opposite sex.[103] It is only fair to point out that his attachment to Elizabeth never wavered, and while it would be naïve to suggest that this was altogether selfless, his letters and general conduct to her give a strong impression that he sincerely liked and admired her. In contrast to the stylized effusions with which her later admirers hailed her, Dudley consistently addressed her in an affectionate manner that had nothing the least arid or contrived about it, and in all his dealings with her, there is an undercurrent of genuine warmth.

Elizabeth could not but be aware that few of her subjects shared her high opinion of Dudley, but it did not trouble her that he was so widely disliked. Far from thinking the worse of him for disdaining to court the goodwill of her people, she would have been alarmed if he had tried to endear himself to them, for this would have implied that he wished to free himself from his utter dependence on her. In his very unpopularity lay the guarantee of his loyalty, for he knew that if she abandoned him, he could draw on no support from elsewhere. It gave her a perverse pleasure that although few others were able to penetrate Dudley's reserve, with her he was affability itself, and she liked to think that he permitted no one else to feel the full force of his charm. There was a definite piquancy in such a conquest, and to her, Dudley was like one of the mettlesome steeds which she insisted on riding, despite being warned of the danger: a high-spirited beast, which she found it exhilarating to handle, but which she did not doubt her ability to control.

Although Dudley's enemies thought him so obnoxious, it is not difficult to see what it was about him that the Queen found so appealing. In the first place, he was immensely attractive physically, and since the Queen "always took personage in the way of affection", this counted for a good deal. At a little under six foot, he was tall by the standards of the day, and possessed of dark and saturnine good looks that earned him the nickname of 'the gypsy'. In his heyday at least, he had a magnificent physique, which he kept in trim with regular exercise, and he certainly conformed to Elizabeth's stipulation that any man who sought to win her "should not sit at home all day amongst the cinders, but should in time of peace keep himself employed in warlike exercises". In particular, Dudley was an expert jouster, and no sooner had he been freed from the Tower in Mary's reign than he had been required to display his sporting prowess by competing in a tournament against Philip's Spanish entourage. After Elizabeth's accession, Dudley continued to make frequent appearances in the tiltyard: he was one of the contestants in the joust that was held to celebrate the coronation, and the following November he and Lord Hunsdon took on all comers at another tournament. The Queen watched from a gallery as eighteen assailants ran four courses each with the defending champions, and at the end of the day, it was thought she had been greatly pleased by Dudley's performance.[104]

To do so well in tournaments called for equestrian skills of a high order, but Dudley had a good eye for horseflesh as well as being a talented rider. In his capacity of Master of the Horse, he made great efforts to raise standards at the royal studs, bringing in Italian experts to advise on breeding techniques, and starting a stud at Greenwich, where barbary horses could be reared. To Elizabeth, such things mattered, for she was known to "take great pleasure in good horses". She was an excellent rider, and had such a good seat on a horse that in February 1560 the Spanish ambassador reported admiringly, "The Queen rides out every day into the country on a Neapolitan courser or jennet . . . She makes a brave show, and bears herself gallantly". Early in the reign, she seems to have experienced problems in obtaining good mounts, for in 1559 Sir Thomas Challoner, her representative in the Netherlands, was instructed to purchase horses for her in Flanders, and the following year she asked Dudley to obtain from Ireland "good strong gallopers which are better than her geldings". The Queen and Dudley also shared a passion for the chase. He was indeed so enthusiastic a huntsman that in his spare moments he was often to be seen "riding about from bush to bush with a crossbow on his back" in the hope of flushing deer out of the thickets, and it was not surprising that Elizabeth found him an ideal companion for a day's sport.[105]

Dudley kept himself active in other ways, being a keen fisherman, an accomplished archer, and an energetic tennis player, but it was not only in outdoor pursuits that he excelled, for his intellectual attainments were by no means insignificant. He was fluent in both French and Italian, and as a young man had shown a considerable aptitude for the classics. To the sorrow of his Latin tutor, however, he had refused to concentrate solely on the humanities, and instead applied himself to studying geometry and related branches of mathematics. After his formal education had been completed, Dudley remained receptive to new ideas, and kept abreast of developments in geography, cartography and astronomy and navigation. Dudley's curiosity about such matters may have been awoken by Dr John

Dee, the celebrated scientist, mathematician and delver in the occult. When Dudley was a boy, Dee had been retained in Northumberland's household, and it has been posited that the Duke engaged him as a science teacher for his children. If so, Dee was evidently an inspiring mentor, for after the Queen's accession, Dudley kept up his acquaintance with the Doctor, and like Elizabeth herself was a regular visitor to Dee's house at Mortlake.[106]

Dudley was also a keen patron of the arts. He gave financial support to numerous poets and dramatists, including Spenser and George Gascoigne. He had his own troupe of actors who performed before the Queen at Christmas 1562 and on many occasions thereafter. He built up an impressive collection of paintings, in which he had an eclectic taste, and patronized the best living artists: he has been credited with having persuaded Federico Zuccaro to come to England in 1575 in order to paint both the Queen and himself.[107]

Attractive, athletic, cultured and intelligent, Dudley was clearly a stimulating companion for the Queen, but perhaps the real secret of his attraction lay in the fact that he made her laugh. As a friend of his remarked later in the reign, Dudley could claim to "know the Queen and her nature better than any man", and no one was more gifted than he at thinking up ways to amuse her. This was important to Elizabeth, who eschewed solemnity whenever possible. "During the meal, we laughed and enjoyed ourselves a great deal", remarked Feria, after dining with Elizabeth in early November 1558, and as Queen she found the strain of conducting business was considerably eased if it was done in a light-hearted fashion. Because of her fondness for "merry tales", ambassadors who were serving her overseas were always told to include in their despatches "one half paper of court news and accidents". As she grew older, her ministers found that the best way of dealing with her notorious reluctance to sign papers was for the Secretary who presented her with a pile of documents "to entertain her with some relation or speech whereat she may take some pleasure" while she worked her way through it. She even liked to introduce some spice of levity into her dealings with foreign powers, and when Mary Stuart sent an ambassador to England in 1564, he was instructed by his mistress "to leave matters of gravity and cast in merry purposes, she being well informed of that Queen's [Elizabeth's] natural character".[108]

In the circumstances one of Dudley's greatest assets was his sense of humour, which so well accorded with the Queen's own. They both derived immense pleasure from exchanging banter with each other and indulging in elaborate teases, as can be seen from the Spanish Bishop de la Quadra's description of an evening he spent with Elizabeth and Dudley on the royal barge in 1561. He reported stiffly that when he engaged them in conversation, "They began joking, which she likes to do much better than talking about business", and before long the pair of them were poking gentle fun at him. With mock-seriousness, Dudley said that the Bishop should marry them forthwith, at which the Queen laughingly queried whether de la Quadra knew enough English. The pompous diplomat did not take particularly kindly to being made the butt of their humour, but as Elizabeth was in such a jolly mood he judged it best "to let them jest for a while", before trying to talk in a less frivolous vein.[109]

Such moments of levity were precious to the Queen, and Dudley provided her with more of them than anybody else. When Kat Ashley had pleaded with Elizabeth to distance herself from Dudley, the Queen had defended herself for seeing so much of him on the grounds "that in this world she had so much sorrow and tribulation and so little joy", and it is significant that she evidently believed that there was no other person in the world with whom she would have so much fun. Dudley alone had the unflagging ability to inject gaiety into her life, and his presence always acted as a tonic to her spirits. This was the real reason why Elizabeth was so devoted to him, and it was this that made her say that it was imperative that she saw him at least once a day.[110]

The Queen's obvious delight in Dudley's company not unnaturally depressed poor Baron Breuner, who feared that Archduke Charles would be elbowed aside by Lord Robert. Throughout the summer of 1559, Breuner nevertheless refused to accept that all was quite lost, for as he wrote to the Emperor in June, "Although the Queen affects a certain strangeness, she is quite otherwise in conversation". He could only regard it as a good sign that one day when he was boating on the Thames, Elizabeth came alongside in her barge and serenaded him with her lute, and he was pleased too that she "often of her own accord began to talk about the Archduke". Whether this would lead to anything he found it impossible to say, for her behaviour was so inconsequential that he was at a loss how to interpret it. As Count Feria had exasperatedly remarked in the spring, "Sometimes she appears to want to marry him [Archduke Charles] and speaks like a woman who will only accept a great prince, and then they say she is in love with Lord Robert, and never lets him leave her."[111]

To add to the general confusion, on 1 October Duke John of Finland landed at Harwich, intent on pressing the suit of his brother Eric, who was the King of Sweden's eldest son and heir. Elizabeth had already rejected one proposal from Eric before she came to the throne, and she had done her best to discourage him from sending his brother to England to repeat the offer, but he was not so easily deterred. Sweden was not a rich country, but Eric was a Protestant, and he hoped that Elizabeth would think this good reason to enter into a union with him. So confident was Duke John, that when he stepped ashore and was greeted by a party of courtiers sent by the Queen, he took their conventional phrases of welcome to mean that she had already decided to marry Eric, and he had to be tactfully corrected. He also antagonized his reception committee by extending his hand to be kissed, but after he had spent some time at court he began to "be a good fellow" and "leave off his high-looks and pontificality". He sought to endear himself to the general populace by scattering silver coins amongst them when he passed through the streets, and he promised "mountains of silver" for them if the Queen were to take his brother. Unfortunately, this was not much of an inducement, for on close inspection it turned out that much of the money he had brought with him was counterfeit.[112]

Baron Breuner found Duke John's flashy ways insufferable, and Elizabeth had to take steps to keep them apart after Breuner accosted the Swede and told him that "his father was only a clown who had stolen his kingdom from the Crown of Denmark". Possibly the Baron would have had less difficulty keeping his temper if he had realized that Elizabeth had no intention of marrying Eric, who became King of Sweden on the death of his father in early 1560. That February Elizabeth wrote to him that she did not doubt his love for her, but unfortunately she could not reciprocate it, and therefore she must turn down his proposal.[113] Eric would not yet give up, and Duke John lingered in England for a few more weeks, but in April he sadly returned home.

"Here is a great resort of wooers and controversy amongst lovers", Cecil had sighed to Throckmorton in October 1559. The Queen obviously relished the situation, but Cecil saw nothing uplifting in the spectacle. "I would her Majesty had one and the rest honourably satisfied", he observed irritably. By this time Baron Breuner was also becoming increasingly downcast about his chances, and was beginning to think that he should admit defeat and return home. Elizabeth kept telling him that she could not possibly marry a man without prior inspection, having been particularly alarmed by false reports that Archduke Charles had "a head bigger than the Earl of Bedford".[114] Since Emperor Ferdinand did not think it seemly for his son to submit himself to her scrutiny, an impasse had been reached.

As it became clear that Breuner was on the verge of departure, Elizabeth grew troubled. There had been a steady build-up of domestic pressure on her to marry, and though until now her subjects had derived comfort from the reflection that she was currently engaged in delicate marital negotiations with the Habsburgs, it did not look as though she would be able to use this excuse much longer. In November Breuner warned the Queen that he saw little point in prolonging discussions further, and it was noticed that immediately after this, Elizabeth was "worried and peevish the whole day, giving no one a gracious answer". She was concerned not least because she knew that if Breuner left England, Dudley would be blamed for the collapse of the negotiations, and he would be more widely reviled than ever. Already, indeed, the bitterness against him had reached alarming levels. Breuner noted, "It is generally stated that it is his fault that the Queen does not marry", and he added smugly, "his own sister and friends bear him ill-will". Feelings were running so high that the ambassador regarded it as "a marvel that he has not been slain long 'ere this".[115]

The most virulent of Lord Robert's enemies was the twenty-three-year-old Duke of Norfolk, the highest ranking nobleman in England, who doubtless would himself have been put forward as a potential husband for Elizabeth if he had not married another lady shortly after the Queen's accession. He abhorred Dudley as an upstart, and found the prospect that he might one day become his king almost unbearably offensive. By November 1559, he was making no effort to conceal his hatred, and at the end of the month he and Dudley quarrelled in public when the Duke angrily upbraided Lord Robert for deliberately obstructing the Archduke's suit. Until now, Dudley had always maintained that it was not his fault that Elizabeth was making difficulties about marrying Archduke Charles, for he personally was well affected to the proposal, but he now abandoned this pretence. Hotly he told Norfolk that "he was neither a good Englishman nor a loyal subject who advised the Queen to marry a foreigner".[116]

As tension mounted at court, Sir Thomas Challoner lamented the way that Elizabeth was wilfully repudiating a match that had so much to be said for it. "The affinity is great and honourable; the amity necessary to stop and cool many enterprises", was how he put it to Cecil, but to the dismay of both men, nothing could stop Breuner from leaving England in January 1560. Despairingly Challoner told Cecil, "This delay of ripe time for marriage, besides the loss of the realm (for without posterity of her Highness what hope is left unto us?) ministreth matters for . . . lewd tongues to descant upon, and breedeth contempt".[117]

Certainly England had need of an ally, for there were signs that the French King, Henry II, had only temporarily shelved his plans to declare Elizabeth a bastard and set Mary Stuart on the English throne. As though to proclaim that in the near future he intended to uphold Mary's claim, he permitted his daughter-in-law to quarter the arms of England on her escutcheon, and when the English ambassador to France dined at court, he was forced to eat off plate that was engraved with a coat of arms that implied that Mary Stuart was his rightful Queen. Far from thinking that this was merely a pointless insult on the part of the French, Cecil was sure that the situation was fraught with genuine menace. It was particularly alarming that Mary Stuart's marriage to the Dauphin had bound Scotland so closely to France, for it left the French ideally placed to mount an assault on England. It would be easy for them to build up their troops in Scotland and to launch an invasion from there, and if another French force were to strike simultaneously against southern England, the success of the attack would be virtually guaranteed. Pinioned between its two ancient enemies, England would be quickly overpowered.

Cecil was therefore greatly interested to learn that an influential group of Scots nobles was becoming disenchanted with their country's close association with France. Because Mary Stuart had left her kingdom when only five years old to go and live with her fiancé in France, her mother, Mary of Guise, was acting as Regent in her absence, and the policies which the Regent had recently been pursuing had annoyed many of the leading men in the kingdom. There was resentment about her attempts to stamp out Protestantism, which had gained many adherents in Scotland over the past few years, and concern had also been aroused by the fact that she had recently imported large numbers of French troops into the country. The nobles feared that her aim was to turn Scotland into little more than a dominion of France, whereas when Mary Stuart had been betrothed to the Dauphin, it had been understood that the two kingdoms would be on a footing of absolute equality.

Cecil had been closely monitoring the situation in Scotland since early 1559, when he had first received information that the Scots nobles were becoming restive, and surreptitiously he had done what he could to inflame their discontent. In May 1559, the anti-French party in Scotland received a great fillip with the return to his homeland of the polemicist and preacher John Knox, one of the Calvinist Church's most doughty champions, who had spent the last few years in exile on the continent. By delivering a series of remarkable sermons, Knox rallied Protestant opinion in Scotland, so that the movement against the French began to assume the appearance of a holy war. Cecil was delighted by these developments, seeing in them an opportunity to put an end to the hostile encirclement of England. He believed if the French were expelled from Scotland, and the Catholic Church there was overthrown, it would open up the way for a trans-formation in Anglo-Scots relations whose significance could scarcely be over-estimated.

The trouble was, that if the Scots did rise up against their present rulers, Elizabeth's approval was unlikely to be forthcoming. For the Queen, rebellion against a prince's divinely constituted authority represented the pinnacle of human wickedness, the ultimate sinful deed, which put its perpetrators beyond redemption. As a monarch she felt strongly that there could be no deviation from orthodox political theory, which propounded that, since princes had been sent by God to rule nations, obedience to one's sovereign was a subject's sacred duty. "Let every soul submit himself unto the authority of the higher powers", admonished one tract on the subject, written some fifty years before the Queen's accession. "There is no power but of God; the powers that be are ordained of God. Whosoever therefore resisteth the power, resisteth the ordinance of God." None was exempt from this obligation, which lay on all individuals within a Christian society, and there were no circumstances in which a withdrawal of allegiance could be legitimate. Even if a prince was evil, or governed unjustly, his people should not rise up against him, for bad rulers were accountable to God alone, and it was for Him to deal with them in His own time. Elizabeth wholeheartedly subscribed to the conventional view that "A rebel is worse than the worst prince, and rebellion worse than the worst government of the worst prince",[118] and it was an article of faith with her that those who resisted their prince, procured their own damnation. It followed that she could not accept that if a prince denied his subjects the right to practise the faith of their choice, this gave them a valid excuse to rise up in revolt. She did not question that a monarch was entitled to prescribe the religion that his people must observe, and in this, as in all else, they must bow to the superior power. For the Queen, therefore, the very suggestion that it was possible for subjects to wage a religious war against their prince was the most grotesque contradiction in terms.

In the circumstances Cecil knew that Elizabeth would recoil from the idea of associating herself with the revolutionary movement in Scotland, when her every instinct would be to condemn it as impious. If she did show approval, she would bring on herself the execration of her fellow monarchs, who would abominate her as an apostate who was undermining the very foundations of the institution which they had been placed on earth to defend. To uphold these values was in no way reactionary or eccentric of the Queen, for they were regarded as nothing less than universal truths, which all but the most searing radicals endorsed. Under normal conditions, Cecil himself would never have dreamt of suggesting that Elizabeth's philosophy was at fault, but in the special circumstances that then prevailed he felt there must be a departure from it. While France was capable of maintaining that Elizabeth was not a true prince at all, but had usurped her throne, the accepted rules of conduct were automatically suspended, for the necessity to protect England from the enemy that was currently perched on her northern frontier was too overwhelming to allow for a rigid adherence to principle. To Cecil's mind there could be no argument that the Scots must be encouraged to rise up against the regime then in power, and that England must aid them to overthrow it: but in view of the Queen's ideological outlook, he knew it would be difficult to persuade her to sanction anything of the sort.

It was particularly unfortunate that John Knox was so bound up with what was happening in Scotland, for Elizabeth utterly abhorred him. Endowed with the zeal and integrity of an Old Testament prophet, Knox was not the sort of man to let outdated concepts that had hitherto determined the nature of government and society interfere with the dynamics of the Calvinist reform movement. As early as May 1554, he had penned in exile an *Admonition to the People of England* that some interpreted as calling for the assassination of Mary Tudor, and four years later he elaborated on this theme with the publication of *The First Blast of the Trumpet against the Monstrous Regiment of Women*. Fierily repudiating the notion that it was God's will that an oppressed people must endure the sufferings inflicted by a tyrant, Knox declared that in some circumstances rebellion could be equated with righteousness, and that it was not necessarily a contravention of the divine law if an ungodly prince was deposed. This was advanced political thought of a sort that no ruler could condone, but not content with this, Knox launched into a virulent denunciation of the very concept of female sovereignty, which to him represented a gross violation of the natural order. Angrily he inveighed against women rulers, quoting from the ancient fathers and citing biblical texts to prove that they were unfitted to wield power, and declaring that in view of the inferior sex's inherent sinfulness and mental frailty, it was "repugnant to nature, contumely to God . . . contrarious to his revealed will and approved ordinance" to permit a woman to have dominion over any nation, realm or city.[119]

Knox's work had been directed primarily against Mary Tudor, who had been on the throne at the time of publication, but obviously the arguments were equally applicable to Elizabeth, and she was outraged by their tenor. In her view, Knox was no better than a seditious firebrand, and she wanted to have nothing whatever to do with the author of this revolutionary tract. Throckmorton might tell her that, in view of the fact that Knox was capable of uniting the Scots against the French, Elizabeth should be prepared to overlook his faults, but the Queen's prejudice against him was much too potent for that. Fearing that her disgust for Knox would reinforce her inclination to remain aloof from the resistance movement in Scotland, Cecil warned a colleague, "Of all others, Knox's name . . . is most odious here; and therefore I wish no mention of him hither".[120]

From Cecil's point of view, it was almost a relief that the French continued to goad Elizabeth in a manner impossible for her to overlook. In July 1559, Henry II of France had died as a result of injuries sustained in a court tournament, and Mary Stuart's fifteen-year-old husband had succeeded him as Francis II. Initially it had been thought that the new King might be more friendly towards England than his father had been, but these hopes soon proved illusory. It became apparent that Francis was dominated by his wife's maternal relations, the predatory Guises, whom one of Elizabeth's advisers described as "a race that is both enemy to God and the common quiet of Europe". They were fanatical Catholics, and were as ambitious as they were religious, and since, in Cecil's words, they were known to nourish "a long old rooted . . . hatred against England", it was hardly likely that they would encourage Francis to stay at peace with

Elizabeth. Under their aegis, Mary Stuart was emboldened to be more assertive about her claim to the English throne. When in company, she was overheard uttering "disdainful speech" against Elizabeth, and from France Throckmorton related that on one occasion Mary had declared, "That as God has so provided that notwithstanding the malice of her enemies, she is Queen of France and Scotland, so she trusts to be Queen of England also". Nor was this an isolated incident, for Cecil heard that when Mary attended chapel, the ushers who preceded her cried out to the spectators, "Make way for the Queen of England!"[121]

In the face of this provocation, Elizabeth agreed that the Protestant nobles in Scotland should receive clandestine financial aid from England, and on 8 August, £3,000 was despatched north to boost the rebel cause. This did not escape the attention of Mary of Guise, and at her request, the French ambassador in London raised the matter with Elizabeth. In absence of proof, however, Elizabeth was able to deny giving the rebels any encouragement, and she professed herself mystified that the ambassador could think that any of her servants would become mixed up with such disreputable people. Indeed, as her resentment towards Mary Stuart gradually neutralised her unease at being in complicity with rebels, she even began to enjoy herself, and when the French ambassador returned to court to make further representations on Mary of Guise's behalf, he reported that Elizabeth had been unable to stifle her laughter, even while she parried his enquiries.[122]

Before long, however, it became apparent that the situation was too grave for it to be treated as a joke. On 21 October 1559, the revolt in Scotland took a step forward when the aristocratic rebel leaders declared that they would no longer recognize Mary of Guise as Regent, but their military situation remained weak, for they were not making headway against Mary of Guise's French troops. Worse still, it was reliably reported that the French were preparing to send reinforcements to the Regent, and it was obvious that in that event the rising against her would be crushed. Elizabeth's representatives on the borders, who were anxiously watching the situation in Scotland, gave a sombre warning that "her Highness must either open and manifest herself on that side, or else they shall not be able to wrestle and strive against the power of France".[123] The stakes in the game were becoming higher by the minute, and Elizabeth no longer regarded it as fun.

Initially, the Council had not been informed that the Scots were receiving covert aid, for Elizabeth and Cecil had made only two or three men privy to the secret, but further consultation was now in order. By 12 November, the Council had been brought up to date with the situation, and they retrospectively endorsed the sending of secret aid. In addition it was agreed that in order to ensure that all would be in readiness if it proved necessary to send an army into Scotland, 4,000 men should be stationed at Berwick on the borders. The fleet was also to be prepared, and the Duke of Norfolk was ordered to Newcastle to take up the post of Lieutenant of the North.[124]

In the ensuing weeks, the situation continued to deteriorate. As the emergency grew more acute, there were urgent debates in the Privy Council, and after it had sat in conference for eight days running, it was agreed on 16 December that the experienced sea captain William Winter should sail north with a squadron of ships. His unofficial instructions were that having entered the Firth of Forth, he was to seize some excuse to attack the French ships moored there, and then to set up a blockade which would prevent the French from sending reinforcements to Mary of Guise.[125]

Cecil did not regard this as sufficient, for he now believed that outright intervention in Scotland was the only way to prevent the French triumphing, but he had a hard time convincing his colleagues on the Council of this. His leading opponent was his brother-in-law, Sir Nicholas Bacon, who argued cogently that England lacked the manpower and financial resources to contemplate such an operation. By 24 December, however, Cecil had managed to win round a majority of the Council to his view, and a memo urging that an army should be sent to Scotland was accordingly presented to Elizabeth. She was not impressed: four days later the document was returned and Cecil sorrowfully endorsed it, "Not allowed by the Queen".[126]

Elizabeth's diffidence was understandable, for as Feria had earlier remarked, the English were "without money, men, armour, fortresses, practice in war, or good captains" which would have enabled them to tackle the enterprise with confidence. Even while advising her to go to war, the Council had admitted that in sanctioning an attack, she would "hazard not only money and men ... but also the state of the crown, the realm, and all that depend thereupon, which is too dreadful to think upon". They argued that inaction would be still more perilous, but Elizabeth could not help dwelling on what would happen if the attempt to eject the French from Scotland proved unsuccessful. She would then have given them the very excuse they needed to surge over the border into England and deprive her of her throne, and without convincing proof that they were planning to do this anyway, she dared not risk a confrontation. Already she had done as much as she thought feasible to help the Scots, and when news arrived that Winter had successfully accomplished his mission, her reaction was that surely this was enough to enable the Scots "to expel the French of themselves, without ... open aid".[127]

Cecil knew that this was not the case, and such was his desperation at seeing that Elizabeth was going to let this unique opportunity slip by, that "with a sorrowful heart and watery eyes", he sent in his resignation. Brokenly he assured Elizabeth, "And as for any other service, though it were in your Majesty's kitchen or garden, from the bottom of my heart, I am ready without respect of estimation, wealth or ease to do your Majesty's commandment to my life's end", but he reiterated that in the present circumstances it was impossible for him to continue as her adviser.[128]

In the face of this ultimatum, Elizabeth gave way, and agreed to enter into a formal alliance with the Scots. Nevertheless, she remained full of misgivings. On 27 February 1560, Elizabeth officially took Scotland into her protection with the signing of the Treaty of Berwick, which stated that since France clearly intended to conquer Scotland and suppress its liberties, Elizabeth would "send men of war there with all speed" to help the Scots repel this threat.[129] The treaty was so worded that Elizabeth could maintain that this did not amount to giving aid to rebels, for it was stressed that the Scots still acknowledged Mary Stuart as their Queen, and that in taking this action they were merely seeking to defend themselves from the encroachments of a hostile foreign power. As Mary was Queen of France as well as Scotland, the argument was somewhat tenuous, but it helped Elizabeth to come to terms with her conscience.

Even though the Queen had been pressured into going thus far, she still hoped that hostilities might be averted, and when the French suggested that it might yet be possible peaceably to settle their differences, she eagerly agreed that they could send over an envoy. Hoping that this meant that the French were now ready voluntarily to withdraw their troops from Scotland, she told the Duke of Norfolk to delay the departure of the English army, which was scheduled to march into Scotland on 25 March. The Council were appalled that the Queen was prepared to be so conciliatory, for they were convinced – correctly as it turned out – that the French were not interested in serious negotiations, and were only trying to keep the English out of Scotland until such time as reinforcements could be sent there in such large numbers that Mary of Guise's position would become impregnable. Gloomily the Council wrote to Norfolk that, although the French were pretending to be reasonable, "Considering their accustomed practices, we have small hope that their meaning agreeth with their fair words. Nevertheless ... her Majesty is pleased, though to her cost, and to some other hindrance of her affairs, to make proof of their intent." Whenever her Councillors tried reasoning with the Queen, her forlorn response was that "it is a dangerous matter to enter into war".[130]

By 12 March, the French representative, Monluc, had arrived in England, but it soon became apparent that he was not empowered to make any proposals which could have formed the basis for an agreement. Throckmorton sent urgent messages from Paris that it was clear the French were planning "with their gay and simple speech to enchant her Highness", but the Queen was most unwilling to break off talks. On 23 March, the Council addressed her a stern memorandum telling her that the time had come to prosecute the war with vigour, but it was not until six days later that Elizabeth hesitantly agreed that her army could advance.

On 31 March, the English army, which consisted of 8,000 men under the command of Lord Grey, crossed the border into Scotland. There they joined with the Scots' forces, who were encamped outside Leith, the port adjacent to Edinburgh where the French troops were based. The town was soon under siege, but still Elizabeth did not seem to be in earnest about the war, for she refused to let her men attack Edinburgh Castle, where Mary of Guise had taken refuge. "These toys and womanish tolerations, these impatient and unwarlike proceedings will hazard all most dangerously and to no purpose!" Throckmorton fulminated angrily. Instead of trying to take Edinburgh Castle by force, Elizabeth agreed that Monluc could go to Scotland and inform Mary of Guise of the terms on which the English would be prepared to make peace. Cecil wrote to Throckmorton lamenting, "In all this great matter ... the Queen is so backward ... as it is [unlikely] that any good can come thereof".[131] He believed that by maintaining contact with the enemy in this way, Elizabeth ran the risk of demoralizing the Scots, but it is only fair to point out that it was this initiative that eventually led to peace talks, so the Queen was probably correct in keeping communications open.

Meanwhile, on 7 May an attempt was made to take Leith by storm. The result was a disaster: the scaling ladders provided were too short, the breach that had been made in the walls proved insufficient to force an entry, and the Captain of Berwick, Sir James Crofts, failed to provide troops in the vanguard of the attack with adequate support. As a result, the French defenders had no difficulty repelling it, and the English casualties numbered about 1,500 men.

When Elizabeth was informed of the setback, she flew into a rage. Unhappily, Cecil wrote to Throckmorton, "The Queen's Majesty never liketh this matter of Scotland ... and now, when we looked for best fortune, the worst came ... I have had such a torment herein with the Queen's Majesty ... " It was feared that the news would cause Elizabeth "to renew the opinion of Cassandra", but in fact, once she had recovered from the initial shock, she realized there could be no question now of giving up the struggle. Making the best of a bad job, she wrote briskly to Norfolk, "We be sorry that the success was no better, but considering the importance of the matter .... the enterprise must needs be achieved ... We mean further so to reinforce this matter with all manner of things lacking".[132]

Fresh troops were sent to Scotland, and the siege of Leith was renewed. Elizabeth's tenacity was rewarded, for as shortage of supplies began to make things difficult for the defenders, a message came from France with an offer to negotiate. Despite the abysmal military record of the English up to this point in the war, religious tensions within France itself were causing domestic unrest and the country was therefore in no fit state to sustain a prolonged struggle outside the kingdom. The siege of Leith was not called off, but at the end of May it was agreed that Cecil should go north to discuss a possible peace settlement with representatives from France.

Before talks could open in Edinburgh, the English had a stroke of good fortune for, at midnight on 10 June, Mary of Guise died. Throckmorton had justly said of her, "She hath the heart of a man of war", and now that she was gone it was hoped that the French would lose much of their will to resist. Yet even so, Cecil's negotiations did not run smoothly. The French representatives refused to accept that the Anglo-Scots agreement concluded at Berwick was valid, for they objected that the Scots should not have entered into a league with another country without the sanction of their Queen. On this point, negotiations nearly broke down, but after great exertions Cecil succeeded in salvaging the talks. By 2 July, unofficial peace terms had been agreed upon, and four days later the Treaty of Edinburgh was formally signed. By its terms, the French promised that in future they would observe Scots liberties and withdraw their troops, and an undertaking was also given that henceforward Mary Stuart would renounce all claim to Elizabeth's throne. Cecil was justly proud of his achievement, for despite the fact that Elizabeth's army had scarcely distinguished itself in the field, England had gained all that it had set out to win at the outset of the conflict. With great satisfaction he wrote, "We think the same very honourable for the Queen's Majesty, profitable for her realm, and commodious for the liberty of Scotland".[133]

He was therefore shattered when the day after peace had been concluded, he received a letter from Elizabeth stating that in view of the provocative conduct of the French, she expected to be compensated by the immediate cession of Calais and a cash payment of £150,000. It was clear to Cecil that in his absence some irresponsible person had been inflaming the Queen, trying to persuade her that, as the French were experiencing difficulties at home, this was the moment to pursue an expansionist policy against them. Fortunately her letter had not arrived in time to prevent peace being signed, and it was too late now to disavow the treaty. Even so, the communication plunged Cecil "into the deep dungeon of sorrow". It profoundly disturbed him that Elizabeth, who had hitherto showed herself so wavering and pusillanimous, and who had had to be dragged kicking and screaming into a struggle on which her very survival depended, should suddenly have acquired the taste for strutting on the battlefield, and now fancied herself as a warrior queen. Instead of contenting herself with the rational pursuit of statesmanlike objectives, she now wished to plunge her country into a war of aggrandisement which it could ill afford. Throckmorton wrote to her recalling, "I heard your Majesty say you have a great longing to do some act in your time that should make your fame to spread abroad in your lifetime and after occasion memorial for ever" and, for the moment at least, it seemed that Elizabeth had allowed herself to be gripped by wild ambition. If the Queen was going to continue to behave in such a wilful and inconsistent fashion as this, the fears of those who had prophesied that a woman's rule would prove catastrophic looked set to be proved correct. Wearily, Cecil prayed, "God send her Majesty understanding that shall be her surety", but on her record so far, there was little reason to suppose that his plea would be granted.[134]

CHAPTER 5

"So great a lady that there could be no hold taken of her"

On Cecil's return from Scotland, his gloom deepened immeasurably. Elizabeth, it seemed, was entirely unappreciative of the way he had employed his skills as a negotiator to obtain the diplomatic victory of the Treaty of Edinburgh. Like the Duke of Norfolk, the Secretary had not been fully reimbursed for expenses incurred while on service in the North, and this rankled a good deal. Much worse than this, however, was the fact that Cecil now found himself excluded from the Queen's confidence, for though Elizabeth still expected him to deal with the routine burden of administrative tasks, he was no longer admitted to frequent consultations with her. His only consolation was that his supporters at Court were loud in their condemnation of the treatment he was receiving. When he confided his woes to Throckmorton, now in France, the ambassador wrote indignantly that he was appalled to hear of the state of affairs in England, where "neither councillor nor conductor was rewarded; that all men that did at this time service, were displeased; that her Majesty would do her pleasure in all things, so as there was none to take the special care of her affairs".[1]

Cecil was particularly concerned that Elizabeth would irresponsibly throw away an historic opportunity to forge a permanent friendship with Scotland. Having loosened the ties that traditionally bound them to France, the Scots nobility (who at present were in effective control of their country, despite the fact that Mary Stuart remained its titular sovereign) looked to Elizabeth to show them firm amity. The Queen nevertheless made little effort to cultivate them, peremptorily refusing to foster goodwill by distributing pensions to leading members of the Scots aristocracy. This drove Cecil to distraction, for he was sure that the French would not hesitate to use financial inducements to regain their lost influence in Scottish affairs, and if Elizabeth failed to match their offers it was obvious that Scotland

would again be seduced into becoming a dependent of France. To Throckmorton, Cecil moaned at Elizabeth's refusal "to bestow somewhat on the
Scots", complaining dismally, "With £1,000 I durst undertake to save
£20,000 in five years, with £2,000, to save £40,000. And yet it is no good
counsel." So despondent was he at the decay of his influence that Cecil
seriously contemplated resignation.[2]

The Queen's neglect of Scottish affairs was not the only, or even the
most important, reason for the Secretary's troubled state of mind, for his
disagreement with her on this issue was merely symptomatic of a more
fundamental cause of tension that had arisen between them. While in
Edinburgh Cecil had written to the Queen hoping that "God would direct
your heart to procure a father for your children, and so shall the children
of all your realm bless your seed",[3] but on his return he had been appalled
to find that there was a likelihood that Elizabeth was going to fulfil his
wish in a manner he had not foreseen. In Cecil's absence, the Queen's
attachment to Lord Robert Dudley had become a great deal more marked,
and she had now reached a point where she gave every appearance of
having fallen madly in love. Earlier in the reign her affection for Lord
Robert had of course excited comment, but in those days she had shown
a comparable degree of favour to others. Besides, the fact that Dudley was
a married man made it difficult to regard him as a serious contender for
her hand. While the crisis with Scotland had been at its height, the Queen
had had little time to waste on flirtation with her Master of the Horse, and
this had lulled Cecil and others into assuming that Dudley had never meant
very much to her. With the conclusion of the war in Scotland, however,
Lord Robert had once again come to the fore, and by the time that Cecil
was back at Court, the Queen was flaunting the delight she took in Dudley's
company in a manner that some thought little short of wanton.

Whereas in recent weeks, Elizabeth's concentration had been riveted on
state affairs, she now devoted herself largely to pleasure. She spent every
day on hunting expeditions with Dudley, riding recklessly, and demanding
to be mounted on the most spirited horses in her stables. The conduct of
business was having to take second place to more invigorating pursuits,
and while it was not, perhaps, inherently reprehensible that a young woman
of twenty-seven, whose life so far had had few carefree interludes, should
give herself up to fun in this way, the change in her habits struck many
people as being far from innocent. To Cecil, whose own dedication to duty
left him little time to pursue his hobbies of gardening and genealogy, the
Queen's temporary abdication of responsibility was indicative of greater
follies to come. Already her reputation was suffering, for the hours she
spent with Dudley were a godsend for the scandalmongers, and nourished
rumours that she was an adulteress. In August 1560, Anne Dowe of
Brentford was sent to prison for asserting that the Queen had a child by

Dudley, but she proved to be the first of many such offenders, and repressive measures of this sort failed to silence the insidious gossip. The Court, of course, was alive with it, and even Cecil, normally so level-headed and discreet, found himself listening to the poisonous whispers.

He was indeed in such an unsettled state that, when he encountered the Spanish ambassador on 7 September 1560, he made no attempt to hide his despair. He frankly told de la Quadra that he was thinking of resigning, even though by doing so he might run the risk of being consigned to the Tower by the Queen. He declared that "It was a bad sailor who did not enter port if he could when he saw a storm coming on, and he clearly foresaw the ruin of the realm through Lord Robert's intimacy with the Queen, who surrendered all affairs to him and meant to marry him". He begged de la Quadra to reason with the Queen about her conduct, and twice repeated "that Lord Robert would be better in paradise than here". More startling still, he concluded by saying "that Robert was thinking of killing his wife, who was publicly announced to be ill, although she was quite well, and would take very good care they did not poison her".[4]

De la Quadra had little sympathy for the Secretary, for it was his opinion that "Nobody worse than Cecil can be at the head of affairs". He nevertheless was ready enough to believe all that Cecil had told him, although in fact panic may well have impaired the Secretary's judgement or led him to exaggerate. At any rate, the Secretary's wild outburst had no chance of simply fading into oblivion, for the very next day the body of Dudley's wife, Amy, was found at the foot of a staircase at Cumnor Hall, the Oxfordshire manor house where she had been staying.

Amy's death at once gave rise to a flood of controversy and speculation, and to this day it remains a celebrated mystery. The immediate cause of death was a broken neck, but how she sustained the injury was the subject of much dispute. It was said that the staircase at Cumnor Hall was insufficiently steep for a fall to have had fatal consequences, and this led to suggestions that Amy had first been murdered and then her corpse had been deposited at the foot of the stairs in hopes of averting suspicions of foul play. Suicide was also put forward as a possibility, for it emerged that in recent weeks she had been in a highly disturbed state of mind, and a maidservant had overheard her mistress praying God to deliver her from desperation. There was little else to bear out this theory, however, which never commanded much support, for even if Amy had been wretched enough to want to kill herself, it was scarcely credible that she should have chosen to do so by throwing herself downstairs.

It is only recently that a truly plausible explanation has been advanced. As early as April 1559, Amy was reported to be suffering from a "malady in one of her breasts", and from this it has been inferred that she was a victim of breast cancer. If this was the case, her bones could have been weakened by cancerous deposits carried through her bloodstream from the cells of the original tumour, so that even the slight exertion involved in walking downstairs could have caused a spontaneous fracture of the spine. Her diseased condition, and the pain it caused her, could also have been the reason for her anguished mental state, although obviously her husband's absence at Court, and the rumours of his infidelity with the Queen, are in themselves sufficient to account for her depression. All in all, the hypothesis that Amy was terminally ill, and that it was this which killed her, is more convincing than any of the theories that were current at the time, but in the sixteenth century the medical knowledge was lacking that would have allowed for such a specialized diagnosis. It occurred to no one that Amy's death was the result of natural causes, and although Lord Robert's friends manfully maintained that her fall should be attributed to "the hand of God", they failed to overcome the widespread conviction that the responsibility for it should be laid at Dudley's door. The whole of England buzzed with the scandal; "even preachers in the pulpits discoursed on the matter in a way that was prejudicial to the honour and interests of the Queen".[5]

Elizabeth and Dudley themselves were under no illusion as to the unpleasant construction that was being put on the tragedy. When news of Amy's death first arrived, the Queen at once grasped that it would be fatal to give the impression that she did not wish the matter to be fully investigated, and accordingly Dudley was sent away from court pending the outcome of an inquest on his wife. Dudley did not even try to pretend that he was particularly sad to have lost his wife in this unexpected fashion, but he was appalled that her death could not be satisfactorily accounted for, and he too realized that his only hope of vindicating himself lay in ensuring that the forthcoming enquiry was as frank as possible. Knowing full well "what the malicious world will bruit", he begged his agent at Cumnor to see that every clue and shred of evidence was laid before the jury, for otherwise it would be assumed that he had something to hide.[6] When the case came to court, a verdict of misadventure was duly returned, but unfortunately the available evidence had been too inconclusive in character for the public to feel that Dudley had been fully exonerated. He was permitted to return to Court, which he found deep in mourning for Amy, but even after he had paid for a lavish funeral for his wife, the suspicions voiced against him were no less dreadful than before.

Despite the hostility which greeted him, Dudley was determined to put Amy's death behind him, taking the robust view that, as his name had been formally cleared, it was perfectly proper for him to embark on a courtship of the Queen. For Elizabeth, the issue was obviously less straightforward. She had always known that a marriage with one of her courtiers would give rise to jealousy and resentment, but if Dudley became her husband, the backlash against her would be magnified tenfold. Not only was he uniquely unpopular, but his reputation had been irreparably smeared by the mysterious death of his wife, and this meant that those who were not prepared to accept him as their king would be able to cloak their selfish objections to his elevation in the guise of outraged decency. The danger that the kingdom would split into hostile factions on her marriage to Dudley was underlined when a servant of the Earl of Arundel's was arrested for having boasted that it would cause "a great stir" among the nobility, as Arundel would ally himself with the Marquis of Northampton, the Earl of Pembroke and Lord Rich against the upstart.[7] It was well known that the Duke of Norfolk was also a bitter antagonist of Dudley's, and with so impressive a list of enemies arrayed against him, it was far from fanciful to predict that if his suit proved successful, it would plunge the country into civil war. It was nevertheless unclear whether Elizabeth had assessed the risks involved, and even if she had, the way she behaved when Dudley was with her made some people think that she would insist on having him, whatever the consequences.

Quite apart from the potential domestic repercussions, by marrying Dudley, Elizabeth would have gone down in the estimation of foreign courts, and England's standing within the international community would have been grievously diminished. In Paris, Throckmorton found himself squirming at the mocking comments passed on his mistress by "the malicious French", and he knew that these would become still more offensive once she had become Lord Robert's wife. He confessed to one colleague that things were being said "which every hair of my head stareth at, and my ears glow to hear", and he claimed that he would rather die than to go on listening to the "dishonourable and naughty reports that are here made of the Queen". Utterly humiliated, he confided to Northampton, "Some let not to say 'What religion is this, that a subject shall kill his wife, and the Prince not only bear withal but marry with him'". The young Queen of Scots had joined in the scornful chorus, making a jibe to the effect that she heard the Queen of England was to marry her horsekeeper, and since Throckmorton knew that this would sting Elizabeth, he made certain that she heard of it. For the moment, Throckmorton did his best to parry the sneers, but he made it plain that his position would become utterly untenable if the marriage rumours proved true. To Cecil he wailed, "We begin already to be in derision and hatred for the bruit only, and nothing taken here on this side more assured than our destruction; so if it take place ... God and religion, which be the fundaments, shall be out of estimation; the Queen our sovereign discredited, condemned and neglected; our country ruined, undone and made prey".[8]

So great was Throckmorton's agitation that in November 1560 he despatched to England his secretary Mr Jones, with instructions to impress upon the Queen the utter folly of taking so unsuitable a consort. Jones carried out this difficult mission with commendable directness and resolve. When granted an audience with the Queen, he found her looking pale and tired, but though it was clear that the tension of the past few weeks had taken its toll in nervous stress, her manner was far from subdued. For one thing, she made it plain that whatever the public outcry, she intended to stand by her favourite. Jones's visit, she insisted, was quite uncalled for, and she became positively irritable when he embarked upon his lecture. "I have heard of this before!" she exclaimed impatiently, but Jones doggedly pressed on, pointing out that Dudley had been implicated in his father's plot to set Jane Grey on the throne, and this had been directed as much against Elizabeth as against her sister Mary. The Queen obviously found such home truths uncomfortable: "She laughed", Jones reported, "and forthwith turned herself to the one side and to the other, and set her hand upon her face", but despite her evident embarrassment, she nevertheless proved tenacious in Dudley's defence. With reference to his wife's death she stated firmly that "the matter had been tried in the country and found to be contrary to that which was reported", and she concluded defiantly "that it fell out as should neither touch his honesty nor her honour".[9] Jones subsequently told Throckmorton that considering the awkward nature of the subject, the Queen had treated him with remarkable patience and consideration, but his account of the interview nevertheless did little to allay Sir Nicholas's fears.

Cecil, in contrast, was growing calmer by the day. Since his indiscreet avowals to de la Quadra, he had relapsed into silent watchfulness, and by the late autumn his observations had instilled in him a cautious optimism that the Queen did not intend to rush into marriage with Dudley. In this he judged aright. For the past few weeks Elizabeth had been in the grip of conflicting emotions, and though it was true that she was strongly attracted to Dudley, her desire for him was not so overwhelming that her judgment had been impaired. However powerful his appeal for her, it was considerably muted by his non-royal status, and Lord Robert also had to contend with her antipathy to marriage in general. Had he been a less controversial figure, he might perhaps have overcome these handicaps, but the stigma which still hung over him as a result of the curious death of his wife helped tip the balance against him.

It was to Cecil's credit that he realized that if the Queen was to summon up the detachment necessary to disappoint her admirer, she must be given time for reflection, and after his first flurry of panic had subsided, he had been careful not to harry her in any way. She clearly resented all criticism of Dudley, and the need to defend him from his detractors had only increased her determination to demonstrate her devotion. For as long as she felt that Dudley was being shabbily treated, the danger remained that she would try to compensate for this by accepting his suit, but provided people ceased to denigrate him openly, her loyalties would not be so deeply engaged. When Dudley was disparaged, he acquired the added lustre of forbidden fruit, but if Elizabeth was left to make her own assessments, there was a better chance that she would accept that Amy's death could never be forgotten, and that her own integrity would be called into question if she married the widower regardless. Realizing that Throckmorton was only making matters worse by tactlessly badgering the Queen, Cecil wrote him a sharp letter, telling him not to meddle in matters that were beyond his sphere.[10]

The recovery of Cecil's nerve owed much to the fact that even when Dudley's favour was supposedly at its height, Elizabeth continued to manifest an aggressive independence of spirit. In November 1560, it was given out that Dudley was to be raised to the peerage, but when the necessary papers had been prepared, the Queen suddenly thought better of it, and taking a knife, she slashed the patent to shreds.[11] This exercise in humiliation was an unmistakeable signal that she would not easily surrender herself to Dudley, and early in the New Year Cecil's morale was further boosted when he himself received a coveted court appointment. The previous December, the Mastership of the Court of Wards had been vacated when Elizabeth's former cofferer, Sir Thomas Parry, had died, and in January the post was conferred on Cecil. It was a highly lucrative position, which put a great deal of patronage at the Secretary's disposal, and the fact that the Queen had given it to him rather than Dudley confirmed that she would not allow Cecil's career to be overshadowed by the rise of a favourite.

By this time Dudley himself was concerned by the courtship's lack of progress, and accordingly he tried a fresh approach. On his instructions, his brother-in-law, Sir Henry Sidney, went to the Spanish ambassador and passed on an assurance from Dudley that once he and the Queen were man and wife, Catholicism would be restored in England. Because of this Sidney suggested that Philip II should try to further Dudley's cause by conveying to Elizabeth that he would be very pleased if she became Lord Robert's wife. It is difficult to know what to make of this curious initiative, for later in the reign, Dudley flaunted strong Protestant convictions. He insisted that he had never deviated from these, telling a Puritan minister of his acquaintance, "I take Almighty God to my record, I never altered my mind or thought from youth touching my religion, and you know I was ever from my cradle brought up in it". Even at this early stage in his career, he had used his influence to benefit radical churchmen, for it has been estimated that no less than six of the Bishops recently appointed by the Queen owed their new positions to Dudley's recommendations.[12] As yet, however, few people were aware of his identification with the Protestant cause, and so his offer to the Spaniards was not inherently implausible.

Whether or not Dudley was really prepared to forsake his religion if this helped him win the Queen is impossible to say. Certainly many of his contemporaries would have believed him to be capable of it, but in all probability he calculated that once he was married he would have little difficulty disavowing earlier promises.

De la Quadra, at least, thought that the overture was sincere, and he persuaded Philip II to believe in it as well. Having secured his master's approval, the ambassador went to Elizabeth and said pointedly that he was glad to hear that she was contemplating marriage. The Queen did not appear in the least displeased that Dudley had managed to enlist the assistance of the Spaniards, and indeed, it may well have been she who had encouraged him to approach de la Quadra in the first place. She had no intention of permitting a change in religion, but she welcomed any move that implied that the situation with regard to it remained fluid, for so long as the Catholic powers entertained hopes of her conversion, she was less likely to face excommunication. Accordingly, she did not hide her pleasure when de la Quadra alluded to Dudley's prospects. "After much circumlocution", she answered coyly "that she was no angel, and did not deny she had some affection for Lord Robert for the many good qualities he possessed." She went on to say that she had not made up her mind to marry Dudley or anyone else, but it was becoming clear that she could not long remain single, and in that case she believed her best choice of husband would be an Englishman. Roguishly she asked what King Philip would think if she married one of her servitors, and de la Quadra took the cue by assuring her warmly that his master would be delighted.[13]

Far from trying to conceal from Cecil Dudley's links with de la Quadra, the Queen herself apprised him of them, apparently not thinking they would cause him concern. By now, Cecil knew better than to object to Dudley's activities, and he pretended that he welcomed the Spanish intervention, going so far as to suggest ways in which King Philip could best demonstrate his support for the match. In reality, however, he was alarmed to find that matters had gone as far as they had. He feared that Elizabeth would have great difficulty disentangling herself from these dealings with de la Quadra, and he was particularly shocked to learn that she was on the verge of promising the ambassador that she would give permission for a Papal Nuncio to visit England. Presumably the Queen was confident that she could receive the Pope's envoy without compromising the position of her Church in any way, but Cecil had no doubt about the risks involved in any form of dialogue with Rome.

Determined to avert the Nuncio's arrival, Cecil took vigorous counter-measures. A Catholic priest detained in Kent admitted to being in the employ of Sir Edward Waldegrave, a former councillor of Mary Tudor's, and Cecil used this as an excuse to place Waldegrave under arrest. The

Secretary also succeeded in uncovering a letter from one of the Marian bishops which alluded to the forthcoming visit of the Nuncio in optimistic terms, and Cecil claimed this highlighted the dangers of permitting a papal agent to enter the country. In this way he managed to create the impression that the English Catholics were becoming dangerously presumptuous, and by implying that it was de la Quadra who had fostered disaffection in them, he effectively discredited the Spanish ambassador. As a result anti-Catholic feeling was aroused at Court, and on 1 May 1561 the Council, carefully shepherded by Cecil, unanimously advised the Queen not to receive the Papal Nuncio. Elizabeth agreed to abide by their wishes, and though she plainly regretted that she had been obliged to adopt this unconciliatory stance, she accepted that now was not the time to appear ambivalent about her religion. Cecil was triumphant: "God and the Queen (the one by directing and the other by yielding) have ended the matter well", he told Throckmorton with undisguised relief.[14]

Dudley was nonplussed to find that his connection with the Spanish ambassador had become more of an embarrassment than an asset, and some of his friends told him frankly that in view of the recent setbacks he had suffered, it would be advisable for him to go and live abroad. He cheered up, however, when the Queen suddenly allocated him apartments at court next to her own, for this allowed him to hope that his next step would be to share the royal bedchamber itself. He nevertheless was quick to learn from past failures, and while he remained confident that he had a good chance of marrying Elizabeth, he now realized that he would never bring this about by posing as a champion of Papistry. From now on, he deliberately advertised his commitment to Protestant beliefs, calculating that these would form a better vehicle for his ambition than the crypto-Catholicism of his earlier years. In May 1561 de la Quadra was dismayed to learn that Dudley was now receiving a course of theological instruction from "the heretic bishops", and thereafter it was Lord Robert's proud boast "that there is no man I know in this realm . . . that hath shewed a better mind to the furthering of true religion than I have done".[15] The shift in his religious affiliations was mirrored by his adoption of a more militant approach to foreign affairs, for henceforward his tendency was to persuade Elizabeth that she should set herself up as the protectress of Protestants abroad as well as in England. Instead of allying himself with the forces of reaction, Dudley now aimed to project an aura of idealism and patriotic fervour, thus outflanking the pedestrian Cecil and commending himself to the Queen. He was careful not to take this policy to extremes, for Elizabeth would not have relished it if he had pushed her too insistently to take a more active role on the continent, but the muscular Protestantism that now became his hallmark enhanced his credibility by enabling him to carve out his own niche within the English political scene, and ensured that he was regarded as much more than a mere minion of the Queen's.

By the late spring of 1561 the first phase of the Dudley courtship was over, but there was no question of his being discarded by the Queen. Lord Robert remained a figure to be reckoned with at court, and as Cecil had no alternative but to learn how to live with him, he did his best to remain on equable terms with the favourite. In the coming years there were frequent periods when the Secretary's nerves were frayed by a terror that the Queen would, after all, accept Lord Robert, but though he never ceased to believe that this would be a disastrous development, his policy on these occasions was to place subtle obstructions in Dudley's path, rather than oppose the marriage openly.

As for the Queen, it is obvious that in the winter of 1560–61 she was genuinely tempted to marry Dudley, but it would be an exaggeration to say that refraining from doing so represented a supreme sacrifice on her part. For one thing, she never gave him a definitive rejection, and she continued to look on him as being very much her own. For years she drew comfort from the knowledge that she could still have him if she chose to, and she was so successful in keeping alight the romance between them that almost two decades elapsed before Dudley could bring himself to acknowledge that she would never be his.

In the summer of 1561 Dudley was still looked upon as the strongest contender for the Queen's hand. It was true that when urged to take him, Elizabeth would "pup with her mouth" and indicate that such a match was beneath her, but outsiders estimated that her affection for him was "now as great as ever". That autumn Lord Robert was still so close to her that it was said, "It seems his favour is just begun", and incidents such as that which took place in November, when the Queen stole out of the palace incognito to watch Dudley compete in a shooting match, ensured that his hopes were kept alive. If court gossip was to be believed, there were even times when he was permitted to treat Elizabeth with a familiarity that threatened to overstep the bounds of propriety. In the morning, he had the right to enter Elizabeth's bedchamber after she had been woken by her ladies, and an enemy of Dudley's claimed that on one occasion he had tried to hand the Queen her clothes as she was dressing, and had attempted to kiss her without being invited.[16]

Despite the fact that such stories were current, it was obvious enough that the Queen knew when to keep her favourite under control. In June 1561 she was irritated to find herself under renewed pressure to make Dudley a peer, and had suddenly shouted that she had no intention of promoting someone to the House of Lords whose family name was synonymous with treason. Dudley had naturally been severely shaken by this outburst, and though partially mollified when Elizabeth patted him on the cheek and, in a reference to his family crest, said tenderly, "No, no, the bear and ragged staff is not so soon overthrown", his pride took some time to recover. At other times, she would use mockery to puncture his pretensions. Some years after this, the French ambassador piqued her by saying that the king his master thought that Dudley would make a fine husband for her, and was very anxious to make his acquaintance. Dudley did not hide the fact that he was delighted by the invitation, but the Queen put him in his place with the sneering observation that it would scarcely be very honourable to send a groom to see so great a king. Laughingly she explained to the ambassador that she could not do without her favourite, for he was like her little dog, and whenever he came into the room everyone at once assumed that she herself was near.[17]

Sometimes she was still rougher with Dudley, for when she sensed that he was getting out of hand, she could lose her temper to devastating effect. On one memorable occasion she exploded in a rage after Dudley had comported himself arrogantly towards a minor court official. "God's death my Lord!" she shouted at him, "I have wished you well, but my favour is not so locked up for you that others shall not participate thereof". Scathingly she warned him, "I will have here but one mistress and no master", and this was a maxim that Dudley was never allowed to forget.[18]

Obviously it was frustrating for Dudley to be reminded of his state of servitude to Elizabeth, but the tantalizing prospect that one day he would exercise a husband's mastery over her ensured that he never dreamt of cutting himself free. There were of course additional compensations for his attachment to her. In the summer of 1561 the Queen awarded him a license to export 80,000 undressed cloths (a privilege which he subsequently sold to the leading London trading company, the Merchant Adventurers) and the following October he was granted a pension of £1,000 a year. These were the precursors of yet more substantial concessions such as the right to farm the customs duties levied on imported sweet wines, silks and velvets, oil and currants. He sublet these at great profit, and the farm of the sweet wines alone brought him £2,500 a year.[19] In June 1563 the Queen bestowed on him the magnificent gift of Kenilworth Castle, a former property of John of Gaunt. Dudley had coveted it for some years, partly as an act of filial piety, for in the reign of Edward VI, his father had briefly owned it, and it had only reverted to the Crown on the latter's execution. It had the additional advantage of being situated only five miles away from Warwick Castle, the country seat of his brother Ambrose, who had been created Earl of Warwick in December 1561. The Queen might once have humiliated Dudley by comparing him to a lap-dog, but she did at least ensure that he was a supremely pampered beast.

Despite Elizabeth's generosity to him, Dudley's spending still exceeded his income, but he had always aimed higher than the mere acquisition of wealth. He used his fortune to live like a *magnifico*, knowing that by

publicizing the fact that the Queen had so enriched him he would automatically enhance his prestige. The lesson was not lost on less fortunate
courtiers, who themselves did not have regular access to the Queen, and
who needed an influential intermediary to represent them at high level, so
that they too could participate in the royal bounty. As a result, Dudley was
besieged by suitors, all anxious for him to secure them promotion, or
wangle them some grant, and Dudley was conscientious about providing
them with assistance. His help did not come *gratis*, however, for he
maintained that anyone who secured a favour through his agency owed
him a debt of gratitude for evermore. In 1585 he was to declare, "I know
none able at this day, nor any heretofore, that have done me any pleasure,
that I have not deserved someways a good turn at his hand", but the fact
that he had so ably exerted himself on behalf of so many people throughout
his career ensured that there was an ever swelling number of men whom
he felt entitled to look on as his dependents.

When those whom he had helped in the past failed to repay his kindness
with the punctiliousness that he expected, his wrath was terrible, and
anyone who had incurred obligations to him was left in no doubt of what
would happen if they were remiss in discharging their liabilities to him.
For example, on one occasion he wrote to Bishop Scambler of Peterborough
(whose career he had furthered in the past) instructing him to reinstate a
certain man who had recently been deprived of a position, and he warned
the Bishop that he must do as he wished, if "you intend to have me
favourable in any your requests hereafter, and as you will give me cause
to continue your friend and think well of you". This was no empty threat,
for when Dudley took umbrage against Bishop Overton of Coventry and
Lichfield in 1582 (by which time Dudley had long since been raised to the
peerage as the Earl of Leicester), his vengeance was fearful. The Earl had
been instrumental in securing Overton his see, but subsequently decided
that the Bishop was guilty of some form of "apostasy" against him. Too
late, Overton realized that he had offended him, and he wrote in terror to
another Councillor that the Earl "hath given, and doth still give great
countenance to those that work all my sorrow; a nobleman as your Lordship
knoweth, far above my power to withstand. And therefore like sure to undo
me, if he will". It would seem that the Earl was encouraging various men
to pursue lawsuits against the Bishop, and Overton wailed that "for fear
of displeasure", his own lawyers "scarce dare encounter him in my causes;
so that almost I may say, I am denied that which every common subject
may claim, the course of justice".[20] This story does something to explain
why men did not lightly run the risk of falling foul of Dudley, and his
adept manipulation of the system of clientage – as this legitimate form of
racketeering was known – ensured that despite his lack of popularity, his
position at court was never one of isolation.

The hubbub aroused by Elizabeth's obvious predilection for Dudley was just beginning to die down when the court was transfixed by a new scandal. Since the beginning of 1560, the Queen had been treating her second cousin, Lady Katherine Grey, rather more kindly than had been the case earlier in the reign. The Spanish ambassador even reported that Elizabeth talked of formally adopting Lady Katherine, although undoubtedly her only aim in saying such a thing would have been to remind the French that Mary Stuart's claim to the throne was only one of many. At any rate, within months Lady Katherine had brought ruin on herself by committing what the Queen regarded as an unforgivable misdemeanour. Shortly before Christmas 1560, Lady Katherine had excused herself from accompanying the Court on a hunting expedition by pleading toothache, and she had then stolen away to marry the Earl of Hertford at his house in Westminster. For over six months the match had been kept secret, but one night in July 1561 a startled Lord Robert Dudley awoke to find a sobbing Lady Katherine kneeling by his bedside, imploring him to acquaint the Queen as gently as possible with the fact that she was not only married but also pregnant. Lord Robert did as he was asked, but he proved incapable of mitigating the Queen's wrath. Hertford himself was bound by familial ties to the Tudors, for he was the eldest son of the late Duke of Somerset, and hence the nephew of Edward VI's mother, Jane Seymour. It particularly irked the Queen that others would say that this dynastic match had only strengthened Katherine's right to succeed her, whereas in her view the fact that the girl had succumbed to a romantic impulse proved that she was peculiarly unfitted to do so.

Lady Katherine was despatched to the Tower, and after her husband had been recalled from France (where he had been sent on diplomatic business in the spring of 1561) he was also incarcerated there in separate lodgings. On 24 September, Katherine gave birth to a son, but Elizabeth saw to it that he at least would have great difficulty staking a claim to be her successor. In May 1562, a commission was held, chaired by the Archbishop of Canterbury, which conveniently concluded that as Katherine could not produce documentary proof that she and Hertford were man and wife, there was no reason to believe that the marriage had ever taken place. Their offspring was thus automatically bastardized, and Katherine and Hertford were sentenced to remain in the Tower indefinitely as a punishment for their "undue and unlawful carnal copulation".[21]

There were many who thought that Elizabeth's attitude was unfair, and that the young couple had been "sharply handled". A sympathetic jailer in the Tower even permitted them to have access to one another, and as a result, in February 1563 Katherine gave birth to a second son, thus putting herself beyond all hope of redemption. A further judicial enquiry was held on the case in the Court of Star Chamber, which ruled that Hertford had compounded his crime of having "deflowered a virgin of the blood royal in the Queen's house" by having "ravished her the second time". The Earl was fined £15,000 (subsequently commuted to £3,000) and thenceforth he and Katherine were never to meet again. In August 1563 an outbreak of plague necessitated their removal from the Tower, and Katherine was committed to the custody of her uncle, Lord John Grey. He was a kindly man, who was shocked by the Queen's unrelenting treatment of his niece, but his pleas to Cecil that Elizabeth should be persuaded "to forgive and forget" Lady Katherine's transgressions met with no success.[22]

The Queen's hostility towards her Grey cousins was only exacerbated when, in August 1565, Katherine's younger sister Mary emulated her by secretly marrying the Sergeant-Porter at court, Thomas Keyes. A pathetic and universally despised dwarf, Mary may have calculated that the Queen would not be interested in the marital arrangements of someone so insignificant as she, but Elizabeth proved her wrong by promptly imprisoning her husband and sending Mary away from Court. For years the Grey girls mouldered in the country, where Katherine's refusal to eat and constant fits of weeping contributed to the steady decline in her health. In 1568 she died of tuberculosis, her crime still unforgiven. Mary Grey was marginally more fortunate, for after she was widowed in 1571 she was permitted to return to court. To the end of her life she continued defiantly to sign herself 'Mary Keys', but she only survived her husband by a few years, dying in 1578, unmourned by the Queen.

In the autumn of 1560 Cecil had complained that the Queen was being incorrigibly frivolous, but there was one item of business that was successfully taken care of at this time. When Elizabeth ascended the throne, the English currency had been grievously undermined by successive debasements in the reign of her father and brother. As a result, the individual coins contained a high percentage of alloy, and were consequently worth less than their nominal value. When merchants made purchases abroad, the foreign vendors refused to accept the debased coinage, and English businessmen accordingly had to pay for the goods in pure gold. This had caused a shortage of gold at home, which in turn had had a disastrous effect on the rate of exchange, and this problem had to be redressed, for as one of the Queen's foremost financial advisers pointed out, "the exchange is the thing that eats out all princes ... if it be not substantially looked unto".[23] Shortly before the death of Edward VI, and again in the reign of Mary, attempts had been made to remedy the situation, but the government's failure to recall all the debased currency in circulation rendered the proposed reforms ineffective.

Determined that this time the matter must be satisfactorily dealt with, in early 1559 Cecil had begun gathering information about the amount of debased currency in circulation, and he asked a small body of financial experts to put forward solutions to the problem. The Queen took a close interest in these consultations, but the majority of the Council were not informed of what had been decided on, for the success of the operation depended on complete secrecy. As it was, there was some leakage, and Elizabeth and Cecil were obliged to bring forward their programme by one day, issuing a proclamation on 27 September 1560 to the effect that all base coins in circulation were to be reduced "as nigh to their value as might be". For example, testons, which were nominally worth sixpence, would now be valued at fourpence halfpenny, and the Queen guaranteed that if base coins were brought into the mint they would be valued at the new rate and exchanged for newly minted coins of an equivalent worth.

This was an undertaking of immense complexity for the Tudor state, and initially it seemed that it would prove too ambitious. There were insufficient quantities of silver at the mint to produce the required amount of new coins, and people who tried to hand in debased currency were being turned away unsatisfied. Disaster was averted by enlisting the services of London goldsmiths, who had the facilities needed to melt down old coins so that the pure metal in them could be extracted and new ones minted in their place. As a result, the project was brought to a successful conclusion: nearly £700,000 of debased currency was returned to the mint and refined, and though Elizabeth had stated in her proclamation that she would share the cost of the operation with her people, the Crown even made a profit of about £45,000 from the whole transaction. Thus did Elizabeth "achieve to the victory and conquest of this hideous monster of the base moneys", which one early seventeenth-century historian considered to be to her "greater, yea greatest, glory". The revaluation greatly helped English merchants by boosting their credit abroad, and although it could not halt the price rise that continued throughout the reign, its pace would have been still more alarming if the coinage had not been reformed. In July 1561 Elizabeth celebrated her remarkable achievement by visiting the mint at the Tower of London, "where she coined certain pieces of gold and gave them away to several about her".[24]

Elizabeth and Cecil could justly congratulate themselves on the resolution of this complex question, but they were alarmed to find that a problem which they had understandably regarded as settled was still giving cause for concern. The French had been supposed to ratify the Treaty of Edinburgh on the Queen of Scots' behalf within sixty days of its initial signing, but the date passed without them showing any sign of doing so. When Throckmorton remonstrated about this to Mary Stuart's uncle, the Guisan Cardinal of Lorraine, the latter responded airily that the confirmation of the treaty "was no great matter among friends"[25] and subsequent efforts to pin down the French were no more successful. It was scarcely a matter that the English could afford to be relaxed about, for unless the treaty was ratified Mary Stuart would still be in a position to put forward her claim to be Queen of England, and there was also no guarantee that the French would not attempt to regain control of Scotland by sending a fresh army there.

The difficulty remained outstanding when, in early December 1560, Francis II suddenly died, and the eighteen-year-old Queen of Scots found herself a widow. In some ways the King's death promised to benefit the English, for his brother who succeeded him as Charles IX was too young to govern France, and the Regency was assumed by his mother, Catherine de Medici, who had no intention of permitting the Guises to dominate her as they had the late King. Delighted by the eclipse of the Guises, the English ambassador in Scotland, Thomas Randolph, said he looked on Francis's demise as being a "great occasion to praise God",[26] but his joy turned to horror when it became clear that the widowed Mary Stuart was contemplating returning to her own kingdom, where she might well wreak untold mischief. While Mary was in France, her hold over her subjects was tenuous at best, and the English hoped that in her absence the Scots nobility would decide that they had a closer natural affinity with the Protestant Elizabeth than they did with their own queen. Once Mary was back in her homeland, however, she would be well placed to restore her kingdom to wholehearted allegiance, and in view of the fact that she had not formally relinquished her claim to Elizabeth's crown, the possibility remained that she would choose to unite her people behind her by urging them to undertake the conquest of England, so that she could be set on the throne.

The very prospect of Mary's presence in Scotland aroused the gravest concern in the English, but at first they hoped that, having been brought up in the most civilized court in Europe, Mary would be reluctant to return to a kingdom so backward and impoverished that one appalled traveller had dubbed it "the arse of the world". Scotland was renowned for being an appallingly difficult country to rule, whose inhabitants were so quarrelsome and unstable that Mary herself was later aptly to describe them as "a people as factious among themselves, and all fachous [troublesome] for the governor, as any other nation in Europe".[27] At this particular juncture it seemed likely that Mary would find them particularly refractory, for since the death of the last Regent, Mary of Guise, they had become accustomed to conducting their own affairs, and it was to be expected that they would resent being subjected to renewed authority from above. Religion complicated the situation still further, for though Mary herself was a practising Catholic, in August 1560 the Scots Parliament had passed a series of statutes outlawing the mass and abolishing the Pope's authority.

In view of all this, the English thought that Mary would be far from eager to take up residence in Scotland, when the odds were that this would only end in confrontation. Cecil for one assumed that she would need little encouragement to remain in France (of which she was now Queen Dowager) so that she could busy herself seeking for a new husband, but in this he misjudged both the Queen of Scots and her people. Mary proved eager to start a new life in her own country, and though perturbed at the prospect of having her back, her leading subjects were scarcely in a position to exclude her. In April 1561 Mary's illegitimate half-brother, James Stewart, was sent to France to act as their spokesman, and he was relieved to find that she was anxious to be conciliatory. It was agreed that on her return Mary would make no attempt to overturn the Protestant Church that had been established in Scotland in the last year, but that she herself would be free to practise her own religion. The appalled Cecil, who had optimistically foreseen a breakdown in relations, could only agree with the comment of one Scots noble that once Mary was installed again in her kingdom, "Here will be a mad world!"[28]

In view of Mary's impending return it was more essential than ever that she should be prodded into ratifying the Treaty of Edinburgh. With this object in mind, Throckmorton had an audience with Mary in February 1561, but though she much impressed him by her composure and maturity, she declined to give him the assurances he wanted. While declaring sweetly that there were many reasons why she hoped that she and Elizabeth would be friends, for they "were both in one isle, both of one language, the nearest kinswomen that each other had, and both Queens",[29] she insisted that she could not ratify the treaty without consulting her advisers in Scotland. This was clearly specious, and to Cecil such prevarication suggested that Mary's real aim in coming home was "to subvert the course of religion, and to withdraw the goodwill of her [country] hitherward".

Elizabeth had a chance to demonstrate how strongly she felt about the treaty when Mary sent an envoy to her bearing a request that the Queen of Scots should be permitted to pass through England on her way to her own kingdom. When the envoy arrived, the Queen received him rudely, and having subjected him to a violent rating, she peremptorily denied the application. Undeniably she was acting under provocation, but it was a futile gesture of ill will, which merely placed Anglo-Scots relations under further strain. There was no question of the English using any form of duress to keep Mary away from Scotland, and in the circumstances it would have been wiser to have been more gracious about her homecoming. As it was, Mary was able to turn the rebuff to her advantage, for she could make out that it was she, rather than Elizabeth, who was now the injured party. With great dignity, she told Throckmorton, "It will be thought very strange amongst all princes and countries that she should first animate my subjects against me, and now being a widow, to impeach me going into my own country". Stoically she announced that since Elizabeth refused to answer for her safety in England, she would travel to her kingdom by sea, and if she was intercepted *en route* by the English navy, then "the Queen your mistress shall have me in her hands to do her will; and if she be so hard-hearted as to desire my end, she may then do her pleasure and make sacrifice of me".[30] Greatly embarrassed, Throckmorton was reduced to mumbling incoherent excuses.

In the event Mary's voyage to Scotland passed without mishap, and on 19 August 1561, she landed at Leith, accompanied only by a few attendants. In some trepidation about the reception that awaited them, the Scots nobility hastened to pay their respects, but their worries were soon dispelled, for Mary was at her most captivating. The English ambassador in Scotland, Thomas Randolph, reported laconically, "All men welcome, all men well received, good entertainment, great cheer and fair words". Over the next few weeks she apparently succeeded in forging a lasting bond with her subjects. Maitland of Lethington wrote lyrically to Cecil, "The Queen my mistress behaves herself so gently in every behalf as reasonably we can require; if anything be amiss, the fault is rather in ourselves". Only John Knox, who professed to see in Mary "such craft, as I have not found in such age", remained unmoved, and relentlessly "thundereth out of the pulpit" against his Queen.[31] Not only did he condemn her for her religion, but he censured her for what he considered to be her unseemly levity, but despite the veneration in which he was held, he failed to turn the tide of adulation.

The enthusiastic response evoked by Mary in her subjects was the less to be wondered at, for those who came into contact with her invariably found her immensely sympathetic. One contemporary explained simply that she was possessed of "some enchantment, whereby men are bewitched",[32] and throughout her life she never lost these compelling powers of attraction. In person, she was physically imposing, being nearly six foot tall at a time when the average height for a man was considerably less, but her exceptional grace and poise ensured that she never appeared ungainly. Her features were aquiline and slender, but one may conjecture her attractiveness lay principally in an indefinable charm of countenance that the portrait painters never managed to capture. She had great dignity of bearing, but her manner was nevertheless delightfully approachable, resulting in a unique blend of regality and warmth that was so winning as to be almost irresistible. She had the knack of appearing confiding without being over-familiar, and after the shortest of encounters, people came away feeling sure that she held them in particularly high regard. This obviously created expectations in them which were not always easy to fulfil, and their disappointment when they subsequently found themselves overlooked, or excluded from her confidence, was in consequence all the more bitter. In the short term, however, these personal qualities operated solely to her advantage, and she understandably regarded her ability to disarm outsiders as being one of her greatest assets.

Unfortunately Mary's unusual stature was not indicative of robust health, for though capable of furious bursts of energy and bouts of high spirits (she herself remarked that having been "brought up in joyousity" in France, she was determined to inject some gaiety into the sombre Scots court), she was frequently troubled by a mysterious pain in her side; and more alarming still was her undue susceptibility to nervous stress. When confronted by seemingly overwhelming challenges she could display remarkable resourcefulness and courage, but her reaction to lesser crises was frequently to dissolve into tears of grief or rage. It was perhaps excessive to declare, as one English diplomat did, that Mary was no more than "a sick crazed woman", but the Scots were certainly puzzled by her habit of spending days on end in bed "for her ease", even when she apparently enjoyed perfect health. At times it even seemed as if over-excitement could bring her to the point of physical collapse: when she rode through Edinburgh for the first time, she felt so faint that she had to be taken off her horse and carried to her lodgings, and the English ambassador was informed that she was always "troubled with such passions after any great unkindness or grief of mind".[33]

Her heightened sensibility had never been moderated by a rigorous intellectual discipline, for though as a child in France she had been carefully tutored in languages and the classics, her erudition was not of a very high order. Unlike Elizabeth, who liked to think that her education left her well-equipped to deal with the wider responsibilities of kingship, learning for Mary was merely to be numbered among her accomplishments, of little more significance than her skill at dancing or embroidery. While it would be wrong to imply that Mary lacked acuteness, she had none of Elizabeth's mental vigour: when the English ambassador in Scotland tried to interest her in theological debate, her only comment was that "she could not reason, but she knew what she ought to believe", and the ease with which she was accustomed to win the approval of others meant that she had a less than sure touch when it came to overcoming resistance to her opinions, or dealing with insubordination. There were times when her reliance on intuition served her well, but in her handling of public opinion she could also show the grossest insensitivity, and one political instinct she manifestly lacked was that of self-preservation.

Safely installed at Holyrood Palace near Edinburgh, Mary seemed determined to pursue a judicious and moderate policy. She declared that she aimed first "to make peace with England; next to be served with Protestants", and in fulfilment of this latter resolution she chose as her principal advisers her half-brother, Lord James Stewart, and William Maitland of Lethington. Peace with England was not so easy to secure, for Mary's offer of friendship was conditional on Elizabeth agreeing to reinstate her in the line of succession. She was accordingly determined not to put her name to the Treaty of Edinburgh until its terms were somewhat modified, for the original text of the agreement not only bound her to refrain from pressing her claim to the throne during Elizabeth's lifetime, but declared that she would "at all times coming abstain from using and bearing the ... arms of the kingdom of England and Ireland". Had she ratified the treaty, this would have had the effect of confirming the arrangements of Henry VIII's will, so that even in the event of Elizabeth dying childless, Mary would have been denied the crown to which otherwise she would have been entitled by hereditary right. It was understandable that Mary was unwilling to make so significant a concession. Already Lord James Stewart had proposed in writing a more equitable arrangement, whereby Mary would promise to abstain from seeking the throne while Elizabeth or her children were alive, but in return the English Queen must make her her heiress presumptive.[34]

Mary was anxious for this matter to be explored further, and at the end of August 1561 she despatched Maitland of Lethington on an embassy to London, where he arrived on 1 September. A few days later he had his first interview with the Queen, and at once he raised the subject of the succession. Elizabeth parried this by saying sharply that the first priority was for Mary to ratify the Treaty of Edinburgh, but Maitland merely replied that he was not authorized to discuss the treaty, and the Queen had to fall back on other arguments. Suavely, she next observed that she failed to see why Mary was in such a rush to force a declaration from her. After all, it was not as if any of her other putative successors were in a position to assert the superiority of their titles over Mary's, and hence the Queen of Scots had nothing to worry about. Elizabeth did not try to hide her utter contempt for every one of the alternative claimants. "You know them all, alas! What power or force has any of them poor souls?" she exclaimed derisively. She paused here to take a swipe at Lady Katherine Grey, whose pregnancy had only recently come to light, and whose offences were therefore particularly fresh in the Queen's mind. Sarcastically she told Maitland, "It is true that some of them has made declaration to the world that they are more worthy of it [the crown] than either she [Mary] or I, by experience that they are not barren but able to have children", but she then implied that Katherine's claim was invalidated on the grounds that her father's treason had disabled her.

Having unburdened herself of these feelings, the Queen said she hoped that Maitland would agree that it was unnecessary for her to make further provision for the succession. "This desire is without an example, to require

me in my own life to set my windingsheet before my eye: the like was
never required of no prince", she declared in indignation. Maitland could
with justice have retorted that, since sudden death was an ever-present
phenomenon in the sixteenth century, it was not unreasonable to expect
Elizabeth to face up to her own mortality, but he confined himself to saying
firmly that it was necessary for both realms for the matter to be resolved.
Accordingly the Queen tried a new tack. With regard to Mary's claim, she
had already told Maitland outright, "I for my part know none better, nor
that my self would prefer to her", but she now reminded him that she was
by no means a free agent in this matter. There was Henry VIII's will to
be considered, and also it was not clear whether Mary's alien status debarred
her from the throne. Before Mary could be named heiress presumptive,
the succession would have to be debated in Parliament, and if opponents
of her claim succeeded in establishing that it was invalid, Elizabeth could
not ignore their findings. She told Maitland frankly, "If there be any law
against her (as I protest to you I know none, for I am not anxious to
enquire), but if any be, I am sworn when I was married to the realm not
to alter the laws of it". It would be better for Mary to sit tight, commending
herself to the English by displaying firm amity to them. In this way the
objections to her title would imperceptibly be smoothed away, and the
possibility that she might one day succeed would cease to arouse controversy. After all, Elizabeth herself had been declared illegitimate, and this
should technically have invalidated her right to the throne, but in the event
her accession had gone smoothly.

Still Maitland would not back down, and Elizabeth now came to what
she considered to be the nub of the matter. Gravely she explained that "if
it were certainly known in the world who should succeed her, she would
never think herself in sufficient surety". With painful honesty she avowed,
"I know the inconstancy of the people of England, how they ever mislike
the present government, and has their eyes fixed upon that person that is
next to succeed". Maitland was full of airy assurances that, when Elizabeth
adopted Mary as her heir, the text of the agreement could contain specific
safeguards to prevent the subjects of either Queen having dealings with
the other, but Elizabeth's own experiences in her sister's reign had convinced her that the temptations involved were too strong to be contained
by legal *impedimenta*. She said if Mary was her heir the danger in some
respects would be all the more acute, "she being a puissant princess and
so near our neighbour", and she remained adamant that "the succession
of the crown is a matter I will not mell [meddle] in".[35]

This, however, was by no means the end of the matter, for Maitland
was able to remind Elizabeth that Mary did not have to accept her decision
without protest. At his second audience with the Queen his tone was much
more brutal, and in barely veiled terms he warned her that, if she did not

voluntarily offer to bequeath the crown to his mistress, Mary would be tempted to snatch it by force. "Although your Highness takes your self to be lawful, yet are ye not always so taken abroad in the world", he cautioned the Queen,[36] and Elizabeth was clearly badly shaken by this outright threat. She was sufficiently disturbed to give a hesitant undertaking that perhaps commissioners could be appointed to review the terms of the Treaty of Edinburgh, and when Maitland returned to Scotland shortly afterwards, he could feel he had made some progress.

Before long, however, Elizabeth was feeling remorseful that she had gone so far, and Cecil was even more disapproving. He was proud of what he had achieved at Edinburgh, and did not want his handiwork tampered with, for Mary's Catholic faith, Guisan antecedents and earlier flaunting of the royal arms all made him view her ambitions with the gravest reservations. On the other hand, it was undeniably risky to do nothing at all to appease her, and by December 1561 Elizabeth had begun to think that the best way out of the impasse would be for her and Mary to meet, so they could resolve their differences in person.

Mary was delighted by the idea. Knowing full well what a favourable impression she generally made on strangers, she was sure that Elizabeth would not be unreceptive to her charm, and she had besides an ardent curiosity to see in the flesh her "dearest sister" and fellow Queen. She bombarded the English ambassador, Randolph, with enquiries concerning Elizabeth's "health ... exercise, diet and many more questions", and scrutinized the portrait that her cousin had sent from England with the liveliest curiosity. She went so far as to wish that one of them was a man, so that the kingdoms could be united by marital alliance, and Randolph reported that whenever the subject of marriage was discussed, Mary invariably declared, "She will [have] none other husband than our sovereign."[37]

Mary's advisers did not share her enthusiasm. According to Randolph, Maitland feared that Mary would prove no match for Elizabeth if they engaged in delicate discussions, for "he finds no such maturity of judgment and ripeness of experience in high matters in his mistress, as in the Queen's Majesty, in whom both nature and time have wrought much more than in many of greater years". It nevertheless proved impossible to dim Mary's ardour, for as Maitland ruefully admitted to Cecil, "I see my sovereign so transported with affection, that she respects nothing so she may meet with her cousin; and needs no persuasion, but is a great deal more earnestly bent on it than her counsellors dare advise her". The thrifty Scots nobility were also far from pleased that Mary remained so set on visiting England, for they would be expected to accompany her, and in order not to look dowdy, they would have to fit themselves out with expensive new wardrobes.[38]

At the English court, people were also grumbling about the money they would have to spend if the meeting went ahead, but besides this, there were other, less frivolous, objections that could be voiced against the proposed encounter. These principally concerned the situation in France, where the Regent Catherine de Medici was struggling to avert civil war. Catherine's coarse and homely features concealed a mind of great subtlety and determination, but for all her ingenuity, the divisions that rent French society had proved too deeply hewn for her to restore cohesion. While the royal family themselves were Catholic, there was a substantial minority of Protestants (known as Huguenots) in France, who were prepared to resort to arms rather than to acquiesce in the extirpation of their faith. In the interests of peace, Catherine had attempted to institute a policy of religious toleration, granting the Protestants a limited freedom of worship in an edict of January 1562. By doing so, however, she had alienated the extreme Catholics in the kingdom, and her policy collapsed when their leader, the Duke of Guise, massacred a congregation of Huguenots at worship. He then marched to Paris, where the massive acclaim accorded him by the populace left Catherine with no alternative but to commit herself and her son to his protection. Convinced that these events would be followed by an offensive against heresy, the leading Huguenot noble, the Prince of Condé, withdrew to the Protestant stronghold of Orléans, and other towns throughout western France signalled their determination to defy royal authority until the Crown had freed itself from the control of the Guises. Desperately, Catherine strove to halt the slide into anarchy, but it was clear that unless she managed to persuade the hostile factions to reach some sort of accommodation, armed conflict would be the inevitable result.

If civil war did break out, and the Protestants fared badly, the prestige of the Guises would be greatly enhanced, and there was an alarming possibility that French foreign policy would thenceforth be shaped and directed by these inveterate enemies of England. To forestall so disastrous a development, it was arguable that Elizabeth should assist the Huguenots in their fight for survival, and it was understandable that many of the Queen's advisers considered this to be an inopportune time for her to meet with Mary, who was, after all, a niece of the Duke of Guise. Throckmorton in particular was anxious for Elizabeth to intervene in France, and was vexed that instead she remained absorbed in plans for her conference with Mary. Gruffly, he told Cecil that the Queen should be giving orders for warlike preparations, rather than immersing herself in "pleasure and hunting matters".[39]

Elizabeth did not agree. She clung to the hope that Catherine would prevent the crisis escalating into civil war, and even tried to promote an agreement by suggesting that she herself should mediate between the two sides. She refused to accept that the situation in France made it impossible for her to extend hospitality to Mary, for she genuinely believed that if they were given a chance to communicate directly with each other, they would manage to obtain an understanding of a sort that could never be achieved if their dealings were always conducted at one remove. Like Mary, she was also intrigued by the prospect of meeting another woman ruler: she had heard so much about her cousin, and though she was always irritated by allusions to Mary's beauty (when one foreign diplomat had thoughtlessly remarked to the Queen that Mary had the reputation of being very lovely, Elizabeth had snapped that "She was superior to the Queen of Scotland"),[40] she did not want to miss this opportunity to inspect her for herself. Above all, she was sure that a personal encounter would make Mary less importunate about the succession, for once Mary was convinced of Elizabeth's goodwill, she would find it easier to accept that there was nothing sinister in the English Queen's reluctance to designate her her heiress. Elizabeth felt confident that if she and Mary were brought face to face she would be able to persuade her cousin that it would be contrary to the interests of both of them to seek formal recognition of Mary's title, and that if the matter was left alone there would be a much better chance of the Queen of Scots' ultimate accession to the English throne.

At the end of May 1562, Maitland was sent to England with instructions to secure a definite invitation from Elizabeth. The Queen welcomed him warmly, but when consulted, the Council were unanimous that it would be inadvisable to let Mary come to England. Elizabeth still disagreed. Having listened to what each councillor had to say, "She answered them all with such fineness of wit and excellence of utterance as for the same she was commended", and "not allowing replication", she declared that unless the situation in France broke down irretrievably, "go she would". "It is both groaned at and lamented of the most and wisest", Sir Henry Sidney glumly informed Throckmorton, but in view of Elizabeth's insistence, preparations for the reception of Mary and her train went on apace. The mayor and aldermen of York busied themselves laying in supplies for the two Queens and their retinues, estimating that between them, they would consume daily a hundred dozen loaves of bread, seventy tuns of ale and beer, and thirty tuns of Gascon wines. "All lusty knights" started practising their tilting in preparation for the tournaments in which they would compete against the Scots, and courtiers resentfully informed their tailors that they would require a series of splendid new costumes to ensure that they put up a good display before their guests. On 7 July, Elizabeth gave Maitland the required assurance that Mary would be welcome, and four days later he left for Scotland bearing a sealed document that stated that the two Queens would meet at York or another town in the North of England, at some date between 10 August and 20 September.[41]

The very next day, Throckmorton sent word that Catherine's efforts to keep the peace in France had failed. Civil war had broken out, marked by appalling atrocities on both sides, and on hearing this Elizabeth accepted that there could be no question of her leaving her capital while there was a danger that the Guises would acquire complete mastery in France. On 16 July Sir Henry Sidney was despatched to Scotland to inform Mary that in view of the tense situation, the meeting with Elizabeth would have to be postponed. Mary received the news tearfully and took to her bed for consolation; it was fortunate that she could not know that though Elizabeth had stressed that the upheavals in France would only temporarily delay their summit, she and her cousin were destined never to meet.

As the arrangements for the pageants and banquets that were to have marked the visit of the Scottish court were quietly shelved, Elizabeth was more willing to listen to those men who were urging her to participate in the struggle that was taking place in France. Foremost among these was Lord Robert Dudley, who stressed that here was a chance to advance the cause of righteousness while covering herself in glory. His arguments, constantly reiterated, did much to erode the Queen's natural caution. Throckmorton was delighted when Dudley sanctimoniously reported, "God be thanked, she doth not so much measure common policy as she doth weigh the prosperity of true religion". In truth, however, Elizabeth was not animated solely by pious zeal. More important was the fact that the Huguenots had secretly offered that if she helped them, they would reward her by giving her possession of the town of Le Havre (or Newhaven as it was known in England), which could be kept as security until such time as the French returned Calais to the English. By 29 August Elizabeth had indicated that she would be prepared to give her assistance on these terms.[42]

As Cecil did not dispute that it would be calamitous if the Guises succeeded in consolidating their hold over France, he agreed that the Queen had no alternative but to go to war, and busied himself with arranging for the transportation of six thousand troops to Newhaven. Not all the Council were in favour of the enterprise, for the Earls of Arundel and Pembroke expressed strong opposition, but by that time Elizabeth was in so militant a mood that she was "quite furious" about their objections. Angrily she told them that "if they were so much afraid that the consequences of failure would fall upon them, she herself would take all the risk and sign her name to it".[43]

Although at one time it was thought that Dudley would command the expedition, the Queen refused to let him leave her side, but his close identification with the project was made clear when his brother, the Earl of Warwick, was appointed in his stead. The choice caused some surprise, for Warwick was not regarded as an especially competent soldier, and it was whispered that he had been "preferred to this high place of charge more by favour of them who were in favour with the Queen, than upon experience, or expectation of his own worth". Apparently oblivious to the hostile comment, on 24 September 1562 Elizabeth published a proclamation announcing that she was sending a force to France, not as an act of war, but to protect the inhabitants of Normandy from the depredations of the Guises.[44] Ten days later, the first English troops landed in Newhaven.

It was at this perilous juncture, just when the nation was nerving itself for war, that Elizabeth was suddenly struck down by smallpox, a dreaded scourge which had recently claimed several illustrious victims at court. The disease had a frighteningly high mortality rate among "aged folks and ladies", and the Queen was held to have put herself particularly at risk because on 10 October, when she had first felt unwell, she had rashly taken a bath.[45] The outlook was the more alarming because at first no spots appeared, and this was generally a sign that the attack was going to be especially severe. By 16 October, Elizabeth was so ill that she had lost the faculty of speech, and the physicians were holding out no hope whatever of her survival.

Despairing of her life, the Council assembled, but their discussions only emphasized the magnitude of the crisis. Of the fifteen or sixteen members present, "there were nearly as many different opinions about the succession to the crown", and it proved impossible to achieve any sort of consensus. The Council was split three ways, with one group upholding the right of Katherine Grey to succeed, another arguing on the Earl of Huntingdon's behalf, while yet a third advocated that the question should be referred to the consideration of the judiciary. Mary Stuart appears to have had no open protagonists, but the judges were believed to harbour Catholic sympathies, and if consulted, they might well have found in her favour.[46] At any rate, the Council's failure to reach agreement proved beyond doubt that the Queen's death would result in political disintegration and utter chaos, and with every hour the grim vision loomed still closer.

Total breakdown seemed a foregone conclusion, when unexpectedly the Queen rallied. She developed a rash after Lord Hunsdon called in the German physician, Dr Burcot. He wrapped the unconscious Elizabeth in scarlet flannel and laid her on a pallet before the fire, and two hours later she regained the power of speech. The Council rushed to her side, but her first words were scarcely reassuring, for she begged that in the event of her death Lord Robert should be appointed protector of the kingdom, and given an annual income of £20,000. Deliriously the Queen rambled on "that although she loved and had always loved Lord Robert dearly, as God was her witness, nothing improper had ever passed between them".[47] Anxious not to cause her unnecessary distress, the assembled councillors solemnly agreed to respect her wishes, although it would have been obvious to all of them that if they did as she asked there would be no chance whatever of averting civil war. Fortunately their intentions never had to be put to the test, for the Queen maintained a steady recovery, and before long she was out of all danger. Nevertheless, Dudley emerged from the crisis with his position at court consolidated, for on 20 October Elizabeth made him a member of the Council. It was not a popular decision, but the Queen skilfully managed to allay the ill-feeling by simultaneously conferring the same honour on Dudley's known enemy, the Duke of Norfolk.

By 25 October the Queen was feeling well enough to attend to business, although as yet her face remained too scabby and inflamed for her to wish to appear in public. Before long, however, her complexion was quite restored, a fortunate escape in view of the fact that smallpox generally left its victims permanently scarred. On 2 November Mary Stuart was able to write the Queen a tactful letter expressing her delight "that your beautiful face will lose none of its perfections".[48]

Elizabeth had cause to be grateful that her illness had not left her permanently disfigured, but in other ways her brush with death was fraught with consequence. The emergency had graphically demonstrated the extent to which the kingdom's stability depended on the Queen's continued survival, and had proved beyond question that, if she were to die prematurely, England would drift rudderless into anarchy and civil war. In the circumstances it was inevitable that Elizabeth would face renewed demands both to name a successor and to marry, and however much she might wish to avoid doing one or the other, her subjects had had too fearful a glimpse of the hideous void that would open up on her death to be prepared to accept continued prevarication on either of these issues.

The Queen looked set to clash with her people on these points, but for the moment at least, the immediate priority was to gain victory in France. Warwick's troops were now all installed at Newhaven, and work had started on improving the town's fortifications to enable it to withstand a long siege. Several ministers noted for their Puritanical zeal had accompanied the expeditionary force to France, and Warwick wrote enthusiastically that the exhortations of these chaplains were having a remarkable effect on morale. The men had even voluntarily given up gambling and swearing, though he had to admit that whoring had proved harder to eradicate. But despite the dedication and fervour of the English troops, they had so far failed to achieve anything which furthered the Protestant cause. The Huguenots had hoped that instead of concentrating all her troops at Newhaven, the Queen would agree that they could assist in the defence of the Protestant towns of Dieppe and Rouen, which were currently under siege from the royalist army. Unfortunately, as Elizabeth was reluctant to diversify her forces, she sent no more than minimal support, and partly in consequence, Rouen had fallen to the enemy by the end of October. The Queen accepted a share of the blame and expressed remorse "that she had not dealt more frankly for it", but despite this, she sent no effective aid to Dieppe, and within three weeks that had capitulated too.[49] Her failure to supply them with the backing they needed left the Protestants feeling aggrieved, and they began to suspect that she was more interested in acquiring territory in France than in helping them to overcome their enemies.

The situation worsened further when on 19 December the Prince of Condé was captured in battle, for though the Huguenots vowed to fight on under the leadership of Admiral Coligny, outright victory now seemed unlikely. The Queen did not desert her allies, sending them more money in February 1563, but it was obvious that before long they would have to seek an accommodation and that, when that happened, they would not be in a position to dictate their own terms. In view of the Huguenots' poor performance in the field, Elizabeth felt they could not complain if they were not granted the universal freedom of worship that they had wanted, but she saw no reason to abate her own demands. Majestically she sent word to Coligny that he should accept any "reasonable accord" that provided for "toleration in some sort ... and we to have our right in Calais",[50] but by now the Huguenots had a different set of priorities. They too had become anxious to make peace, but it was obvious that they would have a better chance of obtaining good terms for themselves if they did not insist that Calais had to be surrendered to the English as a part of the settlement. Elizabeth had not been so supportive an ally that the Protestant leaders felt very badly about leaving her in the lurch, particularly since it was clear to them that her intervention had been motivated principally by nationalistic greed, and not by any true sense of fellowship with oppressed members of her own Church. On 10 March 1563 the Huguenots came to terms with the French government at Orléans, and as a token of reconciliation they agreed that, if Elizabeth refused to withdraw her troops from Newhaven, they would unite with the royal forces to drive the English out.

At the end of April Condé and Coligny sent a message to the Queen, asking that Newhaven should be evacuated. When Elizabeth angrily refused, they indicated that she left them with no alternative but to take the town by force. As the French army assembled outside the walls of Newhaven, Warwick gallantly swore to the Queen that he would retain the town "despite of all France", but it was hard to see how he could make good this pledge.[51]

Meanwhile, the expense of maintaining an army in France had impelled the Queen to summon Parliament, for money was in short supply. Already she had had to sell more than £250,000 worth of Crown lands in order to meet the costs of the Scottish expedition of 1560, and there could be no question of her digging further into her capital to pay for the present expedition. She nevertheless sent out the writs for election reluctantly, for she knew that the Members of Parliament would seize this opportunity to tax her about her failure to marry or settle the succession.

Parliament assembled on 12 January 1563, and even at the church ceremony that was held to mark the opening, the succession was the dominant topic. The Dean of St Paul's, who was making the sermon, took the Queen to task for having so far remained single, upbraiding her for it with a directness that was little short of offensive. Brazenly, he demanded of her, "If your parents had been of your mind, where had you been then?" – a piece of insolence which earned him Elizabeth's fixed dislike. When parliamentary business got under way, however, it was clear that the House of Commons thought that the Dean had spoken very much to the point. There were several lively debates on the same theme, and then on 28 January the Speaker of the House presented Elizabeth with a petition begging her to marry and – above all – to name a successor. The Queen "thankfully accepted" it, and in "an excellent oration" explained that she would give a more full answer to it at a later stage in the session.[52]

On the understanding that they would soon receive a more detailed reply, the House occupied itself attending to other business. This included a statute broadening the scope of the Act of Supremacy by making it compulsory for greater numbers of professional men to take the oath acknowledging Elizabeth as Supreme Governor of the Church. The list now comprehended all in Holy Orders, schoolmasters, lawyers and Members of Parliament, and the penalties for refusal were life imprisonment for the first offence and death for the second. Although opposed by a vociferous minority, the measure obtained a majority in the Commons and went on to pass the Lords with only a few minor amendments, but the Queen obviously thought that its provisions were too harsh. She did not veto the measure altogether, but she saw to it that it was never fully implemented, for Archbishop Parker was directed to send out a circular to all the Bishops, making it clear that if anyone refused to take the oath, it was not to be tendered a second time. As a result of this stratagem, no Catholics were sentenced to death under the terms of this act.[53]

The progress of the anti-Catholic measure had not so absorbed Parliament that the succession issue was forgotten, for on 12 February the Commons sent the Queen a message reminding her that they were awaiting an answer to their petition. Despite their importunity, the session drew to an end without Elizabeth breaking her silence. At the closing ceremony, which the Queen attended, it emerged that she had decided against making a direct answer, and instead Lord Keeper Bacon read out a prepared reply that she had written in her own hand. Like all Elizabeth's compositions, its wording was involved and tortuous, a rich confection made up of layer upon layer of subordinate clauses, studded with metaphor and scholarly allusion. In essence, she was saying simply that she still had not come to any decision with regard to the succession, but the grandeur of her language (as well as its near impenetrability) was supposed to compensate for the statement's disappointing content.

She began by stressing her sincerity: "Since there can be no duer debt than Prince's word, to keep that unspotted for my part, as one that would be loth that the self thing which keepeth merchants' credit from craze should be the cause that Princes' speech should merit blame and so their honour quail, therefore I will an answer give". After this mystifying preamble, she touched briefly on the subject of her marriage, for she said that it had saddened her that they should be pressing her to name a successor when there was still a good chance that she would marry and produce a direct heir. "If any here doubt that I am as it were by vow or determination bent never to trade that kind of life, put out that heresy, for your belief is therein awry", she told them severely, adding that though she personally had little inclination to take a husband, she realized that her duty as Queen might compel her to do so. Having dealt with that, she came to the succession, declaring that she would already have chosen an heir if the matter had not been fraught with such difficulty, but as it was she needed more time for reflection. She begged them to be understanding about this tardiness, promising, "As a short time for so long continuance ought not to pass by rote, as many tell their tales; even so, as cause by conference with the learned shall show me matter worthy of your behoofs, so shall I more gladly pursue your good after my days, than with my prayers whilst I live be mean to linger my living thread". She concluded with an assurance that she was even then seeking to devise ways of dealing with the problem, for when the time came for her to die, she hoped that she would have a clear conscience, and this could not be "without I see some glimpse of your following surety after my graved bones".[54]

Simplicity and directness were not qualities which Elizabeth aimed for in such formal addresses, for she rather prided herself on what her later admirer, Sir Christopher Hatton, described as "the cunning of your Highness's style ... with the conveyance of your rare sentence and matter ... exceedingly to be liked of". With their complex syntax and stately rhythms, her speeches were at once resonant and yet abstruse, requiring detailed sifting before they yielded up their true meaning. The original drafts were frequently subjected to a great deal of revision, as the Queen fashioned her sentences with the care of a craftsman, working on her text until it resembled some elaborate incantation. In doing so, she was not driven solely by her creative instincts, for in demonstrating her mastery of language she was effectively asserting her singularity of mind. Her contemporary John Clapham commented, "Her manner of writing was somewhat obscure and ... affected for difference sake, that she might not write in such phrases as were commonly used",[55] and by eschewing straightforward statements and commonplace phrases she hoped to dazzle her audience with her artistry and convince them that her powers of understanding surpassed theirs. Earlier in the session, she had remarked that reticence and "fear to speak" were qualities becoming to members of her sex, but by showing off her eloquence she was establishing that the normal criteria did not apply to her. Once again, she was reminding the men about her that they were dealing with no mere woman, but an extraordinary being, endowed with gifts that bordered on the sublime.

On this particular occasion, she had taken especial pains with her product, polishing and embellishing it until she judged that the effect was precisely right. Undeniably the end result was impressive, but whatever the strength of her presentation, nothing could shake the conviction of her subjects that it was her duty to make some provision for the future. Now that Parliament had been dismissed, they had no public forum in which they could express their feelings, but it was obvious that if the Queen had not resolved the situation before the next session was held, the pressure on her would become extraordinarily intense.

The weeks in which Parliament had sat had been a trying time for the Queen, but at least it had voted a generous grant of money, and now that the necessary funds had been secured, Elizabeth could devote her full attention to gaining victory in France. Warwick was still optimistic that he would succeed in defending Newhaven, and Elizabeth promised that he would receive the fullest support, writing to him on 25 May that she would take as much care to see that he was as well supplied "as though it were in our own household, for our own diet and food". In early June, however, the English in Newhaven were confronted by a new danger, for an epidemic of plague started to sweep through the town, and by the end of the month sixty soldiers a day were dying of the disease. One of the officers in Newhaven wrote to Cecil that he was "more afraid of this plague than of all the cannon in France", for it was obvious that if the garrison was further depleted it would be too small to hold the town. As it was, the French were threatening to overwhelm them, for a constant battery of the walls had resulted in many casualties, shrinking their numbers still further. Undernourishment was another problem, as the windmills which ground the corn had all been destroyed by cannon fire, and most of the bakers in the town had already died of plague.[56]

Elizabeth was doing her best to help her men. In mid-July, she sent fresh troops and supplies to Newhaven, but the reinforcements promptly fell sick themselves, and adequate revictualling was made impossible when adverse winds prevented access to the town by sea. On 26 July, Warwick received the Queen's permission to surrender on the best terms he could obtain, and three days later he evacuated the town after the French agreed that the English could leave with their possessions. With Newhaven no longer in English hands, there was no chance whatever that in 1568 the French would honour the obligation they had incurred at Cateau-Cambrésis to return Calais to its former owners, for they could plausibly argue that this clause of the treaty had been invalidated when the English violated the peace. At the appropriate time, the Queen did not fail to remind the French that Calais was due to be rendered up, but the very suggestion was received with open hilarity at Charles IX's court.

Worse still, the ill-starred escapade had unfortunate domestic repercussions, for the returning soldiers brought plague with them. A serious epidemic ensued, and according to one contemporary estimate there were over 21,000 fatalities in London alone. Margaret of Parma, who was Regent of England's principal trading partner, the Netherlands, used the threat of infection to justify the imposition of a commercial embargo, and as a result the cloth trade ground to a virtual standstill. Elizabeth sent word to Margaret that unless the stoppage was lifted, the English would find other outlets for their merchandise, but attempts to establish Emden as an alternative trading base on the continent did not prove very satisfactory. As a result, both merchants and cloth weavers suffered financially and the Crown lost revenue in customs duties until the embargo was lifted in January 1565.

The Queen took her setback in France squarely. She accepted that the responsibility for the venture was hers alone and did not try to blame Dudley for having goaded her into a futile action. The episode had also taught her a lesson which she never forgot. While the struggle was in progress Cecil had told a leading French Protestant, "In ye cause of religion I hold no difference between nation and nation, but that we are all of one city and country, that is, Christians of His Church, bound to join together for defence of ourselves against antichristians of what country soever they be", but the way that the Huguenots had turned against their English allies demonstrated that the bond of a shared faith was not strong enough to override nationalist sentiment. Having burnt her fingers so badly in France, Elizabeth acquired a lifelong distrust of reckless forays on the continent, and in this sense at least the experience was a valuable one. At the time, however, it was not easy to draw much comfort from having suffered such a reverse: one disgruntled Englishman commented sourly, "God help England and send it once a king, for in time of women it has got but a little".[57]

CHAPTER 6

"Contrarily threatenings and chidings"

Of all the problems she now faced, Elizabeth regarded the maintenance of good relations with Mary Queen of Scots as being the most intractable. Unlike Elizabeth, the widowed Mary was anxious to marry, for she felt keenly her responsibilities to produce an heir. She was fully alive to the political advantages that marriage with the right man could bring, and expected that it would provide her with both companionship and fulfilment. It was indeed a source of some frustration to her that the matter could not be settled swiftly, for the solitary life told upon her nerves. By the end of 1563 she was prone to bouts of melancholia and fits of weeping, and Elizabeth's ambassador in Scotland, Thomas Randolph, attributed these to her unsatisfied longing to procure herself a partner.[1]

From the English point of view, Mary's eagerness to wed was perturbing, for as she had had a King of France for her first husband, it was probable that she would want her second marriage to be a union of comparable grandeur. It was obvious, however, that if she matched herself with some great Catholic prince, the implications for Elizabeth would be grave. Having contracted such an alliance, Mary would once again be in a position to assert that Elizabeth's throne was rightfully hers, and she would then be able to rely on her powerful husband to supply her with the military backing that would allow her to make good her claim by force. The danger would of course be lessened if Mary took a comparatively insignificant husband, who was well disposed towards Elizabeth, but it was reasonable to assume that she would consider this to be beneath her dignity unless there was a guarantee that she would be compensated for it by being named as Elizabeth's successor. Unfortunately, that was an option that Elizabeth herself regarded as unacceptable.

This, then, was Elizabeth's dilemma, and at times it reduced her to a state of near-despair. On one occasion she wrote to Cecil that she was "in such a labyrinth" with regard to Scots affairs that she had no idea of the right approach to take, and she begged him to think of some way to guide her out of the maze. On this issue, however, there was not much that Cecil could usefully contribute. So far as one can judge, he was considerably more prejudiced against Mary than Elizabeth was herself, for the very idea that a Catholic descendant of the Guises might one day sit on the English throne filled him with alarm. The signs are that, if at this stage Elizabeth had died childless, Cecil would have liked Lady Katherine Grey to succeed her, but he was careful to voice no such preference to the Queen. For one thing, he knew that she regarded this as a matter on which her subjects were not entitled to hold any opinion, but he also fully appreciated that if Elizabeth did anything to exclude Mary from the succession, the latter would surely declare war. As a result, he believed that the only way for the Queen to extricate herself from the impasse would be to marry as soon as possible. He wrote fervently to Throckmorton, "God send our mistress a husband, and by time a son, that we may hope our posterity shall have a masculine succession".[2]

For Elizabeth, of course, the answer was not so simple, and in the absence of any viable alternative she fell back on the unsatisfactory expedient of seeking to delay Mary's marriage for as long as she could. Unfortunately, when dealing with a woman who was genuinely anxious to take a husband, Elizabeth found herself hopelessly out of her depth, for however adept she may have been at spinning out her own matrimonial negotiations, she could not force others to do likewise.

It was in the spring of 1563 that Elizabeth first tried to break the deadlock that prevailed between Mary and herself by suggesting an imaginative – some would say fanciful – scheme. Once again, Maitland had been sent to England in hopes of securing official recognition that Mary was the Queen's heiress presumptive, and in the course of his discussions with Elizabeth the subject of Mary's marriage had naturally loomed large. Maitland was nevertheless caught completely unprepared when the Queen suddenly artlessly remarked that if Mary really wanted to marry, she would do well to take Lord Robert Dudley as her husband. Much embarrassed, Maitland could only stammer that Mary would not wish to deprive her cousin of the joy and solace of Lord Robert's company, but to his dismay, Elizabeth refused to drop the subject. She mused that it was unfortunate that the Earl of Warwick was not so attractive as his younger brother, for otherwise Mary could have married Ambrose while she herself became Lord Robert's wife, but by now the conversation had taken too surreal a turn for Maitland to be prepared to take it seriously. Jocularly he commented that Elizabeth "should marry Lord Robert first ... and then, when it should please God to call her to himself, she could leave the Queen of Scots heiress both to her kingdom and her husband".[3] Having responded to her proposal in what he considered to be an appropriately light-hearted vein, he fervently hoped that the matter would not be raised again.

Maitland's confusion was understandable enough, for Elizabeth's attempt to fob off on his mistress a rejected admirer of her own was arguably little short of insulting. It would be demeaning enough for the Queen of Scots to marry the grandest of Elizabeth's subjects, but Lord Robert was scarcely that, and his putative history of wife murder and adultery made it seem still more outrageous that Mary should be even tentatively invited to take him as her consort. Elizabeth, however, was in no way being facetious, for she was determined that the offer must be fully explored. Obviously, there was a degree of malice in this, for she clearly savoured the delicious piquancy of asking Mary to give serious consideration to a man whom she had once contemptuously dismissed as the Queen of England's horsekeeper, but Elizabeth's motives were far from being wholly disreputable. It pleased her to think that this would be a means of rewarding Dudley for his devotion to her, for despite her own rejection of him, she did not wish it to be inferred that he was in some way unworthy of a queen. More importantly, however, by doing him this kindness, she would provide for her own future security, for she believed Dudley's affection for her to be such that she could depend on him to restrain Mary from trying to seize the English crown in Elizabeth's lifetime. By making Dudley "a partaker of all [Mary's] fortunes", she would make fitting recompense to the man "whom, if it might lie in our power, we would make owner or heir of our own kingdom", while simultaneously freeing herself from the fear of being "offended by any usurpation before her death. Being assured that he was so loving and trusty that he would never permit any such thing to be attempted during her time".[4]

In this way, Elizabeth herself would be a beneficiary from this outlandish triangular arrangement, although undeniably the emotional cost would be high. When the project was in its infancy, however, Elizabeth was insistent that this was of no significance, and she seems to have deluded herself that she would manage to summon up the necessary composure when the moment to part with Dudley came. The great comfort was that this could not possibly take place for some time for, even if Mary showed interest in Elizabeth's proposal, nothing could conceivably come of it without extensive discussions and delay. For Elizabeth, indeed, the principal attraction of the scheme lay in the fact it gave her time. It was only much later, when a marriage between Mary and Dudley no longer seemed so remote, that it emerged that the Queen lacked the will to carry her policy through.

On his return home Maitland declined even to hint to Mary that Dudley had been mentioned as a possible husband for her, but in August 1563 Elizabeth instructed Thomas Randolph to take the matter a stage further.

He was directed to inform Mary that if she agreed "to content us and this our nation in her marriage", Elizabeth would "proceed to the inquisition of her right and title to be our next cousin and heir, and to further that which shall appear advantageous to her". As yet, the exact identity of the man whom Elizabeth had in mind was not to be divulged. Randolph could merely explain that his mistress wished Mary to marry "some person of noble birth within our realm ... yea, perchance such as she would hardly think we could agree unto",[5] and Elizabeth hoped that following this oblique hint, Mary would intuitively divine that it was Dudley who was meant.

Hardly surprisingly, Mary needed further enlightenment before she understood what Elizabeth was trying to convey. When Randolph delivered his message, Mary showed great curiosity to know who her mystery suitor could be, but she made no attempt to supply the answer herself. It was a matter of some relief to Randolph that his instructions did not permit him to be more specific on this point, for he frankly dreaded the moment when the true position was revealed. As he lamented to Cecil, it was asking a lot of Mary's "noble stomach" to "imbase itself so low as to marry in place inferior to herself", but if she did agree to consider an Englishman, she would naturally expect to be offered one of the highest ranking aristocrats in the land. Yet this was far from being the case: "Of all those that are in England it is known who is most worthy!" Randolph groaned,[6] aghast at the very thought of Mary's reaction when ultimately all became plain.

Elizabeth herself still refused to admit that there was anything incongruous in her plan, and after some months had passed without Randolph making any further progress, she instructed him to be less equivocal with Mary. In some trepidation, Randolph nerved himself to tell the Scottish Queen that Elizabeth wished to couple her with Dudley, but though Mary succeeded in keeping her temper under control ("It pleased her Grace to hear me with meetly good patience", Randolph noted with relief), she did not receive the suggestion well. "Is that conform to her promise to use me as her sister?" she demanded sharply of poor Randolph, who hardly knew what to say. Indignantly Mary pointed out that Elizabeth was always urging her to do nothing that would be inconsistent with princely honour, "And do you think that it may stand with my honour to marry a subject?" Overcome with embarrassment, the wretched Randolph could only mumble that "there was not a worthier man to be found" than Lord Robert.[7]

While she did not reject the idea outright, at this stage Mary was not prepared to give it much consideration. She had a more illustrious match on her horizon, and since she believed herself to be on the point of gaining admittance to the most powerful dynasty in Europe, she had little incentive to accept the suit of an impecunious vassal of the English Queen. When

Maitland had last been in England he had sounded out Philip II's ambassador, de la Quadra, as to whether the King would be prepared to see Mary married to his eldest son, Don Carlos, and Mary was currently expecting Philip to authorize the start of detailed marriage negotiations. This would have been the most glittering of alliances for Mary, even though from a purely personal point of view Don Carlos had little to recommend him. He had always been an unpromising youth, but in 1562 his "natural imbecility" had been aggravated by brain damage incurred when he had fallen downstairs while chasing a maidservant. A diplomat stationed in Spain commented, "He is usually so mad and furious that everyone here pities the lot of the woman who will live with him"[8] but, if his character was set aside, the heir to the Spanish throne was undeniably one of the greatest matches in Christendom.

As far as Elizabeth was concerned there could be no more threatening combination than Mary and Don Carlos, and she made this abundantly plain. Having got wind of Maitland's overture to de la Quadra, she told him outright that if Mary went ahead with this marriage, she would regard it as a hostile act. Randolph was subsequently instructed to remind Mary that by taking such a husband, she would cause Elizabeth to "judge that no good is intended towards us", and this could only jeopardize her chances of inheriting the English crown.[9] Mary did not hesitate to ignore these warnings, for she could pertinently reflect that, once she was the wife of Don Carlos, it would be she who would be in a position to menace Elizabeth, rather than the other way round. Fired by visions of greatness, she saw no reason to be conciliatory, and by the summer of 1564, communications between the two Queens were at a virtual standstill.

In the end, however, Mary's Spanish match did not materialize. Initially, King Philip had expressed interest in having Mary for a daughter-in-law, but the negotiations had been entrusted to de la Quadra, and in August 1563 the latter had died before he could give the business his attention. For nearly a year there was no Spanish ambassador at the English Court, and this gave Philip time to reconsider. By June 1564, when Don Diego de Guzman de Silva arrived to replace the dead man, the King had decided that Mary would not, after all, be a good choice of wife for his son. As a result of this setback, Mary began to wonder whether she had been wrong to be so dismissive of Elizabeth's earlier overtures, and in September 1564 she decided to try and heal the rift between them by despatching Sir James Melville on a special mission to England.

Sir James was a good choice of emissary, for he had a sophistication and worldly charm that Elizabeth was quick to appreciate. He was gallant, witty and urbane, with a cultivation and polish far above that of the majority of his countrymen. Delighted to receive a visit from someone so cosmopolitan and entertaining, Elizabeth used all her wiles to make a favourable impression, and on successive days she paraded herself before him, arrayed in the latest fashions from abroad. Melville was something of a connoisseur of these, for he had acquired much of his diplomatic experience at foreign courts, and Elizabeth asked him to say which style became her best. She was very pleased when he pronounced that his favourite was her outfit from Italy, with its elaborate head-dress that showed off to great advantage her red-gold hair.

The Queen subjected Melville to intensive cross-questioning about Mary's accomplishments and appearance, and Sir James was somewhat disconcerted when Elizabeth asked him outright which one of them was the most beautiful. Determined not to be drawn into embarrassing comparisons, he answered guardedly that "The fairness of them both was not their worst faults", but Elizabeth was not satisfied by such smooth evasions. She put the query to him again, whereupon Melville replied that she was the fairest Queen in England, while Mary was the fairest Queen in Scotland, but even this was not good enough. Elizabeth still pressed him to be more specific, driving Melville to concede that she was the paler of the two, but he affirmed that Mary was nevertheless "very lovely".

Evidently piqued that the verdict had not gone more clearly in her favour, Elizabeth next demanded to know whether Mary was taller than her, and on learning that she was, the Queen declared triumphantly, "Then she is too high; for I myself am neither too high nor too low". Having settled that question to her satisfaction, she then enquired whether Mary was musical, and when Sir James answered that his Queen was reasonably proficient on the lute and virginals, Elizabeth felt confident that in this field at least, she could outshine her cousin. That evening Sir James was taken to a gallery that overlooked a room where the Queen was practising at the virginals, and he was much impressed by the skill with which she played. After a while, he made his presence known to her, and Elizabeth pretended that she was embarrassed to have been overheard. Despite this, she did not fail to ask whether she was a better performer than her cousin, and she was duly gratified when Melville answered in the affirmative. By this time, Sir James was beginning to tire of his uncomfortable role as arbiter between rival Queens, but Elizabeth was thoroughly enjoying their exchanges. She did not let him escape until she had showed off her dancing to him, extracting from him the compliment that Mary "danced not so high or so disposedly as she did".

Though much time was frittered away on these pleasantries, business was not entirely neglected, and the upshot of Melville's visit was an agreement that English and Scottish commissioners should meet at Berwick to discuss the possible marriage between Dudley and Mary, Queen of Scots. To try and make Dudley a more attractive proposition, Elizabeth decided that she must do something to narrow the yawning disparity in rank between him and his prospective bride, and on 29 September Melville came to Westminster Hall to see the Queen confer the ancient title of Earl of Leicester on her favourite. As tradition demanded he was raised to the peerage in a stately ceremony, but even on this formal occasion the Queen's mood remained playful. Melville was amused to see that as Dudley knelt in homage before her, she stretched out and surreptitiously tickled his neck.

Such incidents did not exactly corroborate Elizabeth's claim that she looked on Robert as no more than a "brother and best friend", but she remained adamant that she would be very happy to see him married to Mary. As proof of her sincerity, she invited Melville into her bedchamber, and taking a miniature of Mary out of a cabinet where she stored various precious possessions, she kissed it fondly. She feigned bashfulness when Melville asked to see another item in the collection, which she kept carefully wrapped in paper. This bore the legend in the Queen's own hand, "My Lord's picture", and it was only after some importunity that Melville was permitted to inspect what turned out to be a miniature of Leicester. He remarked that this would make an ideal gift for Mary, although he conceded that failing that, she would be very pleased with a massive ruby "as great as a tennis ball" which was another of the cabinet's treasures. Elizabeth was prepared to part with neither: crisply she told Sir James that if Mary followed her advice, "she would in process of time get all she had", but in the meantime her cousin would have to rest content with the present of a fair diamond.[10]

Melville's visit could hardly have gone better, but the meeting between English and Scots commissioners which commenced at Berwick on 18 November, was a much less amicable affair. Mary was represented by her half-brother James (who had been created Earl of Moray in 1562) and Maitland of Lethington, and naturally they wanted to know exactly what steps Elizabeth would take to further Mary's title if she did agree to marry Leicester. To this the English commissioners only gave the vague answer that "There is no better way to further it than this", prompting the angry retort from Maitland that if they could offer nothing better, it "importeth nothing else but a desire in your mistress that ours should not marry great, and herself to be at liberty to do what she will". The following month Maitland and Moray wrote frankly to Cecil that there could be no question of Mary marrying an Englishman unless the succession was settled on her, but it was gradually becoming clear to Cecil that Elizabeth had repented of her earlier offers to do what she could to further Mary's claim. Plaintively he noted, "I see the Queen's Majesty very desirous to have my Lord of Leicester placed in this high degree to be the Scottish Queen's husband; but when it cometh to the conditions which are demanded, I see her then remiss of her earnestness".[11]

Since the Scots would plainly feel aggrieved when it emerged that Elizabeth had led them to have false expectations, it was necessary to think of some way of making them seem in the wrong. When Mary had first been widowed, Cecil had remarked, "The longer the Scottish Queen's affairs shall hang in an uncertainty, the longer will it be 'ere she shall have such a match in marriage as shall offend us", and he still believed that by creating enough confusion, Elizabeth would be able to outwit the Scots. For the moment the Scots were waiting for Elizabeth to make the next move, but if Mary could be prompted to forestall this by coming up with a counter-proposal of her own, this would reduce her to the level of a supplicant, and give Elizabeth a great deal more leverage in any subsequent negotiations. This, presumably, was why Cecil pressed the Queen to let her second cousin, nineteen-year-old Lord Darnley, go to Scotland, calculating that this would cause Mary to seek Elizabeth's permission to marry him instead of Leicester. It does not seem to have occurred to him that Mary might go ahead and marry Darnley even if Elizabeth's consent was not forthcoming. Sir James Melville subsequently commented that Cecil was "not . . . minded that any of the marriages should take effect, but with such shifts to hold the Queen [of Scots] unmarried so long as he could",[12] and this interpretation seems plausible enough.

For reasons of his own, Leicester seconded Cecil's suggestion that Darnley should go to Scotland. From the start he had viewed askance the plan to pair him off with Mary Stuart, regarding it simply as an unwelcome distraction to his courtship of Elizabeth. He believed that she was still attainable, and did not want to wreck his chances by showing any interest in the Queen of Scots. He was sure that Elizabeth saw this as a test of his fidelity, and that she did not seriously intend to bestow him on her cousin, and indeed, if Mary is to be believed, Leicester went so far as to write to her warning that Elizabeth had devised the whole scheme merely in order prevent her marrying at all.[13] Accordingly, he was anxious to sabotage the project, and one way of doing this was to introduce Darnley into the field. What means he used to persuade the Queen that this was sound policy remains unclear, but at any rate, by early February he and Cecil had convinced Elizabeth that Darnley should be given license to go to Scotland.

Tall and athletic, with delicate good looks, Darnley was in some ways the obvious husband for Mary Stuart. His mother was Margaret, Countess of Lennox, and hence, like Mary herself, Darnley was a grandchild of Henry VIII's sister, Margaret Tudor. If he and Mary were to marry together, they would constitute a formidable partnership, for their respective claims to the throne would be merged, and since Darnley had been born in England, this would enable Mary to say that any law regarding inheritance of English property by aliens no longer applied to her. For this very reason, English statecraft had hitherto been directed at keeping the pair apart, for Mary's claim was already dangerously weighty without the added muscle that marriage with Darnley could bring. Having joined herself with Darnley, Mary would be under renewed temptation to try and strip Elizabeth of her crown, and when making such a bid she could rely on all those who were sympathetic to Darnley's pretensions to rise up in her support.

Certainly Darnley himself could not be relied upon to restrain Mary in any way, for he came of thoroughly untrustworthy stock. His mother was a meddlesome and domineering woman, who had already conducted herself in a manner that had led to her being described as a person that "loveth neither God nor the Queen's Majesty". In matters of faith she was regarded as so unsound that one Protestant churchman declared her to be "beyond measure hostile to religion, more violent indeed than even Queen Mary [Tudor] herself". His mother's influence had ensured that Darnley himself had been "grafted in that devilish papistry", and his Catholic upbringing was an additional reason to regard him as a particularly dangerous husband for Mary Queen of Scots.[14]

Religion was not the only area in which Lady Lennox's loyalty had been found wanting, for her naked ambition for herself and her sons had also led her into intrigues that were little short of treasonous. By no means all of these had come to light, but when in 1561 Lady Lennox had left Court to go and live with her husband on their Yorkshire estates, they were already regarded with sufficient suspicion for them to be placed under surveillance. Before long, an agent planted in their household had reported that, after the death of Francis II, Lady Lennox had sent emissaries to France, Spain and Scotland in hopes of bringing about a marriage between Mary Stuart and her eldest son. Elizabeth was also angered to learn that the Countess was in the habit of letting fall some very unfortunate remarks, such as the comment that "Either Queen Mary I, or the Queen's Majesty ... behoved to be a bastard. As for Queen Mary, all the world knew that she was lawful". As a result of these revelations, in November 1561 the Lennoxes had been summoned to London and placed in separate confinement, and though their stout denials of all accusations meant that nothing could be proved against them, they were kept under restraint for over a year. In February 1563 they had been freed, and soon after that they were apparently back in favour at court, but Elizabeth was under no illusion that their devotion to her was anything but superficial.[15]

In view of all this it is extraordinary that Elizabeth should have permitted Darnley to go to Scotland at such a juncture, but she clearly assumed that even once he was over the border, the situation would remain in her control. If this was her thinking, it certainly was too devious for poor Randolph in Scotland, who over the past eighteen months had made such heroic efforts to promote a union between Mary and Leicester. By February 1565 he was just beginning to believe that it would be possible to bring this about, for when he saw Mary at the beginning of the month she had implied that if offered the right conditions, she would be willing to marry the Earl. "What I shall do it lieth in your mistress' will, who shall wholly guide and rule me", she had told Randolph warmly, and in great excitement the ambassador had rushed off a letter informing Elizabeth of this encouraging new development.[16] A few days later, Randolph was shattered to hear from Cecil that just when things were at this particularly sensitive stage, Lord Darnley was being sent north.

By 17 February, Darnley had been received by the Scots Queen, but though Mary treated him in a friendly and attentive manner, Randolph reported in relief that he believed she did so out of courtesy alone. Evidently she was still waiting for Elizabeth to outline the concessions that would be granted if she married Leicester, and in the interval saw no point in permitting her thoughts to wander elsewhere. On 5 March 1565, Elizabeth finally made known her terms, and Randolph passed these on to Mary eleven days later. They could hardly have been more threadbare, for the most that Elizabeth was prepared to do in return for an undertaking to marry Leicester was "to offer to the Queen of Scots all gentleness, etc., but not to meddle with her title until she be married herself or determined not to marry". Having advanced so far to meet what she understood to be Elizabeth's wishes, Mary was understandably resentful at being so soundly snubbed. Cecil heard that "She useth evil speech of the Queen's Majesty, alleging she abused her, and made her spend time".[17]

Since Mary stood to gain so little from marrying Leicester, Darnley was clearly the logical alternative, and when Maitland arrived in England on 18 April to seek official sanction for a betrothal, it should not have afforded anyone the least surprise. Elizabeth nevertheless declared herself to be grievously taken aback by Mary's "very strange and unlikely" proposal, and referred the matter to the Privy Council. Having ascertained that the match was "misliked of all", she announced that Throckmorton was to go to Scotland, "to stop or delay it as much as possible". Throckmorton was instructed to re-offer Leicester to Mary, this time on marginally improved terms, for Elizabeth now said that if Mary proved co-operative, she would "advance our sister's title, as far forth as with one that were our natural brother, and yet not inheritable to our crown, as it might be being our brother on our mother's side". Alternatively, Mary could have her pick of any English nobleman *apart* from Darnley, but if she persisted in demanding the latter's hand, she must realize that in that case, Elizabeth would be unable to "impart to her such fruits of our goodwill, as we can and will with others".[18] At this stage it is probable that Elizabeth was not excessively concerned. She assumed that Mary would not dare marry Darnley without her authorization, and envisaged that there would be another round of protracted negotiations before anything could be decided either way. If Mary insisted on having Darnley in preference to all the other Englishmen on offer, it would appear that it was she who was being unreasonable, and Elizabeth could then say that she could only consent to such a thing on the most stringent of terms. What these would have been remains a matter for conjecture, though Mary would almost certainly have had to waive her demands that her title to the throne be given formal recognition, and might possibly have had to undertake to convert to Protestantism.

These cheerful calculations failed to take into account a disturbing new element in the situation, for Mary had now fallen hopelessly in love. According to Sir James Melville, she had found Darnley attractive from the start, but she had kept her feelings under control until early April, when Darnley had suddenly been smitten by measles. Concerned that this delicious being was going to be snatched from her by illness, Mary let herself be swept away by emotion. She sent the invalid titbits from her own table to tempt his flagging appetite, and insisted on visiting him, despite the danger of infection. By the time that Darnley was out of danger, she was utterly besotted, and she resolved to have him, with or without Elizabeth's approval.

She signalled her new mood of defiance by sending fresh instructions to Maitland. He was now commanded to tell Elizabeth that since Mary had been "so long trained with fair speech and in the end beguiled of her expectation, she did mind ... to use her own choice in marriage, and to take such a one as in her opinion should be fit for her; and that as things fell forth she would no longer be fed with yea and nay, and to depend upon so uncertain dealing". On seeing this letter, Throckmorton was shocked by the violence of her language, which in no way accorded with his previous estimate of Mary's character. "You would have said there had neither wanted eloquence, despite, anger, love nor passion", he wrote to Cecil in alarm. He was amazed at the change that had come over the woman who had formerly so impressed him by her self-control that he had praised the way "she more esteemeth the continuation of her honour, and to marry one that may uphold her to be great, than she passeth to please her fancy ... thereby". In those days he had been more inclined to censure Elizabeth for being "young and subject to affections";[19] now it was gradually becoming clear that this was a description that fitted Mary much better.

When Throckmorton arrived at the Scottish court on 15 May, his worst suspicions were confirmed, for he found Mary "seized with love in fervener passions than is comely for any mean personage". At his first audience with her, he begged her to show some restraint, but he was unable to prevent her from conferring a Scots peerage on Darnley that very afternoon. "She doteth so much ... that some report she is bewitched", was Randolph's gloomy comment, and he registered his disapproval that, instead of Mary trying to hide her feelings, "Shame is laid aside, and all regard of that which chiefly pertaineth to princely honour removed out of sight". By 21 May, Throckmorton had lost all hope that Mary would voluntarily defer her marriage. Sombrely he wrote to Elizabeth, "This Queen is so far past in this matter with Lord Darnley, as it is irrevocable, and no place left to dissolve the same by persuasion or reasonable means, otherwise than by violence".[20]

In England, all was in disarray. On 4 June the Council prophesied that if the marriage took place, it would encourage the English Catholics and embolden Mary to try and usurp the throne, but by now the situation was beyond repair. The Queen tried summoning Darnley home, but was met by flagrant disobedience, for he greeted the news of his recall with the pert comment, "I find myself very well where I am, and so purpose to keep me".[21] Elizabeth may have thought that Darnley would be intimidated by the knowledge that his mother remained in England as a hostage for his good behaviour, but even when Lady Lennox was sent to the Tower on 24 July for having encouraged her son in his undutifulness, nothing whatever was achieved. On 28 July, Darnley was proclaimed King in Scotland, and the following morning his wedding to Mary took place.

From the vantage point of England, everything that Mary did in the next few weeks merely confirmed that she harboured hostile intentions. As early as 21 May, Randolph had complained that Mary no longer used "the counsel of such as can best advise her, nor giveth ear to any than such as follow her fantasy", and having tried to halt her headlong rush into matrimony, the Protestant Moray and Maitland now found themselves excluded from her confidence. The management of affairs passed to David Riccio, a diminutive Piedmontese of undistinguished origins, who had come to Scotland four years earlier in the suite of the Savoyard ambassador. He was "a merry fellow and a good musician", and Mary had been sufficiently appreciative of his talents as a singer to suggest that he remained in Scotland on the departure of his master. From being the fourth member of a musical quartet, Riccio had been promoted to the position of French secretary to the Queen, and was responsible for drafting all her correspondence in that language. As Maitland's career had gone into a decline, Riccio's influence had become much wider, and by 3 June 1565 Randolph was reporting, "David is now he that works all".[22] The English may well have been mistaken in assuming that this was a development that was necessarily malign, but in their present state of panic they were incapable of seeing the situation in terms which were anything other than stark. Riccio was both a foreigner and a Catholic, and little more was needed to make the English regard him as their foe.

Elizabeth was nevertheless not bereft of potential allies within Scotland.

The Earl of Moray had been enraged to find that Mary no longer regarded him as being of any significance, and following her marriage he had withdrawn himself from court to plot against her. He had no difficulty gathering a party of malcontents around him, for Darnley had swiftly alienated many of the Scots nobility by conducting himself in a manner that was both arrogant and overbearing. Teetering on the edge of rebellion, Moray contacted Elizabeth to find out whether he could count on her support, and she replied that if he and his followers were "forced to inconvenience" in their bid to uphold the true religion and maintain amity with England, "they shall not find lack in us to regard them in their truth". At the end of July, Elizabeth sent a special envoy to Scotland to tell Mary that it was imperative that she be reconciled with Moray, but on 6 August, the very day after this message was delivered, the Queen of Scots outlawed her half-brother. Haughtily she told Elizabeth, "Her Majesty desires most heartily her good sister to meddle no further with the private cases concerning him or any other subjects of Scotland than her Majesty has heretofore meddled with any cases concerning the subjects of England". She capped this by arresting Elizabeth's envoy after he left court, to punish him for having disdained the offer of a safe conduct which had Darnley's name on it. When Elizabeth heard of this effrontery she was beside herself with rage, and cried out that she would aid Moray and his cohorts with all the means that God had given her.[23]

Yet when it came to the point, the Queen held back. Apart from sending Moray £1,000, she did nothing to help his cause, for the French ambassador warned that if she intervened in Scotland, his king would not fail to come to Mary's assistance. When the Queen consulted her Council, some members took the view that the French were bluffing, and that Moray should be succoured regardless, but after prolonged wrangling, a majority advised Elizabeth "to do nothing to break peace". On 30 September, she wrote to tell the rebel lords that she could give them no further support, and six days later Moray and his followers sought sanctuary in England. By leading Moray on and then abruptly deserting him, Elizabeth had incurred the obloquy of Mary to no purpose whatever. The Earl of Bedford, Governor of Berwick since 1564, commented searingly, "What has England gotten by helping them in this sort? Even as many enemies as before it had friends". Moray himself complained to Leicester, "By the Queen's Majesty's cold dealing herein, a great part of my friends are ruined, and I and the rest of the nobility here put to this extremity, which we are brought to by following her Majesty's and her Council's advice". Elizabeth nevertheless preferred to forget the part she had played in his downfall. Anxious to distance herself from the whole sorry episode, she inflicted further humiliation on Moray when she received him at court, for in the presence of the French ambassador, she rebuked him soundly for insubordination to his Queen. "Whatsoever the world said or reported of her", she pontificated, "she would by her actions let it appear she would not ... maintain any subject in disobedience against the Prince".[24] While it was obvious enough that her speech was no more than a public relations exercise staged for the benefit of the French ambassador, this can hardly have been much consolation to the wretched Moray.

Despite the Queen's ostentatious efforts to dissociate herself from Moray's rebellion, Mary knew well enough that the English had encouraged it. This gave rise to fears that she would take revenge at the first opportunity and, in October 1565, the suspense was heightened by a fortuitous discovery. At the time of Moray's uprising, Mary had sent an agent to Spain to ask Philip II for financial assistance, but on his way home, her emissary was drowned in a shipwreck. His body was washed up on the Northumbrian coast, and when searched by the English authorities, large quantities of Spanish coins were found upon the corpse. In the jittery mood that then prevailed, this led to the assumption that the money was intended to serve some sinister purpose, and it was even cited as evidence that Mary was now a member of an international Catholic coalition dedicated to the overthrow of Elizabeth. The existence of such a league had been predicated ever since the summer of 1565, when the French royal family had met with the Spanish court at Bayonne in southern France, for the purpose, so it was alleged, of hatching a conspiracy to eradicate heresy throughout Europe. In reality, nothing of the sort had been agreed on at Bayonne, but Protestants everywhere believed in the existence of the conspiracy, and the revelation that Philip II was subsidizing Mary Stuart was taken to prove that she was now a party to the pact. In February 1566, Randolph fuelled the rumours by asserting, "There was a band lately devised in which the late Pope, th' Emperor, the King of Spain, the Duke of Savoy, with divers princes of Italy, and the Queen Mother [of France] suspected to be of the same confederacy, to maintain papistry throughout Christendom. This band was sent out of France ... and is subscribed by this Queen".[25] Although there was little solid fact to support such a statement, it commanded widespread credence within England. To all those who were in the grip of this powerful neurosis, it seemed imperative that Mary was deflected from her purpose, and if this entailed promoting internal subversion within her own realm, then so be it.

By the autumn of 1566, Mary was pregnant, but in every other respect her marriage had turned out disastrously. Within weeks of her wedding, she had ceased to be infatuated by her husband, for though initially passion had blinded her to his faults, on closer acquaintance he was revealed as a contemptible wastrel and degenerate. Petulant and immature, it was not long before he was held in universal execration. Randolph reported in disgust, "Darnley is of an insolent, imperious nature, and thinks that he is never sufficiently honoured", while another estimate of his character summed him up as "wilful, haughty and, some say, vicious". In February 1566 Cecil was told, "Darnley is in great misliking with the Queen. She is very weary of him, and as some judge will be more so 'ere long".[26] His behaviour had become utterly deplorable: he frequently quitted the royal palace to pursue a life of depravity in Edinburgh, and having taken to drinking in excess, he treated his wife insultingly when in his cups. Yet even while showing himself unfitted for the responsibilities of government, he nagged Mary to make him a King in more than name by bestowing on him the Crown Matrimonial. When she refused, he sullenly consoled himself with further debaucheries.

Darnley had initially been on the best of terms with Riccio, but his resentment at having his wishes flouted led him to turn on the little Italian, whom he blamed for Mary's intransigence. Not only was Riccio more influential than he, but Mary clearly preferred his company to that of her husband's, as the Secretary's droll humour and lively charm helped her to forget the miseries of her married life. Having brooded on this for a while, Darnley came to the conclusion – which does not seem to have been warranted – that Riccio and Mary were lovers, and he became avid for revenge. He found ready allies in a wide cross-section of the Scots nobility, for despite their destestation of Darnley, they were ready to collaborate with him in order to rid themselves of a conceited foreign upstart who had infuriated them by monopolizing power and depriving them of the profits of office. Almost all the leading lords in Scotland pledged themselves to secure Riccio's overthrow, and it was agreed that, once this had been achieved, they would force Mary to bestow on Darnley the Crown Matrimonial.

Randolph was kept informed of what was going on, and on 13 February he wrote to the Earl of Leicester, "I know that if that take effect which is intended, David, with the consent of the King, shall have his throat cut within these ten days." He added ominously,"Many things grievouser and worse than these are brought to my ears; yea, of things intended against her [Mary's] own person", but he asked Leicester to keep this to himself. By 6 March Randolph had decided that it was no longer possible to conceal the matter from Elizabeth, and he and Bedford asked Cecil to pass on to her that Riccio's arrest and execution were imminent. There is no record that Elizabeth was perturbed to hear of this, although even if she had been, the letter would have arrived too late for her to have given Mary any warning. At any rate, although she knew, at least in outline, of the design against Riccio, she is unlikely to have realized that he would be attacked in Mary's presence. At it was, Randolph and Bedford seem to have been anxious that Elizabeth should only be given a partial account of what the lords intended to do, for on 8 March, when they brought Cecil and

Leicester up to date with the latest developments in Scotland, they cautiously concluded their letter, "We advertise your Honours thereof to communicate to her Majesty as seems most expedient to your wisdoms".[27]

On 9 March 1566, Riccio was dragged, shrieking and begging for mercy, from a small supper room in Holyrood Palace, where Mary was entertaining an intimate group of friends. Having been hustled away, he was slaughtered in cold blood, his body skewered with a multiplicity of stab wounds. It would hardly have been surprising if this horrific act of violence had caused Mary to have a miscarriage, but though shaken and appalled, she proved unexpectedly resilient. "No more tears now; I will think upon revenge", she had remarked soon after the murder, and she confronted this challenge to her authority with commendable daring and aplomb. Being all too familiar with the defects in Darnley's character, she was now able to exploit them to her own advantage, and before long she had detached him from his partners in crime. She convinced the young man that having eliminated Riccio, his accomplices would play him false, and Darnley weakly agreed to betray his former confederates. At midnight on 11 March, he and Mary effected their escape from Holyrood, creeping down the back passage and into the grounds, where horses were awaiting them. Together they rode the twenty-five miles to Dunbar Castle, a strenuous ordeal for a woman who was six months pregnant, but which passed without mishap. Once at Dunbar, she rallied her supporters, and on 18 March she was able to return to Edinburgh at the head of 8,000 men, Riccio's assassins having ignominiously fled the realm.

From Dunbar, Mary had despatched Elizabeth a vivid account of Riccio's murder and her subsequent escape, and Elizabeth had publicly expressed her horror that her cousin had been subjected to so terrible an experience. In reality, however, the English were highly relieved that Riccio had been eliminated. The Earl of Bedford commented with satisfaction, "Since so great an enemy to religion and the amity of the two realms is now taken away, there is the greater hope that all quietness and good peace shall be established upon these borders".[28] The Earl of Moray had returned to Scotland the day after the murder, and when Mary re-entered Edinburgh, she forgave him for his earlier disloyalty and reinstated him in her Council. By September 1566, Maitland was also advising her again, and now that these two Protestant councillors were once more to the fore, the English fears that Mary was planning to act as the spearhead of the Counter-Reformation began to subside.

In June 1566 Mary gave birth to a son, James, and this too caused her to be looked on with new respect. Whereas only a few months before she had been classified as a religious bigot and potential aggressor, she was now hailed as a prudent ruler who had upheld the Protestant settlement in Scotland and safeguarded the future of the monarchy into the next generation. If Sir James Melville is to be believed, there was at this time an influential body of men in England, including the Earls of Leicester and Pembroke and the Duke of Norfolk, who all thought sufficiently highly of Mary to press Elizabeth to make her her heir.

The Queen was still not ready to take this step, but she was prepared to extend to Mary a pledge of her goodwill. She accepted Mary's invitation to stand godmother to the infant, and in November 1566 the Earl of Bedford travelled to Scotland to represent her at the baptism. Apart from presenting the Queen's godson with a magnificent golden font (unfortunately somewhat undersized, necessitating an explanation from Elizabeth that it was her assumption that the christening would be held before the baby had grown so large that accounted for this niggardliness), he was authorized to tell Mary that provided she undertook not to press her claim to the English throne during the lifetime of Elizabeth or any of her lawful issue, Elizabeth would see to it that no laws were passed in England that were in any way prejudicial to Mary's title. Mary was delighted: in January 1567 she wrote warmly to Elizabeth, "Always have we commended us and the equity of our cause to you and have certainly looked for your friendship therein ... and now we think us fully assured of the same". She declared that as soon as possible she would send an envoy to England to discuss the matter, "For we like well of the motion made by you in that behalf".[29] After years of tension and misunderstanding, at last it seemed that the relationship between Elizabeth and Mary Queen of Scots was going to settle down.

Obviously it was a relief that England and Scotland were no longer on such unfriendly terms with one another, but there were many Englishmen who took the view that the only sure way in which Elizabeth could provide for her kingdom's security would be for her to marry and have a child. In 1563 she had promised Parliament that she would do her best to overcome her aversion to matrimony, and since then a bewildering variety of suitors had been encouraged to pay her court. They had included a Habsburg archduke and a king of France, as well as an assortment of her own subjects, but their combined efforts had failed to produce any result. For three years, therefore, the matrimonial see-saw had soared and dipped in an utterly fantastic fashion: one minute the Archduke Charles would be borne aloft while his French rival plummeted, and the next the position would be reversed, while all the time the Earl of Leicester tenaciously retained his foothold in the centre. The Queen of course had found the spectacle hugely diverting, while simultaneously hugging to herself the knowledge that she was deluding them all, but now that her subjects' patience was wearing thin, the joke had lost some of its savour.

It was in the autumn of 1563 that the Queen had first tried to reawaken the interest of Archduke Charles, at first with no success. Charles's father, the Emperor Ferdinand, was mindful of the way she had previously rebuffed his son, and despite being urged to spare no effort to win "such a Helen, accompanied by such a dowry and so much dignity", nothing could shake his conviction that a fresh attempt to woo her would meet with an outcome as ignominious as the first. It was only when Ferdinand died, in June 1564, and was succeeded by his eldest son Maximilian, that things began to seem more promising. When approached, Maximilian agreed to send a representative to England to see the Queen, although he was insistent that his brother "would not, as on the last occasion, suffer himself to be led by the nose".[30]

Maximilian's emissary was expected in the spring of 1565, but by that time this was not the only illustrious courtship in which the Queen was involved, for since early 1565 the fourteen-year-old King of France had also been numbered among her suitors. The previous autumn she had started hinting to the French ambassador, Paul de Foix, that she would welcome a proposal from Charles IX, and on hearing this, Catherine de Medici had become beside herself with excitement. Nevertheless when the ambassador tendered a formal request for her hand, Elizabeth greeted the offer with distinct reserve. Expressing fears that she was already too old for the King, she said that she would rather die than see herself despised and abandoned as her sister had been. She protested that people would sneer that he had married his mother, just as in Mary's day, people had derided Philip for marrying his grandmother – though in fact the age difference between Elizabeth and Charles was much greater. Piqued that the Queen should have given so negative a reception to an invitation that she had implied would be most welcome, the ambassador said coldly that in that case it would be best not to pursue the matter any further, but this was the last thing Elizabeth wanted. Reddening with temper, she fired back that the French King must have very little regard for her if he was prepared to drop his suit so precipitately. All she wished to do, she explained, was to outline the difficulties she laboured under, so that the French would understand that she could not give her answer without much delay.[31]

In France Catherine de Medici scoffed at the idea that Elizabeth was too mature a bride for her son, and the King was no less eager, telling the Queen's ambassador, "I find no fault: I would she were as well content with me as I with her age". Sir Thomas Smith, who had succeeded Throckmorton as English ambassador in France, opined that the King would make Elizabeth a good husband, for though "pale and not greatly timbered", he seemed "tractable and wise for his years ... and to give wittier answers than a man would easily think". Much enthused, Smith wrote to the Queen, "I dare put myself in pledge to your Highness that your Majesty shall like him".[32]

Despite these glowing references, Elizabeth held back. She told the French ambassador that she could not give a definite answer until she had had further consultations with her nobles, and since de Foix knew that many of them were against her marrying a Frenchman, he drew little comfort from this. It was true that he looked on the Earl of Leicester as an ally, for the latter was always assuring him that he was doing all that he could to promote the King's cause. The ambassador failed to realize that Leicester only affected enthusiasm for Charles IX because he did not want the Queen to devote too much attention to Archduke Charles, who was the rival he really feared. As for Cecil, he could not believe that Elizabeth was really serious about the French marriage, and he therefore looked on the courtship as an unwelcome diversion. However, he did not dare voice any open criticisms, for as he put it, "I, being *mancipium reginae* [the Queen's bondsman], and lacking wit to further so great a matter, will follow with service where her Majesty go before". Other members of the Council were more outspoken, and advised the Queen against accepting the King on the grounds that France would swiftly establish itself as the senior partner in the relationship. The most vehement opponent of the match was the Earl of Sussex, who prophesied that the King was bound to neglect his elderly wife by going home, "and in accordance with French usage live with pretty girls there, and thus all hope of an heir would be rendered nugatory".[33]

Ideally, Elizabeth would have liked to have kept the French waiting much longer, but they insisted on having a prompt answer, and as always when decisions loomed, the Queen grew fretful. Already she was feeling tense and irritable on account of Mary Stuart's marital plans, which she foresaw would result in increased pressure on her to take a husband. One afternoon in May 1565, it all became too much for her, and she suddenly broke down. She started hurling wild reproaches at Leicester, Throckmorton and Cecil, sobbing that all those who importuned her to marry were in reality seeking her ruin. Thoroughly nonplussed by this hysterical outburst, the trio had to soothe her by protesting that no one would force her to do anything against her will, and that whatever course she chose to follow, her subjects would always remain loyal.[34]

At the end of June de Foix was told by the Council that the Queen could not accept marriage with Charles IX on account of the latter's extreme youth. This seemingly cleared the field for Archduke Charles, whose representative, Adam Zwetcovich, had arrived in England in mid-May. The Queen had welcomed him warmly, declaring that she was now resolved to marry, but Zwetcovich was downcast when she named her terms. Firstly, she stipulated that before she accepted him, the Archduke must come to England to be inspected, justifying this on the grounds that "She knew well how the King of Spain had cursed the painters and envoys when first he beheld Queen Mary, and she would not give the Archduke Charles cause to curse". She was also adamant that the Archduke would have to convert to Protestantism, being positive "that two persons of different faith could not live together in one house". Finally she said that she could not marry the Archduke unless he was prepared to make a substantial annual contribution to her household expenses. To Cecil, none of these demands seemed unreasonable, and when Zwetcovich left England in August in order to report them to his master, the Secretary felt that there was cause for cautious optimism. "Common opinion is", he told Sir Thomas Smith, "that the Archduke Charles will come, which if he do, and will accord with us in religion and shall be allowable for his person to her Majesty, then except God shall purpose to continue his displeasure against us, we shall see some success".[35]

For Leicester, this was depressing enough, but that August he was still more irked when the Queen started showing a marked predilection for one of her gentlemen of the Privy Chamber, Thomas Heneage. Heneage was "a man for his elegancy of life and pleasantness of discourse born as it were for the Court", and though he was a married man, Leicester still regarded him as a serious threat. Much disturbed by the unexpected materialization of a rival within his own domain, Leicester retaliated by indulging in a flirtation of his own. He started an affair with Francis Knollys's daughter Lettice, "one of the best looking ladies of the Court", who had been married for about four years to Viscount Hereford. It was a provocative choice, for Lettice had formerly been on close terms with the Queen, and Elizabeth saw it in the light of a personal betrayal. Enraged by Leicester's fickleness, she upbraided the Earl "in very bitter words", whereupon Leicester withdrew to sulk in his apartments. Cecil noted smugly, "The Queen's Majesty letteth it appear in many overt speeches that she is sorry for her loss of time – and so is every good subject", but before long the quarrel was over. Leicester and the Queen had an emotional reunion, at which they shed tears in an ecstasy of atonement, but a certain amount of ill-feeling lingered, for at the end of September it was noted that he and Elizabeth were still not on such warm terms as before.[36]

Within days, however, the atmosphere had so altered that Leicester was again being tipped by the pundits as the man the Queen would choose. By November his prospects looked so promising that the French ambassador dryly observed that some of the Earl's enemies now thought it politic to feign goodwill towards him, although the Duke of Norfolk, for one, remained as bitter an adversary as ever. The Duke's detestation of Leicester had become still more implacable after an incident that had taken place in March 1565, when they were playing tennis together, watched by the Queen. At the end of the game, Leicester, "being very hot and sweating, took the Queen's napkin out of her hand and wiped his face, which the Duke seeing, said that he was too saucy, and swore that he would lay his

The Princess Elizabeth, aged about thirteen.

King Henry VIII, by an unknown artist.

A pair of medals, by the Milanese sculptor Jacopo da Trezzo, of Mary Tudor and her husband, Philip of Spain.

Anne Boleyn, by an unknown artist.

Thomas, Lord Seymour of Sudeley, who was executed in 1549 for attempting to marry the fifteen-year-old Princess Elizabeth.

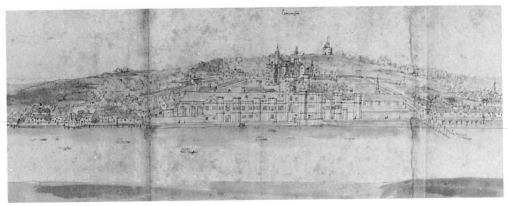

Elizabeth's birthplace, Greenwich Palace, a drawing by Anthony van Wyngaerde.

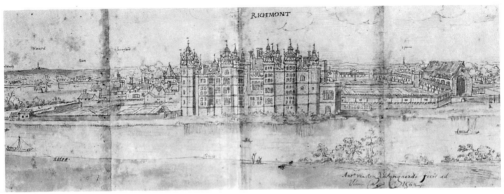

The most comfortable of Elizabeth's palaces, Richmond, built by her grandfather Henry VII.

A drawing by Anthony van Wyngaerde showing the entrance from the River Thames to Elizabeth's principal London residence, Whitehall.

The Englishman who came closest to marrying Elizabeth: Robert Dudley, Earl of Leicester, by an unknown artist.

Mary Queen of Scots in a bonnet; painting by an unknown artist after a portrait of c. 1560–65.

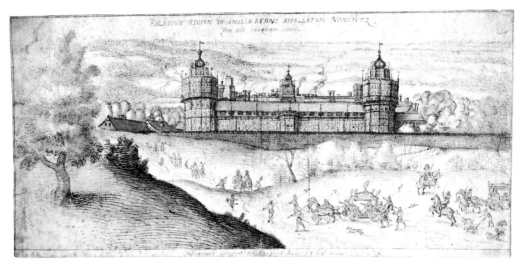

Elizabeth arriving in her coach at Nonsuch, the magnificent palace built by Henry VIII, and which was described as the residence "which of all other places she likes best".

Virginals thought to have belonged to Queen Elizabeth I. To the left of the keyboard the royal arms of England are emblazoned, while on the far right is displayed a falcon perched on a tree stump, the heraldic badge of Anne Boleyn which Elizabeth adopted as her own. Elizabeth "played very sweetly and skilfully" on the virginals.

that the Prince or chiefe (it so please them) doe alight and take
assaye of the Deare with a sharpe knyfe, the whiche is done

Elizabeth out hunting, a sport in which she delighted. After a stag was killed, she was always invited to give it the first cut with the hunting knife.

racquet upon his face". Harsh words had been exchanged, and the Duke's ill-feeling had been aggravated when Elizabeth took Leicester's side, and rebuked Norfolk for threatening violence when in her presence.[37]

Norfolk found a valuable ally in Thomas Radcliffe, Earl of Sussex, whose mother had been the Duke's great-aunt. Sussex had spent the early years of the reign trying to govern Ireland for the Queen, but after his return in 1564, he and Norfolk had gravitated together, bound not only by ties of blood but also by a mutual antipathy towards Leicester. By June 1565, Sussex and Leicester held one another in such hatred that violent clashes seemed likely, for each of them had taken to swaggering about surrounded by armed men. The Queen intervened with strict instructions that neither should molest the other, but she could not heal the rift between them, and in October it was noted that Leicester and Sussex were still "on strange terms".[38]

Leicester was not in the least bit abashed by the hostility he aroused at court, for he prided himself on being a man "that never did depend upon any but merely her Majesty". In December 1565 he was confident enough to press her to marry him during the Christmas festivities, and though she told him that he would have to wait until the February festival of Candlemas for his answer, it seemed that she was giving his proposal serious consideration. As excitement mounted at court, Leicester grew ever more insufferable, encouraging his supporters to express their solidarity with him by donning costumes marked with purple stripes. Within days, Norfolk's friends were kitted out in yellow, and as the normally multi-hued court began to break up into solid blocks of colour, the divisions that rent English society became visible at a glance.[39]

For all Leicester's strutting, the Candlemas deadline came and went without the Queen making any declaration, and it was hoped that this latest setback would force him to concede defeat. Deciding that there was little to be gained by remaining on bad terms with the Earl, Norfolk tried a more high-minded approach, telling Leicester that it was his duty to refrain from pursuing the Queen, as this would make it easier for her to accept the Archduke. Leicester was sufficiently taken aback by this appeal to his better nature – if indeed he had one – to agree to do what Norfolk asked, though he qualified his assent by saying that he could not allow Elizabeth to think that he was relinquishing his suit out of distaste for her, for that might "cause her, womanlike, to undo him". He was nevertheless not prepared to maintain this self-effacing stance when in March Elizabeth began making much of a new arrival at court, the Irish Earl of Ormonde, for this was a violation of his own territory. There was a series of rows, reconciliations and then more recriminations between him and Elizabeth, which culminated in Leicester leaving court in a huff.[40]

In January 1566, a letter had arrived from the Emperor expressing considerable interest in a marriage between his brother and Elizabeth, but nevertheless baulking at her conditions, and he had begged the Queen to modify these. Elizabeth refused to do anything of the sort: "How could she marry ... with a man whom she had to feed and let the world say she had taken a husband who could not afford to keep himself?" she indignantly demanded of the Spanish ambassador, adding that it would give rise to "a thousand inconveniences" if her husband was not of the same religion as herself. To the Emperor himself she wrote loftily, "I do not consider myself so base that I impair the honour of the Archduke when he visits me".[41] In April 1566 Cecil's brother-in-law, Thomas Dannett, was despatched to the Imperial court, ostensibly in order to offer Maximilian the Garter (which the Queen used as a sort of Valentine in these negotiations), but really to explain why it was impossible for her to revise the terms on which she was prepared to make herself available.

Having had an interview with the Emperor at Augsburg, Dannett travelled to Vienna to see the Archduke for himself, and he sent home glowing reports of him. Unfortunately piety was numbered among Charles's many outstanding attributes, and Dannett thought it most unlikely that the Archduke would agree to convert. After the Emperor had asked that his brother should be permitted to attend mass in private, Dannett wrote home urging that "Something must be winked at by the Queen therein",[42] but Elizabeth would not hear of it. Dannett lingered abroad in the hope that his instructions would be modified, but this proved a vain hope, and in August he disconsolately returned home. Despite the disappointing lack of progress, the Queen apparently thought it worthwhile to persevere. Once again, the Garter was brought into play, for Elizabeth gave out that she intended to send some great nobleman to Germany to present the Emperor with the order's insignia, and it was understood that this would provide an opportunity for the match with the Archduke to be reappraised.

Elizabeth had been careful to stress that Leicester was not to blame for the failure of Dannett's mission, as "none about us is more inclining and addicted towards this match in this house of Austria than he is; neither doth any person more solicit us toward the same". In fact, however, Leicester had been in hot pursuit of her all the time that Dannett was abroad. When the Earl had withdrawn himself from Court that spring, there had been rumours that the Queen intended to deprive him of the office of Master of the Horse, but after no more than a fortnight's separation, Elizabeth could bear it no longer, and summoned him to her side. They were reunited on 1 April, and the Queen sunnily declared that never again would she permit him to leave her for so long. For Cecil, who had hoped that Leicester's career had gone into permanent decline, this was a depressing blow. Frustrated by his role of onlooker, he mournfully drew up a table of comparisons which articulated exactly why the Archduke would prove a superior husband for the Queen than would Leicester. Leicester, he noted succinctly, would bring the Queen "nothing ... either in riches, estimation, power", and if Elizabeth married him it would furthermore be "thought that the slanderous speeches of the Queen and the Earl are true". In contrast to the Archduke, who was of royal lineage and well connected, Leicester was penniless, "infamed by the death of his wife", and not even likely to treat the Queen well, for his treatment of Amy Robsart showed that he was not naturally uxorious.[43] Presumably it was a comfort to Cecil's tidy mind to tabulate the contrasts between the two leading contenders for the Queen's hand, but there was of course no question of him showing this savage indictment of Leicester to Elizabeth herself, and having completed the exercise he filed away the document amongst his private papers.

Although Cecil clearly derived satisfaction from compiling his grim catalogue of Leicester's failings, the Queen for one remained blissfully oblivious to them. The Earl continued in high favour, and it was agreed that during the summer progress of 1566, Elizabeth would come to stay with him at Kenilworth. It was a singular honour, and as Leicester immersed himself in preparing the festivities that were to enliven her stay, it was widely conjectured that the celebrations would culminate in the announcement of their engagement. Talk of this was so rampant that at the last moment Elizabeth took fright and threatened not to come, but in the end she relented. The visit went ahead as planned and was pronounced a great success, but Leicester as usual had no luck in wearing down the Queen's resistance, for though she delighted in being offered his hospitality, she was still not ready to accept his hand.

When Parliament assembled on 30 September 1566, the Queen's marital plans remained as hazy as ever, and the stage was set for a major clash over the succession. Not only had she failed to satisfy her subjects with regard to her marriage, but her desperate need of money would compel the Queen to seek a larger grant of tax than in previous years,[44] and this left her vulnerable to criticism from all sides. Since Parliament had merely been prorogued in 1563, rather than dissolved, there had been no necessity for fresh elections, and the men who came to Westminster that autumn were well-versed in parliamentary business and determined to use their experience to circumvent her.

The Queen could not console herself that, if the Lower House proved difficult, the Lords would rally to her side, for her failure to resolve the uncertainty as to her successor had left several prominent peers in a state of acute dissatisfaction. In particular the Duke of Norfolk believed her to be guilty of inexcusable negligence, and in early October he infuriated the

Queen by declaring in Council that she should permit Parliament to discuss her marriage and the succession. The Queen flared up at once, insisting that the responsibility for the succession was hers alone, and that not one of her subjects would be permitted to interfere. Recalling the way in which courtiers and careerists had thronged to see her at Hatfield while her sister's life was ebbing away, she said that she had no intention of being buried alive as the late Queen had been, and added that since they knew that her marriage was imminent, she failed to see they had any cause for complaint.[45] The emotional outburst temporarily silenced Norfolk but failed to placate him in any way, and it was clear that opposition in Parliament would not be so easily subdued.

In the Commons, the discontent aroused by the introduction of the subsidy bill on 17 October was harnessed by a Mr Molyneux, who suggested that the grant of money should be contingent on the Queen making a declaration about her successor, and this "motion was very well approved by the greater part of the said House". The Privy Councillors in the Chamber, who were supposed to supervise the conduct of business on the Queen's behalf, were disturbed by the nature of the bargain that was on offer. Sir Ralph Sadler, who had recently been appointed a councillor, declared that like everyone else he wished the Queen to settle the succession, but "This kind and manner of conditioning with the Prince is not, I think, fit for us to use". The following day, Cecil and Sir Francis Knollys tried to calm the House by assuring them that the Queen was "moved to marriage and that she mindeth . . . to prosecute the same" but the members refused to listen. One of them cried out, "No, no! we have express charge to grant nothing before the Queen gives a firm answer to our demands."[46] Unable to control the members, and sympathizing with their disquiet, the Privy Councillors agreed that the Commons should seek to join with the Lords in petitioning the Queen to settle the succession.

The Lords were duly approached, but initially they were reluctant to hold the Queen to ransom by applying concerted parliamentary pressure. They therefore sent a deputation to Elizabeth suggesting that unless she was prepared to settle the succession promptly, she should dissolve Parliament and thus avoid futile confrontation. However well-meaning their intentions, the Queen was infuriated by the very suggestion that her present position was untenable. Stubbornly she insisted that the succession was too complex an issue to be decided by "a knot of harebrains", and warned that she would not be terrorized into changing her opinion about this. "My Lords, do what you will", she finished contemptuously. "As for myself, I shall do nothing but according to my pleasure. All the resolutions which you may make have no force without my consent and authority".[47]

After the Queen had spurned their compromise solution, on 17 October the Lords agreed to combine with the Commons and petition her to marry and name a successor. Elizabeth regarded this as an act of betrayal, and since she believed it was the Duke of Norfolk who had incited the peers to act thus, she rounded on him at Court, calling him "traitor or conspirator, or words of a similar flavour". At once the Duke's colleagues leapt to his defence: in unison Leicester, Pembroke, Northampton and Howard reproached the Queen, protesting that "It was not right to treat the Duke badly, since he and the others were only doing what was fitting for the good of the country, and advising what was good for her, and if she did not think fit to adopt the advice it was still their duty to offer it". Elizabeth had reluctantly to accept that dissatisfaction over the succession was now at such a peak that she was effectively isolated.

Smarting at her predicament, she lashed out with personal abuse. She told Pembroke that "he talked like a swaggering soldier", and then taunted Northampton, whose first marriage had been dissolved, that "he had better talk about the arguments used to enable him to get married again, when he had a wife living, instead of mincing words with her". As for Leicester, she commented scathingly "that she had thought that if all the world abandoned her, he would not have done so". When the Earl protested that he was ready to die at her feet, she riposted sharply "that that had nothing to do with the matter". So bitter was she at their defection that for a few days Leicester and Pembroke were denied entrance to the Presence Chamber, while the Queen, bereft of allies, sought solace on the comforting shoulder of the Spanish ambassador. She complained in particular of Leicester's behaviour, asking de Silva what he "thought of such ingratitude from him, after she had shown him so much kindness and favour that even her honour had suffered for the sake of honouring him". As she admitted, however, Leicester was far from being the only offender, for her other nobles were "all against her".[48] The ambassador made appropriately sympathetic noises, but apart from him, only the doddering Lord Treasurer ranged himself with the Queen.

Having done herself no good by indulging in wounding attacks, Elizabeth had to acknowledge that mere vituperation would not suffice to ward off the challenge she now faced. A parliamentary committee was already at work on a petition that she feared would inflame the position further, and she decided that at all costs she must forestall them. Accordingly on 5 November she summoned a deputation of thirty members of each House to Whitehall, so that she could put her point of view to them before they had had a chance to state their case in writing. Still seething with anger at the pass she had been brought to, she nevertheless grasped that if she were to emerge from this crisis with her authority intact, she must try to win over at least a section of the political nation, which at present was united against her. Having taken the precaution of excluding her more vociferous critics from the audience, she sought to detach the moderates from their allies by implying that the leaders of the parliamentary opposition were hotheads who did not understand where England's true interests lay. She knew, however, that by mounting too harsh an attack she would alienate her listeners, and therefore she had more than once revised the speech she intended to deliver, toning down some of its more biting phrases to avoid giving universal offence. The final version was consequently somewhat milder than the original, but there was no denying its immediacy and power, for although the Queen had struggled to keep her feelings under control, bitterness and sarcasm still vibrated through every line.

She opened by deploring the way that the subject of the succession had been bandied about in Parliament, showing a particular animus against the bishops, who had evidently led the debates in the House of Lords. She sneered that in long-winded orations these prelates had implied that they were more considerate of the safety of the country than she herself, but she failed to see what grounds there could be for such an assertion. "Was I not born in the realm?" she demanded imperiously, "Were my parents born in any foreign country? Is there any cause I should alienate myself from being careful over this country? Is not my kingdom here? Whom have I oppressed? ... How have I governed since my reign? I will be tried by envy itself."

Having set forth her credentials with these ringing interrogatives, the Queen next alluded to the petition concerning marriage and the succession. With regard to her marriage, she said that she had already informed the Commons via two of her councillors that she intended to take a husband, and she could not understand why so little weight had been attached to this assurance. "A strange order of petitioners, that will make a request and cannot be otherwise entertained but by their Prince's word, and yet will not believe it when it is spoken", she commented derisively. She told her audience that she felt sure that when she did select a husband, many of those who had urged her to do so would find fault with her choice, but despite this, she solemnly reaffirmed her previous undertaking. "I will never break the word of a prince, spoken in a public place, for my honour's sake. And therefore I say again, I will marry as soon as I can conveniently, if God take not him away with whom I mind to marry [a reference to the Archduke] or myself, or else some other great let happen".

Over marriage, at least, the Queen was theoretically prepared to accommodate her subjects, but this was the only comfort on offer, for when she addressed herself to the subject of the succession, she was categoric that this was no business of theirs. She explained that it was not a matter on which they were qualified to adjudicate, for none of them had her personal experience of the intrigues to which the heir presumptive to a crown was invariably exposed. As so often, she invoked the ordeal she had undergone following Wyatt's rebellion, which had left her indelibly marked. "I stood in danger of my life, my sister was so incensed against me", she now recalled. "I did differ from her in religion and I was sought for divers ways. And so shall never be my successor". Warming to her theme, she added that the complexities attendant on ordering the succession were so intractable and diffuse that she knew that if she did agree that the question could be openly debated, it would only give rise to fresh wrangling and bitterness. Nothing would please her more, she said, than to give them liberty to treat of this matter, but she knew that in that event, "Some would speak for their master, some for their mistress, and every man for his friend", and she foresaw that this would cause the most terrible dissension.

Having summed up her reasons for rebuffing them, she uttered a defiant peroration. "As for my own part, I care not for death; for all men are mortal. And though I be a woman, I have as good a courage, answerable to my place, as ever my father had. I am your anointed Queen. I shall never be by violence constrained to do anything. I thank God I am endued with such qualities that if I were turned out of the realm in my petticoat, I were able to live in any place in Christendom".

In conclusion, she repeated that for the moment she regarded it as unacceptably perilous for both herself and the realm if she named a successor. There would in fact always be an element of personal danger in doing such a thing, but when she deemed it appropriate she would none-theless take a calculated risk and announce a decision. She alone, however, "as your Prince and head", must be left to judge the timing of the move, without prompting from her subjects, "For it is monstrous that the feet should direct the head".[49]

The following day, Cecil had to tell the House of Commons what the Queen had said. Fearing that this would provoke an indignant reaction, he did not pass on her speech verbatim, and instead read out an emasculated version of her words. Even so, his rendition was accorded a very frigid reception, for "all the House was silent" as the members digested the unpalatable message. The Queen would doubtless have preferred it if they had remained so, but in fact their taciturnity did not signify acquiescence. On 8 November, William Lambarde, the member for Aldborough, rose and urged the House to continue with its plans to petition Elizabeth over the succession. The Queen promptly countered this move: the following day, Sir Francis Knollys informed the House that she had forbidden them to persist with their suit, but it soon emerged that the Commons were not so easily curbed. On 11 November, Paul Wentworth demanded of the House whether the Queen's command did not run contrary to their tra-ditional liberties, and the question was animatedly debated.

The next morning the Speaker of the House of Commons was summoned to Court, and on his return he announced that the Queen had repeated her prohibition on the suit for the succession, and warned that any member who questioned her order would be summoned before the Privy Council to explain himself. This threat had a steadying effect, but even so, the Commons were not completely chastened. Within a day or two, a committee was busy drawing up a response to the Queen's message of 5 November, respectful but firm in tone. It thanked her for her promise to marry, expressed regret that she felt unable to settle the succession at present, and prayed that it would not be too long before she judged it safe to do so. It went on to say that the Commons had been upset by her command to desist with their suit over the succession, for this had made them think that she wished to deprive them of their privilege of free speech. They claimed that the Queen had been over-hasty in assuming that they intended to persevere with their suit, for though such a move had been suggested, it had not received the sanction of the whole House. They trusted that once Elizabeth understood what a responsible body of men they were she would wish to confirm, or even augment, their liberties rather than diminish them.[50]

In the event, however, this petition was never presented, for Elizabeth pre-empted it with a conciliatory gesture. While determined not to surrender to the Commons on the issue of the succession, she had no wish for a confrontation with them on the question of parliamentary privilege, for here she was uncertain where she stood. It was an accepted feature of the constitution that the members of the House of Commons were entitled to use free speech in debate, and though as it happened the current speaker of the House had not followed the precedent set by Sir Thomas More in 1523 and asked for the privilege to be formally accorded, this in no way invalidated the general principle.[51] But while the Commons' right of free speech was unquestioned, the exact meaning of the term was vague. In the petition that they were in process of drawing up, the Commons defined it as "leeful sufferance and dutiful liberty to treat and devise of matters honourable for your Majesty and profitable for your realm", but it was unclear precisely what such matters were. The Queen for her part held that the Commons should not initiate debates on topics of such fundamental importance as the succession or religion, and that unless she chose to consult Parliament on these questions, she was entitled to control them exclusively herself. She was aware, however, that this interpretation would not command universal acceptance, and that there were members of the House of Commons who believed that their right to freedom of speech was subject to no restriction, and that, if public interest demanded it, there was no area of government in which they could not legitimately intervene. The liberties of the House of Commons were hence a highly sensitive issue, and the Queen had no wish to precipitate a clash on such awkward ground. Accordingly, instead of waiting for the Commons to present their petition, on 25 November she sent them a message declaring that she now understood that although a few men had contemplated pressing forward with the suit on the succession, by no means all of the House had favoured the idea. She therefore acknowledged that she had acted prematurely when she had ordered them to proceed no further, and this being so, she now remitted her command as unnecessary. When this message was delivered to the House it was received "most joyfully", and the atmosphere somewhat eased.

Yet even though the Queen had gone out of her way to appease them, the Commons remained far from tractable. Parliament had only been summoned in the first place because of the urgent need for money, but to Elizabeth's concern the House showed no sign of proceeding with the subsidy bill. To prod them into action, Elizabeth had to send a message remitting a third part of the proposed subsidy, and though the ploy succeeded in prompting the Commons to give the bill their attention, Elizabeth's financial position was too precarious for the sacrifice to be anything other than unwelcome. Worse still, despite the Queen's bene-ficence, the Commons were not disposed to forget that they had been denied satisfaction in the matter of the succession. Accordingly, the preamble to the subsidy bill not only alluded to the Queen's promise to marry as soon as possible, but also reminded her of her undertaking to settle the succession when convenient, for where these matters were concerned there was unde-rstandable scepticism as to the reliance that could be placed upon her words. Having already had some experience of the maddening way that Elizabeth succeeded in forgetting about verbal engagements, they hoped that she would find it impossible to go back on pledges which had been formally incorporated into an act of Parliament. The Queen proved too canny for them, for when she realized what they were about she acted forcefully to block the move. Furiously she scribbled at the foot of the offending document, "I know no reason why any of my private answers to the realm should serve for prologue to a subsidies book. Neither yet do I understand why such audacity should be used to make without my license an act of my words . . . Is there no hold of my speech without an act compel me to confirm?" Subdued by this outburst of princely wrath, the Commons meekly reworded the preamble so that it read more innocuously.[52]

The Queen's troubles were not yet at an end, for having failed to encroach upon Elizabeth's prerogative right to order the succession, the Commons addressed themselves to another taboo area, namely religion. A bill was passed making it compulsory for clergymen to subscribe to the Thirty-Nine Articles which had been passed by convocation three years before, and which encapsulated the Church of England's doctrine and beliefs. When the bill was sent up to the Lords, it was welcomed by the bishops, but since Elizabeth believed that it would be an infringement of the Royal Supremacy if Parliament was permitted to introduce legislation that modified the religious settlement of 1559, she sent orders that the Upper House must proceed no further with the measure. The Commons nevertheless hoped that if enough time elapsed, the Lords, egged on by the bishops, would press ahead with the bill regardless, and they therefore set out to keep Parliament in being for as long as possible. With this aim in mind, they deliberately held up a bill providing for the renewal of various acts which were due to expire when Parliament dispersed. Knowing that the Queen did not want these laws to be wiped from the statute book, they calculated that she would not dismiss Parliament until the bill had been passed, but at this Elizabeth decided to call their bluff. Determined not to be blackmailed, she dissolved Parliament without more ado.

Understandably, Elizabeth was not in the best of tempers when she attended the closing session of Parliament on 2 January 1567. Despite the fact that she had exerted herself to win over the Commons with gracious handling and timely retreats, she had not obtained as much money as she had hoped for, and had failed to secure the passage of important legislation. If she was to avoid experiencing similar humiliations in the future, she could not afford to let such disorderly conduct pass without protest. Accordingly, having listened to the Lord Keeper's closing speech, she rose to deliver a ringing reaffirmation of her rights.

She began by observing that in the present session they had been distracted by discussions on the succession and parliamentary liberties. With regard to the former, she repeated that this was a matter which should be left to a "zealous prince's consideration", rather than providing material for "lip-laboured orations" from lesser individuals. "I think this be the first time that so weighty a cause passed from so simple men's mouths", she told them in her most majestic manner, determined to establish once and for all that she would not permit them to penetrate the highest mysteries of government. As for parliamentary privileges, she insisted that while she had no wish to erode their lawful liberties, "God forbid that your liberty should make my bondage". There was no doubt, she continued, that she had been within her rights when she ordered them to cease their debates on the succession, and though she had subsequently revoked her command, she had done so only out of pity, and not because she thought that she would have otherwise exceeded her lawful powers. She said that it was obvious to her that the dutiful majority of the House had been "sore seduced" by certain "broachers" who were behind the bid to try and force her to declare the succession, and while she could not but regard with suspicion the motives of these troublemakers, she did not blame the rest. Having shown them how they had been misled, she said she did not wish to administer harsher discipline, rather hoping that her words would teach them never again "to tempt too far a prince's patience".[53]

From the Queen's point of view the session had been a nightmare, but she could console herself that it would be some years before she had to face Parliament again, and next time a more malleable bunch of men might be elected. However disagreeable this sitting of Parliament had been, she had at least retained her control over the succession, and although she had given a formal undertaking to marry, Elizabeth knew better than anyone how to extricate herself from such apparently binding commitments. In the past few weeks tempers had been frayed and much friction generated, but she could justly congratulate herself on averting the total fragmentation of the body politic while simultaneously keeping her authority unimpaired.

There were others about the Queen who saw less cause for optimism. In a gloomy memorandum which he drew up for her, Cecil lugubriously listed numerous causes for concern: "The succession not answered; the marriage not followed; a subsidy to be levied; the bill of religion stayed to comfort of the adversaries. Dangers ensuing: general discontentations; the slender execution of the subsidy; dangers of sedition in summer by persons discontented." Nor did things look better on the foreign front: earlier in the year Cecil had written in a confidential paper, "No prince ever had less alliance than the Queen of England hath". Elizabeth's friendless condition seemed all the more disturbing in view of the widespread fears that on the continent, the major Catholic powers were coalescing, preparatory to mounting an offensive against Protestantism. "The Pope ... and all his parties are watching adversaries to the Crown", Cecil noted broodingly, and in the late Parliament Sir Ralph Sadler had not failed to remind the Commons of the dangers that beset England: "We have heard and we hear daily of secret conspiracies and great confederacies, between the Pope, the French King, and other Princes of the Popish confederacy against all Princes Protestant and professors of the gospel, of which the Queen's Majesty is the chief patroness and protectrix at this day".[54] The alarming prospect remained that having failed to resolve the nation's inner tensions at the last session of Parliament, the Queen would in addition soon have to face a threat from abroad.

CHAPTER 7

"The general cause now of Christendom"

At two o'clock in the morning of 10 February 1567, the inhabitants of Edinburgh were awoken by the sound of an immense explosion. The blast reduced to rubble a house on the outskirts of the city named Kirk o' Field, where the Queen of Scots' husband, Darnley, had recently taken up residence to complete his convalescence after a severe illness. When concerned citizens rushed to the scene to discover what had become of him, his lifeless body was found lying in the grounds of the house. It was clear that he had survived the explosion, but had been killed shortly afterwards, having apparently been either strangled or suffocated.

Queen Mary, who was spending the night at nearby Holyrood Palace, was swiftly informed of the fate that had befallen her husband, and she professed herself appalled. She declared that she herself had been the murderers' intended victim, for she had planned to spend the night at Kirk o' Field, and the assassins had doubtless failed to realize that at the last minute she had changed her plans. She wasted no time sending letters to foreign courts, dwelling upon her miraculous escape.

Yet Mary's version of events did not gain widespread credence. It was common knowledge that she had been on the worst possible terms with her husband, for their reconciliation after Darnley had helped the Queen escape from his accomplices in the Riccio murder had lasted no more than a few days. In October 1566 the Earl of Bedford had reported from his vantage point on the borders, "The disagreement between the Queen and her husband continues, or rather increases". Subsequently Mary had discussed with her advisers the possibility of divorcing Darnley, and she had refrained from this step only because it would have automatically bastardized her son. More recently, it was true, it had appeared that Mary wished to try and make a success of her marriage. When Darnley had left Edinburgh in December to go and live with his father at Glasgow, Mary had followed him and begged him to return to the capital, and although Darnley was bedridden with an illness (he may have been suffering from syphilis), he agreed to do as his wife desired. Instead of taking him to Holyrood, Mary had installed him at Kirk o' Field so that he could complete his recovery, but she had frequently visited the invalid, and done all she could to convey the impression that the rift between them had completely healed. Inevitably, however, after Darnley's murder suspicions arose that this had been far from the case, and that Mary had only lured her husband away from his family in Glasgow in order to facilitate his violent despatch. In October 1566 Maitland had written of Mary, "It was a heartbreak to her to think that he should be her husband, and how to be free of him she sees no outgate".[1] Now it appeared that the desired escape route had been found.

It was not long before Edinburgh was abounding with well-informed rumours as to the identity of the men who had carried out the deed. Among the names mentioned was that of James, Earl of Bothwell, who in recent months had established himself as one of Mary's most trusted intimates. There was little doubt that he was capable of the crime: a contemporary described him as "high in his own conceit, proud, vicious and vainglorious above measure, one who would attempt anything out of ambition",[2] and the blowing up of Kirk o' Field was just the sort of audacious ploy calculated to commend itself to his rough nature. Within a week of the murder, anonymous placards had been erected in Edinburgh citing Bothwell as the chief assassin. On 1 March a poster appeared in which Bothwell was represented as a hare (a reference to his family crest) surrounded by swords, and above him the Queen was depicted as a mermaid – the symbol for a prostitute.

It was clear that if Mary wished to exonerate herself of complicity in the murder, she must track down and punish those responsible for it. She was told as much by Elizabeth (who herself had been so careful to observe the correct procedures after the mysterious death of Amy Robsart) in a severe letter written on 24 February. Addressing Mary coldly as "Madame", instead of the more cordial "Ma chère soeur", Elizabeth declared that she had been shocked and afflicted to hear of Darnley's "horrible and abominable murder". Caustically she continued, "Yet I cannot conceal that I grieve more for you than him. I should not do the office of a faithful cousin and friend if I did not urge you to preserve your honour, rather than look through your fingers at revenge on those who have done you such a kindness, as most people say". From France, Catherine de Medici wrote to Mary in even stronger terms, stating that if she did not punish the culprits, the French would not only think her dishonoured, but would be her enemies.[3]

Despite this, Mary did nothing effectual. Every day more and more placards were nailed up in Edinburgh, but Bothwell remained at liberty, blustering "that if he knew who were the setters up of the bills and writings, he would wash his hands in their blood".[4] By the end of March, there were rumours that he and the Queen were planning to marry, despite the fact that Bothwell already had a wife. At this the outcry grew still louder, until even Mary had to accept that it could not be altogether ignored. She agreed that Darnley's father, the Earl of Lennox, could bring a private process in Parliament, accusing Bothwell of being the murderer of his son. Yet this gesture was so perfunctory as to compound the outrage, for Bothwell's 'trial' was an out and out mockery. As the plaintiff, it was illegal for Lennox to bring to court more than six friends, and since Edinburgh was swarming with four thousand of Bothwell's adherents, Lennox did not even dare to enter the city on the appointed day. Realizing that this was his only chance of bringing Bothwell to justice, Lennox begged Elizabeth to make an application to Mary for a stay of proceedings, but when a messenger arrived in Edinburgh at dawn on the day of the hearing, bearing a request to this effect, he was not permitted to see Mary. As Bothwell rode to court, flanked by two hundred retainers, Mary looked on from an upper room of the palace, and in Parliament the case against him was dismissed for want of evidence.

On 24 April 1567 Bothwell staged an abduction of his Queen, carrying her off to the Castle of Dunbar, ostensibly against her will, but few people doubted that Mary had known and approved of his intentions beforehand. There, he made love to her, possibly for the first time and arguably without her consent, and having made sure of her in this way, he obtained a speedy divorce from his wife and married the Queen on 15 May. By dint of bold, decisive actions, and an utter contempt for all legal forms, it seemed that Bothwell had triumphed, but it needed more than mere bravado to control the Scots nobility. Many of them had had foreknowledge of Darnley's murder, and their loathing for the King had been such that they had raised no objection to it, but they had no intention of permitting Bothwell to fill the vacancy he had created.

The breathtakingly quick sequence of events in Scotland put Elizabeth in a quandary. In 1563 Bothwell had been described by Randolph as "as mortal an enemy to our whole nation as any man alive", and it was to be feared that if he were at the helm in Scotland, Anglo–Scots relations would be put under great strain. Elizabeth and her advisers had therefore been relieved by signs that the Scots aristocracy would resist Bothwell's rise to power. In early April several members of the Privy Council had instructed the Earl of Bedford at Berwick to "comfort" all those in Scotland who seemed "to mislike of Bothwell's greatness", and to encourage them to liaise with one another. On 25 April Elizabeth had decided to send Lord Grey to Scotland so that he could inform Mary that she was "greatly perplexed" by the fact that the Queen of Scots had not only failed to punish her husband's murderers, but had also extended manifest favour to "such as have been by common fame most touched with the crime", and notably the Earl of Bothwell.[5] In the event, however, these strictures were never delivered, for Mary was in Bothwell's hands before Lord Grey had even set out, and rebukes from the English Queen became a sad irrelevance.

Elizabeth was shocked to the core to learn that Mary had surrendered herself to Bothwell, and when Mary compounded her follies by marrying her abductor, the Queen's opinion of her plummeted still lower. She told Randolph frankly that she had "great misliking of that Queen's doing, which now she doth so much detest that she is ashamed of her".[6] Mary was dragging monarchy into the mire, and with each successive link in the spectacular chain of events in Scotland, it became increasingly hard to put a generous interpretation on her conduct. When her actions were dispassionately reviewed, the inference was inescapable that, having been seized with an adulterous passion for Bothwell, she had conspired with him to kill her husband so that her paramour could rule in the murdered man's stead. Certainly everything pointed that way, and much as Elizabeth would have liked to believe there was an alternative explanation, none seemed feasible at present. All the evidence that was subsequently shown to her with regard to Darnley's death merely served to confirm her in the view that Mary had deliberately turned her back on the values of civilized society, and that the obloquy heaped on her was richly deserved.

To Elizabeth it seemed incontrovertible that Mary had abused her position, but there could be no question of depriving her of it, for however wicked or unscrupulous she had been, nothing could justify her overthrow by her subjects. Elizabeth was therefore profoundly disturbed when a group of Scots nobles approached Bedford and asked what assistance they could expect from her if they acted to deliver their sovereign from the bondage of Bothwell. As Elizabeth pointed out, it was unclear what was meant by this ambiguous phrase, for once Bothwell and Mary were married their destinies would be permanently intertwined. Since the lords had expressed concern for the safety of young Prince James, Elizabeth suggested that they should obtain custody of him and then send him to England where he could grow up under her protection, but if James was not on offer, she could give them no assistance. Furthermore, she made it clear that she would strongly object if the lords made any attempt to crown James in Mary's place, for this would be "a matter hardly to be digested ... by us or any other monarch".[7]

The lords did their best to make Elizabeth reconsider. In early June they assured the Earl of Bedford that though they could not deliver the prince into Elizabeth's custody, she should not refrain from helping them, for their hostility would be directed against Bothwell alone. Swift action was necessary, for Mary was already carrying Bothwell's child, and if he fathered a son by her his position would be consolidated. As the lords had intended, Elizabeth was shocked to hear that Mary was believed to be pregnant, for it would have been impossible to tell this unless the child had been conceived out of wedlock. She commented dourly that if the news was confirmed, "It will be thought all was not well before", but even so, she still would not commit herself to assisting the lords.[8]

Despite Elizabeth's misgivings, in Scotland opposition to Mary and Bothwell continued to mount. By 6 June 1567, the aristocratic coalition arrayed against the Queen of Scots and her husband was so formidable that the newlyweds had to leave Edinburgh. A week later, they decided to return and confront their opponents, but as they marched towards the capital they did not attract as many supporters as they had hoped. When the two rival armies were drawn up in battle array on the morning of 15 June, it became clear that the royal forces were outnumbered by those of the dissident lords, and as defeat seemed virtually inevitable, Mary agreed to surrender on condition that Bothwell was granted a safe conduct. After Bothwell had galloped away (he subsequently escaped to Denmark, where he was imprisoned by the King, and died insane after eleven years in confinement), the sobbing Mary was hustled off to Edinburgh, while hostile soldiery shouted as she passed, "Burn the whore! burn her, burn her, she is not worthy to live, kill her, drown her!"[9] The following day she was conducted to the island fortress of Lochleven and incarcerated there.

When news of these events reached Elizabeth, she reacted instantaneously. Viewed dispassionately, the downfall of Mary and Bothwell was of course a fortunate development for England. In place of a Catholic queen, who had never renounced her pretensions to Elizabeth's crown, Scotland was now ruled by a clique of Protestant lords who were desperate to be on good terms with their English neighbours. Such a straightforward analysis nevertheless ignored the moral dimension, and Elizabeth was more concerned by the philosophical implications of the political upheavals in Scotland than by potential benefits that might accrue from them. She had no sympathy whatever for Mary as an individual, but her cousin's ill-judged actions could not alter what was due to her as a sovereign, and if the Scots lords were permitted to force their Queen to settle for less, this would effectively diminish the institution of monarchy itself. Elizabeth was outraged by the notion that a queen could be divested of her regal dignity as if it were no more than a tattered old cloak, and felt sure that by accepting so profane a concept, she herself would be eroding the very foundations of kingship. Her conviction that crowned heads must show solidarity with one another transcended her disgust at Mary's personal failings; to have raised no protest at the deposition and imprisonment of a fellow sovereign would have contravened the basic tenets of her creed as a ruler, to which she adhered not merely "because we ourselves are called by God's order to that estate, but that we think it so ordained by God and received for a truth in doctrine in all good Christian government".[10] Shocked and infuriated by the conduct of the Scots lords, she determined to send Sir Nicholas Throckmorton to Scotland to intervene in Mary's favour.

Throckmorton set off on 1 July. He was instructed to see Mary on his arrival in Scotland and to explain that, though Elizabeth had been shocked by her failure to punish the murderers of Darnley, and by her marriage to Bothwell, she had been still more outraged by the treatment Mary had received at the hands of her subjects. She had therefore determined "to aid and relieve her by all possible means for the recovery of her to her liberty, and not to suffer her, being by God's ordinance the Prince and Sovereign, to be in subjection to them that by nature and law are subjected to her". To the lords he was to say that Elizabeth "neither can nor will endure" that Mary should be "imprisoned, deprived of her state, or put in any peril of her person", and to insist that the Queen of Scots should be restored forthwith, albeit on the understanding that she would thenceforth have to rule in conjunction with her council and to agree to try Bothwell for the murder of Darnley.[11]

Throckmorton travelled north in deep depression, for like Cecil he believed that Elizabeth would have done better to welcome the fact that Scotland was now under a new and compatible regime, rather than to chide those who were responsible for this satisfactory state of affairs. Unwilling to reach his destination, he dawdled on the way, and had to be sent a sharp reminder that Elizabeth wished him to make haste. When he eventually arrived, however, it emerged that even had he believed in his mission implicitly, he had been set an impossible task. The lords peremptorily denied him access to Mary, saying that if she believed that the English were behind her, it would only encourage her in her determination not to abandon Bothwell. Far from discussing the terms on which they would allow Mary to resume power, they let it be known that they had not ruled out the possibility of executing her. This was a move that would have been welcome with the populace of Edinburgh, who had been inflamed by the sermons of John Knox, and were openly saying that their Queen had "no more liberty nor privilege to commit murder nor adultery than any other private person".[12]

More alarming still was the possibility that if Elizabeth declined to endorse their actions, the lords would turn their backs on England, and forge a union with Scotland's ancient ally, France. Elizabeth may have assumed that Charles IX would feel an indignation no less potent than her own at the plight of one who was not only one of the Lord's anointed, but also a former Queen of France, but this proved to be far from the case.

Anxious to renew the links with Scotland that for generations had been pivotal to French foreign policy, Charles would let neither sentiment nor orthodox political theory imperil diplomatic objectives, and he wasted no time in sending an ambassador to Scotland in order to woo the rebel lords. Throckmorton could only watch in horror as the French worked to ingratiate themselves with the Scots, noting bitterly "they take it not greatly to the heart how the Queen speed, whether she live or die, whether she be at liberty or in prison. The mark they shoot at is to renew their old league".[13]

In London, Cecil was in despair at the wanton way that Elizabeth was throwing away the fruits of seven or eight years' diplomacy with Scotland. For the moment, however, it seemed that nothing could induce her to modify her stance. She continued to rage against the lords, and if one of her advisers ventured a word in their defence, she turned her fury on him, hurling accusations that anyone who was content to see a neighbouring monarch unseated must be less than dutifully minded towards his own sovereign. "*And where such thorns be it is no quiet treading*", sighed Cecil, who himself had been the recipient of some of the Queen's most bitter jibes. It seemed that not even the most measured advice could prevail in the face of Elizabeth's dogmatic adherence to principle: Leicester told Throckmorton sadly that there was no persuading the Queen to "disguise" or "use policy". All those who urged her to be more pragmatic were greeted with torrents of abuse, and it was scant consolation to those affected that the vigour of her invective may well have owed something to the fact that she was presently in discomfort from a disagreeable crick in the neck. At the end of July, she remained so incensed against the lords that she could contemplate military intervention, instructing Throckmorton to warn them that if they deposed Mary, "We will make ourselves a plain party against them, to the revenge of their Sovereign, for example to all posterity".[14]

Elizabeth trumpeted these dreadful threats in vain. The Scots lords calculated that it was in fact highly unlikely that she would go to war with them, and even if she did so, they were confident that in that event they could count on the French coming to their support. On 24 July, Mary (who had recently miscarried of twins) was pressured into signing an instrument of abdication, and five days later thirteen-month-old Prince James was crowned in her stead. When Elizabeth was informed, she again erupted in a passion: on 11 August Cecil wrote to Throckmorton that that afternoon the Queen had "increased in such offence towards these Lords, that in good earnest she began to devise to revenge it by war". Even as she had uttered her tirade, however, a letter had been brought in from Throckmorton pointing out that, if Elizabeth continued to menace the lords with a forcible restoration of Mary, they might eliminate the danger by executing their captive, and this sobering missive had made the Queen

pause for thought. By 20 August, Cecil could express a hope to Throckmorton that hostilities with Scotland would be avoided, for though the
Queen continued to wax wrathful against the lords, he felt cautiously
optimistic that she would confine herself to verbal attacks.[15]

Sure enough, Elizabeth did not carry out her threat to declare war. On
22 August, Mary's half-brother, the Earl of Moray, was named as Regent
in Scotland, and Elizabeth made no serious efforts to unseat him. She did
agree to subsidize the Hamiltons, a Scottish clan that had vowed to restore
Mary, but after they had accepted money from Elizabeth, they then let her
down by making their peace with Moray. Her hopes that pressure could
be applied on the Scots lords if England and France imposed a joint trade
embargo on Scotland foundered because of French indifference to Mary's
fate, and Elizabeth now accepted that it would be misguided of her to press
ahead with unilateral action. Her indignation at Mary's deposition had
been sincere, but in the absence of any support from her brother monarchs
on the continent, she had realized the futility of giving vent to her annoyance. She still refused to recognize James as King, or Moray as the lawful
Regent, but gradually her enmity towards the Scots lords subsided, and
she came to accept the change of regime as an established fact.

In November 1566, Elizabeth had promised Parliament to marry "as soon
as I can conveniently". Since then, she had frequently declared that she
intended sending a nobleman to Austria to resume marriage negotiations
with Archduke Charles, but for months she had delayed doing anything.
At the end of April 1567, however, she told the Earl of Sussex to make
ready to visit the Habsburg court, ostensibly in order to present the
Emperor with the order of the Garter. Sussex was far from happy about
undertaking the mission, despite the fact that he was all in favour of a
match between the Queen and the Archduke. He was concerned that
Elizabeth was only sending him abroad to stifle complaints that she had
broken her promise to look for a husband, and that once she had wasted
time on protracted negotiations, she would find some pretext to wriggle out
of a betrothal. At a private audience with the Earl, Elizabeth nevertheless
succeeded in allaying his fears, and at the end of June, Sussex set off for
the continent.

In August 1567, the Earl arrived at Vienna, where he found the Emperor
anxious to resume negotiations on his brother's behalf. Nevertheless, the
talks did not go smoothly, for as before the Queen had stipulated that the
Archduke must convert to Protestantism before she accepted him as her
consort, and Charles's conscience was too tender to permit him to give way
on this point. Initially he and the Emperor insisted that, when in England,
Charles should be permitted to worship in public according to Catholic
rites, but when Sussex made it plain that this was out of the question, they

somewhat modified their demands, asking only that Charles could receive mass in a private chapel at Court. Charles agreed that if this was granted, he would refuse to let any Englishman attend his Catholic services, and offered to accompany Elizabeth when she went to church herself, but he was adamant that he could not renounce his faith altogether. Sussex thought this not unreasonable, and at the end of October he wrote home imploring Elizabeth to concede the Archduke the private use of his religion. He also wrote to Cecil, warning bleakly, "The universal opinion is, that if her Majesty will not satisfy him for the use of his religion, she wanteth or meaneth never to proceed in the matter".[16]

In November 1567, Elizabeth consulted her Council as to the advisability of giving way to the Archduke's demands. The Earls of Leicester and Pembroke, the Marquis of Northampton and Sir Francis Knollys all maintained that the Queen could not satisfy the Archduke in this respect. Cecil thought otherwise, but his case was weakened by the fact that the Duke of Norfolk, who also thought that she could not afford to lose this chance of marriage by being inflexible on the religious issue, was away from Court and could only state his case in writing. As the Council was divided, the Queen took some weeks to make up her mind, and suspense at Court steadily heightened as the rival parties strove to win her over to their point of view. Leicester, who was as determined as ever to thwart a foreign match, was believed to be working surreptitiously to inflame Protestant sentiment. He was said to have prompted Bishop Jewel to preach a fiery sermon at Paul's Cross attacking Catholicism, and the Duke of Norfolk complained that after he had written to the Queen urging her to come to an accommodation with the Archduke, Leicester put it about that Norfolk himself had papist leanings.[17]

In Vienna, Sussex, who was waiting impatiently to hear the Queen's decision, was infuriated when he learnt how Leicester was trying to manipulate public opinion. He attributed the Earl's righteous fervour to pure hypocrisy: "If Protestants be but only Protestants I mistrust not a good resolution", he growled in a letter to Cecil. "But if some Protestants have a second intent which they cloak with religion, and place be given to their counsel, God defend the Queen with his mighty hand and dispose of us at his pleasure".[18]

On 10 December 1567 the Queen finally gave her answer, writing to tell Sussex that she could not permit the Archduke to exercise his religion in private. She explained that not only would she be unable to square this with her conscience, but she would have to obtain the consent of Parliament before there could be any modification in the religious settlement of 1559, and she doubted that this would be forthcoming. The first reason was of course nonsense: the Queen's conscience would have been quite supple enough to accommodate the Archduke if she had believed it in her interests to do so, but her fear that it would have unfortunate domestic repercussions if she did as the Archduke required was a far more weighty objection. Uniformity in religion was a bedrock of her policy, for there was no denying that the sixteenth-century state was barely capable of withstanding the tensions generated by religious rivalries. In those countries in which an attempt had been made to bestow official recognition on more than one creed, the invariable result had been internal fissure and civil war. In Scotland, the novel experiment of a Catholic Queen ruling a Protestant country had just ended in signal failure, while in France, Catherine de Medici's attempts to extend a limited toleration to the Huguenots had again recently broken down, and in September 1567 the kingdom had been engulfed in renewed civil war. It was therefore hard to take issue with the Queen when she explained to Sussex that she had reached an unfavourable decision partly because "the present examples round about us upon diversity of religion doth directly move and urge us thereto". Despite the Archduke's professed moderation, it could scarcely have been long before he found it intolerable that his wife's subjects were denied from sharing the consolations of his faith, and conversely his arrival would put fresh heart into the English Catholics, who would not cease to agitate for the same freedom of worship that the Queen accorded her consort. Even the Duke of Norfolk, who had begged the Queen to grant the Archduke's request, did not underestimate the dangers involved, but urged that the risk was justifiable in order to avoid the "certain mischief" that would ensue if the Queen remained unmarried.[19] There was, therefore, much to be said for Elizabeth's assertion that her kingdom's stability would be wrecked if she and her husband espoused different faiths, and she knew too that her subjects would be more understanding about the breakdown in the matrimonial negotiations if they knew that it was religion which was responsible for the impasse. In 1566 Elizabeth had promised that only the death of her intended husband "or else some other great let" could prevent her from marrying, but the religious difficulty certainly qualified as a sufficiently weighty impediment, and Elizabeth was confident that it in no way reflected badly on her if she declared it to be an insuperable bar to a union with Archduke Charles.

In Vienna the Emperor was "much appalled" when he learnt that the Queen was unyielding, and Sussex likewise was shattered. He told Cecil that he was "left in a maze" by Elizabeth's decision, and made it clear that he feared for the consequences. He had already warned that if the Queen did not marry the result would be "the destruction of her own life" and "the bloodshed of her people, perhaps in her own time ... which bloody time threateneth little respect of religion, but much malice and revenge for private ambition on all sides"[20]. Now he had little doubt that these dire prophecies would come true. Despondently he bestowed the order of the

Garter upon the Emperor, and then set out for home, arriving in England in March 1568.

Elizabeth had claimed that her conscience had prevented her from according toleration to Archduke Charles, but when it came to the deposition and imprisonment of Mary Queen of Scots she had held less firmly to her principles. She still withheld official recognition from the new regime in Scotland, but by the spring of 1568, informed observers could discern signs of a thaw in the relations between the two countries. The English and the Scots were co-operating over border security, and in March 1568 Elizabeth had responded positively to a request from Moray that she should write to the King of Denmark and ask him to send Bothwell back to Scotland so that he could stand trial. In April 1568 she was prepared to do business with Moray when he decided to raise money by selling some of Mary's jewels, including some particularly fine pearls, as large as black grapes. The Queen purchased these for 12,000 ecus, much to the annoyance of Catherine de Medici, who had wanted to obtain them for herself. Despite Elizabeth's vaunted refusal to countenance the Scottish revolution, Moray and Cecil were in regular correspondence, and in one letter Moray was confident enough to remark that "although the Queen's Majesty seems not altogether to allow the present state here", he did not doubt "but she likes it in heart well enough".[21]

This cosy situation was disrupted on 2 May 1568, when the half-brother of Mary's custodian, "in fantasy of love with her", aided her to escape from Lochleven. In the ensuing days she gathered together her supporters and was marching with her troops to Dumbarton Castle when Moray decided to give battle near Glasgow on 13 May. Although the royal forces were numerically superior to the Regent's, his were better led, and at the end of the day Mary was forced to flee the field. For three days she rode south, living on sour milk and oatmeal and shaving off her auburn hair to avoid recognition. Many of those loyal to her begged her to remain in Scotland to see if the situation there could be salvaged, or else to sail to France, of which she was Queen Dowager, but Mary refused to listen. She insisted that the best course was to throw herself on the mercy of her cousin Queen Elizabeth, who alone of all European princes had been so vocal in her defence when catastrophe had struck. Failing to realize that Elizabeth had been less concerned for her welfare than to prevent an encroachment on the majesty of kingly office, on 16 May Mary crossed the Solway Firth and landed at Workington, Cumberland.

Her arrival plunged English affairs into a crisis that terminated only with Mary's execution, nineteen years later. Initially, however, it did seem as though Mary's desperate gamble would pay off: in London, the French ambassador heard that at a Council meeting convened to discuss Mary's presence in England, Elizabeth caused consternation by announcing that she wished to receive her cousin at Court with all honour, and to assist her to the best of her capabilities. Once again, this generous impulse was inspired not so much by a belief in the merits of Mary's case, as by Elizabeth's conviction that her cousin's royal dignity must be upheld come what may, and it may well have been at this juncture that she sent Mary an undated letter, coldly declaring "If not for you, yet for your honourable King that fathered you, I shall think all well employed that for his daughter I may do". The French ambassador, for one, was sure that if Mary did come to Court, the Queen and she would fall out within the week "considering the difference in beauty and grace between the two of them", but on the whole he believed that on mature reflection Elizabeth would not let Mary near her.[22] He knew that the Council had not failed to impress upon the Queen that she had compelling reasons to keep Mary at arm's length, and he deemed Elizabeth too politic a princess to ignore these.

It was, after all, obvious that it was scarcely in Elizabeth's interests to restore a Catholic queen with a claim upon the English throne to a neighbouring country that was at present ruled by well-disposed Protestants. It was true that while in Scotland Mary had kept her promise to accept Protestantism as the state religion, provided she herself was permitted to exercise her own faith. On the other hand, she had persistently refused to renounce her claim to Elizabeth's crown, and the fact that a decade before the French had proclaimed her Queen of England still told against her. For all Mary's professed moderation, Cecil and others believed it to be no more than a feint, and that at the first opportunity she would show herself the true product of her Guisan genes by seeking to overthrow her English cousin. In Cecil's eyes, Mary's marriage with Darnley, her advancement of Riccio and her elopement with the Anglophobe Bothwell were all indicative of her real intentions towards Elizabeth, and random pieces of intelligence that had reached him while Mary was on the throne had only confirmed the Secretary in his prejudice against her. In the summer of 1566, a disreputable character named Christopher Rokeby had sent Cecil a description of an audience he had had with Mary at which the latter had allegedly declared that she hoped to win the loyalty of several leading members of the English aristocracy, whom she believed "all to be of the old religion, which she meant to restore with all expedition". She had gone on to say "That after she had friended her self in every shire of England . . . she meant to cause wars be stirred in Ireland, whereby England might be kept occupied: then she would have an army in readiness, and her self with her army to enter England; and the day that she should enter, her title to be read, and she proclaimed Queen". In June 1566 Randolph had also warned that Mary was busily establishing contacts with English Catholics, and he reported that her agent in England had recently sent word to her "that the papists are ready to rise in England, when she will have them". Elizabeth had taken this sufficiently seriously to have sent Sir Henry Killigrew to Scotland to caution Mary against soliciting English subjects to support her title, and also to voice suspicions that Mary was giving aid to Shane O'Neill, who was leading an insurrection against Elizabeth in Ireland.[23]

It was doubtless misguided to assume from such incidents that Mary was intent on usurping Elizabeth's throne. The sensational depositions of paid informers were always suspect, and even if Mary had cultivated the English Catholics, she may merely have wished to ensure that if Elizabeth did die childless, she would be in a strong position to put forward her claim to succeed her. Cecil nevertheless inferred from them that Mary would never be able to resist the temptation to revive her pretensions to the crown, and he had no doubt that while at liberty she would always pose a threat. It was his belief that once Mary was back in power in Scotland, "the friends of England shall be abased and those of France increased", and even if Elizabeth imposed stringent conditions on Mary in return for assisting her to recover her throne, "how they shall afterwards be performed, wise men may doubt".[24] The Queen of Scots had been an uncomfortable neighbour in the past, and might be a committed enemy in the future, and Cecil had no desire to see her restored to the position in which she could inflict the greatest harm. At all costs therefore, it was vital that Elizabeth should refuse to see Mary, for once she had received her, it would be much more awkward to deny her requests for aid. To Cecil's relief it was not long before Elizabeth herself came to see that it would dangerously narrow her options if Mary was permitted to come to Court.

Even Cecil had to admit that if Elizabeth refused to help Mary, the alternative courses of action were scarcely very inviting. It would be acutely dangerous to let Mary go to France, for if the French were instrumental in restoring her to her throne, Mary would be indebted to them, and French dominance in Scotland – with all that that implied – would be successfully re-established. On the other hand, it would be only marginally less perilous to detain Mary in England against her will. As Elizabeth had constantly reiterated, potential successors to the crown formed a natural focus for plots against the reigning incumbent, and Mary posed a particular threat in this respect. In the eyes of Catholics, Elizabeth's claim to the throne was seriously flawed, while Mary's was arguably superior, and the temptation for disaffected papists to push her claim would be the greater because an uprising in her favour might well secure support from abroad. All of the Catholic powers of Europe had good reason to want Mary in Elizabeth's place, and in particular the King of France was under a special obligation to act as her champion. It was true that when Mary had been overthrown he had not lifted a finger in her defence, but that was because he had believed he had much to gain from acquiescing in her captivity, and now that she was in England, the reverse might be the case.

It was clear that the situation admitted of no easy solution. In one respect, however, the English were fortunate, for in December 1568 the Scots lords had announced that they had written evidence that proved that Mary was an accessory to Darnley's murder. As Mary's reputation lay under such a stigma, Elizabeth could use this as a reason to deny her her presence, and should the Queen decide that Mary should be kept in England, the documents in the possession of the Scots might well provide an excuse for putting their Queen under restraint.

If Elizabeth really had contemplated inviting Mary to Court, she changed her mind within days. On her arrival at Workington, Mary had written to her cousin, "I entreat you to send to fetch me as soon as you possibly can, for I am in a pitiable condition, not only for a Queen but for a gentle-woman". She explained that she had arrived with "nothing in the world but what I had on my person when I made my escape", but though she had clearly assumed that her plight could not fail to excite sympathy, the desired invitation did not come. Instead, Elizabeth arranged for Mary to be conducted to Lord Scrope's castle at Carlisle, and when she was installed there, Sir Francis Knollys travelled up from the south to see her. He declared to Mary that Elizabeth was "inwardly sorry and very much grieved" that she was unable to receive her at present on account "of this great slander of murder whereof she was not yet purged". He added that even if Mary could not satisfactorily establish her innocence concerning this matter, he was sure that she could count on Elizabeth assisting her to regain her throne. Taken aback by her cousin's aloofness, Mary "fell into some passion with the water in her eyes", but she was in no position to protest, and so, having wept for a time, "discontentedly she contented herself therewith".[25]

She was not even cheered by the arrival in early June of a fresh supply of clothes that Elizabeth had despatched to her, for when the consignment appeared, it emerged that the Queen had picked out some of the most unprepossessing garments in her wardrobe for her cousin's use. Knollys was so embarrassed that he pretended to Mary that the selection had been made by a maidservant of Elizabeth's, who was under the misapprehension that the clothes were intended for one of Mary's waiting women, but in fact the choice of articles had been no mistake. Elizabeth had assembled the items in a fit of petty spite, and far from being ashamed of her mean-spiritedness, she thought that Mary should count herself fortunate to be in receipt of her charity. When Knollys made no mention of how Mary had reacted, Elizabeth wrote a petulant letter, demanding to know if her gifts had gone down well.[26]

In the meantime, Queen and council had been pondering what to do with

Mary. As ever when faced with a problem, Cecil drew up a memorandum on the subject, outlining with clerkly precision the various courses that Elizabeth could adopt. The first priority, he noted succinctly, was that the evidence concerning Mary's complicity in the murder of her husband should be sent to England. If, on inspection of these papers, it emerged that she was innocent of the crime, then she should be restored to the Scottish throne forthwith. On the other hand, "If her cause prove criminal", then the English had two alternatives: either she could "be restored to her country with some sure limitations and restrictions", or else, "according to the excess and quantity of the crime", she could "live in some convenient place, without possessing of her kingdom, where she may not move any new trouble". There is little doubt that from the first Cecil favoured the latter course of keeping many in England against her will, but the indications are that at this stage Elizabeth contemplated a conditional restoration of her cousin, for in a paper of 30 June Cecil noted that Elizabeth's aim was "to have some good end to grow betwixt the Queen [of Scots] and her subjects . . . by reasonable and honourable condition . . . with sufficient surety for all parties".[27] As the summer progressed, however, Elizabeth's temper hardened, and by late September 1568 it would appear that her attitude to Mary was substantially in line with that of Cecil.

It was nevertheless a far from simple matter to arrange an enquiry into the Darnley murder. An examination could only be held if Mary agreed to send representatives to attend the hearing, for no authority would be attached to its verdict if her case had not been fully stated. Unfortunately, there could be no certainty that Mary would co-operate, for as a Queen she could pertinently claim that she was not subject to foreign jurisdiction, and that Elizabeth had no authority to pronounce on her guilt or innocence with regard to her husband's death. It was therefore necessary to convince her that it was in her interests to let the English preside over the investigation, and for her to participate in the proceedings as wholeheartedly as possible.

Conversely, however, there was the awkward possibility that Moray, who was in possession of the evidence against Mary, would not wish to produce it if he thought that Elizabeth planned to restore her to her throne regardless of whether or not Mary was to blame for Darnley's murder. Before doing so, Elizabeth could in theory make Mary promise that she would not punish the men responsible for her deposition, but it was hard to see how the English would manage to protect Moray once the Queen of Scots was back in power. At Carlisle, Mary was making no secret of the fact that "she would go into Turkey rather than she would have any peace or agreement with the Lord of Moray",[28] and Moray knew that her attitude towards him would be still more venomous if he did anything to blacken her name at a public enquiry.

Realizing that there could be no form of trial until the misgivings of the principals in the case had been overcome, Elizabeth despatched north Henry Middlemore, with instructions first to visit Mary and to persuade her to collaborate, and then to see Moray in Scotland to find out whether he was prepared to come to England in order to accuse his half-sister. Middlemore saw Mary on 14 June, and having explained that Elizabeth could not receive her "until some good trial were made of her innocency", he assured her that provided Mary consented to such a proceeding, the Queen would "do every way for her that which she could desire". Mary did not receive the suggestion well: to Middlemore "She brake forth ... into some piece of choler, and said she had no other judge but God ... She knew her degree of estate well enough". She protested that if Elizabeth had been prepared to hear her explanation of the events surrounding the Darnley murder, she would have related to her the whole story, "But how can that be when the Queen my sister will not suffer me to come at her?" She would not be so open, she added, with any deputies that Elizabeth selected to hear her case, for "If I would say anything of myself, I would say of myself to her, and to none other". "All this was not done, Sir", Middlemore related to Cecil, "without great passion and weeping, complaining of her evil usage and contrarious handling to her expectation".[29] With Mary in her present frame of mind, the chances of holding the sort of enquiry that Elizabeth desired seemed very dim.

In the ensuing six weeks, however, Mary was given no reason to hope that Elizabeth would relent and hear her case in person. On 20 June, the Council confirmed that it would be unthinkable for the Queen either to restore Mary to her kingdom, or to permit her to leave the country unless she previously had been subjected to some form of trial, and Elizabeth did not dissent. A fortnight later, she wrote coldly to Mary that she found it "very strange" that she "would not answer but before myself", and urged her sharply "to have some consideration of me, instead of always thinking of yourself". Mary continued to send affecting pleas, begging her cousin to reconsider ("Good sister, change your mind ... " she implored the Queen in early July. "Alas! do not as the serpent that stops his hearing, for I am no enchanter, but your sister and natural cousin"), but she failed to penetrate Elizabeth's reserve. In the circumstances there was little left for Mary to do, for though on occcasion she lost her temper and raged to Knollys that if the English did not set her free, "we should have much ado with her",[30] she was scarcely in a position to carry out these threats.

Eventually Mary realized that she had little alternative but to agree that Elizabeth's representatives could adjudicate on her case, but she dropped her resistance only after receiving specific assurances from the Queen that she would be restored to her throne, whatever the outcome of the hearing. Towards the end of July, Elizabeth had sent Mary a message promising that if she was cleared of Darnley's murder, she "would absolutely set her in her seat regal, and that by force". She explained that all she would ask in return was that Mary would sign an alliance with England which would preclude her asserting her claim to the throne in Elizabeth's lifetime, and also that Mary would forsake the mass in favour of the Book of Common Prayer. On the other hand, if Moray and his confederates managed to prove that Mary's behaviour had been such that they had been justified in taking action against her ("which her Highness thinks they cannot do", Elizabeth commented in a soothing aside), Mary would still be restored, but would be subject to the restriction that she must keep her half-brother and the other lords as her councillors. Still Mary hesitated, being reluctant to commit herself to renouncing Catholicism, but on 28 July she finally gave in and agreed to "submit her cause to her Highness in thankful manner".[31]

The undertaking which Elizabeth had given Mary could hardly have been more explicit, but to Moray the Queen had expressed herself in entirely contradictory terms. When she had sent word to the Regent that he must come to England to answer for his reasons in deposing Mary, he had been understandably wary, for he had no wish to give a detailed account of the evidence against Mary if there was no guarantee that this would suffice to keep her off the throne. On 22 June he had accordingly written to Elizabeth, asking what she would do if he did denounce Mary, and "in case we prove all that we allege". For nearly three months, during which the Queen was evidently wrestling with her conscience, there had been no reply, but on 20 September Elizabeth finally broke her silence. She wrote to Moray sending him a private assurance that although it was reported that she intended to restore Mary even if she were clearly culpable of Darnley's murder, this was not in fact the case.[32] It was of course impossible for Moray to be sure that Elizabeth would not subsequently renege on her word by forcing him to accept Mary as his Queen, but her affirmation at least gave him some hope that so long as he played his cards aright in this political game of poker, the outcome might prove to his advantage. Much encouraged by this, he signified that he would attend the commission of enquiry.

It was decided that the case should be heard at York, and at the beginning of October commissioners for all parties assembled in the northern capital. Mary herself would not be present, but was to be represented by Lord Herries and the Bishop of Ross, an urbane and wily churchman who had been a member of Mary's Scottish Privy Council, and who was now one of her foremost advisers. The Scots lords' contingent included both Moray and Maitland of Lethington, although the latter had recently come to regret that Mary had been deprived of her throne. Far from numbering himself among Mary's enemies, he had come to York in hopes of preventing Moray from inflicting further damage on her reputation, and was anxious to secure a settlement that was not in the least injurious to her. The English commissioners were the Duke of Norfolk, the Earl of Sussex and Sir Ralph Sadler.

Elizabeth's instructions to her commissioners show that she wanted to encourage the Scots lords to produce their evidence against Mary. The lords were to be given verbal confirmation of her earlier statement that she would think Mary "unworthy of a kingdom" if it could be "plainly proved" that she had been involved in her husband's murder, but they were also to be warned that if the case against Mary was purely circumstantial, then Elizabeth would restore her. This procedure was followed, but Moray was still anxious to do nothing impetuous, and the conference had barely got under way when on 9 October he brought it to a standstill by privately asking the English commissioners whether they were invested with the authority to declare Mary guilty of murder if the case against her proved sound. Furthermore, he made it plain that it was not enough to say that Mary would not be restored if her complicity was established, for he also wanted to know whether she would subsequently be delivered up to the Scots for punishment, or kept in permanent confinement in England.[33] The English commissioners' instructions were too circumscribed to enable them to answer these questions, and proceedings were adjourned while the points at issue were referred to London for the Queen's consideration.

In the meantime, Moray tried to whet the appetite of the English by giving them a foretaste of the sort of material that could be adduced against Mary, for on 11 October he gave Norfolk and his colleagues a private viewing of the infamous "casket letters". These compromising documents, encased "in a little coffer of silver and gilt", had allegedly been recovered from a servant of Bothwell's shortly after Mary had fallen into the Scots lords' hands. In the intervening centuries they have given rise to a historical controversy of immense dimensions, in which their authenticity has been constantly challenged. Mary's defenders have maintained that the lords used trickery to cobble together this incriminating collection of papers, and that among other devices, they inserted forged interpolations into genuine letters of Mary's, and also made use of old love letters which had been written to Bothwell by a former mistress, and pretended that they were the work of the Scots Queen. At the time, however, these ingenious explanations were never put forward in Mary's defence. Mary herself told her commissioners that if the Scots lords produced any damaging letters that purported to be from her, these documents would be "false and feigned, forged and invented by themselves, only to my dishonour and slander". She observed that it was very easy to counterfeit her hand, but did not go into further details, and her blanket repudiation of the letters did nothing to explain how it was they contained matters "in them . . . such as could hardly be invented or devised by any other than by her self, for that they discourse on some things which were unknown to any other than to herself and Bothwell". After his first viewing of them, the Duke of Norfolk wrote in horror that the letters revealed "such inordinate love between her and Bothwell, her loathsomeness and abhorring of her husband that was murdered, in such sort as every good and godly man cannot but detest and abhor the same". When Elizabeth herself subsequently inspected the originals, she evinced not the least doubt that they were genuine, and remarked that they "contained many matters very unmeet to be repeated before honest ears, and easily drawn to be apparent proofs against the Queen".[34]

Norfolk had been appalled by what he had seen, but now that he knew how shocking the letters were, he felt it essential that their contents remained a closely guarded secret. Whatever the Queen of Scots' failings, it could never be forgotten that if Elizabeth died, her crown would in all probability pass to Mary, particularly in view of the fact that Mary's leading competitor, Lady Katherine Grey, had died of tuberculosis in January 1568. Bearing this in mind, Norfolk did not want Mary to be irrevocably discredited by having her letters broadcast, and he thought it would be most irresponsible of Elizabeth to permit her likely successor to be exposed to public infamy in this way.

Norfolk's doubts were artfully exploited by Maitland when the two of them went on a hawking expedition a few days later, for Maitland was himself most anxious to prevent the letters' contents from becoming common knowledge. Maitland told the Duke that it was unfair that Mary was saddled with the blame for Darnley's murder, and then went on to say that he thought it would be in the best interests of all parties if Mary were to obtain a divorce from Bothwell and married Norfolk instead. The Duke (whose wife had recently died) was intrigued by the suggestion, and though at the moment it was not practicable to pursue the idea further, he thought it had great merit. He repaid Maitland for his confidences by revealing that he knew that Elizabeth had no intention of either restoring Mary to her throne or of pronouncing her guilty of murder. All she wanted was to be provided with an excuse to keep Mary in England, and for that reason she wanted the evidence against her to be aired. Once Mary had been disgraced, but not formally condemned, she could be kept in reserve, and if at some later date it suited Elizabeth to hand back the Scottish crown to her, she would still be free to do so. Since Norfolk made it plain that he was opposed to this Machiavellian strategy, Maitland suggested that the Duke should seek out Moray and warn him of Elizabeth's intentions, for the Regent was hardly likely to press forward with his accusation of Mary if there was any chance of her subsequent restoration.[35] Norfolk did as he was bid, and having been alerted to the manner in which Elizabeth was planning to betray him, Moray became more uncertain than ever whether it would be safe for him to produce his evidence against Mary.

In London, Elizabeth was unaware of these manoeuvres, but it was nevertheless apparent to her that the enquiry was not taking the direction she had hoped. Moray was proving hard to coax into producing the Casket Letters, and rumours were also reaching her that Norfolk's integrity was not above reproach.[36] In the circumstances she thought it desirable that the proceedings should be transferred to a location where she could supervise them more closely, and on 3 November she informed Norfolk that the next session of the conference should be held at Westminster, later in the month. To make sure that this time all went according to plan, she added various councillors to the commission, including Cecil and Sir Nicholas Bacon, both of whom were held to be hostile to Mary's cause. When Moray arrived in London towards the end of November, Elizabeth accorded him the privilege of a private audience, at which she presumably strove to reassure him that he would have nothing to fear if he produced his evidence against Mary. Having taken these precautions, she was happy to let the conference proceed, and though she herself decided not to attend, she felt confident that she would be able to monitor the proceedings from nearby Hampton Court.

When the conference re-opened on 26 November, the English commissioners gave Moray an official undertaking that if Mary was found guilty, "which was much to be lamented", Elizabeth would recognize James as King, and would either hand Mary over to the Scots, or else keep her securely in England. Thus reassured, Moray then read out a formal accusation, alleging "that Bothwell was the chief murderer of the late King, and the Queen the chief persuader, commander and maintainer of him", and when Mary's commissioners denied the charge, he promised to produce conclusive proofs. On 3 December, Mary's commissioners requested in writing that Mary should be given permission to appear before the conference so that she could answer the accusations in person, but this was the last thing that Elizabeth wanted. It was obvious that if Mary spoke in her own defence she would assert that she was not the author of the Casket Letters, and in the face of her solemn disavowals it would be difficult to maintain that the letters were nonetheless admissible evidence. Elizabeth therefore smoothly replied that if Mary's commissioners were not permitted to answer on her behalf, it would give rise to the unfortunate impression that the case against her was so strong that her only chance of overturning it lay in making a personal appearance and denying the charges upon her word as a Queen. Solicitously, Elizabeth explained that she did not want Mary to degrade herself in this way, for she was confident that Moray's case would not stand up to scrutiny, and that Mary's name would be cleared without there being any need to resort to such desperate measures.[37]

On 6 December the Bishop of Ross and Herries announced that as the Queen had rejected Mary's request, they were withdrawing from the conference. Since Mary was no longer represented, the hearings should in theory have been terminated, but her commissioners' submission was overturned on a technicality, and the conference was therefore still in being when on 7 December Moray finally nerved himself to produce the Casket Letters.

The letters caused the expected sensation. To maximize the impact, on 14 December Elizabeth assembled her Privy Councillors and all the principal peers of the realm at Hampton Court, and there exhibited to them the controversial documents. All present expressed their shock at the "foul matters" within the text, and agreed that since Mary's crimes were "upon things now produced made more apparent", it was unthinkable for Elizabeth to receive her cousin at Court. Accordingly Elizabeth sent word to Mary that she must either empower her representatives to refute Moray's charges on her behalf, or else make a personal statement to a committee of English noblemen whom the Queen would send north to hear her explanation. Mary rejected both alternatives: "To answer otherwise than in person before your presence, she sayeth she never meant", Knollys informed Elizabeth.[38] This brought proceedings effectively to stalemate, for Mary could not be found guilty until she had put forward a defence and it had been found wanting. On 10 January 1569 Elizabeth therefore declared that she was unable to pronounce for or against the Queen of Scots and, as Norfolk had predicted, matters remained in suspense.

The outcome proved beyond doubt that Elizabeth was a consummate tactician, for she had achieved her aim of disgracing Mary without passing judgment on a Queen. The story is of course a far from edifying one: having been tricked into countenancing the conferences at York and Westminster, Mary had been denied a chance to conduct her own defence, and now was to be kept in England even though nothing had been formally proved against her. Moray also had been deliberately misled by Elizabeth, and both he and his sister had reason to resent their treatment at the hands of a Queen who was fond of averring that there could be "no duer debt than prince's word". Undeniably, "policy had been preferred before truth"[39] in order for things to turn out as Elizabeth wished, but the Queen nevertheless felt that she had emerged from the conference with her honour intact. Only by allowing the evidence against Mary to be ventilated had it been possible for Elizabeth to justify her refusal to restore her, but her aim had been always to vindicate her own actions, rather than to condemn Mary for hers. She had no doubt that Mary was both an adulteress and a murderer, but had managed to avoid formally labelling her as either, and in according her such consideration she prided herself on having treated her cousin better than she deserved.

Now that it had become apparent that Mary's stay in England would not be a brief one, it was necessary to make long-term provision for her maintenance. To his dismay, the Earl of Shrewsbury was appointed Mary's guardian, a burdensome post not merely because of the awesome responsibility it imposed upon him, but also because the allowance from the government which in theory was meant to reimburse him for the cost of keeping Mary and her household, proved quite insufficient to cover his expenses. In January 1569, Mary was removed to Tutbury, the dilapidated Staffordshire castle which, of all the residences between which she was to be shunted in the coming years, she came to loathe the most.

Mary may have been safely ensconced in a Midlands fortress, but the government could not feel that she was truly secure. Despite the imputation of murder which clung to her, sympathy for her plight was not lacking, and even those who did not think that she had been ill-used frequently found their attitude softening once they were in her presence. Sir Francis Knollys himself, a man renowned for his detestation of all things Romish, had shown signs of succumbing to Mary's charm, and if so doughty a Puritan as he could prove so susceptible, it was difficult to rely on anyone remaining immune. "Surely she is a rare woman!" he exclaimed of Mary on one occasion, and after his very first meeting with her he had spoken warmly of her "eloquent tongue" and "discreet head", and noted that she had "a stout courage and a liberal heart joined there-unto". No one knew better than Mary how to make herself agreeable, and Knollys could not help being touched when she fashioned little gifts to be passed on to his wife, or played psalms to him on the virginals and administered "princely medicine" to him when he was ill. When Knollys handed over his charge to Shrewsbury, it was understandable that the Council felt nervous that he might one day be suborned from his loyalty by his beguiling captive, and his instructions contained stern reminders that he "must, by no pretence ... allow her to gain rule over him, or practise for her escape".[40]

Even assuming that Shrewsbury remained incorruptible, Mary would be able to enlist others in her behalf. Knollys had pointed out the danger that "with devices of towels, or toys at her chamber window or elsewhere, in the night a body of her agility and spirit may escape" and it was to be feared that there were all too many people in England who would be prepared to connive at such a scheme. Nicholas White, a government official who stayed overnight at Tutbury in January 1569, counselled Cecil to permit few men to have access to Mary, for contact with her was bound to prove unsettling. "She hath withal an alluring grace, a pretty Scottish accent, and a searching wit, clouded with mildness", he told Cecil (though tactfully he qualified this with the comment that Mary was "not comparable to our sovereign"), and he predicted that "Fame might move some to relieve her, and glory joined to gain might stir others to adventure much for her sake".[41]

Cecil did not take such warnings lightly, for he had an almost superstitious terror of Mary's bewitching qualities. It did not escape him that Mary managed to captivate those most prejudiced against her after only the briefest of acquaintanceships, and he noted darkly, "She is able, by her great wit and sugared eloquence to win even such as before they shall come to her company shall have a great misliking". For Elizabeth, who had the utmost contempt for Mary's character, and who only evinced any regard for her because she had once been a queen, it was particularly galling that Mary should have such striking success on the purely personal level. She once remarked angrily that there must be something "divine about the speech and appearance of the said Queen of Scots, in that one or the other obliges her very enemies to speak well of her".[42] Mary may have assured Elizabeth that she was "no enchanter", but now that her cousin was immured in her realm, Elizabeth would find by bitter experience that her powers of fascination did indeed border on the magical.

It was unfortunate that Mary's internment in England, which could hardly fail to destabilize the realm, should have coincided with several dangerous developments in the foreign policy sphere. For some time now, there had been a growing coolness between England and France: not only were the French annoyed by depredations on their shipping by English pirates, but the renewed outbreak of civil war in France had also given rise to friction, for despite the fact that Elizabeth now knew better than to intervene openly on the Protestants' behalf, Charles IX and his mother were sure that she was sending the Huguenots covert assistance in the form of money and supplies. Mary Stuart's arrival in England had only heightened the tension between the two countries, and if the French had wanted an excuse to declare war, Mary's continued detention furnished them with a ready-made grievance which they could at any time state to be intolerable.

France was of course England's traditional enemy, so there was at least no novelty in the two kingdoms being on less than friendly terms. In contrast, the English had always striven to maintain favourable relations with Spain, but though for the past ten years shared commercial interests and a mutual fear of France had sufficed to keep in being an uneasy understanding between Elizabeth and King Philip, there were ominous signs that the latter was troubled in his conscience at continuing to abet a heretic queen. This suggested that the accord between them would not last indefinitely.

The pressures that could drive England and Spain apart were illustrated by a diplomatic incident that occurred in April 1568, when Philip II refused to give any more audiences to Elizabeth's ambassador at Madrid, Dr John

Man. Earlier that year, Elizabeth had been annoyed to hear from Man that he and his household were not permitted to exercise their religion within the privacy of the embassy building, despite the fact that such a privilege was accorded to the Spanish ambassador in London. She had instructed Man to see the King and obtain a redress of this grievance, but Philip was warned of this in time to deny Man an audience. He justified this on the grounds that Man's conduct in Madrid had been consistently indiscreet, and claimed that on one occasion he had even gone so far as to refer to the Pope as "a canting little monk". Possibly because she suspected that Philip did have some cause for complaint, Elizabeth had initially reacted quite mildly when she heard that Man had been excluded from the royal presence (although from the start Cecil had regarded it as an outrage), but subsequently she came round to the view that it was the King who was at fault, and did not conceal that she found his treatment of her accredited representative highly insulting. Man was recalled from Spain and never replaced, and the Queen's decision that it was more trouble than it was worth to maintain an ambassador at Madrid emphasized that she and Philip were steadily growing more distant.[43]

More serious than the rumpus over Dr Man was Philip's decision to send a new ambassador to England in place of Guzman de Silva, an urbane and reasonable cleric with whom Elizabeth had enjoyed transacting business. He was succeeded by Don Guerau de Spes, and despite de Silva's assurance that Elizabeth would find the new arrival "a gracious and pacific minister", the very reverse turned out to be the case. Don Guerau was both a religious bigot and political incendiary, whose incorrigible tendency to overestimate the forces of opposition to Elizabeth's government led him into irresponsible intrigues and blatant attempts to foment rebellion. Untiring in his efforts to destabilize the realm, even when his superiors urged him to be conciliatory, over the next three years de Spes alone bore much of the responsibility for the widening estrangement between England and Spain.

De Spes arrived in England at the beginning of September 1568, a peculiarly unfortunate juncture in view of the fact that Spanish activities in the Netherlands were at that time arousing universal concern. Although they formed part of Philip II's inheritance, the Low Countries were no mere apanage of Spain. They had a powerful nobility of their own, the most important of whom were members of the Council of State, the institution which gave advice on policy matters to Philip's half-sister Margaret of Parma, whom the King had appointed Regent in 1559. A further check on royal authority lay in the fact that the Netherlands did not constitute a single, unified state, but were made up of a loose confederation of seventeen provinces, known (somewhat inaccurately) as the United Provinces. In some matters these were under the direction of the central government at Brussels, but each province had a representative assembly of its own, as well as a set of local privileges which their ruler swore to uphold. The slightest hint that Philip was thinking of rationalizing these arrangements provoked instant protest. In the early 1560s the King on several occasions had had to retreat before pressure of public opinion, dropping a plan to billet three thousand Spanish soldiers in the Netherlands because of vociferous objections from his subjects, and dismissing his unpopular minister, Cardinal Granvelle, after complaints from the nobles that he was seeking to exclude them from power.

Philip had been prepared to compromise in the administrative sphere, but he would make no concessions in his bid to stamp out heresy in the Low Countries, a problem that he was aware was becoming more acute. Catholicism remained very much the religion of the majority, but Protestant churches were springing up all over the Netherlands, and Calvinist doctrines were being propagated there by French refugees who had fled from the civil wars in their homeland. The fight against heresy in the Netherlands was ruthlessly conducted by a state inquisition, but though its activities were bitterly resented, Philip was deaf to pleas that the persecution should be less severe. Nevertheless, local resistance to the inquisition had effectively hampered its operations, and in April 1566 Margaret of Parma had had to agree that the laws against heresy should not be so stringently enforced. The result was a great upsurge in Calvinism, with vast prayer-meetings, addressed by itinerant preachers, being held in the open air, while the authorities looked on helplessly. Under the influence of inflammatory sermons, the masses became turbulent, and in August 1566 an iconoclastic fury swept the Netherlands, as rampaging crowds stormed through towns, sacking churches, destroying images, and smashing any object that smacked to them of idolatry. In a bid to contain the violence, Margaret granted a limited freedom of worship, but when it became clear the Calvinists would accept no restrictions whatever on the practice of their religion, she accepted that she had lost control of the situation and appealed to Philip for aid.

Incensed by the collapse of religious uniformity, and by the nobles' failure to prevent the iconoclastic excesses, in October 1566 Philip resolved to send an army to the Netherlands. The Duke of Alva was put in command of these troops, but their despatch was delayed until the following spring. By that time, however, Margaret of Parma had managed to recover her authority by sending forces to attack the chief centres of Calvinism, and these had surrendered one by one. By the spring of 1567, Calvinist worship was again prohibited, and Margaret could feel a renewed trust in the leading nobility, for when the unrest of the previous summer had escalated into open revolt, they had rallied to the Regent's side, and helped her to crush all resistance. She duly informed her brother that it was no longer necessary to send Alva, but Philip was now convinced that disaffection had gone too far to be overlooked, and refused to recall the Duke.

Alva arrived in Brussels in August 1567, accompanied by ten thousand Spanish soldiers. At once the purge began: he arrested the provinces' most important nobles, Egmont and Hoorn, and set up the Council of Troubles – swiftly nicknamed the Council of Blood – to try those guilty of religious and political disaffection. In the next five years this institution would be responsible for over a thousand executions, and the death toll would have been much higher if hordes of people (a recent estimate is sixty thousand)[44] had not fled the realm, many of them finding refuge in England.

In England, the official attitude to Alva's appointment was that if Philip wished to restore order in his domains by this means, he was fully entitled to do so. At the beginning of 1567 the Spanish ambassador had notified Elizabeth that Philip would be sending an army to the Netherlands, and the Queen had been most indignant when de Silva had taken the opportunity of saying that there were some rumours that the English had been giving encouragement to the disobedient Calvinists. Hotly she had responded that "If any of her Council were to dare to advise her to such a wicked course, she would hang him as a traitor". A year later, she apparently remained of the same mind, for she told de Silva she was "opposed strongly to such proceedings of subjects against their rulers, and particularly in the case of your Majesty and your dominions, which should never be molested by England, at least while she was Queen".[45]

In reality, however, Alva's presence in the Netherlands could not but be a source of acute disquiet to the Queen. While the provinces retained a quasi-autonomous status, relations between them and England rested on a stable basis, for the two economies were to a large extent interdependent, with both trading partners finding in the other's markets an indispensable outlet for their goods. However, once Philip had succeeded in fashioning the provinces into a mere subject state of Spain, his foreign policy could be shaped without regard to the interests of its inhabitants and, if he so desired, he could ignore their wishes to maintain their ties with England, and instead declare war on Elizabeth. That this was indeed his ultimate aim was a danger that could not be lightly overlooked, for it was to be feared that having stamped out Protestantism within his own territories, and deprived the Netherlands of the last vestiges of independence, he would be tempted to do the same elsewhere. Certainly, after he had subjugated the Netherlands, he would be ideally placed to break with Elizabeth, for the Low Countries could be transformed from a peaceable commercial centre on friendly terms with its neighbours into a military base, bristling with soldiers and sophisticated weaponry, and the forces stationed there could at any time be transported across the Narrow Seas and used for the occupation of England.

By the autumn of 1568, the Duke of Alva seemed well on his way to accomplishing his task. Egmont and Hoorn had been executed and, now that the Council of Troubles had effectively terrorized all sections of the populace, Alva was thinking of ways to consolidate these achievements by instituting a permanent system of taxation. All this had not been done without resistance, it is true, for in the course of 1568 Netherlands patriots had mounted no less than four invasion attempts in the hope of toppling Alva, but all had turned out disastrously. The last incursion had been led by William of Orange, a leading member of the nobility who had wisely fled the realm before Alva's arrival, and despite being routed he vowed to continue the struggle against Spain. For the moment, however, it appeared inconceivable that he had any chance of success, and nothing seemed to stand between Alva and final victory. Elizabeth did not lack advisers who were convinced that once Alva had mopped up the last strands of resistance, he would train his sights on her, one of the foremost of these being her ambassador in Paris, Sir Henry Norris. In September 1568 Norris delivered a sombre warning that "It is ordered and fully agreed that if the Duke of Alva do bring his purpose to desired effect in Flanders he will forthwith invade England".[46]

Neither Elizabeth nor Cecil yet saw the situation in quite such stark terms, but they were well aware of a potential danger, and even at this stage there were times when the Queen believed that action would be necessary to prevent the Spaniards effecting a total conquest. In July 1568 Cecil told one of his correspondents, "The triumph of the Duke of Alva ... hath caused the Queen's Majesty to give some hearing to such as think her security cannot have continuance if the planets keep this course". For the moment, however, she thought the best course was to wait upon events, and she dared give no more than minimal encouragement to Alva's opponents. In the summer of 1568 she did not prevent a band of Netherlands refugees who had settled in England from returning to their homeland in order to fight Alva, but this did little good, for they were swiftly captured and annihilated. A few months before this, she had also given a friendly reception to an emissary sent by William of Orange, and as 1568 progressed she likewise dropped all pretence that she took a benevolent interest in Alva's activities in the Netherlands. When the newly arrived de Spes told her in the autumn that Philip was planning to reinforce his army of occupation there, the Queen exclaimed angrily, "So the King of Spain wishes to torment this people still further!"[47]

Thus it was that at the end of 1568 Elizabeth was feeling in a far from friendly mood towards Spain, and it was at this juncture that she was presented with an opportunity to spite Philip. On 29 November 1568 several Spanish ships that were carrying about £85,000 worth of treasure towards the Netherlands were forced to take refuge in English harbours in order to escape the numerous pirates who were cruising in the Channel at that time. Initially it seemed that Elizabeth was going to accord full protection to the vessels and their cargo, for on 12 December she issued a passport for the treasure to be carried overland from Plymouth and Southampton to Dover, where it could be transported to the Netherlands by sea swiftly and with less chance of capture. In the course of the next week, however, she discovered that the money belonged not to Philip, but to various Genoese merchants, who had undertaken to loan the King the money once it arrived at Antwerp, but were transporting it there at their own risk. Since it was not technically Philip's property, this gave Elizabeth an excuse to detain the treasure in England, although it would be rash to assume that from the outset she had determined to appropriate the cash for herself. As she was aware that Alva intended to use the money to pay his troops, she may have contemplated no more than letting it reach him in instalments – which would hamper his war effort without constituting unbearable provocation – and, almost certainly, the most that she would have dared to do was retain a small portion in the form of a handling charge.[48]

De Spes nevertheless thought otherwise. By 22 December he had already leapt to the conclusion that the Queen intended to filch the money for herself, and the prospect so inflamed him that he at once wrote to the Duke of Alva urging him to confiscate all English property in the Netherlands. When the Queen next saw de Spes, a week later, she remained non-committal about what she planned to do with the treasure, but by that time Alva had already acted, seizing English ships and arresting their crews without waiting to check that de Spes's hunch had been correct. Thus Elizabeth was able to complain that Alva had adopted punitive measures without any justification, and that she was entitled to retaliate in kind. De Spes was accordingly placed under house arrest, and on 7 January 1569 all Netherlandish and Spanish shipping in English harbours was put under restraint. This move more than made up for the forfeitures in the Low Countries, as the contents of the vessels seized by the English proved more valuable than those in Alva's hands.

It soon became clear that Alva regretted his precipitate action, for within a fortnight he sent an envoy to England in hopes of patching up the quarrel. Feeling that she was now in an advantageous position, Elizabeth refused to see him, and as a result in March Alva banned all subjects of the Low Countries from trading with England. This damaged his own position, as it caused serious commercial disruption in the Netherlands, but it did also adversely affect the English: it has been estimated that because of the decline in trade, the Crown lost an average of £4,000 every year that the embargo remained in being. Nevertheless the results were not nearly as harmful as they might have been, because in 1567 Cecil had negotiated an agreement with the port of Hamburg, whereby the leading English trading company, the Merchant Adventurers, were permitted to set up a depot there. In the spring of 1569 a merchant fleet set sail for Hamburg and did good business there, and having found an adequate alternative to the facilities at Antwerp, the pressure was less on Elizabeth and Cecil to find a way of bringing an end to the embargo. At times it even brought unexpected windfalls, for whenever a Spanish ship was blown into an English harbour in the next few years, it was seized and its wares were impounded by the authorities.[49]

Viewed narrowly, therefore, the episode was a profitable one for the English, but the consequences could not be measured in economic terms alone. The seizure of the payships can be said to have ignited a slow-burning fuse, for the incident helped transmute what had been no more than a vague yearning on the part of Philip II to take up arms against the Queen in the name of religion, into a more tangible desire. In the past, Philip had frequently deplored the fact that under Elizabeth's aegis England had become a Protestant country, but until now he had not contemplated remedying the situation by force. In 1565 he had commented that Mary Queen of Scots was "the sole gate through which religion can be restored in England, all the rest are closed", but even so, he thought it too risky for Mary to try and topple Elizabeth from her throne, advocating instead that she waited until she succeeded peacefully to the crown. Even when this prospect receded, after Mary had been imprisoned by her subjects, Philip still could see no merit in adopting a more positive approach. Instead, he left it to God to make Elizabeth see the error of her ways: in February 1568, he told de Silva, "He was, and he always would be the sincere friend of that poor princess, who he trusted would at no distant period return to her senses and for whose conversion he would never cease to labour".[50]

Obviously, once Mary Stuart had arrived in England, Philip had less excuse to be fatalistic about English affairs. His earlier lack of enthusiasm at seeing Mary set up in Elizabeth's place owed much to his fear that the former still viewed herself as a protégée of France, and that it would be the French who would be the principal beneficiaries of her elevation to the English throne. If he helped her in her present plight, however, there would be a better chance that thenceforward she would be permanently beholden to him, and certainly Mary wasted no time conveying to him that she would be ready to reward him for any assistance rendered. In a letter written to Philip's wife in September 1568, Mary declared that if Philip would give her aid, she was prepared "to make ours the reigning religion [in England] or perish in the attempt", and she indicated that in return for his kindness she would arrange for her son to be betrothed to Philip's daughter, the Infanta.[51]

Still, however, the King hesitated, for like all European monarchs, he had been scandalized by Mary's private life, and he remained doubtful as to whether she would prove a fit instrument to effect the spiritual regeneration of England. He did write to de Spes, asking whether he thought it feasible to help Mary in any way, but it was only after the payships' seizure that his attitude perceptibly hardened. De Spes had written back assuring the King that it would be easy to provoke a rebellion in Mary's favour, and on 18 February 1569 Philip replied, "If what you mention about taking the crown away from the Queen were successful, it would be certainly of great moment, and I would assist it most willingly in order to redress religion and shelter and console the good Catholics, who I am persuaded are very numerous". To Alva he wrote in the same way, commenting, "It appears to me that after my special obligation to maintain my own states in our holy faith, I am bound to make every effort to restore and preserve it in England".[52] Undoubtedly, de Spes's sweeping assurances about the facility with which this could be achieved were largely to blame for Philip's new sense of purpose, but the seizure of the payships had also been significant in goading the normally cautious King into a more warlike frame of mind.

Despite Philip's new assertiveness, the Duke of Alva was adamant that this was not the moment to make a move against England, for he believed that the Spaniards could not tackle an ambitious venture of this sort until the Netherlands had been quite subdued. He insisted that for the moment the only option open to Philip was to continue to seek an accommodation with Elizabeth, but the King could draw consolation from the fact that Alva stressed that this need be no more than a temporary expedient, and that there would "be means for fully satisfying your Majesty by and by".[53] Dutifully, Philip accepted that he would have to defer his ambition for a time, but he still looked forward to the day when he could bring it to fulfilment.

The payships row had escalated in a way that Elizabeth and Cecil had hardly intended, and for a time it also appeared as though the domestic repercussions would be severe. It was not immediately apparent that the value of foreign goods seized at the Queen's command would outweigh the losses of English merchants abroad, and it took still longer for there to be any confidence that Hamburg would prove a suitable alternative to Antwerp. In the meantime there was fierce criticism of the way the Government had acted, and the resentment was not confined to the merchant community alone, for the payships incident brought to a head the discontent of a number of nobles who had felt for some time that Cecil had too much power. The most extreme of these malcontents was Thomas Percy, seventh Earl of Northumberland, a northern magnate who had borne a grudge against Cecil since early in the reign, when he had been forced to resign the prestigious border posts of Captain of Berwick and

Lord Warden of the East and Middle Marches. Deeply resentful at his exclusion from power, the Earl had secretly converted to Catholicism in 1567, and now he longed for a return to the days when the people in his county knew "no other prince but a Percy".[54] Northumberland was not alone in nursing a sense of grievance, for he had the support of other northern landowners such as the Earl of Westmoreland and Leonard Dacres, who shared his religious sympathies and had the same feudal cast of mind. By the beginning of 1569 their malaise had reached such proportions that treason itself seemed the only feasible solution.

In January 1569, Northumberland secretly visited the Spanish ambassador and suggested that the recently widowed Philip II should take Mary Stuart as his wife, a course that would have been tantamount to declaring war on Elizabeth. Even de Spes, fiery and incautious as he was, baulked at the idea of Philip committing himself so far: Northumberland later recalled that in reply the ambassador merely "wagged his head, as though ... that could not be".[55] Nevertheless he made it clear that he was pleased that Northumberland should be so eager to serve Philip, and when the Earl left he still hoped that if he did rise up against the Queen, Spanish support would be forthcoming.

De Spes may have found Northumberland's proposals unrealistic, but he was more interested when the Earl of Arundel and the Duke of Norfolk approached him with an independent scheme of their own. The Earl of Arundel's devotion to Elizabeth had slackened a good deal since the days when he had been described as "a most addict subject" to the Queen and had aspired to his sovereign's hand. Hurt by his rejection, in 1564 he had been briefly put under house arrest after he had resigned the prestigious post of Lord High Steward, "with sundry speeches of offence towards the Queen's Majesty". Two years later, he had sulkily gone abroad, but when he had returned in 1567 it had appeared that he had now swallowed his pique, and would in future behave with a greater degree of responsibility. In reality, however, he was vexed that Cecil was more influential than he, and blamed the Secretary for the adoption of policies which he believed to be contrary to the national interest. In particular, he was incensed that Cecil had laboured to prevent a restoration of Mary Stuart, which he himself favoured, for as he sarcastically told the Queen, "One that has a crown can hardly persuade another to leave her crown because her subjects will not obey. It may be a new doctrine in Scotland, but it is not good to be taught in England".[56] Arundel's blunt admonishment must have made Elizabeth wince, but the Earl knew that there was little chance of her heeding his words while Cecil remained in charge. On top of this had come the payships incident, for which Arundel held Cecil responsible, and the Secretary's casual severance of ancient ties that for generations had been thought indispensable left the Earl in a fury.

Arundel's antagonism towards Cecil would have been of little significance were it not for the fact that he had found an ally in the Duke of Norfolk, for as England's premier nobleman and sole remaining duke, the latter commanded great respect in both Court and country. Norfolk was a descendant of Edward I, and held the honorific post of hereditary Earl Marshal, as well as being related to the Queen on her mother's side. His impressive rank was backed by material wealth on an equally magnificent scale: he was described by one contemporary as "the greatest subject in Europe, not being a free prince", and he himself admitted on one occasion that his revenues exceeded those of the crown of Scotland.[57] His position had earned him military command in Scotland at the age of only twenty-three, and a seat on the Council three years after that, but even so, the Duke could still feel that in political terms he was a lightweight. Despite being at the centre of affairs, he had come to resent that the Queen acted on his advice infrequently, and was annoyed that she paid more attention to Cecil's opinions than his own.

In the past, of course, Cecil and the Duke had been allies on the Council, having worked together to promote the Habsburg match, and for his part Cecil had believed that Norfolk had in him qualities of true statesmanship. "For the Duke", he noted in 1565, "I think England hath not had in this age a nobleman more likely to prove a father and stay to his country ... He is wise, just, modest *et timens deum*". Of late, however, their thinking had diverged, for the main reason why Norfolk had been so anxious for Elizabeth to marry into Philip II's family was that this would automatically bring about closer relations with Spain, and he failed to understand why Cecil had now turned his back on the time-honoured conventions of English foreign policy. He was angered, too, that when he and Arundel had spoken up for Mary in Council, their arguments had been ignored.[58]

It was unlucky that Norfolk's former mentor, the Earl of Sussex, had been appointed Lord President of the Council of the North in June 1568, and was therefore stationed in York. Sussex was a sincere admirer of Cecil's, and would have exerted himself to compose the Secretary's differences with Norfolk, but as it was the trouble between them was allowed to fester. In Sussex's absence, Norfolk fell under the influence of Arundel, who successfully inflamed his jealousy, and having previously regarded the Secretary as a valuable bulwark against Leicester's ambitions, Norfolk came to see Cecil as the greatest threat of all. He concluded that unless checked, this upstart would continue to impose his will on the Queen, thereby quashing the legitimate aspirations of those whose birthright entitled them to regard themselves as the true guardians of the national interest.

In February 1569, Norfolk, Arundel, and Arundel's son-in-law, Lord Lumley, sent word to the Spanish ambassador that they were outraged by

Cecil's recent actions, and they announced that they were working to bring about his dismissal. They asked de Spes to see that King Philip maintained the trade embargo with England, and even suggested that the Spaniards should waylay the English merchant fleet that was about to set sail for Hamburg, for the resulting losses would be blamed on Cecil and his position would become more vulnerable. They next set about building up a coalition against Cecil within the Council, and with this in mind, Norfolk managed to settle his quarrel with Leicester. Unscrupulous as ever, Leicester was delighted to pledge Norfolk his support, for though he had endorsed Cecil's recent policies, he knew that the Secretary was implacably opposed to his marrying Elizabeth, and therefore he welcomed his prospective removal from the scene. The Earl of Pembroke followed Leicester into the anti-Cecil camp, and to mark their displeasure against the Secretary, the four members of the Council in the group took to boycotting its sessions. They hoped that in their absence, business would grind to a halt, and that the Queen would conclude that her only hope of dealing with the pressing issues that faced her lay in abandoning Cecil.[59]

Sensing that Court rivalries were becoming more vindictive, the Queen tackled the problem directly. On 22 February 1569, Cecil, Leicester and Norfolk were among those in attendance when she took supper in her chamber, and Elizabeth seized the opportunity to upbraid Leicester for his recent neglect of duty. At this he told her outright that the majority of her subjects were in despair at the way her affairs were run, and that Cecil was to blame. At once the Queen flew into a rage, bitterly castigating Leicester for his attack, but Norfolk then made it plain that the Earl was far from isolated on this issue. As the Queen was shouting abuse, the Duke quietly remarked to the Marquis of Northampton (who was also present), "Look how Lord Leicester is favoured and welcomed by the Queen when he endorses and approves the Secretary's opinions; but now that he quite rightly wishes to state his good reasons for opposing them she looks ill on him, and wants to send him to the Tower. No, no! he will not go alone".[60]

One must admit that this was a pretty feeble performance on Norfolk's part, for he had not dared confront the Queen himself, but Northampton nodded his assent, and there was now no mistaking that feeling against Cecil was running high. The members of the cabal deluded themselves that, having made their position plain, little else would be needed to secure the Secretary's downfall. They reasoned that once Elizabeth was aware that a united and powerful opposition was ranged against Cecil, she would bow to their wishes and disgrace him. Cecil himself had no doubt that he was in the gravest danger, and frantically tried to save himself by attempting to detach Leicester from his associates. He protested to the Earl that if there was a review of government policy over the past few years, it would be found that Leicester himself shared responsibility for much of it, but the favourite answered coldly that he had no worries on this account, and that Cecil would do well to look out for himself. Far from being prepared to relent against Cecil, Leicester and his confederates supposed that they were on the brink of destroying him, being confident that they could bring the Queen, "without great difficulty, to the point which they desired".[61]

This turned out to be a serious misjudgment, for instead of the Queen succumbing to panic, it was the conspirators' nerve that broke. Norfolk and Arundel subsequently admitted to de Spes that on three occasions during April it was agreed that Cecil should be arrested at a Council meeting and despatched to the Tower, but despite the general conviction that "if he were but once imprisoned, means to undo him would not be far to seek", none of his enemies dared carry out the plan.[62] They were confounded by the fact that the Queen showed no sign of turning against Cecil, for unlike her father, she was not prepared to discard a loyal servant simply in order to appease Court rivalries, or to ease pressure on herself. Since the Duke of Alva was not prepared to make things easier for the conspirators by seizing the fleet bound for Hamburg, their schemes collapsed ignominiously. Once the worst danger was past, Cecil worked shrewdly to fend off further attacks: he patched up his relationship with Norfolk by convincing him that his attitude towards Spain was not as antagonistic as had been assumed, and later in the year he managed to strengthen this accord when he presided in the Court of Wards over a case that affected Norfolk's interests, and he was able to find in the Duke's favour.

The conspirators' blithe assumptions that the Queen would stand by while Cecil went to his fate had proved utterly unfounded, but the episode had been disturbing enough for her to think it prudent to modify her policy in some respects. While she agreed with Cecil that it was unnecessary to make concessions to Spain over the payships, she was concerned at having simultaneously alienated France, and felt that a conciliatory gesture would be in order. At a Council meeting in April, she twice stated emphatically, "I don't want war at all",[63] and she now decided that if the French were to be placated, she could no longer afford to keep Mary Stuart prisoner. A few days later she announced that she would, after all, find a way of restoring Mary to her throne, a move designed not only to appease the French, but also to propitiate those at Court who had thought that Cecil was to blame for Mary's recent ill fortune. In Scotland, the hapless Moray was informed that he must prepare himself to take Mary back as his Queen.

Despite the Queen's attempts to clear the atmosphere both at home and abroad, the air at Court remained thick with intrigue. Throughout the summer, concentric circles of conspiracy continued to spin dizzily, and the Duke of Norfolk was at the centre of each one. Norfolk had been fascinated the previous autumn when Maitland had suggested to him that he would make a good husband for Mary Stuart, and the more he had thought about it, the keener he had become on the idea. His interest in it was such that it had proved impossible to keep secret, and by the end of 1568 the proposed match was already prompting gossip at Court. These rumours had reached the Queen's ears, and in December she had taxed the Duke on the subject, asking him if there was any substance in the stories. Norfolk had vehemently denied this: "What!" he had exclaimed in horror, "Should I seek to marry her, being so wicked a woman, such a notorious adulteress and murderer? I love to sleep upon a safe pillow".[64] In reality, however, he was set on making Mary his wife, and in the ensuing months he had underhand discussions with leading men at Court, with the object of reconciling them to the idea. By the spring of 1569, Leicester, Arundel, Pembroke and Sir Nicholas Throckmorton were all in favour of it, and were working secretly to bring about the marriage.

Although the plot against Cecil had fizzled out, Norfolk and the others remained anxious to implement the marriage plan. There was indeed an undeniable logic in the proposed match: if Elizabeth did give Mary back her crown, it would be sensible to marry her beforehand to a loyal Englishman, who could ensure that the Queen of Scots observed the terms imposed upon her as a condition of her restoration. Furthermore, if Mary was given a reliable husband, this would make it safe for Elizabeth to declare her her heiress, and the vexed question of the succession would thus be satisfactorily settled. The Queen, of course, might well take a different view of the matter, and the conspirators were aware that she would probably not share their implicit faith in Norfolk's dependability. He had already declared to her that he found the idea of marriage with Mary personally distasteful, and the fact that he nevertheless wished to persist with the project would suggest to her that he was motivated by ambition alone. By marrying Mary he would become King of Scotland, and in due course he could expect to become King of England too, and the Queen would be mindful of the possibility that his hunger for power would prove such that he would not be prepared to wait for her crown to pass to him by bequest, and instead would succumb to the temptation to seize it by force. For these reasons, the conspirators moved warily, anxious not to alert the Queen to their plans until a time had come when they would be able to convince her that they were acting in her interests.

In May, they secretly established contact with the Bishop of Ross, and asked him to inform Mary of Norfolk's desire to marry her. Mary was delighted to hear about this. Until now, she had believed that her best hope of recouping her fortunes had lain in securing assistance from abroad, and as recently as January 1569 she had sent word to Philip II that with his aid, she could be "Queen of England in three months, and mass shall be said all over the country". So far, however, help had not been forthcoming from that quarter, and Mary now accepted that marriage with Norfolk would present her with a surer way of ending her troubles. She sent a message to the conspirators, saying that provided Elizabeth could be induced to consent to the marriage, she would be happy to take part. Soon she started to correspond with the Duke, addressing him fondly as "My Norfolk", and the pair also exchanged love tokens.[65]

At this stage Norfolk thought it advisable to broaden the basis of the coalition that was striving for the marriage. He therefore informed Cecil of what was afoot, and satisfied himself that the Secretary would do nothing to obstruct his schemes. In reality Cecil had little desire to see Norfolk joined with Mary, but he had only narrowly escaped disaster when he had aroused the Duke's enmity earlier in the year, and dared not run the risk again. The Duke also let the Earl of Sussex in on the secret (who cautioned him to do nothing to displease the Queen) and established contact with those influential figures in the north, the Earls of Northumberland and Westmoreland and Leonard Dacres, and asked for their approval. As it happened, neither Northumberland nor Dacres was very enthusiastic about the plan, for they would have preferred to set Mary free from her prison and then put her on the English throne with the aid of Spain,[66] but as Mary herself now urged them to support Norfolk, they agreed to help him in any way they could.

Norfolk could congratulate himself on having gained the support of a formidable body of opinion, but the difficulty of securing the consent of the Queen still remained. Norfolk tried to make out that this was not a problem: when asked what he would do if she withheld her assent, he blustered that Elizabeth would have no alternative but to fall in with his plans, for "Albeit at the first motion she might stir and mislike ... none would be found to feed her in that humour".[67] In reality, however, he was nervous of tackling her on the subject, and he and his confederates agreed that it would be better if the Earl of Moray were to do the job for them. They therefore contacted Moray and pointed out that if Mary were restored, the outlook for him would be less grim so long as she was married to Norfolk. Not only would the Duke restrain her from wreaking a bloody vengeance on the men responsible for her deposition, but as a Protestant he could be counted on to safeguard the state of true religion in Scotland. Moray apparently accepted these arguments, and said that he would put the idea to Elizabeth. Nevertheless, several weeks passed by, and he showed no sign of doing so.

By the end of July an overwhelming majority of the Council was in favour of the marriage, but at this juncture their schemes received an unexpected setback. They had looked on Moray as an ally, but in early August he suddenly informed Elizabeth that he and the other Scots nobles were not prepared to accept Mary back as their Queen. Elizabeth declared herself incensed, and said that she would press forward with Mary's restoration regardless, but Moray evidently calculated that when it came to the point Elizabeth would not be prepared to go to war on Mary's behalf, and that he could therefore defy her with impunity.

Since Moray had let them down, Leicester now volunteered to act as marriage broker, promising that at a propitious moment he would approach the Queen and persuade her to permit the union to go ahead. To Norfolk's consternation, however, Leicester delayed doing so, claiming that it was vital to time the move correctly and that he must wait till the Queen was in an amenable mood. It was nevertheless obvious that it would be unwise to delay much further, for Norfolk was uncomfortably aware that the projected marriage was already being widely talked of at Court.

Elizabeth herself had in fact been alerted by the chatter of her ladies-in-waiting, and already had an inkling that something was afoot. Anxious to find out exactly what her nobles were up to, the Queen hoped that Norfolk would voluntarily take her into his confidence, but the Duke was too cowardly to make a frank explanation, and unwisely left it to Leicester to do the job for him. Elizabeth first tried to prod the Duke into disclosing the truth in early August, when Norfolk rejoined the Court at Richmond after spending a few days in London. The Queen encountered him as she was walking in the grounds, and seemingly casually, asked whether he brought any news. The Duke said he had nothing to report, whereupon she cried out, "No? you come from London, and can tell no news of a marriage?" Norfolk declined to take the hint, and merely slipped away at the first opportunity. Later that month, while on progress in Hampshire, the Queen tried again by inviting the Duke to dine alone with her. At the end of the meal, she suddenly gave him a pinch and told him meaningfully to "Take good heed of his pillow", alluding here to Norfolk's vehement disavowal of marital intent towards Mary, at the end of the previous year. Still Norfolk remained silent, despite the golden opportunity; he later explained this remissness by saying lamely that he had been "abashed by her Majesty's speech", and that he had "thought it not fit time or place there to trouble her".[68]

Finding herself fobbed off with lies and evasions, it was not surprising that Elizabeth felt uneasy. The atmosphere at Court became unbearably tense as the Queen's nerves steadily tautened. To the French ambassador she remarked balefully that she had tried to act as a good mother to Mary Stuart, but the latter had repaid her by involving herself in intrigue. Spitefully, she added the barbed comment that anyone "who did not wish to treat her mother well, deserved a wicked stepmother". The ambassador tried to reassure her that nothing sinister was going on, to which Elizabeth merely retorted that she knew the identity of the troublemakers well enough, and that she would like to cut off a few heads.[69]

By early September the whispers at Court had reached a crescendo. The Queen's mood was now so savage that both Leicester and Cecil found themselves under attack, as she raved at them that she knew they were scheming on Mary's behalf. To an opportunist like Leicester, the signs were clear that it was time to extricate himself from an awkward predicament. On 6 September, he feigned illness and took to his bed, and then summoned Elizabeth to his bedside and poured out an abject confession, imploring her forgiveness and assuring her that in furthering the marriage plan he had believed himself to be operating in her best interests. Elizabeth was appalled that matters had gone so far: she told Leicester that if Mary and Norfolk had been permitted to marry, she knew that she herself would have been in the Tower within four months of the ceremony. Nevertheless, considering Leicester's delicate state of health, she did not want to be too harsh with him, and she was the more forgiving because he had been so open with her. With Norfolk it was otherwise: the unfortunate Duke was summoned peremptorily to the Queen's presence and there was forced to admit that he had aspired to be Mary's husband. His confession was received with "sharp speeches and dangerous looks" from Elizabeth, who angrily commanded him on his allegiance to put away such thoughts for ever.[70]

At Court the word soon spread that Norfolk was in the Queen's displeasure, and this gave rise to fears that all those who were seen to associate with him would likewise fall from favour. Accordingly the courtiers unanimously shunned him: the Duke subsequently recalled that whereas before, his table was "ever replenished as full of gentlemen as could sit at it, now if I could get three or four to dine with me, it was all". Even Leicester, who might have had the decency to offer some moral support, assiduously avoided his presence.[71] Isolated and insecure, on 16 September the Duke decided to leave the Court for London.

When the Queen discovered that Norfolk had gone without permission, she at once recalled him to Court, but the Duke wrote back saying that he was too ill to travel, and that he could not obey her summons for another four days. This was a lie, for in fact it was his terror that Elizabeth was planning to put him in the Tower that prompted him to stay away. Far from being bedridden, on 23 September he left London and rode to Kenninghall, his house in Norfolk.

The news of his departure caused immense consternation at Court, for it was assumed that such rank disobedience could only be the prelude to the Duke gathering his supporters and breaking into open rebellion. Convinced that a crisis was at hand, the Queen moved to Windsor Castle (which could be more easily defended than any of her other residences) and sent a further summons to Norfolk, but still the Duke pleaded illness and stayed where he was. In reality he was indeed contemplating revolt, and was in communication with the Earl of Westmoreland (who was married to Norfolk's sister) and Northumberland, both of whom had long believed that the best way of attaining their objectives was to use force. They now wrote to tell Norfolk that even if he could not accomplish his purpose with the Queen's goodwill, they were prepared to assist him to the uttermost of their powers.[72]

Initially it seemed that Norfolk was going to take up the sword, for he sent a defiant message to the northern Earls that "he would stand and abide the venture", but he was discouraged to see how few of the gentry in his home county were prepared to offer him their support, and gradually his courage subsided. On 30 September he decided that his best course was to trust to the Queen's mercy, and he set out for Windsor, having previously sent a note to his brother-in-law Westmoreland imploring "that he would not stir; for if he did, he [Norfolk] was then in danger of losing his head".[73] He never reached the Court, however, for on 3 October he was stopped *en route* to Windsor and placed under house arrest, and eight days later he was transferred to the Tower by order of the Queen.

It seemed that Elizabeth had regained control of a dangerous situation. Norfolk was safely in custody, and the Queen now concentrated on extracting confessions from other protagonists in the imbroglio, confining Lords Arundel, Lumley and Pembroke to their Court apartments, and interrogating them closely about the intrigues of the previous summer. Norfolk was also questioned intensively, and while he managed to conceal from the Queen his illicit dealings with the Spanish ambassador and with the northern Earls, the picture that emerged of his activities was quite sufficient to enrage her. Throughout the summer, she had been under intolerable stress, uncertain whom she could trust, and sensing the existence of plots that might threaten her very survival. Now the tensions within her erupted in a terrifying outburst against the Duke, whom she was determined should suffer for the weeks of suspense that she had had to endure. Imperiously she demanded that Norfolk be charged with treason, and it fell to Cecil to explain that as he understood the evidence, it was unlikely that the Crown would be able to obtain a conviction. "I cannot see how his acts are within the compass of treason ... " he told the Queen collectedly, "And if you consider the words of the statute I think you will agree." The French ambassador heard that this rational tone did not go down well with the Queen, and that she shrieked that if the laws of England did not provide for Norfolk's execution she would proceed against him on her own authority. According to the same source, she worked herself into such a frenzy that she fainted, and had to be revived with vinegar and burnt feathers. In time, however, her excitement subsided, and having come to accept that it would be unthinkable to try the Duke on a capital charge, she contented herself instead with detaining him in the Tower without trial. The Duke, for his part, expressed himself deeply penitent and earnestly forswore intrigue, assuring the Queen in December, "Now I see how unpleasant this matter of the Scots Queen is to your Majesty, I never intend to deal further herein".[74]

Yet even though Norfolk no longer constituted a threat, still the Queen could not relax. She had the feeling that throughout the summer she had completely lost her grip on affairs, and in doing so had nearly brought disaster on herself. From now on, she determined to be more vigilant, and when she heard that the North of England was convulsed with rumours that a rebellion was imminent, she set herself to probe the matter further. She therefore sent instructions to the Earl of Sussex, now Lord President of the Council of the North, that he must summon to her Court the Earls of Westmoreland and Northumberland, in order that they could give an account of their recent activities. Sussex was dismayed by these orders, for he feared that the Earls would reason that since Norfolk was already in the Tower, it was probable that a similar fate lay in store for them if they went south, and rather than submitting passively to imprisonment, they were likely to rise up in revolt. Nevertheless, although he felt that by obeying the Queen he was more likely to provoke rebellion than to avert it, he reluctantly did as he was bid.

To the Queen, Sussex's unwillingness to act appeared deeply suspicious. She knew that during the summer Sussex had been let into the secret about the Norfolk marriage, and though Sussex had striven to reassure her that he had been no more than peripherally involved, she still believed him to have been "no small worker in the matter". She knew too, that Sussex was a devoted friend of Norfolk, and this made her doubt his loyalty the more. Furthermore, she could not but think it sinister that throughout the summer Sussex had enjoyed many hunting and hawking parties in the company of Northumberland and Westmoreland.[75] Perhaps sporting pursuits had merely served as a pretext, and the real purpose of these convivial outings had been to plot rebellion against her?

In this Elizabeth did Sussex a grave injustice, for the Earl was a loyal servant. Sir Ralph Sadler gave a true assessment of his worth when he told the Queen, "Her Majesty hath such a treasure of him as few princes have of a subject". Sussex himself declared stoutly, "With my Prince and my friend I deal *bona fide* and know no cunning", and protested at the unfairness of Elizabeth doubting his fidelity when he had "always hitched my staff at her door only". Furthermore, Elizabeth would have done well to have listened to his advice to leave the Earls alone for a time. She was of course quite right to mistrust them, for they had indeed contemplated rising up against her after Norfolk's arrest, but by summoning them now she only spurred them into revolt. Sussex had advocated that the Queen should wait until the dead of winter before calling the Earls to Court, for then the roads and passes in the North would be blocked, and the Earls would be unable to call out their tenantry to support a rebellion even if they felt so inclined.[76] The Queen rejected these arguments, being no longer prepared to play a waiting game. The experiences of the summer had made her so disenchanted that she believed that safety lay in trusting to her instincts alone, and she could even suspect that Sussex was advising delay in order to give the Earls time to mature their plans against her.

As Sussex had predicted, by summoning the Earls to Court, the Queen precipitated the very unrest she had hoped to forestall, for both of them assumed that if they ventured south, they would inevitably be deprived of their liberty, and thought it better to defy the Queen on their own ground. As the messenger who had delivered Sussex's summons to Northumberland left the latter's house at Topcliffe, he heard the bells being rung backwards in the local church as a tocsin for rebellion. Five days later, on 14 November 1569, Northumberland, Westmoreland and the Sheriff of Yorkshire, Richard Norton, rode into Durham accompanied by three hundred armed horsemen. Having entered the Cathedral, they tore down the communion table, ripped up the English bibles and prayer books, and announced that no more Protestant services would be held there. The following morning, they began a southward march, gathering followers from the villages as they went. On 16 November, they issued a proclamation, stating that evil advisers who had "cropen in about the Prince" had secluded Elizabeth from her nobility and introduced laws "contrary to the honour of God and the wealth of the realm", and that they were obliged to have recourse to arms in order to rectify the situation.[77] Despite their attempt to shelter behind the fiction that they were acting against the royal ministers, rather than the Queen herself, this was nothing other than rebellion.

The situation was immensely dangerous, for the Queen's hold over the North was precarious at the best of times. The five northernmost counties of the kingdom were administered by a permanent body of royal officials, known collectively as the Council of the North. The Council was both the supreme executive authority in the North, and its highest court of law, but under Elizabeth its members had made little headway in consolidating Tudor rule in an area that remained economically backward and comparatively lawless. Many of the inhabitants owed a deeper allegiance to local magnates than to the central government in the South, for as Sir George Bowes, a former Marshal of Berwick, noted, "the old good will" of the people in the North was "deep grafted in their hearts to the nobles and gentlemen of this country". Their sense of alienation from the South was only exacerbated by Elizabeth's policy of leasing Crown estates in the area to needy courtiers, for these men were invariably absentee landlords, who inspired little affection in their labourers and tenants. The situation would perhaps have been better if Elizabeth herself had ever visited the

North, but though a progress to York was mooted on several occasions, the proposals always came to nothing. Not least of the reasons for this was that the Queen's advisers viewed with alarm the prospect of her adventuring her person in this remote and undisciplined region, whose denizens were reluctant to admit that the Crown had the first call on their loyalty. In 1564, for example, Sir John Mason had told Cecil agitatedly, "The Queen is expected to go north on a progress, whereunto no good man will persuade her".[78] However, on this occasion, as on others, the representations of those who shared Sir John's misgivings were sufficient to deter her, and that summer she went no farther than Leicestershire.

Religious disaffection was also endemic in the North, where the majority of the populace had only grudgingly accepted the imposition of Protestantism as the state religion, and still hankered for a return to the ancient rites and ceremonies. The Archbishop of York, Thomas Young, had lacked the determination necessary to mount a sustained onslaught on recusancy, and had tended to justify his inaction by pretending that the problem was less serious than was really the case. Others were less complacent, and a few years before the Bishop of Carlisle had frankly admitted that many of the clergy under him were "wicked imps of antichrist, and for the most part very ignorant and stubborn", but so far little had been done to remedy the situation. As far as the laity were concerned, the Council of the North seems to have taken the view that if they tendered the Oath of Supremacy as energetically as they were required to do by law, refusals to subscribe would be so numerous that it would only advertise just how slight an impact the religious settlement of 1559 had made on consciences in the North. In November 1568 Sussex and his Council had been shaken when a survey revealed that "in many churches, there have been no sermons for years past . . . and in most parts the pastors are unable to teach their flock". An attempt was made to combat these deficiencies by sending out a detachment of dedicated preachers to travel round the rural parishes. This nevertheless met with little success, for the following year the situation had not improved. Towards the end of 1569, the veteran Privy Councillor, Sir Ralph Sadler, commented, "There be not in all this country ten gentlemen that do favour and allow of her Majesty's proceedings in the cause of religion, and the common people be ignorant, full of superstition, and altogether blinded with the old popish doctrine". He cautioned that even where Protestantism was outwardly professed, this was no guide to true religious feeling, for "the ancient faith still lay like lees at the bottoms of men's hearts, and if the vessel was ever so little stirred, came to the top".[79]

Understandably, in the circumstances, the Earls calculated that, by placing great emphasis on the religious issue, they would enhance the attractiveness of their cause, and certainly the initial reaction to their resort to arms seemed to confirm that their promise to restore Catholicism would prove a potent rallying cry. Not a dissenting voice was raised as the Earls made their stand in Durham and, when mass was celebrated in the Cathedral, it was attended by a great crowd of worshippers, who knelt bareheaded to receive absolution for having acquiesced in the governmental schism with the Church of Rome. All over the North, the story was the same, as high altars were set up in place of communion tables, the prayer book and the book of homilies were ceremonially burnt, and simple believers sprinkled themselves with holy water to cleanse themselves of their sins. As the rebel army marched south, they held mass every day, thereby gaining much support: Sussex noted in alarm, "The people like so well their cause of religion, they flock to them in all places where they come". Elizabeth herself was concerned the rebel numbers would swell uncontrollably if the leaders of the insurrection succeeded in investing it with the character of a holy war. She wrote urgently to Sussex that in order to prevent their attempts to "make religion the show of their enterprise", he must publish a proclamation asserting plainly that "these rebels have nothing so much to heart ... as the subduing of this realm under yoke of foreign princes, to make it the spoil of strangers". Knowing her people as she did, the Queen did not forget that "The English hate the very name of foreigner",[80] and though many in the North might be tempted to rise up in the name of Catholicism, she trusted that, in the final analysis, their native xenophobia would outweigh their religious zeal.

At York, Sussex was in something of a panic, believing himself to be in such a weak position that he would only be overwhelmed if he tried to resist the rebels. On first hearing that the Earls had taken up arms, he had planned to raise troops locally and confront the rebel army, but he had experienced great difficulty in gathering forces, for even those who had not joined the insurgents had little desire to fight against them. He insisted that, as far as his own wishes went, he would, "for my conscience sake, spend all my lives, if I had a thousand, against all the world that shall draw sword against our religion", but he nevertheless questioned whether it was wise "to hazard battle against desperate men with soldiers that fight against their conscience". His conviction that it would be courting defeat to go into combat surrounded by enemy sympathizers led him to advocate that the Queen should offer to pardon the Earls if they agreed to lay down their arms. "All the wisest Protestants think you should offer mercy before you try the sword", he cautioned his mistress,[81] warning her that if she decided to fight on regardless, she would have to raise an army in the South that could be sent against the rebels.

At Windsor, the Queen had been greatly grieved to learn of the popular movement that had arisen in the North against her. On the verge of tears, she told the French ambassador that she deserved nothing less than such ingratitude from her subjects, and said she found it hard to believe that they could so easily forget the exemplary treatment they had always received from her. Distressed as she was, however, her nerve remained firm, and she refused to accept Sussex's advice that the best course would be to adopt a conciliatory policy towards the rebels. In part this was because she found it hard to grasp that Sussex was truly in great difficulties, and even at this stage she still harboured a lingering suspicion that his reluctance to act stemmed from disloyalty rather than military weakness. Having been invariably greeted with adulation and acclaim when in progress in the Home Counties, East Anglia and the Midlands, she found it incredible that sentiment in the North should be so very different. There was a degree of naïvety in her comment to Sussex that she was surprised by "the doubt you have conceived of the steadfastness of our subjects of that country . . . for although we do well enough consider that amongst a great multitude, some may, perhaps, for private respects, forget their duty towards us, yet doubt we not we have a great multitude of faithful and trusty subjects, both gentlemen and others, in that country". It was only when Sir Ralph Sadler and Lord Hunsdon, who had been sent to York as much to keep an eye on Sussex as to help him deal with the crisis, confirmed that it was proving very difficult to recruit locally the numbers required to defeat the rebels[82] that Elizabeth had to acknowledge the unpalatable fact that her northern domain was not wholly at her disposal.

Dismaying though the discovery was, she did not agree that these disloyal subjects should be placated rather than punished, and she rose to the challenge with vigour. On 22 November, the Earl of Shrewsbury was commanded to remove Mary Stuart south to Coventry, which would diminish the risk that she would be liberated by the rebels and proclaimed Queen. Elizabeth next ordered the Earl of Warwick and Lord Clinton to collect together troops in their home shires, so that they could march northward against the rebel army. Indeed, by now she was so determined to reduce the North to obedience that she decided to despatch more soldiers than Sussex, Sadler and Hunsdon thought necessary, for though they had requested to be reinforced with five hundred cavalrymen and better weapons for those on foot, Clinton and Warwick were authorized to muster ten thousand men in all.[83]

Meanwhile, on 22 November the Earls and their supporters (who by this time numbered 5,000 strong) had reached Clifford Moor in Yorkshire, but here they halted for, despite its size, the rebel army was not in fact a very formidable striking force. The leaders had counted on securing the support of other important northern magnates, such as the Earls of Cumberland and Derby, but to their disappointment both had remained aloof. The gentry had also failed to flock to the Earls in the numbers that they had looked for, and even among their tenants, only a fairly low percentage turned out for them. The bulk of their followers were poor countrymen, who did not possess weapons of their own, and this ill-disciplined rabble excited in the Queen nothing but contempt. Loftily she told her commanders, "As for the footmen with the rebels, her Majesty has at all times heard they are of no value, but vulgar and common people, unarmed, and the less to be considered".[84]

If the rebels had managed to secure the person of Mary Queen of Scots, their cause might have fared better, but as she had been moved beyond their reach, their momentum was effectively checked. Their chances of success were also diminished by the fact that they were chronically short of funds; Northumberland, for example, had so little ready money that he was reduced to pawning part of his Garter insignia in a desperate bid to raise cash. Furthermore, since neither Northumberland nor Westmoreland were capable of formulating clear-sighted military objectives, or adhering to a plan, the rebellion lacked firm leadership. Things might have been different if the Countess of Northumberland had been in charge, for she worked tirelessly to boost her husband's morale, as well as that of the troops. Sir George Bowes reported, "His wife being the stouter of the two, doth hasten him and encourage him to persevere, and rides up and down with their army from place to place, so as the grey mare is the better horse".[85] It was beyond even this virago, however, to instil real backbone in the vacillating noblemen and their comrades. For a time they debated whether they should advance to besiege York, but in the end more faint-hearted counsels prevailed, and on 24 November the army started to retreat.

Now that the rebels were no longer sweeping everything before them, Sussex could feel more confident, and he even detected signs that he would soon be able to assume the offensive. The rebel army was having to live off the country, which forfeited them the sympathy of many local inhabitants, and government propaganda stressing that religion was merely the pretext to disguise naked civil disobedience was also having an effect. "They begin to be odious to such as at the beginning liked them", Sussex noted exultantly at the end of November,[86] and where before men could not be found to fight for him, they now stepped forward to enlist under the Queen's banner.

On 11 December, Sussex finally decided that he now had at his disposal a sufficient number of reliable troops to set out in pursuit of the rebels. Faced with this challenge, the Earls dared not give battle, knowing that their followers were already wearied by weeks on the march without regular victuals or pay. On 16 December, they told their wretched supporters "to make shift for themselves",[87] and within days they themselves fled across the border to Scotland.

The rebellion had proved a pathetic fiasco, and now it only remained for the authorities to enact a grisly retribution. Of the leaders of the rebellion, only Northumberland was brought to justice. In Scotland, he had the ill luck to fall into the hands of the Regent Moray, and after some hesitation the latter handed him to Elizabeth in June 1572. The following August the Earl was executed at York. The Countess of Northumberland managed to escape to Flanders – fortunately for her, for the Queen had noted her active role in the rebellion and remarked that she "behoved to be burnt and merited it well" – as did the Earl of Westmoreland and Richard Norton. For the Queen, who had been cheated of her biggest prey, the only consolation was that Norton's brother and son were taken prisoner, and they were hanged at Tyburn for the edification of Londoners. On the whole, however, it was the poorer followers of the northern Earls who bore the brunt of the government's wrath. The Queen sent "special commandment" that although the more prosperous rebels should be kept in prison until they were tried at the assizes (for if convicted there, their property would be forfeit to the Crown), the "common sort" could be summarily dealt with by martial law, and executed without delay.[88]

The Earl of Sussex agreed that severity was essential. "The example shall be (as it is necessary that it should be) very great", he intoned, estimating that the number to suffer would not be "under six or seven hundred at the least". The French ambassador thought it probable that Sussex was inclined to use such terrible rigour because he believed that his loyalty was still under scrutiny at Court, and he therefore was anxious to impress upon the Queen his great zeal for her service. This analysis seems plausible, and may well account for the way Sussex chivvied his lieutenants throughout the New Year, reproving any that seemed not to be hanging offenders with the necessary despatch. Exactly how many suffered under martial law at this time is difficult to say. As Sussex had forecast, the number marked down for execution was "seven hundred and odd", three hundred and fourteen of them in the palatinate of Durham alone, but in fact a percentage of these succeeded in escaping the hangman. They were aided in doing so by compassionate individuals such as Sir George Bowes, who appears not to have enquired too closely into the whereabouts of all offenders. Neverthless it would seem that the death penalty was inflicted in at least five hundred cases[89] and the number executed would have been even greater if the Queen had had her way.

It has been suggested that since Elizabeth was miles away in the South, she was not aware of the scale of the vengeance that was being enacted in her name. Certainly it is true that communications were bad, and the Queen complained that her commanders were failing to keep her informed of their activities, but the main reason that she was worried by this was her fear that not *enough* was being done to chastise the North. On 11 January 1570, she wrote to Susssex, "We marvel that we have heard of no execution by martial law, as was appointed, of the meaner sort of rebels in the North. If the same be not already done, you are to proceed thereunto, for the terror of others, with expedition". Indeed, if the Queen's instructions had been followed to the letter, men who had not been directly involved in the rebellion would have come within the compass of martial law, for she urged Sussex to proceed against those who had merely remained at home when he had tried to call them up for military service against the rebels. "Have an earnest regard to such, and spare no offenders in that case, but let them come to trial and receive due punishment", she exhorted vindictively.[90]

Nor is there any evidence that when the Queen was apprised of the execution figures, she felt any remorse that such a multitude had paid with their lives for their disobedience. In March 1570, for instance, she spoke with satisfaction of the way an example had been set by the "necessary execution of justice upon a great number of the poorer sort of people that have already worthily suffered death". Even by that time, indeed, her wrath was not appeased: when officials at York, who were conducting the trials of the wealthier rebels, asked that some of those condemned might be reprieved because they had been forced to join the rising against their will, she answered simply, "We are in nothing moved to spare them". Admittedly, she did grudgingly agree that the legal commission in York could have the final word on their fate, and as a result none of those interceded for were put to death, but the Queen had made it abundantly clear that she personally was against extending mercy. She justified this on the grounds that as the poor had already been dealt with so harshly, it was unfair if their social betters received more lenient treatment, but while there was some truth in this,[91] her reluctance to take into account that some of those arraigned had acted under duress is scarcely to her credit.

In assessing these events it is of course well to remember that Elizabeth ruled in an age when even petty felonies were subject to the death penalty, and rebellion was categorized as one of the most heinous crimes of all. A contemporary homily on the subject thundered, "He that nameth rebellion, nameth not a singular and one only sin, as is theft, robbery, murder and such like; but he nameth the whole puddle and sink of all sins against God and man, against his Prince, his country, his countrymen, his parents, his children, his kinsfolks, his friends and against all men universally; all sins I say, against God and all men heaped together, nameth he that nameth rebellion". Yet even by the standards of the time, the extent of the repression does seem to have been excessive. In 1536 Henry VIII had thought it sufficient to execute between two hundred and two hundred and fifty rebels after the Pilgrimage of Grace, a rising which had arguably endangered the Crown far more than that which his daughter had just faced. Under Mary about a hundred offenders had suffered for their part in Wyatt's rebellion, which also compares favourably with the vengeance Elizabeth wreaked. In fact, every Tudor monarch had to cope with rebellion of some sort, but it was Elizabeth who inflicted the severest punishment on her subjects for their disobedience. Elizabeth once told a visiting Spanish ambassador that "one of the things she had prayed to God for when she came to the throne, was that he would give her grace to govern with clemency".[92] On this occasion at least, the Almighty had not seen fit to grant her prayers.

Many of the rebels who had escaped the noose were only pardoned after paying heavy fines, which brought in a total of about £4,800. As the Crown also acquired forfeited lands which were valued at £2,500 a year, this went some way to compensate for the fact that the cost of suppressing the rebellion had wiped out a Treasury surplus of about £30,000 that had been painstakingly accumulated earlier in the reign. To some extent, however, Elizabeth only had herself to blame for the high level of expense. The army raised in the South was far larger than that which Sussex had requested, and while she did have to take into account the possibility that the Earls might receive aid from abroad, the decision turned out to be a costly mistake. The southern army played no part in bringing the rising to an end, for they only arrived in the North after the rebels had scattered. Once there, however, the troops behaved with deplorable ferocity, looting and plundering so indiscriminately that the Queen was vexed to learn that they had pillaged about £10,000 worth of property that she was counting on being forfeited to her.[93]

Depredations such as these, as well as the heavy toll that had been exacted in both lives and fines, ensured that the North did not easily recover from the crisis of 1569. In September 1571, the Vice-President of the Council of the North, Sir Thomas Gargrave, reported, "I have not heard the complaint so general of poverty as it is now. They have been much touched with the late troubles". As a result of forfeitures, or the execution of breadwinners, many families had been rendered destitute, and had to wander about the countryside begging. Furthermore, although the Bishop of Durham had specifically cautioned Cecil that if any of the confiscated estates were bestowed on southern absentee landlords, "The people shall be without heads, the country desert, and no number of freeholders to do justice by juries, nor serve in the wars",[94] this was in fact the policy that was followed.

In view of the fearful reprisals that had been visited on the North, it was perhaps surprising that a spark of resistance remained, but so in fact it was. In the summer of 1569, Leonard Dacres had been the most inveterate of those who had plotted against Elizabeth, for as early as June, he had sent word to Philip II, "that whenever your Majesty pleased to send an army to this country, he and his friends will undertake to provide 15,000 selected troops". However, as he had been absent at Court when the Earls had risen up, he had been unable to offer them any support. This had proved a serious handicap to their cause, for the whole North Country was "so addicted to a Dacre" that he could have brought out great numbers on their side.[95] As it was, all that Dacres could do was to convince the Queen that he wished to assist Sussex crush the rising, with the result that she permitted him to go north, and although he arrived there too late to save the Earls, he undauntedly started gathering together forces, with the aim of starting a private rebellion of his own.

On 13 January 1570 the Queen ordered his arrest, but Dacres promptly entrenched himself in his stronghold of Naworth Castle, which was too formidable to be taken without a sizeable cohort of troops. It was agreed that a detachment under Lord Hunsdon would have to join forces with men commanded by Lord Scrope, but on 20 February, as Hunsdon was marching towards Carlisle to link up with Scrope, he and his party were ambushed by Leonard Dacres and three thousand men. Hunsdon was outnumbered two to one but, for all that, he and his men carried the day. They killed four hundred of the enemy and took nearly three hundred prisoner, and as Hunsdon exultantly informed the Queen, "Leonard Dacres ... was the first man that flew, like a tall gentleman, and as I think, never looked behind him till he was in Liddesdale". The Queen was delighted by her cousin's triumph over "that cankered subtle traitor". Effusively, she told Hunsdon, "I doubt much, my Harry, whether that the victory were given me more joyed me, or that you were by God appointed the instrument of my glory". She observed that Hunsdon's action was "the very first that was executed by fight in field in our time, against any rebels"[96] and she fervently hoped there would be no more.

The North had been brutally pacified, but as Elizabeth well knew, the stability of her kingdom would always be at risk while Mary Stuart – "her whom the world beholdeth to be the principal hidden cause of these troubles", as Elizabeth now balefully referred to her – remained in England. As soon as she had learnt of the plan to marry Mary to Norfolk, Elizabeth had abandoned all thought of restoring her cousin to her throne, and instead she decided that it would be preferable to let Mary's half-brother Moray assume responsibility for her. On 21 September she instructed Hunsdon's son, Henry Carey, to propose to Moray that Mary would be returned into his custody, provided that he guaranteed that she would come to no physical harm while in his charge. Negotiations to this effect were in progress when they were interrupted by the outbreak of the Northern Rebellion, and since Elizabeth held that Mary's intrigues had contributed to the breakdown in civil order, she no longer felt obliged to handle her with any restraint. For the first time, she actually contemplated executing Mary, going so far as to have a death warrant for her drawn up, so that she could be killed in haste if the rebellion looked like succeeding. After the rising had crumbled, Elizabeth reverted to a less intemperate frame of mind, and all talk of Mary's execution ceased. Nevertheless, she remained anxious to hand her back to Moray, and the talks with him on this subject were resumed. Moray made it plain that he would only take control of Mary if Elizabeth rewarded him by sending him money and arms with which to shore up his regime, and by formally recognizing James as King, and the Queen apparently decided that it would be worthwhile to make these gestures if they rid her of Mary's irksome presence. By the New Year, she was on the verge of granting Moray's demands, having finally accepted that it was time to rip off the figleaf of monarchical propriety and brazenly endorse Mary's deposition.[97]

At last it appeared that relations with Scotland were to be set on a satisfactory footing. Yet even if the problem of Mary could be resolved in this way, the future was still overshadowed. The northern rising had revealed that beneath the fragile crust of religious uniformity, divisive passions bubbled. Then, too, there was Spanish hostility to contend with. In 1569 Alva was convinced that his first priority was to pacify the Netherlands, and with that object in mind he had striven to achieve good relations with England. Accordingly, he had carefully refrained from involvement in the Northern Rebellion; "I expect it will all end in smoke", he had commented laconically when he had heard that Northumberland and Westmoreland had taken to arms. Philip himself had been more tempted to act against England, and indeed, when he had heard of the outbreak of the rebellion, he had taken steps to send assistance to the Earls. This was no more than opportunism, for on the whole he accepted that Alva's overall policy was wise, and that for the present it would be injudicious to break with England. Nevertheless he made it clear that he was not prepared to wait indefinitely to revenge himself on a heretic queen who had humiliated and flouted him. To Alva he remarked, "English affairs are going in a way that will make it necessary, after all, to bring that Queen to do by force what she refuses to do by reason . . . We are beginning to lose reputation by deferring so long to provide a remedy for the great grievance done by this woman to my subjects, friends and allies". Neither internally nor externally was England free from danger. As an English Catholic exile put it, when sending an account of the Northern Rebellion to a correspondent in Spain, "This was the first bloody bickering, but is not likely to be the last".[98]

CHAPTER 8

"The rarest creature that was in Europe these five hundred years"

Despite the collapse of the Northern Rebellion, there were not many of Elizabeth's advisers who saw cause for optimism at the outset of the new decade. Sussex in particular was demoralized by the fact that Elizabeth seemed not to appreciate his efforts against the rebels. He was upset that while he had been detained in the north directing "hanging matters", courtiers nearer the Queen had succeeded in obtaining grants from her of some of the rebels' forfeited estates, which he had hoped would be awarded to officers in his army. To Cecil, Sussex lamented, "Blame me not, good Mr Secretary, though my pen utter somewhat of that swell in my stomach, for I see I am kept but for a broom, and when I have done my office to be thrown out of the door". He thought himself so ill used that he even contemplated resigning from the post of Lord President of the Council of the North, and his friends professed themselves at a loss to understand why Elizabeth should treat him with such wilful ingratitude. From Berwick Lord Hunsdon opined, "Either she is bewitched, or this practice of her destruction, which was meant to have taken place perforce and by arms ... is meant to be performed by practice and policy".[1]

The general gloom was intensified by the news of an unexpected calamity, for on 23 January 1570 the Earl of Moray was assassinated, leaving the Protestant party in Scotland effectively leaderless. Elizabeth was devastated by Moray's loss, possibly the more so because she had been so slow to see him as a friend, and she shut herself tearfully in her chamber when the news arrived.[2] There was now a real danger that Mary's supporters would succeed in seizing power in Scotland, and while the outlook was so uncertain Elizabeth dared not compromise herself by formally recognizing James. She feared that even with her backing the King's party would have difficulty surviving, and was reluctant to provoke the French (who had made it plain they wished Mary to be restored) by making a vain attempt to buttress Mary's enemies.

Despite the changed circumstances, few of the Queen's advisers concurred that she should abandon James's party. Their view was that unless she gave some assistance to the King's men in Scotland, they were bound to be annihilated, and once Mary's supporters had regained control of the country it was likely that the French would assist them to invade England and punish Elizabeth for the way she had treated their sovereign. To avert this, they urged that Elizabeth should send an army into Scotland to attack Mary's party in their strongholds, and they argued that, provided the expedition was properly financed and equipped, its objectives could be achieved before the French had had time to make a protest. Elizabeth however did not share their confidence that the French would remain supine in the face of such blatant provocation.

In the early spring of 1570 she agreed that Sussex could lead a force across the borders to harass those of Mary's supporters who were suspected of having given sanctuary to English rebels who had fled royal vengeance in 1569. This action did something to raise Sussex's low spirits, but it was strictly limited in scope, and Elizabeth regretted that she had countenanced even this when the French ambassador informed her that on 12 April 1570 his master had directed him to deliver an ultimatum to the effect that henceforth he would regard Mary Stuart's cause as his own, and that if Elizabeth did not take immediate steps to restore her, he would be forced to declare war.

Greatly perturbed by the new militancy of the French, Elizabeth saw no easy way out of the dilemma. On 29 April she presided over a full meeting of the Council, at which she admitted that she did not know what to do, and implored them all to give her their advice.[3] Yet when a majority of those present declared that the French were probably bluffing and that, instead of restoring Mary, Elizabeth should assist James's party by sending money and men to Scotland, the Queen could not bring herself to heed their words. Although Cecil had been emphatic that she should not give in to French blackmail, Elizabeth came to the conclusion that this was not the moment for defiance, and to the Secretary's distress she instructed him to draw up a series of conditions that could serve as a basis for Mary's restoration.

With a heavy heart Cecil did as he was bid, and by 7 May he had produced a list of articles which could form a starting point for negotiations. These included the demands that prior to her restoration Mary must agree to ratify the Treaty of Edinburgh, to maintain Protestantism in Scotland and to retain in office those lords who were at present trying to govern Scotland in the name of her son. As an additional precaution, it was stipulated that James must be sent to England to complete his upbringing, but despite the severity of these conditions Cecil did not think this afforded any guarantee of Mary's future good behaviour. At a Council meeting on 22 May Cecil bluntly informed Elizabeth that if she persisted with the project for Mary's restoration she would be wilfully endangering her own person. His statement only managed to enrage Elizabeth, already overwrought as a result of weeks of tension. Furiously she raged that, as far as Mary was concerned, the Secretary had never given her any advice that was not "full of passion and hatred", but that on this occasion she was going to pay no attention to Cecil and his "other brothers in Christ"[4] . Shocked by her outburst, for the moment Cecil dropped his open opposition to Mary's restoration, although at heart he remained convinced of the folly of the policy. Having dealt with his objections, on 27 May 1570 Elizabeth informed the French ambassador that she would at once start discussions aimed at setting her cousin back on her throne.

For once it seemed that Elizabeth had embarked upon a determined course of action, and that the threats of the French had finally shaken her out of her habitual irresolution. In reality, however, the situation was very different. Unlike Cecil, Elizabeth was not so set against Mary's restoration that she would rather risk war with France than give Mary back her crown, but she still hoped that events would turn out in such a way that she would not have to do so. She knew that the negotiations concerning Mary's return to Scotland would be both prolix and involved, and Elizabeth trusted that she would be able to spin them out to her own advantage. The outcome of such complex discussions could never be a foregone conclusion, and they could not even be started without a lengthy period of preparation. Throughout the summer of 1570 Elizabeth was able to placate the French by assuring them that she was about to embark on talks with Mary, but simultaneously she was sending assurances to the King's party in Scotland that she would do everything in her power to see that the negotiations came to nothing. At her coronation Elizabeth had remarked, "Time has brought me hither"; now she was hoping that it would have the opposite effect of keeping Mary where she was.

Elizabeth knew well enough that she was playing a very dangerous game, and the constant sense of uncertainty had an adverse effect on her temper. She was ungracious to Sir Nicholas Bacon when he told her it was insane of her to contemplate setting Mary free, but she was no better pleased when Leicester, thinking to win approval, spoke in favour of a conditional restoration. Much to the Earl's surprise, she suddenly accused him of taking Mary's cause too much to heart, at which Leicester was so offended that he withdrew from court in a huff. The Queen soon made it up with him, but nevertheless her mood remained unpredictable throughout the summer, and was not improved when she developed a painful varicose ulcer on her leg, which became even more sore and inflamed when she insisted on going on her usual summer progress.[5]

Already surrounded by perils aplenty, in the summer of 1570 the Queen was suddenly confronted by a new and dangerous challenge. Despite her espousal of Protestantism Elizabeth had never been formally excommunicated, for Pope Pius IV had accepted that it would be inexpedient to put her under sentence of anathema unless one of the Catholic powers was prepared to put the bull into effect by invading England and deposing the Queen. In 1566, however, the Papacy had passed into the hands of Pius V, an austere fanatic who did not accept that political considerations should be permitted to trammel the crusading spirit of the Counter-Reformation. On 25 February 1570 he issued the Bull *Regnans in Excelsis*, depriving "Elizabeth, the pretended Queen of England, the servant of wickedness" of her throne, and declaring that henceforth her subjects were absolved of their allegiance to her.[6] For a time, the English government remained unaware of the papal decree, but on 25 May 1570, it was brought to their attention when an ardent Catholic gentleman named John Felton nailed up a copy of the Bull on the Bishop of London's garden gate.

Up until now the Queen had steadfastly refused to treat her Catholic subjects as enemies of the state. From time to time, Cecil and others had voiced concern that she was being "too easy" on the papists,[7] but on the whole it was recognized that, with gentle handling, there was a good chance that Catholicism in England would die out of its own accord. Because the Pope had not succeeded in making it clear that he wished his followers to boycott Anglican services, many English Catholics had contrived to remain within the law by attending church regularly, but declining to take communion. It was therefore not entirely unrealistic of the Queen to hope that once they had grown familiar with the English service, they would come to feel affection for it, and that this, coupled with the difficulties of finding priests to say mass, would ensure the gradual withering of their attachment to the ancient faith. The Pope may indeed have been spurred into action by the fear that, unless he asserted himself in some way, it would ultimately cost him many souls, and he felt he must make it clear that the chasm that separated Elizabeth and him was too wide to be bridged by the legalistic formula which the English Catholics had adopted in the hope of simultaneously satisfying God and Caesar.

By excommunicating Elizabeth he put her Catholic subjects in an agonizing dilemma, for theoretically at least, they had to examine their consciences and decide once and for all where their loyalties lay. John Felton, for one, had no doubts as to who had first claim on his obedience: arrested a month after he had posted up the Papal Bull, he was tortured and subsequently executed, and on the scaffold he refused to recognize Elizabeth as his Queen. For the moment however, it seemed that he was the exception, for the vast majority of English Catholics simply refused to accept that there was an inherent contradiction in trying to remain loyal to both Queen and Pope. They wished to acknowledge Elizabeth as their sovereign and Pius as their spiritual leader, and they did not see why these two claims on their allegiance should be regarded as mutually exclusive. From an intellectual point of view, however, this position could not be sustained, for the harsh reality was that the Pope had made it impossible to be both a good Catholic and a good Englishman. The Government could never be sure whether in the final analysis the Catholics would put their religion before their country, and uphold papal authority at the expense of that of the Queen. By sanctifying treason, the Pope had thrown down the gauntlet, and this was a challenge that the Queen could scarcely ignore.

Nevertheless, her response was a guarded one. Immediately after the Northern Rebellion, Elizabeth had issued a declaration stating that it was not her intention that her subjects "should be molested either by examination or inquisition in any matter ... of faith ... as long as they shall in their outward conversation shew themselves quiet and conformable and not manifestly repugnant and obstinate to the laws of the realm which are established for the frequentation of divine service". This was a principle that she was determined should still be upheld, seeing no reason why she should be dragooned by the Pope into modifying her policy of permitting freedom of conscience, if not freedom of worship. Earlier in the reign, known recusants had at various times been subjected to random arrest and short terms of imprisonment, but the Queen did not want these haphazard proceedings to be refined into a consistent campaign of persecution. At a Council meeting held soon after the Bull had been made public, she turned down a proposal by some more militant members that all known Catholics should be examined on oath and proceedings initiated against them under martial law if their loyalty was found wanting. She was annoyed, too, that a prominent Catholic of her acquaintance, Sir John Cornwallis, had been arrested and put in the Tower, and on her instructions he was freed and invited to come to court to kiss her hand.[8]

Elizabeth had restrained her Council from resorting to arbitrary action in answer to the Pope's condemnation of her, and for as long as she could she delayed making an official response to the sentence of excommunication. Cecil wanted her to call Parliament so that it could frame legislation to deal with the situation that had arisen, but the Queen was slow to do so. She did not want to be rushed into tightening up the laws against the Catholics, and besides she was worried that a new Parliament, like its predecessor, would importune her to name a successor. Such was her distaste at the prospect, indeed, that although money was needed to pay for the cost of suppressing the Northern Rebellion, she preferred to raise it by having recourse to forced loans (an unpopular device whereby gentlemen of means were called upon to advance the Crown sums of money which were repaid, free of interest, at a later date) rather than to request Parliament for fresh supplies. By the spring of 1571, however, continuing financial pressure had made the summoning of Parliament imperative, and by that time even Elizabeth had come to agree that the Pope's aggressive move must be countered in some way.

Parliament met on 2 April. To a certain extent the Queen's fears that it would prove a difficult and demanding assembly were nullified by the fact that Lady Katherine Grey had died of tuberculosis in 1568 and, with her departure from the scene, Protestant members of Parliament had less of an inducement to press the Queen to name a successor. Whereas earlier Parliaments had been obsessed by the anarchy that would ensue if Elizabeth were to die without settling the succession, recent events had emphasized the dangers that could arise in her lifetime, and there was hence more concern to shield the Queen from these than to guard against purely hypothetical perils.

With the Queen's reluctant consent, two bills were introduced into Parliament extending the definition of treason. The first provided that anyone who introduced a Papal Bull into the realm should henceforth be adjudged a traitor, while the second laid down that in future it would be treasonous to describe the Queen as a heretic, schismatic, or tyrant. To Elizabeth's annoyance, however, Thomas Norton, the virulently anti-Catholic Member of Parliament for London, sought to append to the latter measure a provision to the effect that any person who had laid claim to the Queen's throne in the past should be automatically disabled from inheriting the crown. This would have ruled out any chance of Mary Stuart succeeding Elizabeth, but the Queen had no intention of letting a measure of this sort slip through on the coat-tails of legislation that was designed to counteract any problems that might arise from her excommunication. It would seem that she managed to convey a warning that, if Norton's proposals were added to the treasons bill, she would veto the entire measure at the end of the session, and as a result the offending clauses were altered. In the final version of the Bill, only those who sought to usurp Elizabeth's throne in the future forfeited their right to the succession, and once the measure had assumed this relatively innocuous shape, the Queen was prepared to give her assent to it.

A further anti-Catholic measure gained a majority in both Houses of Parliament, only to be rejected by the Queen at the end of the session. It had sought to make it mandatory to take communion at least once a year, with a heavy fine of 100 marks (£66 13s 4d) being levied on those who failed to meet this requirement. The signs are that the Privy Council were in favour of the bill, as were most, if not all of the Bishops, but at the closing ceremony Elizabeth exercised her power of veto to prevent it from reaching the statute book. Far from wishing to smoke out those "Church Papists", who attended divine service but abstained from taking the sacrament according to Anglican rites, she deemed it unwise to force them to define where they stood, for if it came to a precise allocation of loyalties, who could tell whether or not she would end up the loser? It was the Pope who was striving to upset the uneasy balance that the Catholics sought to achieve between their Queen and their conscience; Elizabeth had no desire to make his task any easier.

Elizabeth had seen to it that no new law had been passed which could have prevented Mary Stuart from succeeding her as Queen of England, but by the spring of 1571 the project to restore Mary to her Scottish kingdom had virtually ground to a halt. The difficulties were not of Mary's making, for though at first she had been shocked by the severity of the terms that had been set as the price of her restoration, her advisers had been swift to reassure her that once she had regained her freedom she need not necessarily adhere to any promises that Elizabeth had extorted from her. Maitland of Lethington, who was now the leader of the pro-Marian forces in Scotland, urged that Mary should "yield to all rather than she remain a prisoner", for as he pointed out in a letter to the Bishop of Ross, "If she were once at liberty I fear not means shall be found to make both England and Scotland loth to enterprise far against her".[9]

Accordingly Mary intimated her acceptance in principle of the proposed conditions, and in September 1570 Secretary Cecil and the Chancellor of the Exchequer, Sir Walter Mildmay, had left for Chatsworth to go over the terms in detail with her. The task was one that Cecil found far from congenial, but as the time approached for Cecil to set off, Elizabeth began to wonder whether even he would remain impermeable to the Queen of Scots' legendary charm. Having grown accustomed to Elizabeth berating him for being so prejudiced against Mary, Cecil was taken aback when she suddenly launched into a jealous tirade against her cousin, angrily demanding whether he too would return lauding Mary's perfections.[10]

Cecil's negotiations with Mary went well enough, although Elizabeth took umbrage when she learnt that in the course of them Mary had suggested that a clause binding her never to do anything to the prejudice of Elizabeth or her issue should be changed to read Elizabeth and "her lawful issue". Hearing this, Elizabeth snorted angrily that though Mary "may, peradventure, measure other folks' dispositions by her own – which we trust in God shall always be far from us", she did not see why she should accept an amendment that implied she might produce a child out of wedlock. Somewhat grudgingly, she eventually agreed that the phrase could be changed to "any lawful issue by any lawful husband", which she felt would not constitute a slur upon her honour.[11]

By the end of 1570 all such difficulties had been successfully ironed out, with Elizabeth and Mary apparently in full agreement as to the safeguards that would encircle the restoration. It only remained for Elizabeth to lay the compact before representatives of young King James's party, and demand that they assent to it, but this was by no means easy to accomplish. None of the King's lords believed that their heads would be secure on their shoulders once Mary was returned to power, and Elizabeth's requests that they send an emissary to England were met by evasions and excuses worthy of the Queen herself. Only in February 1571 did their representative, the Earl of Morton, arrive in England, and discussions with him reached stalemate when on 19 February he announced that his commission did not empower him to accept any proposal which tended to diminish the young King's authority.[12]

Elizabeth pretended to be furious. She declared violently that she was sure that Morton was only being so obstinate because he was receiving encouragement from various members of her Council, and she raged that these men deserved to be hanged outside the palace gate. In reality, however, she welcomed the further respite. She was currently engaged in forging closer links with the King of France, and once they were on better terms with each other, it could well be that the French would become less insistent that Mary must be restored. Matters were not yet sufficiently far advanced for them to have relaxed their pressure on her, so it was a relief to the Queen when the intransigence of the Scots lords afforded her an excuse for further delay.[13]

On 24 March Elizabeth sent word to Mary that Morton had returned home in order to obtain the Scottish Parliament's agreement that she could repossess her throne, but despite assurances that this would not take long, Mary's patience was exhausted. In recent months her frustration had mounted as new excuses had been incessantly put forward to explain why she was still a prisoner and by February 1571 she had concluded that it would be foolish to look for better treatment from Elizabeth. Convinced that her liberation would never be achieved through orthodox diplomatic channels, she now pinned all her hopes on intrigue: on 6 February she wrote bitterly to the Bishop of Ross that "our good sister must pardon us" if, seeing "no furtherance to be had at her hand", she turned to foreign princes for her deliverance.[14]

In pursuit of this resolve Mary enlisted the aid of Roberto Ridolfi, an eloquent and resourceful Florentine banker whose considerable energies had never been fully absorbed by the legitimate business transactions which formed the pretext for his residence in England. In 1569 Ridolfi had been peripherally involved in the intrigues which had culminated in the rebellion of the northern Earls, but though he had been arrested in October of that year he had succeeded in talking his way out of trouble. Indeed, he had vindicated himself so completely that when, in the spring of 1571, he suggested that he might be of some assistance in bringing about a restoration of trade between England and the Netherlands, his offer was gratefully received, and he was even granted a private audience with Elizabeth. The meeting passed off well enough, but the Queen would have been less cordial if she had known that in January Ridolfi had written secretly to Mary Queen of Scots informing her that he was a papal agent, and offering to act as her representative at the courts of Rome, Madrid and Brussels in a bid to stir them into action on her behalf.

Mary was overjoyed, and emphasized that Ridolfi should make it clear to the Pope and King of Spain that, if they did invade England for her sake, they could count on receiving the support of influential members of the nobility. In particular she felt confident that the Duke of Norfolk would not fail her, for she knew he had not relinquished his ambition to become her husband. Mary herself was largely responsible for this, for shortly after Norfolk had been sent to the Tower in 1569 she had succeeded in secretly re-establishing contact with him, and she had set out to convince him that it would be unworthy of him if he did not honour his earlier offer of marriage. "Our fault were not shameful", she wrote coaxingly to him in early 1570. "You have promised to be mine, and I yours. I believe the Queen of England and country should like of it ... You promised you could not leave me".[15]

With his experience, Norfolk can hardly have deluded himself that Elizabeth would ever voluntarily sanction a union between him and Mary Stuart, but the prospect of marriage with her continued to fascinate him. This remained the case despite the fact that in June 1570 he gave Elizabeth a written undertaking to the effect that he did "freely, voluntarily and absolutely grant, promise and bind myself by my bond of allegiance ... never to deal in the cause of the marriage of the Queen of Scots". His humble submission had convinced Elizabeth that it would now be safe to remove Norfolk from the Tower, and instead to place him under house arrest at his London residence, but in fact the Duke did not consider himself under any obligation not to resume his courtship of Mary. Indeed, prior to signing his submission, he had sent Mary a copy of the document. He had explained that he was putting his name to it only because he would thereby obtain a measure of freedom, and she had signified that she approved of his decision.[16]

On 8 February 1571 Mary wrote Norfolk a letter, explaining that Ridolfi was going to tell King Philip that there were many English nobles who would "set themselves in the fields and raise them for me, if the said King of Spain will sustain and embrace my causes". She sought Norfolk's approval, but when the Bishop of Ross had arranged for the letter to be delivered to him, the Duke's instinctive reaction was not to let himself be involved in so dangerous a conspiracy. His secretary subsequently recalled that having read the missive, Norfolk merely commented, "The Bishop of Ross will never be quiet", and then he went into supper. Having already incurred the wrath of Elizabeth, his shrinking and unsteadfast nature quailed at the thought of outright treason, and he was disturbed too, by Mary's warning that if Spanish help was to be forthcoming, it would be necessary for him to convert to Catholicism. Yet at the same time, he could not bring himself to repudiate the enterprise altogether. Having forfeited the favour of Elizabeth, he felt he could not afford to antagonize Mary as well, and he also feared that if he did not assist her, Mary would look elsewhere for a husband. She had hinted in her letter that King Philip's illegitimate half-brother, Don John of Austria, was keen to marry her, and he did not want to lose her in this way. The Bishop of Ross, who was co-ordinating the conspiracy, did his best to exploit the Duke's unease. "Well then, my Lord shall do nothing, and nothing shall come of him", he commented ominously when Norfolk's secretary told him that his master was not interested. "But ... as for the Queen my mistress, she is no castaway; if he will not do for her, there be enough that will".[17] Too spineless to resist such pressure, the Duke agreed to have a meeting with Ridolfi.

Ridolfi came secretly to see the Duke on the evening of 10 March 1571, and he asked Norfolk to sign letters to the Pope, King Philip and the Duke of Alva, volunteering his services. This the Duke refused to do, but nothing daunted, Ridolfi went away and drew up the letters regardless. He also composed a more detailed set of instructions, purporting to be from Norfolk, asking King Philip to send "aid, as well in money as in men, armour and munitions", and designating Harwich as a suitable port at which the invaders could land. After discussions between Ridolfi, Ross and the Duke's secretary, William Barker, it was agreed that Barker should visit the Spanish ambassador and explain that though the Duke dared not put his signature to these documents, he approved of their contents and endorsed the requests. These assurances sufficed to convince de Spes that the plot had Norfolk's backing, and he at once wrote to Spain urging that Ridolfi should be given a good hearing.[18]

On 24 March 1571, Ridolfi set out for Brussels, where he secured an audience with the Duke of Alva and asked him to press King Philip to send an army to England. Alva did not dispute the esssential desirability of the project – in a letter to the King, he remarked that Philip was under an obligation to restore Catholicism in England and that Elizabeth had already done much to provoke him – but he questioned whether now was the time to launch such an enterprise. The King already had his fair share of military commitments in the Netherlands, and a successful invasion of England would also arouse the hostility of France, wary as ever of Spanish aggrandisement. Ridolfi the Duke dismissed as a babbler, whose loquacity had already enabled too many people to penetrate his secret, and he found the Italian's airy assurances that at a pre-arranged moment rebel forces in England would simultaneously manage to free Mary, seize Elizabeth, and take control of the Tower a little hard to digest. Only if Elizabeth was already dead – from natural causes or otherwise – or in custody, did Alva think it worthwhile to despatch troops to England.[19]

The next stage of Ridolfi's peregrinations took him to Rome. There he saw the Pope and secured his blessing for the projected invasion of England, although Pius declined to offer more tangible assistance. In Madrid, however, where Ridolfi arrived at the end of June 1571, he was to have a much more positive reception. Although Ridolfi was the very antithesis of King Philip, the latter's habitual caution inexplicably evaporated when confronted by the irrepressible Italian. Ridolfi was granted "daily, nay hourly" audiences, at which he waxed eloquent on how the English would rise in spontaneous support of a Spanish army that came to capture the Queen, and Philip swallowed it all. He decided that he must seize this opportunity to punish Elizabeth for her heresy and provocative conduct. On 7 July 1571 there was a meeting of the Spanish council, at which a suggestion that Elizabeth should be assassinated by a Spanish agent was overruled in favour of sending a military force under Alva's command from the Netherlands to England, with the aim of placing Mary on the throne. When notified of this plan, Alva protested, but Philip replied firmly that Elizabeth was an enemy who would never overlook an opportunity to do him harm, and that the only way to recover control of the Netherlands would be to deprive her of her crown.[20]

While Philip was engaged in plotting her destruction, Elizabeth had become immersed in a new courtship. She still professed to be "as disgusted with marriage" as ever,[21] but appeared to have accepted that she must subject herself to the nuptial bond for the good of her kingdom. In September 1570 she had blithely attempted to re-open marriage negotiations with the Archduke Charles, only to learn that he had finally lost patience with her and become betrothed to the daughter of the Duke of Bavaria. Having registered her surprise that he had broken faith with her in this way, her next move was to seek a husband from the royal house of France. Like the Archduke, the French King, Charles IX, had also recently found himself a wife, but if he was no longer available he did have a younger brother, the Duke of Anjou, who was still on the marriage market. It was true that Anjou was not an ideal choice of partner for a woman of thirty-seven, for he was only nineteen. Later in life he became renowned for his transvestism and homosexual tendencies, but at this period he was more noted for his promiscuity with the opposite sex, which made it unlikely that he would prove a model husband. His Catholicism presented another difficulty, but the Duke's very youthfulness encouraged hopes that his views on religion had not had time to solidify, and that he would be prepared to embrace Protestantism as well as the Queen. Peace had recently been restored to strife-torn France after the Huguenots there had been granted a measure of toleration, and while such a liberal policy was in being, it did not seem inconceivable that Anjou might convert.

In November 1570 the French ambassador, La Mothe Fénelon, was informed by Leicester that the Queen wished to see him. When he arrived for the audience he noticed that she had taken a good deal of trouble with her appearance, being much more splendidly dressed than usual. The reason for this soon became apparent, for she began to speak of her regret at having remained single for so long. Taking his cue, the ambassador observed that he would like to be instrumental in altering that state of affairs, and that he would deem it a great honour to bring about a marriage between Elizabeth and Anjou. The Queen affected coyness, saying that she was already very old, but when she next saw the ambassador she proved eager to continue the discussion. She still voiced concern about Anjou's lack of maturity, saying that he would always be much younger than her, but she seemed far from displeased when Leicester interposed with a grin, "So much the better for you".[22]

Fénélon passed all this on to Catherine de Medici, who was greatly excited at the prospect of obtaining a crown for her younger son. Unfortunately, Anjou himself proved distinctly less enthusiastic: in February 1571 an agitated Catherine informed Fénelon in the strictest confidence that her son complained that Elizabeth was reputed to be extremely immoral, and said that he would be universally ridiculed if he saddled himself with so depraved a bride. Only when Fénelon wrote insisting that there was no truth whatever in these slurs could the Duke be induced to let the courtship proceed.[23]

In March Elizabeth informed the Council of her dealings with the French. There was general surprise, for hitherto only Cecil (whom the Queen had raised to the peerage as Baron Burghley the previous month) and Leicester had had any inkling of what was going on. One member offended the Queen when he tactlessly enquired whether Anjou was not rather young to be her partner. While relations with Spain were so bad, however, it was obviously desirable to draw closer to the French, and the majority followed the lead of the newly ennobled Burghley, who showed great enthusiasm for a match that would make "the Pope's malice, with his bulls and excommunication, vanish away in smoke".[24]

It nevertheless soon became clear that Anjou's religion might well obstruct the marriage. When he was sounded as to his willingness to renounce Catholicism, he revealed an inconveniently pious streak and declared that he would give up his faith for no one. Burghley was so keen for the marriage to take place, that he begged the Queen to agree that if Anjou came to England he might be permitted to practise his religion in private, but Elizabeth was adamant that any such concession would arouse public feeling in the country against the union. To the disgust of those who desired the match, Leicester supported her firm stand. Previously he had feigned great enthusiasm for the marriage, hoping in this way to rebut allegations that he always schemed to prevent the Queen from marrying anyone other than himself, but the religious issue enabled him to change his stance without being obviously inconsistent. "We are bound to thank God to see her Majesty so well to stand to the maintenance of the cause of religion", he intoned reverently to a colleague, but while these sentiments were in themselves unimpeachable, his enemies were sure that his sanctimonious posture formed a cover for more selfish objections. The Queen's cousin Lord Hunsdon sourly opined that if Anjou "were a Protestant, there would be other devices to hinder it".[25]

It scarcely augured well for the marriage that neither of the principal parties had shed their personal doubts as to the other's desirability. In May 1571 Anjou had gallantly observed to the English ambassador in France, Sir Francis Walsingham, that "For her rare gifts, as well of mind and body" Elizabeth was "the rarest creature that was in Europe these five hundred years", but private information reached the Queen indicating that in reality he was not so sure of her attractions. Fénelon was much embarrassed when the Queen accosted him one day and said she heard that Anjou had been told that she was an old woman with an incurably sore leg. The ambassador naturally pooh-poohed the very thought, and Elizabeth accepted his assurances, but evidently the story still rankled. At a subsequent audience she made a point of telling Fénelon how much she had enjoyed dancing at the Marquis of Northampton's recent wedding, adding archly that she hoped Monsieur would have no cause to complain that he had been tricked into marrying someone lame.[26]

The Queen was clearly piqued that Anjou was being so cool, for in marriage negotiations she liked the reluctance to be on her side alone. At times, however she was ready to admit that the age difference between them was too large to be lightly overlooked. In conversation with one of her ladies, she expressed fears that Monsieur would despise her if she proved incapable of producing children, and said that at present she did not feel strong enough to take a husband. Worries of this sort could nevertheless be voiced by no one else at court. On one occasion the Queen asked for Lady Cobham's opinion as to whether she should press on with her marriage plans, saying that she trusted her more than any woman in the world. Taken in by Elizabeth's confiding tone, Lady Cobham counselled against the match on the grounds that the best marriages were those where the partners were roughly the same age, but that here "there was a great inequality". The Queen was outraged: "There are but ten years between us", she snapped, and though the true figure was in fact eighteen, Lady Cobham knew better than to contradict.[27]

The truth was that neither party seemed to have much enthusiasm for the other, but officially it was only the religious difficulty that stood in the way of an engagement. The Queen still refused to modify her position, and because of this it appeared by August 1571 that marriage with Anjou was out of the question. Francis Walsingham, who had been conducting the negotiations in Paris, suggested that something might be salvaged from the wreckage if England and France were to sign a treaty pledging mutual friendship. At this stage Burghley could see little merit in the idea, for he believed that in the absence of any marital tie such an agreement would be too limited in character to protect England from the dangers which encompassed her. Marriage alone could provide for the succession and obtain for the country at least one friend abroad, but now it seemed that Elizabeth had wilfully spurned her sole means of salvation. On 31 August Burghley told Elizabeth that he would ask the Council to devise alternative solutions for her preservation, adding severely, "And surely how your Majesty shall obtain remedies for your perils, I think is only in the knowledge of Almighty God".[28]

Burghley's gloom was understandable in view of the fact that he was now aware that a Spanish-backed invasion of England was in the offing. He knew too that a prominent English nobleman had promised to give it his support, although as yet the identity of the traitor remained a mystery. These facts had come to light after a young man named Charles Bailly had been stopped at Dover on 12 April 1571. He had sailed from the Netherlands, and on being searched was found to be carrying a packet of letters in cipher. Bailly was arrested, and the letters were meant to be forwarded to Burghley for his perusal, but in fact before they were delivered to him, the Bishop of Ross succeeded in suborning a government official to pass on to him some of the more compromising documents. In their place Ross substituted a collection of much less incriminating papers, hoping that when Burghley inspected them he would not think it necessary to delve further into the matter. Nevertheless, when Burghley read these, he had a hunch that something was being kept from him. To find out what it was, he placed an undercover agent in Bailly's gaol cell, primed to pump the prisoner for further information. By this means the deception was uncovered, for Bailly, "fearful, full of words and given to the cup", proved only too willing to confide in a supposedly sympathetic listener. Having established that Bailly had been entrusted with letters that had never reached him, Burghley had him removed to the Tower and racked. Under torture Bailly revealed that he had been carrying a letter from Ridolfi addressed simply to "40", and said that he had understood this to be the code name for an English nobleman. The letter in question had contained a highly coloured account by Ridolfi of his meeting in Brussels with the Duke of Alva, and in it Ridolfi had quoted Alva as saying that, subject to Philip's approval, Ridolfi "should have all the assistance and aid that he required".[29] In so far as it went, Bailly's confession was of the utmost importance, but no torture, however fearful, could make him reveal the identity of the mysterious peer, for that was a secret with which he himself had not been entrusted. Unable to unmask the traitor, Elizabeth and Burghley knew only that a conspiracy was in existence, while remaining powerless to strike at those who were behind it.

In a bid to penetrate the enigma, the Council ordered that the Bishop of Ross be placed under house arrest. Naturally he was rigorously questioned, but his ambassadorial status preserved him from the inquisitorial methods that had elicited a confession from Bailly, and in any purely verbal contest the wily Bishop was more than a match for his interrogators. He did admit that he had obtained possession of some of the letters that Bailly had brought with him from abroad, but insisted that the correspondence related only to Mary's perfectly legitimate dealings with her supporters in Scotland, and that Bailly was quite wrong to claim that it concerned a projected invasion of England. At Elizabeth's insistence, Mary herself was also interrogated by her custodian Lord Shrewsbury, but she too hotly denied all knowledge of any plot. "Think these of our sister's Council that we have had so small respect for our own weal, or that we were so evil advised in our proceedings as to hazard our action in that sort?" she wrote to Ross in righteous indignation. "No, we are not, thanks be to God, of so weak judgement ... And it had been great folly for us (feeling already evil treatment enough, without cause) to have given such colour of occasion for worse". As the summer of 1571 drew to its close, Elizabeth remained as clueless as ever as to the real name of the elusive "40", and she certainly had no inkling that Norfolk might be the unknown man.[30]

It was only at the end of August 1571 that a fortuitous discovery linked Norfolk with Mary's intrigues. As a former Queen of France, Mary was entitled to a pension from the French Crown, and she had requested that a portion of this money should be transmitted to her supporters in Scotland. The cash had first been sent to the French ambassador in London, who had secretly contacted the Duke of Norfolk and asked him to organize its transportation. This Norfolk agreed to do, arranging that an unsuspecting merchant should deliver the consignment to an agent of his in Shrewsbury, who would undertake the final phase of the journey himself. On his way to Shropshire, however, it struck the tradesman that his load was unusually heavy, and when he investigated further he found that he was carrying

£500 in gold and several letters in cipher. Thinking this strange, he alerted Lord Burghley to his discovery.

As it happened, the incident was in no way connected to the Ridolfi plot as such, but it served to set Burghley on Norfolk's trail. The Duke's two secretaries and his agent in Shrewsbury were arrested, and the rack, or the threat of it, forced out of them disclosures which revealed that Norfolk was much more than the Queen of Scots' courier. These confessions were corroborated when an intensive search of the Duke's London house yielded to Burghley's anxious scrutiny several letters in cipher, one of which proved to be that which Mary had sent to Norfolk in February, recommending Ridolfi to him.

On 7 September 1571 Norfolk was again conveyed to the Tower, and once there successive interrogations reduced to tatters his initial protestations of innocence. By 11 October he had been brought to admit that he had broken his oath to have no further dealings with Mary, and he confessed to having received a secret visit from Ridolfi. He was adamant, however, that Ridolfi had made no mention of a foreign invasion of England, claiming that the Italian merely wanted to raise money abroad which Mary could use to subsidize her party in Scotland. This was the Duke's explanation for why Ridolfi had gone traipsing around the courts of Europe, but he stressed that he himself had declined to have anything to do with the financier's schemes, and made much of the fact that he had refused to sign any letters addressed to Alva, Philip or the Pope. He maintained too that his secretary Barker's visit to the Spanish ambassador had been made without his authorization, but his interrogators could not accept that the Duke's employee had been anything more than "a lewd drudge in this evil service", believing rather that it was Norfolk's "foolish devotion to that woman" that had made him a moving spirit in the whole affair.[31] In this they did the Duke something of an injustice: all the evidence suggests that he was sucked into criminality by characters more forceful than himself, feebly acquiescing in the villainy of others as though his forfeiture of royal favour had simultaneously deprived him of the faculty of free will. Nevertheless, he was pivotal to the conspiracy, and if he had made it clear that his loyalty to Elizabeth was unshakeable, Ridolfi would not have dared to make so free with his name at Brussels, Rome and Madrid.

Norfolk continued to insist that he had never assented to any proposal "which might turn to the prejudice of her Majesty's most royal person, or detriment of her Highness's noble dominions" and this raised the possibility that his fellow peers would be reluctant to convict him of treason if the evidence against him rested solely on the depositions of his servants, extracted under torture. To secure a verdict of guilty, it was desirable that another witness was found to corroborate their stories, but Burghley was confident that, if the Bishop of Ross was forced to make a frank confession, the case against the Duke would be watertight. On 17 October Burghley obtained a ruling from a panel of legal experts that any ambassador who sought to foment rebellion in the realm to which he had been accredited forfeited all right to diplomatic immunity and this gave the Secretary the lever he needed. On 24 October Ross was taken to the Tower and informed that unless he co-operated with the enquiry, he would be put on the rack. The threat proved remarkably persuasive, and Ross's nimble tongue, hitherto so adept at inventing plausible excuses and smooth evasions, now poured forth a flood of damning recollections, each one sufficient to bring the Duke to the block.[32]

Ross confirmed that Norfolk was "40", and explained that after he had gained possession of the letter from Ridolfi that Bailly had carried to England, he had forwarded it to the Duke. He augmented his tale with a wealth of significant detail, going so far as to declare that he found it a relief to rid himself of his burden of guilty secrets. He even wrote a letter of admonishment to Mary, saying that instead of becoming involved in further intrigues she should in future "refer all to God's divine providence and Godly pleasure", for undoubtedly the exposure of this plot had been brought about by heavenly intervention. Not content with this, he gratuitously supplemented his confession by informing his interrogator, Dr Wilson, that Mary was not fit to be a wife, for she had poisoned her first husband, connived at the murder of the second, and then married the murderer in hopes that he would shortly be killed in battle. He added that if she had managed to bring Norfolk to the altar, she would doubtless have capped her career by doing away with him. Dazed by the torrent of allegations that had come tumbling out of Ross, Dr Wilson commented bemusedly to Burghley, "Lord, what a people are these! What a Queen, and what an ambassador".[33]

On 6 January 1572, Norfolk was tried by his peers in Westminster Hall. He pleaded innocent and put up a vigorous defence, but under cross-examination his refutations seemed very lame. He claimed, for example, that Ridolfi had written to him from abroad only because he had previously lent the Duke some money, and he wished to discuss the terms of its repayment, but this was scarcely very convincing. Although he could hardly deny having received the letter from Mary that had been discovered in his London house, he insisted that he had been horrified by its contents, but the Attorney General thereupon pertinently asked him why, in that case, had he carefully preserved the document? Nor were the jury impressed when Norfolk blustered that the case against him rested on the testimony of humble men. "Who is there that accuseth me ... that may spend five marks a year?" he demanded haughtily, but the Prosecution retorted that since his initial betrayal of trust at the time of the York commission Norfolk had freqently committed "wilful perjury" and broken his word to the

Queen. In these circumstances, the prosecuting counsel went on, "it is not for my Lord of Norfolk to stand so much upon the discrediting of the witnesses and advancing of his credit, which himself hath so much decayed".[34] The twenty-six peers sitting in judgement agreed: a unanimous verdict of guilty was returned, and the fearful sentence of death pronounced on England's sole remaining duke.

The Queen had no doubt of Norfolk's guilt, but even so she was very reluctant to execute him. Burghley lamented, "The Queen's Majesty hath been always a merciful lady, and by mercy she hath taken more harm than justice, yet she thinks she is more beloved in doing herself harm". In unison those closest to her lectured her on the need for severity: from Berwick, Lord Hunsdon thundered, "It is small policy, not worthy to be termed mercy, to be so careless of weighty matters that touch the quick so near".These words, and others like it, could not sway the Queen. To Walsingham, Burghley sighed, "I find her Majesty diversely disposed. Sometime when she speaketh of her Majesty's danger, she concludeth that justice should be done; another time when she speaketh of his nearness of blood, of his superiority in honour, etc., she stayeth".[35] On 9 February, Burghley's spirits momentarily soared when Elizabeth signed a death warrant setting the execution for the following morning, but he sank back into despondency late that night when the agitated Queen sent word that she had revoked her decision. Next day, the large crowd that had gathered to witness the Duke's beheading had to content themselves with observing the execution of two much more humble offenders. On three other occasions, the Queen put her name to a fresh death warrant for the Duke, only to change her mind at the last minute, leaving her ministers to fret and chafe at her failure to take action so essential to her safety.

Worse still, Elizabeth viewed with distaste the very suggestion that Mary should be brought to justice for her role in the conspiracy. In the autumn of 1571, Elizabeth had ordered that Mary's household should be drastically reduced, for the Queen of Scots' servants were frequently the filaments in her web of intrigue, but though Mary complained bitterly of the "extreme severity" of the measure, to Burghley and others it seemed woefully inadequate. Certainly Mary made it plain that she would not allow this latest misfortune to bow her down: defiantly she told her custodian, Lord Shrewsbury, "They shall find me to be a Queen, and to have the heart of a Queen". She seemed not in the least disconcerted by the evidence that had accumulated to connect her with Ridolfi's machinations, brazenly denying that it was she who had written the ciphered letter found in Norfolk's home. Shrewsbury reported, "What the Duke of Norfolk and others have done, she saieth she cannot tell; let them answer for themselves, saieth she ... As for the Bishop of Ross, he is, she says, a flayed priest, a fearful priest, who will say whatsoever you will have him to say ... Ridolfi, she says, is a man to her unknown". Far from adopting an apologetic tone, she complained furiously of her wrongs in a series of "uncomely, passionate, ireful and vindictive speeches", and when Elizabeth icily countered that her cousin should think herself fortunate that she had not treated her more harshly, Mary still would not admit that she was in any way at fault. Despite her earlier disavowal of Norfolk's activities, she made no attempt to hide her sympathy for the Duke: she "wept bitterly" when she heard of his condemnation, and then shut herself away to offer up devotions on his behalf. "She thinks, I trow, with fasting and praying to preserve or prolong the Duke's life ... " sarcastically commented Sir Ralph Sadler, who was acting as Mary's guardian while Lord Shrewsbury was in London for Norfolk's trial. "God give her grace to repent and amend her own life, which hitherto have been very loose and dissolute".[36]

Burghley took the view that there was very little chance that Mary would voluntarily amend her life, and his preferred solution was that Elizabeth should act to abridge it. The majority of his colleagues shared his conviction that Mary should be tried and put to death. From France, Francis Walsingham fulminated, "So long as that devilish woman lives, neither her Majesty must make account to continue in quiet possession of her crown, nor her faithful servants assure themselves of safety of their lives", but Elizabeth shrank from applying such harsh logic.[37] She did not question that Mary Stuart was both bad and utterly unscrupulous, but her loathing for her as an individual was subordinated to her reverence for the monarchical order as a whole. For all her shortcomings, Mary remained an honorary member of the fellowship of crowned heads, and to proceed against a Queen as if she was a common criminal was an extreme step from which Elizabeth still recoiled.

In hopes that pressure of public opinion would force her to reconsider, the Council persuaded the Queen that she must ask Parliament to make new laws to provide for her safety. Sure enough, when Parliament assembled in the spring of 1572, the hostility towards Mary was palpable. In a Commons debate of 15 May, one member compared her to Clytemnestra, "a killer of her husband and an adulteress", and his robust advice was that Elizabeth should "cut off her head and make no more ado about her". Another inveighed against Mary as "a Scot, an enemy to England, an adulterous woman, a homicide, a traitor to the Queen, a subverter of the state" and, when Thomas Norton joined in with a vehement speech in favour of Mary's execution, he was interrupted with cries of "Yea! Yea!" from his approving listeners.[38]

By 19 May a committee of both houses had suggested two ways in which the problem could be tackled. The first of these was that a Bill of attainder could be brought in against Mary, convicting her of treason and sentencing her to death. If that option was rejected, a more moderate measure could be introduced, which merely deprived her of her right to succeed to the throne. Somewhat apologetically – for it was clear which alternative was favoured by Parliament – Elizabeth asked them to proceed with the second proposal. Since indignation against Mary was running so high, the disappointment caused by this announcement was intense. In the Commons there were emotional scenes as "many members shed salt tears for her Majesty", and petitions were drawn up imploring the Queen to reconsider.[39] On this point however, Elizabeth was immovable, and so the House of Commons sorrowfully set about drafting the bill of her choice.

With difficulty the Queen had ensured that Mary would survive the session, but Norfolk was not so lucky, for the mood of the Lower House was too fierce to go entirely unappeased. On 30 May Mr St Leger declared that though they had been prevented from proceeding against "the monstrous and huge dragon and mass of the earth, the Queen of Scots", they might yet attain "the execution of the roaring lion, I mean the Duke of Norfolk". The House took up the theme with gusto, drawing up a petition stating that while they would have preferred it if Mary had been the one to suffer, "the striking off of his head shall be at the least half the cutting off of her neck, because though it cutteth not the wisant wherewith she breatheth it shall yet cut asunder the sinews wherewith her head moveth".[40] In the face of this ringing demand, Elizabeth thought it best to give in gracefully. Before the Commons had even had time to present her with their petition, she signed Norfolk's death warrant, and this time she did not rescind it.

On 2 June 1572 the Duke of Norfolk was led out to execution on Tower Hill. Dressed in a black satin doublet, he made a dignified address to the large crowd that had gathered to see him die. "Through great clemency of her Majesty, it has been strange to see a nobleman suffer in this place", he told the onlookers. "It is my fortune to be the first, and I pray God that I may be the last".[41] Moved by his words, several of those present cried "Amen!" but by no means all of his audience can have subscribed to his pious wish that he would be the only person of note to be executed under Elizabeth. Indeed, there were many loyal subjects who cherished the entirely contrary hope that his fate would serve as a precedent, and that he would be followed to the block by Mary Queen of Scots.

By 26 June a bill stating that Mary should never "have, hold, claim, possess or enjoy the dignity and title of the crown of England" had passed both Houses of Parliament, and now it merely needed the royal assent to make it law. It was regarded as a foregone conclusion that Elizabeth would give it her approval, for she herself had seemingly acknowledged that she could do no less. On 30 June she came to Parliament for the closing ceremony, but all present received a rude shock when Sir Nicholas Bacon, speaking for the Queen, announced that "Upon a strange occasion, a strange answer would be given". He explained that Elizabeth applauded the general aim of the bill against Mary, but that some of its details were not to "her whole and perfect liking", and therefore for the moment she would withhold her assent. Since she was unwilling that Members of Parliament should be detained in London during the summer months, she had decided to prorogue Parliament till 1 November, when it could re-assemble and formulate a piece of legislation that would be acceptable in all respects.[42]

The Queen's audacity left men aghast, for in this nonchalant fashion she had made a mockery of their frenzied debates, their hours of committee meetings, and their painstaking efforts to protect her. If Elizabeth's life was snuffed out, Mary was still poised to step into her shoes, and when that happened the outlook for those who had bayed for her blood and spoken of her in such opprobrious terms did not bear thinking about. Few realists attached any weight to the Queen's promise that the bill would be resurrected in the near future, and Burghley summed up the prevailing mood of anger when he described to Walsingham what had transpired. "Now for our Parliament I cannot write patiently", was his bitter comment. "All that we had laboured for, and with full consent brought to fashion ... was by her Majesty neither assented to nor rejected, but deferrred until the feast of All Saints. But what all other wise and good men may think hereof, you may guess".[43] Now that the exposure of the Ridolfi plot had revealed the sort of dangers which menaced the Queen, he and many others were reduced to despair that even in this time of national emergency she apparently thought it more important to preserve intact her right to dispose of the succession as she saw fit than to guard against the crown falling into the wrong hands. They found it incomprehensible that she should shrug off their loyal attempts to neutralize her enemies, and it grieved them immensely that the united will of Parliament had proved insufficient to make her surrender on this point. Nevertheless, the Queen's decision stood. For the moment at least, the only further action she would countenance against Mary was the despatch of a solemn delegation to see her at Sheffield Castle so that they could enumerate Elizabeth's grievances against her, and as Mary rebutted these charges with her usual vigour, there was little reason to suppose that the lecture had had any effect on her.

The Queen's refusal to let Parliament devise measures for her protection led to heightened concern that she would fall victim to an assassination attempt. The fear that her enemies might resort to murder was of course nothing new: as early as April 1560, Sir Nicholas Throckmorton had warned Elizabeth of "a pestilent and horrible device" of the Guises to poison her by means of an Italian named Stephano, "a burly man with a black beard, of the age of about forty-five years". At about the same time, Burghley had drawn up a memorandum entitled "Certain cautions for the

Queen's apparel and diet", suggesting ways in which Elizabeth could guard against being poisoned. Among other recommendations, he had warned her not to accept gifts from strangers of perfume or scented gloves, or anything else "appointed for your Majesty's savour", unless "the same be corrected by some other fume". Now, however, the danger seemed more acute, for the Papal Bull of 1570 could be held by Catholics to justify the Queen's elimination, and the fact that Mary was waiting in the wings was a further incitement to regicide. It was quite right to think that the Queen's life was in jeopardy, for in July 1571 the King of Spain's council had had a lengthy discussion about a possible murder of the Queen, and one of its foremost members had volunteered to go to England to accomplish the deed. In the event the offer was rejected, but the fact that it had been seriously entertained proved that the law of the jungle now governed international relations. The deliberations in Spain of course remained a closely guarded secret, but such intelligence as did reach the English authorities left them in no doubt of the dangers that faced the Queen. In January 1572 the Bishop of London had felt moved to warn Burghley, "The number of obdurate papists and Italianate atheists is great at this time ... both desperate, and grown as it appeareth, to the nature of assassins. Wherefore I should wish that her Majesty should not be so easy of access as she has been, especially to mean strangers; nor walk abroad so slenderly accompanied as she was wont".[44] Burghley would certainly have agreed with this suggestion, but the Queen thought differently, seeing no reason why the threat of terrorism should be permitted to bring about the least modification in her daily routine.

However, it did seem that in one area at least, the Queen would defer to Burghley. Now that the Ridolfi plot had made plain the extent of Spanish hostility, the arguments in favour of a close alliance with France were more telling than ever. Elizabeth apparently acknowledged that she must do everything within reason to bring it about, and in the autumn of 1571 she had taken steps to revive the virtually moribund Anjou marriage negotiations. Because of the urgency of the situation, she agreed that when in England Anjou would be permitted to practise Catholicism in private, a concession that afforded Burghley untold relief. *"Her Majesty was never more earnestly bent to the marriage than now"*, he wrote in great excitement to Walsingham in December,[45] and when at the end of the month Sir Thomas Smith set out on a special embassy to France, Burghley flattered himself that there was every reason to hope he would bring the marriage negotiations to a successful conclusion.

Smith arrived at the French court soon after New Year, and was graciously received, but despite the evident enthusiasm of Charles IX and his mother for the match, it soon emerged that Anjou himself remained full of misgiving. An alarmed Smith reported home that the Duke obviously had little desire to take up residence across the Channel, "where all Englishmen naturally hate Frenchmen", and he was also in the throes of a new love affair, which further disinclined him towards matrimony. Smith, who found it hard to reconcile Anjou's professions of piety with his loose way of living, commented sardonically, "Monsieur is here entangled, and has his religion fixed in Mademoiselle Châteauneuf at first."[46]

It nevertheless soon became clear that religion of a more conventional sort still presented difficulties. Despite the Queen's agreement that after the marriage Anjou and his household could perform their devotions in private chapels set aside for their use, the Duke made it plain that he wanted more. In disgust Smith reported that Anjou was now "extraordinarily papistically superstitious", and when the ambassador had an audience with Catherine de Medici on 6 January 1572, she regretfully confirmed this. She admitted that Monsieur had become "of late so devout that he heard two or three masses every day" and confided that during the previous Lent he had fasted so much that he had "begun to be lean and evil coloured". In his present exalted mood Anjou deemed Elizabeth's grudging concession that he might "have his mass in a corner" to be little better than an insult, for if he abided by her conditions it would imply that he was ashamed of his religion. To avoid such an imputation he insisted that he must be allowed to participate at "high mass and all the ceremonies thereof", and he stipulated that the ceremony must always be performed in public. Smith knew that Elizabeth could never consent to so outrageous a demand: "Why Madam", he expostulated to Catherine, "then he may require also the four orders of friars, monks, canons, pilgrimages, pardons, oil and cream, relics and all such trumperies. That in no wise can be agreed."[47] Catherine could only deplore her son's high-mindedness, but though she "wept hot tears" of frustration, Anjou refused to moderate his demands, and this inevitably terminated the negotiation for his hand.

Elizabeth declared herself greatly offended by the way that Anjou had spurned her, despite her gestures of goodwill, but in reality she could not have been more pleased by the way the business had turned out. In the aftermath of the Ridolfi plot it had been difficult for her to resist the pressure of those who urged that it was her patriotic duty to link herself with a powerful protector, but her temperamental aversion to marriage had remained as violent as ever. Knowing, however, that Anjou was singularly uninspired by the prospect of matching himself with her, she had calculated that in all probability he would decline her hand even if it was extended to him on the most generous of terms. The gamble had paid off magnificently. By making an improved offer to Anjou, Elizabeth had signalled that she was serious about marriage, and when he had declared it unacceptable, all the onus of rejection had fallen on the French. The Queen was now able to assume the guise of injured maidenhood: in martyred tones she declared that since her attempts to find herself a husband had caused her to be so ill-used, she hoped that her subjects would now understand why it was that she preferred to live unmarried.⁴⁸

Astonishingly, however, Catherine de Medici still cherished hopes that Elizabeth could become her daughter-in-law. Two days after negotiations had ground to a halt, she imperturbably observed to Smith that Anjou had a still younger brother, the Duke of Alençon, "whom if the Queen could be content to phantasy . . . would make no scruple" in the matter of religion. Sir Thomas Smith, for one, thought the idea a good one: Alençon, he told the Queen, was "not so obstinate and forward, so papistical and (if I may say so) so foolish and restive like a mule as his brother was". He added that though he couldn't understand exactly why, when it came to the "getting of children", all at the French court implied that Alençon was "more apt than th'other". In short, Alençon was "the more moderate, the more flexible, and the better fellow". "The marriage with this duke . . . is 10,000 times better than the other", Smith enthused,⁴⁹ but he can hardly have expected Elizabeth to be entirely uncritical of a proposal to wed her to a beardless youth of sixteen. As always, however, she was not averse to entering on a new courtship, especially since Anjou's recent behaviour meant that the French were in no position to try and bully her into accepting Alençon. Confident that she would not be called upon to make a decision for an appreciable length of time, the Queen graciously sanctioned a further round of discussions.

As it was clear to English and French alike that Elizabeth was not going to commit herself in haste, both sides agreed that in the interim a more limited form of alliance was desirable, for this would be proof of their solidarity. Tiresomely, however, the reproachful figure of Mary Stuart made the French uneasy about putting their names to such a pact. It was true that while the Anjou marriage negotiations had been in progress, the French had muted their demands that Elizabeth restore Mary to her kingdom, but to acquiesce in her captivity was another matter entirely. Ideally they would have liked Elizabeth to have agreed that Mary could come to live in France, for they feared it would look discreditable if they signed a treaty with a country that was holding one of their former queens against her will. Fortunately for Elizabeth, however, when the French learnt that Mary had employed Ridolfi to solicit aid from their old enemy, Spain, it considerably lessened their sympathy for her. The English ruthlessly exploited this, by sending to France copies of letters which Mary had recently written to the Duke of Alva, but which had been intercepted before they reached him. In these Mary promised that if Philip II sent her aid she would repay him by betrothing her son to his daughter the infanta, and when the French saw this fresh evidence of Mary's reliance upon Spain, they felt free to wash their hands of her. In early April Catherine de Medici made it plain how much she disapproved of Mary's overtures to Spain, telling Smith that Mary evidently "seeketh another way to ruinate herself, to hurt her friends, to deserve no pity nor favour, and sorry we must be for her". Henceforth the French dropped their demands that Mary be set at liberty, requesting only that Elizabeth refrain from executing her, and Francis Walsingham, the English ambassador in France, declared that even this was merely for the sake of appearances, and that if Elizabeth did bring her cousin to justice, the French "would not inwardly be miscontented".[50]

With Mary no longer complicating the agenda, agreement could be reached, and on 19 April 1572 the Treaty of Blois was signed. Its provisions included an undertaking that if either of the signatories was attacked, the other would provide her ally with military and naval assistance, an obligation that remained binding on France even if England was invaded by another power on religious grounds. All in all, the diplomats who had hammered out the terms had every reason to congratulate themselves: a satisfied Sir Thomas Smith wrote to the Queen, "By God's grace ... this league shall be as great an assurance and defence for your Majesty's crown as any that was or may be". He added proudly, "If Spain will now threaten or shew evil offices (as it hath done of late) against your Highness's surety, it will be afraid hereafter, seeing such a wall adjoined. And if it may not, it may sooner feel the smart of evil doings than it would".[51]

There were some men, however, who contended that this defensive pact with France did not go far enough, for in its present form it gave inadequate protection against the might of Spain. In the past, of course, England had traditionally tried to forge links with Spain and the Netherlands in order to combat the ambitions of France, but the Ridolfi plot had shown the need for a bold reversal of policy. England and France shared a common fear of Spain and, although France was a Catholic country, the fact that its king was now extending toleration to Huguenots allowed room for hope that he would be prepared to work with Elizabeth if it was in the national interest to do so. In contrast, Spain was the citadel of Catholic orthodoxy, with a king renowned for his abhorrence of heresy, and recent events suggested that he was set on Elizabeth's destruction. It was true that the failure of the Ridolfi plot had obliged the Spaniards to defer their plans for invasion, but it was far from fanciful to suppose that the respite would be only temporary. Once the Duke of Alva crushed the last vestiges of resistance in the Netherlands – and he was already alarmingly close to achieving this objective – it was all too plausible that Philip would order him to take his army the short distance across the sea to conquer England. If these predictions were correct, the logic of the situation demanded that the English countered the threat by allying with France and mounting a pre-emptive strike against Spain. The necessity for this was the more acute because, for the first time in his reign, Philip II was not distracted by the Turkish menace in the Mediterranean, for in October 1571 a Christian fleet, led by Philip's half-brother, Don John of Austria, had inflicted a crushing naval defeat on the Ottomans at Lepanto. It was to be feared that this victory, which eased pressure on Philip's resources, would free the Spaniards to concentrate on other theatres of war, and one Catholic Englishman living in exile expressed the fervent hope that now that Don John had proved his powers of leadership, "his next enterprise shall be to subdue the English Turks".[52]

The principal exponent of the "First Strike" theory was the English ambassador in France, Francis Walsingham, a Kentish gentleman and brilliant linguist who had been in royal service since 1568. Forbidding in aspect, hard working and outspoken, Walsingham was the most militant of Protestants, and his religious outlook accounted for his contentious views on the conduct of foreign policy. In 1586 a French diplomat described him as "a very skilful man of business, and very clever, but also so impassioned with regard to his religion that for this respect alone, his advice frequently swerves from the paths of temperance and wisdom". He himself once declared that he believed religion was the "matter principally to be weighed by Christian councillors in giving advice to a Christian prince, seeing the prosperity or adversity of kingdoms dependeth of God's goodness, who is so long to extend his protection as we shall depend of his providence, and shall not seek our safety (carried away by human policy) contrary to his word". Because he was sure that war with the forces of the popish Antichrist was inevitable, he took the view that the English must strike the first blow, and he had no patience with those who pleaded that the country could not afford to squander its resources on military adventures overseas. To such critics, Walsingham replied that in the long term, futile attempts to preserve the peace would prove infinitely more costly, and he insisted that, compared to the perils of inaction, the risks involved in pursuing a more aggressive policy were of little account. Time and again he would tell Elizabeth that she must go to the aid of the embattled Protestants on the continent, urging that this was at once a sacred duty and a means of self-defence. A failure to respond would be an inexcusable betrayal of God's cause for, as he ringingly proclaimed in a memorandum written in 1576, "All creatures are created to advance God's glory; therefore when His glory is called in question, no league nor policy can excuse if by all means he seek not the defence of the same, yea, with the loss of life".[53]

Of the hostility of Spain Walsingham had no doubt: in June 1571 he stated succinctly, "Let her Majesty well assure herself that Spain will never forget the injuries they have received, as shall well appear when opportunity of revenge shall be offered". He regarded it as madness on her part to watch idly while the Spaniards re-established their ascendancy in the

Netherlands, for to him it was blindingly obvious that once the Provinces had been subdued, they would be used as the springboard from which an invasion of England would be launched. Obsessed by the need to prevent these developments, in early 1571 he had urged the Queen to give financial support to an expedition against the Spanish forces in the Netherlands, led by William of Orange's younger brother, Louis of Nassau, who had fled to France in 1568. Elizabeth had given the idea some thought, but she had drawn back when she had learnt just how sizeable a sum of money she would have to advance, with little guarantee of repayment.[54] Walsingham made clear his belief that in doing so, she was missing a great opportunity: he declared that if Elizabeth had ventured 50,000 crowns now, it might have saved her 300,000 in the future, and this was a refrain he would constantly repeat over the next few years.

The Queen in no way underrated Walsingham's abilities, but she treated his arguments with caution, for she did not share his apocalyptic vision of events to come. In view of the Spaniards' ill will towards her, she was disturbed by the thought of what might happen once Alva had regained mastery in the Netherlands, but she found it hard to believe that her ideological differences with Philip were so deep that he was now committed to her overthrow. She refused to accept that a war between their two countries was an inevitability, and was reluctant to do anything that would preclude a relaxation in tension at some date in the future. She was mindful that ambitious schemes of the sort advocated by Walsingham had a tendency to miscarry, and never lost sight of the fact that if she lent her support to a venture that failed, she would do nothing to loosen Alva's grip upon the Netherlands, and would only succeed in making Philip intent upon revenge.

It was true that the discovery of the Ridolfi plot showed that her relations with Philip had deteriorated to a point where he would not scruple to exploit disaffection in her subjects. Nevertheless, the Queen could dismiss this as mere opportunism, and now that the blow had been deflected, she thought it unlikely that he would want to try again in the near future. That he had been prepared to go so far could indeed be largely attributed to the unsettling influence of de Spes, whose wild flights of hyperbole about the universal discontent prevalent in England had given his master an entirely misleading impression about her subjects' state of mind. In December 1571 de Spes was accordingly expelled from the country, having been denounced by the Queen as "a person that would secretly seek to inflame our realm with firebrands",[55] and Elizabeth could now hope that more moderate counsels would be listened to in Madrid.

The Queen had been careful not to let herself be drawn into any action she might later regret, but Alva's presence in the Netherlands did occasion her concern, and she was not averse to inconveniencing him if it could be done without bringing trouble on her head. For this reason she had given shelter in her ports to the band of pirates known as the Sea Beggars, who had been authorized by William of Orange to disrupt Spain's maritime route to the Netherlands by preying on Channel shipping. When Alva complained, she justified her action on the grounds that Orange was a free prince of the Holy Roman Empire, whose sovereign powers entitled him to issue letters of marque to privateers, and that the actions of the Sea Beggars were therefore quite legitimate. Nevertheless, the indiscriminate depredations of the Sea Beggars against ships of any flag soon resulted in protests from other powers, and she came to regret that she had given a haven to such brigands. Accordingly, on 21 February 1572 she issued an order expelling the Sea Beggars from her harbours.

Her action had unforeseen consequences: the pirates cruised about for some weeks, until their desperation for supplies led them to attack and take the northern Netherlandish port of Brill, and henceforth they were able to use this as a base for their operations. Heartened by their success, they went on to seize Flushing, which commanded the entrance to the Scheldt, and the feat sparked off similar upheavals all over Holland and Zealand. Throughout the summer of 1572, ardent Protestants succeeded in gaining control of municipal councils in numerous towns, and having engineered these coups, they declared for the rebels. For the first time since 1568, there seemed to be a glimmer of hope that the revolt against Spain could succeed, particularly since the insurgents could count on receiving aid from abroad. In Germany, William of Orange was recruiting mercenaries with the intention of mounting an invasion of the Provinces from the north, while in France his brother Louis had been exerting himself to equally good effect. Having failed to procure aid from Elizabeth in 1571, Louis had next sought the assistance of Charles IX, and it appeared that the French King was ready to provide it. He permitted bands of French volunteers to reinforce the rebels at Flushing and he gave Louis to understand that he was on the point of despatching an army across the border which would enable the Netherlanders to drive out their Spanish overlords. Confident that Charles would not renege on his promises, in May 1572 Louis left France with a small contingent of men, and having succeeded in capturing Mons in the southern Netherlands, he settled down to await the arrival of troops from France.

To Walsingham it seemed grotesque that the Queen was leaving others to shoulder a burden that was rightfully hers, and he passionately implored her to combine forces with France and fight in the Netherlands herself. He was confident that if she did so, she would not go unrewarded, envisaging that once the Spaniards had been ousted, the Netherlanders could show their gratitude by giving England one or two ports on their eastern seaboard, while the French could take possession of a couple of towns near the Low Countries' southern frontier. The proposal earned the approval of the Earl of Leicester who saw in it a rare opportunity to combine high-mindedness with self-interest. "I think her Majesty shall be advised not to lose all these good advantages offered her, specially when they tend both to the setting up of God's true religion, and establishment of her own surety", he commented gravely, when first acquainted with the plan.[56]

In contrast, both Elizabeth and Burghley had serious doubts as to the feasibility of this cosy arrangement. Despite the Treaty of Blois, they did not want to see the power of France increased, and they feared that the French desire to drive the Spanish out of the Netherlands was nourished by a secret desire to possess the United Provinces for themselves. The very prospect of their ancient enemy acquiring a property of such commercial and strategic importance was enough to convince Elizabeth and Burghley that a Spanish defeat was not necessarily a desirable outcome to the struggle now in progress. Burghley explained to Walsingham that he had every sympathy with the Dutch struggle to regain ancient freedoms, but added, "I wish it were rather done by themselves than by others that percase would not suffer them long to enjoy their liberty when it should be recovered; percase it will not be liked here".[57]

In order to keep an eye on what was happening in the Netherlands, the Queen agreed that over a thousand volunteers from England could go and fight on the rebel side. Alva naturally protested, but was told that these men had "departed without either licence or knowledge of her Majesty". That was not true, but their presence in the Netherlands owed quite as much to the Queen's anxiety to prevent the French from entrenching themselves there as her desire to make life more difficult for Alva. Indeed, a memorandum written in June 1572, presumably by Burghley, went so far as to say that if it appeared likely that the French would succeed in gaining control of the Low Countries, Elizabeth should offer to help Alva to drive them back. In that event, however, the Queen would not give her services unconditionally, for in return she could demand that Philip should "discharge his subjects of their intolerable oppressions, restore them to their ancient liberties, reconcile his nobility to him, deliver them from the fear of the inquisition, and continue with her Majesty the ancient leagues for amity and traffic in as ample sort as any others, Dukes of Burgundy, heretofore have done".[58] This indeed would be the ideal solution: the Netherlands would remain in the hands of their rightful owner, but so long as Philip was forced to abide by his constitutional obligations, he would be unable to maintain a large army there, and hence, even if he wished to do so, it would be more difficult for him to mount an attack on England. However, the French menace in the Netherlands was not yet so great that Alva felt any need for outside assistance to help him deal with it, for he was confident that he would be able to regain control of the Provinces on his own terms. In these circumstances there was obviously little hope that the English could have much influence over the nature of any settlement eventually achieved there, and the memorandum rather lamely concluded that until the situation became clearer, "It is like to be best for England to let both sides alone for a time".

In view of the Queen's guarded attitude towards the French, Walsingham's vision that the English should unite with them to strike against the forces of evil as personified by Spain seemed far-fetched indeed. Neverthless, he could at least console himself that while the Alençon marriage negotiations remained in being, hopes of closer co-operation with the French at some time in the future were not utterly unrealistic. The problem was that Alençon himself was hardly the most enticing of baits: originally christened Hercules, he had turned out so puny that this had proved to be an absurd misnomer, and on the death of his eldest brother it had been deemed advisable for him to adopt the less heroical name of Francis. Furthermore, his complexion left much to be desired, for two attacks of smallpox had left him with a severely pitted skin. Sir Thomas Smith found it difficult to believe that this could adversely affect his chances of marriage – pock marks were "no matter in a man", he robustly declared – but Walsingham was well aware of the Queen's sensitivity in such matters. "The great impediment I find", he admitted privately to Burghley, " ... is the contentment of the eye. The gentleman is void of any good favour, besides the blemish of the smallpox. Now, when I weigh the same with the delicacy of her Majesty's eye ... I hardly think that there will ever grow any liking". Sure enough, although every effort was made to assure the Queen that the disfigurement was only slight, she became increasingly concerned about "the absurdity that in general opinion of the world might grow"[59] if she allied herself to this juvenile pock-marked midget. Negotiations continued to proceed at a desultory pace, but by August 1572 an engagement still looked very remote.

This being so, Catherine de Medici could only regret that her son Charles IX had made such large offers of help to Louis of Nassau in the Netherlands. If a sizeable force from France went to the aid of the rebels in the Low Countries, this amounted to a virtual declaration of war on Spain, and Catherine thought it madness to seek a confrontation with so formidable a foe. If Charles's army failed to drive the Spaniards out of the Netherlands, it was obvious that the Spanish would then punish the King for his attempt to do so by invading France, and Catherine believed the country to be in no condition to meet such a challenge. It was true that according to the terms of the Treaty of Blois, the English were bound to assist their ally in the event of an invasion, but the Queen Mother had no confidence that Elizabeth would honour her treaty obligations. If the marriage between Elizabeth and Alençon had gone ahead, Catherine could have felt that the Anglo-French league rested on a solid foundation, but her youngest son was plainly very far from ensnaring the Queen, and in these circumstances Catherine felt sure that the English would cheerfully renege on their commitments and leave France to take on Spain alone.

Catherine's consternation increased as it became apparent that it would not be easy for Charles to change his mind about intervening in the Netherlands. It was the leader of the French Huguenots, Admiral Coligny, who had been largely responsible for the King's original decision to do so, for Coligny had told the King that only if the nation's energies were absorbed in a foreign campaign would it be possible to preserve the internal peace of France. The Admiral still maintained this, and warned that if Charles failed to deliver the promised support, the Huguenots would doubt his ability to enforce the policy of religious toleration proclaimed two years previously. In the council chamber, Coligny threateningly demanded that Charles "weigh whether it were better to have foreign war with advantage, or inward war to the ruin of himself and his estate",[60] but it was Catherine's opinion that either alternative would prove ruinous for France.

In her determination to halt the headlong rush into war, Catherine had no time for conventional morality. She decided that Coligny should be eliminated, reasoning that once the Huguenots were deprived of their leader, they would be too weak to protest if Charles abandoned his plans to invade the Low Countries. On 22 August 1572 Coligny was fired on as he walked down a Paris street, but although he was wounded, he survived the attack. Terrified of what would happen if the Huguenots learnt that it was she who was behind the crime, Catherine justified her action to the King by pretending that she had learnt of the existence of a Huguenot plot against the Crown, and she explained that she had hoped to forestall it by sanctioning an attack on Coligny. However, as the attempt had miscarried, the danger still remained, and she persuaded Charles that his only hope of safety lay in arranging for all the leaders of the Huguenot party to be summarily murdered. This would be easy to do, for the most prominent members of the French aristocracy were then gathered in Paris for the wedding of Catherine's daughter Marguerite to the Protestant Henry of Navarre. The King gave his consent, and in the early hours of St Bartholomew's day, 24 August, Catherine's design was put into action. Coligny and other Protestant nobles were slain according to plan, but the victims were much more numerous than Catherine had envisaged, for when the virulently Catholic Parisian populace learnt what was going on, they added to the carnage by rising *en masse* and butchering all the Protestants they could find. In this way, between two and three thousand Huguenots perished in the capital, and the slaughter soon spread to the provinces, where similar horrors were perpetrated.

At Rome, the tidings were received with joy by the new Pope, Gregory

XIII, who had a special commemorative medal struck in honour of the occasion. Similarly, the normally impassive Philip II could not hide his delight on hearing the news, which made him laugh and dance about his bedroom. In England, however, the reaction was very different, for when the first refugees trickled in from France, bringing tales of streets awash with blood and rivers choked with corpses, it occurred to few people that such atrocities could be attributed to a spontaneous outbreak of savagery. The massacre was hailed as a hellish manifestation of the Counter-Reformation's essential inhumanity, and those who had claimed that the major Catholic powers were engaged in a gigantic conspiracy to exterminate Protestantism seemed vindicated in the light of the Huguenots' awful fate. It was widely credited not only that violence had been long pre-meditated, but also that the French monarchy had previously consulted the Pope and the King of Spain, so that the bloodbath could be carefully co-ordinated with a more general onslaught on heresy in Europe.

Stunned by events so monstrous that they defied rational assessment, Burghley hardly knew how to convey his revulsion, writing falteringly that "These French tragedies and ending of unlucky marriage with blood and vile murders cannot be expressed with tongue to declare the cruelties". As for Walsingham, who had been in Paris at the time and had been lucky to escape with his life, the shock was still more intense, particularly since he had entertained such high hopes of what could be achieved by strong links with France. He had long predicted that Armageddon was on its way, and assumed that the atrocities in France were merely the first phase of a holocaust that would sweep the whole of Europe. Resoundingly he trumpeted, "Can we think that the fire kindled here in France will extend itself no further? That which was concluded at the late Council of Trent, as also that which was agreed on at Bayonne . . . for the rooting out of the professors of the gospel, may in reason induce us to think the contrary. Let us not deceive ourselves, but assuredly think that the two great monarchs of Europe, together with the rest of the papists, do mean shortly to put into execution that which in the aforesaid assemblies was concluded." Burghley was scarcely less pessimistic, noting darkly, "These fires may be doubted that their flames may come both hither and into Scotland, for such cruelties have large scopes".[61] All the painstaking work that had gone into the making of the Treaty of Blois now seemed completely worthless, and French overtures of friendship could be dismissed as nothing more than a cynical ploy designed to prevent their so-called ally Elizabeth from perceiving how vulnerable she really was. It could indeed be said that England's position was in fact more beleaguered than ever, and far from having emerged from diplomatic isolation, the country was in a state of siege, the unwitting target of a combined Franco-Spanish offensive orchestrated by the Holy See.

CHAPTER 9

"The weaving of Penelope"

Since July 1572 Elizabeth and her Court had been on an extended progress. In the course of this she had visited various Midland towns and been sumptuously entertained by a succession of noblemen, including the Earl of Warwick at Warwick Castle, Lord Berkeley at Berkeley Castle, and the Earl of Leicester at Kenilworth. At all these places the Queen's hosts had vied with one another to see who could provide the most lavish hospitality, and Elizabeth had been on excellent form throughout, thoroughly enjoying the banquets, firework displays and "princely sports" that were put on for her benefit. During the daytime she had managed to fit in a good deal of hunting, and the first intimations of the massacre had indeed reached her when she was on horseback. At once the day's sporting activities were cancelled, and for the remainder of the progress there was no more thought of gaiety. A Spanish merchant in London took grim satisfaction in informing the Duke of Alva that the Queen had "sent all her musicians and minstrels home, and there are no more of the dances, farces and entertainments with which they have been amusing themselves lately, as they have some less agreeable things to think about".[1]

Even before the Court returned to London, the Council met daily, anxiously debating what the horrific events across the Channel portended for England. From France itself, letters came from Walsingham, avowing that the breach between the two countries was now so wide that the Queen's wisest course would be to break off diplomatic relations forthwith, for as he put it, "I think less peril to live with them as enemies than as friends".[2] Nevertheless, as the initial wave of panic subsided, the Queen came to take a cooler view, for on closer examination there were signs that St Bartholomew's was not the first stage in a meticulously planned programme of extermination, but a self-contained event, dreadful in itself, but without the wider implications that had been feared.

By the beginning of September the peripatetic Court had reached the royal palace of Woodstock, and the French ambassador hurried west to meet it, anxious to give an official explanation as to why his master had slaughtered his own subjects on such a massive scale. For three days he was kept cooling his heels in Oxford, but at length the Queen agreed to grant him an audience. He had a somewhat unnerving reception, for when admitted he found the Queen surrounded by a daunting array of courtiers and ladies, who eyed him reproachfully, sunk in meaningful silence. Nevertheless, when Elizabeth gravely took him aside for a private discussion, the ambassador was able partially to still her fears. Far from claiming that the King had been justified in proceeding to extremities against heretics, his tone was highly apologetic. He pedalled the line that Charles had had to move against the Huguenots because he had uncovered the existence of a dastardly Protestant plot, and said that had he not acted swiftly the King and all his family would have been assassinated. Naturally Elizabeth did not accept this tale without question: at this and subsequent audiences she pointed out that it did not explain the scale of the violence, and she declared that she had been moved to tears by the grisly reports that had been coming out of France. Nevertheless, she could not but be reassured by the ambassador's protestations that nothing was more important to his master than the alliance with England, and although Burghley was swift to point out, "We have great causes in these times to doubt all fair speeches",[3] she elected not to disbelieve them altogether. Mindful of the need for watchfulness, she agreed that the fortifications of the principal forts on the south coast should be inspected, and that the navy should put to sea in case the French were planning a maritime attack, but for the moment she believed that these precautions would suffice.

Gradually, the tension eased, but while it was a relief to learn that England would not have to fight for her survival in the immediate future, the way ahead was nevertheless still murky. The Queen had tried to safeguard her country through a partnership with France, but though neither party had officially repudiated the other, it would clearly be madness to regard the French as the most stalwart of allies. Since the friendship of France no longer provided her with a protective shield, Elizabeth now had to fall back on more makeshift forms of shelter, and because she could not rely on the goodwill of either of the two major continental powers, her aim was to ensure that they were in no position to do her harm. The standard way of achieving this was to see to it that the Kings of France and Spain were too distracted by unrest within their own dominions to think of becoming involved in action against her, and in these circumstances the Queen acknowledged that it was sometimes in her interest to give discreet assistance to the Protestant resistance movements that had sprung up in their realms. To do so nevertheless ran contrary to her instincts, which were peace-loving and conservative, and although destiny was to thrust on her the role of the guardian of the godly, she found the position an invidious one. Self-preservation dictated that she could not callously ignore the plight of foreign Protestants, but she had little sense of identity with them, and did not feel inspired by the prospect of becoming involved in a universal struggle against a common foe. Far from automatically putting her resources at the disposal of her co-religionists abroad, she scrutinized each appeal for aid on its merits, and generally it was only if it seemed that the international Protestant cause was in danger of total collapse that she was ready to come to its defence. Not only was she wary of antagonizing the Kings of France and Spain more than was absolutely essential, but she also took the view that the situation in Europe was too fluid and unpredictable to warrant the formulation of a set policy and its single-minded pursuit. Instead of anticipating a set of circumstances and taking steps to deal with them in advance, she preferred to cope with emergencies as they arose, relapsing thankfully back into inertia as soon as each crisis was past.

To the more hawkish of her advisers, Elizabeth's grudging and piecemeal response to the calls on her for aid were entirely inadequate to cope with the exigencies of the situation she faced. The most articulate and forceful of those who took this line was Francis Walsingham, whose opinions carried great weight even before he returned from France in April 1573. Thereafter, a period of convalescence temporarily postponed further advancement in his career, but in December 1573 he was simultaneously created a member of the Privy Council and Principal Secretary of State. From this vantage point he incessantly lectured the Queen on the need to face up to unpalatable realities, for he was appalled that she could think that the raging torrents of hatred which engulfed the continent during these years could flow by and leave her untouched. To him it seemed she laboured under a fundamental misconception, deluding herself that after a period of maladjustment Europe would once again assume the aspect of a reasonably balanced community, in which none of the major powers denied the others' right to existence. This ignored the religious dimension, a new and destructive element "incident to the times",[4] which made a nonsense of all such comfortable assumptions, and Walsingham was aghast at Elizabeth's reluctance to take this into account. As he saw it, the scene was already set for a titanic struggle within Christendom, and it was time for the Queen to gauge correctly the scale of the dangers that lay in store. Instead of waiting passively on events, she should shape them to her advantage, and by making common cause with European Protestants she could weaken the evil and reactionary forces that were bent on their mutual annihilation.

Walsingham's viewpoint was best summed up by William Davison, a protégé of his who was frequently employed on diplomatic missions abroad. In 1577 he prepared a memorandum for the Secretary dwelling on the dangers posed by the existence of an international Catholic League, an entity in which he, like Walsingham, firmly believed, and to which he imagined the Pope, the Holy Roman Emperor, the Kings of Spain, France and Portugal, plus "divers other princes and potentates" were all a party. Davison roundly declared that "as they are enemies to all that profess our religion, so is there no doubt but the chief end and mark of their conspiracy tendeth to the overthrow of her Majesty's state, partly for religion and partly for malice and revenge, accompting her the only bridle and stop to their tyrannous purposes. How much, therefore, it shall import her Majesty to look about her, and carefully to entertain her intelligence in France … to look to the state of Scotland, and by all good means to assure herself of the Prince and states of Holland and Zealand, I leave to your honour's judgement!"[5]

Walsingham's most notable supporter within the Council was the Earl of Leicester, who prided himself on being the courtly patron of the Protestant Cause. When the Secretary begged the Queen to intervene in foreign religious wars, he could generally count on the Earl's backing, not least because Leicester envisaged that he would be the General of any expeditionary force that was sent overseas, and this meant that for him evangelical fervour and personal ambition agreeably dovetailed. It was infinitely harder for Walsingham to convince the Queen that a more martial policy would bring either material or spiritual gains, for her distrust of continental entanglements ran very deep, and his frequent inability to convince her that he knew best left Walsingham in a near-permanent state of frustration. Nevertheless, if Elizabeth rarely welcomed Walsingham's advice, she did not lightly disregard it, for though he was too alarmist and doctrinaire for her liking, she did not doubt his shrewdness. There was no question of her ever permitting Walsingham to dominate her, but she admired his incisive mind, and knowing that in her position complacency could prove fatal, she regarded it as a salutary discipline that he should be so remorseless about telling her what she did not want to hear. At times she was goaded beyond endurance by his ceaseless admonishments, and then she would flare up, screaming that he favoured Calvinists and Puritans more than those who had her true interests at heart. When she was in these moods, Walsingham had to stop nagging her for a while, knowing that if he persisted it would "rather hurt than help" his cause. "My state standing as it doth, having no hope to do good, I think it wisdom to forbear to offend," he once commented ruefully when he knew himself to be in particularly ill odour with the Queen. Such restraint was nevertheless uncharacteristic, and soon he was at it again, worrying Elizabeth relentlessly and refusing to let her relax. It was no wonder that she sometimes lost her temper, but on the whole she was very long-suffering in the face of his tirades, and the freedom with which Walsingham was permitted to criticize royal policy was in many ways truly remarkable. He himself acknowledged that he did not always handle her with as much sensitivity as could be required, but expressed the hope that the Queen "seeing the ground of this my zeal, will most graciously incline to pardon this my rude and plain, though dutiful manner". Since Elizabeth knew that it was true that his outspokenness derived from a sincere concern for her well-being, she did her best to endure his fault-finding and reproofs.[6] There was always a certain tension in their relations, but she came to grow quite fond of him, and it was a sure sign of affection that in moments of good humour she would address him by the nickname of "Ethiopian" or "Moor".

Like Elizabeth herself, Lord Burghley held views on foreign policy that were less decided than those propounded by Walsingham. His caution, always profound, had by now attained depths that were virtually unfathomable, for though he was able to identify myriad threats to the nation's security, he felt less confident about suggesting ways of combatting these. As a peer of the realm and man of considerable property, Burghley had further to fall than most if the regime collapsed, and it was perhaps this that led him to harp upon its vulnerability, without venturing to propose remedies for this sorry state of affairs. He continued compulsively to draw up memoranda, outlining dangers, reiterating warnings and prophesying catastrophe, but he shared the Queen's fears that if these complex problems were tackled directly, it would only bring further calamity in its wake. Well might Elizabeth remark that she liked transacting business with Burghley because he "knoweth her mind",[7] for his way of thinking was indeed remarkably similar to hers.

Yet for all his quavering uncertainty, Burghley did recognize some constants that should govern the formulation of English foreign policy, support for the Protestant regime in Scotland being one such bedrock of his statesmanship. To his distress, even here the Queen would not accept that the path to take was clear, for though she sometimes acknowledged the necessity for a closer connection with the lords who were ruling Scotland in the young King's name, she repeatedly aborted negotiations that were designed to bring it about. Aghast that Elizabeth could not bring herself to take a step so fundamental to her safety, Burghley was reduced to complaining about her in terms that Walsingham himself would have thought highly apt. "If her Majesty will continue her delays for providing for her surety by just means given to her by God, she and we shall all vainly call upon God when the calamity shall fall upon us", he wailed to Leicester on one occasion. "God send her Majesty strength of spirit to preserve God's cause, her own life, and lives of millions of good subjects, all which are most manifestly in danger; and that only by her delays, and consequently she will be the cause of the overthrow of a noble crown and realm, which shall be prey to all that can invade it. God be merciful to us".[8]

If at times even Burghley despaired of the Queen, it was acknowledged that of all her advisers he was the best at coaxing a decision out of her. This had been apparent from early in the reign: in June 1560 Sir Nicholas Throckmorton had been appalled to hear that Cecil was being sent to Scotland, for he believed that in his absence Elizabeth would be quite unmanageable. "Who can or will stand fast against the Queen's arguments and doubtful devices?" he had asked in panic, "Who will speedily resolve the doubtful delays? who shall make despatch of anything?" Over the years, Burghley's handling of her had grown still more assured, and at those times when Elizabeth was at her most impossible, his colleagues looked to him to bring her round. In November 1572, for example, she was being particularly refractory about Scottish affairs, and so Leicester begged Burghley to come to court at once. He wrote urgently, "There will little be done while you are away; if I say plainly as I think, your Lordship, as the case stands, shall do her Majesty and your country more service here in an hour than in all the court there will be worth this seven years; wherefore I can but wish you here, yea to fly here if you would, till these matters were fully despatched".[9]

It was universally acknowledged that Burghley was incomparable at dealing with the Queen, but he was not always at hand to deploy his skills, for whereas at the beginning of the reign he had been almost invariably in attendance at court, he was now away much more frequently. In March 1572 the aged Marquis of Winchester had died, and the following July Burghley replaced him as Lord Treasurer. As a result of this promotion he found himself in charge of the Exchequer, the department responsible for the collection of customs and taxes, the administration of crown lands, and the disbursement of all receipts. This did not mean that he now concentrated exclusively on the national finances, for as he rather lugubriously remarked, "I am out of the office of the Secretary ... and yet I am not discharged from my ordinary care",[10] and he continued to concern himself with almost all aspects of state affairs. Nevertheless, much of the day to day business of the realm now devolved upon Walsingham and Sir Thomas Smith, who were appointed joint Secretaries in his place, and as a result Burghley enjoyed more frequent opportunities to snatch time away from Court.

Unfortunately, since neither Smith nor Walsingham were so adept as their predecessor at prising decisions out of the Queen, both were frequently left fuming by her time-wasting ploys. Even when she agreed that letters should be drafted containing definite instructions, or authorizing a change in policy, the Secretaries had infinite difficulty in persuading her to put her signature to the documents, and if she did bring herself to sign, she would then insist that the despatch of the letter was delayed until she had had further time for reflection. At other times she simply avoided seeing the Secretaries, knowing that they would importune her to deal with all unfinished business. "I had somewhat ado to get to the Queen, and more to get anything signed", Sir Thomas Smith moaned to Burghley in January 1573 and two years later his lament remained the same. In exasperation he told the Lord Treasurer that not only was the Queen refusing to make up her mind about Irish affairs, but "I neither can get the other letters signed, nor the letter already signed ... permitted to be sent away, but day by day, and hour by hour, deferred till anon, soon and tomorrow ... This ... indeed maketh me weary of my life, to have no resolution, but still waiting and suspense for that which doth so much import her Majesty's honour, profit and reputation. I would some other man occupied my room, who had more credit to get things resolved, signed, and things necessary resolved in time." Walsingham fared no better in his efforts to persuade the Queen to make up her mind. In November 1576 he indulged in a typical outburst when he wrote to Leicester informing him that Elizabeth was cavilling about sending a diplomatic representative to the Netherlands. His letter bitterly concluded: "The experience your Lordship hath in like cases of our slowness in proceeding in all our doings, whereby the occasion being forestalled, both that we attempt taketh no effect and the charges thereby cast away will ... make your Lordship the less to wonder at this present slackness".[11]

In seeking to justify her near-pathological tendency to procrastinate, Elizabeth herself was to offer the quaint explanation, "Methinks I am more beholden to the hinder part of my head than well dare trust the forwards side of the same", but what really lay behind it was a perfectly understandable reluctance to do anything which might set her on a collision course with her neighbours. Zealots on the council might urge her to adopt a dynamic policy, saying that she could uphold the interests of European Protestants without undue wastage of her resources, but Elizabeth could not overlook that even a brief incursion into the upheavals on the continent brought with it a danger of escalation. As Burghley was to note in 1577, she was not convinced that a confrontation between her and the leading Catholic princes was inevitable, but if she were to give a significant degree of aid to their disobedient subjects, it would "justly irritate" the Kings of France and Spain and cause them "to be revenged of the Queen's Majesty, which otherwise she thinketh they would not".[12]

Always in the forefront of the Queen's mind was the worry about the strain that any sort of military commitment would impose on the economy, for the Tudor state lacked the infrastructure which would have enabled it to pay for a prolonged war. She herself once remarked that in cases of pressing necessity she was always ready to produce money, and "neither did her mind ever move her to spare upon such occasions ... but sorry she is that she is not better furnished to spend". To Walsingham this seemed arrant nonsense, and certainly it was true that by 1571 the Queen's financial circumstances were much more comfortable than had been the case in the early part of the reign. After taking into account the costs of collection and various administrative expenses, Elizabeth's net annual income from feudal and ecclesiastical dues, customs duties and crown lands had then averaged about £200,000, out of which she was expected to find the running costs for her government and Court. As a result of stringent economies effected soon after her accession, these were reduced to just under £135,000 a year, but even so, in the first decade of the reign the Queen still had difficulty paying her way. Apart from defraying her basic expenses, she was also burdened with a debt of nearly £228,000 which she had inherited from her sister, and in addition she had to finance the expeditions sent to Scotland and France and spend an estimated £300,000 on improving national defences. Parliamentary grants had covered a proportion of these costs, but the remainder had to be paid for out of the savings achieved in ordinary expenditure, combined with the proceeds from sales of crown lands. By 1572, however, Elizabeth had settled the most pressing of her obligations and for the remainder of the decade she had no money worries to speak of. It was true that almost all the money raised in that period from parliamentary taxation went on quelling unrest in Ireland, and she had to provide for all other expenses out of crown revenues, but thanks to her prudent financial management she was able to do this and still have £50,000 a year to spare.[13]

To Walsingham it seemed obvious that this surplus ought to be devoted to financing the energetic foreign policy that he believed the country's interests required. He was always telling the Queen that if she followed his advice, it would save her money in the end, for provided she did not let the situation get out of hand, a comparatively modest investment would free her from the necessity of spending much larger sums at a later date. "Surely my Lord", he grumbled to Leicester on one occasion, "this our art of saving £2,000 is accomplished with so many mischiefs like to ensue hereby as I fear will not be put off with the expense of a million". Nevertheless, the Queen was surely right in thinking that Walsingham's schemes would entail much greater expense than he allowed for, and she was certainly not alone in her belief that once she had started meddling in her neighbours' affairs, it would be no easy task deciding when to stop. The Earl of Sussex, for one, cautioned her in 1578 to do nothing which might bring on her the wrath of Spain, for if she did she would "enter into that which my simple head sees no possibility for you to maintain, nor knows no way how to bring you out of it".[14]

It was true that if Elizabeth took measures that were designed to enhance national security she was entitled to ask Parliament to furnish her with larger supplies. In 1579 Burghley noted that "the general excess of the people in purchasing, in buildings, in meat, drink and feastings, and most notably in apparel" led him to believe that they could easily afford to pay more tax, and he was confident that loyal subjects would be glad to do so if they knew it was for their own protection. Predictably Walsingham and his cronies were still more sanguine that the Legislature would be eager to underwrite costly foreign ventures. "As for the charges of war", Davison wrote airily in one memorandum, "she is Queen of a wealthy kingdom, and a people well-affected and willing to employ the means they have for the welfare of her Majesty, themselves and the country". This was scarcely very responsible, for although there was quite enough money in the country to pay for brief campaigns abroad and isolated loans to foreign allies, extended military operations would have a much more debilitating effect on the economy. Walsingham tended not to concern himself with the minutiae of financial affairs, and his only contribution on the subject was to suggest that once the Queen was involved in hostilities she would be able to fund them by selling off the Bishops' temporalities. Burghley's attitude was much less cavalier, for he did not underestimate the demands that would be placed on the Exchequer once the Queen became involved in a major war. "As for charges to her own coffers and to her people", he noted in a pessimistic memorandum written at the end of 1577, "the charges shall be so inestimable as no reckoning can be made thereof, neither will any treasure that she hath serve but a small time, neither shall she without offence of her people get by subsidies that which ought to serve, for her best people shall be themselves so charged as they shall not be able to yield any help".[15] In the circumstances the Queen's desperate efforts to remain at peace were understandable enough.

In the aftermath of St Bartholomew's, English relations with France had sunk into a sort of uneasy limbo. Superficially the two countries were on polite terms with each other, but the friendship forged at Blois had lost all trace of warmth. As a gesture of goodwill, Charles IX had asked Elizabeth to be a godmother to the daughter that his wife produced in October 1572, and despite expressing surprise that he should have extended this invitation to her, "we being of that religion which he doth persecute", the Queen had not declined it. When accepting she had nevertheless commented pointedly that it would be no easy task to find someone suitable to represent her at the baptism, for any English nobleman who was asked to visit France at this time would think she did not value his life very highly. In the end the Marquis of Worcester was sent and came to no harm, apart from having a brush with pirates in the Channel, who were anxious to seize the golden salver that Elizabeth had selected as a christening present.[16]

As for the Alençon marriage negotiations, following St Bartholomew's these were suspended but not entirely dropped. Apparently unruffled by the mayhem she had caused, Catherine de Medici cheerfully suggested that Elizabeth and Alençon should arrange to meet on the island of Jersey, but the Queen was not yet ready for a personal encounter. In the weeks after the massacre the surviving Huguenots had taken up arms in self-defence, and Elizabeth pointed out that since Alençon was currently with the royal forces who were besieging the Protestant stronghold of La Rochelle it was scarcely a very propitious moment for them to become engaged. In July 1573 this obstacle to the courtship was removed when peace was temporarily established between the warring factions in France, but Alençon now became involved in a series of intrigues against his brother Charles IX, and the King and Catherine de Medici were so preoccupied in keeping the Duke out of mischief that they regarded it as less of a priority to provide him with a wife. By April 1574 he was suspected of such disloyalty to his brother that he was placed under restraint at Court, and when the subject of marriage with him was next raised, Elizabeth could comment lightly that she thought it not unreasonable of her to expect that her husband should be a free man.[17]

In May 1574 the death of Charles IX threw Anglo-French relations into fresh confusion. As Elizabeth caustically commented, in some ways the late King could "well be spared, considering his bloody disposition", but it was to be feared that the brother who succeeded him as Henry III would turn out to be a still more terrible scourge of the Protestants. The Queen did not need to be reminded that even when the then Duke of Anjou had been numbered among her suitors he had never seemed very well disposed towards her, and it was particularly ominous that the courtship had had to be broken off because he was so fanatical a Catholic. For the past year he had been ruling Poland after being elected King there, but as he made his way across Europe to take possession of his new kingdom there were reports that he was using the opportunity to forge close links with the other leaders of the Catholic world. This led to speculation that he was planning to mount a concerted attack on Protestantism, particularly when he made a detour to Milan and was received in conclave by the leading Counter-Reforming churchman, Cardinal Borromeo. Greatly alarmed, Elizabeth left no one in any doubt as to her low opinion of the new monarch, for one observer reported that her "best word is to say he is worse than a devil".[18]

Towards the end of 1574 an embassy was sent to France under Lord North to try and gauge whether the new King's intentions towards England were as hostile as had been feared. In the event, however, this fact-finding mission only made matters worse, for on his return North not only reported that he had been treated with scant courtesy while in France, but also said that he had been present when Catherine de Medici had dressed up two of her court dwarves to resemble Elizabeth, and had then mockingly asked Alençon (who was still being kept under close supervision) what he thought of the beauty of his intended.[19] The Queen took this as confirmation that Henry and his mother now bore her ill-will, and this made her more receptive to proposals that she should stir up internal dissension within France, for while the King was struggling to maintain a grip on his own country he would have scant leisure to do anything unpleasant to her.

Despite the patched up peace, the Huguenots had remained restive, and Elizabeth hoped that if she encouraged Alençon to become their protector he could help them to extort concessions from the French Crown that would make it impossible for the King to overwhelm them in the future. In February 1575 she sent an agent to Germany to conduct exploratory talks with the Elector Palatine's brother, Duke John Casimir, a mercenary leader who for a price was prepared to raise an army and come to the defence of the Protestants in France. In the first flush of enthusiasm, Elizabeth even contemplated paying Casimir £45,000 to take an army to France, envisaging that once Alençon was set free it would be possible to obtain a settlement that would not only secure toleration for the Huguenots but would also provide that Calais must be handed back to her. In March 1575, however, Henry III suddenly made the friendly gesture of sending an envoy to England to confirm the Treaty of Blois, and in these changed circumstances Elizabeth began to question whether it was necessary to provide the Huguenots with so significant a degree of support. By May she had decided that she would do no more than provide £15,000 to subsidize the mercenary army from Germany, and even in September, when Alençon escaped from the French court and joined with the Huguenot forces, she was reluctant to give further aid. During the ensuing months Alençon repeatedly entreated her to reconsider, and in the end she might well have succumbed to this pressure, but in May 1576 peace was again restored in France, and for the time being it seemed that the Huguenots were out of danger.

Within six months Alençon had changed sides once more, supporting the King when in December 1576 the latter rescinded the Huguenots' right to freedom of worship which he had earlier accorded them. As a result civil war again broke out, and Alençon busied himself besieging Protestant towns such as Issoire, committing great atrocities on its fall. Leicester and Walsingham were emphatic that it now fell to the Queen to come to the Huguenots' rescue, seeing that theirs was "the general cause now of Christendom", but Elizabeth hesitated to embroil herself with a King who technically at least was still her ally. However, at the end of July 1577 she did offer to raise £20,000 in Germany so that the Huguenots could recruit forces there, but their leaders informed her that this sum would be quite insufficient to meet their needs. Walsingham and Leicester begged the

Queen to be more generous, and towards the end of the summer it seemed she was on the brink of giving way. On 16 August Leicester delightedly informed the secretary that Elizabeth was showing contrition for having "so slenderly dealt for her friends", adding happily, "She is now in a mind to repair the oversight". In the event, however, she did not have to do so, for within a month peace was again concluded in France, and though by this time the Queen was in so militant a mood that she actually expressed regret that the Huguenots had not held out for further concessions, this latest development spared her from the necessity of digging deeper into her purse.[20]

Elizabeth had been reluctant to sever relations with those responsible for the St Bartholomew's day massacre, but at one time it did seem that Mary Stuart would be made the scapegoat for the misdeeds of her French in-laws. Immediately after the massacre, Burghley told the Earl of Shrewsbury, "All men now cry out of your prisoner". Feeling against Mary was fuelled by rumours that she had been very joyous when she had heard what had happened in France, and it was said that she had stayed up half the night to celebrate. In the atmosphere of rage and fear that then prevailed it was thought that if she was permitted to live it would merely enable her to preside over similar sanguinary events in England, and it was universally agreed that her life must be forfeit. At such a time of crisis, the notion that come what may a monarch's life was sacrosanct seemed to have less relevance, even for Elizabeth, although she still wanted to avoid being saddled with the responsibility for putting Mary to death. On 10 September 1572 Sir Henry Killigrew was sent to Scotland, in hopes that with a little prompting from him the Regent Mar would suggest that Mary should be delivered into Scots custody so that she could be executed for crimes she had committed when on the throne.[21]

As things turned out, Killigrew's sensitive mission was a failure, for the Scots were not particularly keen to do Elizabeth's dirty work for her. Instead of grabbing at the chance to dispose of Mary, Mar said that he could not risk doing so unless Elizabeth undertook to convey her to Scotland with an escort of two to three thousand English soldiers, and he stipulated that these troops would also have to be present at Mary's execution. In these circumstances it would have been impossible for Elizabeth to have distanced herself from the event, and accordingly the matter was quietly dropped. Nevertheless the fact that the attempt had been made demonstrated once again that in times of acute stress even the Queen's most cherished ideals could be subject to modification.

Though it had proved impossible to arrange for Mary to be put to death, Elizabeth's advisers were unanimous that she had other effective means at her disposal which would ensure that the Queen of Scots no longer represented a threat. Following the death of the Earl of Mar, the anglophile Earl of Morton became Scots Regent in December 1572, and it was obviously in Elizabeth's interest to assist him to overcome that faction of Scottish nobles who were still hoping to effect Mary's restoration. With the renewal of the Scottish civil war in January 1573, Mary's supporters took refuge in Edinburgh Castle, intending to hold out there until they obtained enough aid from France to enable them to recover the initiative over their opponents. Burghley, Walsingham, Leicester and Smith unanimously echoed Killigrew's pleas that men and munitions should be sent north in sufficient quantities to enable the Regent to take Edinburgh Castle by force, but though at times the Queen seemed amenable, her preferred solution remained that Morton should try and achieve a negotiated settlement with the Marians that would obviate the necessity for English aid. At length, after weeks of nagging, Elizabeth gave in, and on 12 March 1573 she instructed Sir William Drury to take 1,500 men and thirty-three siege guns to Scotland so that they could assist in the reduction of the Marian headquarters. On 17 May the attack on the Castle began, and eleven days later it surrendered. Kirkaldy of the Grange, who had been its principal defender, was hanged shortly afterwards, and Mary's other leading supporter, William Maitland of Lethington, either committed suicide or died of natural causes. With their removal from the scene, Mary no longer had a party in Scotland dedicated to her cause, and this was a development of the utmost significance. When the news was relayed to her in England she confined herself to saying, "I will from henceforth ... be quiet ... and give no more ear to advertisements from Scotland", but the Earl of Shrewsbury could see that the setback had upset her more than she cared to admit. He told Burghley gleefully, "She ... makes little show of any grief, yet it nips her very near".[22]

Since the Queen's association with the Regent and his fellows had proved mutually advantageous, it seemed logical to assume she would wish to develop the links between them. Her advisers recommended that she made a treaty with the Scots guaranteeing to come to their aid if their country was invaded, and also urged that she bound Morton and his supporters to her by the judicious distribution of pensions. "Money will do anything with that nation, as your Lordship knoweth," Walsingham commented drily to Leicester, and he estimated that £2,000 alone would suffice to buy the loyalty of all the leading men in Scotland. Unfortunately, the Queen was as careful with her cash as any Scot, and was not prepared to part with even this insignificant amount. She made it clear that when she had assisted in the capture of Edinburgh Castle, this had been an isolated gesture, which was not to be followed up, implying that it would in some way demean her if she extended protection to Morton's regime. On the death of Charles IX she became for a short time less aloof, for she was concerned

that under their new ruler the French would once again exert themselves
to infiltrate Scotland. In an access of panic she gravely warned Morton of
the danger to them both, and trumpeted, "We think it now full time to
awake", but to the distress of her advisers she swiftly dozed off into her
familiar torpor. Having kept the Scots waiting for almost a year in hopes
of gifts of money from England and the formation of a firm defensive pact,
she finally informed them in May 1575 that these would not be forthcoming
as she did not want to provoke the French.[23]

For the next three years she remained equally obdurate, apparently
unconcerned by the possibility that Morton could be unseated if she did
not provide him with more support. In the summer of 1578 Burghley was
utterly downcast when a Scots ambassador who come to solicit her protection was sent away unsatisfied. He noted that for generations the Queen's
predecessors had striven to secure the northern border "by all means, both
fair and foul and could never attain the same", and yet here was Elizabeth
spurning the opportunity to do so when it was being handed to her on a
plate. "A strange thing it is to see God's goodness, so abundantly offered
for her Majesty's surety to be so daintily hearkened unto!" he exploded.
Although only six years earlier Elizabeth had been willing to send Mary
back to Scotland to be killed, she had by now reverted to an altogether
more lofty frame of mind, justifying her rejection of Scots overtures on
the grounds that it would be inconsistent with her honour to let them sign
a treaty in James's name while his mother was still alive. Walsingham told
her sternly that "such scruples of conscience are rather superstitious than
religious" but this was an area where the Queen felt very sure of her
ground. Relations with Scotland remained uncertain and confused, leading
Walsingham to tell one colleague in fury, "Though the country be cold I
can neither think nor speak of it but in heat".[24]

A somewhat unlikely consequence of the massacre of St Bartholomew's
day had been Anglo-Spanish rapprochement, for since it was impossible
to rely on the friendship of France, Elizabeth could hardly afford to be
simultaneously on poor terms with Spain. As early as October 1572 Burghley had sounded out the possibility of making an agreement with Spain
that would end the trade embargo that had been in being since 1569, and
the Duke of Alva had received these overtures with enthusiasm, being
convinced that it would be difficult for the Spaniards to regain control over
the Netherlands as long as commerce there was in decline. King Philip
was less sure that an accommodation with Elizabeth was desirable, fearing
that "the Pope and all Christianity would blame him for it". To this Alva
protested that he would not have advocated such a course if he had not
thought it of vital importance, for Philip "did not have a vassal who desired
the ruin of Elizabeth more than he". "Sometimes, Sire, it is necessary for

Princes to do what displeases them, as we do all the time", he cajoled his master, pointing out that if Philip did conclude an alliance with Elizabeth he could always forswear it later, for though ideally a ruler ought to keep faith once he had given his word, there were other rules for princes than for gentlemen.[25] As a result of these casuistical arguments, Philip relented. On 15 March 1573 it was agreed under the Convention of Nymegen that trade between England and the Netherlands should reopen on 1 May, and any outstanding difficulties between England and Spain were settled by the signing of the Treaty of Bristol in August 1574.

Having secured at least the nominal friendship of Spain, Elizabeth felt reluctant to jeopardize it by giving assistance to the insurgents in the Netherlands. In November 1572 the English volunteers who had served in the Netherlands under Sir Humphrey Gilbert had been summoned home, and as Alva painstakingly set about recapturing those towns that had declared for the rebels, it seemed that it would only be a matter of time before he crushed the last pockets of resistance. William of Orange had to retreat to the northern province of Holland, which like neighbouring Zealand was still holding out, but though he repeatedly told Elizabeth that without her succour these two provinces would also fall, she seemed unworried at the prospect.

The main reason for Elizabeth's aloofness was that she felt an instinctive distaste towards those she once termed "no better than rebels". Knowing this, Orange declared that he had not taken up arms out of mere disobedience, for he was fighting "neither for ambition nor gain ... but for the defence of religion and of his country and for the lives and liberties of the same". To Elizabeth, however, this was scarcely reassuring, for it implied the existence of a contract between a prince and his people which was nullified if the former failed to observe its terms, a dangerous doctrine, with which she wished to have no truck. Far from accepting that Orange's resistance to the Spanish tyranny was morally justifiable, in April 1575 she even formally expressed her disapproval by proclaiming him a rebel whom she was not prepared to harbour in her realm.[26]

Nor was she mollified by the fact that the struggle was partly religious in origin, for she accepted that Philip was entitled to demand that the only faith that was practised in his dominions should be the one that he himself professed. After all, she herself denied her subjects the right of freedom of worship, and she did not expect Philip to grant a larger measure of tolerance. She only objected to the activities of the Inquisition in the Netherlands, holding that while a sovereign was entitled to require outward conformity to a state religion, it was wrong to pry into the workings of individual consciences, and to prosecute those who were thereby revealed to be of doubtful orthodoxy. This, however, was as far as she was prepared to go, and the demands of the Low Countries Protestants that they should be permitted to worship unmolested met with little sympathy from her. On one occasion she went so far as to say that the inhabitants of Holland and Zealand were always asking her to take their consciences into account, but she did not see what account one could take of consciences that were already damned.[27]

As a reigning monarch it was understandable that Elizabeth should view with suspicion those whose claims arguably constituted an encroachment on the rights of sovereigns, but her aversion to the Hollanders also stemmed from other, less commendable, feelings. Far from being an aristocratic movement, the revolt in Holland and Zealand was sustained by the burgomasters and merchants who served on the town councils, and if Orange himself was patrician enough (and even him Elizabeth once dismissed as "one princelet" with a "passion for reigning against all law and might"), it pained the Queen that the majority of his associates were of an infinitely lower social standing. In 1576 a servant of Lord Burghley's remarked that one reason why the Dutch had met with such disappointing results when they had pressed for English aid was that they had sent "none but townsmen" to present their case. He added that before the Queen or the Council took them seriously, "They would look with what great personages they should deal", and undoubtedly Elizabeth's regal disdain for the worthies of the Netherlands coloured her attitude to the entire revolt. Even in later years, when the geographical base of revolt had broadened so that many nobles from the southern provinces became participants, the Queen remained acutely conscious of class issues. On one occasion she caused complications by trying to bypass the representative assembly of the Netherlands, the States General, in order to deal with the more aristocratic Council of State. At the time it was noted that "Her Majesty taketh this course because she hath a better liking for nobility". Ultimately Philip II was to drive Elizabeth and the Netherlands patriots together, but the Queen never overcame her fastidious dislike at colluding with a rabble of "shoemakers, carpenters and heretics".[28]

The great dilemma for the Queen was that however much she might wish to distance herself from those in revolt against divinely constituted authority, she could not afford to ignore the dangers that would arise either if the Spaniards effected a total conquest of the Netherlands, or if the French gained possession of them instead. In her opinion, the most satisfactory outcome of the struggle would be if King Philip came to an accommodation with his subjects in the Low Countries, whereby they would reaffirm their loyalty to him in return for a recognition of their ancient rights and privileges – though significantly, Elizabeth did not believe that religious liberty was included in these. She repeatedly suggested that she should act as an independent arbitrator at talks designed to achieve a settlement on these lines, but received successive rebuffs from Alva and

Don Luis de Requesens, who succeeded Alva as Governor General in December 1573. Undaunted, in July 1575 Elizabeth sent Sir Henry Cobham to Spain bearing a further offer of mediation, but Philip's cold response left little room for hope that he would accept anything less than an unconditional surrender from his insubordinate subjects.

By the end of 1575 Holland and Zealand were in a desperate condition, and Orange made it plain that if Elizabeth still denied them any succour, he would gladly have recourse to France. Profoundly disturbed, the Queen reiterated that rather than calling in the French, Orange should rely on her to secure a negotiated settlement, but the Prince's response was to despatch an embassy to England with instructions to offer the Queen the sovereignty of Holland and Zealand if she would agree to give them aid.

With the Spaniards poised to repossess the Netherlands, unless the French grabbed them first, it was not easy for the Queen to decline to take responsibility for the Provinces herself. Yet she was scarcely able to decide which alternative she found more unpalatable, and her distress was apparent to all at Court. One onlooker reported, "Her Majesty is troubled with these causes, which maketh her very melancholy, and seemeth to be greatly out of quiet". At times indeed her mood bordered on hysteria: an informant of the Duke of Alva's heard that when the Queen learnt the Dutch ambassadors were on their way, "she entered her chamber alone, slamming the door after her, and crying out that they were ruining her over this business . . . Her ladies-in-waiting and others were much distressed, saying if she did not open the door they would burst it open, as they could not bear her to be alone in such trouble".[29]

Whatever her private inclinations, the Queen knew the situation to be too grave for her to dismiss the Hollanders' appeal out of hand. When the Dutch ambassadors arrived, she steeled herself to give them a gracious reception, promising them "on the word of a prince . . . to deal briefly and sincerely with them", which made them "the contentedest men in the world". On 15 January 1576 the ambassadors were told that the Queen would make one more effort to bring Requesens to the negotiating table; but they were left with the impression that this would be her last attempt at mediation, and that if it failed, she would aid them forthwith. In early March news came that Requesens had died without answering her invitation, and Dutch hopes rose that as there had been no satisfactory response, Elizabeth would now think fit to help them. Knowing that she could not postpone her decision much longer, the Queen became positively distracted with worry. She had several sleepless nights, and was thoroughly disagreeable to everyone around her, berating Walsingham when he pleaded the rebels' cause, and cursing the luckless Lady Warwick when the latter had to explain that her husband was ill and away from court. One evening she was so foul-tempered she even "beat one or two of her ladies".[30]

On 22 March the Dutch were informed of Elizabeth's decision. They were told that instead of offering them anything, the Queen would make another attempt at mediation, and they were given no reason to suppose that if this failed, they could then count on English support. To make matters worse they were peremptorily forbidden to apply to France for aid, for the Queen warned that she would not tolerate a French incursion into the Netherlands. Understandably, the Dutch were "in a marvellous passion" at the verdict: "There where we hoped for salvation, there was the cause of our ruin", one commented bitterly, incensed that the Queen should not only deny them aid herself, but had banned them from seeking relief elsewhere.[31]

The ambassadors went home "satisfied in nothing", and the prospects of the Dutch seemed more hopeless than ever. Predictably, the Queen's offer to mediate was again rejected, and as the rebels were unable to obtain aid from France their capitulation appeared inevitable. The Queen gave the impression of being unconcerned: indeed, in the summer of 1576 she went so far as to talk of taking punitive action on Holland and Zealand herself, after they had vexed her by extorting forced loans from her merchants in the Netherlands in return for letting them navigate the Scheldt.

However, a few months later the rebel cause gained an unlooked-for reprieve. Lack of pay had led to a total breakdown in the discipline of the Spanish troops in the Netherlands, and by the autumn of 1576 their excesses had become so intolerable that even those provinces that had stayed loyal to Philip II decided that this military presence could no longer be endured. They reasoned that by joining with Holland and Zealand they would be able to pressure Philip into withdrawing the soldiers, and talks were already in progress when on 4 November the troops' lust for plunder led them to take Antwerp by storm. A four-day orgy of violence ensued, in which 8,000 of the citizens perished, convincing the entire population that they must unite in order to obtain the troops' expulsion. On 8 November 1576 the Pacification of Ghent was signed, which enshrined a declaration that all the provinces would work together to bring about the removal of the army of occupation. Once this had been achieved, it was agreed that the States General would be summoned to settle the affairs of the Provinces and to draw up a religious settlement that would be acceptable to all.

So long as all the provinces were prepared to resist him, there was no possibility that Philip could weld the Low Countries into an absolutist state, and at last it seemed that there could be a composition between Spain and the Netherlands along the lines that Elizabeth had long desired. To encourage Philip to come to terms she sent Sir John Smith to Spain, once again offering her services as a mediator, and the King was now so disheartened by the state of affairs in the Netherlands that he seriously considered taking up her invitation.[32] Meanwhile in December the States General sent a representative of their own to see Elizabeth, and with uncharacteristic promptness she agreed to loan them £20,000 to pay for their immediate necessities, and promised that she would lend them more if Philip proved intractable.

While Elizabeth waited eagerly for Philip's reply, the States embarked on negotiations with their newly-appointed Governor General, Don John of Austria, the King's illegitimate half-brother, who had arrived at Luxembourg just before the signing of the Pacification of Ghent. The talks established that while Don John was not set against the dismissal of the Spanish troops, he would make no concession in matters of religion. This was awkward, but the leading southern Catholics expressed interest in doing a deal on this basis, despite the fact that Holland and Zealand would clearly not be happy with an agreement that made Protestantism a proscribed faith. The southern nobles felt the more inclined to desert their allies because they knew that Elizabeth did not think it essential that they won religious toleration, and besides, throughout the summer she had been on such hostile terms with Orange and the Hollanders that it was thought she would not object if the latter were not comprehended in a treaty with Don John. In fact, this was not the case: Elizabeth was aware that Orange alone possessed the necessary authority to ensure that, if a settlement was reached, the Spaniards would observe its terms, and she let the States General know that she considered him "the only man fit to be employed in so weighty a cause; without whose assistance she cannot hope that her affairs can take good success".[33] Nevertheless, it proved impossible to prevent the unity of the Provinces from crumbling. On 12 February 1577 the States General concluded the Perpetual Edict with Don John, which secured the withdrawal of the Spanish troops but contained a declaration that the Catholic religion would be maintained and upheld in the Netherlands. Orange refused to sign the pact on behalf of Holland and Zealand, and it seemed all too likely that if Don John failed to win over the recalcitrant provinces, the peace would prove impermanent.

On the continent, Protestantism was under threat from the forces of reaction, but in the view of Popery's most ardent opponents, even in England, true religion did not flourish. Certainly it was undeniable that the established Church in England had many imperfections, and these were widely lamented. When Elizabeth had come to the throne, between ten to fifteen per cent of all the benefices in England lacked a minister, and in a bid to fill these vacancies, numerous unfit men had hastily been ordained. As the reign progressed, repeated efforts were made to raise the standard of ordinands, but as Elizabeth once admitted, men who were "of such lewd life and corrupt behaviour" that they were not "worthy to come into any honest company" continued to find their way into the clergy. Furthermore, while only a minority of ministers were men of truly disreputable character, a far larger number were ill-educated, and lacked the necessary learning to preach at length. Since an emphasis on sermons was one of the hallmarks of Protestantism, this was regarded as the gravest of defects. In addition, pluralism was widespread, for many ecclesiastical livings had such low incomes that they could not adequately sustain a minister, and clergymen were obliged to accept the charge of more than one parish in order to earn enough money to survive. This inevitably gave rise to a good deal of non-residence, and indeed, as a result of these abuses, it has been estimated that during Elizabeth's reign, less than one church in four had a resident preaching minister.[34]

The Queen acknowledged freely enough that the Church was not without blemish: she told Parliament in 1585, "This much I must say, that some faults and negligences may grow and be, as in all other great charges it happeneth; and what vocation without?" When she thought it feasible, she took steps to try and remedy the situation. In 1560, her concern at the lack of good ministers led her to instruct Lord Keeper Bacon to award promising theology students the income from crown prebends, which in effect meant they received scholarships at her expense. On realizing that the North suffered from a particularly acute shortage of vicars, she set aside funds to endow four preachers in Lancashire with stipends of £100 a year. Partly as a result of such measures, the quality of the clergy was higher by the end of the reign that it had been at the beginning, and in London at least, the percentage of ministers who were university graduates had risen significantly.[35] Indisputably, however, there was still a great deal of room for further improvement.

One reason why it had proved so hard to bring this about was that laymen who owned advowsons – which gave them the right to present clergymen to benefices under their control – were often negligent or corrupt in the observance of their duties. In 1594 a preacher at St Paul's attacked those gentlemen who "cry out for a learned ministry ... but willingly present none but such as are base, ignorant and beggarly, because such persons will easily accept of benefices upon unlawful conditions". Possessors of advowsons were known to have sold benefices to the highest bidder, and there were also instances where they deliberately kept livings vacant so their sons could occupy them when they grew older, or bestowed them on incumbents who were under age. In a sermon preached at court in 1569, the hot-gospeller Edward Dering reproached the Queen for permitting such abuses, telling her that though a thousand iniquities covered the priesthood, "Yet you, in the meanwhile that all these whoredoms are committed, you at whose hands God will require it, you sit still and are careless, let men do as they list". Nevertheless, it was scarcely possible for the Queen to monitor appointments at parish level, and although in theory her bishops were entitled to overrride lay patrons if they tried to award a benefice to someone undeserving, in practice, their powers in this regard were limited.[36]

The main problem was that, although so many gentlemen professed concern about the clergy, they were reluctant to underwrite the cost of bringing about improvements, and the resources of the Church itself were certainly not sufficient to sustain a learned minister in every parish. It was calculated that in order to support himself, a minister needed an annual income of £30, but only one in twenty benefices was worth this much. There were 2,000 parishes in England which had livings of only £8 a year. As the Archbishop of Canterbury pointed out to the Queen in 1585, there were 13,000 parishes in England, and it was out of the question to place a learned man in each one. The Queen accepted this: "Jesus!" she exclaimed (not even the presence of the Archbishop could induce her to tone down her language), "13,000! It is not to be looked for". She told the Archbishop that she did not expect all her clergy to be highly erudite, and that she only wanted the parishes to be filled with "honest, sober and wise men, and such as can read the scriptures and homilies well unto the people".[37] In the circumstances, this was probably as much as could be hoped for, but by no means all of the governing class were as realistic as she.

Before Elizabeth had been on the throne for ten years, the "hotter sort of Protestants" who inveighed most loudly against the failings of the Church had already been christened "Puritans". It was not a label they relished: the strongly Protestant Earl of Huntingdon told his son that the epithet 'Puritan' had been dreamt up "either by Papists ... or atheists, or men extremely vicious".[38] Men such as he felt the term implied they were a bunch of isolated extremists, whereas it was their contention that it was widely recognized that the Church was in need of further reform. Yet while it was true that the state of the Church caused great concern to large numbers of the governing classes, there was little consensus as to what should be done to set things right. A majority of the House of Commons would have liked to see a tightening of the sabbatarian regulations that were currently in force, and believed that the standard of the clergy needed to be raised, and on such issues they were at one with Puritan opinion. If given the chance, they doubtless would also have voted for a moderate revision of the prayer book that would have eliminated some rites and ceremonies in the Church services, and it saddened them that the Queen refused to take into account their views on such matters. To the more zealous Puritans, however, measures of this sort would have represented only the beginning, for if their programme had been implemented in full, it would have resulted in nothing less than a radical reorganization of state and society along presbyterian lines. These ideas were too immoderate to be widely endorsed, but the general indignation at the Church's condition meant that Puritan aspirations were viewed with more sympathy than might otherwise have been the case.

One of the Puritans' most fundamental complaints was that the Church as presently established exerted insufficient control over the morals of the laity. Although in theory those guilty of sexual misdemeanors or other transgressions could be summoned before the local bishop's court, offenders were frequently let off with a fine, and Puritans thought it scandalous that "great sins" were "either not at all punished, as blasphemy, usury etc., or else lightly passed over".[39] If discipline were to be maintained, they believed it had to operate at parochial level, for the ministers and lay elders of the nearest church could administer much more effective rebukes to their erring neighbours than could be delivered in the impersonal bishop's consistory.

Even the Queen would not be exempt from the workings of ecclesiastical discipline, but if she sinned she would be liable to excommunication or other penalties. As one leading Puritan put it, princes "be servants unto the Church, and as they rule in the Church, so they must remember to subject themselves unto the Church, to submit their sceptres, to throw down their crowns before the Church, yea, as the prophet speaketh, to lick the dust of the feet of the Church".[40] If this argument was accepted, the Royal Supremacy itself was invalidated, and to rigid Puritans the idea that the Queen could order her Church as she saw fit, even if by doing so she contravened what they regarded as the will of God, was a monstrous aberration.

The senior hierarchy of the Church were under no illusion as to the full implications of the Puritan threat. In 1573, the Dean of York told Burghley, "The supreme authority (you know) was justly taken from the Pope ... and given to the Prince ... but these reformers take it from the Prince and give it unto themselves". Another leading opponent of Puritanism warned the Queen, if she were to "innovate the whole government of the Church" by introducing discipline, "She must submit herself and her sceptre to the fantastical humours of her own parish governors".[41] There was no need to point this out to Elizabeth, for she was fully alive to the inherent dangers of Puritanism. She had no intention of relinquishing control over her Church, or of giving in to pressure for further reform which made no allowance for the views of those whose opinions about religion were less progressive than those of the Puritans. In matters ecclesiastical, she was determined that her subjects should submit to direction from above, and that Parliament should not be permitted to tamper with the ecclesiastical edifice that had been crafted in 1559.

As for the notion that ministers and lay elders of a parish were entitled to regulate religious affairs, she deemed it an absurdity, while the idea that her own authority could be in any way subordinate to theirs was nothing short of revolutionary. As she explained to Parliament in 1585, she knew well enough that it would be "dangerous to kingly rule to have every man according to his own censure, to make a doom of the validity and privity of his prince's government, with a common veil and cover of God's word, whose followers must not be judged but by private men's exposition". Five years later she expressed herself even more strongly in a letter to James VI of Scotland, when she described fanatical Puritans as "A sect of perilous consequence, such as would have no kings but a presbytery, and take our place while they enjoy our privileges, with a shade of God's word, which none is judged [to] follow right without by their censure they be so deemed. Yea, look we well unto them". Being in no doubt as to the anarchic tendencies of a movement which had no respect for the hierarchical structure of society, she told the French ambassador that ultimately Puritans wished to recognize "neither God nor king".[42]

The first dispute that seriously threatened the unity of the Elizabethan Church centred around the vestments that were prescribed by the ornaments proviso in the Act of Uniformity. To stern-minded Protestants, it seemed intolerable that they were expected to minister to a congregation arrayed in garments that savoured "of monkery, Popery and Judaism". They reviled the surplice as "a filthy popish rag", and were no less indignant about the distinctive costume they had to don when going outside. In particular they hated the square caps that they were obliged to wear, angrily dubbing them "woollen horns", which made them "like unto a mass-monger". The Puritanical Dean of Wells, Dr Peter Turner, felt so strongly about this that he trained his pet dog to leap up and snatch the caps off the heads of passing clergymen.[43]

Nowadays the issue might seem trivial, but these early Puritans felt passionately that if their dress was reminiscent of that of the Catholic priesthood, it would confuse the simple and encourage superstition. The Queen, on the other hand, insisted on the retention of vestments precisely because she felt that simple believers would have difficulty identifying with a Church which had discarded too many of the practices associated with traditional religious observance. She could argue that since rites and ceremonial had no bearing on individual salvation, they were a thing 'indifferent' and she was entitled to regulate such matters as she thought best. To this the Puritans could retort that, if vestments were a thing indifferent, it was pointless for her to make such a fuss about them, but they also contended that while it was the duty of princes to defend the Church, they did not possess "a prerogative to burden it with superfluous and hurtful ceremonies".[44]

For the first few years of the reign, the issue of vestments was not too contentious because uniformity was comparatively laxly enforced. By the beginning of 1565, however, Elizabeth had become disturbed by the discrepancies in religious observance that prevailed in different parts of the country, for she feared that if measures were not taken, the Act of Uniformity would be more openly flouted, and "the inconvenience thereof were like to grow from place to place, as it were by an infection".[45] On 25 January she accordingly informed Archbishop Parker that she could not tolerate such disorders in the Church, and that he and the bishops were to put a stop to them.

Having given Parker his instructions, Elizabeth left him to tackle the problem without overt support from her, refusing to put her name to the regulations which the Archbishop drew up in March 1565, setting out in detail the requirements relating to clerical dress. As a result it was Parker and the bishops who were held responsible for the ensuing drive against non-conformists, and many Puritans even laboured under the delusion that if it were not for the episcopate, the Queen would have been anxious for the Church to be further reformed. Nevertheless, although dismayed that Elizabeth expected him to proceed against non-conformists on his own authority, Parker manfully entered the fray. The leading English opponents of vestments were Laurence Humphrey, the Regius Professor of Divinity at Oxford, and Thomas Sampson, the Dean of Christ Church, and when these two adamantly refused to wear the cap and surplice, Sampson was deprived of his post and Humphrey was rusticated. In March 1566, thirty-seven London ministers were suspended for refusing to adopt the regulation dress, but once they had had some time for reflection, the majority of these submitted, and after three months only eight were permanently deprived.

It appeared that the ecclesiastical authorities had successfully quelled non-conformity, but in doing so they had incurred the lasting odium of the Puritans. Whereas before, disaffection within the Church had focused on the "shells and chippings of popery" in the form of vestments, a murmuring now developed against episcopacy itself. In the spring of 1570 a Cambridge professor of divinity named Thomas Cartwright gave a series of lectures in which he maintained that there was no foundation in scripture for the government of the Church by bishops, and that instead its administration should be entrusted to ministers, deacons and lay elders, as in the days of the Apostles. His lectures created an immense sensation: within days, Cambridge was "all in a hurly-burly and shameful broil" over what one don denounced as "such doctrine as is pernicious and not tolerable for a Christian commonwealth".[46] At the end of the year, Cartwright was deprived of his post at the university, and in fear of further punishment he fled to Germany.

As yet, only extremists could contemplate the abolition of episcopacy, and in the Parliament of 1571 an attempt was made to reform the Church

in conjunction with the bishops. On 5 April, Walter Strickland proposed
to the Commons that a committee of the house should confer with the
bishops to devise improvements in the Book of Common Prayer, but when
this meeting took place it became clear that the bishops would not give
their approval to any alterations in the set text. From now on, even
moderate Puritans were less inclined to believe that they could bring about
their aims by an alliance with the bishops.

Undaunted by the lack of episcopal support, on 14 April Strickland
exhibited in the Commons a bill for the reformation of the prayer book,
but the fate of the bill was to demonstrate that the bishops were not the
only obstacles to such measures. Ardent Protestant though he was, Sir
Francis Knollys warned the house "it were not expedient" to encroach on
the royal prerogative by dabbling with matters of religion, and before
adjourning for the Easter recess, the Commons obediently agreed that they
would do nothing until they had petitioned the Queen for permission to
proceed. By the time they returned from their holidays, Elizabeth had
made her position clear, for Strickland had been put in confinement by the
Privy Council "for the exhibiting of a bill in the house against the prerogative of the Queen",[47] and though he was released shortly afterwards,
his bill was heard of no more.

Nevertheless, when Parliament reassembled in 1572 this did not deter
the Commons from giving a reading to a bill proposing that the Act of
Uniformity should be enforced only against Catholics, and that the bishops
should be given powers to permit clergymen to dispense with parts of the
service. At Sir Francis Knollys's suggestion, the bill was made more
moderate in the hope that this would make it acceptable to the Queen, but
even in its toned-down form Elizabeth could not stomach it. Instead she
confiscated the bill and sent a message that in future no measure concerning
religion was to be introduced into Parliament unless it had first been
approved by the bishops.

Because of the Queen's intervention, the Puritans had not managed to
achieve anything through Parliament, and radicals in the movement vented
their anger for this failure on the bishops. In June 1572 there appeared the
Admonition to parliament, a virulent attack on episcopacy, which had been
penned by two Puritan militants named John Field and Thomas Wilcox.
The government of bishops was condemned as "anti-Christian and devilish
and contrary to the scriptures", and the authors expressed their horror at
the way "the Lord Bishops ... and such ravening rabblers take upon
them – which is most horrible – the rule of the Church, spoiling the pastor
of his lawful jurisdiction over his own flock".[48]

When apprehended, Field and Wilcox were jailed for a year, but their
tract was a runaway success. Despite the efforts of the authorities to
suppress it, the pamphlet went through several editions, and was described

as being "in every man's hand and mouth". Even while under confinement, the authors were so lionized by their fellow citizens that the Bishop of London wrote indignantly that they were "esteemed as Gods". To the discomfited bishops, it seemed that they were now the object of universal scorn. In March 1573, Parker wailed to Burghley, "The comfort that these Puritans have, and their continuance is marvellous". The Bishop of Durham described to a colleague how things had escalated, so that "not only the habits, but our whole ecclesiastical polity, discipline, the revenues of the bishops, ceremonies or public forms of worship, liturgies, vocation of ministers or the ministration of the sacraments – all these things are now openly attacked from the press". He added that it was somewhat unfair that "the entire blame is laid upon the bishops, as if they alone, if they chose, were able to eradicate these evils", when in reality they were "under authority, and cannot make any innovation without the sanction of the Queen".[49]

It was true that the bishops were in an unenviable position, for having forced them to carry out her policies the Queen left them to take the consequences. Pinioned between the Supreme Governor and the Puritans, the bishops began to feel that they were "*excrementa mundi*". In the autumn of 1573, however, a lunatic who was believed to have connections with the Puritans stabbed and wounded the sea-dog John Hawkins. He had mistaken him for the Queen's favourite, Sir Christopher Hatton, who was regarded as a vehement opponent of the Puritans, and this made Elizabeth take a more serious view of the situation. As a result, several prominent figures in the Puritan movement were either imprisoned or had to flee abroad. Deprived of its leadership, for the time being Puritanism lost its momentum.

In May 1575 Archbishop Parker died, and the following December the Archbishop of York, Edmund Grindal, was named as his successor. In some ways it was a surprising choice, for Grindal was one of the most radical members of the episcopal bench, and it may be that Elizabeth only promoted him because Burghley urged her to do so. Moderate Puritans hailed his appointment with delight, for it was hoped that he would make an effort to reform the Church from within. In his first year of office he did much to justify these expectations, seeking to improve the quality of the priesthood by tightening up admission procedures, and pioneering various other reforms. In December 1576, however, his innovative activities were abruptly halted when he and the Queen clashed over the suppression of 'prophesyings'.

A prophesying was the name for a conference of ministers who met to hear a dissertation on the scriptures by one of their brethren, whose performance was then subjected to a critical assessment by those present. They were designed to promote learning within the ministry, and were not inherently radical assemblies, being frequently conducted under the supervision of the local bishop. The Queen nevertheless viewed them with suspicion. She was concerned about how the conferences would evolve, fearing that those who met there would not confine themselves to interpreting the scriptures, but would soon begin to elaborate disciplinary procedures of the sort advocated by zealots, and that the prophesyings would form the base on which a nationwide Puritan network would develop. She even viewed askance the educational aspect of the conferences, for she believed it could have an unsettling effect on the less sophisticated members of the audience if too many novel ideas were instilled in their heads. She feared that those who attended the prophesyings imbibed "new devised opinions upon points of divinity ... unmeet of unlearned people ... By which manner of assemblies, great numbers of our people ... are brought to idleness and seduced, and in a manner, schismatically divided among themselves into variety of dangerous opinions".[50] At the end of 1576 she therefore summoned Grindal and told him that henceforth the prophesyings should be banned, and when he defended them on the grounds that they would help to bring about a learned preaching ministry, she retorted that it was quite unnecessary to have more than three or four preachers in any county.

If Grindal had pretended he would do as she wished, and had then evaded her orders, the odds are that Elizabeth would shortly have forgotten about the matter, but as it was, he decided on a direct confrontation with the Queen. He wrote her a remarkable letter, flatly refusing to suppress the prophesyings, which he described as "a thing profitable to the Church and therefore to be continued". As for the Queen's assertion that the number of preachers should be limited, he chided, "Surely I cannot marvel enough how this strange opinion should once enter into your mind", and he reminded her that "Public and continual preaching of God's word is the ordinary mean and instrument of the salvation of mankind". The Queen had maintained that readings from the homilies (improving discourses that had been printed, bound together and circulated to all churches) substituted perfectly well for genuine sermons, but Grindal was categoric that homilies were an unsatisfactory alternative to preaching. In conclusion, he trenchantly requested that in future Elizabeth should "refer all these ecclesiastic matters which touch religion, or the doctrine and discipline of the Church, unto the bishops and divines of your realm ... for indeed they are things to be judged ... in the Church or a synod, not in a palace ... And although you are a mighty prince, yet remember that he that dwelleth in Heaven is mightier ... If you turn from God, then God will turn away his merciful countenance from you. And what remaineth then to be looked for, but only a terrible expectation of God's judgments, and an heaping up of wrath against the day of Wrath".[51]

Never before had Elizabeth been subjected to such devastating criticism from one of her own instruments. The Archbishop begged, "Bear with me, I beseech you Madam, if I choose rather to offend your earthly majesty than to offend the heavenly majesty of God", but the Queen could not tolerate such rank disobedience. Grindal had in effect repudiated the Royal Supremacy, and the hectoring tone he had adopted made his missive still more unpalatable. When he was pressed by the Council to do as Elizabeth bade him, and he still refused to obey, the Queen sent circular letters herself to all her bishops, ordering that the prophesyings must cease. By May 1577 she was in such a fury that she wished to deprive Grindal of his office, and it was only because Burghley warned her that it was not clear whether she was legally entitled to take such unprecedented action that she was prevailed upon to desist. Instead she had to content herself with confining Grindal to Lambeth Palace as a virtual prisoner, and preventing him from discharging his archiepiscopal functions.

The majority of Elizabeth's advisers were aghast that just at a moment when the Catholic threat was growing more alarming, the Queen should weaken the Church by striking down one of its most devoted sons. Walsingham growled to Burghley, "Thus my Lord, you see how we proceed still in making war against God: whose ire we should rather seek to appease, that he may keep the wars that most apparently approach towards us, from us. God open her Majesty's eyes". Burghley agreed that "These proceedings cannot but irritate our merciful God", but despite the disapproval of her Councillors, Elizabeth would not relent.[52] At various times there were rumours that Grindal would be restored to favour, but in fact he remained in disgrace for the next seven years. In 1583 it was agreed that the blind and ailing prelate could resign the following spring, but in September 1583 he died while he was technically still in office.

In the Netherlands the peace effected by Don John lasted no more than a few months. The Governor General had done all he could to endear himself to the leading men in the Provinces, but though it was said that the majority of the nobility were "drunk with his charms", he could not induce Orange to endorse the Perpetual Edict. Furthermore, he himself had come to regret that he had bound himself by its provisions, finding it irksome that he had to have frequent consultations with the States-General, and thinking himself "overmuch controlled by the States, yea almost commanded by them".[53] Having come to the conclusion that the only way of imposing an acceptable settlement would be to take up the sword, on 24 July 1577 he seized the citadel of Namur. The following month King Philip agreed that the troops that had been evacuated from the Netherlands earlier in the year should be sent back to effect their conquest. Shocked by Don John's treachery, the Provinces once again coalesced, and at the invitation of the

States-General, Orange came to Brussels to help conduct the struggle against the enemy.

In September 1577 the States sent the Marquis of Havre to England to ask the Queen to give them aid, and he found Elizabeth most accommodating. One explanation for this was that in the the summer of 1577 Dutch spies had intercepted letters from Don John to the Spanish court begging to be allowed to lead an invading force to England. These letters made it clear that he would have preferred it if the conquest of England had taken priority over the pacification of the Netherlands, but failing that, he wanted to launch an attack as soon as he had gained possession of the harbours of Zealand. The documents had been passed on to the Queen, and having seen for herself "what a benevolent and propitious neighbour" she had in Don John, she was the more inclined to give favourable consideration to the Dutch plea for assistance. On 29 September, after only two days' deliberation, Elizabeth not only agreed that she would lend the States-General £100,000 but also offered to send to the Netherlands 1,000 cavalry and 5,000 foot soldiers under the command of the Earl of Leicester.[54] Leicester was enormously excited by the prospect of leading an army overseas, but against all expectations the States seemed curiously unappreciative of the Queen's generosity. They wrote thanking her for the offer of a loan, but questioned the wisdom of sending an army to the Netherlands at the onset of winter, when it would be difficult to obtain victuals to feed the horses. The Queen shrewdly divined that this cautious response was inspired by a fear that she wanted to annexe a portion of the Netherlands for herself, and not unnaturally was extremely annoyed that her motives were being questioned in this way.

To make matters worse, on 18 October news arrived that jealousy at Orange's ascendancy had led a splinter group of nobles from the Netherlands to invite the Holy Roman Emperor's younger brother, the Archduke Matthias, to become Governor General of the Provinces in place of Don John. Understandably, the Queen was disturbed by such signs of disarray, and all the more so because she was having trouble finding out exactly what the situation in the Netherlands was. The States-General were not taking the trouble to communicate regularly with Havre, and Orange was no more forthcoming, being so reticent that Elizabeth had reason to think that his sobriquet of "William the Silent" was highly apt. In these circumstances even Leicester was momentarily discouraged, commenting, "If they shew themselves thus irresolute, for my own part I [would] rather ... abide the worst at home than to hazard life and hand with such unstable men abroad".[55]

At length, after almost two months of dithering, the States woke up to the fact that all this time Don John had been building up his army and was now poised to attack. On 12 November they wrote to the Queen gratefully accepting her offer of assistance, but not unreasonably Elizabeth was now having second thoughts at involving herself with men who had shown themselves to be so irresolute and divided. On 14 December she told Havre that she would refrain from sending aid until she had made one more attempt to bring about a negotiated peace between Spain and the Netherlands, and she said that she would at once send Thomas Wilkes to Madrid for that purpose. Havre had to agree when the Queen remarked that the States only had themselves to blame for this latest change of mind, but as Elizabeth was adamant that if Philip rejected this fresh offer of mediation she would fulfil her earlier undertakings to the States, he was not unduly downcast. At the end of December he returned to the Netherlands "well satisfied" with the outcome of his mission.[56]

In the next few weeks, however, she came to regret that she had gone as far as she had. While she had to concede that there was a possibility that Philip was planning to invade England in the future, the fact remained that whereas war with Spain was at present no more than a hypothesis, a deeper involvement in the Netherlands might well make it a certainty. In January 1578 her resolve to help the States was further shaken when Don John inflicted a major defeat on their army at Gembloux, for it hardly seemed an opportune moment to enter the fray immediately after so serious a setback. Nor were men lacking who were able to play upon these fears for, while a majority of the Council was in favour of intervention, it appears that there were other individuals with access to the Queen who were telling her that all costs she must avoid a rupture with Spain. In February Walsingham's secretary noted sorrowfully that "of late, such as incline more to the faction of Spain than to her Majesty's safety" had been pressuring her to renege on her commitments to the States. "This has wrought such a coldness ... that she can hardly be moved from that Spanish persuasion", he noted in alarm.[57]

In her anxiety to extricate herself from her unwelcome undertakings, Elizabeth grasped at every sign that suggested that Philip's attitude towards her was not so inimical as had been supposed. She was greatly heartened when Thomas Wilkes sent back a report from Madrid saying he had been well received and "There was never fairer weather made to the English nation in Spain than there is at present". The Queen might perhaps have been less pleased if she had seen the annotations made by Philip on the letter that Wilkes had delivered to him containing her offer of mediation: "It seems to me that ... the Queen wishes to lay down the law for us here; and if I have understood well I can see no good to come from the matter", he had commented coolly. The King's attitude to Wilkes had been positively chilling, for he had noted, "It will be well to send the man off long before his fortnight is up, and this before he commits some impertinence which will oblige us to burn him".[58] The Queen, however, was not privy to these thoughts, and she persuaded herself that Philip intended to avail himself of her offer to be a mediator. She saw it as a further cause for optimism when she learnt that Philip had appointed as his ambassador to England Don Bernardino de Mendoza, a purblind Spanish grandee who had greatly charmed the Queen on a previous visit to England.

However much Elizabeth might want to convince herself that she had nothing to fear from Spain, her Council still thought otherwise and were strongly recommending that the Queen should intervene in the Netherlands without further ado. On 20 February 1578 Walsingham reported approvingly, "We are here now in daily and earnest consultation what is best to be done, in which generally I see my Lordships inclined to one course for her Majesty's safety, if it please God to incline herself to embrace and follow the same".[59] It soon emerged however that the Queen had already shrunk back too far to recover her former sense of purpose. Torn between her own peace-loving inclinations and the stern admonitions of the Council, on 8 March she decided on a compromise solution: instead of sending an expeditionary force of her own to the Netherlands she would subsidize the German mercenary leader John Casimir, paying him £40,000 to take an army of 11,000 men to the Low Countries. In addition she agreed that if the States succeeded in raising a loan on the European money market, she would underwrite the obligations they incurred for any sum up to £100,000.

The Queen did her best to make out to the States that this arrangement was infinitely preferable to that which had been mooted earlier. She stated blandly that though the new plan "may seem somewhat diverse from our former resolution", this was not really the case, and now she would be able to aid them effectually without incurring the suspicion that she wished to appropriate the Provinces for herself. As for John Casimir, she had no doubt that he would be the perfect instrument for her purpose, for he was "a prince for all respects so to be accompted of, that that part may think itself happy to whose succours he shall be pleased to incline". Not everyone shared the Queen's confidence that this indirect approach would be best for all concerned, and Leicester, for one, was utterly disconsolate. He told Davison sombrely, "Our good God hath found us, I fear, too unworthy of his former blessings; it is he alone that can help us, I mean miraculously, seeing the apparent ordinary causes are so overslipt".[60]

The States too felt they could not rely on Casimir alone to secure them victory, and in April 1578 they began negotiations with the Duke of Alençon in hopes of securing more effectual aid from him. Since the outbreak of the revolt it had been a fundamental tenet of English foreign policy that the French must not be permitted to exploit the troubles in the Netherlands to acquire a foothold there, but in her anxiety not to become further embroiled, Elizabeth could now question whether even this hallowed formula could not, after all, be profitably modified. In the spring of

1578 Alençon had sent a messenger to her professing his devotion, and while expressing astonishment "that after two years of absolute silence he should wake up to her existence", she was pleased by this development. Pondering on it further, it occurred to her that if Alençon were to resume his courtship of her, this would give her the perfect means of controlling any activities of his in the Netherlands. As luck would have it, Alençon was currently on very bad terms with his elder brother, and this made it less likely that if he went to the Netherlands he would seek to make territorial gains on behalf of the French crown. Furthermore, if the Duke was to be believed, he was not drawn to the Low Countries in hopes of personal gain, for he was loud in his protestations that he thought of going there solely because "his nature abhors tyranny, and desires only to succour the afflicted".[61]

Unfortunately, it was not altogether easy to trust in Alençon's assurances, for the Queen was reminded that if he were to drive out the Spaniards from the Netherlands he might well "wax straight a greater enemy himself".[62] Elizabeth fondly imagined that she could use him as her stalking horse, but several of her advisers still feared that he might rather turn out to be a Trojan Horse who would seize the Provinces for France. There was also the possibility that while he was in the Low Countries his elder brother would die, and Alençon would mount the French throne ideally placed to extend the borders of his inheritance. Certainly his past record was not one to inspire confidence, for while at intervals he had seemed desirous of throwing in his lot with the French Huguenots, at other times he had been happy to make savage war on them. Indeed with a background such as this, the possibility could not be overlooked that his real aim in going to the Netherlands was to betray the States and assist Don John to overrun the United Provinces.

To Walsingham, these risks were completely unacceptable, and he believed that the only option open to the Queen was to provide effective aid for the rebels herself. He made it plain, too, that he believed that Alençon's protestations of love for Elizabeth were insincere. He stated bluntly that Alençon "entertaineth her at this present only to abuse her", and claimed that the Duke was only making up to her so that she would not object when he took an army to the Netherlands. Leicester had to caution his colleague that this had gone down very badly with the Queen, who did not find it in the least implausible that Alençon should be enamoured of her. Indeed, far from accepting that he might be callously exploiting her affections in order to gain a free hand in the Netherlands, she preferred to believe that he was only thinking of going there because it would give him "better means to step over hither". Leicester told the Secretary, "Surely I suppose she is persuaded he hath more affection than your advertisement doth give her hope of ... I would have you, as much as you may, avoid the suspicion of her Majesty that you doubt Monsieur's love to her too much".[63]

It was perhaps not surprising that Walsingham's tactless observations had ruffled the Queen, but quite apart from this, she was being so extraordinarily difficult throughout the summer of 1578 that almost all her advisers found themselves at odds with her. The fact that for weeks her whole face had been inflamed with toothache in part accounted for this, for instead of dealing with business she spent hours closeted with physicians, who pondered anxiously "how her Majesty might be eased of the grief". Naturally this meant that her temper was more than usually short: Walsingham heard that on one occasion she cried out that he deserved to be hanged, whereupon he merely commented drily that if it came to the worst he only asked that he could be tried by a jury of Middlesex.[64]

The Queen used the discomfort she was in from her teeth as an excuse to deny her ministers access to her, for she knew that at every audience they would merely reiterate their pleas that she take steps to prevent the French from penetrating the Netherlands. "Our conference with her Majesty is both seldom and slender, more than upon necessity is urged", Leicester noted unhappily in August, but even so, as far as possible he and his colleagues remorselessly kept up the pressure. Walsingham congratulated them on the way they had stood up to the Queen, saying that he knew that "no prince could be more faithfully and earnestly dealt withal by councillors than her Majesty hath been by hers". Leicester particularly distinguished himself in this respect, speaking to the Queen "so plainly, so boldly and so faithfully ... against delays and unnecessary used allegations" that an admiring colleague remarked, "I did never hear councillor take the like liberty upon him". It appeared, however, that his frank speech would serve no purpose, for when urged to give fresh injections of cash to the States, the Queen replied that she would do nothing till they had repaid the sums that she had already loaned them. However much her councillors begged her to reconsider, she remained "earnestly resolved and bent not to change her mind".[65]

Then, on 9 August, the position was unexpectedly transformed, for with a sudden thrill of terror the Queen awoke to the fact that, once admitted to the Netherlands, Alençon might prove an even more uncomfortable neighbour than Philip II himself. In a state of virtual frenzy she insisted that letters were drawn up and despatched even before there had been time to make fair copies, offering to send an army of 10–12,000 to the Netherlands and to loan the States a further £100,000 if they refrained from making a league with the Duke. Evidently still bemused by the Queen's latest about-turn, Burghley patiently explained to a colleague that although these instructions might take him by surprise, "Her Majesty is greatly perplexed to think that the Low Countries may become French, and whilst she is in fear hereof, she will hazard any expense".[66]

Elizabeth's change of heart came too late. On 13 August 1578, before her frantic missives had even had time to reach their destination, the States signed a treaty with Alençon. By its terms, the latter promised to furnish them with an army of 12,000 men at his own expense for three months, in return for being declared The Defender of the Liberties of the Low Countries against the Spanish Tyranny, a grandiose title of which the exact significance remained obscure. Elizabeth was incensed, blaming everyone for this development but herself, but perversely she would not listen when her councillors told her that, if she wanted to prevent Alençon attaining too dominant a position within the Netherlands, she should promptly send the rebels there more money, for then they would not be exclusively dependent on French aid. Far from being prepared to come up with extra cash, she now said she would not send the bonds guaranteeing the loans that she had earlier promised to underwrite until the States gave her further security by pledging to her the Burgundian Crown Jewels. In vain her councillors pleaded that it was not only dishonourable to go back on her word in this way, but also dangerous, for the States' financial situation was precarious in the extreme, but they could make no impression on the Queen. Shrewishly she demanded whether the States were seeking her money out of necessity or pleasure. If they were doing so out of necessity, she rasped, then they should not quibble about giving her adequate guarantees, and "if they asked money for pleasure then the lending may be spared".[67] At length, after hours of disputes, she was induced to produce another loan of £8,000 for the States, but she remained adamant that she must have the jewels as collateral.

As it happened, any fears that the French would manage to entrench themselves in the Netherlands proved groundless, not so much because Alençon was intent on honouring his promises of moderation, but because of his incompetence. By the end of the year his army had melted away for lack of pay, and in December he returned crestfallen to France. For the moment there was no danger that the Netherlands would become a French satellite but, though freed of this worry, the English again had cause to dread an overwhelming Spanish victory. Elizabeth's proxy, John Casimir, in whom she had put so much faith, had arrived in the Netherlands in August 1578, but far from being of assistance to the States, he had only aggravated the bitter feelings that threatened to cause a split between Catholics and Protestants there by allying himself with a set of Calvinist extremists in Ghent. By the autumn the Queen was admitting ruefully that "seeing the course he takes she is sorry that she ever brought him into the country".[68]

To make matters worse, in October 1578 Don John had died, and had been succeeded as commander by the exceptionally able Alexander Farnese,

Duke of Parma. The latter not only swiftly pulled off a series of striking military victories but also had great success in weaning away from the rebel cause disenchanted Catholics from the southern Netherlands. In May 1579 he regained control of the key areas of Hainault, Artois and Walloon Flanders after negotiating the Treaty of Arras with the leaders of these provinces, and at this rate it did not seem as though the remaining rebels would be able to hold out against him for very long.

Still the Queen was not prepared to come to their rescue, considering them "ingrate for the benefits they have received", and incapable of using any money she might send them to good effect. Instead, she decided to investigate more seriously the possibility of marriage with Alençon. By matching with him she would not only be better placed to extend her protection to the French Huguenots, but it would improve her chances of bringing about a satisfactory peace in the Netherlands, for Philip II might abandon his attempts to subjugate the Provinces if he thought that by doing so he would bring down on his head the combined wrath of England and France. At the beginning of 1579 Walsingham noted that Alençon's prospects of marriage had received "no small furtherance upon occasion of the decayed state of things in the Low Countries, for that her Majesty, foreseeing that if the King of Spain come once to have his will there, he will prove no very good neighbour to her, thinketh this the best mean to provide for her safety that can be offered".[69]

The courtship began in earnest on 5 January 1579 when Jean de Simier (who was Alençon's Master of the Wardrobe as well as being "chief darling to Monsieur"), arrived in England to woo Elizabeth on the Duke's behalf. Elizabeth was utterly enchanted by her visitor, "a man thoroughly versed in love fancies, pleasant conceits and court dalliances", and was delighted that her life, which of late had been dominated exclusively by wearisome cares of state, should be reanimated by this heady draught of romance. She saw Simier as often as she could, frequently keeping him at court till nine or ten at night, and Lord Shrewsbury was told by his son, "She is best disposed and pleasantest when she talketh with him (as by her gestures appeareth) that is possible". Having agreed that one of her handkerchiefs should be sent to France as a love token for Alençon, the Queen was further beguiled when one day Simier crept into her bedchamber and purloined a nightcap for his master to treasure. It was not long before Simier had been given that sure mark of royal favour, a nickname, for in a pun upon his name the Queen dubbed him her "monkey". Simier repaid her with the graceful compliment that he hoped always to be numbered among her beasts.[70]

There were some courtiers who even questioned whether Simier had used "love potions and unlawful arts" to work his way into the Queen's affections, for there was no denying that he had swept her completely off her feet. Elizabeth made a point of always carrying about with her a little book in a jewelled binding that Simier had brought over as a present from Alençon, and she was always sidling up to him and pressing on him trifling gifts that could be despatched to his master in return such as a miniature of herself, or a handkerchief, or a pair of gloves. At such times she would say that one day she hoped to give Monsieur much more fine and valuable things, but in the meantime these must suffice. Simier noted excitedly that whenever Alençon's name was mentioned, the Queen's whole face lit up, and he heard too that she could not stop talking about him in private. She went so far as to declare that she thought there could be no greater happiness in the world than marriage, and said wistfully that she was annoyed to have wasted so much time. Hardly surprisingly, Simier began to feel optimistic about his chances of success, although he knew enough of the Queen's past history not to permit himself to become oversanguine. To a fellow Frenchman he confided, "I have every good hope, but will wait to say more till the curtain is drawn, the candle is out, and Monsieur in bed. Then I will speak with good assurance".[71]

Sure enough, difficulties arose as soon as negotiations began to take a more serious turn. As always, Elizabeth was insistent that she must see her suitor before she could agree to a betrothal, but the French were reluctant to let Alençon come over if it was not certain that he would win her hand. For the moment the religious issue caused no problem for it was agreed that that could be considered at a later date but, when the terms of a marriage contract were discussed, Simier put forward a series of unacceptable demands. Among other things he stipulated that Alençon should be crowned immediately after the wedding, and insisted that his master should be endowed with a large pension, payable throughout the remainder of his life. The Council refused to concede these points, but when it seemed that as a result talks might be abandoned, the Queen was much distressed, growing so melancholic that some of her favourite ladies had hastily to be summoned to court in order to cheer her up.[72]

This acted as a tonic, and by May her drooping spirits had sufficiently revived for her to feel angry rather than upset that the French should be so exacting. To France she wrote indignantly that their proceedings gave her cause to think that "The mark that is shot at is our fortune and not our person", and that she found this highly offensive. She continued wrathfully, "If they had to deal with a princess that either had some defect of body, or some other notable defect of nature, or lacking of mental gifts of the mind fit for one of our place and quality, such a kind of strainable proceeding ... might in some sort have been tolerated. But considering how otherwise, our fortune laid aside, it hath pleased God to bestow his gifts upon us in good measure, which we do ascribe to the giver, and not glory in as proceeding from ourselves (being no fit trumpet to set out our own praises) . . . we may in true course of modesty think ourself worthy of as great a prince as Monsieur is without yielding to such hard conditions". This outburst did the trick: in June 1579 Alençon offered to come incognito to England later in the summer, and in the meantime he told Simier not to insist on the conditions he had previously put forward.[73]

On 17 August 1579 Alençon arrived at Greenwich on what was in theory meant to be a secret visit. The Queen was thrilled, and any misgivings about his bizarre appearance were swiftly dissipated, for not only had he become "not so deformed as he was" as he grew older, but he made up for his less than handsome features by being blessed with an engaging gallantry and wit that left her quite enraptured. Promptly christening him her "frog", Elizabeth declared fondly that she had never in her life seen a creature who was so agreeable to her, and the next thirteen days were to pass in a delicious whirl of amorous dalliance. Tactfully, her councillors stayed away from Court as much as possible, so that the Queen could devote her full attention to the courtship, and though the unofficial nature of the visit meant that Alençon was unable to appear in public, Elizabeth did her best not to be separated from him for any length of time. When she attended a Court ball, she arranged for Alençon to be stationed behind an arras throughout the evening, and then showed off shamelessly, dancing much more than usual and making signals to the Duke, which the other guests pretended not to notice.[74]

At last the idyll came to an end with Monsieur's return to France. "The parting was very tender on both sides", the Spanish ambassador reported, but at least Elizabeth had the consolation that Simier stayed behind, and she found his company as intoxicating as ever. Having escorted Alençon to Dover, where he took ship to France, Simier painted Elizabeth an affecting picture of the Duke's last night in England, which he had passed sleeplessly, sighing and lamenting, and frequently waking up Simier to discuss the Queen's "divine beauties, and his extreme regret at being separated from your Majesty, the jailer of his heart and mistress of his liberty".[75]

All the signs were that this time the Queen would indeed be brought to the altar, but as an engagement seemingly grew nearer, ripples of anxiety began to spread through the country. Previously her subjects had implored her to marry so that she could beget an heir, but on 7 September 1579 Elizabeth celebrated her forty-sixth birthday, and this made it highly unlikely that she would be capable of producing children. Admittedly, it was said that prior to Simier's arrival the Queen had consulted her physicians over "whether she could hope for progeny, in which the doctors found no difficulty", and the French ambassador certainly claimed to have no worries on this score. "The Queen of England has never been more pretty or more beautiful", he pronounced firmly, "There is nothing old about her except her years". He added confidently that women born under Elizabeth's astrological sign were never barren, and that in England it was anyway commonplace for women of advanced years to produce children. Burghley was equally sanguine as to the Queen's reproductive abilities. He reminded the Queen that the last Duchess of Savoy had been somewhat older than her when she had had her first child, and she was "a woman of sallow and melancholy complexion, in all respects far inferior to her Majesty". How much more, then, could be expected of Elizabeth, "a person of most pure complexion, of the largest and goodliest stature of well-shaped women, with all limbs set and proportioned in the best sort, and one whom in the sight of all men nature cannot amend her in any part"![76]

Doubtless the fact that these comments were to be perused by the Queen largely accounted for the adulatory tone, but even when Burghley adopted a more scientific approach in a memorandum penned for his own benefit, he remained scarcely less optimistic. He noted that not only was the Queen healthy and well-formed, but she had no "lack of natural functions in those things that properly belong to the procreation of children, but contrary wise, by judgement of physicians that know her estate in those things, and by the opinion of women being most acquainted with her Majesty's body".[77] He had evidently made the most careful enquiries, and was presumably correct in thinking that the Queen had not ceased to menstruate, but even so, Elizabeth had now reached an age where it was rash to take this as an indicator of fertility.

Furthermore, even if it turned out that the Queen was capable of conceiving, she might not survive her pregnancy, for death in childbed was frighteningly commonplace. It has been estimated that there was a rate of mortality of perhaps twenty-five deaths per 1,000 births, and as an older woman the risk to Elizabeth would have been even greater. To make matters worse, it was frequently remarked upon that ladies in the upper reaches of society were more likely to die in labour than their social inferiors, for whereas "poor women, hirelings, rustics and others used to hard labours, also viragoes and whores, who are clandestinely delivered, bring forth without great difficulty, and in a short time after rising from their bed return to their wonted labours ... women that are rich, tender and beautiful and many living a sedentary life, as though they partaked of the divine curse after a more severe manner, bring forth in pain, and presently after their delivery lie in an uneasy and dangerous condition". The reason for this was probably that the poor were spared the attentions of the doctors, which meant that unlike their grander counterparts they did not have to undergo such treatments as having their bellies wrapped in the fleece of a freshly skinned sheep, or the skin of a hare flayed alive. The fact that it was standard practice for midwives to stretch and dilate the genital parts, cutting or tearing the membranes with their fingers if they thought it necessary, helps explain why deaths from sepsis and puerperal fever were so appallingly frequent. Even those women who survived the delivery were by no means out of danger, for they were actually weakened by the recommended methods of convalescence, which entailed lying in bed for a long time in a dark hot room, living on liquids and repelling the milk with poultices. The risks of childbirth are illustrated by the fact that in the Queen's immediate family circle, her grandmother Elizabeth of York, and her stepmothers Jane Seymour and Katherine Parr died having babies, and all three of the Duke of Norfolk's wives had succumbed in the same way. It could not be overlooked that if Elizabeth were delivered of a child it was quite likely that she would share their fate. Burghley was inclined to think that it was worth taking the chance, shrugging off the danger of death in labour as a peril "common to the sex", but Walsingham voiced the fears of many that motherhood could have fatal results for the Queen when he remarked grimly that in her case "Madonna may prove *morbe deletior*".[78]

Such misgivings did little to win over to the marriage that section of the populace who anyway thought it obnoxious that the Queen could contemplate matrimony with a Catholic and a Frenchman, for a combination of xenophobia and religious bigotry ensured that many Englishmen were strongly opposed to the match. The ill-feeling had been stimulated by attacks from the pulpit, as for months now Puritan preachers had been heaping invective on the proposed union, and as early as March 1579 the Queen had stalked out of a sermon at Court after the minister had stated baldly that "marriages with foreigners would only result in ruin to the country". By the autumn feelings had become still more inflamed. Lampoons vilifying the Duke were affixed to the Lord Mayor of London's door, and mocking ballads were in circulation such as that which concluded with the refrain,

> Therefore, good Francis, rule at home, resist not our desire,
> For here is nothing else for thee, but only sword and fire.[79]

Worst of all was the attack mounted in an anonymous publication of September 1579, clumsily entitled "The Discovery of a Gaping Gulf whereinto England is like to be swallowed by another French marriage if the Lord forbid not the banns by letting her Majesty see the sin and punishment thereof". This was the work of a Norfolk squire named John Stubbs, whose brother-in-law was the leading Puritan theologian Thomas Cartwright. Despite the author's plea that its contents were inspired "by the affection of my heart which must love my country and my Queen", Elizabeth was roused to paroxysms of fury by this tract, for though literate and well argued, in places its tone was nothing short of offensive. Not only did Stubbs stress the likelihood that the Queen was too old to be successfully delivered of a child, but he stated that it was unthinkable that Alençon could love a woman so many years his senior, and went on to abuse the Duke and his brothers in the coarsest possible terms. Alluding to the rumours of a "marvellous licentious and dissolute youth passed by this brotherhood", he commented, "If but the fourth part of that misrule bruited should be true, it must needs draw such punishment from God, who for the most part punisheth these vile sins of the body even in the very body and bones of the offenders, besides other plagues, to the third and fourth generation". In excoriating phrases he deplored the fact that the Queen could even think of marriage with "this odd fellow, by birth a Frenchman, by profession a papist, an atheist by conversation, an instrument in France of uncleanness, a fly worker in England for Rome and France in this present affair, a sorcerer by common voice and fame ... who is not fit to look in at her great Chamber door".[80]

The Queen reacted promptly: on 27 September she issued a proclamation stating that she would not permit friendly foreign princes to be abused in her dominions, and accusing the author of the piece of attempting to stir up sedition in her realm. She furthermore commanded the Bishop of London to instruct his clergy to deliver sermons lambasting whoever it was who had written the book, but the following Sunday the Bishop had to report that these addresses had not been well-received by city congregations. In one case, as the preacher had warmed to his theme, his listeners had "utterly bent their brows at the sharp and bitter speeches which he gave against the author of the book", and the Bishop unhappily admitted, "I perceive that any that bend their pen, wit, and knowledge or speech against the foreign Prince is of them counted a good patriot".[81]

If so, the Queen seemed set for a head-on collision with public opinion. Around 17 October Stubbs was apprehended, and he and his printer and distributor were sentenced to lose their right hand under an act passed in Mary's day against promoters of sedition. No matter that two judges, Monson and Dalton, contended that the statute was obsolete; the Queen, supported by the Lord Chief Justice, maintained that it was valid, and repaid them for their defiance by depriving one of his post and placing the other under restraint. Stubbs was to be shown no mercy: on the contrary, the French ambassador heard that Elizabeth was upset that a diligent search though the lawbooks afforded her no grounds to prosecute him on a capital charge, and though obliged to accept this setback, she declared that she would rather lose a hand herself than mitigate his punishment.[82]

Despite this, a group of courtiers sought to save Stubbs by going to Simier and asking him to intercede for the gentleman, thinking Elizabeth could not but relent if Alençon's own representative pleaded for clemency. Hearing of these manoeuvres, the Queen acted fast, decreeing that Stubbs should suffer before Simier had had time to approach her. The next morning at eight, the sentence was carried out in front of the Palace of Whitehall. Having had his right hand "cut off with a cleaver, driven through the wrist by the force of a mallet", Stubbs managed to pull off his hat with his other hand and cry out "God save the Queen!" before fainting. The distributor of the book (the printer was pardoned on grounds of old age) showed equal presence of mind: after his limb had been amputated, he lifted up the stump and declared stoutly, "I have left there a true Englishman's hand". Sullen and appalled that the Queen should be so implacable towards men whom many believed had her best interests at heart, "The multitude standing about was deeply silent".[83]

Despite her subjects' evident disapproval, Elizabeth apparently still thought that a marriage with Alençon was desirable, and she looked to the Council for a confirmation of this view. Unfortunately, when she asked them to deliberate on the matter at the beginning of October, their discussions revealed that a majority opposed it, for though Burghley was in favour of the match, he could muster the support of only three of his colleagues. Nevertheless, even those who spoke against it hesitated to make their opinions known to the Queen, for as Burghley pointed out, Elizabeth was obviously greatly taken with Alençon's "nature and conditions", and "seemeth not pleased with any person or with any argument appearing to mislike of the marriage". In the circumstances they agreed that caution was advisable, and having been closeted together on 6 October from eight in the morning till seven at night, they went to Elizabeth next day and told her that they had been unable to reach any conclusion on her marriage, a matter in which "Her person and her own present disposition is principally to be regarded". Warily, they begged her not to call on them to make a firm recommendation until she had given them some further enlightenment about "the inclination of her mind".[84]

The Council could hardly have been more circumspect, but even so the Queen was greatly upset. She had wanted nothing less than a full endorsement of the marriage plan, and these fumbling inexactitudes fell far short of her hopes. For all their reticence, she knew well enough that most of the Council were against her taking Alençon as her husband, and she felt humiliated and betrayed. To the embarrassment of those present, she launched into a lachrymose diatribe, tearfully complaining that she had expected them to agree that there could be no greater "surety to her and her realm than to have her marry, and have a child of her own body to inherit, and so to continue the line of Henry VIII; and she said she condemned herself of simplicity in committing this matter to be argued by them, for that she thought rather to have had an universal request made to her to proceed in this marriage, than to have made doubt in it".[85] Much alarmed, the councillors hastened to reassure her that, if she so desired, they would do everything in their power to further the marriage, but the Queen understood that though they were prepared to defer to her wishes in this way, a majority would not be happy to do so.

Stung by their reaction, in the ensuing days the Queen rounded on those members of the Council who had argued against the marriage from the start, suspecting that if it had not been for their eloquence a majority would have been content to let her proceed. Sir Francis Knollys was one of the match's most notable opponents, taking the view that "the observation of faithful love in marriage has always been despised in the Popish French court", and that the marriage would result in England being in bondage to France, as had been "agreed upon by that holy father the Pope, and plotted out by the serpentine subtlety of Queen Mother's head". Resentfully the Queen taxed him on his attitude, remarking bitterly, "It was a fine way to show his attachment to her, who might desire, like others, to have children". Walsingham too found himself in disgrace, for in a rage Elizabeth denied him the court, telling him to "Be gone, and the only thing he was good for was a protector of heretics". Even Sir Christopher Hatton, an adoring devotee of the Queen's who had been appointed to the Council the previous year, was excluded from her presence for a week because he was known to be opposed to the French match.[86]

The Queen might thrash about in anger but, for all her fierce posturing, her nerve had been shaken by her failure to secure an unequivocally favourable verdict from her Council. The Spanish ambassador recorded, "She remained extremely sad after the conversation [with the Council] and was so cross and melancholy that it was noted by everyone who approached her ... She has been greatly alarmed by all this." Her rancour and spleen stemmed largely from the knowledge that she would ignore at her peril the feelings of those who were ill-disposed to the match, and that however much she might bluster that in this matter she was an entirely free agent, her fear of losing her people's affection was likely to prove an effective curb. By mid-October, Alençon's prospects, formerly so bright, had begun to dim: the Archbishop of York reported confidently that "the French matter was dashed", and predicted that before long "Simier, with that crew" would be leaving the country.[87]

Nevertheless, Simier was not unduly despondent, for he believed that if he were to strike at the Earl of Leicester, he could still salvage the marriage. He reasoned that if he could convince the Queen that Leicester had betrayed her in the grossest fashion he would not only undermine the Earl's influence (which hitherto had been directed against the French match) but he would reduce Elizabeth to a distressed and vulnerable frame of mind, and in this state she would be the more inclined to seek consolation in marriage with Alençon.

When Simier had first appeared on the scene Leicester had tried to make the Frenchman look on him as an ally. He had declared expansively to Simier that he had taken great pains to reconcile various nobles to Alençon's suit, and said that he himself was so enthusiastic that he had already ordered new clothes for himself and trappings for his horses so that he could be splendidly turned out at the coming wedding. However, within a few months of his arrival Simier had deduced that, far from trying to promote the marriage, Leicester was labouring insidiously to prevent it, losing no opportunity to impress upon the Queen that it would be both unpopular and impolitic. Simier accordingly decided that if the match were to go ahead it was vital to discredit Leicester. The Frenchman's familiarity with Court gossip gave him the weapon he needed, for he was able to reveal to the Queen the devastating news that in September 1578 Leicester had secretly married Lettice, Countess of Essex.

It was hardly to be expected that Leicester's devotion to the Queen should have caused him to lead an entirely celibate life in the nineteen years that had passed since the death of his first wife. In 1584 it was indeed alleged in a scurrilous pamphlet attacking the Earl that he was an utter debauchee, and that there were not "two noblewomen about her Majesty ... whom he hath not solicited to potent ways". According to this source, when he could not obtain sexual satisfaction from high-born ladies, he "descended to seek pasture among the waiting gentlewomen of her Majesty's Great Chamber", offering them £300 a night if they would agree to satiate his lust. This was character assassination, pure and simple, and there is in fact little solid evidence to suggest that Leicester was genuinely an incorrigible lecher. Nevertheless, he was plainly attractive to women: in 1573 it was noted that not only the widowed Lady Douglas Sheffield, but also her sister, Frances Howard, were "very far in love with him", and that the Queen "thinketh not well of them, and not the better of him" for encouraging their attentions.[88] Nevertheless, so long as Leicester remained a bachelor she could console herself that she still had first claim on his affections, and so she accepted the situation without protest.

Leicester certainly had a sexual relationship with Lady Douglas Sheffield, for in August 1574 she produced a son by him, but rumours that he went so far as to contract a secret marriage with her, only to disavow it when he deemed it convenient, were almost certainly unfounded. A letter survives from Leicester to an unknown lady (presumably Lady Douglas Sheffield) in which he succinctly explains why it is impossible for him to take her as his wife. The letter begins, "I have, as you well know, long both liked and loved you", but he then reminds the recipient that at the beginning of their affair he had given her an explicit warning that he would never be able to put their relationship on a more official footing. She must not delude herself now that there was any better hope that he would make her his Countess, even though he actually would have liked to marry in view of the fact that his only brother was childless, and unless he fathered some legitimate offspring, his family name would die out. "You must think it is some marvellous course, and toucheth my present state very near, that forceth me thus to be cause almost of the ruin of my own house", he observes, explaining that the truth is that he is uniquely situated, and cannot take a wife without causing "mine utter overthrow". "If I should marry", he goes on, "I am sure never to have favour of them that I had rather yet never have wife than lose them" (here he was plainly alluding to the Queen), and he therefore urges his mistress to seek an alternative husband elsewhere.[89]

It does not appear that Lady Douglas took this advice and voluntarily broke with the Earl, but she was subsequently discarded when Leicester embarked on his affair with the Countess of Essex. Lettice was the daughter of Sir Francis Knollys, and was hence the Queen's first cousin once removed. She had had a flirtation with Leicester as early as 1565. This had not lasted long, but a few years later she had resumed the connection while her husband was absent on active service in Ireland. By December 1575 her affair with Leicester was such common knowledge that there were even wild reports that she had borne him two children, and when the Earl of Essex died of dysentery at Dublin the following September, the credulous did not doubt that he had been poisoned by Leicester. Within two years Lettice (who was an altogether more forceful character than the insubstantial Lady Douglas) had prevailed upon Leicester to make her his wife. Leicester would have put up the less resistance because, as he had admitted to Lady Douglas, he longed for a legitimate heir, and he felt that he must do something about it before it was too late. No longer was he the fine figure of a man he had been at the beginning of the reign: he was now "high coloured and red faced", and had grown so portly that the Queen frequently joked about his bulk. Only recently she had chaffed him that he should cut his daily meat consumption to "two ounces of flesh . . . and for his drink the twentieth part of a pint of wine", though she had conceded that on festivals he could supplement his diet with "the shoulder of a wren, and for his supper a leg of the same".[90] Middle-aged and paunchy, the pleasures of domesticity and family life presumably seemed more inviting to Leicester than ever, and he managed to convince himself that he would be able to enjoy them without the Queen finding out. On 21 September 1578 he and Lettice were married at an early morning ceremony performed at his house in Essex, Wanstead, but the wedding remained a closely guarded secret, and the Queen had been ignorant that it had taken place until Simier had seen fit to enlighten her.

The result was explosive: Elizabeth not only felt anguished and betrayed, but she was also roused to fury by the discovery that, while Leicester had been doing his best to wreck her chances of marriage, he was drawing solace from it himself. In her first transports of rage she even thought of placing him under arrest, for she now called to mind the rumours that he had been previously contracted to Lady Douglas Sheffield, and if these proved true Leicester could be sent to "rot in the Tower" on charges of bigamy. The Earl of Sussex was deputed to interrogate Lady Douglas (who had herself recently remarried), but when questioned as to whether Leicester had entered into a binding commitment with her, she merely said tearfully "She had trusted the said Earl too much to have anything to shew to constrain him to marry her".[91] Reluctantly, Elizabeth had to accept that in marrying Lettice, Leicester had done nothing criminal.

Undoubtedly, however, he had abused her trust in perpetrating so gross a deception, and the Queen had every reason to feel seriously aggrieved. Alarmed by the way that Elizabeth was ranting about his faithlessness to anyone who cared to listen, Leicester sought to justify himself to Burghley on the grounds he was not legally bound to ask the Queen's permission before he took a wife. "Her Majesty, I see, is grown into a very strange humour, all things considered, toward me", he wrote plaintively, adding that though he had always rendered faithful service to the Queen, he had never abased himself "in any slavish manner to be tied in more than unequal and unreasonable bonds". Self-pityingly he continued, "I carried myself almost more than a bondman many a year together, so long as one drop of comfort was left of any hope ... So, being acquitted and delivered of that hope, and by both open and private protestations and declarations discharged, methinks it is more than hard to take such an occasion to bear so great displeasure for".[92]

Ostensibly what he said was reasonable enough, but his argument was disingenuous to say the least, for his shoddy attempt to conceal his marriage showed that he fully realized the enormity of what he had done. Whatever the legal position, his obligations to the Queen were such that he could hardly complain about the fact that she had come to regard him as her property. It was true that she had rejected his proposal of marriage, but she had compensated for this by enriching and ennobling him, and Leicester had been perfectly aware that she did so on the tacit understanding that he would never share these gains with another woman. When he had told her repeatedly that he was deserving of her hand, she had taken this to mean that he would never be content with that of anyone else, and Leicester himself had justified his shabby treatment of Lady Douglas on the grounds that his courtship of the Queen had placed permanent restrictions on his private life.

When the storm first broke, he had feared that the Queen might confiscate everything that she had previously lavished upon him, but in fact his material well-being did not suffer. By the beginning of 1580 the Queen had begun to calm down, and even uttered a few words in Leicester's defence to the French ambassador, saying that the Earl had merely been doing his duty as a councillor when he had urged her against marriage with Alençon. But though he was not formally penalized, for the moment there was no trace of the intimacy that had previously existed between him and the Queen. In April 1580 she remained distant and cold, and though thereafter the warmth gradually crept back into their relationship, the shock of his betrayal had had so corrosive an effect on her feelings that at any moment she was liable suddenly to turn on the Earl and overwhelm him with venomous taunts and reproaches. After one such outburst in July 1580 Leicester was reduced to sighing despondently, "Better for me to sell my last lands than to fall into these harsh conditions". Ultimately, however, his rehabilitation was to prove complete: as late as July 1583 it was observed that he was "in great disgrace about his marriage, for he opened the same more plainly than ever before", but a mere six weeks later he was described as being "grown lately in great favour with the Queen's Majesty, such as this ten years he was not like to outward show".[93] His wife Lettice, on the other hand, was not so fortunate, for she was not permitted to come to Court for the remainder of Leicester's lifetime.

Simier's revelations did not destroy for ever Leicester's influence with the Queen but, at the time he made them, the Frenchman must have been delighted by the impact his tale-telling had. Seeing that Leicester had let personal fulfilment take priority over his duty to her, the Queen decided to follow his example, and put her own happiness first. On 10 November, wearing a veil that was sprinkled with *fleurs de lys*, Elizabeth summoned her principal councillors and "told them she had determined to marry, and that they need say nothing more to her about it, but should at once discuss what was necessary for carrying it out". On 20 November a committee of the Privy Council (from which Leicester was significantly excluded) was formed to discuss the terms of the marriage treaty, and four days later the Queen put her name to the articles that they had drawn up, agreeing among other things that Alençon and his entourage would have the right to practise their religion after the marriage.[94] However, she made one important proviso, stipulating that these articles should not come into effect for a two-month period. During this time, she would try and reconcile her subjects to the match, but if this proved impossible the agreement would be null and void. Even now, the Queen's canniness had not deserted her, and when Simier returned to France on 28 November 1579 it was hard to be specific about what precisely he had achieved.

Once freed of Simier's presence, the Queen was able to view the courtship in an infinitely more rational light. With his exquisite gallantry and fine words, Simier had succeeded in working her into a state of delicious anticipation about Alençon's visit, and the Duke's arrival had done nothing to disillusion her, for despite his unprepossessing appearance, Elizabeth had noticed only that he was blessed in abundance with other, more loverlike qualities. As well as being exhilarated by the attentions of two delightful young men, she was haunted by the knowledge that she was on the brink of the menopause, and this, combined with the heartache she had suffered in learning of Leicester's double dealing, had led her to fancy herself in love with her youthful suitor. The infatuation nevertheless proved transient, and with Simier no longer there to titillate her feelings, it was not long before she descended to a much less exalted emotional plane. The two-month deadline agreed upon with the French drew to a close without the Queen making any move to invite marriage commissioners to England, and at the end of January 1580 Burghley told Elizabeth that though she had made no official announcement, he believed that she was now disinclined to marry, "either of your own disposition, or by persuasion of others whom you trust".[95]

The Queen, however, would not confirm this. Burghley told her that unless she intended to accept the Duke, she should deal squarely with him by saying that the marriage was off, but Elizabeth could not bring herself to discard Alençon completely. Privately she had decided that the best course would be to "keep him in correspondence" for as long as she could, for despite repeated warnings that the French would want revenge once they realized they had been duped, she preferred to spin out her dealings with them to the furthest possible point and then cope with the consequences later.

Accordingly, the pace of the courtship slackened, but it did not halt completely, and even after the expiry of the eight-week deadline the Queen still implied that, if given more time, she would succeed in winning over her people to the match. In the meantime, she did her best to convince the French that she was still madly in love. She wore as an earring an emerald frog that had been embedded in the seal of one of Alençon's love letters, and in her belt she kept tucked another of his little gifts, a pair of gloves which she ostentatiously kissed a hundred times a day.[96] At a Court ball she called over the French ambassador and made a point of reading all Alençon's letters aloud, behaving in so affectionate a fashion that the ambassador believed she intended it as a snub to all those who opposed the marriage. In fact, however, all this was mere artifice: as always when putting on a performance of this kind, Elizabeth was enjoying herself hugely, but her displays of tenderness were shameless fabrications.

In the summer of 1580, the Queen tried to inject fresh life into the courtship, for she could not allow the French to lose interest just when it was becoming ominously clear that the Spanish crown was daily increasing its power and resources. At the beginning of 1580 the aged King of Portugal had died, leaving behind him no direct heir, and at the end of June Philip of Spain had pressed home his claim to be the rightful successor of that throne by sending an army across the Portuguese frontier. By August Lisbon was occupied, and the English had had to watch helplessly as Philip radically shifted the balance of power in Europe by absorbing the enormously rich Portuguese empire into his already extensive dominions. No one could doubt that this was a development fraught with danger for Elizabeth. Sir Christopher Hatton wailed, "When we behold the great prosperity of Spain through his peaceable possession of Portingale, we ought justly to fear that his affairs being settled there ... he will then no doubt with conjunct force assist this devilish Pope to bring about their devilish purpose". When Elizabeth heard of Philip's victory she commented grimly, "It will be hard to withstand the King of Spain now",[97] and as Parma was also making great strides in the Netherlands, the situation seemed doubly menacing. Thoroughly alarmed by the success that was meeting the Spanish army on all fronts, in August 1580 Elizabeth invited the French to send marriage commissioners to England as soon as possible.

By now, however, Alençon had other fish to fry, for since the spring of 1580 he had been involved in discussions with the Dutch, who had offered to make him their sovereign if he would help them to stem the Spanish advance. Feebly, Elizabeth tried to prevent these negotiations coming to fruition, protesting, "I think not myself well used ... if this matter comes to pass ... God forbid that the banns of our nuptial feast should be savoured with the sauce of our subjects' wealth".[98] Alençon had paid no attention, and on 19 September 1580 the Treaty of Plessis-Les-Tours declared him to be the Prince and Lord of the Netherlands. The thought that a French prince might one day acquire suzerainty over the Netherlands had always been an eventuality that had filled the English with dread, but by this time Elizabeth's fear of the Spaniards was such that she scarcely reproached Alençon for taking on his new status. Her first priority now was to prevent him wriggling out of her grasp, and she was therefore much alarmed when for some months the French ignored her invitation to send marriage commissioners to England. To her relief, however, in January 1581 she was told they would soon be on their way.

Alliance with France was one way of countering the growing might of Spain but the Queen had already received comforting proof that Englishmen did not necessarily need foreign support to strike against the Spanish colossus. On 26 September 1580 Francis Drake sailed into Plymouth harbour in a ship laden with Spanish booty, having successfully completed a circumnavigation of the globe. For years the English had felt resentment at being denied any share in the riches and commercial opportunities that had been generated by the Spanish and Portuguese voyages of exploration in the previous century. In 1493, Pope Alexander VI had partitioned the New World, granting all heathen lands to the west and south of the Azores to

Spain, while lands to the east of this meridian went to Portugal. Throughout these territories, a rigid trade monopoly was enforced by the new owners, who forbade foreign merchants to visit or engage in commerce within their recently acquired dominions. These regulations inconvenienced the colonists who went out from Spain to people the settlements in South America and the Caribbean, for their own countrymen proved incapable of furnishing them with all the goods they required, and the temptation for merchants of other nationalities to supply them with what they lacked was therefore considerable. Seeing his opportunity, in 1562 the Plymouth seaman John Hawkins had sailed first to Africa to procure a supply of slaves, and then crossed the Atlantic and found a ready market for them in Hispaniola. He returned home laden with a valuable cargo of pearls, hides, sugar and gold, and since the venture had proved such a success, he was naturally anxious to try again. In 1564 a second voyage was fitted out, and this time the Queen herself was a shareholder, contributing a ship worth £2,000 on the understanding that she would be entitled to a share of any proceeds. Once again Hawkins's business went well, and when he set out for a third time in 1567 the Queen loaned him two of her ships. Elizabeth may have assumed that Philip II would be prepared to sanction a limited degree of trade between England and his colonies, which in many ways was in the interests of all concerned, but in fact the King had no intention of allowing any infringement of his monopoly. In 1568, on his way back from the New World, Hawkins had had to put in to the Mexican harbour of San Juan de Ulua to repair a leaking ship, and while there he was surprised by the arrival of a Spanish fleet, bearing the new Viceroy of Mexico, Don Martin de Enriquez. Although Hawkins could have prevented them from entering the port, he permitted the fleet to come in after obtaining pledges of peace, but once inside the Spaniards broke their word and treacherously attacked. Two of the English ships managed to escape, but there was no time to revictual, and in the rush Hawkins's vessel *The Minion* had to take on so many men that there was no hope that supplies would last throughout the journey home. At their own request, a hundred of the crew were set ashore on the Mexican coast, only to be subsequently delivered up to the Inquisition by the Spanish settlers. Those men who remained on board fared little better, for when Hawkins finally limped into Plymouth in January 1569, thirst, starvation and disease had accounted for all but fifteen of the sailors.

The captain of the other ship that escaped was a stocky Devon man with a ruddy beard named Francis Drake, and he was filled with an abiding sense of grievance by the way the Spaniards had behaved at San Juan de Ulua. He always hoped that on one of his subsequent voyages he would encounter the Viceroy who had been responsible for the dishonourable attack, so that he "might show him how to keep the word of a gentleman".

Until that day, however, he considered all Spaniards to be fair game, saying that though he regretted that Philip II's vassals should suffer for the misdeeds of the King and his Viceroy, he would not rest till he had secured recompense for Hawkins's losses in Mexico.[99]

As a zealous Protestant, who always heeded his chaplain father's injunction to "Make much of the Bible", Drake was the more inclined to regard the Spaniards as his natural enemies, for he felt sure that true religion could not survive in England unless the greatness of Spain was abased. His faith was an inspiration in other ways, for besides being filled with a robust indignation at the pretensions of the Pope ("How can it be endured that kings and princes must kiss the Pope's foot? What a swindle!" he once exclaimed to a shocked Spanish captive), he had no doubt whatever that Providence was on his side. He cheerfully committed himself "to the tuition of him that with his blood redeemed us", and desired his men, "For the passion of Christ, if you fall into any danger you will not despair of God's mercy, for he will defend you from all danger and bring us to our desired haven, to whom be honour, glory and praise for ever and ever, Amen".[100] His belief in divine guidance left him so sure of his own authority that at times it led to charges of arrogance and intolerance (there was a disquieting incident during the voyage of circumnavigation, when Drake had the gentlemanly adventurer Thomas Doughty executed for alleged insubordination, after a summary court martial), but it also helped provide him with the driving sense of purpose and qualities of leadership that were to make his name a legend throughout the world.

After San Juan de Ulua, Drake abandoned all thoughts of trading with the Spaniards, preferring to prey on them instead. In 1572 he had sailed to Panama and there led a daring raid on the treasure house at Nombre de Dios, which was aborted only because his men lost heart after Drake was wounded in the leg. The following year, he successfully ambushed the mule train carrying silver from the mines of Peru across the Isthmus of Panama, and his share of the profits amounted to £20,000 worth of bullion. He returned home in 1573 to find that Anglo-Spanish relations had lately improved and, as his presence was something of an embarrassment, he made himself scarce by going to Ireland for a time. By 1576, however, he was back, full of ideas for a new voyage. During his earlier visit to Panama he had caught a glimpse of the Pacific from the top of a tall tree, and at the time had fervently "besought Almighty God of his goodness to give him life and leave to sail once in an English ship on that sea".[101]

Venturing into the Pacific would not necessarily have involved Drake in clashes with the Spaniards if on his exit from the Straits of Magellan he had sailed south in search of *Terra Australis Incognita*, the great continent whose existence was confidently affirmed by geographers. By the summer of 1577, however, the breakdown of peace in the Netherlands, and the menacing attitude of Don John, made it less difficult for Drake to secure support for the plan that this should be more than a mere voyage of exploration. Sir Christopher Hatton, Lord Admiral Lincoln, the Earl of Leicester and Sir Francis Walsingham all invested in the venture, and Walsingham secured him an introduction to the Queen herself. According to Drake, at this interview Elizabeth told him, "Drake! so it is that I would gladly be revenged on the King of Spain for divers injuries I have received", and Drake declared that the best way of harassing Philip was "to annoy him by his Indies". The Queen, so he said, enthusiastically concurred (although she qualified her assent by saying that "Of all men my Lord Treasurer should not know it"), and Drake claimed she also invested 1,000 marks – about £665 – in his expedition. At various times during the voyage he even flourished a paper purporting to be a signed commission from the Queen, but he did not permit anyone to inspect it closely, and it is in fact extremely unlikely that Elizabeth would have risked compromising herself by putting her name to a document that might well have subsequently fallen into Spanish hands. Indeed, she herself once remarked that one reason why she did not object to Drake's activities was that "the gentleman careth not if I should disavow him". Nevertheless, it seems clear that she approved of his plans in outline, even though she might have envisaged that instead of attacking Spanish settlements in Peru, Drake would concentrate on securing valuable commodities from southern Chile, where fewer Spaniards had penetrated.[102] At any rate, she knew that even if this was the object of the journey, Lord Burghley would not condone it. With his legalistic turn of mind, he abhorred anything that savoured even remotely of piracy, and he feared that ventures such as Drake's only served to bring England into international disrepute.

Drake had set off in December 1577 and by early September of the following year he had passed through the Straits of Magellan. After being buffeted by tremendous storms, he cruised northward up South America's Pacific coast, robbing townships and seizing vessels. Those manning the ships he took were left unharmed (for Drake had little in common with the ruffianly pirates who cruised in the Channel, who had been known to tie up captive crews in the sails and throw them overboard) but Drake helped himself to their cargoes, the richest prize of all being the *Cacafuego*, whose hold yielded twenty-six tons of silver and eighty pounds of gold, as well as a fabulous haul in jewels and precious stones. He continued sailing steadily northward, past Panama and Central America, until he appears to have reached a point just south of Vancouver Island, where cold weather forced him to turn back. Going south, he landed briefly in California, which he claimed for the Queen under the name New Albion, and then headed off for the great journey across the Pacific. At the Moluccas in the Spice Islands his good fortune continued, for he was able to purchase a valuable cargo of cloves, but he only narrowly escaped disaster when his ship *The Golden Hind* struck a submerged rock in the Indian Ocean. After some of the cargo was jettisoned, however, the ship floated free, and by the end of June 1580 he and his crew had rounded the Cape of Good Hope and were back in Atlantic waters. They arrived in Plymouth on 26 September, and Drake's first question on reaching home was whether the Queen was still alive.

His enquiry was not inspired by loyalty alone, for he knew that he was in great need of the Queen's personal protection, as the Spanish ambassador would obviously be clamouring for his head. The attitude of some Englishmen to him was scarcely less hostile, for when the first reports of his exploits had reached home, the merchant community had erupted in anger, saying that trade with Spain would be disrupted as a result, and complaining that it was intolerable that "just because two or three of the principal courtiers send ships out to plunder in this way, their property must be thus imperilled and their country ruined."[103] Elizabeth, however, had no intention of abandoning Drake. On the contrary, shortly after his arrival he was summoned to court, and for six hours he was closeted with the Queen, recounting his adventures. Nevertheless, if Elizabeth did not conceal her delight at the way the voyage had gone, at this stage she remained uncertain whether she dared provoke Spain by hanging on to his plunder. When the Council were consulted, at first it looked as though they would be swayed by Burghley into advising the Queen to refund Drake's haul, but Leicester, Walsingham and Hatton opposed this so vehemently that for the moment the issue remained in suspense.

The Queen nevertheless was determined that Drake's pocket should not suffer, whatever the outcome of the debate. In October 1580 she sent orders that the bulk of the treasure now lying at Plymouth should be sent to London for safe keeping, but before it was removed about £18,000 worth was to be abstracted, so that the crew of *The Golden Hind* could share around £8,000, and the remaining £10,000 was to go to Drake. Thus enriched, Drake began comporting himself like "a right magnifico", "squandering more money than any man in England", in the indignant words of the Spanish ambassador. He gave the Queen a magnificent crown studded with emeralds, "three of them almost as long as a little finger", and on New Year's day, when she wore it for the first time, he presented her in addition with a diamond cross. All this largesse made her have a higher regard for him than ever: it was noted that whenever he came to court she singled him out for attention, warmly conversing with him whenever she had time to spare.[104]

In the end, none of the money was handed back to Spain, a decision which owed much to recent events in Ireland. In July 1579 a small force had landed in Ireland under command of the exiled Irish chieftain

Desmond Fitzmaurice. Officially Fitzmaurice was fighting in the Pope's name, but the English held Philip II responsible for his actions, for the King had permitted Fitzmaurice to recruit men in Spain, and the expedition had sailed from Ferrol. Fitzmaurice himself had been killed shortly after his arrival but, on being pressed by the Pope, Philip had agreed to send more weapons and reinforcements to Ireland. In September 1580 a further eight hundred men had landed at Dingle Bay and had entrenched themselves at Smerwick, but they proved unable to defend the position, and in November they had surrendered to the English. Almost all the captured men were put to death, but their leaders were spared (much to the annoyance of the Queen, who thought it would have been preferable if "as well the heads as the inferiors had received punishment according to their demerits") and the officer in charge had stated that he had come to Ireland on the orders of King Philip.[105]

In the circumstances, the Queen felt she had good reason not to make restitution of Drake's plunder. It is hard to tell exactly what this amounted to, or how much of it went to the Queen. After Drake and his men had received their share, about £70,000 worth of gold and silver was registered as being deposited in the Tower, but clearly the full proceeds of the voyage were much higher. In 1638 one Lewis Roberts claimed he had seen a paper in Drake's hand certifying that all his backers had received a dividend of £47 for every £1 invested, and if the expedition had cost £5,000 to fit out, this would have meant that its total yield would have been £235,000. The fact that this was more than the Queen's net annual revenue puts this figure into perspective, but Spanish estimates put Drake's gains still higher. Mendoza, the Spanish ambassador, was probably exaggerating when he stated that Drake's plunder was worth £450,000, but Spanish merchants may well have been correct when they claimed that the value of Drake's booty was 950,000 pesos, or £332,000.[106]

In April 1581 the Queen blazed her defiance of Spain by conferring fresh honours on Drake. In the presence of the French ambassador, she attended a banquet that Drake gave at Greenwich, "finer than has ever been seen in England since the time of King Henry", and throughout the meal was observed to be in a particularly good mood. After Drake had presented her with a map of the voyage and paintings of the exotic fish he had sighted, members of his crew danced before the Queen in Red Indian dress, and then Drake delivered a discourse on his voyage. To the disgust of the French ambassador, this lasted all of four hours, but the Queen listened raptly. At length, however, she told Drake jocularly that she had "a gilded sword to strike off his head" and then, in order to symbolize that England and France intended to stand together against Spain, she asked the French ambassador to dub Drake a knight.[107]

Before long Drake was a public hero, for though those involved in trade with Spain still grumbled, calling him "the master thief of the unknown world", the vast majority of his compatriots were stirred by his heroism and "generally applauded his wonderful long adventures and rich prizes. His name became admirable in all places, the people swarming daily in the streets to behold him, vowing hatred to all that misliked him".[108] His exploits helped boost the nation's morale, and promoted a spirit of national self-confidence and pride in the skill and daring of English seamen that would do much to sustain the country in its coming struggle with Spain.

By the spring of 1581, preparations were in full swing for the arrival of the French marriage commissioners. Fourteen coaches were ordered for the ladies of the Court, shopkeepers were ordered to sell their luxury cloths at a reduced price, and at the end of March, three hundred and seventy-five men started work on a canvas banqueting pavilion for Whitehall, more than three hundred and thirty feet in length. On 16 April, the commissioners landed in England, and five days later the Queen accorded them the most gracious of receptions. On 25 April there was a splendid feast given in the new pavilion, the roof of which had been painted to resemble a star-spangled sky, and which was festooned with elaborate pendants of holly and ivy, interspersed with exotic fruits and vegetables.

All this was very fine, but as the Spanish ambassador shrewdly observed, Elizabeth was "paying more attention to ostentation and details of no moment than to points of importance for the conclusion of a treaty". It was some time before the commissioners managed to discuss business with the Queen, and when they did, a rude shock awaited them. To their utter amazement Elizabeth breezily announced that not only was she still concerned by the age difference between her and Alençon , but she thought that if he became her husband it would encourage the English Catholics, who had become disturbingly numerous of late. Furthermore, since the Duke now had such extensive commitments in the Netherlands, she feared that by marrying him she might drag the country into war with Spain, and she said that in the circumstances she could only offer to make a looser form of alliance with France, which would not entail marriage. Totally nonplussed, the commissioners stammered that since no difficulties of this sort had been anticipated, their instructions did not empower them to conclude anything other than a marriage treaty, but the Queen insisted that this was the best she could do.[109] Vainly hoping that her attitude might soften, the commissioners lingered in England for some weeks, but in June they finally and disconsolately returned to France.

The following month Elizabeth sent Walsingham to France in hopes of persuading Henry III that it would be "good for all parties, the marriage not taking place, that a confederation should be made between him and her, whereby both the King of Spain might be stayed from his over-greatness, and Monsieur helped". She suggested that England and France should jointly agree to make secret contributions towards the cost of Alençon's operations in the Netherlands, but Henry III was not interested in doing a deal on this basis. He believed that unless Alençon made sure of her by marriage, Elizabeth would not fulfil her side of the bargain, and if he himself were to take on Spain by going to Alençon's assistance, the Queen would then leave him to cope with the consequences on his own. Walsingham explained that Henry did not care for her proposal, "fearing lest, when he should be embarked, your Majesty would slip the collar",[110] and Elizabeth realized that she would have to think again. She had failed to reach the sort of understanding with France that she desired, but she considered it vital that some sort of link was maintained between the two countries, and she decided that she had no alternative but to continue the farce of the marriage negotiations.

Alençon had no objection, for he still believed there was a chance that Elizabeth would accept his suit. More cynically, he thought that even if she did not, the best way of persuading her to part with money to finance his army in the Netherlands would be to keep up his attentions to her. That summer, Walsingham had already persuaded her to contribute £15,000 towards Alençon's costs, and the Duke hoped that by exerting a little pressure he would be able to obtain more. Accordingly, on 31 October he arrived in England once again. It seemed that Elizabeth was no less taken with him than before, keeping him by her side "from the time he rises until supper time", but all his entreaties that he should be allowed to know whether or not she intended to marry him met with evasive answers. Mendoza commented knowingly, "When they are alone, she pledges herself to him to his heart's content, and as much as any woman could to a man, but she will not have anything said publicly".[111] It was nevertheless obvious that the French would not be fobbed off with this treatment indefinitely, and the Queen knew that if she was to keep Alençon on her tail, she would have to do better than this.

On 22 November she made her move. As she and Alençon were strolling down one of the galleries at Whitehall, the French ambassador asked her to make a final decision about her marriage. The Queen replied clearly, "You may write this to the King: that the Duke of Alençon shall be my husband". With that she kissed Alençon on the mouth, and presented him with a ring, and then called together all the ladies and gentlemen of the court and repeated what she had said.[112]

Naturally, the announcement caused a huge sensation. Leicester was distraught, Hatton was in tears, and the ladies of the court became so hysterical that when the Queen retired, they "lamented and bewailed" all through the night, preventing her from getting any rest. All this, of course, was grist to Elizabeth's mill, for it enabled her to point out to the French how upset her subjects were at the prospect of her marrying Alençon, and this gave her an excuse to demand that, before she did so, the French must give her the most stringent guarantees. She still maintained that she wanted to go ahead with the wedding, but when she clarified the conditions on which she was prepared to take him, his family were utterly aghast. Not only was she adamant that she would not contribute a penny towards Alençon's expenses in the Netherlands, but she said the French must agree to come to her defence if England was invaded by Spain. Having been greatly excited when the first intimations had reached them of Elizabeth's decision, Henry III and Catherine de Medici received the news that she had amended the position with "sour countenance and manner of speaking", while Alençon himself was overheard muttering bitter imprecations about "the lightness of women, and inconstancy of islanders".[113]

Elizabeth knew that the French could not possibly accept such terms, which allowed her to make out that it was they who were being unreasonable, and that it was no fault of hers if Alençon and she did not become man and wife. She congratulated herself on having jilted Alençon in the gentlest possible way, and assumed that, provided she gave him some money to pay for his campaign in the Netherlands, they would part on good terms. Anxious now to be rid of him, on 15 December she undertook to loan the Duke £60,000, half of which was to be paid a fortnight after he left England, and the remainder within another fifty days. It was agreed that Alençon would depart for the Netherlands on 20 December, and the Spanish ambassador claimed that, in the privacy of her bedroom, Elizabeth danced with joy at the thought that she would soon be free of him. At the last moment, however, Alençon changed his mind. Evidently concerned that he had undersold himself, he suddenly declared to the Queen that he would rather die than leave England without marrying her. Alarmed by such vehemence, Elizabeth tremulously enquired "whether he meant to threaten a poor old woman in her country?" whereupon Alençon, frustrated and overwrought, burst into tempestuous sobs.[114]

Elizabeth had ruefully to admit that the Duke was not to be so easily fobbed off as she had thought. Artfully, she persuaded Burghley to intimate to him that he would be well advised to take his leave before the New Year festivities, for if he stayed till 1 January he would have to give the Queen an expensive gift. Apparently unshaken by this, Alençon stubbornly clung on, and on New Year's day he imperturbably presented Elizabeth with a jewelled anchor to symbolize his constancy of heart. In some desperation, Elizabeth gave the Duke an advance of £10,000 on the loan she had promised him, hoping that it would stimulate in him so martial a spirit that he would rush off to the Netherlands, but still he refused to budge. Greatly agitated, the Queen began to have sleepless nights and even developed a fever as it seemed that he would be content with nothing less than marriage, but at the beginning of February, much to her relief, Alençon agreed that he would go.

Having gained her object, the Queen felt it safe to indulge in a great show of sorrow that they were to be separated. As Alençon made his way to his port of embarkation at Sandwich, Elizabeth accompanied him as far as Canterbury, and there an affecting scene was played out when she tenderly bid him farewell. One witness reported, "The departure was mournful betwixt her Highness and Monsieur, she loth to let him go, and he as loth to depart. Her Majesty on her return will be long in no place in which she lodged as she went, neither will she come to Whitehall, because the places ... give cause of remembrance to her of him with whom she so unwillingly parted". In public, the Queen continually wept, tearfully telling Leicester and Walsingham that she would not live an hour longer were it not for her hope that she would see Alençon again. She even confided that she would give a million to have her frog once again swimming in the Thames, rather than in the stagnant waters of the Netherlands.[115]

Despite Elizabeth's hopes, the separation turned out to be permanent. Alençon remained in the Netherlands for the remainder of the year, but despite the fact that the Queen loaned him a further £35,000, he proved utterly incapable of stemming the Spanish advance. Blaming the Dutch for his failure, in January 1583 he attempted to stage a *coup d'état* in the Low Countries, but when this proved a fiasco he had to flee the Provinces. Anxious that he should continue to be her proxy in the Netherlands, Elizabeth repeatedly urged the States General to invite him back, but before they could be reconciled with their prince and lord, Alençon died on 10 June 1584 (N.S.).

Elizabeth appeared inconsolable. The following month the French ambassador recorded, "As for the Queen, she is still in appearance full of tears and regrets, telling me she is a widow woman who has lost her husband, and how I know that the late Monsieur was as much to her, and how she ever held him hers, although they had not lived together". The ambassador took all this with a sizeable pinch of salt, commenting sardonically, "She is a princess who knows how to compose and to transform herself as suits her best", but perhaps he was wrong in thinking that Elizabeth's grief was entirely simulated. At an earlier stage in the courtship, the Queen had as usual fished for compliments by telling Henry III that she was no more than "an old woman, to whom paternosters will suffice in place of nuptials".[116] Now that Alençon was dead, and there was no suitor who would step forward to replace him, she had to accept that, in describing herself thus, she had spoken no more than the truth.

CHAPTER 10

The phoenix and her nest

In theory, men came to Court because their adoration for Elizabeth was such that they found it insufferable to live far removed from her. The Earl of Shrewsbury's duties as Mary Stuart's custodian kept him away from Court for long periods, and when applying in 1581 for permission to pay Elizabeth a visit, he wrote to Walsingham, "I neither regard health, travel, time of year or any other thing, in respect of the sight of her Majesty, my greatest comfort; and until her good pleasure may be such, I shall long as one with child, and think every absent hour a year". Fifteen years later, illness forced Lord North into a temporary retirement from Court, and he declared solemnly, "My heart hath been more grieved with this my absence from the presence of her Majesty than my limbs hath been pained with the gout; for the true joy of my heart consisteth more in her Majesty's eyes than in all worldly things else". In 1597, when Robert Carey deserted his post on the Scottish borders in order to come to Court, a friend of his pleaded to the Queen that Carey was not to blame for playing truant in this way, for "not having seen her for a twelvemonth ... [he] more could no longer endure to be deprived of so great a happiness, but took post with all speed to come up to see your Majesty, and to kiss your hand, and so to return instantly again".[1]

The truth, of course, was rather more prosaic. Carey had come to Court not because he had a craving to glimpse Elizabeth, but because he wanted to obtain some form of remuneration for his services on the borders, which had hitherto gone unrewarded. His bid proved successful. The Queen was pleased by the idea that he had been unable to control his desire to see her, and having received him graciously, she ordered that he should be paid £500 for the work he had carried out over the past year. The outcome was satisfactory for all concerned. Elizabeth had not thrown her money away, for Carey was a deserving case, but it suited her purposes that financial demands of this kind should be couched in the language of courtly love.

Obviously Elizabeth's powers of magnetic attraction were much enhanced by the rewards that she could confer on those who secured her favour. These incentives were not necessarily financial, for peerages and knighthoods were bestowed at the discretion of the monarch, and were ardently coveted. Elizabeth nevertheless exercised her rights in such matters with extreme caution. With great deliberation, she "honoured her honours by bestowing them sparingly" for she believed that the prestige attached to titles would be diminished if she handed them out indiscriminately. In the course of her reign, she created only eighteen peerages, and six of these were restorations of titles that had earlier been forfeited as a result of attainders. At her accession, there had been fifty-seven peers in the country, but during the next forty-five years several titles became extinct for lack of male heirs, and on Elizabeth's death the total number of peerages had shrunk to fifty-five. As she grew older, she was subjected to intense pressure to create more peers, but she stubbornly resisted this. When urged to make Robert Sidney a baron in 1598, she refused to do so, even though she acknowledged herself satisfied of his "worthiness and fidelity towards her". "But", she objected, "what shall I do with all these that pretend to titles? I could be willing to call him and one or two more, but to call many I will not."[2]

She was equally reluctant to raise higher in the peerage those who already had titles. In 1572, Lord Hunsdon expressed his annoyance at Elizabeth's failure to make her great-uncle, Lord Howard of Effingham, an earl. She had apparently justified this on the grounds that Howard was not sufficiently wealthy to sustain the honour, but in a snide reference to the Dudley brothers, Ambrose and Robert, Hunsdon pointed out that earlier in the reign she had "made earls of nothing, both without land (saving of her gift), and yet no kin to her". Hunsdon was resentful partly because he himself wanted to be an earl, and he could tell there was little chance of his wish being gratified so long as the Queen maintained her current stance. Eventually, in 1596, when Hunsdon was on his deathbed, Elizabeth sent him word that she intended to make him Earl of Wiltshire, but the irascible old man regarded this as insultingly late. He declined the title with the comment, "Madam, since you counted me not worthy of this honour whilst I was living, I count myself unworthy now that I am dying".[3]

Bestowing peerages cost the Queen nothing, but she also had at her disposal gifts of a more material nature. Awarding annuities to be paid out of crown revenues was one option open to her, and in 1573 some three hundred and fifty men and women were in receipt of such grants. She could also hand out export licenses. In order to boost the weaving industry, the export of unfinished cloth was in theory restricted, but Elizabeth could give permission to courtiers to ship a specified quantity of undressed cloth out of the country. In 1577, for example, the Earl of Sussex was given a license to export 20,000 cloths, and he subsequently sold this to a trading consortium for no less than £3,200. Alternatively, Elizabeth could rent out to favoured individuals the right to collect customs duties on specified items, concessions which often proved highly lucrative. Among those who benefited were the Earl of Leicester, who was entitled to the duties on all sweet wines that came into the country, and Sir Robert Cecil, who in 1598 was granted a lease of the customs levied on all imported silks and satins.[4]

Under the royal prerogative, Elizabeth was entitled to grant individuals monopolies. Early in the reign, these tended to go primarily to foreign craftsmen who had introduced into the country some new industrial process which they wanted patented, but by the 1580s monopolies had become little more than an additional means of enriching courtiers. Members of the Court were also occasionally allocated a share in the profits of justice. In 1580, for example, Sir Philip Sidney was assigned the proceeds of fines levied on certain Catholics who had failed to attend church services. "I think my fortunes very hard that my reward must be based on other men's punishments", he commented mournfully at the time but, however distasteful he found it, he did not fail to collect what was due to him. Apart from this, Elizabeth could award fee farms (perpetual leases of royal land at a nominal rent) or lease lands to courtiers without charging them the premium known as a fine which landlords generally charged when letting their property.[5]

The grant of wardships was another lucrative privilege in the Queen's gift. When tenants of the Crown died and left heirs who were minors, Elizabeth was entitled to the revenues from their lands until the heir reached the age of majority. The Crown could sell this right to others, who were then entitled in their turn to exploit their ward's property and to marry him or her to the person of their choice. The lower the price of the wardship, the more profitable it would prove to the purchaser, and the Queen occasionally issued instructions that wardships were to be sold to specified individuals on particularly favourable terms. Towards the end of the reign, for instance, Elizabeth decreed that Lady Scrope should be permitted to purchase a wardship at a bargain price, "because it was her Majesty's pleasure that she should have good benefit by it, and not pay according to the rates".[6]

Such interventions on Elizabeth's part were comparatively rare, for in general she left it to Burghley, as Master of the Court of Wards, to handle all matters pertaining to wardship. However, she was aware that Burghley frequently sold wardships below the market price, and by suffering such practices she tacitly endorsed them. The purchasers frequently resold their recently acquired wardships to other buyers, obtaining sums which were up to twelve times the amount that they had paid the Court of Wards. The

Queen made no objection for, although profits from the sale of wardships (which totalled about £650,000 in the course of the reign) were a useful increment to her income, she valued the system primarily because of the opportunities it afforded of indirectly rewarding courtiers.[7]

It was a common practice of the Queen to make loans to needy courtiers. This was a relatively cheap way of making them beholden to her, and their fear of foreclosure acted as an additional incentive for their good behaviour. When the date for settlement came, she often agreed to extend the deadline, but it was very rare for her to write off the loan altogether. It was not unusual for courtiers to die heavily in debt to her, and in such cases their heirs had to make repayment. The Earl of Leicester ran up some of the largest debts, but he was by no means exceptional in obtaining credit from the Crown, and many of his colleagues, such as the Marquis of Winchester and the Earls of Huntingdon and Sussex, died owing considerable sums to Elizabeth.[8]

Leicester was perhaps the supreme example of a man whose fortunes were founded exclusively on royal favour, but there were others whose rise was scarcely less spectacular. Christopher Hatton was a handsome Northamptonshire gentleman who first attracted Elizabeth's attention when he danced before her in a masque that was written and performed for her by the law students of Lincoln's Inn Fields. By 1564 he had become one of the Queen's Gentleman Pensioners, an elite corps of royal bodyguards which had been created by Henry VIII in 1539. Hatton was a talented jouster as well as a graceful dancer, and one of Elizabeth's first gifts to him was an expensive suit of armour. This was followed by more substantial endowments. In 1565 she bestowed on him the manor of Sulby, nominally in exchange for his own estate at Holdenby, but he was allowed continued tenure of that, and two years later it was conveyed back to him in fee farm. In 1568 he was made Keeper of Eltham Park, and allocated royal lands in Pembrokeshire, and awards to him over the next three years included property in Yorkshire, Dorset and Hereford. All the time he was becoming closer to the Queen, and in July 1572 he was made Captain of the Yeomen of the Guard, one of the most coveted positions at Court.

As Hatton had started to emerge into prominence, Leicester had done his best to retard his career. When Elizabeth had praised Hatton's dancing, Leicester told her that he knew of a dancing master whose skills were far superior. The Queen was not impressed. "Pish!" she exclaimed scornfully, "I will not see your man. It's his *trade*!" However, in 1573 Hatton fell ill with kidney disease and was obliged to seek treatment abroad, and Leicester hoped that in his absence he would be eclipsed. This proved to be far from the case, for Hatton was a consummate letter-writer, and the Queen was delighted by the tender avowals that daily poured from his pen. In an allusion to *Elizabeth Regina*, he signed his letters, "All and EveR yours, your most happy bondman", and he wrote with an exquisite sensibility of his anguish at being parted from the Queen. He had been absent for only two days when he wrote, "No death, no, not hell, shall ever win of me my consent so far to wrong myself again as to be absent from you one day ... I lack that I live by ... The more I find this lack, the further I go from you ... My wits are overwrought with thoughts. I find myself amazed. Bear with me, most dear sweet lady. Passion overcometh me. I can write no more. Love me, for I love you ... Live for ever".[9] However over-stated such sentiments seem today, Elizabeth was satisfied that this was the language of genuine emotion.

By the autumn of 1573 Hatton was back in England and as high in favour as ever. In time he and Leicester became friends but others remained jealous of Hatton's ascendancy, sneering that he was "a mere vegetable of the Court" who had risen "by the galliard". Elizabeth nevertheless discerned that there was more to Hatton than his decorative exterior. When a diplomat from the Netherlands visited England in 1576, Elizabeth commended Hatton to him, declaring that she could "divine the humour of everyone, and that it was wise for her to make use of the service of all sorts, great and small, and that she knew how to elevate lesser men when they deserved it".[10] Two years later she knighted Hatton, appointed him Vice-Chamberlain, and made him a member of the Privy Council.

Hatton's devotion to Elizabeth never dimmed. Unlike her other favourites, he remained unmarried (although he did produce an illegitimate daughter) and the Queen esteemed him the more highly for this. Energies that might have gone into family life instead went into building an immense mansion at Holdenby, which was "consecrated" to Elizabeth, and which outdid in magnificence even Burghley's "princely seat" of Theobalds. It was described by one contemporary as "altogether even the best house that hath been built in this age", but unfortunately all too little remains of a building that Hatton had hoped would stand for centuries as "a monument of her Majesty's bountifulness to a dutiful servant".[11]

As a public servant, Hatton proved himself worthy of the trust Elizabeth placed in him. He was a distinguished and regular orator in the House of Commons, and he served on several commissions which were set up to conduct the state trials of notable offenders. His able handling of these convinced the Queen that he merited still higher preferment, and in April 1587 she made him Lord Chancellor. Leading members of the legal profession greeted the appointment with "very great distaste", for Hatton had never practised as a lawyer and it is not even clear whether he had ever taken his place at the bar. Characteristically, having committed the Great Seal to him, Elizabeth herself became uneasy at her choice, but when Hatton declared that he would "deliver up the Seal rather than keep it to her discontentment and his disgrace", she would not hear of receiving it back from him. In the end her controversial decision was vindicated, for Hatton's awareness of his limitations meant that when presiding in Chancery he was always careful to consult those who were familiar with the court's procedure and "what he wanted in knowledge of the law, he laboured to make good by equity and justice".[12]

Elizabeth was nearing fifty when another unknown young man had an impact on her comparable to that first made by Hatton. Walter Ralegh had been born and brought up in Devonshire, as was evident from his heavily accented speech, which served to the end of his life as a reminder of his West Country origins. By the time he attained royal favour, he had already had an adventurous career, having fought as a volunteer on the Huguenot side in the French civil wars, and served with the Queen's forces in Ireland. In 1580 he was present at the fall of Smerwick, but the following year he came to Court and swiftly attracted Elizabeth's attention. How he did this is not clear: the story of him laying his valuable cloak over a "plashy place" so that Elizabeth could keep her feet dry as she walked over it is not inherently implausible, but is not authenticated by contemporary evidence. Possibly he was simply presented to her, for he had good connections at Court. It seems that during earlier visits there he had made the acquaintance of Leicester, Burghley and Walsingham, and Ralegh's mother had also been a relation of Elizabeth's old governess, Kat Ashley. Kat had died in 1565, but her husband John was still alive, and would have been a useful contact.

At any rate, once she had noticed him, Elizabeth became greatly taken by this "tall, handsome and bold man" in his late twenties, with a beard that "turned up naturally". From the Queen's point of view, Ralegh's physical attractions were only part of his allure, for he was both a freethinker and a poet, and she found him an exceptionally stimulating companion. "An indefatigable reader, whether by sea or land", Ralegh was immensely versatile without being in the least a dilettante, and Elizabeth so "loved to hear his reasons to her demands" that before long "she took him for a kind of oracle, which nettled them all". Not only was he an original conversationalist, but he was a master of "ditty and amorous ode", and though much of the poetry which he wrote in her honour is now lost (for Ralegh disdained publication), the verse which survives is remarkable for its controlled intensity. Ralegh hailed Elizabeth as "Nature's wonder, virtue's choice/ The only wonder of time's begetting", and while not neglecting to pay the usual tributes to her beauty, it was her intellect quite as much as her appearance which provided him with his inspiration:

> O eyes that pierce into the purest heart
> O hands that hold the highest hearts in thrall
> O wit that weighs the depth of all desert

O sense that shows the secret sweet of all.
The heaven of heavens with heavenly power preserve thee!
Love but thyself and give me leave to serve thee.[13]

In April 1583 Elizabeth arranged for Ralegh to be leased two estates belonging to All Souls College, Oxford. The following March she awarded him a license to export woollen broadcloths, which earned him £3,500 a year, and two months later she conferred on him the right to charge every vintner in the country £1 a year as a licensing fee. The same year Ralegh was knighted, and Elizabeth also allowed him to take up a lease of Durham House in the Strand. A foreign visitor who saw Ralegh at Court in 1584 commented, "She is said to love this gentleman now beyond all others. And this must be true, because two years ago he could scarcely keep one servant, and now with her bounty he can keep five hundred".[14] This was rather an exaggeration but, even so, Ralegh had indisputably arrived.

Few others shared Elizabeth's high opinion of Ralegh, for most people had a violent aversion to him. He was "commonly noted for using of bitter scoffs and reproachful taunts" in everyday social intercourse, and his biting and sarcastic tongue "bred him much dislike". The money he made from licensing taverns and exporting cloth naturally aroused resentment, and when this was coupled with "a pride above the greatest Lucifer that hath lived in our age", it was enough to make him almost universally detested. Far from being disturbed by his unpopularity Ralegh positively exulted in it, but though Elizabeth did not mind that he showed no interest in courting the public, she was less happy about the fact that he sometimes seemed to go out of his way to cause gratuitous offence. He was the sort of man who would "lose a friend to coin a jest" and, for all his brilliance, Elizabeth could see that in some respects his judgment was flawed. This made her wary of entrusting him with weighty responsibilities: she sometimes consulted him about Irish affairs, and as war with Spain approached Ralegh helped co-ordinate defence measures in the West Country, but he was never made a member of the Privy Council. She realized that someone who was once justly described as "insolent, extremely heated, a man that desires to seem to be able to sway all men's fancies, all men's courses" was too intoxicated with his own cleverness to prove much of an asset at the Council table, and that his tendency to stir up animosities by "perpetually differing" for the sake of it, would cancel out any positive contribution he could make.[15]

Denied political influence in his own country, Ralegh had more time to devote to projects to colonize the New World, but Elizabeth never showed more than cautious interest in these. Until this time, North America had been thought of primarily as an inconvenient land mass which barred the way to the East, but Ralegh had the vision to take a more constructive approach. In 1584, he sponsored an exploratory expedition to North America, and on its return Elizabeth agreed that an area near Roanoke island could be christened Virginia in her honour. Two Indians who had been brought back from America were received at Court, dressed in brown taffeta, and when Ralegh fitted out another expedition with the aim of establishing a settlement in Virginia, the Queen put at his disposal one of her ships, the *Tyger*. This, however, was the limit of the assistance which she gave him. By the time this group of settlers returned in July 1586, Elizabeth was already too preoccupied with the struggle against Spain to think of colonization as an important priority. Ralegh persevered, sending a third expedition to Virginia in 1587, but for three years he was unable to provide the settlers with any form of succour, as all available English shipping was required to serve in the war against Spain. When a relief ship finally landed in Virginia in 1590, the colonists were nowhere to be seen.

The careers of men such as Hatton and Ralegh illustrated the potential gains that could accrue from royal favour, but inevitably theirs were exceptional cases, for the Crown would have been bankrupted if Elizabeth had shown comparable generosity to more than a tiny minority. Far from being obliged to distribute her largesse systematically, it was part of her prerogative to hand it out in an arbitrary and erratic fashion, which kept everyone guessing and made it impossible to predict who would be a beneficiary. Obviously this gave rise to injustices: many men who worked tirelessly to uphold the interests of the state failed to grow wealthy, for though it was understood that loyal service would not be disregarded, the timing and nature of the rewards conferred for it remained entirely at the Queen's discretion. Burghley certainly thought that Elizabeth squandered too large a share of her assets on men who did not really merit it, and in a memorandum of January 1580 he urged her in future "to gratify your nobility and the principal persons of your realm, to bind them fast to you with such things as have heretofore been cast away upon them that in time of need can serve you to no purpose". It is hard not to suspect that what Burghley was hinting was that he himself was one of those whose well-being had been neglected, for five years later he could not resist moaning to a confidant, "In my whole time I have not for these twenty-six years been beneficed from her Majesty as I was within four years of King Edward. I have sold as much land in value as ever I had of gift of her Majesty".[16] These complaints were certainly not justified, for despite his extensive building operations at his houses, Burghley and Theobalds, the Lord Treasurer died an extremely rich man, but the majority of his colleagues were a great deal less fortunate.

Among these was Sir Francis Walsingham, who lamented in 1578, "None hath more cause to complain than myself, being rather decayed than advanced by my long and painful service". Despite being granted the outport customs farm in 1585, his pecuniary difficulties grew more pressing towards the end of his career. After Walsingham unravelled the Babington plot in the summer of 1586, Burghley revealed to the Queen that the Secretary's financial situation was parlous, but rather than award Walsingham any share of the chief conspirator's forfeited estates, she elected to bestow these on Sir Walter Ralegh. The following April she did do something to redress the situation by giving Walsingham several royal manors in fee farm but, even so, the Secretary was still being harassed by creditors at his death.[17]

There were others who had to wait many years before their services to the Crown received anything like adequate recognition. During the Queen's first twelve years on the throne, the Earl of Sussex not only performed an arduous spell of duty as Lord Lieutenant of Ireland, but he then went on to play a vital role as Lord President of the Council of the North but, as he pointed out in March 1570, Elizabeth had signally failed to show her appreciation. He protested that as a result he had been forced to sell over £12,000 worth of property, having "spent my whole revenues for twelve years in the Queen's Majesty's service, and to this hour I never received, directly or indirectly, any other benefit than was incident to the ordinary fees belonging to the offices of charge that were committed to me". Elizabeth sought to soothe him by declaring that she was on the verge of making him a substantial endowment, but in fact it was another two years before these promises bore any fruit.[18]

If those who had genuine claims on Elizabeth's gratitude sometimes received less than they deserved, it was hardly surprising that more peripheral figures at Court found it a wearisome and long-drawn-out process to obtain a share of her favour. Without assiduous attendance at Court there was little chance of doing so, for to be out of the Queen's sight was to be out of her mind, and she was unlikely to feel well-disposed towards a courtier unless constantly reminded of his existence. It simply was not good enough for a man to expect to swoop down on the Court and grab something worth having, and Elizabeth certainly did not take it kindly if she suspected that someone was interested not so much in her as in what she had to offer. In 1596 one unfortunate gentleman who presented her with a request was told this in no uncertain terms, for, as he recounted to Robert Cecil, she shouted at him that "I never came to attend her but for my own purposes ... and ... that I had been in hand with her for a suit since my coming to the Court, and was never without something". "As fishes are got with bait, so are offices caught with seeking," Burghley once commented wryly, and those who tried a more abrupt approach netted very little.[19]

Even to gain admittance to the Court required some financial outlay, for no one was allowed into the Presence Chamber who was improperly attired.

Wearing fine clothes was one way for an outsider to make a good impression on Elizabeth, for she was an acute observer of male fashion. Seeing Sir John Harington in a new frieze jerkin, she told him approvingly, "'Tis well enough cut", but when another luckless courtier appeared before her in a tasselled doublet she was less complimentary. Rudely she spat on the fringed cloth, commenting scornfully, "The fool's wit was gone to rags". "Heaven spare me from such jibing!" exclaimed Harington, when recording the story. Elizabeth indeed felt so strongly about what men about her wore that in 1594 she put all her courtiers to considerable expense by issuing an order through the Lord Chamberlain that no one would be admitted to her presence wearing a cloak that came below the knees. "It cometh in a good hour for tailors and mercers and drapers, for all men are settled into long cloaks," commented one aggrieved gentleman, although in fact it is probable that the command had not originated simply out of royal caprice. In July 1586, when walking on Richmond Green, Elizabeth had been warned that an assassination attempt on her might be imminent, and at this "Her Majesty started, and looking about her, blamed her servants present for being without weapon, saying she would banish those long cloaks that were the cause". Presumably, therefore, the sartorial edict issued eight years later was meant to encourage courtiers to wear swords at all times and was intended primarily as a security measure.[20]

Although no one wearing suitable clothing was turned away from Court, only a small proportion of those who came there ever gained access to Elizabeth. The best that many of them could hope for was to establish indirect contact with her through the agency of someone high in her favour and, using that person as a mouthpiece, beg her to show them kindness. Obviously, however, it was better if the intermediary could be dispensed with, for as Sir John Harington put it,

> Trust not a friend to do or say
> In that yourself can sue or pray.

It nevertheless required a nice judgment to be able to tell exactly the right moment to present the Queen with an application on behalf of oneself. Sir John Harington took the view that the most propitious time to tackle her was in the morning, before other business intervened to distract her. He resolved, "I must go before the breakfasting covers are placed, and stand uncovered as her Highness cometh forth her chamber; then kneel and say, 'God save your Majesty, I crave your ear at what hour may suit for your servant to meet your blessed countenance'. Thus will I gain her favour to follow to the auditory". Before making any such appeal, however, it was as well to try and ascertain beforehand some knowledge of Elizabeth's frame of mind. One morning Sir Christopher Hatton emerged from an audience with the Queen and, seeing Harington, kindly warned him, "If you have any suit today, I pray you put it aside. The sun does not shine." To try and ensure that Elizabeth would be in a suitably amenable temper, it was wise to sweeten her beforehand with an offering such as a jewel or item of clothing, but even those who had taken such precautions could never be wholly confident as to how she would react to their importunities. Her mood could be alarmingly changeable, causing Sir Edward Stafford to sigh in 1584, "I know the Queen's disposition, that when she is best pleased, asking somewhat is enough to make her fall out with any man". There were times when, sensing that she was about to receive an unwelcome application, she would seize on some excuse to spare herself from hearing it. "Faugh, Williams! I prithee begone – thy boots stink", she once exclaimed on seeing the Welsh soldier Sir Roger Williams waiting with some petition. "Tut, Madam, 'tis my suit that stinks", retorted Sir Roger drily.[21]

Having overcome the first hurdle by putting a request to the Queen, the suitor invariably had to wait for his response, for in this, as in all else, she refused to be hurried. Until the final moment of rejection, she nevertheless did her best to imply that there were no grounds for pessimism, for it was noted of her, "She suffered not at any time suitor to depart discontented from her, and though he oftentimes obtained not that he desired, yet he held himself satisfied with her manner of speech, which gave hope of success in a second attempt". Once she had made up her mind that an application deserved to be turned down, it was rare for her to deliver the bad news in person, and instead she contrived that some luckless third party was called upon to report her decision. This was an obligation that was not unnaturally resented: "True it is", wrote Burghley wrathfully on one occasion, "that her Majesty throweth upon me a burden to deal in all ungrateful actions, to give answers unpleasant to suitors that miss".[22]

Even when Elizabeth appeared to have acceded to a suit, a verbal promise from her was worthless unless confirmed by a formal warrant. There were numerous instances when suitors who believed themselves to have received a firm commitment subsequently learnt that they had been victims of a misunderstanding. In 1585, for example, John Lyly thought he had had an assurance from Elizabeth that he would become Master of the Revels on the death of the present incumbent, Edmund Tilney. After waiting patiently for more than ten years he was naturally horrified to learn that Tilney's nephew was also expecting to succeed his uncle in the office, and try as Lyly might to fight off this interloper, he never succeeded in establishing that his own claim was valid. The occult philosopher John Dee suffered a similar disappointment, although in this case his own negligence was partly to blame. As a result of repeated pleas from Dee, in 1582 Elizabeth had prevailed upon the Archbishop of Canterbury to confirm Dee in the possession of two rectories which had first been bestowed on him by Edward VI. Dee was so absorbed in his work on the reformation of the calendar that he failed to have the grant sealed within the allotted time limit, and in consequence lost £80 a year.[23]

Elizabeth's unreliability when it came to matching words with deeds put suitors in a delicate position, for once she had verbally assented to a petition, they could hardly press her further on the matter without seemingly impugning her trustworthiness. Few dared tackle her so openly as the "plain northern woman" who apparently obtained all she had asked for when granted an audience with Elizabeth, but still remained visibly dissatisfied. "The Queen, willing to be rid of her, said, 'Why, have I not given you my word you shall have your suit?' 'Alas Madam', said she, 'they say your word is nothing if one have not your hand to it'". Elizabeth had the grace to be quite amused – as well as a little embarrassed – by this naïve reply, but usually she did not like to be reminded that she did not invariably honour her word. One day she was looking out of her window when she saw the courtier Sir Edward Dyer taking a stroll. "Sir Edward, Sir Edward", she called out to him, "what does a man think when he thinks of nothing?" "A woman's promise", Dyer quickly replied, and at this barbed repartee Elizabeth hastily "shrunk in her head, and said to somebody near her, 'Well, this anger would be a brave passion for making men witty, if it was not so base a one as kept them poor'".[24]

One of the great arts of bringing a suit to fruition was to gauge exactly when it would be admissible to remind Elizabeth that a promise of hers had yet to be translated into reality. In 1589 Lord Burghley warned the Earl of Shrewsbury that although the Queen had "given good hope" that she would grant his latest suit, pressure must be kept up, for "until she shall sign the book, I dare not give assurance". Experienced courtiers took this in their stride. "Court actions carry seldom performance without *rencontre* of some crossing thwarts", wrote Lord Hunsdon philosophically to Sir Robert Cecil in 1596, adding robustly that as he was sure that those "pursued with direct course in the end prevail, so I doubt not if you shall please to present her Majesty with a new and resolute assault of my much desired poor bill, but that she will be as pleased to sign it as she was graciously contented to grant it".[25]

For less resilient souls, trying to coax suits from the Queen could prove a dispiriting and degrading business. "To be ... like a child following a bird, which when he is nearest flieth away and lighteth a little before, and then the child after it again, and so *in infinitum*, I am weary of it", wrote Francis Bacon dejectedly in 1595 after his hopes of obtaining high legal office had once again been dashed. "A thousand hopes, but all nothing; a hundred promises, but yet nothing" was how John Lyly bitterly summed up his attempts to pursue a career at Court. Elizabeth did her best to stretch the patronage that was available, but as she once observed, "No prince's revenues be so great that they are able to satisfy the insatiable cupidity of men", and certainly her own wealth was too limited for the parcelling out process to be anything other than highly selective. The great challenge for her was to content a significant enough proportion of those who believed they had a claim on her largesse without either stirring up ill-feeling in the country at large, or irresponsibly diminishing her own resources. Her courtiers' expectations had to be kept artificially high while at the same time only occasionally being realized, and on the whole she showed great skill in achieving this balance. Yet despite her proficiency in carving up what was, in fact, a somewhat undersized cake, the necessity to eke out the crumbs meant that she was under constant strain. There were times when she must have regretted that there were few at Court who subscribed to the Italian proverb that "they that serve well and hold their peace ask enough", and certainly the ceaseless round of importunity sometimes left her disenchanted. In a fit of cynicism she once remarked, "Her own servants and favourites professed to love her for her good parts, Alençon for her person, and the Scots for her crown ... but they all ended in the same thing, namely, asking her for money".[26]

Jobs at Court and in the administration were ardently sought after. Within the royal household itself, there were at least a thousand positions that needed to be filled, but more than four-fifths of these were too menial to be acceptable to anyone of gentle birth. Besides this, Elizabeth had in her gift positions such as the keepers of her various parks or houses, or posts in the Exchequer or Court of Wards, although here she did not enjoy an entirely free hand, as officials such as the Lord Treasurer and Master of the Court of Wards controlled a share of their own departments' patronage. It has been estimated that the Queen could dispose of perhaps "1,200 places worth a gentleman's having" and given that there were within the country approximately 2,500 aristocrats and country gentlemen who were eligible for preferment of this kind (and allowing also for some pluralism), this meant that at most, only forty per cent of the politically conscious classes had a chance of obtaining gainful employment from the Crown.[27] Competition for places became still more cut-throat as years went by, for Elizabeth was reluctant to dismiss servants, however old or incompetent, and vacancies generally occurred only on the death of the existing incumbent.

Even comparatively insignificant posts obtained at the Queen's hands conferred on their holders a definite prestige: on being made warden of Otford Park in Kent, Sir Robert Sidney noted that he thought it of "great value, not for the profit but because it was of her Majesty's gift, and of reputation in his country". This was despite the fact that salaries paid by the Crown were generally negligible and sometimes non-existent: the

Lord Chamberlain, for example, whose onerous duties included allocating lodgings at Court and organizing progresses, was paid rather less than £135 a year. Henry VIII had been conscientious about raising Court salaries in line with inflation, but apart from giving a rise to the Yeomen of the Guard (which Hatton negotiated), Elizabeth did not follow her father's example. On the other hand, official figures for pay were often misleading, for salaries could be supplemented by fees or gratuities. An illustration is provided by the department of the Exchequer known as the Pipe Office, where the messenger who carried leases to be sealed by the Master of the Office was entitled to charge two shillings and sixpence for each lease which he handled. In theory this should have amounted to about £50 a year, but he made much more than this, for anyone who wanted a lease signed quickly knew that the only way of stopping the messenger from dawdling about his errand was to pay him extra. Nor was this the only incidental expense that the hapless leaseholder incurred, for after the messenger had been propitiated, "then the pages at the Court and the waiters in the chamber must have somewhat ... and besides this the Master of the Office never set his hand to anything *gratis*".[28]

In other departments of state the pattern was the same. Office-holders in the Court of Wards could make so much money from gratuities that one applicant for a receivership in the Court was prepared to pay £1,000 to secure it, despite the fact that nominally the post was worth no more than £136 a year, including diet and allowances. Burghley himself, as Master of the Court, in theory received a salary of only £133 a year, but this figure represented only a fraction of his earnings from the post. Indeed, in the last three years of his life he received at least £3,000 in gratuities in return for granting wardships on favourable terms.[29] Nor was it particularly dishonest of him to accept this, for it was understood that office-holders were entitled to at least some incidental benefits. It was true that there were limits beyond which an upright man should not venture, but these were only hazily defined, and the line between legitimate payments and outright bribery was hard to distinguish.

If properly exploited, Court offices could bring high rewards, but they were also valued because of the opportunities they afforded for personal contact with the Queen. Senior members of the royal household were on the inner ring of the Court's charmed circle, and were exceptionally well placed to secure favours from Elizabeth. When Lord Hunsdon was offered the post of Lord Chamberlain in 1596, one of his employees commented that the principal attraction of the post lay in the Lord Chamberlain's "continual presence about her Majesty, to take any advantage of time and occasion for having of suits". Just how much of an asset this could be is demonstrated by the fact that the majority of those who were in receipt of annuities from the Crown in 1573 already held office at Court, and a high percentage of the monopolies granted in the last fifteen years of the reign also went to placemen.[30]

Those whose positions at Court enabled them to see a good deal of the Queen were expected to use this to assist not just themselves, but also their family and friends. In 1598, for example, Lady Huntingdon was criticized for being "with her Majesty very private twice a day", and yet failing to turn this to the advantage of her nephew, Robert Sidney. Those who enjoyed the privilege of "near access" to Elizabeth could either beg her to give an audience to someone who normally would not have been permitted to approach her (as in the case of Anthony Standen, who in November 1593 was promised by a Lady of the Privy Chamber named Mary Radcliffe that she would "procure him private speech with her Majesty") or alternatively present Elizabeth with suits on others' behalf. In return for exerting themselves in this way, they could expect to be given gifts by those who had benefited from their actions. Thus in 1587 the Earl of Rutland was told by a friend, "You are much beholden to Mistress Radcliffe; she daily doth good offices for you. She is worthy to be presented with something". A few years later, Rowland Whyte informed Robert Sidney that he was much indebted to several of the Queen's servants, including the Lord Admiral, and he warned him, "They look for thanks and it is due to them". Presents offered under such circumstances ranged from trifling tokens such as boar pies to more substantial items like a set of tapestries or a pair of horses.[31]

The vast majority of Court employees, from great officers like the Lord Chamberlain to more lowly individuals such as the sergeant of the bakehouse, the bread bearers, yeomen harbingers and grooms of the leash, were male, but Elizabeth also had a full complement of ladies-in-waiting. At the outset of the reign there were a total of fourteen ladies who had permanent positions in the Bedchamber and Privy Chamber, and who received salaries of 50 marks a year (just over £33). In addition there were certain ladies "extraordinary of the Privy Chamber" who attended the Queen when her regular ladies were ill or on leave, and who were paid only when they were working. There was also a number of noblewomen who were more loosely attached to the household, and who came on duty too infrequently to receive any kind of salary. Like all the Queen's ladies-in-waiting, however, they were sometimes given gowns that their mistress had discarded (a generous gift in view of the fact that many of these were lavishly bejewelled and embroidered) or alternatively Elizabeth sometimes presented them with dresses that she had had made up specially by her tailors. Even the Queen's dwarf, Thomasina, was allowed to appear at Court in old dresses of Elizabeth which had been altered to fit her.[32]

Besides her ladies of the Bedchamber and Privy Chamber, Elizabeth employed six maids of honour, unmarried girls of good birth whose function was largely decorative. They were always in the Queen's suite when she processed to chapel on Sundays and were in attendance when she received foreign dignitaries at Court and was anxious to put on a good show for them. They were also called upon to dance before Elizabeth, who derived "marvellous pleasure" from watching them. In her youth the Queen herself had loved to dance, preferring energetic Italian dances such as the galliard and volta to the "grave measures" of the stately pavane. She never gave up dancing altogether, but as she grew older she preferred looking on while other people performed. During the 1600 Christmas festivities it was reported, "Almost every night she is in the Presence [Chamber] to see the ladies dance the old and new country dances with the tabor and the pipe". She was an exacting taskmaster, for in 1597 a visiting diplomat observed, "When her maids dance she follows the cadence with her head, hand and foot. She rebukes them if they do not dance to her liking and without doubt she is mistress of the art".[33]

The duties of the Queen's ladies included looking after her clothing and jewellery and serving her her meals, which Elizabeth generally ate in the seclusion of her private apartments. Their job was far from being a sinecure for, like all members of the royal household, Elizabeth's ladies could not absent themselves from Court without her permission. In 1575 Lord Cobham heard from a friend that his wife was hoping to join him in the country "to rest her weary bones awhile, if she can get leave", but clearly it was quite possible that this would not be forthcoming. Certainly if Elizabeth felt so inclined, she did not hesitate to deny her ladies time off. When Sir Francis Knollys was sent north in 1568 to take charge of Mary Queen of Scots, he requested that his wife might be allowed to join him, but since Elizabeth "loved Lady Knollys above all other women in the world", she refused to be parted from her. Unfortunately, shortly after this Lady Knollys sickened and died and, though in her final illness she was "very often visited by her Majesty's own comfortable presence", this cannot have compensated for being forcibly separated from her husband at such a juncture.[34]

Obtaining temporary leave of absence from Court was hard enough, but far worse was the obligation which rested on all of Elizabeth's unmarried ladies-in-waiting to obtain her permission before taking husbands. Ideally, Elizabeth would have preferred it if more of her female attendants had followed the example of ladies such as Blanche Parry and Mary Radcliffe and remained single. Not only did she resent the upheavals that her ladies' marriages caused in her own domestic arrangements (although in point of fact many of those who did take husbands resumed their places at Court shortly after their weddings) but she failed to see why they needed the fulfilment of family life any more than she did. She would "much exhort all her women to remain in virgin state as much as may be", and even on those occasions when she pretended that she would not mind if they married, and asked her ladies if they had anybody in mind, "the wise ones did well conceal their liking thereto, as knowing the Queen's judgment in this matter".[35]

It is not particularly surprising that promiscuity was always dealt with severely at the Elizabethan Court. When maids of honour such as Mary Fitton and Anne Vavasour became pregnant out of wedlock, both they and the prospective fathers were imprisoned for short periods, and the girls were never readmitted to Court. The Queen's intolerance of such lapses is understandable enough, for when she appeared in public, flanked by her ladies, it was a spectacle designed to impress observers and to enhance her own prestige, and by surrounding herself with wantons she would have turned herself into little better than a spinsterish figure of fun.

Her fury when her ladies married without permission is perhaps rather less easy to explain. On hearing, for instance, that the Earl of Southampton had secretly married the maid of honour Elizabeth Vernon, the Queen was "so much moved she came not to chapel", and both Southampton and his "new coined Countess" were incarcerated in the Fleet prison. Yet by the standards of the day, Elizabeth's anger would not have seemed excessive, for all responsible persons accepted that it was inappropriate for individuals of unequal wealth and status to marry one another. There was widespread agreement that if young people were allowed independence in their choice of marital partner, it would undermine the social hierarchy and erode parents' rights over their children, and the Queen was not alone in treating it as a serious matter when these were infringed. To name two examples, in 1602 the poet John Donne was imprisoned by his employer, Lord Keeper Egerton, because he had married Ann More without obtaining her father's permission, and in 1573 the Privy Council intervened when a Mr William Huberson complained that one of his servants had "sought privily to contract himself" to Huberson's daughter.[36]

Elizabeth herself denied that she took an unduly restrictive line towards her servants' marriages. She maintained "she hath always furthered (in good sort) any honest and honourable purposes of marriage or preferment to any of hers when without scandal and infamy they have been orderly broken unto her". She could point out that in the course of her reign no less than thirteen of her maids of honour contracted prestigious marriages within the peerage, and this might seem to justify her claim that it was only unsuitable matches of which she disapproved. Elizabeth could even assert that she did her best to promote unions which she felt had something to commend them. In 1582, for example, she intervened in negotiations instigated by one of Sir Francis Knollys's sons for the hand of the heiress daughter of Lady Rivett. Lady Rivett had maintained that the marriage was out of the question, owing to "the perverse disposition of the maid, who by no means can be wrought to like of a husband and especially of Mr Knollys". It was an attitude with which Elizabeth might have been expected to sympathize but, on the contrary, Lady Rivett was warned that she would incur the Queen's displeasure if she encouraged her daughter in her disobedience.[37]

Nevertheless, it is not possible to acquit Elizabeth altogether of the charge of being (as Sir Edward Stafford once put it) "angry with any love", however respectable, for on occasion she could be unreasonably obstructive even when her ladies wished to contract marriages to which there could be no rational objection. When her cousin Catherine Carey became engaged in May 1563 to Lord Howard of Effingham's son Charles, Elizabeth peremptorily dismissed them from Court. Since the match had the full approval of all the rest of the young couple's family, they went ahead with it regardless, and after a time the Queen was reconciled to the marriage and took Catherine back into her service. Later in the reign, the Countess of Rutland was so terrified that Elizabeth would refuse to let her maid of honour Lady Bridget Manners marry her fiancé, Mr Tyrwhit, that the Countess decided that the only thing to do was to hold the wedding without consulting the Queen beforehand. This of course was a serious offence, and Bridget and her young husband were subsequently put into confinement, but undoubtedly Elizabeth partly invited such disobedience by being so unyielding. Even on those occasions when the Queen had consented that a marriage could take place, it was not unknown for her subsequently to create difficulties in order to delay the nuptials. In 1600 the dowager Lady Russell wrote to Robert Cecil explaining that Elizabeth had agreed that her maid of honour Elizabeth Russell could marry the Earl of Worcester's son, Lord Herbert. Lady Russell stressed that "my conscience beareth me witness that I did agree to no conditions of marriage before, as became me, I had her Majesty's royal consent", but she was evidently concerned that Elizabeth was still not fully reconciled to the prospect of losing her maid of honour. Lady Russell wanted the ceremony to take place as soon as possible, and since her daughter's eyes were giving her trouble she wanted to take the girl away from Court to give her a chance of making a full recovery before her wedding day. However, fearing that the Queen would think that she was being unduly hasty, Lady Russell thought it best not to mention that this was the reason for removing her daughter, and instead she suggested to Cecil that Elizabeth be told that her maid of honour would be embarrassed to remain at Court "and do her Majesty no service, her eyes being so bleared".[38]

Elizabeth had been on the throne for no more than a few days when she "made a speech to the women who were in her service, commanding them never to speak to her on business affairs". In fact, however, they were by no means wholly without influence. It was true that Sir Robert Cross was cautioned by a friend that he would be unwise to depend upon "women to solicit for me, and that the Queen would give them good words, yet they should never affect suit". He ignored this warning, but subsequently admitted that he had found it to be well-founded. Similarly, when Sir Robert Sidney asked his aunt Lady Warwick to do what she could to persuade the Queen to appoint him Lord President of Wales, she told him that "she would find some means or other to feel her Majesty's disposition", but added that in her opinion he would be better advised "to get some man of greatness and authority to do it". Nevertheless, it is clear that the intercessions of Elizabeth's ladies frequently proved effective. In 1572, for example, Sir Thomas Smith told Walsingham that Elizabeth had decided that Francis Carew should take Walsingham's place as English ambassador to France. Smith was sure that the Queen would not change her mind about this, even though Carew was making "great labour to the contrary by the ladies of the Privy Chamber", but in fact, in late December Walsingham learnt to his chagrin that Carew had managed to "slip his head out of the collar".[39]

The Queen's housekeeping expenses were on an awesome scale. In 1593, the Crown had to pay for the board of no less than one hundred and thirty-three Court officials who were entitled to dine and sup with their servants at tables in the Great Hall. Vast quantities of food were served at each sitting, with 'diets' being carefully graduated according to rank. The Queen was never offered fewer than twenty dishes to choose from, but even lesser members of the household, such as the locksmiths, porters and scourers, were provided with a selection of two or three meat dishes, twice daily. In the course of a single year, the Court consumed 1,240 oxen, 8,000 sheep, 310 pigs, 560 flitches of bacon, 13,260 lambs, 2,752 pullets and capons, 1,115 dozen chickens, 1,360 dozen pigeons, 1,428 dozen rabbits, 60,000 pounds of butter, and 600,000 gallons of ale.[40]

Just over £40,000 of the Queen's annual revenue was set aside to meet the costs of maintaining her domestic establishment, but at no time during the reign was she able to keep within this sum. The budget was indeed unrealistically low, for both Edward VI and Mary had spent more than this on their households, and it was no mean feat of management that in the early years of Elizabeth's reign, the spending limits were only modestly breached. The Queen's outgoings would have been far higher had it not been for the fact that each county was bound to supply the Court with goods below the market price, an obligation that was not unnaturally resented. Towards the end of the reign the system was rationalized, for in a bid to free themselves from the activities of purveyors – royal officials who travelled the country compulsorily purchasing supplies for the Court – many counties came to an agreement with the Crown, whereby they contracted in advance to supply a specified quantity of produce at fixed prices. It was an arrangement that worked to the advantage of all concerned, for in 1597 it was estimated that the new system saved the Queen £19,000 a year, but gains of this kind were offset by price increases due to inflation, and at the end of the reign household charges were running at £48,000 a year.[41]

Inflation was by no means the only reason why household expenditure exceeded estimates, for corruption and waste were endemic. Elizabeth herself was a frugal eater: she habitually eschewed rich food and watered her wine, and was apt to attribute her strong constitution to the fact that she was "not tied to hours of eating or sleeping, but following appetite; nor delighted in belly cheer to please the taste". It was therefore surprising that the costs of her table were always far greater than anticipated. When Burghley investigated in 1573, he found that the daily menu provided for the Queen was twice as large as that specified in the Book of Diets, a development that had occurred not at Elizabeth's request, but because others wished to feast themselves on the large quantities she left untouched. Catering arrangements at other levels of the Court were subject to comparable abuses, perhaps the worst of which stemmed from the fact that many Court officials preferred to eat in the comfort of their private apartments, rather than at the communal tables provided. At their request, food would be sent up to them in their chambers, but meanwhile the meals to which they were officially entitled were still being served in the Great Hall, and were consumed by individuals who had no right to eat there. A great deal of the food prepared at Court was also taken away and eaten off the premises, a practice that not only made it impossible to keep track of who was living at Elizabeth's expense, but which also resulted in embezzlement of much of the vessel and plate that had been carried outside the palace. Misappropriation and fraud were well nigh impossible to control, and indeed were effectively encouraged by the system of perks that made even the lowliest household job an attractive proposition. The cooks, for example, could sell all salmon tails and lambskins that otherwise would have gone to waste, while the pantrymen could dispose of the crusts removed from all loaves before they were served at table. In theory this should not have been a particularly valuable concession, but in 1597 it was alleged that so much crust and crumb were being cut away that only a few morsels remained, and at mealtimes the Queen was being offered slices of bread so insubstantial that they "might be thrust through with a finger".[42]

The Lord Steward was the officer with overall responsibility for the Queen's household below stairs, but in practice his role tended to be limited. There were several periods during the reign when the post was left vacant, and the majority of noblemen who did occupy the position did not take their duties particularly seriously. More than anyone else it was

Burghley who deserved the appellation once given him of "her Majesty's housewife", for he took a keen interest in all aspects of household management. The accounts of almost every department at Court were subject to his scrutiny at one time or another, and he was tireless in instituting savings. He reduced the number of dishes that were meant to be served to Court officials, and tried to lessen the Queen's wine bill by obtaining supplies direct from France. When it came to his notice that Elizabeth's kennel expenses had increased in the course of the reign, he compensated by pruning payments to the royal falconers. Similarly, on discovering that the Queen employed more violinists and lute players than she had at the beginning of the reign, he laid off a corresponding number of flautists and sackbut players.[43]

In theory, Burghley's efforts to cut costs had Elizabeth's wholehearted backing, but she herself had some extravagant habits which did not make his task any easier. Twice a week the Court was supposed to serve only fish, but Elizabeth frequently deviated from this rule, and the cost of the additional meat dishes prepared for her on those days amounted to £646 a year. Then again, instead of moving frequently during the winter, she tended to stay at houses for such long periods that all the provisions in the area were used up, and the necessity to transport supplies from further afield resulted in an increase in carriage expenses. In 1576 Burghley drew up a memorandum requesting, among other things, that in future the Court should more frequently shift location, but on reflection he evidently realized that Elizabeth was unlikely to take the suggestion kindly, let alone to act on it, and he crossed this section through.[44]

It was only after Burghley's death that Elizabeth began to take a really active interest in the running of her establishment, and then she too took alarm at the way costs were escalating. Calling to her Richard Browne, a clerk controller of the household, she berated him about the excesses that were daily being perpetrated in his domain. Angrily she told him, "I will not suffer this dishonourable spoil and increase that no prince ever before me did, to the offence of God and great grievance of my loving subjects, who, I understand, daily complain, and not without cause, that there is increase daily of carriages of provision taken from them at low prices, and wastefully spent in my Court to some of their undoings". She announced that there must be a thorough investigation to see if more people had succeeded in securing lodgings at Court than were entitled to be housed there, and to discover why such an unwarranted quantity of food was being consumed. "With very bitter words" she declared "that she would cleanse the Court", and that steps must be "taken to abridge all messes of meat and other expenses more than the book signed doth allow", but before these reforms could be implemented, she died.[45]

In the early years of the reign, the ballads and verses that were written in honour of the Queen depicted her above all as a Protestant heroine who, having nearly fallen victim to Popish repression, survived to deliver her people from it. Inevitably, however, as time went by, the memory of her ordeals in Mary's reign faded and ceased to have such relevance, and in view of Elizabeth's disapproval of Puritanism, and her reluctance to champion the cause of Protestantism on the continent, it became less appropriate to celebrate her primarily in terms of her religion. As a result, other themes began to be discernible in the works of art that she inspired. Great stress was laid upon her ancestry which, so it was said, dated back to the Trojan Brutus, who had fled to England after the fall of Troy and founded London. King Arthur was alleged to be another of Elizabeth's distinguished forebears, for the Tudors' Welsh origins enabled them to claim that they were descended from those Britons who had retreated into Wales to escape the Saxons' advance. Elizabeth was not the first member of her family to draw attention to these links with the past, for her grandfather Henry VII had also thought them significant. The hall of Richmond Palace (which he built) was decorated with pictures of Brutus and Arthur, and Henry had also christened his eldest son Arthur. In Elizabeth's reign these ideas were taken up and elaborated on, and the antiquity of her title was affirmed in rather more sophisticated ways. When Elizabeth visited the Earl of Leicester at Kenilworth in 1575, her connections with Arthur were constantly alluded to. On her arrival she was greeted by the Lady of the Lake, "famous in King Arthur's book", and then a fanfare was blown by giant trumpeters. Presumably these were real men, concealed within pasteboard representations, "and by this . . . it was meant that in the days and reign of King Arthur, men were of that stature". In case Elizabeth had not interpreted the symbolism correctly, she was accosted a few days later while out hunting by a Savage Man, clad in ivy, who explained that the trumpeters had served

> King Arthur, man of might
> And ever since this castle kept
> For Arthur's heirs by right.[46]

Elizabeth's descent from Brutus and Arthur is also one of the recurring themes of Spenser's *Faerie Queene*, for just as it was a function of Virgil's *Aeneid* to pay tribute to Augustus Caesar, so in his great epic poem Spenser set out to portray Elizabeth as the predestined ruler of a chosen people. In Book II, the genealogy of Elizabeth's literary *alter ego*, Gloriana, is exhaustively delineated, beginning with the confident assertion that

> Thy name O soueraine Queene, thy realme and race,
> From this renowned Prince [Arthur] derived are,
> Who mightily upheld that royal mace,

> Which now thou bear'st, to thee descended farre,
> From mightie kings and conquerours in warre.

The Arthurian tradition was merely one strand in a complex web of imagery, allegory and myth that was spun around Elizabeth in order to romanticize her and endow her with an aura almost of divinity. Once she had reached an age where it ceased to be realistic to look on her as a prospective wife and mother, it became important for her to cultivate for herself some form of alternative identity, which would capture the popular imagination and become a part of the national culture. In the development of such an identity, her virginity was to prove one of her greatest assets, for it set her apart from the common mass of humanity and could be represented as an essential part of her mystique. Moreover, by adopting as part of her personal iconography many emblems which in mediaeval literature had been associated with the Virgin Mary – the rose, the moon, the ermine, the phoenix and the pearl – Elizabeth may, perhaps unconsciously, have diverted onto herself some residue of that devotion which in Catholic times had been accorded the Queen of Heaven, and for which the Protestant faith afforded no outlet. Towards the end of the reign, indeed, the poet John Dowland went so far as to urge that there should be an explicit transference of affection, and that Elizabeth's subjects would do well to substitute "*Vivat Eliza!* for an *Ave Maria!*".[47]

Since Protestants condemned the idolatrous worship of the Virgin Mary as one of Popery's most pernicious abuses, the parallel between her and Elizabeth could not be taken too far. On the whole, the blurring of their two identities remained at a purely subliminal level, but poets and painters were able to make freer use of themes from classical mythology which could be adapted in order to idealize Elizabeth. In poetry, references began to abound to chaste Astraea, last of the immortals, who had fled the earth in the face of mankind's wickedness, and who had since resided in the heavens as the constellation Virgo. The implication was that Elizabeth was the reincarnation of this just virgin, whose return had long been foretold, and whose reign would coincide with a golden age of peace and plenty. Thus, in 1588, the students of Gray's Inn presented a pageant in honour of Elizabeth, and in the prologue they declared themselves the servants of "Dame Astraea" or Justice. The play concludes:

> Let Virgo come from Heaven, the glorious star,
> The Zodiac's joy: the planet's chief delight ...
> That virtuous Virgo born for Britain's bliss:
> That peerless branch of Brute: that sweet remain
> Of Priam's state: that hope of springing Troy ...
> Let her reduce the golden age again
> Religion, ease and wealth of former world.[48]

But Astraea was also a synonym for the moon, and in an extension of this idea, Walter Ralegh took to addressing Elizabeth in his verse as the goddess of the moon who, confusingly, also went under the names of Diana and Cynthia:

> Praised be Diana's fair and harmless light,
> Praised be the dews wherewith she moists the ground;
> Praised be her beams, the glory of the night,
> Praised be her power, by which all powers abound.
> Praised be her nymphs, with whom she decks the woods,
> Praised be her knights, in whom true honour lives,
> Praised be that force, by which she moves the floods;
> Let that Diana shine, which all these gives.
>
> In heaven Queen she is among the spheres;
> In aye she mistress-like makes all things pure;
> Eternity in her oft change she bears;
> She beauty is, by her the fair endure.
>
> Time wears her not, she doth his chariot guide,
> Mortality below her orb is placed;
> By her the virtue of the stars down slide;
> In her is virtue's perfect image cast
> A knowledge pure it is her worth to know;
> With Circes let them dwell that think not so.

By the end of the 1580s, Ralegh's "fine and sweet inventions" had been taken up by others. The gifts presented to Elizabeth at New Year 1587 included a jewel from Lord Admiral Howard shaped "like half moons, garnished with sparks of rubies and diamonds pendants", and a red and white feather fan from Sir Francis Drake, "the handle of gold enamelled with a half moon of mother of pearls". In several paintings and miniatures, Elizabeth is depicted wearing a crescent moon in her hair, and the poets continued to employ lunar imagery to glorify their mistress. A late example of the genre is the ode *Of Cynthia*, probably written either by John Lyly or John Davies, and which was commissioned by the Earl of Cumberland to be read to the Queen at a tournament held at Court on Mayday 1602:

> Lands and seas she rules below,
> Where things change, and ebbe, and flowe
> Spring, waxe olde and perish;
> Only Time which all doth mowe
> Her alone doth cherish.[49]

In the past Elizabeth had frequently been compared to the sun, but the properties of the moon, remote and yet enticing, chaste but not sexless, in many ways made it a more appropriate metaphor for the Queen than the sun, with its scorching intensity. Furthermore, the moon ruled the tides, and for the purposes of men like Ralegh and Drake it was a peculiarly apt analogy, as it was intended to convey to Elizabeth that her destiny lay in using seapower to promote exploration and to found a mighty empire. Others sought to express the same idea in different ways. In particular, the link between virginity and imperialism forms the theme of the "sieve portrait" of Elizabeth, painted by the Flemish artist Massys the younger around 1579. The sieve was an allusion to the story of the Vestal Virgin Tuccia, whose purity was vindicated when she miraculously carried water in a sieve without any leakage. Behind the Queen is a globe, with most of the surface in darkness, but England is illuminated, and ships can be seen setting out from it westwards. To the left of Elizabeth is a column with several roundels on it, depicting scenes from the *Aeneid* relating to the story of Dido and Aeneas. The implication is that, just as Aeneas forsook Dido and went on to found Rome, so Elizabeth must renounce love in order to fulfil her destiny as ruler of an empire. Standing in an arcade in the background are several gentlemen pensioners, one of whom has been tentatively identified as Sir Christopher Hatton, and from this it has been conjectured that it was Hatton who commissioned the work. It is a plausible hypothesis, for as a leading patron of Drake and shareholder in the voyage of circumnavigation, Hatton was at the forefront of those at Court who believed that the nation's future depended on imperial expansion. The emphasis on virginity also fits in with the theory, for Hatton was one of the foremost opponents of the Alençon match, currently under discussion, and it would have been in character for him to choose this pleasing way of conveying to Elizabeth that the way to attain true greatness was to turn her back on marriage and devote herself to realizing imperial ambitions.[50]

By no means all paintings of the Queen were so successful as Massys's sieve portrait. While on his way to Vienna in 1567, the Earl of Sussex had admitted frankly to the Regent of the Netherlands that the portraits of Elizabeth which were currently on sale throughout London "did nothing resemble" her. The problem was very largely of Elizabeth's own making, for until then she had proved very reluctant to sit for her portrait, and it was only when she subsequently agreed to pose for artists of the calibre of Nicholas Hilliard and Federico Zuccaro that lesser artists had satisfactory prototypes on which they could base their own works. Even so, the demand from "all sorts of subjects both noble and mean" for portraits of the Queen was such that it continued to outstrip supply, and throughout the 1570s there continued to be official concern that unqualified artists were exploiting the situation by "counterfeiting" unsuitable pictures of the Queen.[51]

One reason why the authorities had such difficulty in controlling the way that Elizabeth was represented in art was that she was not prepared to pay for the services of a Court artist who would have been solely responsible for the production and distribution of likenesses of her. In 1563 there were so many debased images of Elizabeth in circulation that a proclamation was drafted, declaring that "some special person" would shortly be employed to paint a picture of the Queen which could serve as a pattern to all future painters and engravers, but in the event no such appointment was made. It was only in 1581 that the artist George Gower was given the post of Sergeant Painter to the Queen, and though he did paint several portraits of her, the bulk of his time was spent applying decorative paintwork to the interiors of the royal palaces. Indeed, throughout the 1580s it was the brilliant miniaturist Nicholas Hilliard, rather than Gower, who was much the most prolific producer of images of Elizabeth.

Elizabeth had always had a great fondness for miniature paintings. In the early years of the reign, the principal practitioner of the art at Court had been Lavinia Teerlinc, the daughter of the Flemish illuminator Simon Benninck. Lavinia had accompanied her husband to England in 1546, and since then she had occupied the official position of Gentlewoman of the Privy Chamber to both Mary Tudor and Elizabeth. Until her death in 1576, Lavinia regularly presented Elizabeth at New Year with miniatures that she had painted of the Queen either on her own or surrounded by her Court. Elizabeth was so delighted by these offerings that, instead of entrusting them for safe-keeping to one of her ladies-in-waiting, as was customary with such gifts, she kept two of them permanently in her possession. Nicholas Hilliard may well have been a pupil of Lavinia Teerlinc, but his abilities as a miniaturist far surpassed hers. Elizabeth was reluctant to award him an official position at Court, but despite this Hilliard was kept busy throughout the 1580s with a stream of commissions to execute miniatures of the Queen. Elizabeth liked to dole these out to courtiers whom she held in particularly high esteem, and the recipients took to encasing these trophies in jewelled lockets so that they could be worn at all times. Indeed, such was their pride in possessing these objects that several courtiers – including Sir Francis Walsingham, Sir Thomas Heneage, Sir Christopher Hatton and Sir Francis Drake – commissioned portraits of themselves in which they were shown displaying on their persons miniatures of the Queen. Lesser individuals, who could not afford original miniatures by Hilliard, could obtain from his workshops medallions in base metals which could likewise be worn around the neck.[52]

By the early 1590s, Hilliard was past his prime, and Elizabeth experimented by sitting for a promising young miniaturist named Isaac Oliver. The result was not a success, for Elizabeth did not appreciate Oliver's stark portrayal of her ageing features, and thenceforth he received no more commissions from her. Instead she reverted to using Hilliard as her miniaturist, although the portraits he produced of her in the final years of the reign were not painted from life, but were more highly idealized than ever. The Queen was depicted still as a young woman with a pristine complexion and flowing virginal tresses, a portrayal which by this time bore little relation to her true appearance. Unfortunately, pirate versions of the Queen's portrait continued to be produced, causing Elizabeth "great offence". In 1596 a proclamation was issued, ordering the destruction of all those works of art that failed to conform to Hilliard's supremely flattering vision, but the official machinery to enforce this decree was lacking.[53]

Despite the increasing emphasis on Elizabeth's virginity, the image she sought to project was hardly one of nun-like simplicity. It was true that early in the reign Bishop Aylmer had praised the young Elizabeth for habitually wearing understated clothes and eschewing rich jewellery, but as she grew older she ceased to have any inhibitions about indulging her taste for finery. In appearance she became the very embodiment of chaste splendour, for not only did she love clothes for their own sake, but also she appreciated the part which external magnificence could play in propagating an image of regality and power while nevertheless emphasizing her essential femininity. Not everyone applauded her for dressing so elaborately. Towards the end of her life, one of her bishops – it may even have been Aylmer – preached a sermon before her at Court, criticizing the vanity of decking the body too finely. The text did not go down well with the Queen: sourly she told her ladies that "If the bishop held more discourse on such matters, she would fit him for heaven, but he should walk thither without a staff, and leave his mantle behind him".[54]

The Queen's dresses were made up of a large number of component parts, laboriously pinned or tied together every time they were worn. The separate items – ruff, sleeves, stomacher (a piece of material fastened to the front of the bodice that descended in a point some inches below the waistline), kirtle (skirt), forepart (a triangular piece of material glimpsed beneath the opening at the front of the skirt) – did not invariably have to be used in conjunction with the same pieces, but could be assembled in a vast range of permutations. Yet even if they had not been interchangeable, the variety of the Queen's wardrobe would still have been enormous. In an inventory taken in 1600, she was listed as owning, among other items, 102 French gowns (which had small dipping trains), 67 round gowns (which had level hems that formed a circle round the wearer's feet), 100 loose gowns (non-waisted housecoats), 125 kirtles, 136 foreparts, 99 mantles (short-sleeved surcoats), and 99 cloaks. The materials used were invariably luxurious - cut velvets, satins, taffeta and sarcenet – and frequently slashed and pinked to reveal colourful glimpses of contrasting fabrics underneath.

She owned numerous gowns and accessories encrusted with pearls, spangles and precious stones, or exquisitely embroidered, often in gold and silver thread. The motifs employed were astonishingly diverse, and included roses, honeysuckles, pansies (her favourite flowers), suns, clouds, rainbows, caterpillars, sea monsters, snails, flies and spiders, ears of wheat, feathers, mulberries and pomegranates. Even the loose gowns, which were for wear on comparatively informal occasions when comfort was at a premium, were decorated with a bewildering array of designs in silken thread, and trimmed with different furs such as miniver, ermine and mink.[55]

Quite apart from the lavish ornamentation that was a feature of so much of Elizabeth's clothing, the styles she wore tended to become progressively exaggerated and fantastic. This was largely a reflection of what was being worn on the continent, for as far as fashion was concerned Elizabeth was a follower rather than an innovator, and as always it was the French who were the leaders in such matters. At the beginning of the reign, ruffs were no more than modest figure-of-eight frills in cambric or lawn that neatly hugged the chinline, but the introduction of starch to England by the Dutch Mrs Van der Plesse in 1564 inaugurated a fashion revolution. Ruffs became steadily larger in diameter, until the appearance they produced was likened to looking at John the Baptist's head on a platter. Pleats were produced by heating 'poking sticks' of bone, metal or ivory, and inserting them into folds in the material. By the 1580s, ruffs had increased to such a size that not even the most intensive starching could have prevented the more unwieldy specimens from collapsing under their own weight, unless they had received additional support from wire frames known as 'under-proppers' or 'supportasses'. The production of starch became a boom industry, and even in years of harvest failure the Privy Council proved incapable of preventing large quantities of grain from being "expended in that vain matter". Towards the end of her life, Elizabeth showed a preference for fan-shaped ruffs, worn with low-cut dresses, and which stood upright to frame the back of the head rather than encircling the neck.[56]

Just as sleeves became preposterously swollen in the course of the reign – sometimes being padded with flax or wool or bran to plump them out to the desired dimensions – so skirts became progressively more distended and misshapen. At Elizabeth's accession, the cone-shaped Spanish farthingale (which may have been introduced to England by Catherine of Aragon, although it certainly did not become popular till years later) was in common use. It was the precursor of the Victorian crinoline, and consisted essentially of a hooped petticoat which artificially puffed out the skirt. The hoops – which got progressively wider between the waist and the hemline – were made at this date either of cut osiers or strips of material rolled so tightly that they became virtually rigid. Of its very nature the farthingale was an unwieldy and inconvenient garment: when a banquet was given at Court to honour the French ambassador in May 1559, the farthingales of the ladies took up so much space that not everyone could be fitted at table, and several of the Queen's household were obliged to eat sitting on the floor. Even Elizabeth, who had been accustomed to wearing farthingales from her early teens (in the picture of her as Princess in the Royal Collection, she is wearing a Spanish farthingale), sometimes found herself defeated by them, and in 1565 a particularly uncomfortable one had to be sent back to her dressmaker to be remodelled. In 1567 Elizabeth took on John Bate as her personal farthingale maker, presumably in the hope that his specialized skills would enable him to produce farthingales that were rather more light and supple.[57]

The late 1570s probably saw the introduction of the dome-shaped French farthingale, which was still more cumbersome than its predecessor. The bell-like effect was produced by wearing padded hip rolls in addition to hoops, resulting in skirts that were absurdly oversized and clumsy. Mendoza reported that when the Queen tried to have a quiet discussion with him on one occasion in 1579, it proved impossible for them to understand one another until she had "raised her farthingale in order that I might get closer to her and speak without being overheard". Even now, however, the farthingale had not reached the final stage of its development. In 1580, whalebone started to be used for constructing the hoops, a technological advance that made farthingales less weighty, and this paved the way for the bizarre drum-shaped skirts of the Queen's later years.[58]

It was a long established tradition that on New Year's Day, the monarch exchanged gifts with leading subjects, but early in the reign the majority of the nobility marked the date simply by giving Elizabeth sums of money. Only a few individuals had the imagination to come up with rather more personal offerings. For example, in 1562 the Earl of Warwick gave her, among other things, a smock wrought with black silk, while Lady St Loe produced a pair of cambric sleeves embroidered in silver gilt, and from Kat Ashley Elizabeth received twelve handkerchiefs, edged in gold and silver thread. Compared to the gifts she received in subsequent years, these were trifling objects, but the pleasure Elizabeth took in them was evidently sufficiently marked to convince observers that this was a practice worth copying. In subsequent years, the New Year's gift lists always included numerous articles of clothing, ranging from small but costly items (such as the white satin forepart presented by the Countess of Bedford in 1579, embroidered in black silk and gold and garnished with Venetian gold lace and seed pearls) to complete outfits, like Sir Thomas Leighton's gown of black velvet, with a slashed bodice and sleeves, and a lining of white sarcenet embellished with gold aglets.[59]

Despite the size of her wardrobe, Elizabeth was genuinely delighted when it was embellished with some choice new offering. In 1575, the

Countess of Shrewsbury was particularly anxious to give the Queen something which would be to her liking, and she therefore consulted Ladies Cobham and Sussex as to what would be the ideal present. Lady Cobham was no use at all, making the unoriginal suggestion that the Countess should give Elizabeth £40 in cash or a cup of gold, but Lady Sussex knew her mistress better. She urged Lady Shrewsbury to give the Queen a cloak with matching accessories, "embroidered with pretty flowers and leaves with sundry colours". The principal colour scheme should be blue, trimmed with carnation velvet, a combination which would suit Elizabeth, but which was nonetheless unusual. Lady Sussex was confident that "these fantastical things will be more accepted than cup or jewel", and events proved her right, for after the cloak had been duly presented to Elizabeth a friend assured Lady Shrewsbury, "Her Majesty never liked anything you gave her so well; the colour and strange trimming of the garments with the ready and great cost bestowed upon it hath caused her to give out such good speeches of my Lord and your Ladyship as I never hear of better ... If my Lord and your Ladyship had given five hundred pound, in my opinion it would not have been so well taken".[60]

Walsingham declared in 1578 that Elizabeth was "not so much affected to the buying of jewels as her father was", but though she may have spent less on their purchase, in other ways her passion for them equalled Henry's. People were often astounded by the profusion of jewellery with which she loaded her person. In 1582, when a recently painted portrait of her was exhibited at the French Court, the ladies there marvelled "very much at the number of those great pearls wherewith her gown is set forth and beautified; supposing that all the other princes of Christendom had not the like quantity of pearls of that sort". Fifteen years later, a visiting French diplomat was scarcely less impressed by the "innumerable jewels" she wore, "not only on her head, but also within her collar, about her arms and on her hands, with a very great quantity of pearls round her neck and on her bracelets. She had two bands, one on each arm, which were worth a great price". Similarly, in 1601 an Italian observer was dazzled when he saw her at Court "dressed all in white, with so many pearls, broideries and diamonds, that I am amazed how she could carry them".[61]

The bulk of Elizabeth's jewellery collection was inherited, but throughout the reign it was supplemented with gifts from courtiers. In particular, she was showered with costly jewels on New Year's Day. Besides the obvious earrings, bracelets and rings, she received scores of brooches and pendants in figurative designs which reflected the age's passion for symbolism. Among the gifts she received at the start of 1573, for example, was a jewelled dolphin from Lady Cheke and a golden pelican, "garnished with small rubies and diamonds", from Lady Mary Sidney. The significance of these would have been obvious to the Queen. The dolphin was the king of sea fishes, and hence an especially appropriate gift for one who ruled over another element, while the pelican was always depicted rending its breast in order that its young could be nourished with drops of its own blood, and thus epitomized Elizabeth's readiness to sacrifice herself for her people. Like the phoenix – a symbol of virgin regeneration – the pelican was indeed one of the Queen's favourite emblems, although perhaps Lady Mary's was a somewhat inferior sample of the genre, for shortly afterwards Elizabeth handed on her present to the Countess of Huntingdon.[62]

Other jewels had messages which were more difficult to unravel. At New Year 1578, an unknown person gave Elizabeth a "jewel of gold like a circle of pansies, daisies and other flowers, garnished with sparks of diamonds and rubies, having therein a butterfly of mother of pearl, garnished with sparks of rubies and a crab holding the same". What might have seemed at first sight a somewhat arbitrary assortment of flora and fauna was in fact a carefully worked-out design, loaded with significance. The crab represented caution, while the rash butterfly was its very antithesis, and when paired together the two were supposed to illustrate the motto "Make haste slowly" – a sort of latter day equivalent of the fable of the hare and the tortoise. Precious objects fashioned for the Queen could also have political connotations. At the start of 1587 she received a "jewel of gold having two hands, the one holding a sword, the other a trowel, both garnished with sparks of diamonds and between the hands a garnishment of opals". The key to the meaning of this curious device has been found in an illustrated work popular at the time, entitled *A Choice of Emblems*. This included a design identical to that described above, and the accompanying caption explained that it was intended to convey that the interests of national defence required that "for war or work we either hands should arm". Without such clues, however, other items in the Queen's collection are rather harder to interpret. What, for instance, is one to make of the piece described in an inventory of 1600 as "one fern branch of gold, having therein a lizard, a lady cow and a snail"?[63]

The Earl of Leicester's annual offerings to Elizabeth posed fewer con-undrums. These were of course exquisite objects in their own right, but they were also intended to serve as charming evocations of his undying love for her. They usually incorporated some reference to his family crest of a bear holding a ragged staff, as in 1574, when he gave Elizabeth a splendid ostrich feather fan. On one side of the golden handle was "a white bear and two pearls hanging", and on the other, "a lion ramping, with a white muzzled bear at his foot".[64]

The Court was a peripatetic institution which came into being wherever Elizabeth happened to be residing. Elizabeth had inherited nearly fifty houses and about sixty castles, but many of these were in a ruinous condition and she visited them seldom or never. In general she divided her time between her main "houses of access", in or near the capital. Four of these were riverside palaces, conveniently situated on the banks of that great thoroughfare, the Thames. Both Hampton Court and Whitehall, the Queen's principal London residence, had been surrendered to the Crown on the fall of Henry VIII's great minister, Cardinal Wolsey. The largest of her palaces, Richmond, had been built by Elizabeth's grandfather, Henry VII, and was distinguished by its proliferation of turrets topped by onion-shaped domes. Greenwich was somewhat smaller than the others, but no less stately, designed so that all the principal rooms overlooked the Thames and with a great bay window in the Privy Chamber that used eighty foot of glass. In addition she generally resided at Windsor Castle for some part of the summer, and she often ended her progresses with a visit to Oatlands, "a cheerful hunting box" in Surrey.

Unlike her father, who, in the words of one recent authority, was "profuse in everything, from matrimony to architecture", Elizabeth did not embark on any extravagant building projects. However, in 1592 she did repossess Nonsuch, Henry VIII's most magnificent creation. When Henry had started work on this in 1538, he had set out with the conscious intention of rivalling Francis I's palaces at Blois and Chambord, and the result had been suitably grandiose. On completion, the south front measured two hundred feet, and at either extremity was an octagonal gatehouse, five storeys high. More striking still was the inner courtyard, whose walls were covered in exquisite plaster mouldings, set in frames of carved and gilded slate. It was a fitting monument to Henry's megalomania, although oddly enough the King seems quickly to have tired of the project. He visited the site infrequently while work was in progress and possibly only stayed there once after construction was completed. In the reign of Mary Tudor, it had ceased to be Crown property. Plainly regarding the place as an absurdity, Mary had actually contemplated demolishing it on her accession, but in the end she had sold it to the Earl of Arundel. Elizabeth, in contrast, regretted that the house had passed out of royal ownership. She formed a great affection for the place when she was entertained there by Arundel and by his son-in-law Lord Lumley, who was bequeathed the house by his father-in-law. In 1592 she jumped at the chance to take Nonsuch in exchange for cancelling Lumley's debts to the Crown, and she derived great pleasure from her acquisition. She visited it frequently, and in 1599 Nonsuch was described as the residence "which of all other places she likes best".[65]

From an architectural point of view, Whitehall was a shambles, sprawling haphazardly over twenty acres and consisting, at one estimate, of as many as 2,000 rooms. Many of these were poky and ill-favoured, but the main apartments were commodious enough. The layout of these was the same as in the Queen's other leading palaces, progressing in sequence from Great Hall to Guard Chamber, Presence Chamber and Privy Chamber. Anyone suitably dressed could gain admittance to the first three, but the Privy Chamber, with its great mural by Holbein of Henry VIII, was rather more difficult to penetrate. It was guarded at the door by an usher of the Black Rod, and only peers and those in special favour were permitted to pass. Beyond the Privy Chamber lay the innermost sanctum of Elizabeth's private apartments, and naturally when she was in residence, access to those was confined to a tiny handful of privileged men and women. However, when she was staying at another of her houses, visitors were sometimes given guided tours of the whole palace, and might even be shown her bedroom. One tourist was rather disappointed by this, as it was small and rather dark and stuffy, with only one window. Her bed itself, on the other hand, was unashamedly magnificent, "ingeniously composed of woods of different colours, with quilts of silk, velvet, gold, silver and embroidery".[66]

The furnishings of Hampton Court were still more lavish. "All the walls of the palace shine with gold and silver", commented one awed traveller, while in 1592 another foreign visitor produced a more detailed description of its splendours. "The tapestries are garnished with gold, pearls and precious stones ... not to mention the royal throne, which is studded with very large diamonds, rubies, sapphires and the like ... Many of the splendid large rooms are embellished with masterly paintings, writing tables with mother of pearl, and musical instruments, of which her Majesty is particularly fond." As in all Elizabeth's palaces, colour and ornamentation abounded. The ceilings were either covered with 'fretwork' – carved intersecting ribs with pendants – or sprouted 'bullions and buds', which were flowers of carved wood with leaves of gilded lead. All wooden surfaces were either gilded or painted in strong colours – red, vermilion, blue, green or ochre among them – or alternatively *trompe l'oeil* techniques were used to make panelling resemble stone, marble, brick or even drapery.[67]

Elizabeth showed great interest in the upkeep of the gardens and parks attached to her houses, for she liked walking in agreeable surroundings. At Greenwich, special benches carved and painted with the royal arms were set up "for her Majesty to sit on in the garden", and on fine days Elizabeth might even have meetings in the open air with ambassadors and envoys. A feature of all her gardens were the wooden carvings of heraldic beasts which were set atop tall poles, thus ensuring that even in winter the grounds were ablaze with colour, but more conventional horticulture was not neglected. At Whitehall a new orchard was created in 1561, and twenty-four years later there was a further bout of activity, with "making of borders and setting and sowing divers kinds of trees and herbs to bring it to the full perfection of a garden". In 1583 "a certain Frenchman very skilful in planting and setting" was employed to "reform our gardens and orchards at Hampton Court". The improvements he effected, at a cost to the Crown of £420, included laying out hedges, making beds of lavender, double primrose and daisies, and planting holly, bay and musk trees. As well as using the garden at Whitehall when in London, Elizabeth could also go for walks in St James's Park, where gates and bridges were specially erected to facilitate her passage. Even when the weather was bad, she did not like to forego her exercise, and at both Windsor Castle and Greenwich special covered walkways were erected, which protected her from the rain, or afforded shade when the heat was oppressive.[68]

The Queen changed residence at regular intervals primarily for reasons of hygiene, for an intolerable stench permeated any house that had been occupied by the Court for more than a few weeks. Naturally, everything possible was done to alleviate the situation: at Hampton Court, sewage and waste from the kitchen were channelled into the Thames, and presumably the same system was in use at Elizabeth's other riverside palaces. Nevertheless these arrangements were insufficient to overcome the problem. Elizabeth's godson, John Harington, once observed that "even in the goodliest and stateliest palaces of our realm, notwithstanding all our provisions of vaults, or sluices or gates, of pains of poor folks in sweeping and scouring, yet still this same whoreson saucy stink, though he were commanded on pain of death not to come within the gates, yet would spite of our noses". The Queen might use lidded portable close stools, whose contents could be disposed of by her ladies, but lesser denizens of the Court had to make do with facilities such as "the great house of easement" at Hampton Court, or the "common jakes", or even to relieve themselves in a palace courtyard.[69]

For Elizabeth, the pervasive odours must have been particularly disagreeable, for her olfactory sense was highly developed. Before presenting her with samples of their work, bookbinders were warned not to use pungent oils to cure the leather, "for that her Majesty could not abide such a strong scent", and in 1578 the Company of London brewers volunteered to burn only wood in their furnaces after learning that Elizabeth had been "greatly grieved and annoyed with the taste and smoke of the sea coals" that had hitherto been used. After receiving a French ambassador who suffered from halitosis she was overheard exclaiming, "Good God! What shall I do if this man stay here, for I smell him an hour after he has gone!" When some unkind soul passed this on, the unfortunate diplomat felt obliged to leave England without seeing her again. In view of her sensitivity to smells, great efforts were made to prevent her houses becoming too malodorous. In 1567, Lord Treasurer Winchester recommended that the kitchens at Hampton Court should be relocated, for at present they were sited immediately under Elizabeth's private apartments, with the result that "her Highness cannot sit quiet nor without ill savour". The air in the Privy Chamber in all the Queen's palaces was perfumed with rosewater, but obviously such expedients could not wholly mask offensive aromas, and once these had become too rank the only option was for the Court to move elsewhere.[70]

By the standards of the day, Elizabeth was particular about her own personal hygiene. She is known to have had bathrooms at Whitehall, Greenwich, Windsor Castle and Hampton Court, and it is likely that they had been installed at her other main residences. She also owned a travelling bath, which was carried back and forth between the palaces, although its purpose seems to have been primarily medicinal, being only used twice a year on doctor's orders. Elizabeth kept her teeth clean by using fine toothcloths, and at New Year she frequently received gifts of gold and jewelled toothpicks. Unfortunately the present lists also feature offerings such as sugar loaves or chess boards made out of marzipan, and her liking for sweet things meant that in time her teeth became badly decayed. When not in use, her dresses were kept in storage at the Tower of London and, to prevent them getting musty, they were sprinkled with sweet powder in such quantities that in 1584 alone her wardrobe personnel used up twenty-four pounds of the stuff. Obviously it was difficult to clean costly and bejewelled fabrics, but next to her skin Elizabeth always wore washable smocks, chemises, ruffs and cuffs, and the fact that her outer garments scarcely came into contact with her body helped prevent them from becoming too dirty.[71]

The calendar of the Court was punctuated by a succession of traditional festivals – Candlemas, Shrovetide, Maundy, St George's day, and so on – but after Elizabeth had been on the throne for several years her accession day began to be celebrated with as much verve as any of the former. It seems that it was in the immediate wake of the Queen's excommunication that 17 November began to be an occasion for national rejoicing, marked by bell ringing, bonfires, church services and processions. Such evidence as there is suggests that initially these loyal demonstrations were spontaneous in origin, but before long the government, appreciating the propaganda possibilities, began to take control, and by 1576 an official order of service for use on that date had even been issued. To a certain extent, habit played a part in promoting a carnival atmosphere, for according to the old Catholic reckoning, 17 November was St Hugh's day, and since time immemorial church bells had been rung in his honour. At any rate, whatever the festival's antecedents, Elizabeth was remarkably successful in appropriating the day for herself, and in turning it into "a holiday that passed all the Pope's holidays".[72]

At Court, a great tournament was held at Whitehall to celebrate the anniversary, attended by up to 12,000 spectators, who paid a shilling for admission. As befitted a putative descendant of King Arthur, Elizabeth presided over a scene reminiscent of the knights of the Round Table, and which helped keep alive in England the code of chivalry. In Henry VIII's day, the king had been a frequent competitor in Court tournaments, which had served as a useful reaffirmation of his athleticism and prowess, and the jousting itself had been taken extremely seriously, with different points being awarded according to whether a contestant splintered his lance on an opponent's helmet or body. Under Elizabeth there was a change of emphasis: tournaments were still valued for training courtiers in "those exercises of arms that keep the person bright and steeled to hardiness", but in order that the Queen, a mere spectator, should be the centre of attention, more importance came to be attached to the pageantry which took place beforehand, than to the contest proper.

After Elizabeth and her ladies had taken their places in the raised gallery overlooking the tiltyard, the various contestants rode into the arena, flanked by their trumpeters, grooms and servants in matching liveries. Each knight had selected his own theme for the day, and would be wearing an appropriate disguise over his armour. These trappings were generally gorgeous and costly: in 1593 Robert Carey spent £400 on fitting out himself and his retinue in elaborate caparisons. An observer of a tournament held in 1584 reported that some of the contestants "were disguised like savages or like Irishmen, with the hair hanging down to the girdle like women, others had horse manes on their heads, some came driving in a carriage, the horses being equipped like elephants".[73]

The knight rode to a spot beneath where Elizabeth was sitting, and then one of his servants mounted the stairs that led from the tiltyard to the gallery. Having presented the Queen with a gift, he handed to her the knight's impresa, a painted shield bearing on it a device that was in some way relevant to the knight's chosen theme, and superimposed with an appropriate Latin motto. The servant next addressed Elizabeth in verses that were meant to be at once graceful and witty, and which cast enlightenment on the subject pictured on the impresa. Sometimes this took the form of an oblique request for support for, though in theory the chivalric ethos enjoined knights to serve their mistress without thought of reward, a delicate reminder that their fidelity merited recognition was not considered out of place. More often, however, the knight simply sought to find some new and picturesque way of conveying his devotion. In 1580, for example, the Earl of Oxford appeared in the guise of the Knight of the Tree of the Sun, and it soon became apparent that this tree from which he took his name was a metaphor for the Queen herself. Oxford's page explained that while on his travels his master had been dazzled by a magnificent tree which housed a virgin bird in its midst, "whereat Cupid is ever drawing, but dare not shoot", and this had so inspired Oxford that he had thereupon "made a solemn vow to incorporate his heart into that tree" and "to live or die for the defence thereof". Fifteen years later, another knight created a stir by riding into the tiltyard dressed as a South American prince, who had come to pay homage to Elizabeth after being informed by an oracle that,

> Seated between the old world and the new
> A land there is no other land may touch,
> Where reigns a Queen in peace and honour true,
> Stories and fables do describe no such.

Having found the object of his pilgrimage, the prince reverently presented her with three precious offerings: the gift of being ever young, liberty to fly from one admirer to another, and a bow and arrow "to wound where you please".

Christmas was another highlight of the year at Court, and was generally passed at Whitehall or Hampton Court. The Puritans thought it shocking that Christmas should be an excuse for merriment, observing dourly that "it was made rather a feast of Bacchus than a true serving of the memory of Jesus Christ", but, although on Christmas Day itself Elizabeth set time aside for prayer and meditation, she celebrated the remaining eleven days with gusto. She could rely on there being a good turnout for the festivities, for though courtiers generally tried to spend some time at home with their families, they knew better than to absent themselves for the whole holiday period, "lest the Queen take offence". The exchange of presents on New Year's Day was an important part of the proceedings, when Elizabeth received not only the fabulous articles of clothing and jewellery from the uppermost ranks of society, but also humbler offerings from more menial servants, such as the eighteen caged larks that Morris Watkins produced in 1579, or the quince pie from John Dudley, her Sergeant of the Pastry. Apart from this a great deal of dancing and gambling went on, with Elizabeth sometimes taking a place at the tables. Some courtiers played very high, particularly towards the end of the reign (at Christmas 1602 Robert Cecil was said to have lost over £800 at a single sitting), but Elizabeth wagered only moderate amounts. Lord North was among those who tried his luck against her at cards, and his accounts show that he regularly lost sums to her ranging from £28 to £70. There is no record of him ever taking any winnings off her, but it would be uncharitable on that account to credit the playwright Ben Jonson's allegation that she cheated.[74]

The baiting of bears and bulls with mastiffs invariably featured among the Christmas entertainments, for Elizabeth found this hugely diverting. Such cruel spectacles were an unattractive feature of the age, and Elizabeth was typical of her countrymen in seeing nothing wrong with them. The sufferings of the animals involved were looked on as highly comical, and it was deemed "a sport very pleasant" to see "the bear with his pink eyes leering after his enemy's approach, the nimbleness and weight of the dog to take his advantage, and the force and experience of the bear again to avoid the assaults. If he were bitten in one place, how he would pinch in another to get free; that if he were taken once, then what shift, with biting, with clawing, with roaring, tossing and tumbling he would work to wind himself from them; and when he was loose to shake his ears twice or thrice with the blood and the slaver about his physiognomy was a matter of goodly relief." To Elizabeth, all this was a source of unfailing amusement, and when in 1591 it was noted that the theatres were drawing the audience away from bear baitings, the Council responded by shutting down the playhouses for two afternoons a week, as it was essential that bear baiting "and like pastimes" were "maintained for her Majesty's pleasure if occasion require".[75]

Such action should not be taken as signifying any hostility on Elizabeth's part towards the dramatic profession, for in general she was one of the theatre's most devoted patrons. Numerous plays were put on at Court throughout the Christmas holidays, sometimes as many as eleven in one season. These might be performed by young choristers from the Chapel Royal, or by the Children of Paul's, another juvenile company, but adult troupes of actors were also invited to Court on occasion, and by the end of the reign these were appearing more frequently before the Queen than the boy companies. The Puritans regarded Elizabeth's interest in drama as utterly reprehensible, for to them actors were a contemptible breed, and playhouses were little better than brothels. One Puritan preacher went so far as to declare, "The cause of sin is plays", and in 1569 a pamphlet attacking the Children of the Chapel Royal lamented that "Plays will never be suppressed while her Majesty's unfledged minions flaunt it in silks and satins ... These pretty upstart youths profane the Lord's day by the lascivious writhing of their tender limbs and gorgeous decking of their apparel in feigning bawdy fables gathered from idolatrous heathen poets." Fortunately, a combination of royal and aristocratic support was sufficient to insulate the players against such onslaughts, for in order to save themselves from being victimized by puritanical city authorities, professional theatre companies took to inviting powerful men at Court to act as their protectors. In 1559, the then Lord Robert Dudley was prevailed upon to lend his name to a company of players, and other leading noblemen subsequently did likewise, including the Earls of Worcester, Oxford and Derby, and the first and second Lord Hunsdons. These men were close enough to the Queen to alert her if the dramatic companies were being unduly harassed, and such cases generally prompted royal intervention. In 1574, for example, Elizabeth was annoyed to hear that the city fathers had turned down a request from Leicester's Men that they might be permitted to perform in recognized places in London. Later in the year she overturned this decision by issuing a licence empowering the company "to use, exercise and occupy the art and faculty of playing ... stage plays ... as well for the recreation of our loving subjects, as for our solace and pleasure". Armed with this document, the leading actor of the company, Richard Burbage, was able to start work in 1576 on a playhouse in Finsbury Fields, completed the following year, and known simply as the Theatre.[76]

In 1583 a scaffold collapsed onto the audience at a bear baiting, causing eight fatalities, and the city authorities used this as an excuse to close all playhouses in the interest of public safety. Once again, royal action saved the day, for Elizabeth responded with the formation of her own theatre company, the Queen's Men. According to one account it was at the suggestion of Walsingham (who, notwithstanding his puritanical leanings, was a staunch defender of the stage) that Elizabeth decided to recruit twelve of the best actors from existing theatre companies and, having sworn them as her servants, permitted them to wear her livery. Certainly it was Walsingham who wrote to the Lord Mayor in the name of the Privy Council in December 1583, asking that the newly-formed company should be licensed to perform in the city every day except Sundays, as "without frequent exercise of such plays as are to be presented before her Majesty, her servants cannot conveniently satisfy her recreation and their own duties".[77]

The star performer of the Queen's Men was Richard Tarlton, a comic genius who "for a wondrous plentiful extemporal wit was the wonder of his time". He had such a droll appearance that "the people began exceedingly to laugh the instant that Tarlton peeped out his head", and his particular speciality was improvising doggerel verse on any subject the audience cared to name. Elizabeth herself found him utterly hilarious: a description survives of her collapsing into such helpless giggles at a Court performance of Tarlton's that she "bade them take away the knave for making her to laugh so excessively, as he fought against her little dog, Perrico de Falda, with his sword and long staff, and bade the Queen take off her mastiff".[78]

Tarlton died in 1588, causing the Queen's Men to go into irreversible decline. In the 1590s the theatrical scene was dominated by the Lord Chamberlain's Men, the company to which William Shakespeare belonged. Having come to London from Stratford around 1587, Shakespeare had established himself as one of the company's leading actors, and on consecutive nights in December 1594 he appeared before the Queen at Greenwich in "two several comedies and interludes". The names of the plays are not recorded, but Elizabeth was sufficiently impressed with his performance for his fee of £13 6s 7d to be raised to £20, "by way of her Majesty's reward". By this time Shakespeare was writing his own plays, and before long these were being regularly presented before the Queen. *Twelfth Night* was specially written for a Court performance, after the Lord Chamberlain had let it be known that the play staged after the Twelfth Night feast of January 1601 must be "furnished with rich apparel, have great variety and change of music and dances, and of a subject that may be most pleasing to her Majesty". According to tradition, Shakespeare also wrote *The Merry Wives of Windsor* at Elizabeth's behest, as she had been "so well pleased with that admirable character of Falstaff in the two parts of Henry IV that she commanded him to continue it for one play more and show him in love".[79]

Drama was not the only art form which was protected by the Queen, for choral music might well be unknown in Britain today had it not been for her intervention. It was standard for anyone with remotely puritanical leanings to object to "all curious singing and playing of the organ" in church, but Elizabeth held them to be uplifting usages. The injunctions of 1559 laid down that for the "comforting of such that delight in music" there could be sung during church services "an hymn, or such like song, to the praise of Almighty God, in the best sort of melody that may be conveniently devised". The music in the Queen's own chapel was superb, not least because two of her organists, Thomas Tallis and William Byrd, were among the greatest composers of sacred music England has ever known. Both were crypto-Catholics, but in recognition of their genius Elizabeth kept them in her service and protected them from the full rigour of the recusancy laws. Singing was performed by the salaried choristers of the Chapel Royal, a department of the Court subject to the jurisdiction of the Lord Chamberlain rather than the Archbishop of Canterbury, and financed by the Exchequer. In addition to the thirty-two gentlemen of the Chapel Royal, there were never less than twelve children, recruited nationwide by the Master of the Chapel Royal, who was empowered to travel the country in order to "take up and bring such children as be thought meet to be trained for service to her Majesty".[80]

When on good form, the harmonies they produced were of a superlative quality. In 1592, a foreign visitor was immensely impressed by what he heard in the Chapel Royal at Windsor. "The music, especially the organ, was exquisitely played ... " he wrote, "and then there was a little boy who sang so sweetly amongst it all, and threw such charm over the music with his little tongue, that it was really wonderful to listen to him". He concluded, "In short, their ceremonies were very similar to the Papists", but it was for this very reason that Puritans roundly condemned such practices. The Puritan theologian, Thomas Cartwright, spluttered, "The Queen's chapel and those [cathedral] churches which should be spectacles of Christian reformation, are rather patterns and precedents to the people of all superstition", but Elizabeth had no intention of taking account of such prejudices. Her support for church music never wavered, and it was no exaggeration when in 1572 one clergyman commented that "If it were not the Queen's Majesty did favour that excellent science, singing men and choristers might go a-begging, together with their master on the organs".[81]

Music not only played an essential part in the religious life of the Court, but featured largely in its day-to-day existence. Elizabeth employed about thirty musicians in her orchestra, rather fewer than in her father's days, but continuity with the past was provided by the fact that many of them were members of immigrant families such as the Ferraboscos, Bassanos and Van Welders, who had served the Tudors in a musical capacity for generations. Apart from providing the accompaniment for dances, the musicians always played while the Queen was being served her midday meal. One foreign visitor who watched her food being set out in the Presence Chamber, prior to being carried into the secluded room where she dined, reported that while this happened, "twelve trumpets and two kettle drums made the hall ring for half an hour together".[82]

Like her father, Elizabeth was highly musical, for in addition to possessing a good ear, she was an accomplished player on the lute and virginals. She practised with such regularity that in her first ten years on the throne she spent £75 replacing broken lute strings, but in 1564 she claimed to Sir James Melville that "she used not to play before men, but when she was solitary, to shun melancholy". In fact, this was false. Not only was Sir James afforded an opportunity to hear her on the virginals (although Elizabeth claimed this was an oversight on her part) but in 1572 she performed on the same instrument for the ambassadors who had come to England to ratify the Treaty of Blois. Nine years later, she gave a recital on the lute and virginals to another set of French ambassadors. Clearly she had no small ability, for not only was Melville impressed by her talent but, after listening to her on the virginals, the Duke of Wurttemberg declared that she "played very sweetly and skilfully".[83]

For much of the year Elizabeth rarely ventured more than twenty miles out of London, but at the height of summer she liked if possible to go further afield. Accompanied by a baggage train of between four hundred to six hundred carts, the Court would laboriously uproot itself to accompany her on her peregrinations. In the course of her reign she traversed across perhaps a third of her kingdom, covering an area which extended westwards to Bristol, southwards to Southampton, eastwards to Norwich, and with Chartley in Staffordshire at its northernmost extremity. The object of the exercise was partly pure pleasure: whereas her predecessors had broken cross-country journeys by staying in residences of their own, or putting up at monasteries, Elizabeth regarded it as a treat to accept hospitality from her subjects. She did not, however, set off on her travels solely for her own gratification, for she recognized that progresses served as an invaluable means of interaction between subject and sovereign. If she had led a more sedentary existence, the only contact with the Court vouchsafed to the vast majority of her people would have derived from their dealings with her purveyors, and she believed that they deserved to be introduced to a more positive side of royal government. Her tours were designed to let her reach as wide an audience as was possible in an age which lacked sophisticated means of mass communication, and she embarked on them with the deliberate intention of transforming the monarchy from a remote and faceless entity to a living presence.

The Queen's passage through town and countryside made an impressive spectacle. Whenever she entered or left London, she would be the centrepiece of a magnificent procession, with her household officers, ladies-in-waiting and the mayor and aldermen all forming part of her escort. A French ambassador who witnessed one such ceremonial entry in 1579 was transported by the sight of her, "more beautiful than ever, bedizened like the sun, and mounted on a fine Spanish horse; and with so many people before her that it was a marvellous thing. They did not merely honour her, but they worshipped her, kneeling on the ground, with a thousand blessings and joyful remarks". "If your Majesty come to the city of London never so often, what gratulation, joy, what concourse of people is there to be seen!" reflected the Archbishop of Canterbury in a letter written in 1576. "Yea, what acclamations for your long life, and other manifest significations of inward and unfeigned love, joined with most humble and hearty obedience, are there to be heard". The Archbishop subsequently marred this affecting testimonial by asserting that it was the beneficial effect of good sermons that accounted for these joyous manifestations, but undoubtedly Elizabeth deserved much of the credit. She had an instinctive way with crowds, delighting them with the evident pleasure she took in their acclamations, but being careful not to cheapen herself by descending into vulgarity. A contemporary memoirist commented, "I believe no prince living that was so tender of honour, and so exactly stood for the preservation of sovereignty, was so great a courtier of the people, yea of the commons, and that stooped and declined lower in presenting her person to the public view, as she passed in her progresses and perambulations".[84]

The pace she travelled at was excruciatingly slow, for she regarded it as important to take time to acknowledge the plaudits of the crowds that gathered on the waysides to watch her go by. Even so stern a critic of Elizabeth as Guerau de Spes was impressed by the warmth of the reception she met with as she passed through the home counties in 1568. He noted that she was hailed "with great acclamations and signs of joy as is customary in this country; whereat she was extremely pleased and told me so ... She ordered her carriage to be taken sometimes where the crowd seemed

The "sieve portrait" of Elizabeth, c. 1579, by the Flemish artist Massys the Younger, a painting full of symbolism intended to convey that Elizabeth must renounce marriage in order to fulfil her destiny and found a mighty empire.

Sir Christopher Hatton. In his hand he holds a miniature of Elizabeth.

Sir Francis Walsingham, a portrait after J. de Critz the Elder.

Francis, Duke of Alençon at the age of thirty-one, painted by Clouet.

James VI of Scotland in 1574, attributed to Rowland Lockey.

Sir Walter Ralegh, a portrait designed to illustrate his love for Elizabeth. Pearls were a symbol of virginity, and hence one of the Queen's favourite emblems. The moon in the top left-hand corner is a reference to the moon goddess Diana, whom Ralegh used as a synonym for Elizabeth in his poetry.

Den VIII february werde onthalst Maria

Stuart Schots Coninginne s tervende Roomsch Catho-
lyck hebbende gesocht veel onrust te aen te richten haer selven
meet ter te maecken van Engelant t' dwelck haer vanden raet
ofte parlement volcomelyck wende vertoont, Anno 1587.

℃· Metren XIII fol XIII en XIIII b℈

The execution of Mary Queen of Scots at Fotheringay.

The English pursue the Spanish fleet east of Plymouth, 1588. This engraving by John Pine of a tapestry commissioned by Lord Admiral Howard of Effingham shows the crescent-shaped formation of the Spanish fleet.

(*Left*) Medallion that could be worn as a pendant, c. 1585–90, probably after a design by Nicholas Hilliard.

(*Below*) Queen Elizabeth playing the lute, a miniature c. 1580 by Nicholas Hilliard.

(*Below*) A double portrait of William Cecil, Lord Burghley, and his son, Sir Robert Cecil.

A miniature by Nicholas Hilliard of Robert Devereux, Earl of Essex, dressed for a Court tournament.

A miniature of Elizabeth c. 1592, by Isaac Oliver, designed to be used as a pattern for future studies of her. Elizabeth was not pleased with the result.

A more flattering miniature of Elizabeth in old age by Nicholas Hilliard. The arrows in her ruff and the crescent-moon in her hair are references to Diana, virgin goddess of the moon.

A portrait of Elizabeth by Marcus Gheeraerts the Younger, probably painted in honour of the Queen's visit to Sir Henry Lee's house, Ditchley, in 1592. The Queen stands on a globe of the world and her feet are placed on Oxfordshire, where Ditchley was located.

thickest, and stood up and thanked the people." On every progress she would also visit two or three major towns, and the great civic receptions that were held in her honour provided her with further opportunities to put herself on view to her public. Always, the masses who turned out for her were delighted by the inimitable grace with which she accepted their homage, and by the trouble she took to show she did not take their affection for granted. Again and again she took part in scenes such as those which occurred during her visit to Worcester in 1575, when "the people, being innumerable in the streets and churchyard, crying to her Majesty, 'God save your Majesty! God save your Grace!' unto whom, she rising, showed herself at both sides of her coach unto them, and oftentimes said, 'I thank you, I thank you all'".[85]

For the towns, the Queen's visits were not necessarily just passing excitements, for if properly exploited, direct contact with the sovereign could yield solid advantage. Obviously a note of discontent could not be allowed to mar the proceedings, but all the loyal speeches of welcome and flattering rhetoric afforded excellent opportunities for articulating grievances, and municipal authorities knew how to make the most of these. When Elizabeth went to Stafford in 1575, for instance, she was told by one of the city magistrates that the town was in decline partly because the county assizes were no longer held there, and she promptly promised that in future they would be. Similarly, during a visit to Coventry ten years earlier the Recorder of the city mentioned in his speech to the Queen that the town had been unjustly deprived of lands which Henry VIII had set aside for the purposes of founding a free school there, and Elizabeth asked to be given more details about this.[86]

On nearly every official engagement she was required to sit through hours of laboured orations and tedious pageantry, but if she ever felt bored or oppressed at the prospect, she was too good mannered to betray it. No matter how unpolished and provincial the reception that awaited her, she understood that time and effort had gone into its planning, and she did not fail to single out for special notice those who had contributed. Having listened in 1578 to a Norwich schoolmaster deliver a laudatory address in Latin, she exclaimed loudly, "It is the best that ever I heard!" although it is hard to believe that the performance of this rustic pedagogue really compared so favourably to those she had heard during her visits to the universities of Oxford and Cambridge. At Coventry in 1572 she congratulated the Recorder of the city for having plucked up the courage to utter a formal greeting, calling out to him when he had finished, "Come hither, little Recorder. It was told me you would be afraid to look upon me, or to speak boldly, but you were not so 'fraid of me as I was of you". The following year she visited Sandwich, and went out of her way to show her appreciation to the various local ladies who had cooked a banquet of a hundred and forty dishes. Throughout the meal, the Queen was "very merry and did eat of divers dishes without any assay, and caused certain to be reserved to her and carried to her lodging".[87]

Almost everyone at Court dreaded going on progress. Being constantly on the move was an exhausting business, and even when Elizabeth settled somewhere for two or three days, this afforded little respite to those who were accompanying her. It was all very well for the Queen, whose hosts naturally took immense trouble to accommodate her "for her best ease and liking, far from heat or noise of any office near her lodging", but others had to put up with conditions of the utmost discomfort. At somewhere like Burghley's Theobalds, which had been specially enlarged in order to cater for royal visits, the Queen's servants might not fare too badly, but few houses were equipped to handle such a sizeable influx. When Elizabeth announced her intention in 1574 of staying with the Archbishop of Canterbury at Croydon, the officer in charge of sorting out accommodation arrangements had terrible trouble squeezing in all those he was supposed to provide for. In some agitation he wrote to his superior, "I cannot ... tell where to place Mr Hatton, and for my Lady Carewe there is no place with a chimney for her but that must lie abroad by Mrs Parry and the rest of the Privy Chamber. For Mrs Shelton here is no rooms with chimneys, I shall stay one chamber without for her. Here is as much as I have any ways able to do in this house."[88] Yet even if they ended up in quarters that were cramped and inconvenient, the people he named could at least be sure of being provided with a roof over their head, whereas the vast majority of the Court had no such security. Apart from the Queen's ladies, only the heads of household departments, great officers of state and leading favourites had lodgings commandeered for them by the Lord Chamberlain, and less fortunate individuals had to shift for themselves by finding rooms in nearby hostelries. As for menials like the kitchen staff, they generally were reduced to sleeping out under canvas.

One reason why the Queen so enjoyed her progresses was that they alleviated the pressure on her from petitioners, for it was an established principle that while she took what was, in effect, her annual holiday, nothing could be "moved to her but matter of delight and to content her". From her courtiers' point of view, this was, of course, a major inconvenience. In August 1600, for example, Rowland Whyte had a request he wished to put to Elizabeth, but he was told that it was "no time to trouble her Majesty, who had taken that little progress of purpose to pass away the time in sports". Indeed, because the Court was never in one place for more than a few days at a time, it was difficult to transact any form of business, causing Sir Thomas Smith to grumble in 1575, "This trotting about in progress makes many things to be unprofited and longer deferred than is convenient". Three years later, Edward Tremayne confessed to experiencing similar problems. He wrote apologetically to Walsingham that he was having great difficulty keeping up with his correspondence, because "leisure be never so scant with me in this time of progress, when we consume half the day to and from the Court, and the rest not much better, in places not fit to write in".[89]

In years when the international situation looked particularly threatening, the Council would sometimes seek to convince Elizabeth that it would be irresponsible of her to stray too far from the capital, but she was always reluctant to listen. In 1576 she did contemplate cutting short her progress on account of the unstable condition of the Netherlands, but in the end she pressed ahead with it as planned. By the following July tension had, if anything, heightened, but nothing the Council could say could stop her from setting off for East Anglia. In July Leicester wrote mournfully to the Earl of Sussex, "We do all we can to persuade from any progress at all, only to remain at Windsor and thereabouts. But it much misliketh her not to go somewhere to have a change of air. So what will fall, yet I know not, but most like to go forward since she fancieth it so greatly herself".[90]

Burghley disliked progresses, not simply on account of the disruption they caused but also on grounds of expense, for he estimated that it cost Elizabeth up to £2,000 a year to go travelling about the country. Despite the savings made when she stayed with other people, she generally spent some time on progress at outlying properties of her own, and since these houses were generally kept empty, they had to be specially furnished and made habitable before her arrival. Officers had to be sent ahead to strew floors with rushes, and to set up makeshift kitchens and larders, and even though the Crown paid carters only twopence a mile, instead of the market price of tenpence, the costs of transportation remained enormous. Then too, Elizabeth kept late hours, and the fact that she frequently arrived at one of her homes after darkness had fallen "causeth great expense in wax, white lights etc."[91] To all this Elizabeth could justly have retorted that progresses were invaluable public relations exercises, and that the benefits of keeping in touch with her subjects could not be measured in monetary terms alone, but Burghley, with his book-keeper's mentality, could not have appreciated such arguments.

Costs were pushed up by Elizabeth's chronic indecisiveness, for the timetable of the progress was subject to constant revision. In July 1576 Gilbert Talbot wrote to his father, "Since my coming hither to the Court, there have been sundry determinations of her Majesty's progress this summer. Yesterday it was set down that she would go to Grafton and Northampton, Leicester and to Ashby, my Lord Huntingdon's house, and there to have remained twenty-one days . . . but late yesternight this purpose altered, and now at this present her Majesty thinketh to go no further than Grafton; howbeit there is no certainty, for these two or three days it hath changed every five hours". Such vacillations on her part were by no means untypical, and wreaked havoc with Burghley's budgetary calculations. When plans were changed, beer, wine and food that had been sent ahead to places that Elizabeth had originally intended to visit either went to waste or had to be disposed of at a loss. In a memorandum of 1576, Burghley expressed the wish that in future it might "please her Majesty to keep the day appointed for removing in time of progress. And that the alteration of place may be avoided as near as may be: which causeth great expense in the sudden fetching of provision, wage, necessaries etc.". It would take more than this mournful plea to break Elizabeth of the habit of a lifetime.[92]

The bills incurred by the Queen's hosts were often enormous. The Earl of Leicester probably spent the most on entertaining her, for the hospitality he extended to her at Kenilworth became legendary. When Elizabeth visited him for the third time in 1575, staying with him a total of eighteen days, he set a standard that no one thereafter managed to equal: one guest declared afterwards, "For the persons, for the place, time, cost, devices, strangeness and abundance of all ... I saw none anywhere so memorable". Nevertheless, it was Burghley who held the record for entertaining the Queen most frequently, for in the course of the reign she visited him at Theobalds thirteen times, and on each occasion the cost ran into hundreds of pounds. Her stays there were often quite extended, as in May 1591, when she and her Court descended on Theobalds and stayed there ten days, by the end of which time Burghley had laid out just under £1,000, including £100 spent on a magnificent gown for the Queen.[93]

Building expenses also had to be taken into account, for Burghley claimed that he had originally envisaged that Theobalds would be a modest sized house, and that it was only "enlarged by occasion of her Majesty's often coming". According to him, she had left him with little choice in the matter, for on her first visit to Theobalds there had been "fault found with the small measure of her chamber", even though he had considered it to be perfectly adequate for her. Prior to Elizabeth's visit to Elvetham in 1591, the Earl of Hertford also added two new wings to the house in her honour. Even with these new extensions, the house still was not large enough to provide all the accommodation that was needed, and so in the days before her arrival Hertford engaged three hundred workmen to erect pavilions for the Queen's guards and footmen, and to construct a temporary great kitchen, with four ranges and a scullery.[94]

Feeding the Court for even a day or so was always a major operation. In 1602, Lord Keeper Egerton spent a total of £1,260 12s 4d entertaining Elizabeth for four days at Harefield, of which roughly £240 went on provisions. In addition he had to buy 48,000 bricks with which to build ovens, and employ a total of a hundred and twenty-one artisans "about the dining room and other rooms about the house". The Queen's three-day visit to his house at Kirtling in 1578 cost Lord North £762, which was not particularly surprising in view of the fact that during that time there were devoured 64 hogsheads of beer, 67 sheep, 32 geese, 273 mallards and young ducks, 26 dozen quails, 4 stags, 16 bucks, 2,522 eggs, a barrel of anchovies, 2 horseloads of oysters, and 400 red herrings. Very little of all this was consumed by the Queen herself, for her appetite on progress remained as modest as ever. During her 1575 stay at Kenilworth, for example, Leicester laid on "an ambrosial banquet" of 300 dishes, but it was observed that throughout it, "her Majesty ate smally or nothing". Rather more successful was the gastronomic treat provided for her at Belington by Sir Francis Carew, who presented her with late cherries from a tree whose fruiting he had retarded by erecting a tent over it to ward off the sun's rays. Apart from being a delight to the palate, this was a graceful symbolic gesture, for not only was the cherry the emblem of virginity, but the unseasonal gift could also be taken as a manifestation of that perpetual abundance that was said to be a feature of Astraea's rule.[95]

An essential part of the hospitality extended to the Queen was the magnificent gifts offered to her by her hosts. At the end of her 1573 progress, her haul of trophies included a gold salt-cellar from the Archbishop of Canterbury; a tankard of alabaster and a gold cup from Lord and Lady Cobham; a parrot of crystal and gold with sparks of rubies and emerald from Lady Chandos; a ruby and diamond salamander and phoenix from Sir John Young; and a falcon preying on a fowl with a great emerald in her breast from Sir John Thynne. Costly articles of clothing were also regarded as acceptable gifts. During her visit to Sir Julius Caesar at Mitcham in September 1598, Elizabeth's host presented her with "a gown of cloth of silver, richly embroidered, a black network mantle with pure gold, a taffeta hat with several flowers, and a jewel of gold set therein with rubies and diamonds".[96]

Obviously only the most wealthy could afford such generous presents, and some allowance was made for this. When Elizabeth decided to go and stay with Burghley's secretary, Michael Hicks, the Lord Chamberlain sent him a reassuring message that if Hicks's wife presented Elizabeth with some comparatively insignificant item, such as a waistcoat or fine ruff, "it would be as acceptably taken as if it were of great price". From the better-off, however, Elizabeth expected nothing but the best. The Earl of Nottingham was felt to have made rather a poor show of things when he entertained her at the end of 1602, for his presents were not "so precious as was expected, being only a whole suit of apparel, whereas it was thought he would have bestowed his rich hangings of all the fights with the Spanish Armada in '88". Lord Keeper Egerton had done much better than this when Elizabeth visited him at Kew in 1598. On her arrival, she received from him "a fine fan" with a diamond handle, and this was followed by a nosegay, which turned out to have "a very rich jewel", worth at least £400, nestling within it. After dinner Egerton gave her a pair of virginals and also a costly gown, but the Queen was not yet sated, and before her departure she helped herself to a salt-cellar and cutlery set of agate which had caught her eye. Even this was not the end of it, for like everyone else who had Elizabeth to stay, he was expected to provide gifts for members of her entourage ranging from the ladies and grooms of the Privy Chamber to the footmen and Yeomen of the Guard.[97]

Clearly, entertaining the Queen was an effortful and expensive business, but this did not stop many of those called upon to do so from being honoured and excited at the prospect. In July 1598 Vice-Chamberlain Sir Thomas Heneage wrote earnestly to Robert Cecil from Copthall in Essex, "I hope her Majesty will hold her determination towards end of progress time to visit this poor lodge, which I love for nothing so much as that she gave it me, and that I hope 'ere I die to see her Highness here, though not pleased as my heart desires, yet contented with such mean entertainment as my most power can perform with most goodwill". Far from being relieved at being spared an unwelcome ordeal, in September 1582 Lord and Lady Norris were heartbroken to learn that Elizabeth had cancelled her forthcoming visit to their house at Rycote. The following year, the Earl of Northumberland could have been forgiven if he had asked to be excused from having the Queen to stay, for his wife had "stirred not out of her chamber this month, nor is not like to do in another". Despite this a correspondent of Walsingham's emphasized that "Notwithstanding as this is very true, yet it may not be advertised, lest it might be thought to give impediment to her Majesty's coming, whereof I perceive my Lord very glad and desirous".[98]

Obviously, however, for those who were short of money, a visit from the Queen only added to their problems. In 1601, Burghley remarked that it was unfortunate that Elizabeth had decided to inflict herself upon Sir William Cornwallis, as the latter was "in the diet, and ... his purse is likewise, and if her Majesty go hither, she is like the physicians that giveth the wrong medicine". He consoled himself that once Elizabeth "knoweth his disease, she is able to cure him, which I hope her Majesty will do", but there could be no certainty of this. Cornwallis would hardly have been encouraged if he had seen a letter written a year before to Robert Cecil by Sir Henry Lee, on hearing that Elizabeth was planning a visit to Oxfordshire. In the past Lee had entertained her both at Woodstock (of which she had appointed him comptroller) and his own house at Ditchley, but at present he felt that he could not afford to do so again. In consternation he wrote to Cecil that he understood "her Majesty threatens a progress and her coming to my houses of which I would be most proud as oft beforetime, if my fortune answered my desire, or part of her Highness's many promises performed. My estate without my undoing cannot bear it. My continuance in her Court has been long, my charge great, my land sold and debts not small. How this will agree with the entertaining of such a prince your wisdom can best judge".[99]

For those who quailed at the prospect of Elizabeth turning up on their doorstep, the best way to deflect her was to enlist the support of some great man at Court, who could tactfully intimate that it would be inadvisable to visit somewhere where she might be rather uncomfortable. The first thing Sir William More did on learning that Elizabeth was minded to take over his house at Loseley was to alert his courtier friend Sir Anthony Wingfield, and the latter did his best to extricate Sir William from his predicament. He went to the Lord Chamberlain and told him "what few small rooms" Loseley had, "and how unmeet your house was for the Queen's Majesty". In 1570, the Earl of Bedford likewise asked Sir William Cecil to dissuade Elizabeth from coming to his house at Cheynies, explaining that as there was insufficient time to render it in a fit condition to receive "so noble a guest and so large a train, I . . . repose my trust in your friendly solicitation". Eleven years later a panic-struck gentlewoman named Anne Askew begged Sir Christopher Hatton to deliver her from the threat of a courtly infestation. Beseechingly she wrote, "Sir, this short warning and my unfurnished house do ill agree; for besides her Majesty's diet there be many things which I know to be fit for her ease that I want; wherefore if her Majesty's pleasure would otherwise determine, my shame were the less and my bond to you the greater".[100]

Though not always successful, such behind the scenes manoeuvering was a better way to prevent one's house being overrun by the Queen than the tactics adopted by the Earl of Lincoln in 1601. Hearing that Elizabeth purposed to avail herself of his hospitality, he decamped to the country, and when the Queen and her retinue arrived outside his house in Chelsea, it proved impossible to force an entry. Much put out, Elizabeth declared grimly that she would return the following week to dine there, and Robert Cecil and the Earl of Nottingham wrote to tell Lincoln that they would make the necessary arrangements. They explained that it would be necessary to order large quantities of food and also to buy Elizabeth an appropriate present, but they assured Lincoln that they would "moderate expenses as if it were for ourselves". Nevertheless, when Lincoln subsequently received the bill, he was appalled to find that the total "amounteth to as much as seven noblemen's subsidies".[101]

Elizabeth did not make things any easier for her hosts with her incorrigible irresolution, for her reluctance to stick to a pre-arranged itinerary meant that it was hard for them to have everything in readiness for her arrival. In 1583, for example, the Earl of Northumberland had reserved "great provision for the receiving of her" when the news that Elizabeth was not coming on the date originally mentioned forced him to cancel the order. A few days later he received very short notice that she would be appearing at any moment. Desperately, he started to stock up afresh, "as well within the realm as beyond the seas", but he feared that lack of time would make it difficult to obtain all he needed. He was by no means alone in experiencing such difficulties. Six years earlier, the Earl of Buckhurst had written anxiously to Lord Chamberlain Sussex, begging to "know some certainty of the progress". Apologetically he continued that the "time of provision was so short, and the desire he had to do all things in such sort as appertaineth so great, as he could not but thus importune his Lordship to procure her Highness to grow to some resolution". His difficulties were compounded by the fact that all available supplies in the area had already been snapped up by the Earl of Arundel and Lord Montague (who were also expecting a royal visit) and, in order to acquire sufficient quantities, Buckhurst thought he would have to send over to Flanders.[102]

Indisputably Elizabeth was an exacting guest, but entertaining her was not without its satisfactions, for her gratitude at being so warmly fêted was always plain for all to see. On numerous occasions she is described as being "well pleased with all things", or as having "made very merry" and "expressed an extreme delight" at everything that was offered her. After visiting the decrepit old Lord Treasurer Winchester at his house at Basing in 1560, "she openly and merrily bemoaned herself that the Marquis was so old, 'For else, by my troth', said she, 'if my Lord Treasurer were but a young man, I could find in my heart to have him for my husband before any man in England'". Less preoccupied than normal with cares of state, and freed from the constant importunities of suitors, progresses generally found her at her most relaxed and good-humoured, but even when she was on less than sparkling form she took care not to hurt her hosts' feelings. In 1600 Elizabeth spent the day at Penshurst with Robert Sidney and his family, and after she had been shown round the house, it became obvious that she was somewhat wearied. Nevertheless Sidney reported she "seemed much pleased at what we did to please her. My son made her a fair speech to which she did give a most gracious reply ... The Queen was much in commendation of our appearances, and smiled at all the ladies." Nine years before this, she had spent a gruelling five days at the Earl and Countess of Hertford's and, however much she had enjoyed their hospitality, she cannot have been anything other than worn out when she finally took her leave. Nevertheless, as she drove away in appalling weather, she saw that some of those who had taken part in the entertainments put on for her were waiting at the roadside to bid her farewell, so "notwithstanding the great rain, she stayed her coach and pulled off her mask [which all ladies wore when travelling, to protect their complexions], giving great thanks".[103]

However much Elizabeth strove to be gracious and agreeable to those who were offering her hospitality, some of them nevertheless found it an unnerving experience. Having satisfied himself that his house was in readiness to receive Elizabeth, Burghley's secretary, Michael Hicks, was waiting to greet her with a carefully rehearsed speech of welcome, only to be overcome with shyness when the moment came for him to deliver it. He confessed that when he saw her, "the admirable majesty and splendour of her Majesty's royal presence and princely aspect did on a sudden so daunt all my senses and dazzle mine eyes, as for the time I had use neither of speech nor memory". Elizabeth was mystified by his taciturnity, and to his horror poor Hicks heard that "her Majesty took some conceit and more towards myself for my silence, although in her princely favour it pleased her to like of my house, and of the mistress of the house and of all things besides". The unfortunate man consoled himself with the reflection "that men of good spirit and very good speech have been speechless in the like case, as men astonished and amazed at the majesty of her presence", but even so, he found it hard to forgive himself for his gaucheness. Mournfully he concluded, "Though I shall like the better of my house and my wife (because it pleased of her Majesty to like of them) yet I know I shall like the worse of myself as long as I live".[104]

On every progress Elizabeth found time for a great deal of hunting, for this was something of which she never tired. A herd of deer would be driven into an enclosure, with the Queen either following on horseback or watching from a raised platform. Once the animals were trapped she would pick off three or four with her crossbow, or alternatively look on while they were savaged by greyhounds. As far as cruelty to animals was concerned, her sensibilities were no more refined than the overwhelming majority of her contemporaries. There is one occasion when she is recorded as having spared a deer that had been cornered by her hounds, but even then, "the watermen held him up hard by the head while, at her Highness's commandment, he lost his ears for a ransom".[105]

Bloodsports could be relied upon to keep Elizabeth happy, but her hosts also exerted themselves to provide her with less bucolic amusements. Sometimes contortionists or acrobats were hired to divert her, or rustics were called upon to give demonstrations of country dancing. At Warwick Castle in 1572, the fireworks lit in her honour were so exuberant that flying sparks caused the house of a neighbouring poor man to burn to the ground, and he had to be hastily compensated. Three years later the Earl of Leicester was responsible for an even more spectacular display, of which "the noise and flame were seen a twenty mile off", although fortunately the Italian pyrotechnician who organized it was dissuaded from carrying out his original plan of sending live cats and dogs spinning into orbit.[106] To conjure up an atmosphere of enchantment, a strong element of fantasy was introduced whenever possible, and wherever Elizabeth went she would be accosted by creatures from myth and folklore – nymphs, sybils, mermaids, tritons, gods and goddesses, the Lady of the Lake and the Fairy Queen – who extolled her superlative qualities and serenaded her in music and verse.

Many of the entertainments presented before Elizabeth had been commissioned especially for the occasion from poets and dramatists such as George Gascoigne, John Lyly and John Davies. At Kenilworth in 1575, Leicester had intended that one of the highlights of the proceedings would be a masque, "for riches of array of an incredible cost" written by George Gascoigne, but in the end the production had to be cancelled because a banquet held beforehand had gone on longer than expected. Perhaps this was just as well, for Leicester still deluded himself there was a chance that Elizabeth would accept him as her husband, and in keeping with this, the masque had taken as its theme the joys of marriage. Juno, goddess of marriage, was represented as superior to Diana, goddess of chastity, and at the end of the play Juno's messenger apostrophized Elizabeth with a plea,

> That where you now in princely port
> Have passed a pleasant day,
> A world of wealth at will
> You henceforth will enjoy,
> In wedded state, and therewithal
> Hold up from great annoy
> The staff of your estate.
> O Queen, O worthy Queen,
> Yet never wight felt wedded bliss,
> But such as wedded been![107]

More to Elizabeth's taste were entertainments which held up virginity as an ideal state. Having left Kenilworth, the Queen moved on to spend a few days at Woodstock with Sir Henry Lee, and among the pageants and devices that he put on for her delectation was a masque that relayed a story of patriotism triumphing over love. This was a moral that Elizabeth could happily endorse, and according to the author, the play was "as well thought of, as any thing ever done before her Majesty".[108]

By the end of the reign it was virtually *de rigueur* for entertainments presented before the Queen to glorify virginity in one way or another. When Elizabeth visited Robert Cecil in December 1602 she was treated to "a pretty dialogue of John Davies's twixt a maid a widow and a wife". As they made their way towards Astraea's shrine, this trio engaged in a debate on the relative merits of their own conditions, and not surprisingly it was the maid who came out best from the altercation. Twelve years earlier, the daughters of the dowager Lady Russell had welcomed Elizabeth to Bisham by taking the parts of two virgin shepherdesses whom the lustful god Pan was trying to seduce. Showing no interest in his advances, they ward him off with the rebuke, "Thy words are as odious as thy sight, and we attend a sight which is more glorious than the sun rising ... This way cometh the Queen of this island, the wonder of the world and nature's glory, leading affection in fetters ... By her it is that all our carts that thou seest are laden with corn, when in other countries they are laden with harness".[109]

The year before this, the entertainment put on by the Earl of Hertford at Elvetham had been rather more burlesque in character. In front of the house a crescent-moon-shaped pond had been dug out in anticipation of Elizabeth's coming, and on her second afternoon there, the Queen sat under a green satin canopy to watch as a pinnace bearing three virgins playing jigs on the cornet floated into view. Then "a pompous array of sea persons appeared ... all attired in ugly marine suits and each one armed with a huge wooden squirt in his hand". After they had sported for a time in the water, the bestial God of the woods, Sylvanus, materialized on the bank. Wearing a horned head-dress and kidskin breeches, and with the top half of his naked torso stained with saffron, this monstrous apparition declaimed of his love for Cynthia. To extinguish Sylvanus's "wanton fire", Nereus the sea prophet ducked the presumptuous divinity in the pond, and after a certain amount of horseplay, Sylvanus was ignominiously put to flight.[110]

In 1601, an Italian visitor to England declared that he did not think he would "ever see a Court which, for order, surpasses this one", and Elizabeth had legitimate cause to congratulate herself for presiding over an establishment that was "at once gay, decent and superb". Some affected to despise the Court for its shallowness and insincerity, but though a strong-minded individual like Lord Willoughby might absent himself from it with the comment "that he was none of the reptilia ... and could not brook the obsequiousness and assiduity of the Court", he was a rarity. However fashionable it was to deride the Court as "a glittering misery", "full of malice and spite", few who had experience of it succeeded in tearing themselves away. Initially they had come there in pursuit of "ambition's puffball", but even those who met with nothing there other than "empty words, grinning scoff, watching nights and fawning days" still tended to look on it as a place replete with opportunity and excitement. To a certain extent this was a question simply of cultural conditioning, but undoubtedly the presence of a very remarkable woman at its centre helped account for the Court's enduring fascination. In the words of a fictional 'hermit' who featured in an entertainment presented before the Queen at one of the accession day tournaments, there was "very little in that place [the Court] ... to make an honest man much to love it, or a wise man long to tarry in it, but only one, and that was the mistress of the place".[111]

CHAPTER 11

"The blood even of her own kinswoman"

In October 1578 an alarmed Leicester wrote to Lord Burghley from his country house in Warwickshire, "I do assure your Lordship, since Queen Mary's time, the Papists were never in that jollity they be at this present time in the country". The Earl was not alone in thinking that Popery was becoming more widespread, for other observers had noted the same phenomenon. Only the year before, the Bishop of London warned Walsingham that he was receiving reports from bishops all over England "that the Papists marvellously increase both in numbers and in obstinate withdrawing of themselves from the Church and service of God". He was adamant that the only way of countering this disturbing trend was to formulate legislation that would make the Catholics' lot more unpleasant, and although he was aware that the Queen would not welcome such changes he stressed that "Her Majesty must herein be made to be *animo obfirmato*, or else nothing will be done, and all our travail turned into a mockery".[1]

In the early years of the reign, the authorities had tended to be somewhat complacent about the problem posed by Catholicism. There was little effort made to compile accurate statistics for recusancy, and such figures as there were were often misleading, for churchwardens were reluctant to report the offence when their neighbours failed to come to church. Further confusion arose from the fact that many people who regarded themselves as Catholics did not feel guilty about being present at Anglican services, for they were unaware that the Pope expected them to break the law by staying away. It was in fact only in 1564 that a committee of the Council of Trent had issued a directive to this effect, and a large proportion of English Catholics remained unaware of the decision that had been reached. Even in 1580, many of them were surprised to learn of the stand the Pope had taken.

For more than fifteen years after Elizabeth's accession, Catholics had a hard task finding priests who could minister to their needs, although recent research suggests that the shortage was not so chronic as was once supposed.[2] Not only did many of the priests who had suffered deprivation under the Act of Uniformity continue secretly to receive confessions and administer the sacraments, but in outlying areas especially, parish clergy who had contrived to hang on to their livings conducted services that differed very little from the mass. Obviously these men did much to keep alive Catholic sentiment, but whatever their contribution, it was assumed that they could only temporarily stem Protestantism's insurgent tide. One by one, the Marian clergy would surely die, and with their passing the Catholic priesthood in England would become extinct. This, at least, was what the government expected, and they were therefore disagreeably surprised that during the mid 1570s, when Catholicism should have entered into irreversible decline, instead it experienced a new resurgence.

The phenomenon owed much to the efforts of one man, Dr William Allen, the exiled former principal of St Mary's Hall, Oxford, who had founded a seminary for Catholic Englishmen at Douai in 1568. Originally he had envisaged that the college would be a purely academic institution, with no other object than to give its students a higher education in theology. This would ensure that, when the Catholic Church was re-established in England (an event which Allen assumed would occur before long), there would be trained men available to serve as priests, but after a few years the college started to become overcrowded. It occurred to Allen that if some of the surplus graduates were sent to England as missionaries, they could be instrumental in bringing about a restoration of Catholicism, rather than merely waiting for this to happen. In 1574, Louis Barlow was the first of the Douai ordinands to land in England, and by the end of the reign some five hundred priests had followed him there.

Within a couple of years, the seminary priests had made their presence felt. In December 1575, one recent arrival in England wrote triumphantly to Allen at Douai, "The numbers of Catholics are increasing daily, so abundantly that even Lord Burghley ... is looking decidedly askance at the wonderful and constant growth. In secret he has confessed to a certain noble, that for one staunch and constant Catholic at the beginning of Elizabeth's reign, he was sure there were now ten". The following summer another priest declared with understandable pride, "The heretics are as much troubled at the name of the Anglo-Douai priests – which is now famous throughout England – as all the Catholics are consoled thereby".[3] Even while conceding that the priests may have been prone to exaggerate their achievements in order to boost the morale of those who were planning to join them in England, it is clear that there was already a good deal of official concern at their activities.

The Council took what steps it could to stem the advance of popery. In

1575–76, efforts were made to weed out from the magistracy any Justices of the Peace who were suspected of entertaining Catholic sympathies, and the surviving Marian bishops were once again taken into custody. In October 1577, the Council sent a circular to the bishops asking them to draw up lists of recusants in their dioceses, but this only heightened the level of disquiet, for when the returns came in they proved much higher than expected. When the Queen went on progress in East Anglia in the summer of 1578, the Council summoned prominent local recusants to appear before them at Norwich, and several of them were subsequently sent to prison. The following year, special detention centres for Catholics were set up at various points throughout the country, the most important of which was Wisbech Castle.

By this time executions of priests had already started. Cuthbert Mayne had been the first to suffer, for when arrested in Cornwall in 1577 he had on him a papal Bull of Jubilee, and by the terms of the anti-Catholic act passed in 1571, this constituted treason. After he had been convicted, the Privy Council were evidently uncertain as to whether the death sentence should be upheld, but at length they decided to proceed with the execution, "for a terror to the Papists".[4] On 30 November 1577, Mayne was hanged, drawn and quartered at Launceston. The following February two more priests, named John Nelson and Thomas Sherwood, suffered the same fate.

These harsh measures proved of little avail. In 1579 another college for English priests was founded in Rome, and the authorities in England proved incapable of staunching the flow of missionaries into the kingdom. In December 1579 the Spanish ambassador, Mendoza, announced to Philip II, "The number of Catholics, thank God, is daily increasing here, owing to the college and seminary for Englishmen which your Majesty ordered to be supported in Douai, whence there has come in the last year (and from the college in Rome) one hundred men ... Of the old ones [Marian priests] very few remain ... This was a cause for the great decay of religion and there was no one to teach it ... This is being remedied by means of those who have recently come hither".[5]

In June 1580 the Counter-Reformation in England entered a new phase with the arrival in the country of the Jesuits Robert Parsons and Edmund Campion. Like Parsons, Campion was a former Oxford man, who had abandoned a singularly promising academic career to enrol at the Douai seminary. From thence he had gone to Rome and become a Jesuit, and after spending seven years as a missionary in Bohemia, he had been directed back to his native land. The English Government first became aware that the Jesuits had entered the competition for the nation's soul when a manifesto written by Campion came into circulation. The piece – which became known in Protestant circles as "Campion's Brag" – contained the following ringing challenge: "Be it known unto you that we have made a League, all the Jesuits in the world ... cheerfully to carry the cross you shall lay upon us, and never to despair your recovery, while we have a man left to enjoy your Tyburn, or to be racked with your torments, or consumed with your prisons. The expense is reckoned, the enterprise is begun; it is of God, it cannot be withstood".[6]

Numerically, there were always far fewer Jesuits than secular priests working in England, but the Jesuits' contribution to the English mission was disproportionately large. Before their arrival, the mission had been disorganized and lacked direction, but they helped to build up a network of contacts and safe houses in which priests could find refuge. Because of their efficiency, the authorities in England came to look on them with a peculiar dread. In September 1581, for example, Sir Francis Knollys warned, "Those Jesuits, in going from house to house to withdraw men from the obedience of her Majesty unto the obedience of the false Catholic Church of Rome, hath and will endanger her Majesty's person and state more than all the sects of the world, if no execution shall follow upon the traitorous practisers that are for the same apprehended".[7]

Later in the reign, the Jesuits Henry Garnet and Robert Southwell supervised the dissemination of priests all over England, with Southwell remaining in London to look after new arrivals, while Garnet rode around the country, finding houses where they would be welcome. This system, whereby priests worked primarily "in private houses after the old example of the Apostles in their days", was not without its drawbacks. Inevitably it meant that they concentrated mainly on drawing the gentry back to Catholicism, and failed to cater to the needs of their social inferiors. One priest justified this on the grounds that it was best "to bring the gentry over first, and then their servants, for Catholic gentlefolk must have Catholic servants", but the result was that Catholicism lacked a genuinely popular base. There was evidently a feeling that simple believers would lack the strength of character to withstand persecution, but it is at least arguable that the priests were misguided to adopt this elitist approach.[8]

There were failings too in the geographical distribution of priests, most of whom tended to cross the Channel from Calais and land at Dover and Rye, with the result that much of their work was carried out in the south and east, where there were fewer recusants than further north. In consequence, areas such as North Wales and Cumbria, which early in the reign were regarded as hotbeds of popery, were left bereft of priests, and by the end of the reign Catholicism there was on the wane. Having said this, it is clear that the efforts of the Jesuits ensured that priests were more widely dispersed over England than would otherwise have been the case, and in 1596 Henry Garnet could note with pride, "Many persons who saw a seminary priest hardly once a year now have one all the time".[9]

The influx of Jesuits and seminary priests so alarmed the government that in the Parliament of 1581 stern new measures were introduced to try and contain the Catholic threat. Sir Walter Mildmay prepared the ground by pointing out that compared to Mary Tudor, Elizabeth's treatment of religious dissidents had been clemency itself, "but when by long proof we find that this favourable and gentle manner of dealing ... hath done no good ... it is time for us to look more narrowly and straitly to them lest ... they prove dangerous members ... in the entrails of our common-wealth".[10] The result was the notorious "Act to retain the Queen's Majesty's subjects in their due obedience", which subjected the Catholics to a rigorous penal code. By the terms of this statute, anyone who deliberately induced a person to withdraw allegiance from Elizabeth by converting that person to Catholicism was guilty of treason, as was the convert who allowed himself to be so persuaded. Furthermore, those convicted of saying mass were subject to a heavy fine of two hundred marks (approximately £133) and anyone caught hearing mass was liable to be fined half that amount. The penalty for refusing to attend Anglican church services was increased to a fine of £20 a month, a savage financial penalty, which even the wealthiest Catholic would find hard to support.

This was a hard law, but when first drafted, it had been still more stringent. Not only had it originally been proposed that saying mass would rank as a capital crime, but the financial penalties for recusancy were to have been progressive, so that with every month's absence from church, the offender's fine would have increased. It has been contended that one reason why the bill was subsequently modified was that the House of Commons reacted unfavourably to its more punitive sections, but this is not inconsistent with the view that the Queen also thought that the first bill was too harsh, and that it was toned down partly in deference to her feelings.[11]

Certainly several of the Queen's counsellers took the view that her attitude to the Catholics was far too lenient. In 1582, Leicester decried the way that "Her Majesty is slow to believe that the great increase of Papists is of danger to the realm. The Lord of his mercy open her eyes." Ten years before that, Burghley had admitted that it worried him that "Her Majesty has from the beginning showed her natural disposition to be such towards her subjects in the cause of religion that they who have been repugnant or mislikeous of her religion have not lacked her favour". Unlike some of her more inflexible advisers, she could not accept that "Popery and treason went always together", and she went out of her way to protect individual Catholics who were within her Court circle. When she learnt in 1598 that Lady Katherine Cornwallis, widow of a favoured Court official, was being harassed because of her recusancy, the Queen gave orders that she "would not have the Lady Katherine molested for not attending church".[12] Catholic peers such as Lord Montague and the Earl of Worcester were not deprived of her favour and, although William Byrd was known to be a Papist, he kept his position as organist of the chapel royal. Obviously, it would not do to make too much of such cases. In the very nature of things, they were exceptional, and the average Catholic was a good deal less fortunate. Lacking any personal animus against the Catholics, the Queen had staved off penal legislation for as long as she dared, but after more than twenty years on the throne she accepted that the threatening international situation, combined with the spiritual offensive of the seminary priests, left her with no alternative but to adopt repressive measures.

By bringing the priests' proselytizing activities within the compass of the treason laws, the government aimed to avoid the stigma of persecuting in the name of religion. It was laid down that priests would be guilty of treason only if they converted anyone with the deliberate intent of withdrawing them from their allegiance, but in practice the wording of the statute afforded the priests no protection, for when cases came to court it was taken that all conversions automatically entailed a withdrawal of allegiance and hence were treasonous. Understandably, the priests denounced it as monstrous that they should be deemed to have committed a political offence, when in fact their only interest was the cure of souls, and they maintained that despite the government's legal sophistries, it was manifest that they died as martyrs. In his 'brag', Campion stressed that his mission was purely spiritual, and he explained that before he set out, the Pope had given explicit instructions that he was to remain aloof from matters of state, "as things which appertain not to my vocation, and from which I do gladly restrain and sequester my thoughts". Tragically, however, such arguments rested on the false premise that religion and secular affairs could in some way be segregated, when the reality was that, at that time, they were indissolubly linked. As one Protestant propagandist put it, "Religion and politics in England are, through God's singular blessing, preserved in life as with one spirit; he that doth take away the life of the one doth procure the death of the other".[13]

Catholicism had of course been twinned with treason ever since Elizabeth had been excommunicated by Pius V. It was true that before Campion and Parsons set out from Rome, they obtained from Pius V's successor, Gregory XIII (who had become Pope in 1572), a clarification of the Bull of excommunication, which somewhat moderated its rigour. Under the new dispensation, Elizabeth remained excommunicated, but it was no longer incumbent on her Catholic subjects to refuse to recognize her as their Queen, "except when public execution of the said Bull becomes possible".[14] From Elizabeth's point of view, however, this scarcely constituted an improvement on the original, for it was clear that if an army of invasion landed on her shores, the Pope would still expect good Catholics to give it their assistance.

There were many English Catholics who were uncomfortable at the way that the Pope presumed to exercise a secular authority over them. In 1585, a group of prominent Catholic gentlemen, led by Sir Thomas Tresham, addressed a petition to the Queen explaining that though they thought it necessary to their salvation to have access to a priest, they would not hesitate to turn over to the authorities any priest who advocated resistance to her rule. By that time, an English army had entered the war in the Netherlands on the rebel side, and even in Catholic circles it caused profound shock when William Allen wrote a tract stating that good Catholics had no right to fight the Spanish forces there. Nevertheless, the fact remained that in a crisis Catholics could only side with the Queen by wilfully blinding themselves to the Pope's wishes. In truth, the dilemma that confronted them was too excruciating to admit of a simplistic solution, and however much they might deplore this, Catholic loyalism remained, in effect, a contradiction in terms. Even Sir Thomas Tresham, with his much vaunted protestations of fidelity, privately doubted the legitimacy of recognizing Elizabeth as his Queen.[15]

It was the more understandable that popery came to be equated with disobedience in view of the fact that by no means all priests could resist the temptation to meddle in secular affairs. When in England, Robert Parsons certainly did not confine himself to administering spiritual comfort, for after he returned to the continent, at the end of 1581, he stated that he knew that English Catholics would welcome an invasion by a foreign power "from what many had declared when he treated with them of their consciences". It was true that Parsons was an exception in this respect, and the majority of priests heeded the instructions of their superiors that politics were no concern of theirs. William Allen made much of the fact that his students were expressly forbidden to discuss "questions and controversies concerning the Pope's pre-eminence", and stressed that the rules of his seminary laid down that "no matter of depriving or excommunicating princes should be disputed, no, not so much as in generalities, and much less the particularizing of any point on our Queen's case". Allen's case was weakened, however, by the fact that he himself engaged shamelessly in political intrigue, and his ultimate ambition was to secure the overthrow of the Queen. Not only that, but in the event of an invasion of England by a Catholic power, he envisaged that the priests serving there would play an important supportive role. In 1585 he wrote confidently to the Pope, "We have now ... almost three hundred priests in the households of noblemen and men of substance, and we are daily sending others, who will direct the consciences and actions of the Catholics in this affair [the invasion] when the time comes".[16]

On 17 July 1581, Campion was captured at a country house in Berkshire and removed to the Tower of London. From there he was taken to the Lord Chancellor's residence, York House, and interrogated by Leicester and Hatton, but it is not true (as has often been said) that the Queen herself was present and personally questioned Campion. Since the Councillors were dissatisfied with his answers, they ordered that further questions should be put to Campion in the Tower, and that he should be tortured if he evaded these. In the Tower, Campion remained silent when asked where he had said mass, whose confessions he had heard, and what his opinion was of the Queen's excommunication. He was thereupon repeatedly racked and, according to one report, spikes were driven into his fingers and the nails torn out. Through it all, Campion managed to avoid making any statements that could be damaging to the Catholics. He refused to discuss matters such as the Queen's excommunication, on the grounds that he was under orders to abstain from politics, and declared himself to be "an insufficient umpire between her Majesty and the Pope for so high a controversy".[17] He insisted that on such issues his mind was blank, but neutrality of this sort was a luxury the age did not permit. On 20 November, Campion was tried for treason in Westminster Hall. Initially, it had been intended to rest the case against him on the fact that he had converted numerous people while in England, but there was clearly a loss of nerve on the part of the authorities, and in the end false evidence was concocted, alleging that he had conspired to murder the Queen. He was duly found guilty, and on 1 December he was executed at Tyburn with two other priests.

Catholic sources claimed that these hangings engendered a wave of revulsion in England, and Walsingham was quoted as having said "that it would have been better for the Queen to have spent 40,000 gold pieces than to put those priests to death in public". It was alleged that Lord Howard, who had witnessed the execution and heard Campion pray for the Queen on the scaffold, told Elizabeth that the priest had been "innocently done to death", and that the Queen had thereupon tried to shift responsibility for his execution onto the judges.[18] There is little firm evidence, however, to suggest that the Government repented of the decision to hang Campion. The following year, eleven more priests were publicly executed, and in the Parliament of 1585 the laws against the Catholics were made still more savage. Henceforward, any priest found in England could automatically be tried for treason, and the aiding of priests by laymen was likewise declared to be a capital crime.

In all, one hundred and eighty-three Catholics were executed during Elizabeth's reign. One hundred and twenty-three of them were priests, and of the sixty lay victims three were women. By no means all captured priests were put to death, for in about three out of four cases they were either imprisoned or banished. To a certain extent their fate was dependent on the political situation, for in years when national security was in the greatest jeopardy the number of victims increased. The death toll was highest in the Armada year of 1588, with twenty-one priests and sixteen laymen dying for their religion. The decision whether or not the death sentence on priests should be carried out was frequently influenced by the answers they gave to certain key questions that were put to them at their trials or after conviction, and which included a demand whether the accused would fight for the Queen in the event of a foreign invasion. This became known as the 'bloody question' by Catholics, for an incorrect answer sealed the doom of many priests, but even some of those who averred that they would resist the invading army did not escape the death penalty. In 1588, for example, John Hewett swore at his trial that he would take the Queen's part, but he was hanged, regardless of that.[19]

When priests were executed, the people who came to watch occasionally manifested sympathy for them, particularly if the victims prayed for the Queen on the scaffold. If in these cases the executioner made to cut down the victim too early, there were instances when the crowd shouted, "Let him hang!" in hopes of sparing the condemned man the agonies of being disembowelled alive. On the other hand, there were also occasions when the spectators seemed distinctly hostile towards the victims. When six priests and eight Catholic laymen were hanged at a mass execution in 1588, a crowd accompanied the prisoners to the gallows with "incessant shouts ... uttering all manner of harsh and savage abuse". If a priest was defiant on the scaffold, or refused to ask pardon of the Queen, this caused general outrage. There would then be cries of "Away with him!" and demands that the priest should at once "be hanged like the traitor he was".[20]

In general, government propaganda that the priests merited death sentences as traitors seems to have been successful, but there was clearly more unease about the tortures that were regularly inflicted on priests. The use of torture on state prisoners was in theory illegal. In his book *De Republica Anglorum*, Sir Thomas Smith stated proudly, "Torment ... which is used by the order of civil law and custom of other countries ... is not used in England. It is taken for servile". Nevertheless, in exceptional cases warrants for torture were issued, signed either by the Privy Council or the Queen herself. In the course of the reign, fifty-three such warrants were issued, authorizing the torture of more than ninety individuals. By no means all of the victims had committed offences relating to religion; in fact, twenty-one of those named in the warrants were accused of burglary or murder and, on one occasion, some gypsies were ordered to be tortured "for their practices". The torturers had a variety of methods at their disposal. Apart from the rack, which caused its victims such "insufferable agonies ... it is not possible to express, the feeling so far exceedeth all speech", there was the Scavenger's Daughter, an iron hoop that brought together its victim's head, hands and feet, so they were "rolled up together like a ball, and so crushed that the blood sprouted out at divers parts of their bodies". Equally dreaded were the manacles, from which the victim was suspended with his feet barely touching the floor, and which was described by one sufferer as occasioning "an excruciating pain that distends the limbs unbearably".[21]

Torture sessions were usually conducted or supervised by Thomas Norton, and after his death in 1584 by Richard Topcliffe or Richard Young. Topcliffe was an unspeakable sadist who was driven by a fanatical hatred of Catholics. He liked attending priests' executions, and whenever possible he gave orders that the wretched men should be cut down prematurely, so they were conscious while they were being mutilated. It would appear that while he tortured his victims, he engaged in sexual fantasies, for one of them, a priest named Pormort, caused him considerable embarrassment by recounting at his trial that Topcliffe had told him during one interrogation that "he was so familiar with her Majesty", that he had often touched her "between her breasts and paps and in her neck".[22]

The Queen knew of course that torture was used on the priests and she accepted that it was a necessity. She was personally acquainted with Norton, Topcliffe and Young and clearly valued their services. Topcliffe once joyously recalled, "Unspeakably has her Majesty bound me with her sacred conceit and defence of my credit in the desperate times I have lived". One letter from Topcliffe to the Queen does suggest, however, that she had reservations about the policy of torture, and that she had to be prodded into sanctioning it. In June 1592, Topcliffe wrote asking for permission to torture the Jesuit Robert Southwell, who had recently been apprehended, and whom he had already unsuccessfully examined once, without using violence. "May it please your Majesty to see my simple opinion, constrained in duty to utter it", he wrote in a wheedling tone. " ... It is good forthwith to enforce him to answer truly and directly, and so to prove his answers true in haste, to the end that such as be deeply concerned in his treachery may not have time to start." He went on, "If your Highness's pleasure be to know any thing in his heart", the best way was to "stand [Southwell] against the wall, and his hands but as high as he can reach against the wall", which would "enforce him to tell all, and the truth proved by the sequel". This innocuous sounding process was a euphemistic way of describing the manacles (which accordeth to Topcliffe "hurteth not"), and by dint of this grotesque misrepresentation, he prevailed on Elizabeth to let him proceed.[23]

Elizabeth's evident reluctance to permit Topcliffe to have a free hand may have arisen partly from the fact that there had already been adverse comment about the cruelties inflicted on priests while in custody. When

Campion was in the Tower, several ballads had appeared deploring the use of torture, with verses like the following:

> If instead of good argument
> We deal by the rack
> The Papists may think
> That learning we lack.

A more serious attack on government policy came in 1583, when the strongly Protestant Clerk of the Council, Robert Beale, published a denunciation of the use of torture, condemning all racking as cruel, barbarous and contrary to law and English liberties. To counteract the ill-feeling, the government issued propaganda tracts, such as *The Declaration of favourable dealing of her Majesty's commissioners for the examination of certain traitors* (which was probably the work of Thomas Norton) and *The Execution of Justice in England*, written by Burghley himself, and published in 1584. To modern ears, however, the arguments expressed here seem very thin, especially that put forward in Norton's tract that those in charge of torture sessions were under instructions to use the rack "in as charitable manner as such a thing might be". It may have been the strength of public opinion against torture in the Tower that was responsible for the increasing use of the manacles in preference to the rack, for though both caused their victims unbearable agonies, the manacles did not disfigure the body so badly, and this lessened official embarrassment when the sufferer next appeared in public. At the trial of Southwell in 1592, Topcliffe actually denied that the prisoner had been subjected to undue violence, and challenged him to produce evidence of torture. The Jesuit bitterly retorted, "Let a woman show her throes".[24]

So long as Catholic laymen did not harbour priests, they were in little danger of being prosecuted under the treason laws, but financial ruin was an ever present threat. When the law increasing the fine for recusancy had been passed in 1581, it had seemed that it might have only a limited effect, for initially it had not been rigorously implemented. The majority of recusants successfully evaded the summonses to quarter sessions where they would have been penalized for their offences, and in the first five years after the act came into force, only sixty-nine recusants had to pay fines, totalling no more than £8,938 1s 11d. Because of this laxity, in the Parliament of 1585–86 an effort was made to close up the loopholes in the penal code. Henceforth, if an alleged recusant managed to avoid being served a summons, they were deemed to have been given adequate warning of a forthcoming case against them if a notice was posted on the church door. If they failed to turn up in court, they could be convicted in their absence by proclamation, and after they had been found guilty of recusancy they could be repeatedly fined for the same offence, without further indictments. Those recusants who failed to pay their fines forfeited to the government two thirds of their lands. As a result, the yield from Catholics went up considerably, totalling £36,322 9s in the next five years, and by 1592 the sums involved were large enough to necessitate the establishment of a special recusancy department at the Exchequer. Even so, a significant proportion of recusants escaped lightly. When recusants fell behind with the payment of their fines, and hence were theoretically liable to be deprived of two thirds of their property, local juries tended deliberately to undervalue their lands, so that they forfeited less to the Crown. It has been estimated that less than two hundred people had to pay recusancy fines on a regular basis, and the worst burden fell on a few wealthy individuals who were singled out as an awful warning to others. Harsh as the recusancy laws undoubtedly were, the aim was that they should serve as a deterrent, rather than reduce all Catholics to total insolvency.[25]

The Counter-Reformation in England can be accounted a failure in that it did not reclaim the nation for the Pope, but the fact that Catholicism was not stamped out altogether demonstrates the essential limitations of the Elizabethan regime. It was true that by the end of the reign, only about one and a half per cent of the population could be accounted true Catholics, but perhaps as much as a quarter of the gentry were Romanists, as well as a smattering of the aristocracy. Life had been made so unpleasant for recusants that many of the more apathetic Catholics had been driven to conform, but a hard core remained whose devotion to their faith was only intensified by repressive measures. The sufferings of the martyrs, and of those who were brought to the verge of financial ruin, served as an inspiration rather than a warning to them, with the result that throughout the reign recusancy figures remorselessly continued to rise. There was even a school of thought that held that the severity of the penal code actually increased the number of Catholics. In 1597, one Jesuit ventured the opinion, "The rigour of the laws, and the severe execution thereof these ten or twelve years has been the foundation of our credit ... The only thing that is to be feared ... is a report about liberty of conscience at home ... What rigour of law cannot compass in many years, this liberty will effect in twenty days".[26]

It was a harsh fact that in the sixteenth century religion and politics could not be satisfactorily isolated from one another, but above all it was the presence in England of Mary Stuart that ensured that Catholicism and treason were inextricably meshed. In one of his memorandums dwelling on the dangers that faced Elizabeth, Burghley balefully described Mary as "the instrument whereby the perils do grow". Bearing in mind "the opinion of the present title that the papists allow to the Queen of Scots, and disallow the Queen's Majesty's right", Mary was clearly the principal hope of those who were working for the "recovery of the tyrannous estate to the Church of Rome". He was sure that many of them aimed at nothing less than the "eviction of the Crown of England from the Queen's Majesty", for "changing of the state of England to popery ... cannot be accomplished whilst the Queen's Majesty liveth, nor so assuredly and plausibly compassed as by placing the Queen of Scots in the seat of this crown".[27]

With the execution of the Duke of Norfolk, Elizabeth's feelings for Mary had become stonier than ever. When Mary wrote to the Queen, she refused to reply, saying shortly, "Either her letters required no answer or else she saw no cause to grant her requests". In August 1573, however, Burghley had prevailed upon Elizabeth to let the ailing Mary visit the famous spa at the Derbyshire village of Buxton, so that she could partake of the well waters there which were renowned for their curative properties, and Mary decided that this meant that there was still hope that Elizabeth would unbend towards her. In 1574, she took to sending the Queen little gifts, such as a crimson satin petticoat that she had embroidered, sweetmeats and a wig, and although at least one courtier warned that the presents might be poisoned, Elizabeth did not spurn these offerings. By this time indeed, it seemed that Mary had settled down in England, and had become accustomed to her tranquil existence as a prisoner. She whiled away her time by reading and doing endless embroidery, and surrounded herself with pets, which helped to enliven the tedium of her captivity. Behind her apparent resignation, however, lay hope: she confided to a correspondent that she was looking forward to the day that Elizabeth died and she succeeded her as Queen, "which I will wait for patiently, without getting myself into any trouble".[28]

Inevitably, however, as the years passed and Elizabeth showed no sign of obliging her by dying or setting her free, Mary's patience wore thin, and plots and intrigues began to take up more of her time. She hoped that the Duke of Guise would be willing to act as her deliverer, and wrote feverish letters to France, exhorting her relatives there to action. From time to time this secret correspondence fell into Walsingham's hands, alerting him to her designs, and obviously such discoveries were hardly calculated to soften Elizabeth's attitude towards her prisoner. Indeed, in 1578, when an ambassador from France ventured to speak in Mary's favour, the Queen burst out that Mary was "the worst woman in the world, whose head should have been cut off years ago", and she added that Mary "would never be free as long as she lived".[29]

By now it seemed that the King of France had resigned himself to the fact that Mary would remain in permanent detention. He even sent Elizabeth a message that he was "well pleased she keep the Scottish Queen as safely as she will", so long as Mary was "treated with honour and courtesy". Elizabeth could justly claim that she fulfilled this proviso, for Mary was held in conditions of some grandeur. Officially, she was allowed thirty servants to attend to her needs, but this number was not rigidly adhered to, and in 1584 her household numbered forty-eight people. At meals, she was served two courses consisting of sixteen dishes each, and these generally included "four or five dishes of the daintier sort". Other creature comforts were not neglected: the Earl of Shrewsbury reported that each year the household consumed over £1,000 worth of wine, spices and fuel. Naturally enough, Mary still felt she had cause for complaint. Her letters were full of protests that the accommodation provided for her was damp and draughty, that she wasn't allowed to employ extra servants to look after her when she was ill, or that she was prevented from moving residence as frequently as was desirable, so that the house she was currently occupying became smelly and insalubrious through over-use. Nevertheless, as it could be plausibly asserted that Mary had not been "so well entertained, when she lived at her own will in her own country",[30] Elizabeth saw no reason to treat her with greater generosity.

In truth, the Queen begrudged every penny spent on Mary's maintenance, and did her best to shift the burden onto the shoulders of the luckless Earl of Shrewsbury. When Mary had first been entrusted to his care, Shrewsbury had been assigned an allowance of £52 a week, but despite the fact that this sum failed to cover his expenses, in 1575 his weekly stipend had been reduced to £30 a week. Shrewsbury complained that he spent more than twice this amount keeping Mary and her retinue, but for all his protests his allowance was further cut in 1580. Walsingham remonstrated that it was madness to alienate Shrewsbury in this way, and that "to have so special charge committed to a person discontented, everybody seeth it standeth no way with policy",[31] but the Queen would not listen.

Ideally Walsingham would have liked Mary to be put in the care of a more rigorous custodian than Shrewsbury, who would be more efficient at preventing her from secretly communicating with the outside world. Certainly vigilance over Mary was more necessary than ever, for in Scotland her son James was nearing maturity, and the attitude he took towards his mother would clearly have a crucial bearing on Anglo-Scots relations. By the time he entered his teens, James had grown into a gawky boy with slightly bulbous eyes, and now that he was reaching the age where he could assert himself as an independent force in Scottish politics, he might well decide that his mother had been badly treated, and that he should redress the wrongs that she had suffered. As yet, his outlook was undefined. He was immensely erudite, having been taught by the stern Calvinist scholar George Buchanan, but although he had been brought up as a Protestant, there could be no certainty that he would not one day turn his back upon the Kirk, and restore Catholicism in Scotland. His intentions in this regard were all the more difficult to fathom because, having been surrounded since infancy by self-seeking nobles, who had used him as a pawn in their struggles for power, he had been well-schooled in duplicity. Understandably, perhaps, he prided himself on his cunning, for as king of an impoverished and small country that was in constant danger of succumbing to foreign domination, honesty was not a quality that he could put at a very high premium.

James was at pains to declare himself well-disposed to Elizabeth, but no reliance could be put on his words, for it soon emerged that he was equally prodigal in his professions of friendship to her enemies. When James was barely fifteen, Lord Hunsdon commented that Elizabeth would learn to her cost "that the King's fair speeches and promises will fall out to be plain dissimulation, wherein he is in his tender years better practised than others forty years older than himself". As an expert dissembler herself, Elizabeth had no intention of being taken in by a novice at the art: on one occasion she scornfully cautioned James, "You deal not with one whose experience can take dross for good payment, or one that easily will be beguiled; no, no, I mind to set to school your craftiest counsellors. I am sorry to see you bent to wrong yourself in thinking to wrong others".[32] Nevertheless, the bewildering shifts and upheavals that characterized the Scottish political scene made it more difficult for her to control its wayward young king, and Elizabeth could not overlook the possibility that one morning she would awake to find that she had been outwitted by this provoking teenage upstart.

James's impressive academic accomplishments, and his hard apprenticeship in the tortuous by-ways of Scots politics had left him with an overweening belief in his own cleverness, but his loveless and austere childhood had left him marked in other ways. All his life he craved the affection of glamorous members of his own sex, a susceptibility that was first revealed when his cousin Esmé Stuart, Sieur d'Aubigny, came over from France to Scotland in September 1579. Utterly captivated by this handsome older man, the thirteen-year-old James made no attempt to hide the pleasure he took in his company. From Berwick Lord Hunsdon disapprovingly reported that James was "in such love with him [Stuart] as in the open sight of the people oftentimes he will clasp him about the neck with his arms and kiss him".[33]

Moral considerations aside, the English had good reason to be concerned at d'Aubigny's ascendancy, for he was believed to be a Guisan agent who had been instructed to convert James to Catholicism and draw him into dependence on France. At the end of 1580 Elizabeth's alarm increased immeasurably when the Anglophile Earl of Morton, who had acted as Regent in the last years of James's minority, was suddenly arrested on trumped up charges of complicity in the murder of the King's father. The

Queen cautioned James not to proceed any further against Morton, but was unable to decide whether it would be best to restrain him by sending an army across the border, or despatching commissioners who could restore stability in Scotland by peaceable means. In the end she did nothing, and Morton was executed on 2 June 1581. Shocked to find that James could be so ruthless, the Queen was overheard muttering, "That false Scotch urchin for whom I have done so much! . . . .what can be expected from the double dealing of such an urchin as this?"[34]

In France, the partisans of Mary Queen of Scots were delighted by d'Aubigny's meteoric rise, which was capped by James creating him Duke of Lennox in August 1581. Mary's ambassador in France, the Archbishop of Glasgow, saw to it that a Jesuit priest named Father William Creighton was despatched secretly to Scotland to sound out Lennox about his willingness to become the deposed Queen's champion. When approached by Creighton, Lennox indicated that provided he could count on the financial and military support of the Pope and Philip of Spain, he would be prepared to lead an army to England to liberate Mary and restore the Catholic religion. Creighton then returned to France and secured an undertaking from the Duke of Guise that he would mount an invasion of southern England at the same time as Lennox attacked from the north. Armed with these assurances, he next set out for Rome to solicit papal aid, while his fellow Jesuit, Father Robert Parsons, travelled to Spain in hopes of obtaining King Philip's support for the venture. Meanwhile, Lennox wrote secretly to Mary, telling her of the plans that were afoot. "Courage!" he concluded. "I ask nothing of you, only that if this enterprise be successful your son should still be acknowledged as king".[35]

By the summer of 1582 intimations had already reached England that Lennox was meditating hostile action. In June Walsingham's somewhat shadowy suspicions were given substance when a Jesuit priest disguised as an itinerant tooth drawer was stopped by English border officials as he was making his way to Scotland. Having been searched, he was allowed to go on his way, but his equipment was confiscated, and a closer inspection of a looking glass that he had been carrying revealed that letters to Lennox concerning the so-called "Enterprise of England" were secreted within it. In the circumstances it was hardly surprising that Elizabeth was willing to listen when approached by disgruntled Scots nobles who resented Lennox's pre-eminent position with the King. She avoided giving them any written undertakings, but sent verbal assurances that she would reward them if Lennox was overthrown, and as a result, on 22 August 1582 James was seized by a clique of nobles who went under the name of the Lords Enterprisers. After lingering for some months in hopes of rescuing the King, Lennox was forced to leave Scotland the following December.

To guarantee that James was kept under firm control, both Burghley and Walsingham urged the Queen to give generous subsidies to the Lords Enterprisers, but once Lennox had fallen she proved reluctant to pension those who had so conveniently wrought his eclipse. Elizabeth's ambassador in Scotland, Robert Bowes, commented irritably "that this present husbandry shall at length be found like the housewifry of Calais", but though at this time it does seem that the Queen was being excessively careful of her money, she could at least allege sound reasons for her parsimony. Having driven Lennox away, the Lords Enterprisers had started to fall out among themselves, and this made it more likely that before long James would manage to shake off their tutelage and rule his country as he saw fit. While the situation in Scotland remained so liable to fluctuation, Elizabeth feared she might be squandering money to no purpose if she subsidized the Lords Enterprisers, and she began to wonder if it would not be better to stabilize Anglo-Scots relations by using Mary Stuart as the medium through which she could achieve an understanding with James.

The idea came from Mary herself. In the autumn of 1581 she had informed Elizabeth that James was anxious to secure her blessing for his continued tenure of the throne in Scotland, and she had warned the Queen that even if the English tried to prevent her from reaching an agreement with her son, "this matter ... shall by other means be brought to pass". To Elizabeth it seemed highly plausible that a combination of filial instincts and self-interest should make James desirous of being on better terms with his mother, and she was anxious that the pair of them should not reach an accommodation without reference to her. Accordingly she had sent Robert Beale to discuss the matter with Mary, with the result that in April 1582 the Queen of Scots had suggested that a tripartite treaty should be concluded between Elizabeth, James and herself. She proposed that although she would remain in England, she and James would be recognized as joint sovereigns of Scotland, and providing that Elizabeth agreed to treat her more honourably than in the past, she would recognize her as Queen and ensure that James upheld the Protestant religion in Scotland.[36] Elizabeth had lost interest in these proposals after James had been seized by the Lords Enterprisers but, about the spring of 1583, she had devoted fresh thought to the matter, ruminating whether perhaps, after all, a settlement along the lines Mary had proposed would be beneficial to all concerned.

In May, Sir Walter Mildmay was entrusted with the task of conducting negotiations with Mary. His own opinion was that Elizabeth should seize this chance of settling her differences with her cousin, but just when agreement seemed within reach, the Queen drew back. On paper Mary's promises looked fine enough, but Elizabeth was not happy to take it on trust that Mary would abide by them for, as Walsingham remarked, "where the faith of contractants is doubtful, there is it hard to make sound foundation of any contract".[37] Elizabeth was still hesitating when, at the end of June 1583, James transformed the situation in Scotland by escaping from the Lords Enterprisers' clutches. The indications were that now that he was again a free agent, James would pursue a policy hostile to Elizabeth, and in these changed circumstances she could see no point in trying to do a deal with him such as that which had been earlier explored. The talks with Mary were indefinitely suspended, and the chances that this painful saga might have a happy ending once again diminished.

Mary stormed and wept at the injustice of it all, but that autumn Elizabeth received confirmation that, even while she had posed as an instrument of concord, Mary had been engaged in practices against her dearest sister's state. Despite the downfall of Lennox, Walsingham had remained convinced that England was still the target for a Catholic-inspired invasion. Stray bits of intelligence kept reaching him, concerning a projected enterprise but, although he had no doubt that the menace was very real, he remained in ignorance as to the direction from which the attack would come. Speculating that the King of France was behind it all, Walsingham had the French embassy watched, and in this way he learnt that one Francis Throckmorton was in the habit of visiting it under cover of darkness. Spies were set upon Throckmorton and, in November 1583, after he had been under surveillance for six months, Walsingham ordered his arrest. When the government agents burst into his house, Throckmorton dashed upstairs to destroy a letter that he was even then writing to Mary Stuart, but a list of ports and havens that an invading fleet could use remained in evidence against him, and Walsingham felt sure that after a thorough interrogation the young man would yield up full details of any design against Elizabeth.

Incarcerated in the Tower, Throckmorton sent word to a fellow conspirator that he would "endure a thousand deaths rather than accuse anyone", and even when handed over to the rackmaster, he remained as good as his word, refusing to divulge under torture anything of consequence. Walsingham bided his time, quietly confident that if forced to undergo a second session on the rack, Throckmorton's endurance could not last. "I have seen as resolute men as Throckmorton stoop, notwithstanding the great show he hath made of Roman resolution", he commented knowingly. "I suppose the grief of the last torture will suffice without any extremity of racking to make him more conformable than he has shown himself".[38]

This proved to be the case. Next day, Throckmorton was again strapped to the rack, but "before he was strained up to any purpose", his resistance gave way. He made a full confession, admitting that he had been told by his contacts in France that the Duke of Guise was planning an invasion of southern England, which had as its object the depriving of Elizabeth "of her crown and state", and the substitution of Mary in her place. Guise was still waiting to hear whether the Pope and Philip of Spain would provide him with support, but Throckmorton explained that the Duke was confident that it would be forthcoming, for Philip's ambassador in England, Mendoza, had insisted that the venture would receive Spanish backing. When Throckmorton had learnt all this, he had established contact with Mendoza (who was directing the conspiracy from the English end), and at his request had drawn up the list of ports and havens that had been found at his house. He had also written to Mary, telling her of the plans to mount an invasion in her favour. The Queen of Scots had replied that she was already aware of these, and had asked Throckmorton to assist the cause by sounding out the degree of support that could be expected from the English Catholics when Guise led his army ashore.[39]

Throckmorton suffered at Tyburn for his treason, and the Earl of Northumberland (brother of the man who had led the Northern Rebellion fourteen years before) committed suicide in the Tower after he was accused of being involved in the conspiracy. As the government was well aware, however, the real impetus behind the plot came from overseas, and one of the most disturbing aspects of the case was that it revealed just how determined Elizabeth's foreign enemies were to settle ancient scores. There was, perhaps, some comfort to be derived from the fact that the King of France had had no part in the design for, despite the fact that the projected invasion was to be led by the Duke of Guise, Henry III had been kept in ignorance of all that was being planned. The Spanish, however, had been so deeply compromised that it was no longer possible for Elizabeth to maintain diplomatic relations with a power whose ambassador had spent so much time plotting her overthrow. On 19 January 1584, Mendoza was summoned before the Council and told to pack his bags, but he appeared not in the least abashed at being caught out in this outrageous breach of diplomatic convention. Insolently he blustered, "Don Bernardino de Mendoza was born not to disturb kingdoms but to conquer them".[40]

Elizabeth was filled with cold anger to find that, even while negotiations had been on foot to secure Mary's liberation, the Queen of Scots had been seeking "to provoke the Pope and other foreign potentates to attempt somewhat against us and our realm".[41] Surprisingly, however, Mary's complicity in the so-called Throckmorton plot did not mean that no more was heard of the proposals that she should be allowed to share the Scottish throne with her son. Rather, the very evidence of her duplicity once again highlighted the dangers that arose from detaining her in England against her will, and made an amicable settlement seem more attractive. Besides, Elizabeth was obsessed by a nagging fear that James was working underhand to reach an accommodation with his mother, and she thought it imperative that, if an agreement was made, she should be a party to it.

In May 1584 Mary was again given to understand that Elizabeth would approve if she resolved her differences with James by a process of carefully supervised negotiation. By the autumn, Mary appeared to have genuine grounds for optimism, for it was agreed that her secretary could go to the English Court in order to expound to the Queen the terms which Mary believed could form the basis of any settlement. His visit coincided with that of an emissary from the Scottish court named Patrick, Master of Gray, a young man who had formerly been in the service of Mary's ambassador to France, but who had recently returned to Scotland and successfully ingratiated himself with James. Naturally Mary thought it a good sign that James had chosen as his representative someone who had formerly been in her own employ, but a cruel disillusionment awaited her. Her faith that James would ultimately prove himself "a natural child, who would recognize all duties to his mother",[42] was understandable enough, in view of James's past readiness to convey her loving messages and promises of devotion, but she had been mistaken in thinking that these denoted a sincere attachment to her. In reality, James felt no warmth for a mother he could not remember ever having met, and he had only feigned affection for her because he calculated that she would abstain from stirring up trouble for him in Scotland so long as she supposed that he was solicitous for her welfare. Having just begun to taste the joys of wielding supreme power, James was not enamoured of the idea that he should now share it with a woman who meant nothing whatever to him as an individual. He was much more interested in reaching an understanding with Elizabeth that excluded Mary, and it was for this purpose that he had sent Gray on his mission. Despite the latter's earlier connection with Mary, James knew Gray would have no qualms about disavowing her if he deemed it advantageous to do so.

For Elizabeth, who had been completely taken in by Mary's oft-averred insistence that she and her son "were all one, that both are to be had or none", it came as an agreeable surprise to perceive that James was prepared to do business without raising any awkward questions about his mother's status. "We begin to conceive some good hope of the Master of Gray's negotiation", Walsingham excitedly confided to a colleague in December 1584. " . . . The Association between that Queen and her son, so constantly avowed . . . is now discovered not to be so forward as was given out to serve her turn". Having returned to Scotland, Gray was able to declare to Elizabeth that James's goodwill was now "such to your Majesty as though he were your natural son", and he gave her a categoric assurance that there was no longer any prospect that the Scottish sceptre would be placed under dual control.[43]

For some weeks Mary was kept in ignorance that her only child had thus cast her off, but in March 1585 she was undeceived when James himself wrote to inform her that he thought it utterly futile to seek an alliance with one who – as he callously put it – was "captive in a desert". To the wretched Mary, her son's defection came as a shattering blow, and she gave vent to her anguish in a heart-rending missive to the Queen. "Alas! was ever a sight so detestable and impious before God or man, as an only child ... despoiling his mother of her crown and royal estate?" she demanded emotionally. One thing, however, was plain from the letter: whereas a lesser woman might have been driven to distraction by the ignominious collapse of precious maternal delusions, Mary had plenty of fight left in her. She set it on record that as it now seemed unlikely that she would find a saviour in Scotland, she would again turn her eyes to the continental powers to achieve her deliverance. If James persisted in his perfidy, he would incur her perpetual malediction, and by depriving him of her goodwill, she would not only render his present position in Scotland more precarious, but would ensure that his eventual chance of succeeding to the English throne became impossibly remote. "In all Christendom I shall find enough of heirs who will have talons strong enough to grasp what I may put in their hand", she snarled at Elizabeth, undeterred by the possibility that the Queen would treat her still worse for adopting this position. Savagely she stormed that she knew her outspokenness might prompt Elizabeth to order her execution, "But as to any fear or apprehensions of such like accident, I would not take a single step, or say a single word more or less; for I had rather die and perish, with the honours such as it pleased God I was born to, than by pusillanimity to disgrace my life by prolonging it by anything unjust and unworthy of myself and my race". The only way in which she qualified what was in effect an open declaration of hostility was to say that she would never condone an assassination attempt on Elizabeth, for she claimed to abhor "more than any other in Christendom such detestable practices and horrible acts".[44] Time, however, would reveal that this was not really the case, and that her hatred for Elizabeth was untrammelled by any such reservation.

Although untruthful, Mary's denial that she harboured murderous intentions was certainly not irrelevant for, as the scale of persecution against the Catholics climbed higher, so the danger that Elizabeth might fall victim to an assassin rose in proportion. With the steady widening of the ideological rift between the churches, political theory had begun to be modified to an extent where even regicide, which previously had been branded the zenith of iniquity, could be condoned by the highest authorities. In 1580, an English gentleman had sought the opinion of the papal Secretary of State, Cardinal Como, as to whether it would be a sinful act to murder Queen Elizabeth. After conference with the Pontiff, the Cardinal had mellifluously pronounced, "Since that guilty woman of England rules over two such noble kingdoms of Christendom and is the cause of so much injury to the

Catholic faith, and loss of so many million souls, there is no doubt that whosoever sends her out of the world with the pious intention of doing service, not only does not sin but gains merit". Nor was the official endorsement of terrorist acts confined to the Vatican: in May 1583 the Spanish ambassador had hinted to Philip II that the Duke of Guise was thinking of having Elizabeth murdered and, when a few weeks later the diplomat wrote to confirm that Guise had indeed been contemplating a "deed of violence" against the Queen's person, Philip nonchalantly annotated the letter, "It was thus I believe that we understood it here; and if they had done it, it would have been no harm".[45]

In the hopes of obtaining forewarning of any proposed attacks on Elizabeth, the secret service was expanded and given greater financial backing so that, whereas in 1582 Walsingham had received only £750 to spend on an espionage network, within four years the sum set aside for it had risen to approximately £2,000. It was subsequently claimed that Walsingham had agents stationed "in above forty several places" throughout Europe, but one effect of this was merely to exaggerate the dangers that faced Elizabeth. Many of the men who entered the secret service were dubious characters from the fringes of the Elizabethan underworld who had turned into professional scaremongers in the hopes that there was money to be made from the peddling of sensational information. Because of the difficulties of verifying intelligence, the most outrageous reports sometimes gained credence: in December 1583, for example, the Queen told the French ambassador (apparently in all seriousness) "that there were more than two hundred men of all ages who had conspired at the instigation of the Jesuits ... to kill her".[46]

Such reports may have been excessively alarmist, but it was impossible to dismiss them as wholly imaginary. In November 1583, for example, a crazed Warwickshire gentleman named John Somerville was apprehended on his way to London after he was overheard shouting that the Queen was "a serpent and a viper" and "that he meant to shoot her through with his dag [pistol], and hoped to see her head set on a pole". The lethal results that could sometimes be achieved by a solitary fanatic were graphically illustrated in July 1584 when William of Orange was mortally wounded at his town house in Delft by a Catholic serving man named Balthasar Gerard. Even while Protestant England was still reeling from shock at the sudden snuffing out of the great Dutch leader, there came a disturbing report from the Netherlands that a friar had been overheard praising the way that a Burgundian had eliminated Orange, and opining confidently, "Another Burgundian will not be wanting to kill that wicked woman".[47]

The Queen professed not to be intimidated by the possibility that a violent end awaited her. At an audience granted to a deputation from the Netherlands she proclaimed firmly, "They are seeking to take my life, but it troubles me not. He who is on high has defended me until this hour, and will keep me still, for in Him do I trust". This was the line she consistently took in public utterances on the subject, but her ministers were sometimes shown a different side of her character, when she expressed a desire to eschew provocative policies on the grounds that they put her life in still deeper jeopardy. Thus, in the spring of 1586, she told Burghley that her desire to withdraw her troops from the Netherlands stemmed from her fear that their presence there made it more likely "that somewhat will be attempted against her own person".[48] Just how much such worries troubled her is difficult to assess. Undoubtedly her nerves *were* frayed by the feeling of being constantly stalked, and by the knowledge that death might be waiting for her in the most innocuous guise as she took the air in the privy garden, or made her way to chapel. On the other hand she was not above exploiting the concern for her safety to achieve her own ends: when troubled about a prospective course of action, she could always claim that it would result in her life being forfeit, and her councillors could scarcely brush aside this argument without appearing callous and disloyal.

Whatever her inward fears, she would not allow the pervasive presence of danger to impose on her a more restricted way of life. She acknowledged that "there be no cause why I should willingly come amongst multitudes, for amongst many some may be evil", but she throve too much on public adulation to seclude herself from all but a privileged circle of intimates. God would preserve her, she constantly averred, preferring to rely on the protective powers of Providence than to adopt security measures which would have left her less vulnerable to sudden assault. If she went for a stroll, as she would do often when she was residing out of London, her retinue consisted mainly of ladies, and those gentlemen who did accompany her were "but slenderly weaponed". Even indoors, danger might lurk, for anyone who was suitably dressed had the right of entrance to the outer apartments of the royal palaces, and it was impossible to be certain of the loyalty of those who were permitted still nearer the Queen. Leicester thought that at the very least Elizabeth ought to remove the right of access to court from all those who were suspected of papist leanings for, though he acknowledged that many of them would draw the line at murder, he believed "there is no right papists in England that wisheth Queen Elizabeth to live long, and to suffer any such in her court cannot be but dangerous".[49] To his regret the Queen would not issue the necessary orders, and in the absence of any proper vetting procedures the councillors could only nervously survey the jostling horde of gentlemen that thronged the galleries at Whitehall or Hampton Court, and wonder how many killers lurked within the crowd.

The perils that surrounded the Queen were not without their compensations, for fears for her safety only enhanced her loyal subjects' devotion to her. In 1583, just after the exposure of the Throckmorton plot, the French ambassador accompanied Elizabeth to Hampton Court, and he was much impressed by the multitude of people who turned out to acclaim her on the way. They knelt as she passed, wishing her "a thousand blessings, and that the evil disposed who meant to harm her be discovered and punished as they deserved". The Queen appeared touched, frequently pausing to thank them for their affectionate demonstrations, and as she observed drily to the ambassador, "She saw clearly that she was not disliked by all". It was perhaps to be expected that Elizabeth's courage in the face of danger should arouse such crude emotions in the masses, but even in more sophisticated social circles, feelings ran very high when the Queen's safety was at stake. In 1585 a Member of Parliament was so relieved when he heard that another murder plot had been foiled before Elizabeth came to any harm that he noted solemnly in his journal, "It makes my heart leap for joy to think we have such a jewel. It makes all my joints to tremble when I consider the loss of such a jewel".[50]

In view of the Queen's reluctance to be "more circumspect of her person", an indirect means of safeguarding her had to be found. However easy it might be to kill Elizabeth, there might be fewer volunteers for the task if there was reason to believe that her murder would be an act of utter futility. At present, if Elizabeth was done away with, Mary looked set to ascend the throne, a prospect so inviting to the Catholics that it was no wonder that there were desperate men amongst them who would resort to murder in order to make it a reality. To reduce the temptation, it would be necessary to convince them that if they sought to deliver themselves from the scourge of Elizabeth, Mary would be unable to come forward as their saviour, a state of affairs that could only come about if Mary's survival was made dependent upon that of the Queen.

At a Council meeting of 19 October 1584, Burghley produced the document that was intended to deal with the problem. At its inception this instrument (which became known as the Bond of Association) had been no more than a declaration to the effect that any wicked person who procured the death of the Queen would be ineligible to inherit the throne. However, successive revisions by Burghley and Walsingham had broadened its scope and made it more indiscriminate in the application of its penal powers. The final draft provided not only that such a person would be put to death, rather than merely disabled from wearing the crown, but stated that the penalty would be enacted even if the party concerned was unaware that a murder plot had been formed with the object of elevating him or her to the throne. Furthermore, the retribution that was to be exacted for such a murder bid was to extend unto the next generation, for the signatories of the Bond undertook to "act the utmost revenge" on the heir of the pretender to the throne. Thus it was that the measure, which as originally envisaged would have been directed primarily against Mary (although her name was nowhere mentioned in the text) was adapted to comprehend James as well, for while the latter's commitment to Protestantism was so shaky, he stood to benefit from Elizabeth's elimination by Catholic conspirators almost as much as did his mother.

Whatever the injustices of a system whereby Mary and James would be punished for their inability to restrain their followers, rather than for actions of their own, Burghley believed the emergency to be too great to allow of a more equitable arrangement. His colleagues agreed. With the exception of William Davison (a somewhat ironical one as events were to turn out), all the Council put their names to the deed, binding themselves "to prosecute . . . to death", "as well by force of arms as by all other means of revenge", not only those directly involved in a murder attempt on the Queen, but also "any that have, may or shall pretend title to come to this crown by the untimely death of her Majesty so wickedly procured". Their pledge was in no sense a secret undertaking, for Burghley was anxious to harness for propaganda purposes the public sense of outrage at the terrorist threat, and realized that the Bond provided him with a fine symbolic means of demonstrating national solidarity on this issue. Within twenty-four hours of the Council having signed the Bond, "divers good and well-affected subjects" had already petitioned for permission to do likewise, and Walsingham also sent copies to leading noblemen throughout the country, accompanied by a pointed suggestion that all loyal subjects would surely wish to subscribe to so "necessary and dutiful" an instrument.[51]

It is clear that in some circles there was unease about endorsing a measure which showed scant respect for the rights of individuals as established in common law. Sir John Harington recorded that when the Bond was set before a gathering of Somerset Justices of the Peace, some were heard "whispering . . . in mislike of it", and it was only after the waverers had been cautioned that it would be "a thing ill taken by the state" if they withheld their support that all present agreed to sign. Obviously it was difficult for conscientious objectors to the Bond to register their dissent, but although there is no way of knowing how widespread such incidents were, it does seem that the Somerset JPs were atypical in their commendable upholding of libertarian principles. Certainly in other areas the Bond elicited an overwhelmingly positive response. Thousands queued up to attest their devotion to the Queen, vowing destruction to her enemies with exemplary fervour. In some places special church services were organized, where gentlemen knelt bareheaded to take the oath, and in York so many seals were fastened to the document that it became too bulky to send by post. There was comparable enthusiasm elsewhere, for although it had been originally intended that only those in the upper echelons of society should be signatories, public interest was so widespread that in some counties the list of subscribers included even illiterates who had bound themselves by their mark. The Queen subsequently claimed that all this time she had been unaware of the Bond's existence, but after all the names had been gathered, the sheaves of subscribers were exhibited to her at Hampton Court, and she accepted the offering gratefully as a "perfect argument" for her people's "true hearts and great zeal to my safety".[52]

The Queen of Scots was also shown a copy of the document so that she could be left in no doubt that she would be engulfed in the wave of vengeance that would sweep England if any harm came to Elizabeth. With grim satisfaction, Walsingham instructed her custodian to have "some good regard . . . both to her countenance and speech after the perusing thereof",[53] but if he had hoped that Mary would be abashed to see what primitive passions had been aroused in the name of the Queen's safety, he was in for a disappointment. Far from being discomfited, with typical aplomb Mary appended her own name to the document.

The reaction to the Bond had been all that the Council could have wished, but they conceived of it as being no more than an interim measure, which would be superseded when its principles were translated into statute. At the end of November 1584, Parliament assembled, and three weeks later a bill designed to avert violence against the Queen was given its first reading in the Commons. In some respects it was a milder measure than the original Bond, for while the heir of the individual who inspired an attack on the Queen was still debarred from acceding to the crown, there was no obligation to pursue him to the death, as the Bond had required of its signatories. Yet even this diluted version was too strong for the Queen's liking. With the visit to England of the Master of Gray there were grounds for thinking it wise to make a distinction between Mary and her son, and certainly this was a far from opportune moment to try and menace James. At Elizabeth's request, the clauses under which a claimant's heir could be penalized were "clean dashed out".[54]

Against Mary, however, the same stern temper prevailed. Even while the bill was being redrafted to take account of Elizabeth's objections, the need for deterrent legislation was underlined when another murder plot came to light, causing all the more sensation because this time a member of the House of Commons was accused of being behind it. Today it seems obscure whether Dr William Parry really did intend to kill the Queen. Certainly he had talked of doing so when travelling on the continent, but on his return to England he had seen the Queen and told her that he had merely posed as an assassin in order to penetrate Catholic circles overseas, and that his real aim had been to spy on her enemies. Elizabeth was impressed, and rewarded him with a pension, but this failed to cure Parry of the habit of engaging in talk unbecoming in a loyal subject. He sounded out an associate as to whether he would be willing to despatch the Queen, possibly intending to gain kudos by denouncing the fellow if he expressed any interest in the project. As it turned out, however, it was Parry himself who was entrapped after his suspicious activities were reported, and though at his trial he fiercely proclaimed his innocence, he was convicted and sent to the gallows.

In the overwrought atmosphere caused by Parry's arrest, the revised bill for the Queen's safety had an easy passage through Parliament. In its final form it established the legal machinery by which Mary Queen of Scots was subsequently tried, stating that if Elizabeth's life was sought "by or for" a claimant to the throne, not less than twenty-four commissioners were to examine the evidence against that person. If they reached an unfavourable judgement, the individual concerned was to be disabled from inheriting the throne, and if found to be assenting and privy to the plot then it would be incumbent upon all subjects "by all forcible and possible means [to] pursue to death every such wicked person".[55]

Elizabeth's tears for Alençon had flowed all the more freely in the knowledge that his death would put her under fresh constraint to intervene in the Low Countries. With the murder of the Prince of Orange in 1584, the pressure on her became greater still, for the rebel provinces were now leaderless and disunited, and the military outlook for their forces was dire. In the autumn of 1584, the major town of Ghent fell to the Spaniards, leaving the great commercial centre of Antwerp menaced by the same fate. For some months Elizabeth clung to the hope that Henry III would take over his dead brother's responsibilities in the Netherlands, for she had reached the stage where she would have actually been thankful to see a King of France installed as sovereign of the Provinces if he had thereby relieved her of the necessity of taking on the Spaniards herself. At the end of February 1585, however, Henry had definitely rejected the Dutch offer to make him their king, and Elizabeth had reluctantly to face the fact that she alone could stand in the way of the Spaniards' relentless advance.

On 24 June 1585 commissioners from the Netherlands arrived in England, bearing that offer of sovereignty that had so recently been hawked around France. This Elizabeth would by no means accept, for she was determined that her role in the Low Countries would be confined to that of trustee, intending merely to look after the Provinces until such time as King Philip showed himself sufficiently cognizant of his responsibilities to be reunited with his property. For the moment, however, the Low Countries had to be kept out of his hands, and it seemed that Elizabeth had finally come to terms with the fact that it was she who must become protectress of the States. When the Dutch commissioners implored her aid, she replied with the confidence that came from years of seasoned mendacity, "It is not my custom to procrastinate, and upon this occasion

I shall not dally ... but let you have my answer very soon". For once it seemed that she would be as good as her word. Admittedly, the Council had to work hard to disabuse her of the notion that it would be enough to give the States underhand aid in the form of money and munitions, but when they formed up to her in a solid phalanx, she abandoned this last line of resistance.[56] To the end she haggled unmercifully with the commissioners, baulking at the number of troops they were asking her to send, but her hard bargaining was understandable in view of their reluctance to give her adequate security that the expenses she incurred in their defence would ever be reimbursed. The States' record in such matters was not good, for in the past they had failed even to keep up with the interest payments on loans she had underwritten for them. Negotiations were not protracted unduly as a result of her quibbling, for on 10 August, a little less than six weeks after she had first received the commissioners, the Treaty of Nonsuch was signed.

The agreement came too late to avert the fall of Antwerp, which had surrendered three days earlier. The news only arrived at court on 15 August, but though "greatly troubled" – for she had delayed sending a relief force to the beleaguered city after being assured that it would withstand a much longer siege – it apparently only redoubled her determination to shore up the rebel cause.[57] Within a fortnight she agreed to increase the number of troops that were to be sent to the Netherlands, so that under the final terms of the agreement, she was to provide at her own expense 5,000 foot soldiers and 1,000 cavalry, as well as garrisons to man the 'cautionary' towns of Flushing and Brill that were to be handed over to the English until such time as the Dutch indemnified them for their military expenses.

The first detachments of troops left for the Netherlands on 16 August under Colonel John Norris, but the Dutch had made it plain that as soon as possible they wished a great English nobleman to be put in overall command. During his lifetime William of Orange had succeeded in preserving some semblance of unity in the Provinces by working untiringly to counteract the divisive effects of localism, class conflict and religious passion which had sapped the will to resist the Spaniards from the start. Unfortunately, rapid disintegration had followed on his death, for he alone had possessed the ability to weld into an effective war machine the competing interest groups that made up the power structure in the Netherlands. The problems of raising money for the struggle or forcing through administrative decisions were compounded by the fact that the deputies in the States General had to refer back for authorization at local level before raising taxes or agreeing to innovations. Orange had been incomparable at manipulating this unwieldy constitutional system, but a loss of direction had become apparent as soon as he was no longer there to massage sensitive egos and inflame patriotic sentiment. The very commissioners who came to negotiate the Treaty of Nonsuch admitted that the government of the Provinces abounded with "confusion, fraud, negligence and disobedience, to great advantage of the enemy", and they were adamant that only a great magnate from England would possess the necessary authority and prestige to sort out the general anarchy.

From the start, the Earl of Leicester was the favourite candidate for the post of commander-in-chief. It was true that he had not been on military service since Mary Tudor's reign, but not only did he fit the bill as "one of the greatest account in England", but there was no doubting his enthusiasm for a cause of which he had been the foremost exponent at Court for well over a decade. By 28 August he had heard that the Queen had decided that he was the man for the job, and with great gusto he threw himself into warlike preparations, fitting himself out with expensive suits of armour and steel saddles that would protect him and his horses from enemy fire. He arranged for these and other necessaries to be conveyed to the Netherlands in a specially commissioned fleet of merchant ships, but within days there were ominous signs that all this bustle had been uncalled for. Not unnaturally, Leicester's wife had come up from the country to help him to make ready, and the flurry caused by her unexpected arrival in town caused such "great offence" to the Queen that she talked of stripping the Earl of his command. This fit of pique did not last, but was succeeded by a more fretful turn of mind, for the constant worries of recent weeks had told upon her health, and at such a juncture she was loth to be parted from her favourite. Leicester described to Walsingham how the Queen had come to see him "and used very pitiful words to me of her fear she shall not live", and though the Earl had made strenuous efforts to comfort her, his consolatory words made precious little impact. She remained so troubled that at the end of September she sent him a message in the middle of the night, instructing him to suspend his preparations altogether, plunging Leicester into a state of utter despair. "This is one of the strangest dealings in the world", he burst out to Walsingham. "... What must be thought of such an alteration! For my part I am weary of life and all".[58]

With the coming of daylight the Queen relented, and the relieved Leicester could once again concentrate on equipping himself out in the style of a true warlord. For the moment, however, he was still unable to leave England, for the States had not yet ratified the Treaty of Nonsuch, and the Queen had no intention of letting her general go beyond the seas till she had received official confirmation that they would abide by each and every clause that she had had inserted in its text. It was unfortunate that the vessel bearing the countersigned treaty was detained in the Netherlands by adverse winds, for this only accentuated the Queen's conviction that she was dealing with a people who were as unreliable as they were disobedient. In October, Walsingham was disconcerted to hear that the Queen was making known to all sorts of people "the great mislike she hath of her own resolution taken in this cause of the Low Countries". Having failed to persuade Leicester to remain with her because she was in less than rude health, she came to see his imminent departure in the light almost of a betrayal, treating him so disagreeably that his morale inevitably began to droop. To Walsingham, Leicester was driven to complain, "Her Majesty I see will make trial of me how I love her and what will discourage me from her service, but resolved I am that no worldly respect shall draw me back from my faithful discharge of my duty towards her, though she shall show to hate me, as it goeth very near, for I find no love or favour at all".[59]

One reason for Leicester's dejection lay in the fact that Elizabeth was adamant that his official position in the Netherlands should be no more than Lieutenant-General of the Queen's forces, a somewhat misleading term considering that the Earl was not meant to concern himself with military matters alone, but was also supposed to supervise the general conduct of affairs in the Provinces. Behind the Queen's insistence on this point there was a purely personal element: already her misgivings at the way Leicester's new responsibilities had enhanced his self-esteem had caused her to burst out that in going abroad he sought rather his "own glory than her true service", and if granted higher office she feared his pride would become insufferable. But there were also weighty political arguments to justify the prohibition, for if Leicester accepted a more inflated title it would imply that she regarded him as her viceroy in the Netherlands, which would amount to a tacit avowal of sovereignty over the Provinces. Yet she had taken the utmost pains to stress that the English presence there owed nothing whatever to territorial ambitions. In October she had published a "Declaration", insisting that in sending aid to the oppressed people of the Low Countries, "We mean not ... either for ambition or malice ... to make any particular profit to our self or to our people". She wanted only to deliver the inhabitants from the Spanish army of occupation and to obtain "a restitution of their ancient liberties and government by some Christian peace, and thereby a surety for ourselves and our realm to be free from invading neighbours".[60] Her war aims, indeed, could hardly have been more modest, for she hoped that once the Spaniards found they were no longer making progress in the Netherlands, they would become discouraged and seek a negotiated settlement within the year. Titular recognition of the sort Leicester desired would be incompatible with these limited objectives, and would give an air of permanence to the English presence in the Netherlands that the Queen wanted above all else to avoid.

It is true that Leicester could put forward cogent reasons why he needed the added *gravitas* that a more imposing style of address would bring. His instructions stated blandly that he must "use all good means to redress the confused government of those countries", by limiting the number of people who had a say in the formulation of policy, and insisting that "the deputies of the several provinces may have authority to consult and conclude" without the constant reference to local assemblies that at present hampered the conduct of the war.[61] But these were large reforms, which could hardly be pushed through by one whose standing in the Provinces was ill-defined, and it was questionable whether Leicester would be able to achieve anything of the sort unless he occupied a position of the greatest eminence. These arguments did not move the Queen. She reiterated that Leicester must cut through the confusion, but would not let him take on the authority that might have facilitated his task.

Thus, when Leicester finally sailed for the Netherlands on 8 December 1585, accompanied by the "flower and chief gallants of England", he was ranked only as the Queen's Lieutenant General, but he could at least console himself that he travelled in a style that befitted a great prince. Nearly seven hundred cavalry went with him, and a hundred ships were needed to take over his baggage and train, which included a troop of actors who would enliven his leisure hours. When the fleet anchored off Flushing it was given a tumultuous welcome, and having landed Leicester embarked on a triumphal progress through the major cities that remained in the rebels' possession. At Middleburg armed bands of burghers lined the streets, discharging volleys of shot as Leicester passed through their serried ranks. Fireworks and bonfires were lit in his honour, and towards the end of his stay, the town treated him to a great banquet, where the "sugarworks and devices" that adorned the high table were pronounced "most brave and sumptuous" by one appreciative English gentleman. The story was the same elsewhere: on Leicester's entry into The Hague, the streets were decked out in material covered in Tudor roses, and the galleries that overlooked the city's main thoroughfare were occupied by maidens who prostrated themselves as Leicester went past. Not to be outdone, Leiden put on seven different pageants in the Earl's honour, including one in which the city itself was portrayed by "a fair maiden", menaced by various allegorical figures. After fending off their attacks for as long as she could, she rushed from the stage and took refuge under Leicester's cloak, and the Earl entered into the spirit of the festivities and "led her to his lodging".[62]

The Earl was overcome by the adulation accorded him. "Never was there people I think in that jollity that these be", he commented enthusiastically a few days after his arrival. From Delft he wrote lyrically, "There was such a noise, both here, at Rotterdam and Dordrecht in crying 'God Save Queen Elizabeth' as if she had been in Cheapside". His elation had not had time to subside when on New Year's Day 1586 a deputation from the States-

General presented themselves at his lodgings at The Hague, and pressed him to accept the title of Governor General of the Netherlands. A mere three weeks' absence from the Queen had so emboldened Leicester that he felt ready to defy her express prohibition against doing any such thing, trusting that if he presented her with a *fait accompli*, her acquiescence would follow. Having accepted the States' invitation on 14 January, he wrote sunnily to Burghley, "It is done for the best, and if so her Majesty accept of it, all will be to the best". The following day he was inaugurated in his office at a solemn ceremony.[63]

In his letter to Burghley, Leicester had said that he planned to send William Davison to England to explain to the Queen why he had acted as he did, but unaccountably he dallied. Davison did not leave The Hague until late January, and then he was further delayed when adverse winds at Brill prevented him from sailing to England. He only reached London on 13 February, by which time the news had already percolated all over the Court, and Elizabeth had learnt of Leicester's disobedience from other sources.

She had reacted with an eruption of such fury that all past outbursts of temper seemed mere tremors in comparison. She was consumed with anger at the way that Leicester, whom she had felt able to count on as "a creature of our own", should not only have deliberately flouted her wishes, but had then justified himself to Burghley and others, while keeping her in the dark. Contrary to Leicester's calculations, she resolved to deal firmly with this insubordination: on 10 February she gave instructions to Sir Thomas Heneage that he was to go to the Netherlands and inform Leicester that he must publicly resign the honour that had been wrongly bestowed on him. Heneage was also to deliver to Leicester a blistering letter from the Queen, lambasting him for his violation of her orders. In biting phrases the Queen let fly at Leicester: "We could never have imagined, had we not seen it fall out in experience, that a man raised up by ourself, and extraordinarily favoured by us above any other subject of this land, would have in so contemptible sort broken our commandment, in a cause that greatly toucheth us in honour; whereof although you have shewed yourself to make but little account ... you may not think we have so little care of the reparation thereof as we mind to pass so great a wrong in silence unredressed".[64]

One of Leicester's cousins wrote suggesting that he try and appease the royal anger by splashing out on "some rare thing for a token to her Majesty", but the Queen had passed the stage when even the most expensive propitiatory offering could have won her over. Burghley and Walsingham were doing their best to calm her down but, apart from persuading her to delay for a few days Heneage's despatch, their soothing words made no impression. When Davison eventually arrived at Court, she would not listen to his explanations, and merely railed at him "in most bitter and hard terms". Her rage was only exacerbated by a report that the Countess of Leicester was planning to join her husband in the Netherlands accompanied by "such a train of ladies and gentlewomen, and such rich coaches, litters and side saddles as her Majesty had none such". Wildly the Queen shouted "with great oaths, she would have no more courts under her obeisance than her own", and if Lady Leicester had intended to go abroad (which Leicester's supporters denied), her plans had to be quickly shelved. Even so, on 6 March the Earl of Warwick sadly informed his brother that the Queen's "rage doth increase rather than any way diminish ... Her malice is great and unquenchable"[65], and she categorically refused to modify Heneage's instructions before sending him on his way.

On 14 March Leicester had to endure "matter enough to have broken any man's heart" when he stood by as Heneage informed the Council of State in the Netherlands that their Governor General would have to resign his title. The Council of State wrote begging the Queen to reconsider, assuring her that Leicester's elevation in no way conflicted with her repudiation of the sovereignty, for it was the sovereign will of the Dutch people that had conferred the position on him in the first place. At home, Burghley remained tenacious in Leicester's defence, going so far as to threaten to resign if Elizabeth persisted in making him lay down the title. In the face of such entreaties, Elizabeth began to soften, and at the end of March she agreed that Leicester should continue to be designated Governor General "until we shall consider what further order were meet to be taken in that behalf". Sir Walter Ralegh sent Leicester the comforting information, "The Queen is in very good terms with you, and thanks be to God, well pacified, and you are again her 'Sweet Robin'".[66]

A month later, however, she suddenly worked herself into another rage, and went back to her former ruling that Leicester should be demoted. Once again Burghley and Walsingham remonstrated, saying it was "both perilous and absurd" to discredit the Earl in this way, and again the Queen backed down. Utterly worn out by the Queen's contrariness and inconsistency, Burghley told a colleague, "This matter hath been more cumbersome and more severe to me and others ... than any whatsoever since I was a counsellor".[67]

The Queen was being difficult in other ways. Despite the fact that Walsingham thought that she herself was "daily more and more unapt to embrace any matter of weight", she refused to let the Council debate matters relating to the Netherlands, obviously fearing that it would result in unpalatable advice. She also became incensed when she learnt that Heneage had sought to remove the bad impression created in the Netherlands by her treatment of Leicester by assuring the States-General that she would never make peace with Spain without their assent. This was scarcely a very controversial statement, for in a subsidiary clause to the Treaty of Nonsuch the Queen had given an undertaking to this effect, and besides at the beginning of April she had actually written to Heneage empowering him to assure the States, "that we for our part are resolved to do nothing that may concern them without their own knowledge and good liking". By the end of the month all memory of this appeared to have been erased from her mind. Indignantly, she rebuked Heneage for exceeding his orders, writing, "It is enough that I injure not their country nor themselves in making peace for them without their consent ... I am utterly at squares with this childish dealing".[68]

The truth was that Elizabeth's longing for an end to the war had grown so intense that she would have considered peace terms which the States-General would never have endorsed. She had been delighted to hear from Burghley that an Italian merchant who resided in the Netherlands had offered to act as an intermediary if she wished to sound out the Duke of Parma's attitude to peace talks. Throughout the spring and early summer of 1586, Elizabeth remained hopeful about the outcome of this unofficial initiative. Even when the merchant warned that Philip would never accept peace conditions that gave freedom of worship to the Protestants in the Netherlands, Elizabeth appeared unconcerned. She declared that she would not expect him to grant a wider degree of toleration than he could square with his conscience, a statement which could have been taken to mean that Philip need make no concessions whatever in the religious sphere.[69]

Rumours soon reached the Netherlands that the Queen was contemplating making a peace underhand, but though Leicester complained that this gave rise to mistrust and adversely affected his relations with the States-General, Elizabeth persevered with her informal approaches to Parma. The results, however, proved disappointing. She had hoped that Parma would respond by giving some indication of the terms that Philip would regard as an acceptable basis for a negotiated settlement, but Parma was not prepared to commit himself so far. In a letter which he wrote to the Queen in June 1586, he made it plain that it was she who must make the first move by formally suing for peace, and then he would do his best to see that Philip was amenable. Unwilling to cast herself in the role of supplicant, Elizabeth wrote back fiercely, "We hope our actions have not led the world to believe us of so base a mind as to seek him who has first offended us", and for the moment she regretfully abandoned her hope of an early peace.[70]

The Queen's anxiety to entice the Spaniards to the negotiating table was the more understandable in view of the fact that the war in the Netherlands was proving even more ruinously expensive than she had anticipated. Elizabeth had estimated that it would cost her just over £126,000 a year to maintain her expeditionary force, but this figure was rendered obsolete when Leicester learnt that men were being awarded a lower rate of pay than had been given to those who had served in the Irish wars, and he had accordingly upgraded it without reference to the Queen. Even so, Elizabeth's outgoings in the Netherlands should have totalled no more than approximately £134,000 a year, but in fact they were considerably greater; indeed, in the period between the signing of the Treaty of Nonsuch and October 1586, she paid out £20,000 over and above this sum.[71]

Where the money went was a mystery, but certainly not much of it reached the soldiers. The majority of these were impoverished wretches who had been pressed into the army and sent overseas against their will, despite the fact that this was technically an infringement of their rights. By law, every able-bodied Englishman between the ages of sixteen and sixty was liable for service in the militia, but a statute dating from the reign of Edward III stated that no one was to be obliged to serve outside his county except in time of foreign invasion. If the Government had abided by this ruling, the army would have been hopelessly undermanned, for the common soldier's lot was so unenviable that there were few volunteers for military service abroad. Pay was irregular, for instead of being paid on a weekly basis, soldiers had to manage on bare subsistence wages, known as imprests, until such time as the Treasurer-at-War received a large enough sum from England to give them the balance of what was owed them. Since privates had to feed and clothe themselves while on active service, this system hit them hard. In March 1586, Leicester painted an affecting picture of the condition of his men: "There is much due to them. They cannot get a penny; their credit is spent; they perish for want of victuals and clothing in great numbers".[72]

But none of this was the Queen's fault. It was unfortunate that she had refused to send out a Treasurer-at-War to the Netherlands until the States-General had ratified the Treaty of Nonsuch, for as a result a large backlog of pay had built up by the time Leicester arrived, but thereafter Elizabeth made great efforts to pay off the arrears. It was difficult for her to understand why the soldiers remained in such penury in March, for £52,000 had already been sent out to supply their wants, but in view of Leicester's urgent pleas for money a further £24,000 was then despatched. This should have been sufficient to bring the men's wages fully up to date, but failed to do so; consequently another £45,000 was sent out in August, and a further £30,000 followed in October, but still the situation was not brought under control.[73]

The reasons why the money failed to go so far as was expected were manifold. Apart from the forces that the Queen had agreed to maintain, there were additional companies of Englishmen serving in the Netherlands whom the States-General should in theory have supported. In fact, some of the money that the Queen sent out was diverted to pay for the upkeep of these men. Furthermore, these companies had been transported to the Netherlands at English expense, on the understanding that the States General would make prompt recompense for the levying costs, but in fact the States put off paying what was due. When pressure was applied, they said they had discharged their obligations by advancing money and supplies to the Queen's troops, but the inadequate records they had kept of these transactions meant that the Treasurer was unable to amend his accounts accordingly. Indeed, the prevarication and evasiveness of the States was such that the Treasurer was moved to comment hotly that his dealings with them were "the greatest pain of all my service besides."[74]

Nevertheless, it was the Queen's own subjects who defrauded her the most, for at every level of the army corruption was rife. The Queen's forces were customarily split up into companies of up to one hundred and fifty men, and among the worst offenders were the captains who were in charge of these units. The wages for an entire company were always entrusted to its captain for distribution, but frequently he doled out only a small portion of the money, and pocketed the balance himself. In June 1586 Leicester claimed that several captains "do owe all their whole wages for soldiers", and that the more experienced they were, the worse they fleeced their men. Another of their swindles was to make out that there were more men in their company than was really the case, so that there were no deductions made for depletions in the ranks caused by death or desertion. In August 1586 it was reported that some companies had been numbered at one hundred and fifty heads, when a third of that figure was the true amount. It was even alleged that some captains deliberately exposed their men to unnecessary dangers so that they could appropriate their wages after they were killed. It would have been easier to expose such abuses if regular musters could have been held, but the men were meant to be paid after each muster and, as they would have grown mutinous if dismissed empty-handed, it was impossible to assemble them if the money supply was low. Even when musters did take place, captains frequently managed to bribe the muster-masters to accept their inflated estimates of manning levels, or filled up the gaps in their ranks by paying "churls" to masquerade as soldiers.[75]

It had been specifically laid down in Leicester's instructions "that the abuses of captains and their under officers be narrowly looked into and severely punished", but he proved completely unequal to the task. Indeed, when one muster-master rigorously checked the captains' faulty assessments, and paid them only what they could prove they were entitled to, the officers complained to Leicester, and he ordered his subordinate to hand over much of the money that he had withheld. Towards the end of his life Leicester confessed, "I ... have always lived above any living I had", and certainly he showed no greater sense of financial restraint as

Governor General of the Netherlands than he did in the handling of his private affairs. He blamed everyone but himself for the mismanagement and peculation, being especially scathing about the Treasurer-at-War. Accordingly the Queen summoned the Treasurer home and mounted an enquiry into his dealings, but the accounts were so confused that it proved impossible to work out whether he was at fault, and Elizabeth thought it unfair to dismiss him without proof that he was guilty of embezzlement. "You know my old wont that love not to discharge from office without desert. God forbid", she told Leicester, when sending the man back out to the Netherlands.[76]

The Queen was much troubled to learn of the privations endured by her servicemen as a result of the dishonesty of their superiors, telling Leicester, "It frets me not a little that the poor soldier, that hourly ventures life, should want their due, that well deserve rather reward". By the autumn of 1587 Elizabeth was said to be "greatly grieved" on learning that many of the men who returned from the Netherlands were "in lamentable case", and that October she had a chance to see their plight for herself when thirty bedraggled soldiers waited outside the Court gates to complain of lack of pay. "To stay the report of any more to come to Court to offend her Majesty, they were dismissed with sharp speeches", and threatened with the stocks, but the Queen did give orders that two of them should be permitted to air their grievances before the Council. She was sufficiently disturbed by what emerged to demand that there should be further enquiry. As a result, the following December the Council decreed that, if there were any others in the latest batch of conscripts who had been discharged without receiving their wages, "they should, upon their repair to Court, be fully satisfied thereof".[77]

As the Queen well knew, however, matters would never be truly set to rights unless she could check the fiddling and malversation that went on in the Netherlands. This greatly preyed on her mind. One afternoon in June 1586, when ill health had confined Burghley to his bed, she appeared at his chamber door and proceeded to berate him about "her charges in the Low Countries". Burghley reported to Walsingham, "I had much pain ... to satisfy or rather pacify her Majesty's discontent", for though he had pointed out that there had been great efforts made to tighten up the financial administration of the war, Elizabeth remained convinced – and rightly, as it turned out – that the reforms were "not sufficient to stay the errors". "I had long speeches hereof, too long for me to write, for I was fully wearied at this speech", Burghley concluded glumly.[78]

The Queen's anguish was the more understandable because already the involvement in the Netherlands was putting a severe strain on the national finances. In 1585 Parliament had made a generous grant of taxation, payment of which was to be spread over three years. As a result £9,000 was collected in 1585, and a further £90,000 came in the following year, but in 1587 the Queen had to apply to Parliament for another subsidy even before the final instalment of the previous one had arrived in the Exchequer. Again Parliament was responsive, but the Queen still had to top up their contributions by delving into the surplus of almost £300,000 that she and Burghley had laboriously accumulated in the years of peace. By the end of 1587 it was down to £154,000, and it was clear that if the war lasted much longer, nothing whatever would remain. Nor could Elizabeth console herself that her subjects would cheerfully pay for the shortfall when her savings were no longer available: already in July 1586, Walsingham had warned Leicester, "Our people in this realm, by the malicious practices of the ill-affected, begin to murmur at the wars".[79]

Well might the Queen exclaim of the war, "It is a sieve, that spends as it receives to little purpose", for despite all the money lavished on her forces, Leicester was making little headway in the Netherlands. The military outlook had not improved, for he had been unable to prevent Parma from capturing several strategically important towns, and besides this he had landed himself in political difficulties by falling out with the States-General. The Queen's angry disavowal of Leicester after he had accepted his title at their hands certainly contributed to the waning of their confidence in him, and moreover they were undoubtedly a very difficult body of men, but Leicester handled them with so little finesse that relations between them soon became unnecessarily fraught. "I did never deal with such heady people as these States are", he testily complained when they held up proposals that he favoured. Instead of trying to wear down their objections, he allowed his manner to become choleric and dictatorial, declaiming furiously that he would never let himself be "overbearded by these churls and tinkers".[80] Having failed to secure their co-operation, he took to working with a faction of religious extremists, but his new protégés only exacerbated his problems by their antagonistic attitude towards all those who did not subscribe to their own peculiarly rigid brand of Calvinism. To make matters worse, the States claimed that Leicester had exceeded his rights by appointing these men to positions of high trust without their consent.

In the circumstances the Queen could be forgiven for becoming frantic when Leicester told her in July that the only way of gaining better results to the war would be to accept the sovereignty of the Low Countries and send a still larger quantity of troops there. "This doth marvellously distract her and make her repent she ever entered the action", Walsingham reported, but the recent collapse of all peace initiatives did at least force her to acknowledge that it was both self-indulgent and impractical to adopt so unconstructive an attitude. She remained adamant that she would never take on a responsibility that would bring with it only perpetual war and enormous expense, but she did her best to see that Leicester was not unduly demoralized by her refusal, and in an affectionate letter she sent on 19 July, she even came close to apologizing for the way that her vagaries and idiosyncrasies had made his task more complicated. "Rob", she opened fondly, "I am afraid you will suppose by my wandering writings that a midsummer moon hath taken large possession of my brains this month, but you must needs take things as they come in my head, though order be left behind me". Having explained that she was sending out Thomas Wilkes to help him with his administrative difficulties, she tenderly concluded, "Now will I end, that do imagine I talk still with you, and therefore lothly say farewell . . . though ever I pray God bless you from all harm and save you from all your foes, with my million and legion thanks for all your pains and cares. As you know, ever the same, E.R."[81]

Buoyed up by the Queen's affectionate words, in September 1586 Leicester laid siege to the Spanish-held town of Zutphen, and it was in a skirmish outside its walls that his nephew Sir Philip Sidney was fatally wounded. Sidney had never been a personal favourite of the Queen: not only had he annoyed her by writing an outspoken letter advising her against marriage with the Duke of Alençon, but he had also incurred her displeasure by identifying himself too closely with the Protestant cause in the Netherlands in the years when she had hoped it would be possible to remain out of the war there. As recently as July, Walsingham, whose daughter Frances was married to Sidney, had noted that the Queen was "very apt upon every light occasion to find fault with him". Nevertheless, although she had never felt great affection for him, she had valued Sir Philip as an asset to the Court, and had been pleased when he used his poetic talents to pen a graceful entertainment in her honour, or outshone all challengers in the tiltyard, arrayed in armour of blue and gold. At first it had been thought that there was good hope that Sidney would recover, and in relief the Queen had at once written him a comforting letter in her own hand, but subsequently the wound had putrefied, and death was unavoidable. Elizabeth was greatly distressed, as she never failed to be when her courtiers were killed on active service. At the outset of the Netherlands campaign she had actually tried to minimize such casualties by sending a directive that "the young gentlemen of best birth" should be "spared from all hazardous attempts", but commendably this had been ignored. "Much afflicted with sorrow . . . for the loss of her dear servant, Sir Philip Sidney", the Queen's disenchantment with the war was only increased by his death.[82]

There was indeed little reason to feel optimistic about the situation in the Netherlands. In September Wilkes had returned to England painting an appalling picture of the mess Leicester had made of things. Hitherto, Elizabeth had been inclined to lend an ear to Leicester's allegations that the States-General were being wilfully obstructive, but this latest report left her in little doubt that it was the Earl's own tactlessness and incompetence that was largely to blame for the sorry state of affairs. At the end of the month, Wilkes was sent ricochetting back to the Low Countries bearing a letter from the Queen castigating her Governor General. Having rebuked him for quarrelling with his subordinates and for choosing advisers who had infringed the very constitutional privileges of the Netherlands that she had been called in to protect, she told him not to irritate the States any further, "for that they be wise men". Leicester was naturally downcast to find himself the object of such censure: he remarked that he could hardly do worse than to be thought "careless, negligent and improvident in so weighty a place and service as your Majesty hath placed me; to cast away your people and vainly consume your treasure". Nevertheless, he knew that it would take more than this to eradicate the Queen's affection for him, and having made some attempt to defend his record, he concluded, "My trust is that the Lord hath not quite cast me out of your favour".[83]

In this he hoped aright, for although his lacklustre performance had proved all too clearly that the Queen had grievously overestimated his abilities, in the final analysis he could always count on her indulgence. For all his failings, she longed to see him again, for not only was she missing him badly but she had an underlying fear that his health would not stand up to a second winter in the damp and marshy Low Countries. She therefore willingly agreed when Leicester asked if he could have a period of leave, and on 15 November the Earl began his homeward journey, leaving Lord North to carry on the struggle against Spain in his absence. Safely back in England, Leicester wrote complacently to a colleague, "Never since I was born did I receive a more gracious welcome".[84] It was not only the Queen who had been pleased to see him, even though in normal circumstances Burghley and Walsingham might have urged that Leicester should remain at his post until things began to go better in the Netherlands. Just now, however, they wanted him back at home, so that he could support them in what was now the dominant issue of the day – to wit, whether the Queen should agree to the execution of Mary Queen of Scots.

By the spring of 1585, no one remained under the delusion that Mary Stuart would manage to regain her Scottish crown through diplomatic processes, and since Elizabeth now had to assume that she would have Mary on her hands for years to come, she took steps to make her cousin's confinement more secure. Nine months earlier, Sir Ralph Sadler had relieved the Earl of Shrewsbury as Mary's custodian, but this had been no more than a temporary measure, and for some time Elizabeth had been looking for a replacement. Although Lord St John had been pressured to take the post, no amount of coercion could induce him to do so, but eventually Elizabeth found a viable alternative in the forbidding shape of Sir Amias Paulet, an austere Puritan who took charge of Mary in April 1585. Mary was upset not only that she had been entrusted to a man of "no higher quality than a knight", but also because when Paulet had been English ambassador in France ten years earlier, he had been involved in a plot to kidnap her agent in Paris, Thomas Morgan, and Mary correctly inferred from this that Paulet's attitude towards her was one of settled enmity. It was not long before her forebodings proved justified, for within days of his arrival Paulet (whom Mary was to describe as "one of the oddest and most *farouche* men I have ever been acquainted with") was arousing resentment because of the "rigours and alterations" he imposed on Mary's household. He forbade Mary's coachman to go on excursions without his permission, and would not allow her to give alms to poor people in the neighbourhood, an injunction that Mary thought "barbarous".[85]

Despite these precautions, Paulet still thought that the security arrangements at Tutbury (the dilapidated Staffordshire stronghold where Mary had been incarcerated since February) remained inadequate, for there were several laundresses on the staff who lived outside the castle walls, and he was worried that Mary might suborn them to smuggle her secret correspondence. He warned that "unless the women be also stripped unto their smocks" every time they passed the gates, he could not undertake to prevent this, but he ruefully agreed that considering how many soldiers were about, it would hardly "be comely" to subject the washerwomen to this indignity as regularly as he would wish. In December 1585, however, the problem was solved when Mary was moved to another house in the neighbourhood, Chartley, within whose moated precincts the laundresses could be safely lodged. Triumphantly Paulet declared, "I cannot imagine how it may be possible for them to convey a piece of paper as big as my finger".[86]

Despite Paulet's proud assurances, Walsingham was not happy. Experience showed that however closely she was supervised, Mary was adept at opening up secret channels of communication with the outside world. Should she succeed in doing so, he had no doubt that she would use this means to foment rebellion and destabilize the realm and, if he remained in ignorance of what she was about, a conspiracy in her favour might catch him unprepared. In the circumstances he thought that, instead of leaving Mary to her own devices, it would be advisable to arrange for her to have a controlled outlet of correspondence, as this would enable him to monitor all her intrigues.

In December 1585, one Gilbert Gifford travelled to England from France, and on landing he was at once apprehended and taken to see Walsingham. This man, whom one acquaintance described as "the most notable double and treble villain that ever lived", had already had a chequered career. Having been expelled from the English seminary at Rheims, he had for a time led a reprobate life on the continent, before being readmitted to the college and becoming a deacon in the Catholic Church. After that he had gone to Paris, where he had been taken up by Mary's agent Thomas Morgan, and had agreed to take over to England various letters on Morgan's behalf. Nevertheless, when confronted by Walsingham, he undertook to work for him instead, for as one of nature's turncoats, who "played upon all hands in the world",[87] he had no qualms about changing allegiance time and time again.

On Walsingham's instructions, Gifford went to the French embassy, the repository of much correspondence intended for Mary, for those who wished to communicate secretly with her invariably sent their letters there, in the hope that the ambassador would find a way of forwarding them to their rightful destination. In the past year a great deal of mail had accumulated there, for the protective shield erected around Mary had worked so well that nothing had managed to penetrate it, but Gifford claimed he had devised a foolproof method of delivering letters undetected, and offered to act as courier. The ambassador agreed to test the system, and at the end of January 1586 Mary was delighted to receive a letter from him, the first unauthorized communication to have reached her for more than a year. She replied at once, urging the ambassador to put full trust in Gifford, and thenceforth this was the pipeline that was used to convey all secret correspondence to and from Chartley.

Mary was not aware that whenever Gifford was entrusted with letters from the French embassy, he at once delivered them to Walsingham's office. There a crack decoder, Thomas Phelippes, deciphered them, and once their contents had been ascertained, the originals were handed over to another expert, Arthur Gregory, whose speciality was re-sealing letters with such precision that it was impossible to tell that they had been tampered with. Meanwhile Gifford had ridden north, and once he was in the neighbourhood of Chartley, the freshly made-up packet was rushed to him by express messenger. Then the letters, encased in a little wooden box, were given to the local brewer, who slipped them into one of his barrels and carried them into Chartley when he delivered the weekly consignment of beer. There they were retrieved by the cellarmen, and given to Mary's secretary, and from thence they reached the hands of the Queen of Scots herself. When Mary replied to any communication that had reached her in this way, the whole process worked in reverse. Blissfully oblivious that every letter she sent or received passed under Walsingham's scrutiny, Mary made free use of the system. In London, meanwhile, the Secretary, who could justly congratulate himself on the ingenuity of these arrangements, sat back and awaited results.

In May 1586 a seminary priest named John Ballard travelled to Paris to see Don Bernardino de Mendoza, who had been accredited Spanish ambassador to France after his expulsion from England. Ballard told Mendoza that there was a plot afoot to murder Elizabeth, and asked what assistance the English Catholics could expect to receive from Spain, if they took up arms against their Queen. Mendoza gave the priest an encouraging reply, and Ballard thereupon returned to England and sought out Anthony Babington, an immensely rich and well-born young Catholic, who had occasionally acted as a delivery boy for Mary in the days when she had been in the Earl of Shrewsbury's custody. Ballard informed Babington that a Spanish invasion was planned for that summer, and that to assure its success it would be necessary to kill Elizabeth. The priest revealed that one John Savage had already undertaken to murder her, but he and Babington agreed that the plot would have more chance of working if Savage was assisted in the task by five other gentlemen. When the attack was to be mounted on Elizabeth, Babington would be waiting near Chartley with a hundred supporters so that Mary could be swiftly freed from captivity. Throughout June, Babington gathered together a group of associates he could rely on, and consulted with them as to the best way of despatching the Queen. Though no final plans were made, it was agreed that it would be possible to ambush Elizabeth in her coach, or as she rode or walked in the park, or even in the Presence Chamber itself.[88]

By the beginning of July, the plot had reached a stage where Babington thought it possible to take Mary into his confidence. Accordingly he wrote to her, addressing her as "My dread sovereign and Queen", and informing her that he and his confederates would do all in their power to assist the projected invasion. He left Mary in no doubt about the fate that lay in store for Elizabeth, for he declared, "For the despatch of the usurper, from the obedience of whom we are by excommunication of her made free, there be six noble gentlemen, all my private friends, who for the zeal they bear to the Catholic cause and your Majesty's service will undertake that tragical execution."[89]

This letter reached Mary just at the time when she learnt that her son had so completely abandoned her that he had concluded an alliance with Elizabeth in return for receiving an annual pension of £4,000. Until then Mary had still cherished a flicker of hope that James might repent of his behaviour towards her, but this treaty extinguished that last fitful spark. Her secretary subsequently deposed that the news afforded her "the greatest anguish, despair and grief with which I have ever seen her seized", and her tormented state of mind made her the more inclined to sanction the desperate measures that Babington had delineated. On 13 July she sent him a message that she was still cogitating on his letter, and would reply to it as soon as possible. When deciphering this note for Walsingham,

Thomas Phelippes wrote gloatingly, "We attend her very heart at the next".[90]

On 17 July Mary replied as fully as even Phelippes could have wished. In a businesslike tone, she stated to Babington that there were various preconditions that must be fulfilled before he and his associates made any move. Having calculated exactly how much support their rebellion would receive from the English Catholics, they must work out a foolproof way of setting her free, and it was only after they had received the most categorical assurances of foreign aid that they should set about arming their followers. Having dealt with these preliminaries, Mary came to the heart of the matter: "The affairs being thus prepared and forces in readiness both within and without the realm, then shall it be time to set the six gentlemen to work, taking order, upon the accomplishing of their design I may be suddenly transported out of this place".[91]

By 19 July Phelippes had a transcript of all this, and he wrote to Walsingham that since Mary had incriminated herself beyond recall, there was no point in further delaying Babington's arrest. He was anxious that Babington should be apprehended before he had time to burn Mary's letter, for then, "If it please God to inspire her Majesty with that heroical courage that were meet for avenge of God's cause and the security of herself and this state", it could be used in evidence against Mary at her trial.[92] Walsingham nevertheless dared not move too fast. He thought it misguided to arrest Babington until the names of the six would-be regicides had been uncovered for, if they remained at large, they might strike down the Queen before their identities had been wrung out of the ringleader of the conspiracy. To solve this dilemma Walsingham instructed Phelippes to add to Mary's "bloody letter" a forged postscript, purporting to be from Mary herself, asking Babington to tell her who the six gentlemen were. It was an unfortunate, if understandable move, for the fact that Walsingham had not scrupled to amend the letter in this way later gave rise to unfounded allegations that it had been still further tampered with, and that those passages in which Mary authorized the murder of the Queen were not genuine, but had been subsequently interpolated by Phelippes.

The letter reached Babington on 29 July, but possibly the forged postscript aroused his suspicions, for in his reply to Mary he gave no clue as to the names of his accomplices. He was still more alarmed when Ballard was taken into custody on 4 August, for though it was given out that he had been arrested simply because he was a priest, Babington rightly divined that this meant the net was closing around him. Feeling that time was running out, Babington went to Savage and urged him to murder the Queen that day. Savage declared himself willing, but said that he could not go to Court at once because his clothes were so shabby that he would be denied admission. At this Babington gave him his ring to sell, saying that Savage could buy a new suit on the proceeds. Before Savage could strike, however, Walsingham acted. In order to keep track of Babington, the Secretary had ordered one of his agents to befriend him, and Babington was unsuspectingly dining in a tavern with his new acquaintance when a message came from Walsingham that he was to be arrested. By chance, however, Babington caught a glimpse of these instructions, and so, without taking his rich sword and cape, he nonchalantly left the table on the pretext that he was going to settle the bill. Once out of sight, he managed to make his escape.[93]

It was nevertheless impossible for him to remain at large for long. Ballard by now had revealed the names of all the conspirators, and a nationwide manhunt was set in progress. The authorities were aided by an extraordinary act of hubris on the part of Babington, for in the belief that there should be a fitting "memorial of so worthy an act as attempting her Majesty's person", he had commissioned portraits of himself and his six main accomplices, and copies of these were now posted all over England. Desperately, Babington fled London, and in a bid to avoid recognition "sullied the natural beauty of his face with the rind of green walnuts", [94] but on 14 August he was nevertheless found skulking in the thickets of St John's Wood. Next day he was carried in triumph to London, passing through crowds of jubilant citizens who rejoiced and lit bonfires to celebrate Elizabeth's escape.

Noting the depth of feeling against the conspirators, the Queen began to wonder whether wickedness of such an order did not merit a still more terrible penalty than the standard form of punishment for treason. She had some reason for thinking that public opinion would be gratified if the most refined cruelties were inflicted on the prisoners for, when William Parry had been accused of plotting to murder her in 1585, two members of Parliament had petitioned that the normal procedure for traitors should be modified to ensure that his death should be both hideous and lingering. At the time the Queen had not seen fit to grant the request, but in the present climate of opinion she thought it appropriate that truly excruciating torments should be devised for Babington and his associates. She told Burghley that in view of their "horrible treason against her . . . own person", she desired that after their conviction, "the manner of their death for more terror be referred to her Majesty and her council". Burghley was against this departure from precedent, not on humanitarian grounds, but because he saw it as a wholly unnecessary innovation. Although the prescribed punishment for treason was that of hanging, drawing and quartering, on the whole the victim was allowed to hang until unconscious or even dead before being disembowelled. As Burghley pointed out, however, if the sentence was interpreted literally, the offender died in the most fearful agony. To Hatton he explained carefully, "I told her Majesty that if the fashion of the execution shall be duly and orderly executed, by protracting of the same, both to the extremity of the pains in the action, and to the sight of the people to behold it, the manner of death would be as terrible as any new device could be".[95]

Somewhat reluctantly, the Queen accepted his advice, and in the event Burghley was proved correct. When Babington and his six principal accomplices were publicly executed on 20 September, the hangman saw to it that their sufferings were frightful, for the wretched men "hanged never a whit" before they were taken down and had their "privities cut off and ... bowels taken out alive". Ironically, it turned out that the Queen had overestimated the ferocity of her people, for the spectators registered "some note and touch of the cruelty", and made it plain they could not stomach such savage butchery. As a result, when a second batch of conspirators were executed the following day, the Queen gave orders that they should not be taken down and mutilated until they were dead.[96]

Elizabeth had made a dreadful example of Babington and his followers but, in the opinion of the Council, the revenge exacted on these men would be meaningless unless the Queen of Scots was also made to pay for her part in the conspiracy. To their relief it appeared that this time Elizabeth was prepared to instigate formal proceedings against her cousin. To prevent Mary from destroying any evidence that could be used against her, she had initially been kept in ignorance that the plot had come to light. Then, on 16 August, she had been permitted to go on a hunting expedition, and it was while she was on the moors that she had been placed under arrest. Once the weeping Queen of Scots had been carted off to a neighbouring house, her closets at Chartley were ransacked, yielding up three coffers full of private correspondence that were sent to London for inspection.

Elizabeth heard of the way that Mary had been tricked with grim satisfaction. She returned heartfelt thanks to Paulet, telling him, "If you knew, my Amias, how kindly, besides dutifully, my grateful heart accepteth and praiseth your spotless actions, your wise orders, and safe regards performed in so dangerous and crafty a charge, it would ease your travails and rejoice your heart". As for Mary, she bade him to "Let your wicked murderess know how with hearty sorrow her vile deserts compelleth these orders; and bid her from me ask God forgiveness for her treacherous dealings towards the saver of her life many a year". Peremptorily, she ordered that any money in Mary's possession should be confiscated and that all her servants should be dismissed, refusing to rescind these commands even when she was warned that the resultant distress might make Mary seriously ill.[97] Indeed, she would have been relieved if Mary's health had given out under the strain, for that would have spared Elizabeth the ordeal of bringing her to trial.

At the beginning of September, there were many discussions as to where the hearing against Mary should be held, and as the Queen "flatly refused" to accept her councillors' advice that the Tower of London would be the most appropriate venue, let the Tower of London be used, Fotheringay Castle in Northamptonshire was hit on as an acceptable alternative. On 25 September Mary was brought there, and in the ensuing fortnight the thirty-six commissioners who were to try her (among whom were included Burghley, Walsingham, Hatton and other leading councillors) arrived there too. They then embarked on the delicate task of persuading Mary to give some semblance of legitimacy to their proceedings by gracing the hearings with her presence, for it was only to be expected that she would claim that Elizabeth had no right to try another sovereign princess. Sure enough, when it was put to her that "in England, under her Majesty's jurisdiction, a free prince offending is subject to her laws", Mary would have none of it, crying out violently that "She was no subject and rather would die a thousand deaths than acknowledge herself a subject".[98] Thereupon, she was warned that if she stuck to this line she would be tried *in absentia*, and Sir Christopher Hatton pleaded that, for the sake of her reputation, she should take this opportunity to clear herself of the imputation of wanting to murder the Queen. These arguments had their effect. On 14 October Mary relented, and the trial began.

On entering the hall and seeing the commissioners arrayed before her, Mary exclaimed, "Alas! here are many councillors but not one for me!" but despite the fact that she was denied a legal representative and was not allowed to inspect the evidence against her, she conducted her defence very ably. Initially she denied having had any communication with Babington, but had to change tactics when the Prosecution produced copies of various other letters she had sent abroad in which she alluded to the fact that she had given Babington "a full statement of my opinion on all points of the execution of the enterprise". Thereupon she tacitly admitted having written to him, but insisted that when doing so, she had never "consented to the destruction of the Queen". Adroitly she contested that the Prosecution could not prove otherwise unless her original letter to Babington, written in her own hand, could be produced, and this was indeed a weak link in the case against her, for Babington had burnt her letter soon after receiving it. Nevertheless, before doing so, he had shown it to several of his accomplices, and all of them had confessed that it contained an authorization from Mary to murder the Queen. Furthermore, Mary's secretaries had admitted copying out the letter for her, and though she said irately "the majesty and safety of all princes falleth to the ground if they depend upon the writing and testimony of secretaries", the weight of evidence told against her. What Burghley described angrily as her "long artificial speeches" did have some effect, for on the evening of 14 October there was "great debate ... with great estimating" among the commissioners as to

Mary's guilt, but by the end of the second day's hearing, Burghley believed it had been established beyond doubt.[99]

Nevertheless, the proceedings were left up in the air, for at the last moment the Queen sent word that she wished to be consulted before a verdict was reached, and that the hearing should therefore be adjourned for ten days. Walsingham was convinced that this showed that Elizabeth would never steel herself to bring Mary to book, commenting angrily, "I see this wicked creature ordained of God to punish us for our sins and unthankfulness". In the event, however, this proved no more than a temporary delay. On 25 October the commissioners reconvened in the Star Chamber at Westminster and, after a recapitulation of the evidence against Mary, all but one of them (Lord Zouch was the exception) pronounced that she was guilty of the "compassing, practising and imagining of her Majesty's death".[100]

As yet however, there was no sign that the Queen would be prepared to act upon their findings, for she would not even allow the sentence against Mary to be publicly proclaimed. Nevertheless Burghley and Walsingham did not despair, for Parliament assembled on 29 October, and they hoped that leverage from that quarter would oblige Elizabeth to order Mary's execution. As was only to be expected, when Sir Christopher Hatton summarized the case against Mary to the House of Commons, there were strident calls for her head. One member denounced Mary as "the daughter of sedition, the nurse of impiety, the handmaid of iniquity", and having warmed to his theme, he declared that her destruction would be "one of the fairest riddances that ever the Church of God had ... She ought indeed to die the death".[101]

Contrary to her normal practice while Parliament was in session, Elizabeth was residing at Richmond, being reluctant, as she said, to remain in the capital and "hear so many foul and grievous matters revealed and ripped up". Nevertheless feelings in Parliament were running too high to allow her to remain undisturbed, and on 12 November a deputation from the Lords and Commons waited on her in order to present a petition begging that Mary should be put to death. To their disappointment, the Queen explained that she was unable as yet to make a decision on the matter – a reply that Burghley claimed "drew tears from many eyes"[102] – and two days later she sent a message to Parliament asking whether they could not devise a way of procuring her safety that would obviate the need to execute Mary. The reply was uncompromising, for on 24 November another parliamentary delegation had an audience at Richmond and declared that, in the view of both Houses, the only option open to her was to put Mary to death.

Despite this unanimous appeal, the Queen still longed for another way out, and in a remarkable oration she sought to convey that while she did not make light of their wishes, deferring to them would cause her unimaginable pain. She observed that, when faced with hard decisions, she did not normally bemoan her lot in public, but on this occasion she had "just cause to complain that I, who have in my time pardoned so many rebels, winked at so many treasons, and either not produced them or altogether slipped them over with silence, should now be forced to this proceeding, against such a person". Already, she wryly reminded them, she was condemned as a monster of cruelty in Catholic countries, so it was difficult to imagine what the reaction would be "When it shall be spread that for the safety of her life, a maiden Queen could be content to spill the blood even of her own kinswoman". She said that she knew full well that in preserving Mary she would "cherish a sword to cut mine own throat", but she pointed out that it was not uncommon for men to give their lives to save that of a prince, and that it was therefore not so odd that she should contemplate making a similar sacrifice. She stressed that she did not undervalue their love for her, and that she would never cease to be grateful for it, but "As for your petition: your judgement I condemn not, nor do I mistake your reasons, but pray you to accept my thankfulness, excuse my doubtfulness, and take in good part my answer answerless".[103]

Her audience could scarcely fail to be moved at the Queen's obvious torment at being confronted with this supreme crisis of conscience, but they remained determined that whatever the emotional cost, she must face up to her responsibilities as a ruler. Burghley lamented that, if the Queen staved off a decision for much longer, the people would label this session "a Parliament of words, or otherwise nickname it a vain Parliament".[104] To his relief, the suspense was soon broken when Elizabeth agreed that the sentence against Mary could be embodied in a formal proclamation. On 4 December, it was read out in public, and the bonfires that blazed all over London attested to the citizens' joy at the announcement.

Even so, there was no guarantee that Mary's head would be forfeit, for Elizabeth had still to sign the death warrant, and already powerful forces were being brought to bear that might yet stay her hand. For a start, there was the possibility that an appeal from Mary herself might move the Queen to clemency, for Elizabeth had signified that if her cousin wished to write to her, she would receive the letter. Mary had been informed that she had been sentenced to death on 19 November, and exactly a month later she took up her pen to thank Elizabeth for the "happy tidings" that she was to come "to the end of my long and weary pilgrimage". Having asked that her servants should be permitted to witness her execution and that afterwards her corpse should be sent to France for burial, she concluded that she wished to die in perfect charity with everyone, "Yet while abandoning this world and preparing myself for a better, I must remind you that one day you will have to answer for your charge, and for all those whom you doom, and that I desire that my blood and my country may be remembered in that time". Sir Amias Paulet, who nourished hopes that Mary would be executed before Christmas, was reluctant to forward a letter that might hinder the signing of the death warrant, but though he delayed sending it for as long as he dared, Elizabeth had seen it by 23 December. To the relief of Mary's enemies, it still seemed that the Queen was going to stand firm: Leicester told Walsingham that the letter "hath wrought tears, but I trust shall do no further harm". After this scare, Paulet did not allow Mary to write to Elizabeth again.[105]

It was not possible, however, to stifle protest from abroad, for both countries of which Mary had been Queen had reacted vigorously to the prospect of her execution. On learning that his sister-in-law's life was at risk, Henry III had despatched to England a special ambassador, M. de Bellièvre, who had arrived in England on 20 November. He had been unable to prevent Elizabeth from having the sentence proclaimed, but the next day he had remonstrated with her so successfully that she had promised to defer carrying it out for at least twelve days. Pressure from Scotland was more intense still, despite the fact that King James's personal feelings towards his mother remained as hard-hearted as ever. When he had first heard of Mary's involvement in the Babington plot, he had callously indicated that he would not object if she was kept much more strictly, saying "it was meet for her to meddle with nothing but prayer and serving of God". Nevertheless when it became clear that Mary faced death, James took alarm, for it would scarcely be consistent with his honour to let her fall victim to the axeman. He also could not afford to ignore public opinion in his kingdom, which was becoming dangerously inflamed, for the death sentence passed on her had transformed her into the heroine of many of those who had reviled her most strongly in the past. The Scots nobility urged James to declare war if his mother came to any harm, and as James somewhat plaintively told Elizabeth, feeling among the populace was so strong that he scarcely dared "go abroad for crying out of the whole people; and what is spoken by them of the Queen of England, it grieves me to hear".[106]

Warnings were sent to England that if Mary's "life be touched or her blood be meddled with", James could "no longer remain on good terms with the Queen or estate of that realm",[107] but Elizabeth felt safe in treating these threats with scepticism. James did not have much in common with his mother, but his desire to inherit the English throne was every bit as intense as hers had been, and Elizabeth thought it unlikely that he would jeopardize his chances of being her successor by defying her on a point of principle.

It was true that outwardly at least, James was playing to perfection the part of a dutiful son. Although Archibald Douglas was already acting as his representative in England, on 20 October he had also sent south William Keith, with instructions to press the Queen vigorously to spare Mary's life. Thinking that plain speaking was called for, James told his ambassadors to give Elizabeth a letter from him in which he stated, "King Henry VIII's reputation was never prejudged but in the beheading of his bedfellow", but the King could hardly have chosen a more unfortunate approach. Far from being moved at the implied parallel between Mary and Anne Boleyn, Elizabeth was incensed that James had had the effrontery to touch on this taboo subject, and a shaken Keith told the King that when the letter was shown to her, she "took such a chafe as ye would wonder".[108]

If James had really wanted to save his mother, he could of course have sent Elizabeth an ultimatum to the effect that he would at once declare war if she went ahead with Mary's execution, but he was never prepared to go so far as this. Indeed, on 8 December the Earl of Leicester asked Archibald Douglas outright whether James would renounce his alliance with England if his mother was killed, and Douglas replied that he was sure that the King would not do so, provided he was not provoked in other ways. Correctly interpreting this to mean that the King would resort to hostilities only if Elizabeth sought to exclude him from the succession, Leicester gave warm assurances that she would never seek to tamper with James's rights.[109]

Douglas reported this conversation to the King, and James made little effort to counteract the impression that he would make no move if Mary was to die. All he did was send yet another embassy to England, led by the Master of Gray, but the latter was not empowered to tell the Queen that Mary's execution would result in the immediate outbreak of war. Instead, when Gray saw the Queen on 6 January 1587, he put forward a proposal that made it seem as though James was seeking to make capital out of his mother's predicament. The ambassador smoothly suggested to Elizabeth that there would be no need to execute Mary if the latter were prevailed upon to invest her son with any claim she had to the English crown, for as James was a Protestant there could be no danger that Catholics would plot to murder the Queen on his behalf. Elizabeth was not able to swallow this. "By God's passion", she swore, "that were to cut my own throat!" and she bluntly told the ambassador that "She would not have a worse in his mother's place". Somewhat nettled, Gray and his colleagues asked that even if the Queen would not discuss this idea, she would at least delay the execution for a time, if only for a week. "Not for an hour!" the Queen snapped back, and swept from the room.[110]

It appeared that remonstrances from France would fare no better. When de Bellièvre handed the Queen a letter from Henry III saying that he would "look upon it as a personal affront" if Mary was executed, Elizabeth wrote back defiantly that, far from intimidating her, such a threat was "the shortest way to make me despatch the cause of so much mischief". Yet behind this bold façade, she was in inner turmoil at the prospect of having to turn predator on one of her own kind. In different circumstances, indeed, she would have enthusiastically applauded when James demanded, "What law of God can permit that justice shall strike upon them whom he has appointed supreme dispensators of the same under him, whom he hath called Gods, and there subjected to the censure of none in earth ... What monstrous thing is it that sovereign princes themselves should be the example givers of their own sacred diadems profaning?" Despite the Queen's harsh phrases to them, the Scots ambassadors divined that she was not yet "resolved of herself" to proceed with Mary's execution, and that her councillors had not been able to wear down her reservations, "albeit indeed they are very extreme in this".[111]

It was true that her councillors were sparing no effort to stiffen the Queen's resolve. In desperation, some even turned antiquary, dredging up cases from as far back as ancient Greece (Menelaus's revenge on Paris was one example cited) that could serve as precedents for Mary's execution. Burghley based his arguments more firmly in the present, arguing that as the Queen of Scots had been responsible for every single attempt to trouble Elizabeth's estate, "Were it not then more than time to remove that eyesore?" He argued that Mary's sex and status could have no bearing on the case, and tried to make the Queen straighten out her priorities by telling her that it was she herself who was a lady, a queen and a sovereign, whereas as for Mary, "What she is or has been, I forbear for respect to say". All this could not suffice to make Elizabeth sign the warrant. It was apparent to William Davison (who in July 1586 had been promoted to the position of Joint Secretary of State) that, as far as Mary was concerned, Elizabeth was going to "keep the course she held with the Duke of Norfolk, which is not to take her life unless extreme fear compel her".[112]

In the circumstances, the councillors were ready to seize on anything that heightened the Queen's perceptions of being in acute danger. To keep Elizabeth on edge, they fed to her reports that Mary had escaped, that arsonists were at work in the City of London, or that Spanish troops had landed in Wales. On 8 January, events took an even more sensational twist when the resident French ambassador, M. de Châteauneuf, was placed under house arrest for having allegedly conspired to murder the Queen. The background to this incident is murky. One William Stafford had apparently told the ambassador's secretary that he could arrange for Elizabeth to be killed, and as Châteauneuf failed to denounce Stafford to the authorities, he was accused of having countenanced the murder proposal. Two months later, however, the English took the line that the whole episode had been a misunderstanding, and as no proceedings were ever initiated against Stafford, there are grounds for suspicion that he was an *agent provocateur*, who was sent to entice the ambassador into an intrigue in order the keep the Queen's nerves at full stretch.

If this was the case, the technique worked. On 1 February, after a conversation with Lord Howard about "the great danger she continually lived in", the Queen ordered William Davison to bring her Mary's death warrant. Having calmly signed it, she went into various details as to how she wished the execution to be carried out, specifying that Mary should be beheaded in the hall at Fotheringay Castle, rather than the courtyard. Davison subsequently claimed that she also instructed him to send the warrant to Fotheringay with such expedition that she "would not hear any more thereof till it was done", but it is impossible to know whether his memory of their conversation was accurate. At any rate, Davison's pleasure at finding her in so resolute a frame of mind was short-lived. Just as he was about to take his leave of the Queen, clutching the warrant, he was again plunged into uncertainty when Elizabeth suddenly demanded that he should write to Sir Amias Paulet and suggest that he arrange for Mary to be quietly murdered. Greatly disturbed, Davison told her he was sure Paulet would never perform so unworthy a deed, but after consultation with Walsingham he reluctantly did as the Queen had asked.[113]

The fact that the Queen was still groping after an unorthodox solution made Davison wary about despatching the warrant to Fotheringay, particularly since she appeared displeased when she learnt on 2 February that the warrant had been sealed, and therefore could at any moment be put into effect. On the other hand, Elizabeth made no attempt to cancel the warrant, as she had done when the Duke of Norfolk was due to be executed. In some perplexity, Davison consulted Hatton and Burghley, and on 3 February the latter convened a meeting of the Council. There the councillors bound themselves to take joint responsibility for sending off the warrant so that Davison alone would not be accountable when it was carried out. Fearing that if there were any further delay, the Queen might be taken by some "new concept of interrupting and staying the course of justice", they agreed that "it was neither fit nor convenient to trouble her Majesty any further therewithal".[114] The warrant was entrusted to Robert Beale, who departed with it to Fotheringay on 4 February.

The Queen meanwhile was still revolving in her mind the possibility that Mary could be secretly done away with. She again alluded to the matter on 4 February, suddenly remarking to Davison that she had been much upset by dreaming that Mary had been executed. Davison thereupon enquired whether she still wanted the warrant to be carried out, to which she replied in the affirmative, but voiced the reservation "that it might have received a better form". The following day, however, the Queen had a disappointment, for a letter from Paulet arrived vehemently rebutting the proposal that he should assassinate his prisoner. Elizabeth was much put out, for Paulet had been eager enough to sign the Bond of Association, which should have salved his conscience at committing such a crime. Heatedly, she "blamed the niceness of those precise fellows ... who in words would do great things for her surety, but in deed perform nothing".[115]

Nevertheless it appears that the Queen would not relinquish all hope that Mary's death could be contrived without the bother of an execution. On 7 February she commanded Davison to write "a sharp letter" to Paulet, rebuking him for the fact that "it was not already done". Davison (who himself admitted that as he was inexperienced in dealing with Elizabeth, "he might easily mistake the Queen's meaning") understood by this that she wanted Paulet to proceed with the execution, but more likely the Queen had wanted Paulet to be prodded into murdering Mary. She must have been crestfallen when Davison stolidly returned that it was a formal warrant and "not any private letter from me that must be [Paulet's] direction in that behalf".[116]

Elizabeth has been censored for seeking to rid herself of Mary underhand, but she had sound enough reasons for thinking it more seemly to proceed by stealth. If Mary was quietly eliminated, it could be given out that she had died of natural causes, and nothing more need be said. If on the other hand she was executed, Elizabeth would have to justify an act which she regarded as theoretically indefensible and which would be an affront to all reigning monarchs. She accepted that it was essential that Mary be put to death, but her own concept of morality did not allow her to take comfort from her advisers' assurances that provided due legal process was observed, such an act rested on a legitimate foundation. In her own eyes and those of God, nothing could alter the fact that the killing of a Queen was wrong, but since circumstances forced her to countenance such a deed, she took the view that an evil committed out of sight was less obnoxious than one performed brazenly before all the world.

By this time, however, matters had been taken out of her hands. On 7 February 1587, Mary was informed that her execution was scheduled for the following day, and at 8 o'clock the next morning she went to her death. She met her end with moving dignity, for though in later years she had become corpulent, double-chinned and lame, physical decrepitude could not rob her of her regal grace, or destroy the mental fortitude that came from the knowledge that her execution would elevate her to the status of a martyr queen. In her last utterances, she carefully perpetuated the myth that she was dying for her faith, rebutting the Protestant Dean of Peterborough's offer to comfort her on the scaffold with the words, "Mr Dean, trouble not yourself nor me; for know that I am settled in the ancient Catholic and Roman religion, and in defence thereof by God's grace I mind to spend my blood". When the Dean nevertheless insisted on praying aloud, she drowned his words with Latin orisons. With great composure she submitted to having her outer garments removed by the two executioners, remarking only "She never had such grooms before to make her unready, nor ever did put off her clothes before such a company". Having assured the axeman that she forgave him, she knelt down and resolutely laid her head on the block. In Latin she cried out, "Into Your hands, O Lord, I commend my spirit", and then her head was struck off with two blows of the axe. Her lips continued to move for almost a quarter of an hour afterwards, but the disembodied head was scarcely recognizable as Mary's, so great was the alteration now that her features were no longer lit up by that singular charm and animation that had made her countenance so unique.[117]

The news was carried to court by the Earl of Shrewsbury's son, Henry Talbot, and by the morning of 9 February Burghley knew that the execution had taken place. The Lord Treasurer tried to keep the news from the Queen, but by evening she had learnt of it "by other means". At first it did not seem that she was unduly shaken, but overnight she worked herself up, and the following morning she furiously upbraided Hatton for his role in the affair. As yet, however, the Council saw no cause for serious alarm, and Davison's colleagues merely cautioned him to stay out of her way for a couple of days. Their consternation was therefore intense when the Queen suddenly declared that Davison must go to the Tower for his disobedience, refusing to relent even when they begged her on their knees to reconsider. Davison was duly placed in confinement on 14 February, but the Queen's agitation showed no sign of subsiding; indeed, by now she was in such a state that there were fears for her health, as she was not touching her food, and was getting no sleep. After Davison, the brunt of her anger fell on Burghley, who had chaired the fateful Council meeting at which it had been agreed that the warrant should be sent. To his infinite alarm, Burghley found himself denied her presence, and being already in great pain from his bodily infirmities, his condition grew more pitiable on account of this added grief of mind. Desperately he wrote to the Queen begging that he might "be laid upon the floor near your Majesty's feet" in hopes of soaking up "some drops of your mercy to quench my sorrowful panting heart" but Elizabeth refused even to read this quavering appeal.[118]

As the days went by and the Queen continued to brood on the enormity of what had been done, her temper grew more savage. By 25 February Burghley was in a state of utter panic, for he heard that Elizabeth was possessed of a notion that it would be a legitimate exercise of her prerogative if she had Davison hanged without trial, having apparently prevailed upon one of her judges to pronounce that she would be within her rights in resorting to arbitrary action. She was intending to seek the opinion of the remainder of the judiciary, and Burghley desperately sent a message to the judges that they should weigh their words with care, for the consequences could be horrendous. "I think it a hard time if men, for doing well afore God and man, shall be otherwise punished than law may warrant with an opinion gotten from the judges that her prerogative is above the law", he bleated unhappily.[119]

The Queen's fury with Davison was exacerbated by the reaction that Mary's execution provoked abroad. From Paris, the English ambassador in France reported, "I never saw a thing more hated by little, great, old, young and of all religions than the Queen of Scots, death, and especially the manner of it. I would to God ... she had died and no more". He continued to send in descriptions of shrieking crowds, howling for Mary's canonization, and how the entire nation seemed to be clad in mourning, until Walsingham had to send him a sharp letter telling him to desist, for his account "increaseth the more her Majesty's offence against her Council".[120]

Scotland had also been convulsed with rage when Mary's fate was known, and for a time it looked as if the English had been underestimating James in thinking that he would not lift a finger to avenge his mother's death. The first intelligence that filtered through the border reported that when he learnt the news, James "gave out in secret speeches that he could not digest the same nor leave it unrevenged". Lord Hunsdon's son, Robert Carey, was given the unenviable task of delivering to James a letter from the Queen explaining that Mary had been executed contrary to her wishes.[121] If granted an audience with James, Carey was supposed to elaborate on this theme, presumably by saying that Elizabeth had only signed the death warrant in order that Mary could be executed if an emergency arose, but the King refused to let Carey cross the border into Scotland, let alone receive him.

He did, however, agree to read Elizabeth's letter, and as the dust began to settle there were encouraging signs that he himself was anxious to avoid war. It nevertheless remained possible that pressure from his subjects would oblige him to be more belligerent. One Scots noble came to court wearing full armour, and when James told him reproachfully he should be in mourning for Mary, the noble replied acidly that armour was the correct mourning attire for the late Queen. The Scots populace were equally clamorous that Elizabeth should be punished for her presumption. One Scot sent a report to England that the King was unable to "stay the rigour of his people, who ... are so wicked bent and evil given that libels are daily set up in the open street and cast into the pulpit". Some of these lampooned the King for his cowardice, but the worst were those directed against Elizabeth, which were "very odious and detestable". The more pacific of James's ministers were genuinely concerned that the King would be hustled into a war against his will. The Master of Gray wrote frankly that if Elizabeth really hoped to convince the Scots that it was not her fault that

Mary had died, she should at least execute whoever was responsible as a sop to Scots public opinion.[122]

In fact, however, Elizabeth had abandoned all thought of executing Davison for his part in Mary's death. She remained determined that he should be punished, but agreed that the case against him should be heard by the Court of Star Chamber, which had no power to impose a death sentence. On 28 March Davison was accused of having deliberately disobeyed an order from the Queen to keep the signed death warrant in his possession, and of having misled the Council into thinking that Elizabeth did not wish to be consulted before it was sent to Fotheringay. Davison denied these charges, but the commission, chaired by Sir Walter Mildmay, found against him. Having declared him guilty of "a great contempt and misprision", they sentenced him to be fined 10,000 marks and to be detained in the Tower at the Queen's pleasure. In the event however Davison's punishment was commuted, for he never had to pay his fine and he was released from the Tower in September 1588. Till the end of the reign, he continued to draw his salary as Secretary, and for as long as Walsingham was alive he still received the financial perquisites that supplemented the Secretary's official pay. The Queen must have known that he was in receipt of these sums, and though she would never hear of employing him again in any official capacity, it is to her credit that she refrained from ruining him totally. As scapegoats go, Davison was relatively fortunate.[123]

Before the end of February the Queen lifted her ban on Burghley writing to her, but the Lord Treasurer remained in disgrace for nigh on four months. In March he returned to Court to advise the Queen on Low Country matters, but far from having forgiven him, Elizabeth berated him with such venom about Mary that he thought her anger had now "settled and increased". In April he again absented himself from Court, but had to return when Lady Cobham wrote saying he was making matters worse, as "Others here in presence do speak for themselves and do excuse that which is done in putting their hands to the letter, as that they knew not what they did, nor what was therein committed". Perhaps it was this that kept the Queen's resentment alive, and as late as June she was still antagonistic towards him, flaring up on one occasion and using "marvellous cruel speeches . . . calling him traitor, false dissembler and wicked wretch". This, however, was one of the last outbursts he had to endure on the subject. Within a fortnight, Burghley's heart was gladdened by the Queen's renewed "favourable usage" of him, which afforded him "great comfort" after his long period in disfavour.[124]

The Queen had not been prepared to shed blood in expiation of Mary's death, but in minor ways she tried to make amends. After the execution, Mary's body had been embalmed and encased in lead, but for over six months the coffin had lain unburied at Fotheringay. By mid-June it had become something of a health hazard, for it was emitting such "a very noisome savour" that it was unpleasant to enter the room where it was kept. Clearly it would have to be interred, and as a palliative to James, Elizabeth decreed it should be given an extremely grand funeral. On 30 July the coffin was borne by torchlight procession to Peterborough Cathedral, and two days later a stately ceremony was held. The Countess of Bedford headed an impressive list of mourners, which included the Earls of Lincoln and Rutland, the Bishops of Peterborough and Lincoln, and one hundred poor women, who had all been supplied with mourning garments at Elizabeth's expense. Nevertheless the fact that Mary was buried with full honour as a Queen only emphasized the indignity of the treatment meted out to her at Fotheringay, and it would take more than this grotesque charade to salve Elizabeth's conscience. She did not regret that Mary had been killed, but deplored the official nature of the deed, for even though it had been unavoidable to do violence to an anointed Queen, it would have been preferable if it had been done unwitnessed and on the sly. Much as Elizabeth had detested her cousin, she was speaking no more than the truth when she told the French ambassador in May 1587 that "this death will wring her heart as long as she lives".[125]

CHAPTER 12

"I myself will take up arms"

"I never found Her Majesty less disposed to take a course of prevention of the approaching mischiefs towards this realm than at this present", lamented Walsingham in the spring of 1587. The Queen's army in the Netherlands remained unpaid, the situation in France and Scotland was menacing, and worst of all, there was intelligence that the Spaniards were making "very great and puissant" preparations for war. Walsingham saw nothing to indicate that Elizabeth intended to address herself to these problems, and he was not alone in having worries on this score. Lord Buckhurst, who had been appointed to the Privy Council the year before, told the Queen in April, "If ever prince had cause to think himself beset with doubt and danger, you, sacred Queen, have most just cause not only to think it, but even certainly to believe it. The Pope doth daily plot nothing else but how he may bring to pass your utter overthrow... The King of Spain armeth and extendeth all his power to ruin both you and your estate... Will not Your Majesty, beholding the flames of your enemies on every side kindling around, unlock all your coffers and convert your treasure for the advancing of worthy men for the arming of ships and men of war to defend you?"[1]

Despite such forceful pleas, it was hard to feel confident that the Queen grasped the urgency of the situation; at times, indeed, it seemed that she felt more enmity towards her councillors than she did towards Philip of Spain. She was still obsessed by their conduct at the time of Mary Stuart's execution, and this matter tended to absorb her to the exclusion of all else. Walsingham noted that her displeasure with her leading advisers "hindereth the necessary consultation that were to be desired for the preventing of the manifest perils that hang over this realm", and it reduced him to despair that, instead of setting herself to deal with future perils, "Her Majesty doth wholly bend herself to devise some further means to disgrace her poor Council . . . and in respect thereof she neglecteth all other causes". Her dark mood was mirrored by the mourning garments she still wore for her cousin, and as Walsingham told Leicester, her irascible frame of mind made "every man weary of attendance here".[2]

Those who believed that the Spaniards were set on war were correct in their assessment. For years, the plight of the English Catholics had gnawed at King Philip's conscience, and Drake's depredations in the New World had sharpened his desire to punish Elizabeth, or "the Englishwoman", as he coldly referred to her in communications with his ministers. Yet however much he longed to humble her, in recent years his extensive military commitments in the Netherlands had impeded him from launching an invasion against England. His general, the Duke of Parma, had consistently advocated that the King dealt with unrest in his own dominions before embarking on any further ventures abroad, and Philip had believed he had no option but to heed this advice. In October 1583, when Pope Gregory XIII urged him to invade England, the King tersely annotated the letter, "This proposal is out of the question, the more so as I . . . [have] so many obligations already that I cannot fulfil them as I ought". As late as the summer of 1585, Philip could not envisage attacking Elizabeth in the near future, for he noted, "There is little to be said about the English idea". This did not mean, however, that he ruled out the possibility of invading the country at a later stage in his reign. On the contrary, he was clear that "in the case . . . of the pacification of Flanders, I will not fail to furnish such aid". He asked only that the English Catholics continue "to be patient, for something will be done at some time",[3] and he looked forward to the day of reckoning with keen anticipation.

At the end of 1585 Philip decided that he could wait no longer to revenge himself on his heretical neighbour to the north, for his patience had finally snapped when he learnt that Elizabeth had despatched an army to the Netherlands. On 29 December 1585 Philip wrote to Parma that an invasion of England would be "the only means of putting an end to the evils which they are preparing over there against God's service and my own". He asked Parma to supply plans for the conquest, but while Philip was waiting for the reply, his redoubtable admiral, the Marquis of Santa Cruz, independently sent the King a plan of his own for the invasion of England. Santa Cruz wanted to assemble a fleet with a large army on board, which would first be ferried to Ireland and effect a landing there. After two months, during which time the enemy's energies would be absorbed in repelling this threat, Santa Cruz proposed withdrawing his forces from Ireland in order to launch an assault against the mainland of England itself, which would now be only scantily defended, and would not be capable of putting up a good resistance. The resources needed for such an enterprise were of course enormous. Santa Cruz estimated that he would require a fleet numbering 510 ships, capable of carrying 94,222 men, and the cost would be almost a million pounds. Such was Philip II's determination, however, that he did not allow considerations of cost to put him off, and on 2 April 1586, the order went out that naval preparations should begin in Lisbon and elsewhere.[4] On 20 June, matters were thrown into confusion when the King was delivered a letter from the Duke of Parma, outlining an alternative strategy for the invasion of England. Parma stated that provided the enemy was taken by surprise, he would be able to seize England with only minimal support from the Spanish navy, for he proposed under cover of darkness to ship his army in the Netherlands across the Narrow Seas in a flotilla of flat-bottomed barges. Having digested these proposals, Philip decided not to adopt them in their entirety, but instead he sought to incorporate some of Parma's ideas into Santa Cruz's original plan. He decided that once Santa Cruz had distracted the enemy with an attack on Ireland, Parma would have less difficulty sallying forth in his barges and landing in England, but by involving Santa Cruz's navy to such a significant extent Philip destroyed all chance of taking the English unawares, and Parma had always stressed that surprise was of the essence. In trying to combine two incompatible strategies, Philip had ended up with an absurd hybrid of a plan which had few merits in its own right and which was beset by crucial weaknesses.[5]

Preparations for the invasion were already well under way when Philip was informed that Elizabeth had executed Mary Queen of Scots. From Paris Mendoza wrote, "As God has so willed that this accursed people, for his ends, should ... against all reason commit such an act as this, it is evidently his design to deliver those two kingdoms into Your Majesty's hands". Until now, the official object of the invasion had been to set Mary up as Queen in Elizabeth's place, but it had always been Philip's intention that the English crown should pass to him or one of his daughters on Mary's death. He had felt a little diffident, however, at the prospect of explaining this to the Pope, for he feared that the Pontiff might think that his decision to invade was attributable to acquisitiveness rather than religious zeal alone, and that he would disapprove of such base motivation. Mary's death nevertheless relieved him of all embarrassment, for he felt that he was entitled to regard himself as her heir. In May 1586, Mary had written to Mendoza that, "considering the obstinacy and perseverance of my son in heresy", she had decided that unless James changed his religion, she would "cede and give by will my right to the succession of this crown [of England] to the ... King your master". Although there was no evidence that Mary had in fact left a will to this effect, Philip took the letter as being a clear declaration of intent. Quite apart from this, Philip believed that he had a good claim to the English throne in his own right. Edward III's fourth son, John of Gaunt, had married Constance of Castile, and as Philip was descended from a daughter of this couple, he could argue that in view of Elizabeth's illegitimacy, he was in fact the rightful King of England.

Despite the fact that he stood to gain a kingdom from it, Philip was emphatic that this had nothing to do with his decision to go to war, and he insisted that the invasion should be viewed in the light of a crusade. In the circumstances he felt justified in seeking papal aid for it, and the King's ambassador in Rome, the Count of Olivares, was instructed to press the Pope to make a substantial contribution towards the cost of the enterprise, and also to issue a brief recognizing Philip's title to the English crown. Nevertheless, Olivares's task was far from straightforward, for in 1585 the Neapolitan Cardinal Felice Peretti had become Pope Sixtus V, and he was a virulent Hispanophobe. It was true that one of his first acts as Pope had been to press Philip to attack Elizabeth, and he had even volunteered to provide one third of the costs of the expedition, but since then he showed every sign of having forgotten this generous offer. He even seemed to nourish a sneaking admiration for Elizabeth, and certainly he spoke of her in much warmer terms than he usually did of Philip. "She is a great woman", he said on one occasion, "and were she only a Catholic, she would be without her match, and we would esteem her highly". Philip was mortified to discover that even after being informed that an invasion was in the offing, the Pope had made an unsuccessful attempt to persuade Elizabeth to rejoin the Church of Rome, using Henry III of France as an intermediary. Olivares attributed the Pope's lack of enthusiasm for the invasion to meanness, as Sixtus knew he would be called upon to pay for part of it, and as the ambassador explained to Philip, "When it comes to getting money out of him, it is like squeezing his life blood". Nevertheless, however much it might pain him, as head of the Catholic world, the Pope could hardly withhold his blessing from an enterprise designed to lay low the woman who was the leading light of European Protestantism. On 29 July 1587 (N.S.) a treaty was signed between Spain and the Papacy, whereby Sixtus agreed that after the conquest of England Philip could bestow its crown on whomsoever he pleased, providing that the new ruler undertook to restore Catholicism. He also promised to contribute a million scuti (just under £250,000) towards Philip's expenses, although this would be payable only after Spanish troops had landed in England. Olivares did his best to persuade Sixtus to advance a portion of this money, but on this point the Pope proved immovable.[6]

Meanwhile, on Philip's orders, armaments and shipping continued to accumulate at Lisbon and other ports on the southern coast of Spain, and the process had not gone unobserved. By the winter of 1586–87, reports were pouring into England that "great numbers of ships and other provisions for the sea" were being put in readiness by Philip, and from this it was clear that he was planning some grand offensive. It was less easy to tell whether the fleet being assembled would ultimately be directed against England or some other target, but such intelligence as there was suggested that the former was the case. The most significant items of information came from Rome, for Philip had insisted that the entire college of cardinals were told of the impending invasion, fearing that Sixtus V might die, and his successor as Pope would pretend that he was under no obligation to give the venture financial support. As the King desired, all the cardinals swore that they would carry out any undertaking secured from the present Pope, but having been let into the secret about the coming attack on England, they were woefully indiscreet. Soon the story was all over Rome, where it was picked up by spies and relayed to England.[7]

Evidence such as this was too telling to be ignored, and the Queen found it hard to resist calls for her to take steps to ward off the danger. Although she had misgivings about affording Philip further provocation, on 15 March 1587 she signed a commission authorizing Drake to mount a punitive expedition against Spain. She agreed that Drake could take a small fleet (which included six of her own ships) to the coast of Spain, and there do what he thought fit to impeach the Spanish war effort, including attacking Spanish ships in harbour, if the opportunity offered. Within a month of having given her permission, however, Elizabeth began to regret that she had been so rash. The most recent intelligence from Spain claimed that Philip was slackening his warlike preparations, and she persuaded herself that he was ready to treat for peace. On 9 April she altered Drake's instructions, commanding him to confine his attacks to Spanish shipping that was already at sea, and expressly forbidding him "to enter forcibly into the said King's ports or havens, or to offer violence to any of his towns or shipping with harbouring, or to do any act of hostility upon land".[8] But her change of heart had come too late: when her messenger reached Plymouth, he found that Drake had put out to sea on 2 April, and by now he was beyond recall.

On 19 April 1587, Drake sailed into Cadiz harbour, and burnt or captured some thirty-seven vessels that were anchored there. He then proceeded to Cape St Vincent and, having captured a nearby fort, he based himself there for some weeks. This enabled him to prey on all Spanish shipping in the vicinity, and Drake estimated that during this time, over a hundred enemy vessels fell into his hands. He burnt all their cargoes, including tons of hoops and pipe staves that would have been used to make the casks in which water and victuals for the Spanish fleet could have been stored. Drake foretold that Philip would have the utmost difficulty replacing these goods, and indeed, when the Armada sailed, its food supplies were stored in casks made of unseasoned timber, with the result that great quantities of victuals rotted and rapidly became inedible. Furthermore, Drake's presence at Cape St Vincent meant that Philip dared not permit those ships that were in ports on the southern coast of Spain join with the main body of his fleet at Lisbon, for as yet none of them were armed, and they would therefore have been incapable of fending off an attack by Drake. The assembly of the Armada was thus delayed, an achievement of which Drake was justly proud. He wrote home exultantly, "This service, which by God's sufferance we have done, will (without doubt) breed some alteration of their pretences".[9]

At the end of May, Drake left his base at Cape St Vincent and sailed for the Azores, with the intention of picking up a rich prize. He succeeded in capturing the *San Felipe*, a great Spanish merchantmen, loaded with spices, bullion, jewels and silks, which he brought back in triumph to Plymouth on 26 June. Its cargo was valued at £114,000, £40,000 of which formed the Queen's dividend on her investment in the venture. The triumph of the voyage was complete.

The Spaniards were unaware that Drake had gone home, and in a bid to protect his merchant ships in the Atlantic, Philip ordered Santa Cruz to put to sea. As a result, Spanish energies remained absorbed by Drake for months after he had reached England. Santa Cruz only returned to Lisbon in September 1587, and by then his ships needed to be refitted and revictualled before they could again leave port. Philip had hoped that his fleet could set off for England that autumn, but his admiral informed him that the necessary repairs would take so long that it would be December before he could set sail, and the weather then would be dangerously wintry for a naval campaign. Reluctantly, Philip agreed that Santa Cruz could stay in harbour until the following spring.

By singeing the King of Spain's beard – as Sir Francis memorably described his attack upon Cadiz – Drake had procured the Queen a valuable respite, but it remained to be seen whether she would make good use of it. "I assure Your Honour, the like preparation was never heard of, nor known, as the King of Spain hath and daily maketh to invade England", Drake warned Walsingham, but despite the impending danger Elizabeth remained in a less than bellicose frame of mind. One way of striking against Spain would have been for the English to step up operations in the Netherlands, but far from consenting to measures of this sort, the Queen made it plain she regretted even her present limited involvement in the Low Countries. As she was unwilling to have another long parting from Leicester, she had sent Lord Buckhurst to the Netherlands in March 1587, promising that Leicester would follow when Buckhurst had sorted out the difficulties that had previously arisen between Leicester and the States. To her horror, Buckhurst had written home suggesting that she should agree to a plea from the States-General that she should loan them an additional £50,000. In reply, the Queen had stormed, "We marvel at your preferring such a request, being not ignorant how greatly we stand charged otherwise, and how unable we are to furnish such a sum ... Your duty was to dissuade them from propounding so unreasonable a demand". Walsingham thought that by withholding further investment, Elizabeth was losing an excellent opportunity to make real progress against Parma, but the Queen's resentment at these further calls on her purse was understandable enough, in view of the fact that in the last eighteen months she had already spent £60,000 more than she had budgeted for on her forces in the Netherlands, and had had precious little to show for it.[10]

At length, she unwillingly agreed to advance the States a further £15,000 to pay 5,000 extra troops for two months, and this money was entrusted to Leicester in June, when he finally resumed his post in the Netherlands. Nevertheless, the extra cash proved insufficient to prevent further military setbacks, for on 26 July the town of Sluys fell, a disaster for which Leicester's incompetence and the States-General's niggardliness were alike to blame. The Council warned Leicester that the fall of Sluys had disillusioned the Queen still further with the war, and made her long more than ever for a negotiated peace.[11]

Although some of her advisers held that the Queen was refusing to face facts if she thought that an end to hostilities was attainable, by the summer of 1587 she did in fact have good reason for believing that a peace conference would prove productive. In October 1586, Andreas de Loo, the Italian merchant who had previously acted as an unofficial emissary for the Queen, had succeeded in re-establishing contact with the Duke of Parma. Following this meeting, he assured Elizabeth that Parma was not only anxious for peace, but that he had Philip II's permission to negotiate a settlement. He did stress that Parma and others had warned that Philip would never grant the exercise of the Protestant religion in his dominions, but Elizabeth had not been unduly discouraged by this. She had repeated that she would "stand no further on the point of religion than to obtain from the King so much toleration for Holland and Zealand as he may be able to concede on his conscience and honour". It subsequently transpired that what the Queen meant by this ambiguous statement was that she thought that it would form an acceptable basis for a peace if Philip agreed to tolerate Protestantism in the Netherlands for two years, after which time the States-General should be permitted to draw up a religious settlement that would be enforced throughout the United Provinces.[12]

It was true that the Calvinists of Holland and Zealand might well feel that these limited concessions would scarcely make their long struggle against Spain seem worthwhile, but Elizabeth trusted that in time they would become amenable. Prior to his departure, Leicester had been instructed to try and incline the people to peace, a task he found most uncongenial, for he personally believed that the Queen was deluding herself in thinking that the Spaniards were prepared to come to terms. "Surely you shall find the Prince [of Parma] meaneth no peace", he chided Walsingham. "I see money doth undo all; the care to keep it and not upon just cause to spend it ... Her Majesty will rue the sparing counsel at such times". Walsingham of course agreed, but he told Leicester that when he cautioned Elizabeth against trusting Philip or Parma, his warnings were "offensively taken", "so strong a conceit are we grown to have of both their sincerities, contrary to the opinion of all men of judgement".[13] Hardly surprisingly, the States-General also declared themselves resolutely opposed to peace talks when Leicester admitted to them that the Queen wished to start negotiations.

As it happened, Leicester and Walsingham were right in thinking that the Spaniards' apparent willingness to negotiate was no more than a sham, for Philip was determined not to cancel the invasion of England. The fall of Sluys, which had so demoralized Elizabeth, had served to put fresh heart in Philip, and he refused to be discouraged by the delays to which the enterprise of England had been subject. Instead he merely modified his original plan of action, dropping the requirement that Santa Cruz should land in Ireland prior to Parma launching his attack on England itself. Parma had already warned the King that, because there was now no question of catching the English unprepared, he would need Santa Cruz's protection during a sea crossing, and Philip accordingly decided that in order "to extirpate this evil thing at its roots",[14] his army and fleet would have to work in close co-operation. According to the revised plan, the Armada was now to sail directly up the English Channel and anchor somewhere off Margate. When the fleet was at hand, Parma would be able to put to sea in his flat bottomed boats, and while his army was being ferried to the mouth of the Thames, the Armada would be ideally placed to protect his craft from attack by the English navy.

In the meantime, Philip was happy enough that the English should be distracted by peace talks but, as he confided to Parma, he had no intention that these should lead to a treaty. "On the contrary ... " he wrote, "all this is done ... to deceive [the English] and cool them in their preparations for defence, by inducing them to believe that such preparations will be unnecessary. You are well aware that the reverse of all this is the truth, and that on our part there is to be no slackness, but the greatest diligence in our efforts for the invasion of England".[15]

Those who shook their heads over Elizabeth's attempts to disengage herself from the struggle in the Netherlands, could draw no comfort from the situation in France. That kingdom had been gravely de-stabilized by the death of the Duke of Alençon, for Henry III had no son and, in the absence of any brother to succeed him, the heir to the throne was the King's Protestant cousin, Henry of Navarre. The Guises, however, had not been prepared to see a Huguenot on the throne of France. In December 1584, the Duke of Guise had concluded the Treaty of Joinville with Spain, whereby in return for a subsidy of £125,000 a year from Philip, Guise had promised to do all in his power to prevent a heretic becoming king. In March 1585 Guise had called all true Catholics to arms, and as Henry III lacked the forces to resist his over-mighty subject, he had to give in to all of Guise's demands. In July Henry had rescinded his earlier grant of toleration to the Huguenots, and an edict had been issued debarring Navarre from inheriting the throne. Navarre had started to gather together his followers in order to resist this infringement on his rights, and in September civil war had again broken out in France.

The Queen's principal advisers were agreed that she should assist Navarre. At length, in January 1587, she had given £30,000 to the ever-obliging John Casimir on the understanding that he would take a mercenary army to France to fight on Navarre's behalf. This army only arrived in France in September 1587, and it soon disintegrated for lack of pay. Both Burghley and Walsingham entreated the Queen to send more funds to Casimir, but they were unable to prevail upon her to do so. As Guise tightened his grip upon France, Walsingham commented angrily that the money spent on mercenaries had only served for the glorification of the Catholic League.[16] The future of Protestantism in that country now looked bleaker than ever.

Small wonder, then, that as 1587 drew to a close, there were many Englishmen who were nervous of what the coming year would bring. Their fears were accentuated by the ancient prophecies that stated that 1588 would be "a year of wonders", "afflicting mankind with woeful destiny". The best known of these prophecies was that penned by the fifteenth-century mathematician and seer Regiomontanus, whose reading of the heavens had led him to conclude that in 1588 there would be "either an universal consummation and final dissolution of the world, or at least a general subversion and alteration of principalities, kingdoms, monarchies and empires". These prognostications were "rife in every man's mouth", and to the superstitious, signs were not lacking that Nature was in turmoil, confirming that some great cataclysm was imminent. For example, much was made of the fact that "on the window of the Queen's Presence Chamber at Court, were found a vast number of fleas collected together; and thirty great fish, commonly called porpoises, came up the river to the watergate of the Queen's Court".[17]

Such was the public concern that the Privy Council authorized the learned Dr John Harvey to publish a book denying that there was any cause for alarm. In this work, Harvey insisted that it was not in the least bit worrying that during 1588 there would be one solar, and two lunar eclipses, and he accused those who claimed that "Bloody Mars" would dominate the heavens that year of misreading the stars. He told his readers that if the position of Mars was examined carefully, "Shall you not find his violent affection to be bridled and qualified in such sort that he is greatly unlike to infect, terrify or astonish the world with any such sanguinary or horrible garboils as otherwise he portendeth?"[18] Not even this respected authority, however, could assuage prevalent fears, and despite Harvey's measured phrases, the murmuring continued.

Certainly, if Mars was truly pre-eminent in the heavens, he seemed to be having remarkably little effect on Queen Elizabeth, for she remained determined to treat for peace in the Netherlands. In February 1588 she sent word to the Dutch that, regardless of whether or not they were prepared to participate in negotiations, she intended to send peace commissioners to Flanders. Later in the month, the English delegation, headed by Lords Derby and Cobham, crossed to the Low Countries. Nevertheless, little progress was made towards peace. For weeks, the English commissioners haggled with Philip's representatives about where the peace talks should take place, and when at the end of May Bourbourg was finally settled as the location, there were further disagreements as to whether a cease-fire should be declared while negotiations were in progress. By this time, the evident reluctance of Philip's commissioners to get down to business had roused the suspicion of their English counterparts, with the exception of the near senile Sir James Crofts, who had accepted a secret pension from Spain when Mendoza was in England, and who repeatedly assured the Queen that an accommodation was imminent.

Parma's utter lack of sincerity concerning the peace talks was highlighted in June. Preparatory to the invasion of England, Sixtus V had issued a Papal Bull excommunicating Elizabeth afresh, and this Bull was printed at Antwerp and circulated widely. At the same time there was published a book by William Allen, whom the Pope, at Philip's request, had made a cardinal the year before, and who had been promised the posts of Archbishop of Canterbury and Lord Chancellor of England if Elizabeth was defeated. In this latest piece of propaganda, Allen urged the people of England to join with Philip's army when it arrived on their shores, and to depose the Queen in the name of the Catholic religion. He asserted that they were absolved of their oath of allegiance to Elizabeth who was "a most unjust usurper ... an infamous, deprived, accursed, excommunicate heretic; the very shame of her sex and princely name; the chief spectacle of sin and abomination in this our age". With Leicester "and divers others", Elizabeth had indulged in "unspeakable and incredible variety of lust", and "made her Court as a trap, by this damnable and detestable art, to entangle in sin and overthrow the younger sort of the nobility and gentlemen of the land, whereby she is become notorious to the world, and in other countries a fable for this her turpitude". Allen concluded, "If any case may fall in which a prince may justly be forsaken or resisted by his subjects ... here all causes together do concur in the person of the pretensed".[19]

The Queen demanded that her commissioners challenged Parma about these publications, insisting that, if he claimed they had been distributed without his authorization, he had the printers punished. Parma failed to satisfy these demands, but even so, the Queen did not break off the peace negotiations. By now, however, she had ceased to hope that any good would come from them, and she only continued with the charade in order to give her country more time to improve its defences. Only Sir James Crofts remained under the illusion that peace was still within reach. Indeed on 23 July, as the Armada was sailing up the Channel, Crofts assured Burghley that his "discretion and experience" left him in no doubt that Philip was anxious to avoid war.[20]

The Queen has been criticized on the grounds that her blind desire for peace enabled Philip and Parma to make her their dupe, but it was understandable and even praiseworthy that she resisted being sucked into war without thoroughly examining the alternatives. When Walsingham grumbled, Burghley pointed out, "As God will be best pleased with peace, so in nothing can her Majesty content her realm better than in procuring of peace, which, if it cannot be had, yet is she excused before God and the world ... In short, seek peace but prepare for war".[21] This was a maxim that the Queen followed.

Elizabeth had not been so optimistic of concluding an agreement with Philip that home defences had been neglected. On the contrary, indeed, her navy was in a better condition than at any previous time in her reign. The Queen herself possessed no more than twenty-five warships (and in time of peace the majority of these were left unmanned in dock), but when war threatened the towns in maritime counties were expected to fit out ships for the national defence, and Elizabeth could also charter ships from trading companies and private individuals. Obviously however it was the Queen's own galleons that formed the kernel of the fleet, and by 1588 these constituted a formidable fighting force. The upkeep of the royal fleet was entrusted to the Navy Board, and in November 1577 the old sea-dog, John Hawkins, had joined this body as treasurer. From the start he had set himself to stamp out corruption and obtain value for money for his mistress. When he became treasurer, the Queen was spending £6,000 a year on routine maintenance for her ships, and on top of this had come the expenses for heavy repairs. In 1585 Hawkins had undertaken to perform both branches of maintenance for a mere £5,714, a considerable saving for the Queen. She had invested it in new ships, such as the *Ark Ralegh* – subsequently christened the *Ark Royal* – which she purchased from Sir Walter Ralegh in 1587, and which was adopted as the flagship of the fleet the following year. As a result of this programme of modernization and expansion, when the English navy went to war in 1588, eleven of the Queen's warships had been constructed in the last four years.

Hawkins had also presided over a revolution in the design of English ships. Traditionally, these had been equipped with lofty superstructures known as "castles", which towered above the decks, affording some shelter to the fighting men aboard. Hawkins did away with these, and he also commissioned ships which were less wide in relation to their length than was customary. These reforms, which produced ships that were "low and snug in the water", meant that there was more room for artillery on the decks, and also ensured that the ships manoeuvred well at sea. Not only were all the ships that had been brought into service in recent years built along these lines, but twelve of the older vessels in the fleet were remodelled according to Hawkins's specifications, greatly improving their performance.[22]

By eliminating the graft that previously had bedevilled naval administration, Hawkins had hit the pockets of several of his colleagues on the Navy Board, and hence made enemies. In revenge they claimed that he himself was cheating the Queen, by building new ships with rotting timbers, or skimping on repairs. The charges proved groundless. For much of 1588, the Queen's ships were at sea in the most arduous conditions, and they bore it remarkably well. Elizabeth's Lord Admiral, Lord Howard of Effingham, proudly affirmed that his mistress had "the strongest ships that any prince in Christendom hath".[23]

On land, defence preparations had also been set in motion. In each county there was meant to be a core of trained men who could be called upon in the event of invasion, for at the annual musters, at which all ablebodied males were supposed to be present, the fittest specimens were picked out and given instruction on how "to use, handle and exercise their horses, armour, shot and other weapons". In the present emergency, however, not only were these men put on alert, but "the whole strength of the shire" was told to prepare themselves "to their utmost power, for defence". In February 1587, orders had been sent to the Lords Lieutenants, who were responsible for military organization in the counties, telling them to contact their subordinates "and charge them without delay to warn all persons under their charge, from man to man, to be ready in their armour and weapons" for inspection the following month. Once these troops had been reviewed, special care was to "be taken to cause them all to be trained and taught to march in all sorts of marching" and those men who were equipped with firearms were "to be taught to shoot at certain marks to be devised with boards to be set up to shoot at, which the captains may see weekly done".[24]

The Lords Lieutenants of the maritime counties were instructed to make a survey of those "places as may appear most dangerous for any number of enemies to have landing", and to do what they could to make them tenable. If necessary, ramparts, earthworks and parapets were to be erected to protect the defenders, "ditches and pits of good depth" were to be dug, and stakes were to be implanted on the beaches. Meanwhile, ammunition and cast iron ordnance were to be despatched to the coastal counties, with instructions that field pieces were to be kept with sufficient powder and shot on special gun carriages, so they could be moved to wherever the Lord Lieutenant of the county desired. Cart horses were also to be kept in readiness, so that they could move this artillery "when and where need of service shall require". Already, throughout the nation, braziers on poles had been set aloft on suitable hilltops, ready to be ignited in warning of the enemy's approach, and now the Justices of the Peace were given firm reminders "to see to the beacons' guarding and good usage".[25]

In November 1587 a report that the Spaniards were on their way had occasioned a flurry of activity. Merchant ships were requisitioned, and the navy had mobilized with commendable speed. By January the scare was over, and the crews of the Queen's ships had been reduced to half strength. Walsingham, needless to say, thought that Elizabeth was being lax. "Here we do nothing but honour St George", he growled to a friend, when the Queen was absorbed in arrangements for the annual garter ceremony, but these strictures were somewhat unfair, for land defences were not being neglected. At the beginning of the year it had been agreed that measures should be adopted in London "for the training of 10,000 men in better sort than they had been afore times", and by the spring it was a common sight in the city to see these troops being drilled. In January the Queen had also sent orders to the county authorities to draw up a list of local recusants, "and thereupon to cause the most obstinate and noted persons to be committed to such prisons as are fittest for their safe keeping. The rest that are ... not so obstinate to be referred to the custody of some ecclesiastical person, and other gentlemen well affected". Following the recommendations of a committee which included Lord Burghley, Sir John Norris and Sir Walter Ralegh, a list of probable landing places for the Spaniards was drawn up, and these positions were fortified.[26]

In April 1588 letters were sent to thirty-seven towns in the maritime counties instructing them to supply fully equipped ships to reinforce the first line of defence. There was some protest at this. Tewkesbury refused to pay a share of Gloucester's costs in fitting out ships, and York was equally reluctant to help out Hull. The Mayor of Southampton complained that the town was in the depths of a severe trade depression. The subsidy had just been gathered with difficulty, and the townsfolk had also been burdened with providing powder and munitions for the militia. When he had revealed to the people that they must raise a further £500 for fitting out a ship, they began "greatly to murmur and grieve thereat".[27] Incidents such as these proved that the Queen had been right in supposing that her subjects would not take kindly to supporting the financial strain of war, and justified her attempts to stave it off for as long as possible.

The Queen could pride herself on having done everything possible to strengthen the nation's defences, but by the spring of 1588 she was receiving advice that it was not enough to wait for the enemy's arrival and to repel an attack when it came. Instead, Drake and others wanted to seize the initiative by taking a fleet to the coast of Spain so that the Armada could either be destroyed as it lay in port or attacked when it put to sea. Drake declared to the Queen, "The advantage of time and place in all martial actions is half a victory", and he promised the Council, "With fifty sail of shipping we shall do more good upon their own coast than a great many more will do here at home". Elizabeth was nevertheless uneasy at the idea, fearing that the Armada might succeed in eluding her ships and would then descend upon England at a time when the country was bare of naval defences. Despite her misgivings, however, on 10 May it was agreed that Lord Admiral Howard could dispose his fleet in any way he saw fit.[28]

It was still by no means certain that Drake's strategy would be adopted, for at the outset Howard had shared the Queen's scepticism about it. This can only have strengthened Drake's conviction that he himself should have been given overall command of the fleet, rather than having to defer to a man who, by his standards at least, was little better than a landlubber. Charles, Lord Howard of Effingham was a cousin of the Queen's who came from a long line of Lord Admirals, and in May 1585 he had succeeded the late Earl of Lincoln in the post. The appointment had much to commend it, for Howard had commanded royal fleets in the past. In 1583 he had also chaired a commission investigating administrative abuses in the navy, and no other nobleman at court was so well qualified to assume overall responsibility for all marine causes. Nevertheless, compared to Drake, Howard was vastly inexperienced, and since Sir Francis was far from being the most biddable of men, the potential for friction between them was obvious. It was fortunate that Howard was keenly aware of his own deficiencies, and having "skill enough to know those who had more skill than himself", took great care not to be more assertive than was absolutely necessary. He later said that it had been his policy to "yield ever unto them of greater experience", and despite the fact that initially he had been against going to Spain as Drake had suggested, before long Sir Francis had managed to convince him of the merits of the plan. Relieved to find that he had someone so pliable for a superior, Drake in his turn "gave an example of singular self-mastery", and conducted himself so "lovingly and kindly" towards the Lord Admiral that he "dispelled all vain fears that might have been entertained about this doubtful union".[29]

On 30 May Howard and his fleet set out for Spain from Plymouth, but a week later they were driven back to port by storms and high seas, for the weather was "as boisterous and bad as if it were December". "We have danced as lustily as the gallantest dancers in Court", Howard told Walsingham wryly, but despite this he was anxious to get back to sea as soon as possible. He was therefore greatly downcast when the Queen suddenly changed her mind about letting her fleet go to Spain. She could not shake off her fear that the Armada would be able to slip past her fleet and make for England, and on 9 June she sent orders that, instead of sailing for Spain, the ships under Howard's command should "ply up and down" in waters nearer home.[30]

Howard was furious. Sarcastically he wrote, "I must and will obey; and am glad there be such there, as are able to judge what is fitter for us to do than we here; but by my instructions which I had, I did think it otherwise".[31] Stung by his remonstrances, Elizabeth relented, but in the event her ships never reached the Spanish coast. Having been delayed by adverse winds, Howard had again set sail on 8 July, but two days later the wind changed to a southerly. Hastily the Lord Admiral returned to Plymouth for fear that while his ships battled against a head wind, the Spaniards would be blown past him and on to England.

It was just as well that Drake's plan was never put to the test. Although his thinking was strategically sound, the Queen was right to worry about what would have happened if the Armada had succeeded in slipping past her navy, for Philip II had given specific orders that his fleet was not to turn back even if it was reported that the English were on the Spanish coast. On the other hand, if the English had encountered the Spaniards as planned, they might well have found themselves at a disadvantage, for the difficulties of fighting a naval engagement in waters far from home were immense. The ships in the English fleet carried considerably less ammunition than those in the Armada, for whereas the Spaniards allowed fifty rounds of shot per gun, it has been estimated that the English were provided with an average of only twenty or thirty rounds of shot per gun. When they met with the Armada in the Channel, they found themselves running short of ammunition after only two engagements with the enemy, and had urgently to replenish their stocks from supplies on shore.[32] If they had been fighting off the coast of Spain, this option would obviously have not been open to them, and the Spaniards might well have succeeded in carrying the day.

Meanwhile for the Armada itself, all had not gone smoothly. In February 1588 Philip's admiral, Santa Cruz, had suddenly died, and the Duke of Medina Sidonia, who replaced him, had only a limited experience of seafaring. His appointment was nevertheless a shrewd move on the part of the King. As Captain-General of Andalusia, Medina Sidonia had proved himself a man of considerable organizational abilities, and had played a conspicuous part in the arrangements for the Armada's assembly. He also had a good military record, having distinguished himself during the conquest of Portugal in 1580. He himself protested to the King that he possessed "neither aptitude, ability, health nor fortune" for his new position, but it would be misguided to take him at his own evaluation, not least because he subsequently admitted that he had only tried to turn down the job because he did not believe that the Armada would be capable of defeating the English.[33] Santa Cruz's death was thus not so serious a setback for the Armada as has sometimes been supposed, but it did mean that the fleet was subjected to further delays. Philip had hoped that it would set sail by 1 March at the latest, but on assuming command Medina Sidonia insisted on being given more time to ensure that the force was properly equipped. It was 18 May before the Armada left Lisbon, and then a combination of a shortage of victuals and appalling weather forced it to put in at Corunna to refit. A lengthy interval elapsed before the fleet was in a fit condition to sail, but on 12 July 1588 "the most fortunate Armada" finally left harbour and made for England.

A week later, the Armada was sighted off the Cornish coast. Having laboriously worked their way out of Plymouth in the teeth of an adverse wind, the English managed to slip past the enemy fleet on the night of 20 July, with the result that next morning they were lined up to the west of the Spaniards, and had the wind behind them. This gave them the advantage of being able to choose when to start an engagement but, while they could congratulate themselves on their seamanship so far, they cannot have felt happy when they saw the Spanish fleet spread out in its full majesty, "the ocean groaning under the weight of them".[34] The Spaniards now adopted a complicated defensive formation, whereby the slow and poorly armed supply ships in their fleet were screened by rows of warships. On the left and right of the main body of ships, a line of galleons protruded like horns towards the English, so that to them the Armada assumed the appearance of a huge crescent.

Somewhat daunted by this formidable array, the English moved up and opened fire on the ships in the 'horns'. In this first engagement, which only lasted about two hours, the Spaniards suffered little damage. One Englishman admitted, "the majesty of the enemy's fleet, the good order they held, and the private consideration of our own wants did cause, in mine opinion, our first onset to be more coldly done than became the value of our nation and the credit of our English navy". It would appear that the English had been unduly optimistic about the effectiveness of their long range ordnance, and that they had hoped that they would be able to inflict severe damage on the Spanish fleet without venturing too close. The first day's action proved that this was illusory. Two Spanish ships were disabled that day, but only because one suffered an explosion on board and the other collided with another member of her own fleet. When the rival navies had their next engagement, on 23 July, the story was the same, for despite expending the most "terrible value of great shot", the English did not destroy a single Spanish ship. It was obvious that if they were going to beat the enemy they would have to close the range between them, and on 25 July, when there was another exchange of fire off the Isle of Wight, a Spaniard noted, "They came nearer than the first day".[35]

Throughout the week the English fleet trailed the Armada as it maintained a stately progress up the Channel towards its junction with Parma, only occasionally pausing to do battle. But though their fleet remained virtually intact, the Spaniards were far from satisfied with their own performance, for they had no chance of crippling the English navy unless they managed to come to close quarters with their opponents during sea fights. Ideally, the Spaniards would have liked to approach within grappling distance of the enemy, for then the numerous soldiers on board their own vessels could have leapt onto the decks of the adjacent ships and taken them by storm. In every engagement, however, the Spanish had found that there was no question of this, for the English ships wheeled and turned with a precision and ease that left them astounded. Ton for ton, the Spanish galleons were roughly on a parity with those of the English, but the Spanish ships looked much more imposing, being heavily built up above the decks. They were also weighed down with quantities of supplies and ammunition needed for the projected campaign on land, and this affected their sailing performance. As a result, the Spanish vessels were much less weatherly and nimble than the English ones, and this meant that, however hard they tried to get alongside, the English could always dodge away, their "ships being very swift and well handled, so that they could do as they liked with them".[36]

Yet this was not Medina Sidonia's greatest worry for, though he had tried to warn Parma of his approach, he had not heard when the latter intended to leave the coast of Flanders and make the crossing to England. The grim truth was that it was not possible for Parma's barges to leave the havens where they were moored, for Philip's grand conception was fatally flawed. For one thing, Parma had made it clear that the wind and weather would have to be favourable before he could adventure his flotilla on the high seas and, as it was, conditions could hardly have been more adverse. Then too, there was the problem that the waters round the Flemish coastline were so shallow that the Armada could not come within twelve miles of it, and hence could offer no protection to Parma until he was well out to sea. This meant that Parma would be exposed to onslaughts by the flyboats of the Dutch navy, and he knew that his barges would be helpless in the face of attack from these small, but well-armed craft. It would appear that Philip had discounted the possibility that the Dutch would assist the English in this way, and certainly he had made no contingency plans to deal with the problem if it arose. Parma himself had tried to lessen the danger by tricking the Dutch into believing that he was planning an offensive against Holland or Zealand, and the ruse was partially successful, for there were fewer flyboats patrolling the waters off Dunkirk (which would have been Parma's port of embarkation) than would have been the case if it had been certain that Parma was going to move against England. Nevertheless if he had ventured out, there was a sufficient quantity of Dutch ships at hand to have seriously impeded his passage, and it is a matter of conjecture whether he would have managed to make it to England. Furthermore, he had only succeeded in practising this deception by keeping the majority of his troops stationed inland, and this meant he needed six days' warning to move his men to the coast and carry out the embarkation. Unfortunately, he only received Medina Sidonia's message that the fleet was approaching on 27 July, and by the time Parma was ready to set off, the Armada was no longer in the vicinity.[37] Parma therefore remained bottled up in port, unable to sally forth and "join hands" with the Armada as had originally been envisaged.

Meanwhile, Medina Sidonia, who was not aware of Parma's predicament, had anchored off Calais on 27 July in hopes that Parma would shortly emerge. This had given the English the opportunity they needed. Eight of the more insignificant vessels in their fleet were selected and converted into mobile incendiary devices by dint of stuffing them with whatever combustible materials were at hand. About midnight on 28 July, these fireships were sent floating towards the Spanish, in the hope of dislodging them from their anchorage. The ruse worked. At the sight of the approaching fireships, "the whole sea glittering and shining with the flame thereof",[38] the Spaniards were thrown into confusion, for not only did they fear that the burning vessels would spark off a general conflagration, but they wrongly assumed that the fireships were packed with explosives which would detonate once in amongst their fleet. In panic, they cut their cables and scrambled out to sea.

Next morning, off Gravelines, Medina Sidonia turned to face the English whilst his scattered fleet did its best to re-form and come up to support him. By this time, however, the English had the advantage of him. They had now attained numerical superiority, for as they had sailed up the Channel, fresh ships had come from every port to reinforce their fleet, which at present numbered about one hundred and forty sail. Furthermore, they could be confident of outgunning the enemy, for previous engagements had revealed that the Spaniards seriously under-used their artillery. The English mounted their ordnance on wheeled gun carriages which could be pulled back on deck each time the gun was fired, thus facilitating reloading. Spanish artillery, on the other hand, was much more cumbersome to move, which meant that their cannon were so difficult to reload that frequently they were fired only once or twice during an engagement. This gave the English the edge over their opponents, and at Gravelines they exploited their superiority to the full. While remaining out of reach of the Spaniards' grappling irons (much to the fury of the enemy, who shouted angrily that they were "cowards" and "Lutheran chickens") the English sailed so close to the ships in the opposing fleet that they were "most times within speech one of another".

As a result the Spanish took a fearful battering. Medina Sidonia's flagship was so badly holed in the hull that it was only the frantic exertions of two divers plugging the leaks that kept the vessel afloat. Two Spanish ships were reduced to so helpless a condition that it was impossible to prevent them running aground off the Zealand coast, while another sank with two hundred and seventy-five men on board, some of whom were seen clinging desperately to the rigging and spars as she went down.[39] Worse still, from the Spaniards' point of view, was the fact that the English had forced them so far to leeward that it appeared that the winds and tide would finish off the job by driving the entire Armada to destruction on the sandbanks of Zealand.

At the last minute, however, the wind changed, driving the Spaniards northwards with their opponents in pursuit. To their infinite regret, the English had to abandon the chase once the Armada was beyond the Firth of Forth, for their ammunition was quite exhausted, and victuals were also running low. Although disappointed by their inability to pulverize the enemy as completely as they would have liked, the English captains drew solace from the knowledge that the Spanish ships were now so weakened that they would have difficulty surviving the journey home in the strong winds that currently prevailed. One English mariner noted exultantly, "Many of them will never see Spain again; which is the only work of God, to chastise their malicious practices, and to make them know that neither the strengths of men, nor their idolatrous gods, can prevail when the mighty God of Israel stretcheth out but his finger against them".[40]

There was little danger that the Spaniards would be able to avail themselves of safe havens on the Scottish coast, for James VI had already written to Elizabeth assuring her he would give her whatever assistance she needed against her enemies. It was true that until recently there had been uncertainty as to whether he would adopt a friendly attitude towards the Queen in her hour of crisis. Diplomatic relations between England and Scotland, which had been broken off following Mary's execution, had been resumed as early as June 1587, but for months after that there was concern that James's intentions remained hostile. In January 1588 Lord Hunsdon had affirmed, "I dare assure her Majesty that this king means to revenge the death of his mother if ever he be able, and that what fair speeches or promises soever are made of him, her Majesty shall find it but plain dissimulation". James had done his best to exploit English concern on this score by implying that he might ally with the Spaniards unless Elizabeth took material steps to allay his grievances against her. On the whole, the Queen had consistently taken the view that James was bluffing, but for safety's sake a special ambassador had been despatched to Scotland as the Armada approached. In some anxiety that James really was contemplating throwing in his lot with the Spaniards, the envoy desperately promised the King that Elizabeth was planning to bestow a dukedom on him, and to award him a pension of £5,000 a year. Once the invasion crisis was over, the Queen had no compunction about disavowing these offers, claiming that her ambassador had exceeded his instructions, but in the short term these inducements had proved wonderfully persuasive. Contrary to Philip II's confident prediction that James could hardly offer succour to Elizabeth when "the blood of his murdered mother is not yet congealed",[41] on 1 August 1588 the King had written to her volunteering to do all in his power to repel the invaders.

Although so far all had gone well for the English, they could not be sure that the Armada would not return, or that Parma would not attempt the crossing to England without the benefit of naval support. On land, therefore, forces remained in readiness. The Earl of Leicester, who had returned from the Netherlands the previous December, had been named as "Lieutenant and Captain General of the Queen's armies and companies", and about 21 July he had started assembling troops at Tilbury in Essex. In the initial stages, all was in chaos at the camp, for there were no provisions to feed the first detachments that gathered there, and Leicester made matters worse by wasting time quarrelling with his experienced subordinate John Norris. Gradually, however, the confusion lessened, and by early August Leicester could proudly claim that his men were now in such good order that they appeared to be "soldiers rather of a year's experience than of a month's camping".[42]

How these troops would have acquitted themselves if faced with Parma's veterans is naturally open to question. At the time there were many who thought it a foregone conclusion that the Spaniards would emerge victorious. Medina Sidonia, for example, told Philip that he envisaged success on land would be "quite easy when we have beaten the enemy at sea. Everybody says this and your Majesty is better aware of it than anyone". Howard took an equally dim view of the landsmen's abilities, warning that it would "breed great danger" if they had to face combat with the enemy. Parma's troops were renowned for being "the best soldiers at this day in Christendom", and while the English militia machinery in theory should have ensured that there was a large body of trained men ready to oppose them, the Council did have to admit in December 1587 that the musters often "served more, as it is thought, for fashion, than for substance of discipline".[43]

On the other hand, Parma himself was far from sanguine about how he would fare on landing. Apart from the 30,000 men he had hoped to ship to England, he had counted on being reinforced with 6,000 soldiers from the Armada, and he had stressed that he would not be happy with less, for 50,000 men would not be an excessive number with which to try and conquer England. By the summer of 1588, however, he had fewer than 18,000 troops at his disposal, for in the months that his army had awaited the arrival of the Armada, disease had worked havoc in the ranks. In theory at least, the English were capable of setting many more men in the field. Leicester's army at Tilbury was estimated at about 12,500 men, and in addition 6,000 Kentish troops stationed at Sandwich were also under the Earl's command. The Queen had named Lord Hunsdon as the commander of a still larger army that was to be assembled "near unto us for the defence and surety of our own royal person against the attempts and powers of any manner foreign forces". By early August approximately 17,000 troops from the shires were on their way to London to reinforce the 9,000 members of the city's trained bands, although in the event these forces were never united, as the difficulties involved in provisioning such an influx led the Council to send the countrymen back to their counties on 7 August.[44]

Astonishingly, Philip II himself felt less than total confidence about the prospects of the expedition on which he had lavished so much effort and expense. Medina Sidonia had carried from Spain a sealed document which was to be handed to Parma on his landing in England. This contained instructions from Philip that "If (which God forbid) the result be not so prosperous that our arms shall be able to settle matters", Parma could enter into negotiations and agree to withdraw from England in return for limited concessions. Philip stated that if better terms were not forthcoming, Parma could conclude peace with Elizabeth on condition that she granted her Catholic subjects the free use and exercise of their faith. "I have thought well to say thus much", Philip cautiously concluded, "but I hope that God, whose cause it is, and to whom I have dedicated the enterprise, will not allow you to fail, but will aid us to convert England, as we desire, for His greater glory".[45]

On 27 July, Leicester invited the Queen to come and inspect her troops at Tilbury, declaring warmly, "You shall (dear lady) behold as goodly, as loyal and as able men as any Prince Christian can show you". Some of those about the Queen had expressed fears that her life might be endangered if she paraded herself before such a crowd, but Leicester pledged that he could guarantee "your person to be as sure as at St James's, for my life".[46] Elizabeth was pleased to accept his judgment, and her belief that these soldiers would prove as trustworthy and devoted as Leicester had promised was subsequently to form the opening theme of her most famous speech of all.

On 8 August 1588 Queen Elizabeth travelled to Tilbury by river, and having spent the night at Edward Ritche's nearby house, Saffron Garden, she reviewed her troops next morning. In keeping with the martial mood of the gathering, she was dressed "as armed Pallas" for the occasion, wearing a silver breastplate over her white velvet dress, with "a truncheon in her hand". After she had seen her soldiers march past, she made her celebrated address, "most bravely mounted on a stately steed". "My loving people", she began, "We have been persuaded by some that are careful of our safety, to take heed how we commit ourself to armed multitudes for fear of treachery; but I assure you, I do not desire to live to distrust my faithful and loving people. Let tyrants fear. I have always so behaved my self, that under God, I have placed my chiefest strength and safeguard in the loyal hearts and goodwill of all my subjects, and therefore I am come amongst you, as you see, at this time, not for my recreation and disport, but being resolved in the midst and heat of the battle, to live or die amongst you all, to lay down for my God, and for my kingdom, and for my people, my honour, and my blood, even in the dust. I know I have the body but of a weak and feeble woman, but I have the heart and stomach of a king, and of a King of England too, and think foul scorn that Parma or Spain, or any Prince of Europe should dare to invade the borders of my realm; to which, rather than any dishonour shall grow by me, I myself will take up arms, I myself will be your general, judge and rewarder of every one of your virtues in the field. I know already for your forwardness, you have deserved rewards and crowns; and we do assure you, in the word of a Prince, they shall be duly paid you".[47]

As she came to the end of this "most excellent oration", her troops "all at once a mighty shout or cry did give", and Leicester declared that her words had "so inflamed the hearts of her good subjects, as I think the weakest among them is able to match the proudest Spaniard that dares land in England". The review over, Elizabeth went to dine in Leicester's tent, and while she was still there a report reached the camp that Parma was on his way to England. Naturally Leicester urged her to return to the safety of London, but the Queen valorously declared that she would not think of deserting her men at such a time. It was only as "night approached nigh" – by which time it was clear that the rumour about Parma had been false – that Elizabeth could be prevailed upon to take her leave.[48]

As the days passed, and there was no sign of the Armada's return, the Queen could begin to hope that for the time being at least, the Spaniards had been kept at bay. As the English began to review their achievement, complaints were not wanting that insufficient supplies of ammunition "hath bereaved us of the famousest victory that ever our navy might have had at sea", and there were also some regrets that so few Spanish ships had fallen into English hands. Indeed, after the Battle of Gravelines, the Council had sent to ask Howard why none of the Spanish ships had been grappled with and boarded, showing such total incomprehension of the tactics that had brought victory that the Lord Admiral must have ground his teeth in rage. These criticisms could not detract from the fact that the Queen had gained a great triumph, and Elizabeth did not try to hide the satisfaction she took in it. To James VI she wrote jubilantly, "For my part, I doubt no whit that all this tyrannical, proud and brainsick attempt will be the beginning, though not the end, of the ruin of that King, that most unkingly, even in the midst of treating peace, begins this wrongful war. He hath procured my greatest glory that meant my sorriest wrack".[49]

Once persuaded that the immediate danger was past, Elizabeth wasted no time in reducing her outgoings on her armed forces, despite warnings from Drake and others that demobilization was as yet premature. On 17 August she gave orders that the camp at Tilbury was to be dissolved, and ten days later orders were sent that most of the navy should be likewise discharged. As a result, whereas on 1 August, one hundred and ninety-seven ships had been registered as being in royal service, by 4 September, only thirty-four remained officially in commission.[50]

The men of action might frown, but the Lord Treasurer could only applaud the Queen's regard to thrift, for money was desperately short. Expenditure on defence preparations had proved so burdensome that in January 1588 Elizabeth had had to resort to raising £75,000 in forced loans from wealthy subjects, and this had had to be supplemented by a loan of £30,000, obtained from the City in March, at a ten per cent rate of interest. The Queen contributed what she could, and in 1588 another £100,000 was swallowed up of the surplus that had been set aside in more prosperous years. Even so, by the summer, more cash was needed to finance the state of emergency. Having failed to obtain a loan abroad, Burghley had to turn to the City to plead for another loan of £40–50,000, and eventually succeeded in raising £26,000 from this source. It was not a viable option to turn to Parliament to fill the gap, for the subsidies granted in 1587 had not yet been collected in full, and besides this the public had to bear the expenses of the county militias and ship money. Burghley had a shrewd suspicion that it was the poor who had to shoulder a disproportionate part of these burdens, while the well-off managed to evade payment, and he was worried that any further impositions would provoke a great outcry. Already, in August, he had warned Walsingham, "I see a general murmur of people, and malcontented people will increase it to the comfort of the enemy".[51]

Lack of funds made it difficult to pay what was owed to the sailors who had fought against the Armada. The official rate of remuneration was ten shillings a month, and from Dover Howard passed on to the Council the "great discontentments of men here ... who well hoped after this so good service to have received their whole pay, and finding it come but this scantly unto them, it breeds a marvellous alteration among them". To make matters worse, on its return to port, the fleet had been ravaged by disease. Out of approximately 15,000 men who had been in naval service at the time of the Armada, it was estimated that only a hundred or so had fallen in battle, but now typhus, scurvy and food poisoning accounted for hundreds more. Much distressed, Howard reported that his men were sickening one day and dying the next, but there was little that could have been done to avoid such fatalities, for as he remarked, "It is a thing that ever followeth such great services".[52]

Painful though these losses were, the sufferings endured by the Spaniards as they tried to struggle home were infinitely greater. Having been driven north of Scotland, their only hope of return lay in turning west and making for the Atlantic, where they could set a course for Spain. Victuals and water supplies were at such a low level that stringent rationing had to be imposed, and even so, the survivors on board the ships that limped back to harbour in the autumn of 1588 were in a famished and parched condition. "The troubles and miseries we have suffered cannot be described to your Majesty", Medina Sidonia wrote simply to Philip on arriving back at Santander in September. "They have been greater than have been seen in any voyage before".[53]

In one respect at least Medina Sidonia could count himself fortunate, for the vast majority of those who had set out with him in May never completed the homeward journey. After Gravelines, many of the Spanish ships had received such a pounding at English hands that they were in no condition to cope with the violent storms and hazardous seas they encountered off Ireland. It has been estimated that twenty-six Spanish ships were wrecked off the Irish coast, with the loss of some 6,000 men through drowning. Of those who made it to the shore, about 1,000 were either murdered by Irishmen in English pay, or were hunted down and killed by the Lord Deputy of Ireland, Fitzwilliam, and his officers. Several hundred of those shipwrecked had only given themselves up on the understanding that their lives would be spared, but as the Government lacked the facilities to deal with numerous prisoners of war, the authorities in Ireland had no qualms about reneging on their word. In all, of the 30,000 men who had sailed with the Armada, roughly 20,000 are estimated to have perished, and of the one hundred and thirty ships that had made up the fleet, no more than sixty could subsequently be accounted for.[54]

News of the disaster only gradually filtered through to Philip. At first, indeed, he had received reports indicating that the Spaniards had gained a great victory, sinking forty English ships and taking prisoner Francis Drake. Nevertheless, the true state of affairs slowly became apparent, and outwardly at least, Philip accepted the setback with a composure worthy of a man whose mother had declared while in labour with him, "I may die, but will not cry out". In a rare public utterance on the subject, he confined himself to commenting, "In the actions of the Lord, there is no loss or gain of reputation; one should simply not talk about it". Privately, however, he was shattered by the blow. To his confessor he confided, "I promise you that unless some remedy is found ... very soon, we shall find ourselves in such a state that we shall wish that we had never been born ... And if God does not send us a miracle (which is what I hope from him) I hope to die and go to him before all this happens". Yet notwithstanding his deep depression, Philip was in no way prepared to abandon the struggle against England, which he actually felt had "become all the more necessary because of what happened". At the beginning of November, the Venetian ambassador in Spain noted, "In spite of everything, his Majesty shows himself determined to carry on the war".[55]

When the grim catalogue of shipwreck and loss of life was known in England, on the other hand, the nation's mood became ebullient. On 24 November the Queen processed through streets hung with blue cloth and thronged by cheering crowds in order to attend a service of thanksgiving at St Paul's Cathedral. She had composed a special prayer for the occasion, and at the ceremony she read it out in person.

All this time, however, the Queen was labouring under a private sorrow. At the end of August Leicester, whose health had for some time been less than robust, had set out to visit the baths at Buxton in Derbyshire, in the hopes that a course of spa water would do him some good. *En route*, he had stopped at Rycote near Reading, a house which he and the Queen had visited together in former years. From there the fifty-five-year-old Earl had taken up his pen to write a brief letter to Elizabeth, "to know how my gracious lady doth, and what ease of her late pains she finds; being the chiefest thing in the world I do pray for, for her to have good health and long life". As for his own infirmities, he assured her that he was taking the medicine that she had had made up for him, "and find it amend much better than any other thing that hath been given to me". He ended, "With the continuance of my wonted prayer for your Majesty's preservation, I humbly kiss your foot ... P.S. even as I had written this much, I received your Majesty's token by young Tracy". Continuing on his way, he broke his journey again at Cornbury Park, near Woodstock, being "troubled and stayed with an ague".[56] There, his condition grew steadily worse, and at 4 o' clock in the morning of 4 September 1588, he lost his struggle for life.

His death afforded the Queen the profoundest sorrow. Her relationship with Leicester had not been without its traumas, but he had still meant more to her than any other man. Of late they had become closer than ever, for during that last summer she had frequently invited him to dine with her alone, a signal honour that occasioned much comment at Court. In July she had shown her true esteem for him by making him commander of her army, though typically she had tortured him by delaying her decision on the matter for as long as possible, and had not formally signed his commission until the Armada was half way up the Channel.[57]

Now he was gone, and though few of her people shared her sadness at this loss (Camden remarked icily that public joy about the defeat of the Armada was not "anything abated by Leicester's death"), the Queen mourned him sincerely. An informant of Mendoza's reported, "She was so grieved that for some days she shut herself in her chamber alone, and refused to speak to anyone until the Treasurer and other Councillors had the doors broken open and entered to see her". Possibly this was an exaggeration, but certainly she did seclude herself for a while, for on 7 September Walsingham told a correspondent it was impossible to do business with the Queen by "reason that she will not suffer anybody to [have] access unto her, being very much grieved with the death of the Lord Steward".* Her emotion showed plainly in a letter she wrote to her "very good old man", the Earl of Shrewsbury, in reply to one of his that had both congratulated her for the defeat of the Spaniards, and offered condolences for her recent bereavement. Having thanked him for his felicitations, the Queen went on brokenly, "As for the other matter contained in your said letters, although we do therein accept and acknowledge your careful mind and good will, yet we desire rather to forbear the remembrance thereof as a thing whereof we can admit no comfort, otherwise by submitting our will to God's inevitable appointment, who, notwithstanding his goodness by the former prosperous news, hath nevertheless been pleased to keep us in exercise by the loss of a personage so dear unto us". To the end of her life she treasured the note Leicester had sent her from Rycote, reverently inscribing upon it, "HIS LAST LETTER". In November it was observed that the Queen was "much aged and spent, and very melancholy", and those who knew her best affirmed that Leicester's death was to blame.[58]

---

* Leicester had been made Lord Steward in December 1587.

CHAPTER 13

"The only wonder of time's begetting"

For Elizabeth, Leicester's death had been a grievous blow, but she could at least find some consolation in the company of Leicester's twenty-two-year-old stepson, Robert, Earl of Essex. Vibrant, dashing and charismatic, Essex was tall, handsome and (like his mother, who had so annoyed Elizabeth with her marriage to Leicester) auburn-haired. His pedigree was impeccable: on his father's side he could trace his ancestry back to Norman times, while through his mother he was related to the Queen. Unfortunately, he was far from being as wealthy as he was well-bred. His late father had effectively ruined himself when, in 1573, he had volunteered to take an army to Ireland on the understanding that if he pacified the northern province of Ulster, he would be granted vast tracts of land in what is now County Antrim. He and the Queen were to share the costs of the venture, and to finance the expedition he had mortgaged his lands and borrowed £10,000 from the Crown. In Ireland he had failed to meet his objectives, and his debts remained outstanding when in 1576 he had died of dysentery in Dublin Castle. His father's death left his ten-year-old son "the poorest Earl in England", and on reaching maturity Essex had compounded his pecuniary difficulties through his own incorrigible extravagance.

His depleted inheritance nevertheless did not make him ineligible to pursue a successful career at Court, for in some ways indigence was an essential qualification for an aspiring royal favourite. It suited the Queen to bestow her largesse on men who had no fortune of their own, for in consequence they found themselves wholly beholden to her, and she trusted that this would guarantee that they would accord her the devotion and service that she demanded in return. In the case of the Earl of Leicester (whom Elizabeth had once gone so far as to describe as "a creature of our own") the arrangement had worked well, for Leicester was sufficiently

realistic never to forget that his dependency on her was absolute, but with
Essex it was to prove otherwise. "Money and land are base things but love
and kindness are excellent things",[1] he once grandly informed the Queen,
and he expected Elizabeth to be as profligate with all these commodities
as he was himself. Generosity came so naturally to him that he took it for
granted in others, and this made him incapable of valuing Elizabeth's
affection for him at its true worth.

When the eighteen-year-old Earl had first come to Court in 1584 he had
made a dazzling début, for almost instantaneously his "goodly person, and
a kind of urbanity and innate courtesy, combined with the recollection of
his father's misfortunes, won him the hearts of both Queen and people".[2]
As for Leicester, he had been swift to spot the young man's potential,
and having successfully exerted himself to overcome his stepson's initial
aversion to him, he had deliberately thrust his new protégé forward.
Knowing the Queen as he did, he had guessed that she would find Essex
exceptionally appealing, and he hoped that the young Earl's appearance on
the scene would have a detrimental effect on the career of Sir Walter
Ralegh, of whom Elizabeth had as yet shown no signs of tiring.

By August 1585, when Essex accompanied Leicester to the Netherlands,
he could already congratulate himself on having made a favourable
impression on the Queen, but it was only on his return, in early 1587, that
it became clear how greatly she was taken with him. Even those who
had prophesied great things for him were surprised by the speed and
completeness of his conquest, for in the months following Mary Stuart's
execution, when Elizabeth was at her most surly and irascible, she seemed
completely rejuvenated in his presence. In May one courtier reported,
"When she is abroad, nobody near her but my Lord of Essex, and at night
my Lord is at cards, or one game or another with her, that he cometh not
to his lodgings till birds sing in the morning".[3] Already it was being noised
abroad that Essex was set to replace Leicester as Master of the Horse but,
though Leicester let it be known that he had no objection to making way
for the younger man, the Queen was reluctant to appoint Essex to the place
until it was possible to install his stepfather in a still more senior niche at
court. Before long, this problem was overcome, for in December 1587 the
Lord Stewardship became vacant, and having conferred that post upon
Leicester, the Queen had no more qualms about letting Essex succeed him
as Master of the Horse.

Elizabeth had been careful to avoid giving the impression that Leicester
had in any way been relegated in her favour, but even so, Essex was fearful
that his stepfather would be offended when the Queen proposed that he
should use the Lord Steward's vacant apartments when the latter was
absent from Court. At the end of August 1588 Essex wrote anxiously to
his stepfather, "Since your Lordship's departure her Majesty hath been

very earnest with me to lie in the Court, and this morning she sent to me that I might lie in your Lordship's lodging". He promised that he would try to resist the move till he had received Leicester's sanction for it, but warned that the Queen was being so insistent that she might well "force me to it" before it was established that Leicester did not mind.[4] In fact, as Leicester was dead within days of this letter being sent, such worries became immaterial, and with a clear conscience Essex was able to occupy Leicester's former suite of rooms at Whitehall, which were so conveniently close to the Queen's own apartments.

There was of course no suggestion that there was anything remotely improper in the Queen's relationship with Essex and (provided one discounts the maidservant of Sir Robert Sidney who was whipped in 1601 for saying Elizabeth had had a child by the Earl)[5] his meteoric ascent gave rise to none of the bawdy speculation which had accompanied the burgeoning of earlier favourites. Nevertheless, although the Queen was Essex's senior by more than thirty years, she would not have wished it to be thought that they were linked together by no more than the warm affection that might well spring up between an engaging young man with his way to make in the world, and a fascinating older woman who could radically transform his prospects. Instead, courtly convention dictated that Essex adopted the pose of a lovesick swain in pursuit of an elusive mistress, and if the disparity in their ages gave a decidedly grotesque twist to this mannered pantomime, neither protagonist gave any sign of seeing the slightest incongruity in the spectacle. Far from seeming discomfited at his unlikely casting, Essex played his part with panache, projecting the image that was required of him without appearing unduly obsequious or false. It was true that at least one of his contemporaries held that the compliments he paid the Queen had something constrained about them, but the Queen herself voiced no such complaints, for on the whole the Earl's air of candour and imaginative turn of phrase gave conviction to a performance which in less gifted hands could have descended into bathos.

Essex's naturally lively mind had been refined by the exacting discipline of a full renaissance education, and the tributes that he spouted had a classical elegance about them while yet retaining a freshness of their own. A contemporary subsequently recalled, "The Earl was a very acute and sound speaker when he would intend it, and for his writings they are beyond example, especially in his familiar letters and things of delight at Court". Essex's facility with language more than compensated for his ineptitude on the dance floor, where he was described as being "no graceful goer". Now that Elizabeth was growing older, she had less need of agile dancing partners, and instead found it more pleasurable when Essex decided "to evaporate his thoughts in a sonnet (being his common way) to be sung before the Queen". In prose too, the Earl showed no less artistry, and Elizabeth did not hide her delight when, for example, he took advantage of a few days' absence from Court to address her a letter like this: "Madam, the delights of this place cannot make me unmindful of one in whose sweet company I have joyed as much as the happiest man doth in his highest contentment; and if my horse could run as fast as my thoughts do fly, I would as often make mine eyes rich in beholding the treasure of my love as my desires do triumph when I seem to myself in a strong imagination to conquer your resisting will".[6]

Essex not only expressed himself with the eloquence of a poet, but he showed equal flair in devising elegant contrivances which gracefully drew attention to his putative sufferings from the pangs of unrequited love. It has been plausibly conjectured that it was Essex who commissioned Nicholas Hilliard to paint the well-known miniature, "Young Man amongst Roses", and that the picture was intended to illustrate his own lovelorn plight. Dressed in the Queen's tiltyard colours of black and white, the young man in the miniature leans disconsolately against a tree, whose trunk is twined around with white eglantine. To those accustomed to looking for such things, it would have been obvious that the tree trunk symbolized constancy, while the briar rose that encircled it was not only the flower of Venus, but also the Queen's flower, and hence could be taken to represent Elizabeth herself.[7] Certainly it would have been the sort of intricate yet pointed compliment that the Queen so greatly relished, and which Essex was unparalleled at delivering.

At the festivities which marked the anniversary of the Queen's accession day, Essex's contribution was always the highlight of the proceedings, "and done in costly sort, to her Majesty's great liking". Not only did he distinguish himself against all comers in the jousting, but during the preliminaries to the day's sporting events he always delighted both Queen and crowd by coming up with some new and inventive way of illustrating his enamoured state. At the accession day tournament of 1594, for example, the speeches uttered on his behalf to the Queen were delivered by "certain scholars", who had been brought to London from Oxford for the occasion, and dressed by Essex in specially designed liveries. The following November, he had recourse to the services of three professional actors, who accosted Essex as he entered the tiltyard and begged him "to leave his vain following of love [of the Queen] and to betake him" to more responsible pursuits. A fourth actor, disguised as the Earl's squire, rebutted their pleas, declaring "that this knight would never forsake his mistress's love, whose virtue made all his thoughts divine, whose wisdom taught him true policy, whose beauty and worth were at all times able to make him fit to command armies". A few days later a member of the audience reported to a friend, "My Lord of Essex's device is much commended in these late triumphs".[8]

Unfortunately, although Essex was brilliant at conveying in symbolic form his enslavement to the Queen, in real life he found it less easy to prostrate himself to the royal will. He was incomparable at perpetuating the falsehood that Elizabeth was an eternally youthful being, possessed of goddess-like endowments, but while this idealization of her was supposed in theory to enhance the Queen's mystique, it may have had the entirely contrary effect of diminishing her in Essex's eyes. Her apparent susceptibility to flattery, and her outwardly uncritical acceptance of his declarations of passion led him into the fatal mistake of supposing that she would be as easy to manipulate in other ways, and although he was capable of making the imaginative leap that enabled him to celebrate his ageing monarch in romantic terms, he had little insight into her real strengths of character, and had insufficient respect for her intellectual powers. Being himself of vehement and impulsive temperament, he was out of sympathy with the leisurely workings of the Queen's mind, dismissing as weaknesses the caution and circumspection that had served her so well in the past. He once acknowledged to Elizabeth, "I do confess that as a man, I have been more subject to your natural beauty, than as a subject to the power of a king",[9] and certainly it was true that, for all his superficial veneration of her, he never understood just how authoritative a figure she was. Essex was, in a sense, the High Priest of the cult of Queen Elizabeth, but ironically, even while elevating her to a level that was semi-divine, he underestimated her as a woman.

In both the Court and the country at large, previous favourites of the Queen had been the object of widespread dislike, and the animosity that they inspired served as a constant reminder to them that if Elizabeth abandoned them, they would sink without trace. Leicester had even taken a perverse pride in acknowledging that he excited a great deal of antipathy, declaring complacently, "I have many ill-willers, and I am none of those that seek hypocritically to make myself popular". Essex, in contrast, was held in great affection by the public, and he courted them assiduously, fostering their goodwill with "affable gestures, open doors, making his table and his bed ... popularly places of audience to suitors". When he appeared in the tiltyard, or rode through the streets, he was enthusiastically acclaimed by the crowd, and when Essex showed his appreciation by modestly bowing, or doffing his hat to them, it redoubled the applause. Although at times Elizabeth had been pained by the hostility aroused by earlier favourites such as Leicester or Ralegh, it was not an altogether welcome development that Essex enjoyed such startling success in endearing himself to her people. Essex was "so beloved by the commons, so followed and honoured by men of all sorts" that he was not vulnerable in the way his predecessors had been.[10] His standing in the country would remain high, irrespective of whether or not he managed to preserve the

Queen's esteem, and this made it more difficult for her to keep him under control.

At Court, Essex was always at the centre of a close-knit coterie of admiring clients, who latched on to him in the hope of furthering their careers. It was a responsibility which the Earl was happy to accept, for one of his most attractive characteristics was his "forwardness to pleasure his friends", and when closeted with Elizabeth he spared no exertion to secure his supporters titles, court offices or favours of other kinds. This was hardly unusual conduct in a favourite, but Essex took it to extremes, and what was both novel and disturbing about him was that if Elizabeth turned down his requests, he took it as a personal affront. As a contemporary observed, "The Earl was the worst philosopher, being a great resenter and a weak dissembler of the least disgrace". Well might Elizabeth tell the young man that he must learn to "be content when you are well, which hath not ever been your property", for his demands on her were insatiable, and instead of permitting her to regulate the flow of her favour in her accustomed fashion, Essex "drew in over fast like a child sucking a too uberous nurse".[11]

Time and again, Elizabeth would lose patience at the way Essex sought to abuse her goodwill, but even when she delivered herself of the most stinging rebukes, the young man refused to admit the justice of her case. Instead he would storm from the Court, vowing never to return, and Elizabeth's attachment to him was so deep that she could not remain entirely calm in the face of these threats. Essex was fond of saying that prior to his arrival at Court, "He had taken such a taste of the rural ... that he could well have bent his mind to a retired course" and, knowing this, the Queen did not lightly dismiss warnings that if she handled him too roughly, Essex would never have more "to do with Court or state affairs", but would rather "retire to some cell in the country, and to live there, as a man never desirous to look a good man in the face again".[12] Her relief was always transparent when Essex consented to a reunion, and she was so quick to forgive him for any hasty words that he had used in their recent altercations that Essex formed the impression that he would in future be able to commit similar transgressions with impunity.

If Elizabeth sought to avoid an open rupture by gently turning down his requests, Essex would take this as encouragement, reflecting optimistically, "She doth not contradict confidently, which they that know the minds of women say is a sign of yielding". Because he lacked all sense of proportion, he allowed the most trivial disagreements between him and the Queen to escalate into major confrontations, ignoring warnings from his wiser friends that, even if "he did wring out of her Majesty some petty contentments" by this means, such victories were principally injurious to himself. During one period of estrangement from the Queen it was pointed out to him that "if you draw her to forget her powers and yield in her affection to what she is unwilling, your peace will have a matter of new difference", but such counsels of moderation were anathema to the Earl. Much as Elizabeth might long for the day when Essex would mature sufficiently for the pleasure she took in his company to be unalloyed, the Earl's self-destructive streak was too strong to allow of this. In a rare moment of self-awareness he once admitted to the Queen that there were all too many occasions when "instead of being a contentment and entertainment to your Majesty's mind, I have been a distaste and disquiet", but though he then promised that "For the time to come ... I am resolved not willingly to offend your Majesty in matter of court or state, but to depend absolutely upon your Majesty's will and pleasure", such fits of penitence proved all too fleeting.[13]

If Essex was indefatigable when it came to promoting his friends, he was also a man who made enemies easily. His secretary once admitted ruefully, "He can conceal nothing: he carries his love and his hatred on his forehead", and certainly once he had taken a dislike against someone he saw no reason to show them even elementary civility. Worse still, he could not abide it if the Queen was gracious to men whom he abhorred. There was an unpleasant incident in the summer of 1587 when Elizabeth visited the Earl of Warwick's house, North Hall. Essex had understood that during this visit the Queen would receive his sister Dorothy, who had been banned from Court ever since her clandestine and unseemly marriage to Thomas Perrott. However, when Elizabeth arrived and learnt that Dorothy was present, she at once sent a message instructing the girl to keep to her chamber. Choking with mortification, Essex leapt to the conclusion that Sir Walter Ralegh, whom he detested, was responsible for the Queen's change of heart, and at once he confronted Elizabeth and said as much to her. When she defended Ralegh from the charge, Essex cried out that it afforded him no "comfort to give myself over to the service of a mistress that was in awe of such a man".[14] Instead of dealing firmly with such insubordination, Elizabeth then became involved in an undignified shouting match with the Earl, demeaning herself by making an insulting reference to Essex's mother. At this, Essex stormed from the house and, taking horse, he galloped towards the coast. He had intended to cross to the Netherlands and join the English forces there, but at Sandwich he was overtaken by Robert Carey, who had been sent after him by the Queen. He prevailed upon Essex to come back to Court, and when he and Elizabeth were reunited, their differences were soon forgotten.

The lull was only temporary, however, for nothing could induce Essex to be less quarrelsome. He was livid when the personable young courtier Charles Blount was rewarded for a distinguished performance in the tiltyard by being given a golden chessman by the Queen. "Now I see every fool must have a favour", he commented sourly, and when the derisory remark was passed on to Blount, he challenged Essex to a duel. During the resulting swordfight, the Earl was pinked in the thigh, and on hearing this the Queen said it served him right. "By God's death!" she exclaimed roundly, "It was fit that some one or other should take him down, and teach him better manners, otherwise there would be no ruling of him". It was an implicit admission that she herself had so far proved unequal to the task, and despite her hopes that his behaviour would now show an improvement, Essex remained as turbulent as before. In December 1588 he challenged Ralegh to another duel, and though the Privy Council intervened to prevent it coming to a fight, the commotion was said to have "troubled her Majesty very much".[15]

It was Essex's belief that Elizabeth did not really object when he clashed with other men at Court, for he once told the French ambassador, "She takes pleasure in beholding such quarrels between her servants". This was a misconception which others shared, and after the Queen's death the courtier Sir Robert Naunton would assert, "The principal note of her reign will be, that she ruled much by faction and parties, which she herself both made, upheld and weakened, as her own great judgment advised". In reality, however, it was not true that the Queen deliberately fostered divisions within the court, for it was precisely in order to keep jealousy and bitterness to a minimum that she had guarded against allowing any single individual or grouping to establish too great a preponderance there. While Elizabeth would not necessarily have been pleased if all her courtiers had been on such friendly terms that their strivings for her favour had lacked a competitive edge, she wished it to be clearly understood that she was the ultimate arbiter of their rivalries, beyond whom there could be no appeal. She strove to prevent the formation of sharply delineated factions, electing rather to "use her wisdom in balancing the weights than in drawing all to one assize",[16] but no amount of intervention from her served to keep Essex's feuding in check. However much individual courtiers had disliked each other in the past, their feelings of hostility had impinged remarkably little on state affairs. Largely because of Essex, personal issues now came very much more to the fore, and the Court began to assume a character that was dangerously sectarian.

If Essex's wilful and unruly nature afforded the Queen some worries from the start, in the autumn of 1588 the war with Spain was her most immediate and pressing problem. The Queen was anxious to follow up the victory over the Armada by assuming the offensive, and as early as September 1588 there were plans for an expedition to be sent against Spain early the following year, under the leadership of Drake and Sir John Norris. As it was assumed that any ships of the Armada that survived the homeward journey would reassemble in Lisbon, that city was originally conceived of as being the most suitable target for an attack. Once that had been designated the objective, it seemed sensible to broaden the scope of the operation, for a landing in Portugal would afford an opportunity to provoke a native uprising against Spanish rule in favour of the pretender to the Portuguese throne, Don Antonio. Once that had been tried, the fleet could sail to the Azores and lie in wait for the treasure ships which carried across the Atlantic the annual consignment of silver from Spain's South American mines. It was emphasized, however, that these goals were strictly subsidiary to the expedition's *raison d'être*, which was to destroy enemy shipping as it lay in harbour. By the end of September reports were coming in that instead of making for Lisbon, vessels from the Armada were straggling into ports on the northern coast of Spain, and the Queen accordingly revised the original plan of action to take this into account. She stressed to her commanders that their top priority was to wipe out any remnants of the Armada before they had had time to refit for further action, and it was only after accomplishing this task that they should proceed either to Lisbon or the Azores.

Having clarified these aims, the Queen agreed to contribute six of her ships and £20,000 towards the cost of the expedition. The remaining ships and supplies were to be furnished by private investors who would be prepared to sink capital into the venture in the hope that it would yield a sizeable profit. There was no reason to think that this would result in the expedition being under-financed. On the contrary, indeed, Norris and Drake told the Queen that there was such a healthy interest in the venture that her initial investment need be no more than £5,000, and that it was only after they had raised £40,000 from other sources that they would call upon her to contribute her remaining £15,000. In the event, their confidence proved misplaced, for individuals who had undertaken to subscribe proved slow to produce the promised sums. As a result, Norris and Drake had to ask the Queen to stump up her full amount, and Burghley persuaded her she had no alternative but to agree.

Unfortunately, even this proved insufficient for, after unforeseen complications had arisen, the Queen had to lend additional money to Norris to pay for the wages of troops who had been withdrawn from the Netherlands in order to man the expedition. Then the fleet was kept in port by adverse winds for some weeks, and as Norris and Drake had taken aboard a much larger number of volunteers than had been allowed for in the original estimates, the victuals provided to feed the men were speedily consumed. The Queen had therefore to advance still more money to purchase fresh supplies, and as a result, before the expedition had even left port, she had had to expend over £49,000, an increase of nearly one hundred and fifty percent on the sum initially allocated for it.[17]

Small wonder, then, that Elizabeth was vexed, and her mood was scarcely improved when in early April the Earl of Essex absconded from Court in order to join the expedition. Despite his success with the Queen, he regarded his life in England as sadly aimless and, since his debts now amounted to as much as £23,000, he hoped to redeem the situation by sharing the profits which it was assumed would be accrued in the course of the campaign. Incensed that a venture that had already cost her so much money should now deprive her of Essex's company, the Queen sent his uncle, Sir William Knollys, to apprehend the truant, but neither Sir William nor those who followed him managed to track down the runaway. Essex's friend Sir Roger Williams had already commandeered one of the ships that the Queen herself had provided for the expedition, and having slipped out of Plymouth, where the rest of the fleet was moored, he had taken Essex aboard at Falmouth. By the time the Earl's pursuers reached that port, Essex was already at sea. Such was the Queen's fury that she even talked of having Sir Roger Williams executed, and she was also far from pleased with Norris and Drake, for she justly questioned how it was that Williams had contrived to escape from port in one of her own vessels without being detected. One adventurer indeed believed that Elizabeth was so disgusted that she would forbid the expedition to sail, as "Her Majesty's favour, by means of the Earl of Essex's departure, is withdrawn in such sort from the action".[18]

This was far from being the case. In the past few weeks her frustration at the setbacks and bad planning that had plagued the project from the first may have caused her to bombard her commanders with "contrarily threatenings and chidings", but she had never lost sight of the fact that the expedition had a vital function to fulfil. In the instructions issued to Norris and Drake on 23 February 1589, the Queen had again laid great stress on what was the primary purpose of the voyage, for in them it was explicitly stated that "Before you shall attempt either Portugal or the Azores, our express pleasure and commandment is that you distress the ships of war in Guipuzgoa, Biscay and Galicia". Already, however, there were ominous signs that Elizabeth's commanders did not attach as much importance as she did to the attack on Philip's ships. The fact that they had taken on board so many volunteers suggests they were thinking principally in terms of a land operation, and intended to concentrate their energies on the offensive in Portugal. Certainly that part of the enterprise had been much more attractive to potential investors in the expedition, for while there was not much profit to be looked for in sinking the Spanish navy, a successful campaign ashore might well yield rich plunder. One speculator actually agreed to lodge funds with Norris and Drake "upon foundation only of a direct course and voyage to Lisbon or the Islands".[19] Such conflicts of interest were inescapable at a time when the state lacked the resources to provide proper financing for its own war effort, for, once individual capitalists were involved, profitability tended to take precedence over public service. As a result of this shift in emphasis, the Crown forfeited control over actions which it may have instigated, but which soon acquired an independent character of their own.

When the fleet finally set sail on 18 April 1589, it made for Corunna, a port far to the west of those destinations specified in the instructions. Norris and Drake had put much faith in intelligence reports which claimed there was a big build-up of shipping there, but these proved without foundation. When they arrived at Corunna on 24 April, only "four ships, divers barks", were at anchor there. The English quickly accounted for these, but they failed to capture the town's citadel on high ground, and by the time they left Corunna on 9 May, not only had clashes with the Spaniards resulted in several hundred casualties, but epidemic diseases were carrying off many more.

The Queen was greatly angered on learning that Drake and Norris had led her forces to Corunna, a place she rightly dismissed as "being of no importance and very hazardous in the attempt". Darkly she commented, "They went to places more for profit than for service",[20] and on 20 May she wrote upbraiding them for having perverted the primary object of the expedition. She reiterated that they must deal with the Spanish shipping in harbour before going elsewhere, but even as she wrote this, her forces were advancing across Portugal.

Having met up with Essex off the Portuguese coast, the fleet landed at Peniche, which was about forty-five miles from Lisbon, and 6,000 men were disembarked. It was agreed that they would march overland to the capital, and once they were in position, Drake would sail up the Tagus to give naval support for an attack upon the city. Unfortunately, the soldiers' hot and tiring journey proved appallingly deleterious. By the time the force encamped in the suburbs of Lisbon, a high proportion of the troops has already succumbed to fatal illnesses, which in many cases had been aggravated by over-indulgence in local wines. Furthermore, contrary to English hopes, there was no sign that the native population was prepared to rise in support of Don Antonio. Worse still, Drake did not appear, having unaccountably remained at the mouth of the Tagus, and lack of artillery meant that there was no chance of the English taking Lisbon without his aid. In frustration, Essex rode up and thrust his pike into the city gates, challenging the Spaniards inside to personal combat in Elizabeth's name, but this was a futile if chivalrous gesture. On 29 May Norris ordered the army to rejoin the fleet, and since adverse weather conditions precluded all chance of recouping the expedition's fortunes by going to the Azores, by the end of June the remnants of the once proud force were back in England.

On his return Norris admitted that it was probable that "Her Majesty will mislike of the event of the journey", but he pleaded in mitigation that what they had done redounded so greatly to her honour that in any other country it would have been hailed with bonfires and public rejoicing. Whether he genuinely believed this is hard to say, but it is not easy to think of any kingdom which would have derived much comfort from so ill-fated a venture. Apart from the money that had been wasted, huge numbers had been killed overseas, with estimates of English losses ranging from 3,500 to as high as 11,000 men. In October Drake and Norris were asked to justify their conduct before the Privy Council, and though neither was formally disciplined for their disregard of the Queen's orders, Elizabeth did not see fit to entrust Drake with further military responsibility for some years. And indeed, the opportunity lost through disobedience was a real one, for an English spy subsequently reported that, if Drake had gone to the Biscayan port of Santander, "he had done such service as never subject done; for with twelve sail of his ships he might have destroyed all the forces which the Spaniards had there, which was the whole strength of their country by sea. There they did ride all unrigged and their ordnance on shore, and some twenty men only in a ship to keep them. It was far overseen that he had not gone thither first".[21]

For the next few years there were no further opportunities to mount operations in the Iberian peninsula, for the English were kept fully occupied in another theatre of war. In France, the situation was critical, for there was now a real chance that the militant organization which had Spanish backing, and which was known as the Catholic League, would succeed in overrunning the country. In May 1588, the League's leader, the Duke of Guise, had entered Paris in defiance of a royal ban, and when Henry III had tried to mobilize his palace guard against Guise, the citizens had risen against the King and forced him to flee the capital. Despite thundering injunctions from Elizabeth to wage all-out war on Guise, Henry had decided that his only chance of retaining his throne lay in coming to terms with his over-mighty subject, and he had done so that July. This deal had put Guise in effective control of the kingdom, but the defeat of the Armada had put fresh heart into the King. On 23 December 1588 (N.S.) he had had Guise murdered, but Henry had miscalculated in thinking that by this means his authority would be restored. To his dismay, the Catholic League swore to avenge the death of its leader by fighting against the King with the continued support of Spain. At the behest of the League, Henry had earlier repudiated the right of the Huguenot Henry of Navarre to succeed him on the throne, but now it was obvious that they needed each other, and in March 1589 the King and his cousin swore that they would fight the League together. By the summer the pair were besieging Paris, and the city looked set to fall to them when, on 22 July, Henry III was assassinated by a Capuchin monk.

Navarre succeeded the murdered monarch as Henry IV, but the League refused to acknowledge him as King, and it was uncertain whether he would manage to settle himself on the throne in the face of this resistance. Not only was the League still receiving funding from Spain, but the new King enjoyed less internal support than his predecessor, for many moderate Catholics who had assisted Henry III in his struggle against the League were not prepared to fight in the army of a Huguenot. Furthermore Henry was in such dreadful financial straits that in early September 1589 he was reduced to selling off his gold chains in order to pay mercenaries from Switzerland, and it was obvious that such expedients could not suffice to keep him afloat for very long. Utterly destitute, and with his cause on the verge of collapse, he begged Elizabeth to come to his assistance.

Appeals for aid were never welcome to the Queen, but Henry did his best to make his demands more palatable by infusing them with a savour of romance. His predecessor had likewise been aware of the necessity to humour her in this way, but for him, perhaps, the procedure had been rather more of a strain. In the spring of 1588, Mendoza had maliciously described Henry III's reception of a flowery letter from the Queen, which had prompted from him the weary comment, "The Queen of England thinks that everyone must be in love with her; I will answer this letter myself".[22] Henry IV, in contrast, was shameless in his approach. Whereas the late King had been a transvestite who had surrounded himself with young male favourites known as mignons, Henry was an inveterate womanizer, and his exhaustive practice in writing love letters stood him in good stead in his communications with the Queen. His pleas for aid were generally couched in the most seductive of terms, as he assured Elizabeth that he loved and revered her more than anyone in the world, and claimed to have eschewed marriage for her sake. He pretended that the sight of her portrait had sent him demented with passion, and that he longed to witness her beauty at first-hand, and such assurances were very acceptable to the Queen. She preened herself on his flattery, and while she of course knew that Henry was being so ingratiating for reasons that were materialistic enough, her self-esteem required that their dealings should be overlaid with this pleasing gloss.

All the flattery in the world could not have induced the Queen to intervene in France were it not for the fact that her own fate was bound up with Henry's welfare. As it was, she could not allow him to go under, for if the League overran France in conjunction with the Spaniards, that kingdom would become "a highway for Spain to tyrannize the whole world", and it was essential that this was prevented. On the other hand, her own financial situation was too straitened to admit of her pledging

Henry unlimited aid, and she also had to bear in mind the possibility that, once she had helped him to regain control of his kingdom, Henry would perfidiously come to terms with Spain, and then unite with that country in waging war on England. It was true that recent years had seen a diplomatic revolution that had caused Burghley to exclaim in wonder, "The state of the world is marvellously changed when we true Englishmen have cause for our own quietness to wish good success to a French King and a King of Scots", but it would be naïve to assume that these new alignments would necessarily remain fixed. Elizabeth herself once observed to Henry IV, "You are so wise a prince that I am assured you will not forget that our two nations have not often accorded so well but they would remember their ancient quarrels, not considering themselves of the same country, but separated by a mighty deep".[23]

In September 1589 Elizabeth agreed to lend Henry £20,000 and undertook to send 4,000 troops to France for a month under command of Lord Willoughby. At the end of that time she extended their stay for another two months, having received an assurance from Henry that he would pay their wages. She admitted that she was sceptical that he would keep this promise, and ingenuously confessed, "We were, we know not how, overcome and enchanted by the King to yield thereunto".[24] Sure enough, Henry failed to honour his commitment, and the troops in consequence endured terrible privations, but this did not stop them from playing a crucial part in Henry's campaign. By the end of December, only about a quarter of the original 4,000 were alive, but with their assistance Henry had recovered such vast tracts of north-western France that he was now in a position to proceed to final victory over the League.

In the expectation that Henry would be able to vanquish his opponents without further assistance from her, Elizabeth recalled her troops. Throughout 1590, the only way she demonstrated her solidarity with Henry was by making the odd supportive gesture, such as sending him the carcase of a deer that she had shot out hunting. By the end of the year, however, the situation had changed so radically that it seemed inevitable that she would have to do more than present Henry with the occasional gift of venison. In the summer of 1590, the King had laid siege to Paris, and the city had been on the verge of capitulation when in August the Duke of Parma had come to its relief with his army from the Netherlands. Now that Spain was directly involved in the conflict, the character of the war was transformed. Henry was forced into retreat and, though Parma returned to the Low Countries in November, the previous month a new threat had materialized when a force of Spaniards had landed in Brittany and entrenched themselves there.

This raised the spectre that, having gained control of France's western seaboard, the Spanish would use it as a base from which to terrorize the

English. Naturally Elizabeth implored Henry to do all in his power to dislodge the invaders, but the wily King correctly inferred that, if he remained inactive, the Queen would have no alternative but to do the job for him herself. The Queen might bluster that if Henry wilfully neglected his seaports, the only help she could give him would be to remember him in her prayers, but when more Spaniards arrived in Brittany in March 1591, she knew that it was incumbent upon her to make some response. On 3 April she signed a contract with the French by which she bound herself to send 3,000 soldiers to Brittany, although she specified that Henry must match this by sending an equal number of his own troops to the area. This was an obligation that Henry felt free to disregard, and in the ensuing months Elizabeth's forces had to bear the brunt of hostilities in Brittany. Time and again she contemplated revoking her troops, but in the end the perilous consequences of permitting Brittany to become a Spanish enclave always deterred her.

Not content with the Queen's efforts on his behalf, Henry next asked her to supplement her forces in France by sending soldiers to Normandy, so that they could assist him to capture Rouen. Understandably Elizabeth was reluctant, but Burghley overcame her reservations, telling her that in some respects Rouen was of more strategic importance than Paris itself. On 25 June the Queen consented to send at her own expense 4,000 men to Normandy, but she stipulated that they could only remain there for two months, and that they were to be used for no other purpose than the siege of Rouen.

The Queen's next task was to choose a commander for this force, and at once the Earl of Essex began to agitate for the job. His career had continued on its upward trajectory on his return from Portugal, for Elizabeth had speedily forgiven him for his desertion of her, which was "esteemed but a sally of youth". "He grew every day more and more in her gracious conceit", and in 1590 the Queen had demonstrated her regard for him by agreeing that he could be the recipient of all taxes levied on imported sweet wines during the next ten years. It was one of the most valuable awards in her gift, and during Leicester's lifetime had constituted his major source of income. The Queen was not even seriously put out when that autumn it transpired that Essex had secretly married Philip Sidney's widow, for after being disagreeable about it for three weeks, her ill-humour had subsided. Yet however devoted she was to Essex, she hesitated to entrust him with wider responsibility. She had a high opinion of his abilities, and conceded that he had distinguished himself on active service in the past, but she regarded him as "too impetuous to be given the reins". Essex was nevertheless indomitable in overcoming her reservations, pleading with her on his knees for hours at a stretch and, when Henry IV himself said that he wanted Essex to be appointed, Elizabeth relented. The

Earl's commission was signed on 21 July, but the Queen remained uneasy about having given in to him in this way. Not only was she dejected at the prospect of being parted from him, but she was worried that he would expose both himself and his men to unnecessary risks in the field, and she took the precaution of writing to Henry IV, cautioning him against Essex's reckless streak. She acknowledged that she "must appear a very foolish creature" to Henry, whose own courage under fire was legendary, but she stressed that her commander would "require the bridle rather than the spur".[25]

At the beginning of August Essex landed in Normandy, eager for the fray, but to his chagrin found himself condemned to enforced idleness. Despite Henry IV's earlier insistence that he gave the highest priority to capturing Rouen, he was now pursuing other objectives, and was currently engaged in laying siege to Noyon, in north-eastern France. Without French support, Essex could not invest Rouen, and the Queen's army – whose services had been promised to Henry for a mere two months – remained uselessly encamped outside the city walls.

Chafing at this inactivity, Essex accepted with alacrity when the King invited him to visit him in his camp, disregarding the fact that as this entailed a long and hazardous journey across enemy territory, he would be endangering himself without good reason. He reached his destination safely at the end of August, and from a social point of view, the meeting with Henry was a great success. The King royally feasted his guests, and Essex distinguished himself in a jumping match against the French, but nothing worthwhile was achieved. Henry did promise that part of his army would shortly be diverted to Rouen, but explained that he himself was planning to set off for Champagne, to liaise with mercenaries who were arriving from Germany. By the time that Essex returned to Normandy, he had been in France over a month, and his forces had not even begun to tackle the task they had been set. Restless and fretful, he permitted some of his men to become involved in a skirmish with the enemy outside Rouen, and during this pointless encounter his brother Walter was killed.

The Queen meanwhile was fuming. While Essex had been on his jaunt, she had spluttered, "Where he is, or what he doth, or what he is to do, we are ignorant also", for she had no means of communicating with him. The only thing that was clear to her was that her expensive army had not yet been deployed, and such wastage naturally made her seethe. She now bitterly regretted having sent out her troops, and on 22 August wrote angrily to her ambassador in France that she had always suspected that Henry was not being sincere when he had assured her of his eagerness to start the siege of Rouen, "Yet such was the importunity of the King and his ambassadors here, and the inclination of our Council to give more credit to the promises than we ourselves hoped to be performed . . . as we were in a mannner led thereunto against our own opinion". When three more weeks elapsed without any sign of progress, the Queen's fury at being made to look a fool was not to be contained, and she vented her rage on Essex. At her direction, the Council wrote Essex a letter on 13 September which read as a terrible indictment of his leadership. Not only was he castigated for having sanctioned the escapade that cost his brother his life, but Essex's visit to Henry was classified as "an undutiful act", and worse than this, he was told that the Queen "thinketh that the government committed to you hath been evil disposed". Because Essex had assured her that Henry's forces were now on their way to assist in the siege of Rouen, the Queen did grudgingly agree that her troops could remain there for longer than the two months originally specified in the contract, but her disgust with Essex was such that she issued orders for his recall.[26]

Undoubtedly the Queen had ample cause to be annoyed, but it was somewhat unreasonable of her to heap all the blame on Essex. It arguably had been foolhardy of him to go and see Henry, but the fault lay principally with the King for having been absent in the first place, and Essex could hardly be held accountable for the fact that the Queen's army had not yet been properly employed. Elizabeth's peremptory recall of her general may have owed less to the belief that he had shown himself unfit to lead her soldiers than to her desire to have him safely back at home. Certainly Burghley suspected as much, for he disapprovingly commented to a colleague, "God forbid that private respects should overrule public". One of Essex's friends wrote to him from Court describing how in his absence, "Love here is almost banished", and he explained, "All wise men doth wish your Lordship to tarry and serve for the safety of our country ... But ladies and gentlewomen, not respecting the honour of war nor the public good, wisheth your Lordship at home, saying that a man of such a personage should be here in England".[27] The Queen, one may surmise, felt this no less strongly than the rest, and had allowed her yearning to see her favourite to influence her judgment.

If this was so, she soon recovered her self-control, for at the beginning of October she agreed under pressure from Burghley and others that Essex could remain with his men. By this time, however, he was already on his way home, and this meant that, after all, he and Elizabeth were briefly reunited. Within days he was back at his post, but his stay had encouraged Elizabeth to be less negative about military intervention in France, and when it was confirmed that Henry's army were finally in place before Rouen, she sent over a thousand reinforcements to assist them in its siege. Through no fault of the Queen, however, the city was now less vulnerable than before, for Henry's delays had given its inhabitants time to revictual. The siege turned out to be a very laborious affair and, as the weeks passed, disease inexorably eroded the numbers of English troops. By the beginning of January, only a bedraggled rump remained and, after the Council told Essex that it was dishonourable for one of his rank to be in charge of so motley a body of men, he returned to England.

Yet even now, the Queen tenaciously adhered to her goal of gaining Rouen. In December news had come that Parma had again surged with his army into France, and by February 1592 he was advancing towards Rouen, but Henry IV was categoric that this would not cause him to raise the siege. On 19 February Elizabeth therefore agreed to send him 1,600 more troops, supplementing this offering with the gift of a miniature of herself. Henry was effusive in his thanks, saying he would always carry it with him into battle, "in the sight whereof, he would fight with the more resolution against Elizabeth's enemies and his own".[28] Unfortunately, possession of the royal image proved of little use to Henry that April, when Parma suddenly materialized before Rouen. Not daring to risk a confrontation with his opponent in open field, the King had ignominiously to withdraw.

The men and money that Elizabeth had poured into the Normandy campaign had all been squandered to no purpose. The Queen was rightly incensed at the way her ally had consistently deceived and abused her, and the more so because Henry was still failing to make good his promises to send troops of his own to Brittany. She was scarcely mollified when in September 1592 Henry presented her with an outsize love-token in the shape of an elephant. On top of all her other worries, the last thing she wanted was to have to concern herself with the welfare of an animal which had already grown by a third that year, and was expected to continue growing "this eight years yet". Coldly, she let it be known that "Her Majesty was not content with the sending of the elephant".[29]

Understandably disenchanted with King Henry, the Queen was reluctant to send more men to Brittany to bolster the position there. As it became clear that the English could not provide him with limitless aid, Henry began to despair of defeating the League by purely military means, and decided that he must find an alternative way of ending the civil war. He knew that provided he could tap nationalistic sentiment, it would not be hard to unite his kingdom against Spain for, even in the eyes of numerous French Catholics, that country had started to take on the aspect of a predator.

Philip II was currently pressuring the leaders of the League to declare his daughter Queen of France, and a foreign female on the throne was difficult for any Frenchman to stomach, no matter what his religious persuasion. It was only the King's Protestantism which prevented so many of his Catholic subjects from giving him their allegiance, and Henry correctly judged that if he were to convert now, large numbers of his rebellious subjects would willingly renounce their links with Spain and recognize him as their King. Having sounded out the Pope, he started secretly receiving instruction.

When rumours reached the Queen that Henry's conversion was imminent, she declared herself appalled. Piously she warned him that he who did not keep his eyes fixed unwaveringly on the King of Kings could hardly expect his worldly affairs to prosper; but, despite her exhortations, Henry formally abjured his faith on 5 July 1593. Elizabeth reacted emotionally: "Ah, what griefs, what regret, what groaning I feel in my soul at the sound of such news", she wrote at the time, but in fact Henry's apostasy did not have a particularly adverse effect on his relations with England. The Queen was reassured when Henry re-issued the toleration edicts for Protestants, and gave her a formal undertaking that he would not make peace with Spain without consulting her. It was undeniable, too, that his conversion had transformed his position in France. Most members of the League hastened to acknowledge that he was their King, and in March 1594 he triumphantly entered Paris. But though Henry was no longer at odds with his own subjects, the war with Spain continued, for Philip II would not relinquish his attempt to make his daughter Queen of France. Much as it went against the grain, Elizabeth could hardly abandon King Henry while he remained locked in conflict with her foremost enemy, and in the autumn of 1594 she sent an expedition to Brittany which resulted in the Spaniards being ousted from their base near Brest. Henry was hopeful that she would be equally generous in assisting him to eject the Spaniards from their remaining strongholds in France, but the Queen's assessment was that he was now capable of doing this by himself. Determined not to be exploited as she had been in the past, for the next two years she steadfastly refused to do anything further for "the most ingrateful King that liveth".[30]

It was reasonable enough that Elizabeth was reluctant to dole out more to the needy King of France, for her own financial position was dire. The victory over the Armada had cost an estimated £161,000, and in the course of the next few years the Queen not only had to pay for her part of the cost of the Portugal expedition, but also to finance operations in the Netherlands and France. By 1590, Burghley had so successfully cut down the corruption that had riddled the administration of the army in the Netherlands that costs there were reduced to no more than £106,162 per annum, but this was still a burdensome sum to produce, year after year. Intervention in the French wars was also prohibitive, with the Queen spending nearly £145,000 propping up the royalist cause in the two-and-a-half-year period from September 1589 to June 1592.[31]

In addition to the involvement on the continent, operations at sea placed a further strain on the Exchequer. The aim of these was generally to intercept the Spanish treasure fleet that sailed from Havana each year and, if the plan had succeeded, it would have yielded a fabulous return. Unfortunately, the treasure fleet proved far from easy prey. In the summer of 1590, John Hawkins and Martin Frobisher lay in wait for it at sea, but Philip II frustrated their intentions by forbidding his treasure fleet to sail. Indirectly this benefited the English, for as a result of being deprived of its annual injection of silver the Spanish economy was badly dislocated, and this hampered Philip's war effort. The following year another English fleet positioned itself near the Azores in hopes of catching the Spaniards on their transatlantic route. Ralegh, Howard of Effingham and Lord Thomas Howard had all invested in the venture, but the Queen also provided a total of nine ships, at a cost of between £18,000 and £20,000. By this time, however, King Philip had taken steps to protect his bullion imports, and off Ferrol the English were surprised by a fleet of Spanish warships. With the exception of Sir Richard Grenville's *Revenge*, which was captured after an epic fight, the English ships all managed to escape. Nevertheless, it was an unsatisfactory outcome to an expedition which had been designed to net vast riches, and which in fact barely covered its costs.

Then, too, there was the cost of defence preparations to take into account. At a time when it was true to say that "every sudden rumour produces a suspicion of invasion because of want of perfect intelligence", these were much increased by frequent mobilizations in response to false reports of impending attacks. There were invasion scares in 1590, 1591, 1592 and 1594, all of which proved to be without foundation.[32] Conversely, however, in 1595 a small Spanish force landed without warning near Penzance and ravaged the Cornish village of Mousehole, and the fact that the English had been taken completely by surprise emphasized the need for constant vigilance.

Inevitably the Queen was heavily dependent on Parliament to help her to pay for all this, and once the war was under way, the legislature was summoned much more frequently than had been the case in peacetime years. Parliament met in February 1589 and responded generously to a rousing oration from Lord Chancellor Hatton in which he reminded the members that, since England's enemies were "caring of means to continue their offence, we must likewise consider of good means to continue our defence". They doubled the standard grant of tax of pre-war Parliaments, though payment was spread over four years instead of the customary two. When finally collected, this brought in a total of £320,000, but the last payments had no sooner been deposited in the Exchequer than the Queen had again to summon Parliament in February 1593. This time a triple subsidy was granted, and as before this was paid in yearly instalments over the next four years. Even so, the sums raised were nowhere near sufficient to finance the war. Although more subsidies were being granted, each individual levy brought in progressively less than those collected earlier in the reign, and it has been estimated that parliamentary taxation provided less than fifty per cent of wartime expenditure.[33]

In order to find the remainder, the Queen was frequently driven to extort forced loans from her wealthier subjects, a highly unpopular expedient to which the Crown resorted only when money was really tight. Forced loans were levied in 1588, 1590, 1591 and 1596, but resistance and evasion on the part of those called upon to pay frequently meant that the yields were disappointingly low. In theory, the sums advanced were meant to be reimbursed after a few months had elapsed, but in 1592 the Crown fell behind in its schedule of repayments, and this only heightened the resentment that this method of raising money aroused. In 1598, when word went round London that another forced loan was in the offing, many of the citizens were seen to "shrink and pull in their horns", and some even moved to the country, in hopes that they could avoid payment that way.[34]

In a desperate bid to raise money, one of the realm's leading merchants was sent to Germany in February 1589 with instructions to try and borrow £100,000, but these efforts came to nothing. The Queen was more successful in maximizing her ordinary sources of income, such as the customs and royal estates. Earlier in the reign, the customs had been collected by 'farmers', who paid the Crown a rent and pocketed any profits that they could make on top of that. By 1590, however, receipts from the customs were being collected directly by crown agents, and as a result, yields were improved by nearly twenty per cent. In 1589 rents for crown lands were also raised, and thanks to devices such as these, the Queen's gross annual revenue had risen by the end of the century to some £360,000. Unfortunately, ordinary expenditure was also higher, amounting to about £260,000, and the balance of £100,000 was not enough to cover Elizabeth's annual outlay on the war. To make matters more difficult, the war tended to accentuate any inflationary tendencies in the economy, and prices rose faster during the 1590s than at any previous time in the reign. Because of such pressures, the Queen could not avoid liquidating a significant amount of capital, and in 1590 alone she sold £125,000 worth of crown lands.[35]

The Crown did its best to make money out of the war by engaging in privateering, a form of licensed piracy that flourished in these years. On obtaining a permit from the Lord Admiral, private individuals were entitled to fit out vessels in order to prey on Spanish shipping on the high seas, and profits from these activities did much to compensate those who would otherwise have suffered losses as a result of wartime disruption of trade. Prize goods were liable to customs duties, but in order to maximize its gains from this lucrative practice, the Crown itself turned buccaneer, and the Queen's ships frequently participated in privateering ventures. The problem was that, even when these went well, Elizabeth's share of the profits bore little relation to the value of goods seized, for it was impossible to prevent the crews of any ship involved in the capture of a great prize from taking the pick of the plunder.

In 1592 Elizabeth had a ship in the syndicate that captured the *Madre de Dios*, a great merchantman loaded with a fabulous cargo from the East Indies. Its contents included Turkey carpets, porcelain, raw silk, jewels, ivory and spices, and the total value of the goods aboard might have been as much as £500,000. Nevertheless, by the time the vessel was docked at Dartmouth, no more than £140,000 worth remained, for the mariners who had taken her had pocketed a mass of valuables, intending to dispose of them ashore. The Queen sent agents to the West Country to try and recover the stolen loot, but by the time they arrived much of the hoard had already been snapped up by jewellers and London merchants, who had been on the scene in a trice. As a result, only a fraction of the contraband goods was ever recouped. Furious at being cheated, Elizabeth revenged herself by defrauding her partners out of their full share of what remained. Her original stake in the voyage entitled her, at most, to about twenty per cent of the proceeds, but to the fury of the other shareholders, such as Ralegh and the Earl of Cumberland, she appropriated almost half.[36]

The struggle against Spain was not only costly in financial terms, but it also swallowed up men at an alarming rate. Between 1589 and 1593, 17,800 men were sent out of the country to fight abroad, and by 1592 Burghley was anxiously noting, "The realm here is weary to see the expense of their people for foreign services". Military service overseas was unpopular with the soldiers themselves, and many absconded from their regiments at the first opportunity. By 1592, there was a serious influx of deserters from France, some of whom returned "using most slanderous speeches of those her Highness's service and entertainment". Even those who were officially discharged found it hard to find employment on coming home, and frequently ended up as vagabonds. By 1593 these unfortunates had become so numerous that they constituted a serious nuisance, for it was sorrowfully reported, "The Queen is troubled wherever she takes the air with these miserable creatures".[37]

Discontent and lassitude at home were exacerbated by a sequence of poor harvests in the mid 1590s, and by 1596 there was a serious shortage of corn. The Queen held that hoarding was partly responsible for this: in 1596, the Privy Council recorded, "Her Highness doth verily think the fault thereof in part to be the covetous disposition of such as are farmers and corn masters, that not acknowledging God's goodness, do seek immoderate gain by enhancing the prices of corn and grain to the great oppression of the poorer sort". If it was true that the crisis was the fault of unscrupulous capitalists, the Tudor state lacked the necessary mechanisms that would have enabled it to control these vested interests. In times of shortage, Justices of the Peace were in theory meant to monitor the sale of grain, and having calculated how much corn farmers needed for home consumption and the sowing of next year's crop, they were supposed to compel them to sell the rest at reasonable prices. In practice, however, these regulations were completely unworkable, and the harsh truth was that when harvests failed, the poor went hungry. This increased the likelihood of domestic unrest. In 1596 the authorities discovered that an insurrection was being planned in Oxfordshire, where between two and three hundred men were plotting to rise up and "pull the corn out of rich men's houses".[38] Numerous executions ensured that the conspiracy never progressed beyond the embryonic stage, but such disturbing incidents were symptomatic of an alarming trend.

The Government had shown itself ruthless in stamping out unrest among the underprivileged, and by the mid 1590s repressive measures had also come close to wiping out dissent within the Anglican Church. During the seven years of Archbishop's Grindal's sequestration, Puritanism had not remained dormant, for before he died the beginnings of an underground Puritan network had come into existence. By May 1582, about sixty ministers from Essex, Cambridge and Norfolk were meeting at Cockfield to confer with one another, and towards the end of the year comparable assemblies of Puritan clergymen sprang up elsewhere in the country. As at the prophesyings, one purpose of these meetings was to be uplifted by an exposition of the scriptures, but time was also set aside for discussing "profitable questions", such as which parts of the Book of Common Prayer "might be tolerated, and what necessarily to be refused in every point of it".[39] The aim was to prevent non-conformist ministers from feeling isolated, and to iron out inconsistencies in the attitudes of Puritans towards the Anglican Church. As such the meetings were potentially subversive, for the implication was that whoever had the backing of these autonomous bodies was authorized to defy laws laid down by the Queen in Parliament.

But if the Puritans were developing a more elaborate organization during these years, the bishops were simultaneously evolving the weapons that would enable them to crush their enemies. While Grindal was in disgrace, the Bishop of London, Aylmer, had been entrusted with the task of eradicating non-conformity and, under his supervision, the ecclesiastical commission which had come into being following the passage of the Act of Uniformity became a much more formidable body. Whereas earlier in the reign its functions had not extended much beyond administering the oath of Supremacy, or arranging for the supervision of Catholic recusants in time of crisis, Aylmer made much more frequent use of it. He refined its procedures and developed its powers to a point where it came to be looked on as a court, with the imposing title of the High Commission. It had the authority to imprison or fine those who came before it, and hence was an institution well fitted to combat the menace of presbyterianism.

Puritan sympathizers on the Council, such as Leicester, Mildmay and Walsingham, were naturally aghast at Aylmer's activities, and even Burghley, who was less indulgent to the Puritans, was highly critical of the Bishop. The Queen, in contrast, was delighted with the way that the senior Church hierarchy was developing the machinery which would enable it to combat Puritanism without applying to her to strengthen their hand. When Grindal finally died in 1583, she chose as his successor the Bishop of Worcester, John Whitgift, a stern disciplinarian whom she knew she could count on to implement a still more energetic drive against the Puritans. Already, he had the reputation of being one of their most dedicated foes: not only had he been called upon in 1572 to write a reply to John Field's *Admonition to Parliament*, but two years earlier he had been instrumental in bringing about Thomas Cartwright's expulsion from Cambridge, and he was known to be an inveterate opponent of anything that smacked of "T.C., his platform".[40]

One of Whitgift's first acts as Archbishop of Canterbury was to compile a set of articles to which all clergymen would be required to subscribe, and which included the statement that the prayer book contained nothing in it contrary to the word of God. There was a significant number of ministers who could not swear to this in good conscience and, in the first six months of 1584, between three and four hundred clergymen in the province of Canterbury were suspended after refusing to subscribe. The Queen seemed unconcerned by the great swathes that Whitgift was making through the ranks of the clergy, but the Council protested so vigorously about it that a few months later Whitgift agreed to modify the formula for subscription, so that it would be acceptable to a higher proportion of the clergy. Even so, this was far from the end to his onslaught on non-conformity. Henceforward, clergymen who were suspected of Puritan leanings could be summoned before the High Commission, and without being formally charged, they could be examined on oath regarding their attitudes towards the Church. In many cases, they involuntarily compromised themselves during these hearings, and if their answers were not satisfactory, they were deprived of their livings.

To those men within the Council who most strongly deplored the imperfections of the Church, it seemed incomprehensible that Whitgift should be able to instigate this campaign against the very men who were trying hardest to bring about a religious regeneration. Passionately, Sir Francis Knollys declared to Burghley, "It grieves my heart to see the course of popish treason to be neglected, and to see the zealous preachers of the gospel, sound in doctrine (who are the most diligent barkers against the popish wolf ...) to be persecuted and put to silence as though there were no enemies to her Majesty and to the state but they". Burghley shared his concern, and in July 1584 wrote in remonstrance to Whitgift. Having examined a list of the questions which could be put to ministers summoned before the High Commission, he described them as "so curiously penned, so full of branches and circumstances as I think the inquisitors of Spain use not so many questions to comprehend and to trap their preys". Whitgift was undeterred by this reproof. In his reply, he merely reminded Burghley, "I neither do, nor have done anything in this matter . . . which her Majesty hath not with earnest charge committed unto me".[41]

When Parliament met on 23 November 1584, there was a palpable current of anger against Whitgift's high-handed proceedings. If the Queen had had her way, however, the members of the House of Commons would not have been able to give vent to their feelings. At the opening session of Parliament, the Lord Chancellor announced that Elizabeth had given her customary favourable answer to the Commons' request to be accorded the privilege of free speech, "only she restrained the cause of religion to be spoken of among them".[42]

Despite the ban, indignation was running too high among members of Parliament for them to heed this command, and the Privy Councillors in the House did little to restrain them. A Commons committee was formed to consider abuses in the Church, and this body agreed to petition the Queen to implement various reforms. Some of the requests incorporated in their petition were unexceptional enough, but they included pleas that all ministers recently deprived should be reinstated, that the prophesyings should be restored, and that no oath should be administered to the clergy other than those prescribed by statute. The petition was shown to the Queen during the Christmas recess, and when Parliament reconvened, in February 1585, Burghley and Whitgift informed a deputation from the House of Commons of Elizabeth's reaction. Burghley explained that the Queen had agreed it would be desirable if some of their proposals were put into practice, but others she had rejected out of hand, "as requiring innovation and impugning the Book of Common Prayer". This was disappointing enough, but when Whitgift spoke, he made matters much worse by adopting an arrogant and self-righteous tone. He bluntly announced, "They that are deprived are justly deprived; that which is done is justly done, and so will be avowed". This "insufficient and opprobious answer" left the Commons seething.[43]

Once again, a Commons committee met, and produced a report which sought to establish that Whitgift's proceedings in the High Commission were unconstitutional and unwarranted. Dealing point by point with the Archbishop's recent statement to the Commons, the report queried Whitgift's assertion that the ministers had been justly deprived. "We would be glad to know by what law," ran one passage, "for as we take it, they are not deprived by any Common Law or Statute Law of this realm".[44]

Convinced that the bishops had abrogated to themselves powers which exceeded those allotted to them in the Act of Uniformity, the Commons were seeking to establish that the bishops could not wield an authority that was independent of Parliament.

To the Queen this was utterly inadmissible. Before the committee's report could even be read in the lower house, she sent a message reminding the Commons of her earlier command not to "meddle with matters of the Church, neither in reformation of religion or discipline". In the strongest possible terms, she reaffirmed that she would not permit the religious settlement of 1559 to be modified, for "resolutely she will receive no manner of innovation, nor alter or change any law whereby the religion of the Church of England standeth established at this day". [45]

Eighteen months elapsed before Parliament met again, and in the interim, the radical wing of the Puritan movement made efforts to ensure that any reforming legislation that was put before the next session would receive a favourable reception. Under the direction of John Field, the Puritan conferences scattered across England conducted a survey of the clergy in their areas. By the time that Parliament reassembled in October 1586, they had produced a report that covered more than 2,500 parishes, and which read as a sorry indictment of the English priesthood. Among the ministers who featured in its pages were individuals variously described as "an alehouse haunter, a companion with drunkards"; "consumed by carding, dicing and gaming"; "a drunkard and a whoremaster".[46] Statistical information of this sort gave the Puritans the ammunition they needed, for they calculated that Members of Parliament who saw it would be outraged that men such as the above-mentioned should be permitted to remain unmolested in their livings, while Whitgift drove out from the Church ministers who were infinitely more conscientious and God-fearing.

Having seen to it that the parliamentary climate was favourable, a small group of radical Commons members sought to bring before the house a remarkable programme of legislation. On 27 February 1587, Anthony Cope made a speech lamenting the shortcomings of the clergy, and with the aim of procuring "the amendment of things amiss in the ecclesiastical state", he proposed to read a bill and book. Mindful of Elizabeth's displeasure when the house concerned itself with such matters, the Speaker of the Commons begged its members not to proceed, but by a prearranged plan, Cope's allies in the house whipped up a cry for the measure to be read. In the face of such pressure, the Speaker acquiesced, but because it was late, it was agreed that the reading should take place the following day. Next morning the eager house reassembled, only to learn that overnight the Queen had confiscated both bill and book.

The Puritan clique had anticipated this, and they had their response ready. On 1 March, another of Cope's supporters, Peter Wentworth, made a speech asking whether the Queen had acted in a manner that encroached upon the freedoms traditionally accorded the house. He demanded that the matter should form the subject for a debate, but the Speaker of the House said he needed time to consider this request. While he was doing so, the Queen took pre-emptive action. That afternoon, Wentworth was summoned before the Council and sent to the Tower, and the following day Cope and some of his confederates joined him there. Their offence was to have banded together outside of Parliament to discuss ways of introducing their legislative programme, for in the days when the concept of "Her Majesty's Loyal Opposition" did not exist, such political man-oeuvering was looked on as subversive.

In order to curtail the Commons' indignation at these arrests, on 4 March Sir Christopher Hatton made an impressive speech, explaining just how shocking a proposal Cope's bill had been. Not only had it provided for the substitution of the Calvinist Genevan prayer book in place of that now used, but it had declared "utterly void and none effect" all "laws, customs, statutes, ordinances and constitutions" relating to Church government. Having thus wiped the slate clean, the existing ecclesiastical hierarchy would have been replaced by the presbyterian form of Church government specified in the Genevan prayer book. It was not difficult to discredit a proposal that has been described by one recent authority as "perhaps the most immoderate measure ever to have come before the House of Commons". Hatton shrewdly drove the thrust home by warning the members that if the bill took effect, gentlemen would lose their right to present clergymen to livings, and the lands they had accumulated since the dissolution of the monasteries would probably also be confiscated to pay for the upkeep of the Church. Having heard this, the Commons were no longer minded to protest at Cope's imprisonment.[47]

Parliament had failed the Puritans and, to the extremists in their party, it seemed that if reform could not be brought about by constitutional means, the obvious alternative was to precipitate a church revolution from below. As John Field remarked to a follower, "Seeing we cannot compass these things by suit nor dispute, it is the multitude and people that must bring the discipline to pass which we desire".[48] Already Cartwright's colleague Walter Travers had written the so-called *Book of Discipline*, which set out in great detail the way that the Church should be structured. According to this blueprint, ministers and elders were to meet regularly in local assemblies, known as 'classes', and every so often representatives from these bodies would be called upon to attend provincial or national synods, which could settle all matters of contention that arose within the Church. Throughout 1587, this book was disseminated to the various Puritan cells throughout the country, whose members were requested to give a formal declaration that they would put its provisions into practice as soon as possible. Many of those called upon to take this step nevertheless hesitated to take the law into their own hands in so bold a fashion. Several of the conferences deferred making a decision about it for the time being and even in cases where Puritans collectively subscribed, they frequently qualified this by stating that they did so only so far as was agreeable with the law. Although the underground Puritan network had sinister implications for the Royal Supremacy, very few of its members shared the revolutionary convictions of John Field.

1588 was a bad year for the Puritan movement. Not only did it see the death of John Field and the Earl of Leicester (the Puritans' "greatest stay and aid" within the Council), but in October the first Martin Marprelate tract appeared, which ultimately was to bring nemesis on the Godly. Martin Marprelate was the pseudonym adopted by the author of a series of savagely satirical attacks on the bishops, or "the horned masters of the convocation house", to use his terminology. His identity has never been conclusively established, but whoever he was, his witty, railing style and his irreverent denunciations of "that swinish rabble" ensured that his works were vastly popular. They were rendered more amusing by his intimate knowledge of each bishop's personal failings: he knew which of them was prone to swearing, or to breaking the sanctity of the sabbath by playing bowls on Sunday. He wrote mockingly, "You see, my worshipful priests of this crew ... Master Marprelate ... understands all your knavery, and it may be, keeps a register of them". When Bishop Cooper (who was notorious for being cuckolded by his wife) wrote a reply to Martin, the latter responded with another broadside at the bishops, and in this he gleefully alluded to "Dame Cooper's gadding". But although Martin was read with enjoyment by a wide audience, he himself had to admit that many of the most sincere Puritans were strongly condemnatory, "because I am too open, because I jest". They knew that by disseminating such pernicious abuse, Martin would bring the whole Puritan movement into disrepute, and they feared that this would provoke a reactionary backlash.[49]

In this they were correct. The Queen saw nothing remotely humorous about these diatribes against the bishops, and in November instructions were issued that the secret press responsible for issuing the tracts must be tracked down. While the hunt was on, scores of ministers were interrogated all over the country, and *agents provocateurs* thronged the churchyard of St Paul's, hoping to glean from unwary Puritans some idea as to Martin's whereabouts. Martin and his accomplices kept relocating the press to ward off detection, but in August 1589 the printers were run to earth near Manchester. On the Queen's express instructions, the principal printer was tortured,[50] but he refused to reveal Martin's true name. As a result Martin was never caught, and he even managed to publish one final tract after the apprehension of the printers, but this was to be the last word from him.

Already, however, he had done irreparable damage to the Puritan movement. In the course of their enquiries about Martin, the authorities had for the first time uncovered evidence that alerted them to the existence of the underground Puritan network and, with the Queen's support, Whitgift saw that it was dismantled. In 1590, nine of the ringleaders, including Cartwright (who had been back in England since 1585), were summoned before the High Commission, and when they refused to take the oath tendered to them, they were imprisoned for contempt. In June 1591 their case was referred to the Court of Star Chamber, where it was attempted to prove that they were guilty of conspiring to alter the religion established by law, and to set up in its place a presbyterian church, with a discipline and organization of its own. It proved impossible to make these charges stick but, if the evidence had allowed, Cartwright and his fellows would have been prosecuted for sedition, which was a capital crime. As it was, they were merely kept in prison for a time, and were only released because they agreed that in future they would not hold any further "prescript and set meetings".

Cartwright and the others had at least escaped with their lives, but the leaders of an even more extreme Puritanical sect of separatists were not so fortunate. In view of the Church of England's manifold failings, they refused to be a part of an institution which they condemned as unlawful, superstitious and anti-Christian. At least fifty-nine individuals were arrested for holding these views, ten of whom died in jail. Two leaders of the movement named Barrow and Greenwood were tried in March 1593 and, having been convicted of producing seditious writings, they were hanged the following month.

Together the Queen and Whitgift had triumphed over Puritanism. The conferences were no more, and although a few Puritans still found ways of keeping in contact with their brethren, it was now accepted that there could be no question of reforming the Church in Elizabeth's lifetime. In 1591, the Queen had shocked Sir Francis Knollys by telling him that in her opinion, the Puritans represented just as grave a threat to her as did the Catholics, but already by that time the movement had effectively been crippled. As Elizabeth had all along intended, the Church of 1559 was handed intact to her successor.

Within two months of his return from France, Essex had grown restless, for as a man who was "wholly inflamed with the desire to be doing somewhat", he found a routine Court existence unbearably tedious. In contrast, many of his greatest admirers felt that the time had come for him to settle down, and that instead of seeking to distinguish himself as a general, it was "domestical greatness" to which he should aspire. They had applauded when Essex had taken up his command in France, which they had expected to enhance his prestige, but the disappointing outcome to that campaign had proved that leading armies was not a sure way of winning the Queen's esteem. A political career might lack the excitement of soldiering, but it also had fewer pitfalls, and Essex's friends calculated that if he were to concentrate on consolidating his position at Court, he would be better placed to serve them. Hitherto, the Earl had been content to be regarded as a man of action first and foremost, but his supporters were clear that he must now balance this by setting himself up as "a great man in the state".[51]

It was a good moment for Essex to try and make his mark as a statesman, for in April 1590 Walsingham had died, and though Burghley remained "the chief pillar of the welfare of England", it was assumed that before long the Queen would find it necessary to take the opinions of younger men into account. Essex's prospects seemed brighter still when Sir Walter Ralegh committed a serious misdemeanour, thereby forfeiting all chance of further advancement. Ralegh had embarked on an affair with Bess Throckmorton, a maid of honour to the Queen, and by the summer of 1591 the girl was carrying his child. That autumn he had secretly married her, but Bess had nevertheless carried on working at Court, successfully concealing her pregnancy from the Queen. In February 1592 she absented herself from court on some pretext, and a month later had given birth to a son at her brother's house, but even then the Raleghs kept their marriage quiet. When Ralegh was warned that he was rumoured to have taken a wife, he indignantly denied it, maintaining proudly, "There is none on the face of the earth I would be fastened unto".[52] At the end of April Bess brazenly resumed her place at Court, but the deception could not be kept up for much longer. By May the secret was out, and Ralegh was put under house arrest.

Between them the Raleghs had made Elizabeth look a fool, and she naturally took exception to this. Until now she had been under the impression that Ralegh's devotion to her remained absolute, and the depth of his duplicity was only underlined by the fact that as recently as January 1592 she had granted him Sherborne Castle. But Ralegh was guilty of more than a mere breach of trust: by seducing a maid of honour, and then marrying her without her mistress's consent, he had laid himself open to punitive action on two counts, and the cynical way in which he had sought to deceive the Queen made it especially unlikely that she would be lenient about his offence.

At first Ralegh seems not to have appreciated the gravity of his position, assuming that if he addressed the Queen in his familiar devotional strain, she would overlook what he termed his "one frail misfortune". Clearly hoping that his letter would be shown to Elizabeth, he sent a colleague an extravagant description of his distress at being denied her presence, "I, that was wont to behold her riding like Alexander, hunting like Diana, walking like Venus, the gentle wind blowing her fair hair about her pure cheeks like a nymph". The preposterous hyperbole came dangerously close to parodying the language of courtly love, and Sir Walter soon found out that Elizabeth's mood was too grim to be appeased by such a facile paean of praise. In August 1592, he and his wife were sent to the Tower, and though both were released before the end of the year, neither was readmitted to court for years to come. Too late, Ralegh became "greedy to do anything to recover the conceit of his brutish offence", but all his blandishments fell flat. He had alienated too many people with his arrogant ways for his plight to arouse much sympathy and, now that the Queen was no longer his friend, he found himself "like a fish cast on dry land, gasping for breath, with lame legs and lamer lungs".[53]

Ralegh's eclipse gave Essex the better chance to shine, and the more so because in November 1591 Lord Chancellor Hatton had died, worn out with kidney disease and worry. Financial difficulties had undermined his peace of mind, for during his tenure of the woolsack he had borrowed £42,189 out of the receipts of ecclesiastical taxation which had been paid into his department and, when called upon to repay the money, had proved incapable of doing so. As it became clear that his health was failing, the Queen visited him and administered "cordial broths with her own hands",[54] but her own financial circumstances did not permit her to waive the debt. When Hatton died he was still doing his best to scrape together the cash, and there were some who said that the Queen had harassed him into the grave.

Death was inexorably thinning the ranks of the leading men at court, but Essex was very far from having the field entirely to himself. In particular, Burghley's second son, Robert Cecil, was being tipped to achieve high office. Cecil was two years older than Essex, and was described by one contemporary as having been "a courtier from his cradle". Physically, he was a poor specimen: in infancy he had sustained a spinal injury when dropped by his nurse, and even as an adult he remained undersized and bent. His intellect nevertheless made up for his hunched and puny frame. Burghley's eldest son, Thomas, had been something of a disappointment to his father, for after a wild youth he had developed into a bluff country gentleman with neither the inclination nor the aptitude to concern himself with affairs of state. In the younger brother, however, Burghley had early detected much promise, and had taken great pains to bring him up "as near as might be like unto" himself, schooling him personally in the intricacies of diplomacy and statecraft. By 1584, when the twenty-one-year-old Robert went to complete his education in France, Burghley could justly congratulate himself on the way his son had turned out. The elder brother Thomas had also been sent to Paris after leaving school but, whereas he had spent his time there chasing women and running up debts, Robert occupied himself during his stay by writing a memorandum which analysed the problems surrounding the succession to the French throne.[55]

This is not to say that father and son were identical in character, not least of the differences between them being that Robert had a genuine sense of fun. His humorous side shone through clearly in the letters he sent his father's secretary, Michael Hicks, when he was in the Netherlands with the English peace commissioners in 1588. At one point he wrote teasingly, "Your nose would drop off i' faith, Don Michael, if you were as cold as we have been. Not a fair woman, nor an honest".[56] It is not easy to imagine Burghley finding time for such merry asides in his private correspondence, but even in Cecil's case, business always came first. He had inherited his father's formidable powers of application, and had the same memory, and ability to master details. His aptitude for business was complemented by a skill in handling people, for he had the finely tuned antennae of one who knew that his appearance told against him, and who had therefore had to commend himself to the world in other ways. This stood him in good stead in his dealings with the Queen, for he became adept at divining her moods, waiting for the days when she would be amenable to cautiously phrased suggestions, but never contradicting her, or pressing her too far. Perhaps it was learning to cope with his disabilities that had instilled in him his quiet determination and self-control, but certainly his air of professionalism was never allowed to lapse, and just as he successfully masked his irritation when the Queen unkindly dubbed him her 'pygmy', he betrayed no impatience when promotion did not come to him as fast as he had hoped.

Physically and mentally, Essex and Cecil were the complete antithesis of each other, but initially Burghley does not seem to have anticipated that a serious rivalry would grow up between them. When Essex's father had died, Burghley had become the young Earl's guardian and even after Essex had attained his majority, the Lord Treasurer had continued to look on his former ward with a favourable eye. In July 1591, a Court observer reported that Burghley was clearly "inclined" towards Essex, but the latter was not responding well to his benevolence, for "such old and sour wine is not good drink". Rather than looking on Burghley as a friend and mentor, Essex was "impatient of the slow process he must needs have during the life and greatness of the ... Treasurer",[57] and though he was careful to treat him with the honour that was due to one of his advanced years and position, he was reluctant to accord Robert Cecil even this grudging respect.

When Burghley understood that Essex believed himself to have no need of his goodwill, his own hackles rose, and he did what he could to circumscribe the Earl's influence at Court. Determined to safeguard his

son's future, he tried to limit the numbers of Essex's adherents by deliberately withholding his favour from men who were too closely associated
with the Earl. Thus in October 1591 it was reported that Sir Thomas
Bodley and Sir Edward Norris had "fallen into the high indignation of my
Lord Treasurer ... in effect for nourishing a dependency upon others,
besides his Lordship, which will be hardly put up". Three years later,
there was a revealing exchange between the Lord Treasurer and Anthony
Standen, who had recently come back to England from abroad and had
been taken up by Essex. When Burghley offered to present Elizabeth with
a memorandum on foreign affairs that Standen had recently written,
Standen explained that Essex had already shown it to the Queen. "The
Lord Treasurer hereupon began to start in his chair and to alter his voice
and countenance from a kind of crossing and wayward manner ... into a
tune of choler ... saying that Mr Standen having dealt in that affair with
the Earl of Essex, he would do well to persevere; wishing that the Earl
might do him good and that it should no way offend him". Naturally,
when Essex learnt that the Lord Treasurer was penalizing his friends in this
way, it hardly made him better disposed, and he retaliated by vehemently
opposing the advancement of those men whom he regarded as being tainted
by their connections with the Cecils. Between them, Essex and Burghley
were to drive the Court into two mutually exclusive camps, and by 1597
the demarcation line between the factions was so pronounced that "it was
a thing notorious to all the Court" that "a man who was of the Lord
Treasurer's party was sure to be among the enemies of the Earl".[58]

When Walsingham had died in 1590, Burghley had been anxious for
Cecil to be made Secretary in his place. By December it was believed that
the Queen was on the verge of doing as he wished, and that Cecil would
be "sworn Secretary before Christmas", but nothing came of these hopes.
Cecil nevertheless remained in the running for the job, and when the
Queen visited Theobalds that spring there was a general expectation that
she would confer it on him then. Once again, however, Burghley was
disappointed, and on that occasion Cecil had to content himself with being
dubbed a knight. Two months later, he was made a member of the Privy
Council, but higher office still eluded him, and by August Elizabeth
appeared to have decided that he was too young to be given such a key
position in the state. For a time she contemplated letting Sir Edward
Stafford and Thomas Wotton share the post, but in the end she found it
preferable to keep the place vacant, and let Burghley "seal and despatch
all business" that normally devolved on the Secretary. Naturally the Lord
Treasurer grumbled at the extra work that this entailed, but in fact the
situation suited him quite well. It allowed him to delegate a great deal to
his son, and with every day that Robert spent unofficially discharging the
Secretary's responsibilities it became more likely that the Queen would

ultimately award him the post. By the autumn of 1591 Cecil was already doing so much for his father that it was noted that "the whole management of the Secretary's place is in his hands", and no one doubted that Burghley hoped that the experience he was acquiring in this way would subsequently serve as "a means to install him into the place".[59]

In some ways, this informal arrangement worked well, but on balance it was probably misguided of the Queen to keep things thus in limbo. As long as the Secretaryship remained unfilled, Essex hoped he would be able to persuade the Queen to appoint a nominee of his to the post, and obviously this deepened the rift between him and the Cecils. Hoping to convince her that Cecil was not up to the job, he also set up at his own expense a private intelligence network, which was designed to show up the shortcomings in the Cecils' methods of gathering information. The spies who had formerly been on Walsingham's payroll were delighted when Essex offered them work, particularly since he subsidized their activities in a lavish way that the more frugal Cecils could never hope to emulate. Skilled agents such as Thomas Phelippes now deployed their talents in Essex's service, and he received a stream of reports from informers on the continent. By 1596, his office was inundated with so much business that he had to employ four secretaries to deal with all the paperwork and keep him permanently briefed.

In February 1593, when Essex was twenty-six years old, Elizabeth made him a Privy Councillor, and for a time it seemed as if his new responsibilities would have a steadying effect on him. A week after the decision had been announced, one courtier reported, "His Lordship is become a new man, clean forsaking all his former youthful tricks, carrying himself with honourable gravity, and singularly liked of both in Parliament and at the Council table for his speeches and judgment". He remained, however, as intolerant as before, and sitting at the same Council table as the Cecils did not serve to heighten them in his esteem. Leicester had once remarked, "Among councillors there may and must rise by way of argument divisions in opinion ... and oft doth without any causes of mislike at all",[60] but instead of seeing the Council chamber as a forum for orderly debate, Essex tended to view it as another arena in which the Cecils must be challenged.

One way in which Essex sought to isolate the Cecils was by placing clients of his own in the principal offices of Court and state, but he did not have an easy time convincing the Queen that his recommendations in such matters should be followed. In 1593 he clashed with her over the appointment of a new Attorney General, which he wanted to be given to Francis Bacon, son of Elizabeth's first Lord Keeper. For her part, the Queen believed that Edward Coke would be the better man for the job and, despite the fact that Bacon was Burghley's nephew, the Lord Treasurer concurred with her in this. Coke was older than Bacon, and had practised more extensively in the courts, and Bacon had also recently offended Elizabeth by arguing in Parliament that the payment of the latest subsidy should be spread over six years rather than four. His inopportune speech had resulted in the Queen barring him from Court, but Essex did not accept that this made him ineligible for high office, or indeed, that any of her other objections to Bacon's promotion were valid.

True to his conviction that "there is not so much gotten of the Queen by earnestness as by often soliciting", Essex set himself to wear down her resistance. Having first broached the subject in the summer of 1593, he pestered her relentlessly, but to his disgust she remained "stiff in her own opinion". This merely caused the Earl to redouble his entreaties, until the exasperated Queen was provoked into shouting "that she would be advised by those that had more judgment in these things". By December the dispute had given rise to such friction between them that for a short time the Earl withdrew from court in protest. He was back at the Queen's side for the Twelfth Night celebrations, but though on that occasion he was amiability itself, within days he was nagging her as obsessively as before.[61]

To Robert Cecil's sane and orderly mind it appeared that if the parties involved were prepared to adopt a rational approach, the matter could be resolved to the satisfaction of all concerned. When the opportunity arose, he put it to Essex that if he were to acquiesce in the appointment of Edward Coke as Attorney General, Francis Bacon could then be put forward for the subordinate position of Solicitor General, an arrangement which "might be of easier digestion to her Majesty". Essex would not hear of the compromise. "Digest me no digestions!" he heatedly cried out, "for the Attorneyship for Francis is that I must have, and in that will I spend all my power, might, authority and amity, and with tooth and nail defend and procure the same for him against whomsoever".[62] This effectively terminated the discussion, which had served only to confirm Cecil in the belief that Essex was a man with whom it was scarcely possible to do business.

Essex was in this excitable state of mind when he stumbled across what he took to be a plot to murder the Queen. It had been Walsingham's belief that once Mary Stuart was dead, there would be no further Catholic assassination attempts on Elizabeth. Intermittent reports continued to come in that Elizabeth's life was being sought, but although in the Queen of Scots' lifetime he had never failed to alert Elizabeth when he received intelligence of this sort, after Mary's execution he merely warned the Council of what he had heard. He justified this on the grounds that such reports "do always breed fearful apprehensions" in the Queen, and now that Mary was out of the way, he was reluctant to allow his mistress to be disturbed.[63] However, since Essex was so anxious to prove to Elizabeth how well his intelligence service worked, it was not in his best interests that she should believe herself to be safe. He wanted to gain credit for his vigilance by exposing plots against her, and to convince her that only he could provide her with the protection she required. The net result was that the Queen's security became bound up with the struggle to dominate the Court.

Essex was first alerted to the supposed design on the Queen's life in January 1594, when two servants of the Portuguese pretender, Don Antonio, were arrested on suspicion of being double agents in the pay of Spain. While they were being questioned, it emerged they had had some dealings with Dr Roderigo Lopez, a Portuguese Jew who had been the Queen's physician since 1586. Lopez was thereupon examined at Burghley's house by Essex, Cecil and Burghley and, though Essex was not satisfied with his explanations, the doctor succeeded in convincing the Cecils that there was nothing sinister in his connections with the arrested men. When Robert Cecil told the Queen that Lopez was in the clear, Elizabeth became irritated that he had been detained in the first place. At her next encounter with Essex, she had burst out that he was "a rash and temerarious youth, to enter into the matter against the poor man, which he could not prove, but whose innocence she knew well enough".[64] Furiously Essex flung himself away to sulk in his chamber for two days, and the Queen could only coax him out by agreeing that he might, after all, pursue his enquiries further.

Lopez was removed to the Tower, and further pressure was applied to Don Antonio's servants, and after much prodding they volunteered evidence which incriminated Lopez. One of them deposed that Lopez had sent "obscurely worded" letters to Spanish agents, promising "to do all the King required", whereupon his colleague capped this by saying that Lopez had agreed to undertake the Queen's murder for a payment of 50,000 crowns. Lopez himself had staunchly maintained his innocence in the face of a remorseless interrogation, but when confronted with these claims, he broke down and confessed "that he had indeed spoken of this matter [the Queen's murder] and promised it, but all to cozen the King of Spain".[65] He said that it was at Walsingham's behest that he had established contact with the Spanish Court, and explained that the Secretary had used him to pass false information to the enemy, but unfortunately Walsingham was not available to confirm the Doctor's version of events.

To Essex, the facts were clear. He wrote jubilantly to a friend, "I have discovered a most dangerous and desperate treason. The point of conspiracy was her Majesty's death. The executioner should have been Dr Lopez; the manner poison. This I have so followed as I will make it appear clear as noon day". And indeed, when Lopez went to trial in February 1594, the fact that he claimed to have made his confession under fear of torture did not prevent him being found guilty and having "judgment ... passed against him, with the applause of all the world". The Queen, however, still seems to have had her doubts about Lopez's guilt, and for three months his death warrant remained unsigned. On 7 June he was finally executed, but the fact that Elizabeth agreed that Lopez's widow could retain a valuable lease, which theoretically should have been forfeit to the Crown on his conviction, suggests that she continued to be troubled by his fate.[66]

Having performed so notable a feat of detection, Essex had hoped that his suit on Bacon's behalf would gain an added impetus, but in April 1594 Sir Edward Coke's appointment as Attorney General was officially announced. For Essex, who had previously so roundly dismissed the idea that Bacon should make do with the position of Solicitor General, it was a real mortification to have to admit that his friend could hope for nothing better than that. It soon emerged, however, that even in trying to secure this lesser office for Bacon, Essex was aiming too high, for in Elizabeth's eyes the matter of Bacon's advancement now represented a crucial test of will. When Essex brought up the subject – which he did at every opportunity – he still had no luck in overcoming her objections, but typically, he would not be deterred. He recounted proudly how on one occasion he harried her so remorselessly that the Queen "in passion bade me go to bed if I could talk of nothing else". Instead of being concerned at having provoked her in this way, he promised Bacon he would be no less importunate in future.[67]

After the Queen had been subjected to more than nine months of this treatment, she was overheard muttering that she would "seek all England for a solicitor" rather than take Bacon on, and in November 1595 Thomas Fleming was given the job. It was a devastating setback for the Earl, and typically he held others responsible for it, asserting darkly that "all came from his Lordship's mighty enemies". In fact, both Burghley and Cecil had favoured Bacon for the job, and the decision not to appoint him had been very much a personal one of the Queen's. But though the Cecils had not been responsible for Essex's humiliation, indirectly they benefited from it, for the Earl had been so open in his support of Bacon that his reputation had become "much engaged", and his failure to impose his will on the Queen badly damaged his standing at Court. The episode had demonstrated that no one could hope for a more vigorous and determined patron than Essex, but it had also underlined that the Queen had to be handled with a subtlety and restraint that were entirely alien to his nature. As Bacon's mother drily observed, "Though the Earl showed great affection, he marred all with violent courses", and the lesson was not lost on those onlookers who were wondering whether they ought to attach themselves to Essex or his rivals. One courtier told Robert Cecil that if ever he had a suit to put to the Queen, he would always approach her through Burghley, "from whom one commendation in cold blood and seeming to proceed of judgment shall more prevail with the Queen than all the affectionate speech of my Lord of Essex".[68]

In December 1595, preparations began for a major new offensive against Spain. It was to be a joint Anglo–Dutch effort, with eighteen of the Queen's warships being matched by an equal number from the Dutch navy. Additional ships were supplied by English coastal towns, or fitted out by private individuals, so that, when finally assembled, the fleet numbered one hundred and fifty sail.

This was a force formidable enough to change the whole complexion of the war, which otherwise was not going particularly well. The previous summer the Queen had contributed six of her ships towards an expedition fitted out by Sir Francis Drake and John Hawkins. The plan was to attack Panama and other Spanish settlements in Central America, but from the start the voyage had gone badly. Times had changed since the days when Drake had first preyed on ill-defended outposts of the Spanish empire, and the ports on which they swooped were all more strongly fortified than they had anticipated. After a series of quarrels with Drake, Hawkins fell mortally ill at Puerto Rico, but Drake carried on without him, insisting desperately that "We must have gold before we see England". He had refused to return home even when dysentery carried off many of his men, but on 27 January 1596 he himself succumbed to it and was buried at sea. When the survivors reached home, they brought with them only a few pearls and some miscellaneous booty that was valued at £4,205, a miserable return for a voyage in which the Queen had invested £28,000.[69]

In March 1596, the Queen announced that the command of this new expedition was to be jointly entrusted to Essex and Lord Howard of Effingham. Essex threw himself into the preparations with his customary vigour, running himself still further into debt by investing heavily in the venture. In his elation at his new charge, he even lost interest in the feuds and squabbles with rivals which had so preoccupied him the previous year. He had a reconciliation with Cecil and, when Sir Walter Ralegh joined the expedition, Essex welcomed him with the warm assurance that "This is the action and the time in which you and I shall both be taught to know and love one another".[70]

By April, preparations were complete, but suddenly everything was thrown into confusion when news arrived from France that a troop of Spaniards had arrived unexpectedly before Calais and were currently laying siege to it. Henry IV could do little to defend it, and it was clear that unless Elizabeth went to its aid the town would fall. At first it seemed that the Queen did not dispute that this must be averted by employing the men and ships already assembled to relieve Calais. Before long, however, it emerged that she had only given Henry a conditional offer of aid, and that in return for saving Calais she was demanding to be given possession of it, until such time as Henry discharged his debts to her. Essex was incredulous that she could be so mercenary, and Burghley was scarcely less censorious, noting that, if the town was lost, the blame would be laid squarely on her. On 14 April the Queen finally accepted that Henry could not be blackmailed into ceding Calais, for as he remarked, if he could not have the town, it was all one to him whether it was in Spanish or English hands. From Greenwich, where she could hear the Spanish ordnance pounding away at Calais, the Queen exhorted Essex to hasten to its relief, but her action came too late. On 15 April, as Essex was embarking his troops, news came that the town had been taken. Her dreams of repossessing Calais rudely shattered, Elizabeth now had to contend with the reality of having the Spaniards perched on her doorstep.

Never had it been more imperative to deliver a straight thrust against the enemy, but this latest setback merely prompted the Queen to be still more negative in her approach to the war. Now that the fleet was no longer going to be diverted to Calais, the object of the expedition had reverted to being an attack on a Spanish port, but Elizabeth was behaving as if she repented having sanctioned any such thing. When Essex took his leave of her on 25 April, she used him ungraciously, and when difficulties with the wind prevented the fleet from sailing on the scheduled date, there were fears that the Queen would use this as an excuse to countermand the whole expedition. She could not find a good word to say about Essex, snarling that he was opinionated, wilful and rash, and while her comments were true enough, this was scarcely the right moment for her to deliver herself of such strictures. As Essex complained, he had been unstinting in his efforts to ensure that all went well, "And yet am I so far from receiving thanks as her Majesty keepeth the same form with me as she would do with him that through his fault or misfortune had lost her troops".[71]

Worse was to come, for on 16 May Elizabeth suddenly sent orders that Howard and Essex were to hand over command to their subordinates and return to Court. At this, however, there were impassioned protests from all the most important officers in the fleet that a change of leadership at this stage would be fatal, and this made the Queen reconsider. Mercifully, this turned out to be the last of her quibbles, and henceforward her attitude was more supportive. Her parting present to her commanders was a prayer for their safe return which she herself had composed, and she appended an affectionate postscript to a letter to Essex, expressing a hope "that your return may make you better and me gladder". Her improved frame of mind did wonders for morale, and shortly before setting sail Essex wrote jubilantly to Cecil, "Here is such joy in all the fleet, both of soldiers and mariners ... as it would please her Majesty well to see th'effect of her own work".[72]

In some ways, the outcome of the expedition lived up to the highest expectations. Having left Plymouth on 3 June, the fleet appeared before Cadiz seventeen days later. After a successful naval action, in which two of Philip's largest warships were destroyed, and two others captured, Essex led his men ashore, and by the next morning Cadiz was in English hands. During the ensuing fortnight, it was stripped of all goods of value, and before the English left on 5 July much of the town was razed. On the other hand, a rich merchant fleet, containing goods valued at three million pounds, had lain at anchor in the town's inner harbour, and through negligence the English had lost this. As one participant had frankly admitted, "Our men being busy in sacking the town", insufficient attention had been given to securing the defenceless vessels,[73] and rather than let so rich a prize fall into enemy hands, the Spanish military authorities gave orders that the fleet should be fired.

Even so, Cadiz had yielded a rich haul of plunder, but the Queen did not see much of it, for though in theory all valuable items taken should have been surrendered to the Crown, a great deal of loot inevitably went astray. A royal official named Sir Anthony Ashley had actually been sent to Cadiz with instructions to prevent such wholesale spoliation, but as it turned out, far from acting to protect the Queen's interests, Ashley had "well fleshed" himself in the town's sack. As the fleet was on its way home, port officials in the West Country were put on the alert to search all incoming ships for stolen booty, but the dishonesty was so widespread that the measures they took were of little use. One wag at Court commented that, after the action at Cadiz, Elizabeth "should not be hereafter troubled with beggars, all were become so rich" but, as was painfully apparent, she herself had not been allowed to share in the bonanza.[74]

It was of course some consolation that the expeditionary force had covered itself in glory. Those involved could congratulate themselves on having given "battle to the enemy at his own door, defeated and destroyed a war and merchant fleet in one of his harbours [and] captured and pillaged the fairest port in that part of Spain". It was nevertheless understandable enough that the Queen was more inclined to dwell on the opportunities that had been lost than on what had been achieved. As she had always feared, a voyage which should have been hugely remunerative had been "rather an action of honour and virtue against the enemy, and particular profit by spoil to the army, than profitable to ourself".[75]

She was also furious that many of those she suspected of having defrauded her had come back with knighthoods, for between them Essex and Howard had dubbed sixty-eight new knights. Essex had been in trouble for this before, for at Rouen he had handed out twenty-one knighthoods, in direct contravention of orders to give the rank to no one who was "unable by living to maintain the countenance thereof". Elizabeth herself was so sparing with knighthoods that, in the first twenty-five years of the reign, the number of knights in England had actually halved, and this had been deliberate policy on her part. Realizing that the whole concept of knighthood would be devalued if the honour was indiscriminately awarded, she had sought to maintain its prestige by keeping the order exclusive. These latest creations made a nonsense of her policy of restraint. After Essex had been so profligate with the honour at Rouen, it was noted, "Great mockery was made of the Earl of Essex's . . . knights", and Elizabeth had no doubt that this latest batch from Cadiz would be treated with equal derision.[76]

Essex had looked forward to being hailed as a hero on his return, and certainly with the public his standing had never been higher. The Queen, however, did not want his popularity to become too overpowering, and she took steps to damp down the adulation. When Essex commissioned a pamphleteer to write an account of the action of Cadiz which glorified his own part in those events, the Queen saw to it that it was not published, thus denying the Earl the acclaim he craved. Essex was piqued enough by this, but infinitely harder for him to swallow was the fact that, on 5 July 1596, the Queen had taken advantage of his absence and created Robert Cecil Secretary of State. Now that the Cecils, father and son, were "joined in power and policy", they were a still more formidable duo, and Essex was incensed by what he regarded as the underhand way in which Robert Cecil had gained advancement while he was overseas, risking his life. Essex's rapprochement with Ralegh had already been wrecked by the Earl's suspicion that Ralegh had tried to grab a share of the glory that he had earned at Cadiz; now his old bitterness against the Cecils − or "the omnipotent couple", as they were known in the circles in which he moved − was likewise reanimated in full.[77]

Essex might be under the delusion that he was becoming hemmed in by enemies at Court, but in reality his position was by no means so beleaguered as he made out. The Queen's irritation that she had gained no solid advantage from the action at Cadiz had caused her to be cool with him when he first arrived back, but by October her attitude had thawed. Furthermore, now that Robert Cecil was "fully stalled in his longed for Secretary's place", Burghley felt he could afford to behave less guardedly towards Essex, and he stretched out a hand of friendship to his former ward. He wrote to tell him that he was wrong to take him for an enemy when in fact he had consistently upheld his interests, but though Essex responded politely, not for a second did he think that the Lord Treasurer was sincere. The more irresponsible of his friends encouraged him to believe that Burghley had only been so conciliatory because he feared that the Queen would no longer tolerate it if he continued to treat Essex unfairly, and that it was self-interest alone which had "made the old fox to crouch and whine" in this submissive manner.[78]

Not everyone who surrounded the Earl was guilty of encouraging him in his excesses, for in October 1596 Francis Bacon sent his patron a letter imploring him to waste less time in factious wrangling. But though Essex was magnanimous enough not to resent such a lecture, he was incapable of profiting by it. His conviction that he was being outflanked by the Cecils gave a new intensity to the factional struggles at court, and far from being more relaxed over the way patronage was distributed, he now became positively frenzied about such matters. The catalyst which precipitated him into fresh conflict with the Queen was the death in March 1597 of Lord Cobham, who had occupied the lucrative position of Lord Warden of the Cinque Ports. On his deathbed he had pleaded that his eldest son should now be given the post, and Elizabeth was inclined to grant him his final wish. Essex, however, had other ideas, for he detested the new Lord Cobham, and wanted his own follower, Sir Robert Sidney, to be appointed in Cobham's stead. With his usual tenacity, he urged the Queen to gratify him over this, refusing to listen when she said that Cobham's claims to the office were hard to overlook. At a Council meeting, Essex declared his position in a manner that came close to challenging the Queen's ultimate prerogative to distribute patronage as she saw fit. "I made it known unto them", he wrote proudly, "that I had just cause to hate the Lord Cobham for his villainous dealing and abusing of me ... If therefore her Majesty would grace him with honour, I may have right cause to think myself little regarded by her".[79]

When the Queen ignored this, Essex took to his bed like a spoilt child, threatening to leave Court for his estates in Wales. Elizabeth raged at this ultimatum, bellowing that she would "break him of his will and pull down his great heart",[80] but in reality Essex still retained the upper hand. The Queen was miserable that they should once again be locked in combat, and it baffled her that one of the principal beneficiaries of the present system of patronage should plunge the court in turmoil in protest at the way she operated it. To put an end to the unpleasantness, on 10 March she called Essex to her and announced that she was going to make him the Master of the Ordnance. It was a sop which she trusted would reconcile him to Cobham's advancement, but though ostensibly Essex had emerged from the tussle in a stronger position than before, his latest appointment was something of an own-goal. Elizabeth had adopted this solution to appease him, but she resented having been subjected to such constraint. Increasingly, it was being borne in upon her that Essex was a maverick whom it was her duty to subdue, and inevitably this had a corrosive effect on her feelings for the Earl.

No matter how much energy Essex devoted to these contests with the

Queen, he looked on overseas adventures as a welcome distraction, for as he put it, "The Court is the centre, but methinks it is the fairer choice to command armies than honours".[81] It was only by striking against Spain that the English could hope to avert the threat of invasion, for however humiliating Cadiz had been for Philip II, it had signally failed to paralyse the Spanish war effort. In October 1596, another armada had sailed from Lisbon, intending to liaise with a further contingent of ships off Cape Finisterre, and then to proceed to Ireland. Before the rendezvous could be effected, however, a violent storm had arisen, wrecking fifty-two of the ninety-eight ships, and obliging the remainder to make for home ports. News of this disaster reached England in December, when it had been in a state of alert for over a month, but Elizabeth knew that this had only given her a temporary respite. The ships that had weathered the storm were being refitted at Ferrol and Corunna, and it was imperative to disable them before they were ready for further action. Plans were already in existence to send a comparatively modest expedition against Spain the following year, but Elizabeth now accepted that a supreme national effort was called for. She had already agreed that ten of her ships were to sail with the expeditionary fleet, but as reports poured in of the activity in the shipyards of northern Spain, she decided to double this number. A further ten warships were supplied by the Dutch, and by the spring a fleet had been assembled which totalled one hundred and twenty sail, with 6,000 men on board. It was not in Essex's nature to remain aloof from an enterprise such as this. Ignoring those who told him that his place was at Court, he volunteered his services, and in May 1597 he was named as the expedition's commander.

His absorption in these new responsibilities made Essex more ready to set aside old feuds. Hearing that Ralegh wanted to come on the expedition, the Earl welcomed him as a comrade-in-arms, and in April Essex, Ralegh and Cecil dined together with every sign of cordiality. Previously Essex had done everything he could to keep alive the Queen's anger against Ralegh, but when Elizabeth signified that she was now ready to forgive Sir Walter, Essex made no protest. In June, Ralegh was granted an audience with her, and was given her pardon, and after five years of being excluded from Court, he was once again able to come "boldly to the Privy Chamber, as he was wont". Elizabeth was immensely relieved that her courtiers were no longer at each other's throats, and it was hoped that in this new friendly atmosphere her "continual unquietness will turn to contentments", but in reality the truce rested on fragile foundations. From the start it was threatened by pressure from below, for Essex's followers were not happy that he was neglecting their concerns, and were all "in a mutiny at these late courses he holds".[82]

For the moment, however, the emphasis was on fighting the Spaniards.

It was true that in May the Queen started having qualms about permitting the fleet to sail, fearing that in its absence her kingdom would be vulnerable to hostile attacks, but her misgivings proved comparatively easy to allay. Once she had put these worries behind her, she even became quite cheerful about the expedition: when Essex left Court to take up his position with the fleet she sent after him love tokens and "sweet letters", one of which contained an assurance that he need not fear her censure, even if the expedition had disappointing results. Fondly she urged him, "Remember that who doth their best shall never receive the blame that accidents may bring, neither shall you find us so rigorous a judge as to verdict enterprises by events; so the root be sound, what blast soever wither the fruits, no condemnation shall light in their share".[83]

On 10 July the expedition put to sea, but almost immediately ran into storms which scattered the fleet, necessitating its return to port. Essex's ship was among the last to come in to harbour, and the Queen was in such a fever of anxiety that he had been lost at sea that when news at last arrived that he was safe, "with joy the water came plentiful out of her eyes".[84] Repairs to the battered ships had then to be carried out, and when on 17 August the fleet was at last able to set out, fresh storms caused further difficulties. Elizabeth had agreed that once her forces had put the Spanish navy out of action, they could make another attempt to seize Philip's treasure fleet, but in his eagerness to get his hands on that, Essex happily jettisoned the first stage of his mission. Originally it had been planned to mount a fireships attack on Ferrol, but when a message arrived from Ralegh (who had been separated from the fleet during the storm) that the Spanish navy had now left Ferrol and were making for the Azores, Essex gleefully set sail for those islands himself.

At the Azores all degenerated into shambles. Having arranged that his own and Ralegh's squadron should mount a joint attack on the island of Fayal, Essex delayed putting the plan into effect. Instead of sailing direct to the agreed destination, he cruised about in hopes of capturing a rich prize, and by the time that Essex turned up Ralegh had already captured Fayal. The Earl was so enraged at being left out of the action that he threatened to have Ralegh court-martialled and sentenced to death, and it was only with the utmost difficulty that the matter was smoothed over. Essex then compounded his earlier follies by failing to position his ships so that they would be well-placed to intercept the silver fleet, whose arrival was expected at any moment. As a result, when the Spanish fleet approached, the English were engaged in a pointless attack on an outlying island in the archipelago. Too late they abandoned what they were doing, but they were unable to prevent their quarry from safely entering harbour. The treasure fleet was carrying a cargo of bullion valued at nearly three and a half million pounds and, if this huge sum had been in English hands, the Spaniards would have had little alternative but to seek peace. As it was, the only prizes taken in the course of the voyage were six merchant ships, and such paltry gains would obviously have little bearing on the outcome of the war.

On 15 October, the English sailed for home, little realizing that a Spanish fleet, numbering one hundred and forty vessels, was currently bearing down on England. As the Queen furiously observed, the 'Islands Voyage' had left her "in much worse case than when the action did begin, not only in point of honour and charge, but also for safety". Ralegh's assertion that the Spanish navy had been despatched to the Azores had proved totally unfounded, for in fact all this while they had been refitting at Ferrol, unmolested by the English. On 13 October Philip's fleet set sail, intending to intercept Essex's ships on their way home from the Azores. These would have been easy prey, for they had been so long at sea that they would have been in no condition to ward off an attack, and the English were very fortunate that the Spaniards ran into such appalling storms in the Bay of Biscay that their ships had to turn back and head for home. For some time, however, it was not realized in England that the danger had passed, and the Queen still believed herself to be in the invidious position of being caught virtually defenceless while an invading force approached her shores. It was an eventuality she had always dreaded, and she held Essex responsible for her predicament. She wrote angrily to him that by taking her navy to the Azores "upon an uncertain probability that no army would come forth of Ferrol till March, you have given the enemy leisure and courage to attempt us, and left us unprovided to resist them with that provision which is necessary for so important an action".[85]

When Essex reached Plymouth on 26 October he found it in a state of full-scale alert, and having hastily refitted, he once again sailed out to meet the Spaniards. It was only when they failed to materialize that it was grasped that the crisis was over but, while this was a relief, Essex scarcely deserved the credit for it. The Earl himself took the view that he had discharged his responsibilities perfectly adequately over the last three months, declaring defiantly, "We have failed in nothing that God gave us means to do; we hope her Majesty will think our painful days, careful nights, evil diet and many hazards deserve not to be measured by the event". It was true that Elizabeth had promised beforehand that she would be understanding about any failures, but though Essex thought it monstrous that "others that have sat warm at home ... do now descant upon us", the ineptitude he had displayed, and the way in which he had allowed personal enmities to interfere with a venture of national importance, were hard to excuse. As one contemporary commentator remarked of this voyage, "And though chances and accidents are nowhere more ordinary than at sea, yet their errors may seem to have been voluntary and wilful, and the disappointments wrought by some men's emulations amongst themselves, while they endeavoured to prevent each other of a little glory".[86]

The 'Islands Voyage' was to be the Queen's last attempt to win a decisive victory over Spain, and from now on, her war aims were less ambitious. In a treatise written some years after the Queen's death, Sir Walter Ralegh asserted that it was Elizabeth's fault that the war did not go better, for "Her Majesty did all by halves, and by petty invasions taught the Spaniard how to defend himself". This was hardly fair. In less than a decade, she had launched three major amphibious expeditions against Spain, all of which represented a formidable investment in terms of both shipping and manpower. It was unjust to criticize her, as one contemporary did, for permitting her forces to be partially "levied by merchants". "In matters of this kind, princes ought to have employed themselves", moralized this commentator, pointing out that the investors' determination to recoup their money tended to override all other considerations, and meant that "nothing was performed or put in execution according as had been resolved in Council". As it was, however, the Crown's resources were grievously overstretched, and since the Queen had no means of raising additional finance, it is hard to see how she could have underwritten the cost of war by herself.[87]

Perhaps Elizabeth's worst failing as a war leader was the way she sapped morale by threatening to cancel projected expeditions, or to put different men in charge, for this was obviously irksome and inconvenient for her commanders. In the final analysis, however, she never withdrew her support from a naval venture to which she had earlier committed herself, and the only time that her irresolution and inconstancy can be said to have had truly serious consequences was when Calais fell to the Spaniards in 1596. In some respects she had a firmer grasp of strategy than the men to whom she had to entrust the conduct of the war, and certainly much more damage was caused by her commanders' failure to adhere to carefully formulated instructions than by Elizabeth's vacillation or attempts to economize. Once in action her generals were all too likely (in the Queen's own words) "to be transported with an haviour of vainglory", and to forget the objectives for which they were meant to fight, and it was a source of permanent frustration to the Queen that in the military sphere she had to delegate so much responsibility to others. However, as a Scots correspondent of Elizabeth's had remarked years before, this was a problem common to all Queens, "whose sex will not permit them to advance their glory by war".[88]

When Essex returned to Court in November 1596, he found much to displease him. Not only did Elizabeth accord him a frigid reception but, in his absence, Sir Robert Cecil had been made Chancellor of the Duchy of Lancaster, and the Earl's obvious jealousy at this promotion led observers to conclude, "Surely the peace concluded between the Earl of Essex and Cecil ... will burst out to terms of great unkindness". What irked him most of all, however, was that Lord Howard of Effingham had recently been created Earl of Nottingham. As a result of this elevation, he was permitted to take precedence over Essex at Court, for in the hierarchy of Court offices, the Lord Admiral was superior to the Master of the Horse, and only the fact that Essex had ranked higher in the peerage had entitled him to walk ahead of Howard on official occasions. Worse still, in the patent which conferred the earldom upon Howard, specific reference was made to the distinguished service he had rendered during the capture of Cadiz, and since Essex "challenged that glory wholly to himself", he regarded this as an intolerable provocation.[89]

Determined not to endure this slight, Essex withdrew from Court, writing sulkily to the Queen, "I had rather retire my sick body and troubled mind into some place of rest, than living in your presence come now to be one of those that look upon you afar off". Parliament was then in progress, but Essex refused to attend debates in the Lords, or to take his place at the Council table. Disturbed that the Earl should have sequestered himself in this way, Lord Burghley wrote three successive letters, trying to coax him back, but Essex remained sullenly at his house at Wanstead. When the Queen asked Lord Hunsdon what was the matter with the Earl, he explained that Essex was ill, but added that if Elizabeth commanded her favourite to come to Court, he would obey her summons. The Queen was no longer prepared to demean herself in this way. Angrily she snapped that his duty and place should have been sufficient to bring him to court without any orders from her, and that "A prince was not to be contested withal by a subject".[90]

In mid-December, Essex at last agreed to come to Court, but even after an audience with the Queen he remained effectively on strike, for he still declined to be present at Council meetings, and would offer no advice on state affairs. He announced that he would continue to withhold his services in this way unless Nottingham's patent was reworded, so that the offending passage relating to the action at Cadiz was deleted. He even spoke of challenging Nottingham to a duel, and he demanded that an official commission was convened to examine what really happened at Cadiz, thus establishing that Nottingham deserved no credit for the success achieved there. Since Elizabeth could hardly sanction this, the dispute dragged on past Christmas, and business ground to a standstill while the attention of everyone at Court was riveted on this demented struggle.[91]

At last, on 28 December, a solution was reached. The Queen summoned Essex to her and appointed him Earl Marshal, an honorific post that had been in abeyance since the death of the Earl of Shrewsbury. By virtue of this, Essex's lost precedency over Nottingham was restored. The latter promptly left court in a huff, but Essex now had no cause for complaint, and he resumed his place in the Council without further ado. So well disposed was he now to his colleagues, that Sir Robert Cecil managed to engineer a reconciliation with him, by virtue of having urged the Queen to let Essex dispose of some of the merchandise captured during the Islands Voyage. Cecil wanted the pact to be a lasting one: in February 1598 he wrote to the Earl, "I hope now God has disposed us to love and kindness, we shall overcome all petty doubts about what the world may judge of our correspondency; our souls are witnesses that nothing is so dear to us as her Majesty's service, which prospered the worse through our pleasing our followers through contrariety in ourselves".[92]

Before long, however, the tranquillity of the court was again disrupted by bitter rifts that arose in regard to whether the war with Spain should be continued. Despite the fact that in 1596 Henry IV had signed a treaty with England formally binding himself to make no peace with the Spaniards without Elizabeth's consent, he was not prepared to tolerate further delay in seeking a negotiated settlement with Spain. His recapture of Amiens in September 1597 had made him confident that he could gain favourable terms, and he was anxious to secure the withdrawal of the Spaniards so that he could address himself to the task of repairing the ravages of almost half a century of civil war. At the end of 1597 he had sent the Sieur de Maisse to England to see whether Elizabeth would join him in suing for peace. De Maisse found opinion at Court divided. Burghley made it plain that he wanted an accommodation, telling de Maisse that he "wished for nothing else before death", and he was backed in this by the Earls of Buckhurst and Nottingham. However, as the Lord Treasurer sombrely put it, "the Earl of Essex was young and desired war", and the latter had a large enough following on the Council to prevent de Maisse from receiving the assurance he wanted.[93] On 10 February 1598 Robert Cecil was sent to France to try and dissuade Henry IV from making a separate peace but, even while he was there, the French were engaged in secret talks with Spain, and on 2 May (N.S.) the Treaty of Vervins was signed.

Now that the French were no longer in the fight, the Council had to resume its debates as to whether the Queen should follow Henry's example and seek peace. Those against the proposal argued that, even though Henry IV had reneged on his obligations, the tripartite treaty signed in 1596 between England, Holland and France bound the Queen not to enter into unilateral negotiations with Spain, and they added that if England did desert the Dutch, there would be no chance of being repaid the sums that had been advanced to the rebels over the years. This of course was an argument that told heavily with the Queen, but even so, when a Dutch delegation arrived in England on 15 May to try and convince her that she must remain in the war, knowledgeable observers thought that she would show herself "deaf on that side, and no music will please us, unless it be to the tune of peace".[94]

Certainly when the Dutch commissioners were granted an audience with the Queen, she gave the impression of being set on peace. Cholerically she swore, "By the living God!" that she would have no more to do with such people, saying that she regretted having thrown away her money on such ingrates. When the leader of the Dutch delegation protested at these harsh sentiments, she shrieked in reply, "How am I to defend myself? How are the affairs of Ireland to be provided for? How am I ever to get back my money?"[95]

Naturally the Dutch were dejected by the Queen's apparent determination to cast them off, but in reality her commitment to them still hung in the balance. While she pondered what to do, the disputes in the Council grew more venomous, with Burghley complaining bitterly that Essex "breathed forth nothing but war, slaughter and blood". Far from seeking to find some common ground with his opponents, Essex widened the breach by publicizing the points on which the Council were divided, and he sought to force everyone at Court to state where they stood on this issue. He accosted Lord Grey and demanded that he declare himself "either his only, or friend to Mr Secretary and his enemy, protesting that there could be no neutrality". Grey, however, was not to be intimidated by "this great patron of the wars". Loftily he answered that his first loyalty was to the Queen, and that he "would never hold dependency save from her princely throne". Lesser men than Grey nevertheless found it hard to resist such pressure on Essex's part. When the Earl accused a young man called Clifford of being divided in his loyalties, his mother hastened to assure Essex that her son would never be "so base as to be a neuter, or to offer by letter or conference to any man living ... but your Lordship".[96]

In the end, it was the war party within the Council that triumphed, but only because the Dutch were prepared to make generous concessions to avoid being abandoned by the English. They agreed that if English troops were kept on in the Netherlands, they would pay for their upkeep, and furthermore they would repay the money they had borrowed from the Queen at the rate of £30,000 a year. At one time it seemed that even this would not be enough for Elizabeth, for when informed of the Dutch offers, she cried out that her ministers were "great beasts" if they could be satisfied by such terms. However, after some slight modifications to the proposals, she found them acceptable, and a formal agreement was signed between England and Holland on 6 August 1598.[97]

The alliance was forged less than a month before the death of Philip II, who for the last few years had been enduring torments every bit as ghastly as those of the martyrs he had had executed in the name of religion. This most fastidious of men had become a living corpse, unable to control his bodily functions, and covered in stinking worm-ridden sores. Even for one who did not share Philip's certainty of salvation, death could only have come as a relief, but when his sufferings finally came to an end, on 13 September 1598 (N.S.), it did not benefit England. His twenty-year-old son succeeded him as Philip III, and the war against England continued in his name.

In theory, the decision to continue the war with Spain should have been a great triumph for Essex, but he was not at Court to savour it. He had been so maddened by the possibility that Elizabeth would opt for peace that his behaviour had become increasingly unbalanced, and this had culminated in a shocking scene before the Queen. On 1 July Elizabeth had been conferring in the Privy Chamber with Essex, Robert Cecil and Nottingham and, as usual, Essex was contending that the war must be prolonged. Tempers had already grown short about this, when the subject was brought up of who should be appointed the new Lord Deputy of Ireland. The Queen thought that Essex's uncle, Sir William Knollys, was the man for the job, but Essex did not want to be deprived of the company of a man who consistently supported him in the Council. Instead he put forward the name of Sir George Carew, with whom he was on bad terms, and whom he would have been happy to see consigned to the bogs of Ireland. Impatiently Elizabeth spurned this suggestion, whereupon with studied insolence Essex turned his back upon her. Provoked beyond measure, the Queen cuffed him violently on the ear, bidding him to "Get him gone and be hanged!" The unthinkable then happened, for Essex clutched convulsively at his sword, and the Lord Admiral had hastily to step forward to interpose himself between Queen and subject. Essex's sword remained in its scabbard, but nothing could restrain him from expressing himself with the utmost violence. Shouting that "He neither could nor would put up with so great an affront and indignity, neither would he have taken it from King Henry VIII his hands", he stormed from the room.[98]

Convinced that he was the injured party, Essex withdrew to his country house. He genuinely believed that Elizabeth owed him an apology, and even wrote to tell her that she had not only "broken all laws of affection, but gone against the honour of your sex". Perturbed at seeing Essex progress still further down the road to perdition, Lord Keeper Egerton sought to introduce some sense of perspective into the Earl's distorted vision of events. "The difficulty, my good Lord, is to conquer yourself, which is the height of all true valour and fortitude", he wrote sorrowfully, warning Essex that by estranging himself from Court, he harmed himself, disquieted the Queen and let down his friends. He urged that, even if Elizabeth had given Essex cause for offence, "Policy, duty and religion enforce you to sue, yield and submit to your sovereign", but Essex would not heed this friendly admonition. He respected Egerton, and recognized that his intentions were beneficent, but he unhesitatingly rejected his advice. Worse still, his reply contained signs that his recent vicissitudes – which in all conscience had been slight enough – had caused him to embrace a political philosophy that was little short of revolutionary. He expostulated to Egerton, "When the vilest of all indignities are done unto me, doth religion force me to sue? Or doth God require it? Is it impiety not to do it? What, cannot princes err? Cannot subjects receive wrong? Is an earthly power or authority infinite?" Essex might not have thought that he was being unduly controversial when he told Egerton, "Pardon me, pardon me, my good Lord, I can never subscribe to these principles", but in even posing such demands, let alone answering them as he had, he was manifesting an independence of spirit that was fundamentally irre-concileable with any system of monarchical government that was then in existence.[99]

On 4 August 1598, while Essex was absent from Court, Lord Burghley died, at the great age of seventy-eight. He had never retired, and even though of late his son had eased many of his responsibilities from his shoulders, the amount of work that Burghley had still dealt with personally had remained phenomenal. Despite increasing deafness, he had remained mentally alert to the end, but physically he had long been tormented by what was diagnosed as gout, and for long periods he had suffered "pain without remission". At times the Queen had worried that Burghley was taking on more than was good for him, particularly since she knew that it hurt him to hold a pen. In October 1597 the Lord Admiral had passed on to Burghley a plea from Elizabeth "that you will forbear the travail of your hand, though she is sure you will not of your head for her service. Her Majesty ... prayeth your Lordship to use all the rest possible you may, that you may be able to serve her at the time that cometh". The Lord Admiral had added that the Queen had said a great deal more, and though he could not remember her exact words, "I protest my heart was so filled with her kind speeches as I watered my eyes".[100]

Even in July 1598 Burghley had managed to attend two sessions of the Council, as well as transacting business in the Exchequer and the Court of Wards. By this time, however, it was apparent that the end could not be far off, and soon afterwards he took to his bed. The Queen frequently enquired after his condition, and on one occasion she delighted him by visiting him and administering him his broth "with her own princely hand". Gamely, Burghley told his son, "If I may be weaned to feed myself, I shall be more ready to serve her on the earth; if not I hope to be in Heaven a servitor for her and God's church". It turned out that there was nothing more he could do for her in this world, for within a month of writing this letter, he was dead. His passing was scarcely unexpected, but

Elizabeth had performed in tandem with him for too long for the dissolution of their partnership to be anything other than a dreadful wrench. She took the news "very grievously, shedding of tears", and then shut herself away from all company to indulge her sorrow in private.[101]

Essex had sworn that he would not come to Court until he had received a specific invitation from the Queen, but he realized that if he wanted to be a beneficiary of the general reshuffle of Court offices that would follow upon Burghley's death, it would not do for him to remain absent. A disaster in Ireland gave him the excuse he needed to come out of retreat without appearing to have compromised his principles. Since 1595, the Irish chieftain Hugh O'Neill had been in revolt against the Crown, and by the summer of 1598 he had been menacing one of the principal English strongholds in northern Ireland, the Blackwater fort. Sir Henry Bagenal had been marching to relieve it when he had been ambushed by O'Neill at a spot known as the Yellow Ford. Bagenal and his force were annihilated, with perhaps as many as 2,000 men being killed. When the news reached London, one comment was that this was "the greatest loss and dishonour the Queen hath had in her time".[102]

Essex was confident that, if he volunteered to assist Elizabeth to overcome the crisis, it would not entail a loss of dignity, and he therefore came posting up to London to offer his services. To his dismay, however, the Queen flatly refused to receive him, giving it out that the Earl had "played long enough upon her, and that she means to play awhile upon him, and to stand as much upon her greatness as he hath upon stomach". Time and again, Essex had been warned that if he misbehaved too often, "Provoked patience may turn to fury", and it seemed that this moment had finally come.[103]

To work his way back into royal favour, Essex adopted tactics that had served Leicester well in the past, and feigned serious illness. The ploy worked. The Queen had been intending to send him a message "That she looked for a better answer ... of submission" before she would agree to see him again, but when she was told that these harsh words might cause the Earl to suffer a relapse, she changed her mind.[104] Instead, she sent her own physicians to tend Essex, and under their ministrations he made a speedy recovery. As soon as he was strong enough, he was given his usual right of access to the Queen, and Essex assumed that the rupture between them had been repaired.

In reality, however, the Queen was placing him on probation, for Essex's misdemeanours had been too flagrant to be consigned so readily to oblivion. At one time it was rumoured that she intended to mark their reunion by bestowing on him Burghley's most lucrative office, the Mastership of the Court of Wards, and Essex was certainly so confident of being given the post that he began to make enquiries as to exactly how much he could hope to make if he exploited the position for all it was worth. For the time being, however, the Queen decided to leave the office vacant. Instead of swallowing his disappointment, Essex had the temerity to write to her in protest, and this letter showed just how indelible his faults were.

Dissatisfied with how he was faring at Court, Essex looked on service in Ireland as a means of restoring his credit. After Tyrone had defeated Bagenal at the Yellow Ford, the whole island had risen in revolt, and a large army had to be sent to Ireland to deal with this threat. The difficulties that faced a commander there were horrendous, but the prestige of conducting a successful campaign would be correspondingly immense, and Essex was reluctant to allow another man to earn such kudos. Elizabeth had contemplated sending Lord Mountjoy to lead her army in Ireland, but Essex insisted that he was too inexperienced for the job. When asked to name the qualifications that the officer in charge should have, Essex replied that the general must be a nobleman whom the soldiers would respect, and who had commanded an army before. Alone of all men in England, he fitted this description. Elizabeth honestly doubted his capacity for the task, as she questioned whether "good news could accompany him that would follow no good direction here",[105] but no one else wanted to take it on, and Essex therefore found he had talked himself into the job.

Having saddled himself with this awesome responsibility, Essex began to appraise the prospect before him in a more realistic light, nervously confiding to a friend that the Queen had assigned him "the hardest task that ever gentleman was sent about". He also began to be obsessed with the fear that in his absence he would be undermined by enemies at home, who would conspire to prevent adequate supplies being sent to him, or denigrate him to the Queen. Possibly hoping that Elizabeth would reverse his appointment, he demanded that the terms of his commission should be much more generous than those normally accorded to commanders, and several months elapsed while he and Elizabeth haggled over this. As late as 1 March 1599, it was reported, "New difficulties arise daily about his commission, as touching the time of his abode, touching his entertainment, and touching the disposing of places and offices, upon which points he is so little satisfied that many times he makes it a question whether he should go or not". While the matter remained unsettled, the Earl spent his time moodily gaming in the Presence Chamber, but on 12 March his commission was finally signed. All his demands were satisfied, and even Essex had to admit, "I have the best warrant that ever man had". On 27 March he set off from London, cheered on his way by excited crowds. The day had started off fine, but Essex was barely beyond Islington when a sudden thunderstorm broke, "which some held an ominous prodigy".[106]

CHAPTER 14

"The tribute of all mortal creatures"

> He which England means to win,
> With Ireland first is to begin.

It was on account of the message embodied in this grim little couplet that Elizabeth showed such concern for the state of Ireland, which otherwise she would have gladly ignored. Indeed, had it not been for strategical considerations, few Englishmen would have ventured near a place which was uniformly held to be barbarous and ill-fated. Even Walsingham, who normally had no difficulty prescribing solutions for tricky problems, expressed the view that "God's curse upon that country will suffer nothing to take place that tendeth to the reformation thereof". Sir Walter Ralegh, who had extensive personal experience of Ireland, referred to it despairingly as "This lost land ... this commonwealth, or rather common woe". As for the Queen, she often "grew weary with reading the Irish despatches", but she knew that she could not be altogether unheedful of an island which was once described as "the principal key of her royal state". To the end of her life, she was mindful of the words of her first viceroy there, the Earl of Sussex, who had told her in 1560 that she must give the highest priority to seeing that Ireland was secure. He explained that he urged her to do this, "Not so much for the care I have of Ireland, which I have often wished to be sunk into the sea", but because it would be catastrophic for the Queen if one of her enemies gained possession of it.[1] Ireland would make an ideal base from which to launch an attack on England, and it was their terror of seeing Ireland occupied by a hostile European power that made the English so grimly determined never to relinquish control of it.

Almost without exception, the Elizabethans regarded the native inhabitants of Ireland as loathsome savages. Among other faults, they stigmatized them as primitive, bloodthirsty, ungodly, dishonest, filthy, promiscuous and lazy. They were appalled by their outlandish appearance, complaining of the way that Irishmen sported "glibs" – "a thick, curled bush of hair hanging down over their eyes". The English disapproved of this hair-style not only for its "savage brutishness and loathly filthiness", but also because glibs served as "fit masks ... for a thief, for whensoever he hath run himself into that peril of law that he will not be known, he either cutteth off his glib quite, by which he becometh nothing like himself, or pulleth it so low down over his eyes that it is very hard to discern his thievish countenance".[2]

When in 1562 the Irish chieftain Shane O'Neill came to England to obtain pardon from the Queen for his disobedience towards her, his own appearance, and that of his followers, created a sensation. He was surrounded by a ferocious-looking guard of axemen, "bare-headed, with curled hair hanging down, yellow surplices dyed with saffron ... whom the English people gazed at with no less admiration than nowadays they do them of China and America". Prostrating himself before the Queen, Shane was forgiven after he had "confessed his crime and rebellion with howling".[3] This was taken as a sign of true contrition, but shortly after returning to Ireland, Shane rose up against the English once again.

With so wide a divergence in cultures, it was hardly surprising that English and Irish had little understanding of one another. About the only thing the Elizabethans were prepared to concede was good about Ireland was Irish whisky, "the best in the world of that kind". Even here, however, they criticized the natives for indulging too much in it, "and that not for hilarity only (which would be praiseworthy), but for constant drunkenness, which is detestable".[4]

Worst of all, from the English point of view, was the fact that the Irish were virtually ungovernable. In theory, Ireland was ruled by a viceroy – who had the title of Lord Deputy or, more grandly, Lord Lieutenant of Ireland – and his Council, who were selected by the Queen. In reality, however, the only places where the English could count themselves the undisputed overlords were the Pale, a semi-circular area around Dublin, which "exceedeth not the bigness of some two shires of England",[5] and a few towns dotted about the countryside. In outlying areas, power was wielded for the most part by great magnates – who were often the descendants of those nobles who had been granted land by Henry II when he had carried out the conquest of Ireland in the twelfth century – or lesser chieftains of pure Irish origin. Only by their sufferance could English officials hope to exert any influence in the territory they controlled and, as their allegiance to the Crown was by no means firm, their co-operation was not guaranteed.

In Ulster, the most northerly of Ireland's four provinces, the situation was least satisfactory of all, for the chieftains there were virtually autonomous, seldom deigning to acknowledge the supremacy of the Queen. When their behaviour became too unruly, the only way of bringing them to heel was to send a military expedition to Ulster, for none of the Queen's viceroys or officials even dared visit the province without the backing of a substantial army. On taking up his post, one Lord Deputy confessed frankly that he thought he could do no more than "look through his fingers at Ulster as a fit receptacle of all the savage beasts of the land", and an eminent lawyer practising in Ireland admitted that Ulster was "as unknown to the English here as the most inland part of Virginia".[6]

The truth was that, outside the Pale, Ireland was in a permanent state of lawlessness, and sometimes the endemic unrest flared into open revolt. Apart from the rebellions of Shane O'Neill in Ulster between 1560 and 1567, the most serious of these were the Fitzmaurice rising of 1569–73, and the Desmond rebellion of 1579–83. These outbreaks were countered with savage repression by the English, which took a ghastly toll on the civilian population. In 1569, for example, Sir Humphrey Gilbert "killed man, woman and child, and spoiled, wasted and burned by the ground all he might" when he was sent to suppress the Fitzmaurice rebellion in southern Ireland. It was Sir Humphrey's practice to decapitate the corpses of rebel soldiers and to set the heads up in lines outside his tent, so that anyone who came to see him had to pass through a lane of these grisly trophies. One English soldier commented approvingly, "It did bring great terror to the people when they saw the heads of their dead fathers, brothers, children, kinsfolk and friends lie on the ground before their faces".[7] Far from being accused of undue cruelty, Gilbert was generally commended by his compatriots for having restored the locality to order in a matter of months by using tactics of this kind.

When the Earl of Desmond rose in Munster, ten years later, it was the local populace that once again bore the brunt of the counter-insurgency measures. A scorched earth policy was pursued by the English with such devastating effect that, between March and September 1582, an estimated 30,000 Irish perished from starvation. The poet Spenser, who was secretary to Lord Deputy Grey at the time, subsequently recalled how the inhabitants of Munster "were brought to such wretchedness as that any stony heart would have rued the same. Out of every corner of the woods and glens they came creeping forth upon their hands, for their legs could not bear them. They looked anatomies of death, they spake like ghosts crying out of their graves, they did eat of the dead carrions ... yea, and one another soon after, in so much as the very carcases they spared not to scrape out of their graves".[8]

The English seem to have experienced few qualms about inflicting such sufferings on non-combatants, for the prevalent view was that the Irish were a virtually subhuman species, who warranted no compassion. In 1575 the Earl of Leicester advocated that any sign of disobedience on their part should be met with the utmost ruthlessness, for "temporizing wars are to be used with civil and expert men, but savages and those rural rascals are only by force and fear to be vanquished". The Queen, it is true, occasionally exhibited more tender feelings towards her people there. When in 1573 the first Earl of Essex was about to go to Ulster, with the hope of bringing that province under firmer control, Elizabeth told him that she believed its inhabitants were potentially loyal subjects, "and therefore wished them to be well used". However, when Essex encountered resistance in Ulster, the Queen agreed that leniency would not be appropriate. In July 1574 she remarked approvingly that although Essex had been prepared to "bring in that rude and barbarous nation to civility and acknowledging of their duty to God and to us by wisdom and discreet handling [rather] than by force and shedding of blood ... yet when necessity requireth, you are ready also to oppose yourself and your forces to them whom reason and duty cannot bridle". Perhaps it was this which encouraged Essex to enact a bloody revenge on a local notable named Sir Brian Macphelim, and certainly this atrocity went uncensured by the Queen. In November 1574, Macphelim and his dependents were lured to a banquet in Belfast Castle, given by Essex, but after three days of feasting, the English sprang upon their guests, and put "men, women, youths and maidens to the sword". Macphelim, his wife and brother were not killed on the spot, but were carried off to Dublin to be hanged, drawn and quartered there. Essex justified this inhospitable conduct on the grounds that Macphelim was in the habit of murdering loyal subjects and then sticking their heads on poles with their privy members in their mouths, but a Gaelic chronicler commented of the incident, "This unexpected massacre, this wicked and treacherous murder ... was a sufficient cause of hatred and disgust of the English to the Irish".[9]

One reason why the general populace suffered so frightfully even when they were not directly involved in hostilities against the English was that it was exceptionally difficult for English troops to defeat Irish men–at–arms using the methods of conventional warfare. Sir Calasthenes Brook, an officer who was serving in Ireland in 1597, commented that forty years' service in the best European army could not teach a man anything useful about methods of combat in Ireland. Irish insurgents did not occupy towns or strongholds which the English could set themselves to reduce, and the English rarely had an opportunity to meet their opponents on open ground, where they could do battle and deploy their cavalry to good effect. Instead, the Irish made the most of their native terrain, which consisted of large tracts of bog, mountain and forest. This gave them ample opportunities to mount ambushes on advancing troops, and then to melt away before the enemy had time to respond. When the second Earl of Essex went to Ireland in 1599 he soon had to admit that these guerilla tactics were remarkably efficacious, and he wrote home in despondency, "This people against whom we fight hath able bodies, good use of the arms they carry, boldness enough to attempt, and quickness in apprehending any advantage they see offered to them ... The rebels fight in woods and bogs where horse are utterly unserviceable; they use the advantage of lightness and swiftness in going off when they find our order too strong for them to encounter".[10]

The average English soldier (who anyway had generally been pressed into the army against his will) dreaded serving in Ireland above all other places. Not only did he have to cope with an unpredictable enemy, who materialized out of a hostile landscape, but the climate of Ireland was known to be particularly unhealthy, with the "Irish ague" (malaria) and the "Irish looseness" (dysentery) carrying off scores of troops. As one officer remarked, when it came to hardship, "All the soldiers of Christendom must give place in that to the soldiers of Ireland; and so much difference for ease ... as is between an alderman of London and a Berwick soldier". It was said that the troops were "half dead before they came there, for the very name of Ireland do break their hearts, it is grown to such misery". Because of the difficulties of recruiting sufficient numbers to serve in Ireland, the English frequently resorted to enlisting native Irishmen into the army, but these were even more likely to desert than troops from home. Worse still, they might defect to the rebels, taking their weapons with them, and in such cases the English found themselves in the invidious position of having "trained and furnished Irishmen to serve the enemy's turn".[11]

At various times the Queen was told that, if she really wished to subjugate Ireland, she should curb the independence of the great magnates by setting up lesser men as sheriffs and JPs. These would be able to administer justice on the English model, and would also act as buffers between the chieftains and the general populace. The drawback was that such fundamental reforms would be exceptionally costly to implement and, as it was, the Queen begrudged the amounts she had to spend on Ireland. To take one example, in the five-year period 1569–73, annual revenue from Ireland averaged £6,481, but expenditure during that time came to approximately £43,000 a year. In the first thirty years of the reign, a total of £940,933 was spent on the forces in Ireland, and it was figures such as these that elicited from Elizabeth the bitter remark that "The like burden and charge is not found in any place in Christendom". The Queen had too many other calls on her cash to enable her to contemplate pumping the additional sums into Ireland that would have been needed to bring about stability there. In 1584, for example, Lord Deputy Sir John Perrott told the Queen that if she steeled herself to invest £50,000 into Ireland for three consecutive years, he could guarantee that at the end of that time, the island could be governed infinitely more easily and cheaply than heretofore. In reply, he was told that the Queen was on the brink of intervening in the Netherlands, and therefore could not spare any extra money for Ireland.[12]

One way of bringing Ireland under more effective control, at minimal cost to the Crown, was by promoting colonization, or the planting of English settlers there, whose loyalty was undoubted. However, as many of those who emigrated to Ireland soon found out, settling there was fraught with difficulties, for the native population feared that if colonization proved successful they would be driven off their lands to provide fresh waves of settlers with large estates. As a result, the new arrivals were greeted with hostility. In 1572, for example, Secretary of State Sir Thomas Smith sent his bastard son and a group of adventurers out to Ulster, in hopes that they could found a settlement there. On landing they found that a local chief had pulled down all stone buildings for miles around which could have afforded them shelter during the winter. Smith nevertheless managed to survive the winter months, only to be murdered the following summer by his Irish employees, who first stabbed him to death and then "caused Master Smith to be eaten up with dogs after he had been boiled".[13]

After the Desmond rebellion had been crushed in 1583, the Earl of Desmond's estates in Munster were confiscated and parcelled out to English settlers. Sir Walter Ralegh took up 12,000 acres to be sublet to English tenants, and the poet Spenser acquired 3,000 acres, which he intended to farm directly. These ventures failed to prosper. Spenser had to cope with being terrorized by the Anglo-Irish Lord Roche, a local landowner who did his best to make the settlers' lives uncomfortable. When he heard that a local smith had mended a settler's plough, he punished the man by killing one of his bullocks, and he likewise killed an Irish peasant's cow, "because Mr Spenser lay in his house one night as he came from the Sessions at Limerick".[14]

The settlers struggled on in the face of such difficulties but in the summer of 1598 disaster struck, for the news of the English defeat at the Yellow Ford encouraged the Irish in Munster to rise up in revolt. The settlers' homes and plantations were burnt, and many of them were killed as they fled for the safety of the nearest towns. There were reports of horrific atrocities, with "infants taken from the nurse's breast and the brains dashed against the walls; the heart plucked out of the body in the view of the wife, who was forced to yield the use of her apron to wipe the blood off from the murderers' fingers".[15] One of Spenser's children was burnt to death when his house at Kilkolman was set on fire; he had been all too prescient in naming his castle 'Haphazard'.

Not only did the Irish regard the English as unwelcome interlopers in their country, but by the late sixteenth century tension between the two nationalities was exacerbated by religious differences. The Church in Ireland was not rich enough to support a ministry of the calibre required to reconcile the Irish to Protestantism. Spenser admitted that the clergy in Ireland were "generally bad, licentious and most disordered", and that ministers who came there were "either unlearned or men of some bad note, for which they have forsaken England".[16] Even in the rare cases when a minister was sufficiently well-educated to be able to preach decent sermons, he could make little impact on the Erse-speaking natives.

The Catholic missionaries despatched to Ireland were men of a far superior stamp to their Protestant counterparts. As the reign progressed the Anglican bishops in Ireland had to admit that they were failing to win over the population to Protestantism, and that every day more and more of their flock were reverting to the old faith. Bishop Lyon of Cork reported in 1595 that when he had been appointed to his see, thirteen years earlier, he could attract a congregation of a thousand when he preached, but now the best he could hope for was an audience of five.[17]

Devotion to Catholicism helped rally the disaffected, and gave Irish insurgents the stirring battle-cry of "Papa aboo!" ("Up with the Pope!"). The Queen took the view that religion was merely being used as an excuse for disobedience, for as she pointed out, Irish Catholics could not complain of being persecuted for their faith. Sir Robert Cecil said that she hoped to bring about their reformation "rather by prayer to God than by violent compulsion" and, when the first Earl of Essex was about to set off for Ireland in 1573, she had specifically cautioned him that he "should not seek hastily to bring people, that hath been trained in another religion, from that which they have been brought up in". It was true that towards the end of her life there were times when she felt it had been a mistake to be so conciliatory on the religious issue. In 1599 she somewhat unfairly censured the Council in Ireland for having been "the greatest causes of that corruption in matter of religion (whereof the contagion reigneth in that kingdom) by your former suffering (nay favouring) Popery". However, in general she prided herself on having treated the Irish with great tolerance, and she was incensed when one leading rebel claimed that the principal thing he was fighting for was liberty of conscience. Angrily she exclaimed that what he really wanted was "liberty to break laws, which her Majesty will never grant to any subject of any degree". The truth was that she was sceptical that the Irish were as attached to their faith as they claimed, and on one occasion she went so far as to say that they were of "neither one nor other religion, but given to bestiality".[18]

It was the Queen's misfortune that, just when the war with Spain was sapping national resources, a great leader should manage to unite Ireland in its struggle against the English. Hugh O'Neill, Earl of Tyrone, had spent much of his upbringing in England. After his return home, he had remained loyal to the Queen for some years, and even incurred a wound in the thigh when helping the English to quell unrest in Ulster. With hindsight, however, the English came to believe that he had volunteered his services only so that his men would benefit from training by English captains. As a result, by the time he turned traitor he had an army that not only possessed the traditional skills of Irish guerrilla warfare, but was also well schooled in modern combat techniques.

It was in 1595 that Tyrone had first broken out in rebellion, but as yet it was not clear that he was a confirmed traitor. Soon after, he had sued for pardon, and the Queen had been disposed to be conciliatory, even though one of her commanders in Ireland, Sir Thomas Norris, had urged her to crush Tyrone while there was time. In the ensuing three years, Tyrone had repeatedly violated the peace in Ulster, but always followed this up by once again submitting to the English. During this time, however, he entered into correspondence with Spain, asking Philip II to send him military aid, and he also established contacts with other disaffected chieftains throughout Ireland. In 1598 he threw off all pretence of loyalty, and after his victory at the Yellow Ford he set about fanning all four provinces of Ireland into revolt. One of his lieutenants, Tyrell, was sent to Munster to stir up rebellion there, while O'Donnell brought out Connaught, and in Leinster the O'Moores rose up against the English. A plot was even hatched to take Dublin by subterfuge, but was uncovered just in time. In abject terror the Irish Council addressed Tyrone a grovelling letter, begging him to desist from further hostilities, but Elizabeth was furious when she saw a copy. "Never was read the like ... for baseness," she snorted,[19] and though in the past she had shown herself anxious to reach an accommodation with Tyrone, she now became bent on his destruction. This was the task with which Essex had been entrusted, and which he had assured the Queen he would be able to carry out.

No effort was spared to give Essex all he needed. His army numbered 1,400 horsemen and 16,000 foot soldiers, 2,000 of whom were veterans from the Netherlands. In the words of one commentator, these were "the most flourishing and complete troops that have been known to have been sent out of our nation in any late memory", and it was further agreed that every three months, 2,000 reinforcements would be sent over to Ireland to make good any losses. Essex's personal prestige was boosted by him being given the title of Lord Lieutenant, rather than Lord Deputy, an honour that had been accorded to only one of the Queen's previous viceroys. To ensure that the troops were paid promptly, a new treasurer-at-war accompanied Essex to Ireland, well furnished with cash. Great efforts were made to procure the Lord Lieutenant the munitions he desired. Twelve great pieces of ordnance, costing £23,000, were put at his disposal, and though Essex complained on his arrival that the army suffered from a shortage of swords, the Privy Council at once set themselves to remedy the deficiency by despatching a consignment of 3,000 rapiers. 21,000 suits of clothing were sent over for the troops, and in a bid to establish good communications, a new postal service was set up between England and Ireland, costing over £900 a year.[20]

Essex still found much about which to complain. To his chagrin, the Queen forbade him to appoint Sir Christopher Blount (whom his mother had married within a year of the Earl of Leicester's death) to the Irish Council. Elizabeth doubtless felt that nothing in Blount's largely undistinguished earlier career suggested that he was fitted to serve in so important an advisory capacity, but Essex implied that Blount's contribution would have been so indispensable that without it he was fatally disadvantaged. In injured tones he told the Council in England that he hoped that since "her Majesty ... grants not the ability, she will not expect nor exact great performance". Petulantly, he insisted, "It is not Tyrone and the Irish rebellion that amazeth me, but to see myself sent of such an errand at such a time, with so little comfort or ability from the court of England to effect that I go about".[21]

Essex might claim that Tyrone was the least of his worries, but he certainly showed himself remarkably reluctant to come to grips with him. In this he showed a great change of heart. When the English Council had discussed how Ireland could best be pacified, Essex had been utterly positive as to the approach that should be adopted. He had criticized all previous commanders who had allowed themselves to become distracted by subsidiary operations in Connaught, Munster and Leinster, when the overwhelming priority was to vanquish Tyrone within Ulster itself. Once Tyrone had been crushed, Essex had passionately maintained, his auxiliaries could be dealt with without difficulty. As the Queen was subsequently to remind Essex, "Before your departure, no man's counsel was held sound which persuaded not the main prosecution in Ulster: all was nothing without that, and nothing was too much for that". In words that would return to haunt him, he had proclaimed at the Council table that anything "that was done in other kind in Ireland was but waste and consumption".[22] So convincing had he been, that he had persuaded the Queen that his was the right policy, and it was on the express understanding that Essex's forces would be employed for an immediate confrontation with Tyrone that she had supplied him with an army that was so large and well equipped.

Nevertheless, having arrived in Ireland on 13 April 1599, the Earl came to think that the showdown with Tyrone should be deferred. Prior to leaving England, he had been dismissive of the Irish Privy Council, saying that he would find "not one able assistant" among its members. Nevertheless, when they advised that if he led an expedition to Ulster so early in the year he would have great difficulties finding forage for the horses, he did not oppose them. Instead, on 28 April he informed the Privy Council in England that the invasion of Ulster was to be postponed, and that in the meantime he would march south from Dublin to pacify unrest in Leinster, "the heart of the whole kingdom".[23]

If Essex had succeeded in quieting southern Ireland, and had then tackled Tyrone in midsummer, the policy would have had much to be said for it, but the next eight weeks were totally wasted. Essex marched about Leinster and then progressed on into Munster, revictualling a few forts, and placing garrisons in the odd stronghold. Occasionally he paused to make ceremonial entries into loyal towns, where the streets were bestrewn in his honour with rushes and herbs, and the citizens hailed him with Latin orations. A few insignificant rebels came in to ask for pardon, and the Castle of Cahir, which Essex boasted was "accounted the strongest place in Ireland",[24] was captured with minimal resistance. Yet all the time, Essex's army was dwindling, with a few men being lost in inconclusive skirmishes with rebels, and many more falling victim to fatal illnesses. By the time he returned to Dublin on 2 July, he had only about 11,000 men at his disposal.

Nothing worthwhile had been achieved. The Earl had to admit that although he had left behind a large body of troops in Munster, this did not "make us anywhere in that province absolutely masters of the field, but so soon as the garrisons stir, the rebels are upon them". As for Leinster, which was the most loyal area in Ireland, even there "the rebels are so strong ... that everywhere they burn, spoil and prey". Well might the Queen burst out that she had been paying Essex £1,000 a day to go on progress![25]

Back in Dublin once again, Essex assured the English Privy Council that as soon as possible he would go to Ulster to "look upon yonder proud rebel", declaring that, even if outnumbered three to one, "Yet will I by God's grace dislodge him". On the whole, however, he felt less confident than this missive would suggest, for he was still haunted by the paranoid delusion that hostile forces were working against him at home. In a letter to the Queen he suddenly demanded, "But why do I talk of victory or success? Is it not known that from England I receive nothing but discomforts and soul's wounds?" He made no secret of his belief that Lord Cobham and Sir Walter Ralegh were trying to sabotage his mission, and he raved at the Queen for showing them favour "when they wish the ill success of your Majesty's most important action".[26]

Elizabeth had no time for these histrionics. There was no need for Essex's enemies to belittle him to her, because the facts in her possession were quite sufficient to erode her goodwill. Quite apart from his disappointing performance as a commander, he had annoyed her in a variety of lesser ways. She had been particularly irritated to hear that Essex had made the Earl of Southampton his General of the Horse, despite the fact that she had vetoed the appointment because Southampton had offended her by contracting an unauthorized marriage with one of her maids of honour. When she learnt that Essex had defied her on this matter she ordered the Council to tell him that Southampton must be stripped of his position, but Essex refused to demote his friend on the grounds that such an action would adversely affect the troops' morale. Naturally enraged by such disobedience, the Queen had furiously berated him in a letter of 19 July. She had reiterated that Southampton must be dismissed, and expressed incredulity that Essex could "dare thus to value your own pleasing in things unnecessary, and think by your private arguments to carry for your own glory a matter wherein our pleasure to the contrary is made notorious".[27] Her indignation was compounded by reports that Essex was conferring numerous knighthoods in Ireland, despite the fact that his commission had made it clear that he should be very circumspect about rewarding his men in this manner.

Her main cause of complaint, however, was the way that Essex had frittered away time, money and men on his southward march, and it was for this that she reserved her most biting strictures. Scornfully she demanded of him, "What can be more true . . . than that your two months' journey hath brought in never a capital rebel, against whom it had been worthy to have adventured one thousand men?" She stressed that she would not have been so critical if Essex had acknowledged that his performance so far had been undistinguished, and had held out hopes that it would improve, but "we see your pen flatters you with phrases, that here you are defeated, that you are disgraced from hence". In palpable disgust, she flung at him that in reality he had nothing to whine about, for "you have all, and more than, that which was agreed on before you went". This being so, she repeated that she expected him to go and confront Tyrone in Ulster without further ado.[28]

Her letter reached Dublin too late, for on 22 July Essex had again set off from the capital, but this time marching westwards in the hope of ejecting rebels from the newly colonized lands on the fringes of the Pale. He burnt crops and captured a thousand head of cattle belonging to the rebellious O'Moores and O'Connors, but by the time he returned to Dublin in early August, he was no nearer subduing them than before, and he had merely succeeded in reducing still more the forces at his own disposal. The Queen, who had been aghast at this further delay, was dumbfounded to learn that the Irish Council was now advising Essex that, since his army was so depleted and the season so far advanced, it would not be wise to attempt an expedition to Ulster at all that year. Quite beside herself with rage, she told Essex on 10 August that she would tolerate no more excuses, and that she expected "to hear by the next it is begun and not in question". When Essex continued to indicate that for the moment there was little he could do, she unleashed a stinging attack on him, mercilessly lambasting him for his inexcusable dilatoriness in taking on Tyrone. Stormily she wrote, "If sickness in the army be the reason, why was not the action undertaken when the army was in better state? If winter's approach, why were the summer months of July and August lost? If the spring were too soon ... and the summer that followed otherwise spent ... surely we must conclude that none of the four quarters of the year will be in season for you and that council to agree of Tyrone's prosecution, for which all our charge is intended". Remorselessly she continued that his failure could not be attributed to misunderstanding, or lack of means, "For you had your asking, you had choice of times, you had power and authority more ample than ever any had".[29]

In Dublin, Essex pondered how best to salvage his reputation. If he went to Ulster as the Queen desired, he did not envisage that a campaign there would have a successful outcome, and instead he began to contemplate a desperate alternative. To Sir Christopher Blount and Southampton he talked wildly of taking two or three thousand men to England, assuring himself that when he landed in Wales, "his army would have been quickly increased by all sorts of discontented people",[30] and the Queen would then be obliged to treat him more sympathetically than in the past. As yet, however, neither Southampton nor Blount were prepared to countenance treason, and they dissuaded Essex from the venture.

Unable to think of anything better to do, Essex fell back on the idea of taking his army to Ulster, although he was pessimistic as to his chances of inflicting a decisive defeat on Tyrone. The number of serviceable men at his disposal had now fallen to a mere 4,000, and Tyrone's army out-numbered his by more than two to one. As he set out on 28 August, he was hazy about his exact intentions, vaguely informing the Privy Council in England, "I will draw the army so far, and ... do as much as duty will warrant me and good will enable me".[31]

It turned out that Essex's concept of dutiful conduct was far from conventional. As the Earl was marching somewhat aimlessly along the River Lagan, it became apparent that Tyrone was shadowing him on the opposite bank, accompanied by between ten and eleven thousand men. On 5 September, Tyrone sent a message that he wished to confer with Essex. Two days later, Essex agreed to have a private talk with the rebel, arranging to meet him at a ford on the River Lagan. There he and Tyrone conversed for half an hour, and since none of their followers were permitted to come within earshot, there were no independent witnesses who could verify Essex's account of what passed between them. The following day a truce was agreed upon, and Essex's army withdrew to Dublin.

On 16 September Elizabeth was apprised of the ceasefire, but in his letter to her Essex did not elaborate on the terms which had formed the basis for this agreement. In great concern, the Queen wrote to Essex the following day, asking him to give her a written account of precisely what had occurred, and warning him to make no further undertakings to Tyrone till she was in full possession of the facts. Doing her best to remain calm, she assured him that "We that trust you with our kingdom are far from mistrusting you with a traitor", but she acknowledged that she scarcely knew what to make of his conduct. "Only this we are sure of ... " she told him bleakly, "You have prospered so ill for us by your warfare as we cannot but be very jealous lest you should be as well overtaken by the treaty".[32]

Already, however, Essex had decided that nothing less than a personal interview would suffice to reconcile the Queen to what he had done. Apparently untroubled by the fact that Elizabeth had formally denied him the right of returning home without prior permission, on 24 September he departed for England. By daybreak on 28 September he had reached London, but instead of breaking his journey there, he rode at a furious pace to the court at Nonsuch, which he reached about ten o' clock in the morning. Despite the fact that his journey had left him "so full of dirt and mire that his very face was full of it", he did not pause to change his clothes, but instead strode resolutely through the palace until he had reached the door of the Queen's bedchamber. Marching inside, he found Elizabeth "newly up", and in a state of partial undress, with her wig not yet fixed in place and the thinning remnants of her own hair straggling "about her face".[33]

The Queen's shock at this unheralded intrusion can well be imagined. Quite apart from the indignity of being caught in a condition which so cruelly shattered the fable that time had left her unscathed, she could not know if Essex was accompanied by armed men, or whether his apparition in her bedchamber would be the signal for a palace revolution. Despite this, she kept her composure. Realizing that it would be unwise to be too peremptory with Essex until she had established whether he had laid contingency plans to take the Court by storm, she talked to him kindly for a while, and then told him to go and change. An hour later, when both of them were more appropriately attired, she received him again, and was scarcely less gracious to him than before, only asking him to leave when it was time for her midday meal to be served. Greatly heartened, Essex dined himself, regaling those who came to greet him with his impression of Ireland and the Irish. Having eaten, he had a third interview with the Queen, only to find her a changed woman. By this time she knew that he had made no preparations for a *coup d'état*, and she therefore began to chide him for having left his post without her warrant, angrily brushing aside the explanations he offered for his conduct. The same afternoon, Essex had to endure the first of many painful interrogations from the Council, and at ten o' clock that evening, he was instructed to confine himself to his room.

At another session of the Council the following day, further instances of misconduct were alleged against him. Apart from his unauthorized return and his "overbold going ... to her Majesty's presence", he was censured for his mismanagement of the Irish campaign, and for having created so many knights during it. The Queen was particularly irate about this last point, because Essex had ignored her warning of 19 July to be more discriminating about bestowing titles, and he had indeed subsequently created thirty-nine more knights. The Irish rebels had jeered that "he never drew sword but to make knights",[34] and he had been so lavish with his creations that by this time more than half the knights in England owed their rank to Essex. In addition to the consideration that many of these men were so impecunious that they would have difficulty supporting themselves in a manner befitting their rank, Essex's numerous creations laid him open to the charge that he was deliberately seeking to form a sizeable cadre of military men who were beholden to him, and whose support he could enlist in a crisis.

On 1 October, the Queen ordered that Essex should be confined to York House, the residence of Lord Keeper Egerton, but it was widely assumed that the Earl would not be kept under restraint for very long. Cecil declared to a correspondent that "though for example's sake, her Majesty hath kept this form with him", her displeasure would soon be assuaged. Contrary to these expectations, however, her wrath against Essex only seemed to grow. She became still more angry with him when Essex informed the Council of the proposals which Tyrone had put forward in their discussion, and which the rebel had apparently intimated could form a basis for peace talks. Amongst other things, Tyrone had suggested that the Pope should be declared head of the Church in Ireland, that all major offices of state there should be held by Irishmen, and that all lands forfeited to the Crown by Irish rebels in the last two hundred years should be restored to their original owners. On perusing the list, the Queen commented furiously that these conditions were "both full of scandal to our realm and future peril in the state",[35] and if Essex had entertained them, even for a second, it merely highlighted his utter lack of judgment.

Nevertheless, although there was plenty of evidence that Essex was guilty of folly and incompetence, the Council did not find his offences were such as warranted the preferring of charges. By 21 October, they had more than once given the Queen a collective recommendation that Essex should be set free, but Elizabeth was adamant "that such a contempt ought to be publicly punished". "Her Majesty's anger towards him seems to be appeased in nothing", reported one observer, who professed himself mystified as to why she was being so unforgiving.[36]

Perhaps the Queen's implacable attitude merely arose from the conviction that she had been too indulgent towards Essex in the past, and that in order to bring him to anything approaching a state of grace, the discipline she now administered would have to be severe. On the other hand, after Essex had been executed, Elizabeth told the French ambassador that when he had returned from Ireland, she had hidden from her Council the full extent of his disobedience. What she meant by this is a matter for conjecture, but certainly there are stray bits of evidence that suggest that Essex had been in contact with Tyrone even before he set out for Ulster in August, and that he was guilty of collusion with the enemy.[37] If the Queen had any inkling that this was so, her treatment of Essex was extraordinarily forbearing, and shows that, even now, she could not bring herself to abandon hope of his reform.

If Elizabeth did protect Essex by covering up evidence of his malfeasance, her reticence was not altogether wise for, in the eyes of the Earl's ever-adoring public, it came to seem that he was being unfairly treated. A sinister underswell of sympathy began to manifest itself on his behalf, and in city taverns and other centres of gossip, there was much talk of his ill-usage. Particularly vocal in his defence were that disreputable class of adventurers who had lionized Essex because they stood to make most from him, the sort who "had no living, but they went brave, and lived some by the sword and some by their wits". To the Queen's indignation, "traitorous monsters" abused her with "railing speeches and slanderous libels", and broadsheets reviling her were scattered about town. Feeling against Cecil was also running high, for it was thought that he had inflamed the Queen against Essex, and soon he dared not go abroad without the protection of an armed bodyguard.[38]

In a bid to stifle criticism, the Queen directed the Council to call together all Justices of the Peace who were then in London, so that any misconceptions regarding Essex could be dispelled. On 29 November, the assembled magistrates were addressed in turn by the Lord Keeper, the Earl of Buckhurst (who had succeeded Burghley as Treasurer) and Secretary Cecil, all of whom stressed the heroic efforts made by the Queen to bring order to Ireland, and the degree to which Essex had let her down. None of this did any good, for those "turbulent spirits" who had stirred up feeling before, now "gave out that this was to condemn a man unheard, and to wound him on his back, and to leave justice her sword and take away her balance, which consisted of an accusation and a defence".[39]

Sympathy for Essex became still more pronounced when it was learnt that he had fallen ill and he was on the verge of death. The Queen herself was sufficiently concerned to send her own physicians to treat him, but her compassion for him diminished when several London ministers used his ill health as an excuse to lead the public in prayers for him. By January 1600 Essex had recovered, but he stood no better with the Queen than before. The following month it was announced that the Court of Star

Chamber would sit in judgment on his conduct. A humble letter from Essex entreating Elizabeth that "that bitter cup of justice might pass from him" at length induced her to cancel the hearing, although not without considerable misgivings as to whether such a course was wise.[40] Towards the end of March, the Queen agreed that the Earl could move from York House to his own residence on the Strand, but he was still strictly guarded, and allowed no visitors save his wife.

Though Elizabeth had spared Essex the ordeal of a full judicial hearing in Star Chamber, she was loth to let him free without formal censure being passed on him, particularly since it was popularly believed that Essex had not had to appear in Star Chamber because of "want of matter to proceed against him".[41] On 5 June 1600 Essex was therefore called before a panel of Councillors and leading judges that had been convened at York House. Having had to kneel bare-headed while his delinquencies were listed, he was told that though his loyalty to the Queen was not in question, he was guilty of gross contempt and disobedience. At the end of the proceedings the Lord Keeper declared that, if his case had come before Star Chamber as planned, he would have been sentenced to perpetual imprisonment in the Tower and fined an unprecedented sum; as it was the tribunal exercised their more modest powers merely to strip him of all his offices other than that of Master of the Horse.

After this humiliation, Essex was returned to his custodian, for the Queen still did not think he had suffered enough. Three weeks later she suddenly conceived an idea that all the knights that Essex had recently created should be stripped of their titles, causing a dreadful flurry among those gentlemen, who shuddered to think what their wives would say if they had to revert to calling themselves "Mistress", rather than using the prefix "Lady".[42] Eventually Cecil persuaded Elizabeth that such a course would be unconstitutional, but her annoyance at having to drop her scheme delayed Essex's release for some weeks. Only on 26 August was he given his liberty, and even then it was specified that he must remain away from Court.

Taken aback to find that the Queen was still holding herself aloof, Essex wrote beseeching her to give him permission to "kiss your Majesty's fair correcting hand", declaring that until he was admitted to her presence, "time itself is a perpetual night and the whole world but a sepulchre to your humblest vassal". Elizabeth nevertheless could not fail to be aware that his desperation to see her stemmed primarily from money worries. At the end of September his farm of sweet wines, the mainstay of his finances over the past ten years, was due to expire, and if it was not renewed, ruin stared him in the face. Despite Elizabeth's generosity to him, his debts had continued to pile up, for not only had he spent lavishly at home, but he had always emerged with catastrophic losses from the expeditions he had led overseas. So far, the only reason that the Earl had not been bankrupted was that the consortium of merchants to whom he had sublet the right to collect the duties on sweet wines had advanced him money, but if his lease was not renewed they would call in their debts. Desperate to stave off total insolvency, Essex could not prevent a worldly note from creeping into his letters to the Queen. "That farm is both my chiefest maintenance and mine only means of compounding with merchants to whom I am indebted", he wrote anxiously to her, and his sympathizers at Court likewise implored her not to withdaw from the Earl his sole means of support. In the face of these entreaties, the Queen remained non-committal, which several of Essex's friends thought was a good sign. Perhaps they would have been less optimistic if they had overheard Elizabeth tell Francis Bacon sourly that Essex "had written unto her some very dutiful letters ... and she had been moved by them, and when she took it to be abundance of the heart, she found it to be but a preparative to a suit for the renewing of the farm of sweet wines".[43]

When the lease duly expired, Elizabeth kept the matter in suspense for a month, and then decided that, for the time being, the revenue from sweet wines should revert to the Crown. Essex took her action to mean that she had discarded him for ever. He had told friends that if his lease was not renewed, "he should judge what was meant him", and having satisfied himself of the Queen's settled antagonism, he decided to shape his actions accordingly. Already, he had toyed with the idea of rebellion, and even as he had been declaring to the Queen, "Mine uttermost ambition is to be a mute person in that presence where joy and wonder would bar speech",[44] he was envisaging an encounter of a very different sort, in which he would forcefully articulate to her a series of demands, and she would submissively listen.

When Essex had first been put under confinement at York House, Sir Christopher Blount, Southampton, and others among his wilder cronies had talked of helping him to escape to France, but Essex had rejected the proposal out of hand, saying "he would rather run any danger than lead the life of a fugitive". For a more constructive solution to his problems, he looked to his sister's lover, Lord Mountjoy, the man whom the Queen had chosen to take command of the army in Ireland when the truce with Tyrone expired. Before going to Ireland, Mountjoy had been so concerned at Essex's predicament that he had secretly contacted James VI of Scotland, to see if the King would do anything to assist the Earl. He suggested that James should assemble an army so that he could "do that which was fit in establishing such a course as should be best" for England, and promised that if the King did take action of this sort, he could count on being backed by the forces that Mountjoy commanded in Ireland.[45]

James had sent word back "that he liked the course well and would prepare for it" but, when apprised of this, Essex was reluctant to incur the obloquy of having invited a foreign monarch to bring an army into England. He thought it preferable to employ Mountjoy's forces alone, and in April 1600 Southampton crossed to Ireland to request Mountjoy to confirm that he was prepared to put his troops at Essex's disposal. By this time, however, Mountjoy was not interested. From his own experience in Ireland he could already see that the problems there were not insurmountable, and besides being anxious to concentrate on the task in hand, his sympathy for Essex had lessened as it became apparent to him that the Earl had brought nemesis on himself. Mountjoy rebuffed Southampton and, when that summer Essex sent Sir Charles Danvers to Ireland to press the point, Mountjoy told him that he had only contemplated drastic action because he had thought there was a possibility that Essex might be executed. Now that the Earl's life was clearly in no danger, Mountjoy said he "would not enter into an enterprise of that nature" merely "to satisfy my Lord of Essex's private ambition".[46]

Clearly no help could be expected from that quarter, and Essex thought it impracticable to call upon a Scots army to invade on his behalf. Nevertheless he felt confident that James VI could provide him with valuable assistance. Essex's connections with the Scots King went back a long way, for as early as 1589 the Earl had been writing secretly to James, assuring him of his service and fidelity. Essex's sister Lady Rich had gone so far as to tell James that Essex looked forward to the day he ascended the throne, being "exceedingly weary, accounting it a thrall he now lives in, and wishes the change". At that stage James had appeared indifferent to these overtures, but by 1594 he was on friendly enough terms with Essex to send him a message that he was "happy in his acquaintance there . . . He desires the continuance of his affection and promises to reward it in proper time and place".[47]

As James drew closer to Essex, he was simultaneously becoming more suspicious of the Cecils. In 1593 he had been angered when Elizabeth had given asylum to a Scots nobleman whom James alleged had used witchcraft to try and murder him, and the King believed that it was Burghley who had persuaded the Queen to shelter the fugitive. Such incidents convinced James that Burghley was as hostile towards his claim to the succession as he had been towards that of Mary Stuart, and he saw no sign that Robert Cecil was less inimical to him than his father. Since 1595 there had been several occasions when James had cautiously approached Cecil through trusted emissaries, and if Cecil had been willing to enter into a correspondence it might have led to a mutual growth of trust. As it was, however, Cecil had consistently spurned these advances, saying he could not cultivate a connection with the subjects of another sovereign. His attitude was of course very proper, but as James subsequently recalled, it was "continually beaten" into him by Essex that Cecil's aloofness was a sign of "unquenchable malice". In their communications with the King, Essex and his faction were so successful in convincing James that Cecil was working for his exclusion from the throne that James even came to believe that, in order to bring about peace with Spain, Cecil wanted Philip II's daughter, the Infanta Isabel Clara Eugenia, to be accepted as Elizabeth's successor. It was said that Cecil continually commended the Infanta to the Queen, and that he counted on using Ralegh's influence in the West Country, and Lord Cobham's control of ports in the South East to ensure that as soon as Elizabeth died, the Spaniards could land unopposed.[48] Of course this was utter nonsense, but James swallowed it all.

On Christmas day 1600, Essex wrote to the King that the time had come for him "to stop the malice, the wickedness and madness of these men, and to relieve my poor country which groans under her burden". He said his action would be in the best interests of the Queen, for if she went on "believing none nor hearing nothing but as they direct", she "must needs be led blindfold into her own extreme danger". He asked James to send an ambassador to England, the plan being that once Essex had effected his *coup d'état*, the ambassador would complain to the Queen about the men in whom she had formerly put her trust, and this would put additional pressure on her to initiate proceedings against them.[49] James sent word that he would do as Essex bid, and the Earl set about finalizing his preparations.

At the beginning of February, Essex's leading associates met at Southampton's lodgings to draw up a plan of action. Apart from Southampton, the Earls of Rutland and Bedford, and Lords Sandys, Monteagle and Cromwell were among those who pledged Essex support. It was agreed that once Essex had gained control of the Queen, he would force her to call a Parliament which would impeach his enemies such as Cecil, Ralegh and Cobham, clearing the way for his own adherents to be installed in their places. The conspirators nevertheless were unsure of what Essex should do to secure the Queen's person. One plan that was canvassed was that of taking the Court by stealth. Men could be posted at the palace gates, in the hall, the Presence Chamber and other key points, and at an agreed signal they could take control of these stations. Once potential opponents had been disarmed, Essex and Southampton would make their way to the Queen and, kneeling before her in feigned humility, would make known to her their demands. It was generally anticipated that resistance would be slight, and Essex himself took the view that "when he came to the Court, he should come in such peace as not a dog would wag his tongue against him".[50]

Once he had committed himself to rebellion, Essex's general demeanour became increasingly wild, and he took to railing against the Queen in a frenzied manner that suggested to some of his acquaintances that he was no longer altogether sane. After one alarming conversation with Essex, Sir John Harington recorded in his journal that the Earl "shifteth from sorrow and repentance to rage and rebellion so suddenly as well proveth him devoid of good reason or right mind. In my last discourse, he uttered strange words bordering on such strange designs that made me hasten forth and leave his presence ... His speeches of the Queen become no man who hath *mens sana in corpore sano*."[51]

Harington was scared away, but others were not so prudent, and a disreputable assortment of swaggerers and rowdies were only too happy to attach themselves to Essex. Essex House was thronged by this unsavoury crew for, in an effort to attract more of a following, the Earl had his "doors set open to all comers, Meyrick his steward entertaineth at his table all sword men, bold confident fellows, men of broken fortunes, discontented persons and such as saucily used their tongues in railing against all men".[52]

It was an odd way to go about a conspiracy, for inevitably the hubbub attracted the attention of the authorities, and drove them to intervene. On 7 February 1601, Essex was ordered to present himself before the Council, who wished to protest at the way he was abusing his liberty. Essex declared that he could not come just then as he was "in bed and all in a sweat" after playing a game of tennis. Clearly, however, the Council could not be long fobbed off with so paltry an excuse, and although Essex had intended not to rise up in revolt until the new Scots ambassador had arrived in London, the Council's summons precipitated him into action. That night he called together his supporters at Essex House, telling them that Ralegh and Cobham were planning to murder him, and that he was in urgent need of protection.

The following morning, 8 February, the Queen sent four Councillors to repeat that Essex must appear before the Council. The quartet found the courtyard of Essex House filled with unruly men in a state of high excitement. Essex was asked to account for this assembly, and he again maintained that he was in danger of being murdered, and claimed his friends had gathered to defend him. At Essex's invitation, the Councillors then followed him into the house, whereupon to their surprise they were locked up in his library. Outside, the mob in the courtyard roared its approval, and some of the wilder elements in the crowd shouted, "Kill them, kill them!"

Having secured these hostages, Essex and about two hundred men surged out into the streets, armed only with rapiers. There were cries of "To the Court! To the Court!" but Essex did not see how he could take Whitehall by storm with so small a band of followers. He was nevertheless confident of recruiting a sizeable number of supporters in the City, for the previous evening he had received a message purporting to be from the

Sheriff of London, Thomas Smyth, offering to put a thousand armed men at his disposal. Anticipating that he would be able to return with an eager crowd at his heels, Essex set off for the City.

As he headed towards Sheriff Smyth's house in Fenchurch Street, Essex cried to the bystanders, "For the Queen! For the Queen! A plot is laid for my life", but though his reception was friendly enough, scarcely anybody stepped forward to help him. With mounting desperation he shouted that "The Crown of England was sold to Spain", only to meet with the same blank stares. Shaken to meet with such indifference, he lurched on in obvious agitation, becoming "almost molten with sweat". By the time he reached Smyth's house, he was so drenched with perspiration that he had to call for a clean shirt. There was no comfort to be had from Smyth, for if the Sheriff had earlier been prepared to support him, he had now repented of the idea. He only admitted Essex into his house with the utmost reluctance, and at the first opportunity he slipped out of the back door to join the Mayor, who had already received a message from the Queen to call all loyal citizens to arms.

In frustration, Essex issued out into the street again, to find that he had been publicly proclaimed a traitor. "Pish! the Queen knoweth not of it, that is Secretary Cecil", he blustered, but though some of his followers swore, "Wounds and blood! ... they cared not" for any proclamation, others were seen to slink away. Rallying those men that remained, Essex decided to withdraw from the City, but at Ludgate found the way blocked by a troop of militia. Discharging their pistols, his men tried to force their way through, but the defenders returned their fire, and Essex ordered a retreat when his young page was shot dead. Leaving most of his followers to save themselves, Essex and his leading associates scrambled aboard boats at Queenshithe, and having had themselves rowed upriver they re-entered Essex House by its watergate.[53]

The four Councillors who had earlier been detained had already been set free by one of Essex's more faint-hearted colleagues, and hence could not be used as pawns in negotiations with the Government. By late afternoon, Essex House was surrounded by loyal troops under the Earl of Nottingham's command, and it was clear that its occupants would be unable to defend it. When called upon to surrender, Essex swore that he would "the sooner fly to Heaven", but when Nottingham warned he was preparing to blow the house up, Essex accepted he had no alternative but to yield. For the past few weeks he had constantly carried about his person a black taffeta bag, which probably contained his correspondence with James VI. This he now consigned to the flames, swearing it "should tell no tales to hurt his friends".[54] Then, at about ten in the evening, he and his friends emerged from Essex House and humbly offered up their swords.

The news was carried to the Queen at Whitehall, for she had said she would not go to bed until she knew that Essex had been taken. Apart from retiring somewhat later than customary, she had tried not to allow the day's events to disrupt her normal routine. When the alarm had first been raised, a barricade of coaches had been hastily erected to block the approach from Charing Cross to Whitehall, and armed citizens had flocked in from Westminster to defend the palace. One gentleman volunteer described how there "was such a hurly burly ... at the Court as I never saw" but, despite the general pandemonium, Elizabeth herself had remained utterly unruffled. She dined at her usual hour, and Cecil proudly reported that "even when a false alarum was brought to the Queen that the City was revolted with them, she never was more amazed than she would have been to have heard of a fray in Fleet Street".[55]

As preparations were set on foot for Essex's trial, there was a last convulsive spasm of resistance. One of the more ruffianly of Essex's followers, Captain Thomas Lee, planned to burst in on the Queen as she took her supper in the Privy Chamber, and then to keep her "pinned ... up, till he had forced her to sign a warrant for the Earl's delivery out of the Tower". An associate betrayed him, and on 12 February he was arrested while lurking near the Privy Chamber door. When interrogated, he insisted that he had meant no harm to Elizabeth, and that he had intended "only to have angered her one half hour, that she might have lived the merrier all her life after".[56] His defence was not accepted, and he was hanged at Tyburn four days after his arrest. His ill-conceived attempt only served to seal Essex's fate, for while he lived others might be tempted to emulate Lee's example.

The Queen seemed not in the least unsettled by these challenges to her authority. When the French ambassador congratulated her on her escape, she calmly expressed her satisfaction that "a mad ingrate had at last made apparent what he had so long hidden in his mind". Having admitted that she blamed herself for having indulged Essex for so long, she began to hold him up to ridicule, jeering at his absurd progress through the City, which had ended in him beating so ignominious a retreat. She told the ambassador that if Essex had managed to approach the palace she would have gone out to confront him, "in order to know which of the two of them ruled".[57]

On 19 February, Essex and Southampton were tried by their peers in Westminster Hall. Despite the solemnity of the occasion, Essex appeared in a positively jaunty mood, evidently thinking a show of flippancy would go down well with the spectators. During the reading of the indictment, a smile was seen to be playing about his lips, and as he was charged with having conspired "to deprive and depose the Queen's Majesty from her royal state and dignity, and to procure her death and destruction", he ironically raised his eyes to Heaven. Both Earls pleaded not guilty, with

Essex maintaining that it had been their intention simply to prostrate themselves before the Queen and to beg her to dismiss those men "who abused her ... ears with false informations". Essex said that to convince her that this was desirable he would "have bended my tongue, my brain and my best endeavour with all diligence, but without purpose of harm to her Highness", but the Prosecution questioned whether his intentions had been so innocuous. As was pointed out by Essex's old friend Francis Bacon (who was one of the lawyers acting for the Crown), it was hardly normal for petitioners to come to the Queen armed and guarded, or "to consult, to execute, to run together in numbers ... Will any man be so simple to take this as less than treason?"[58]

It was an unanswerable argument and, after retiring briefly, the Lords returned a verdict of guilty on both prisoners. Even after being sentenced to death, Essex still kept up his carefree front. He begged that Southampton might be accorded mercy, but added that, while he would not have wished it to be thought that he despised the Queen's clemency, "I shall not, I think, be found to make any cringing submission to obtain it".[59]

When the Dean of Norwich visited Essex in the Tower and urged him to make a more detailed confession to the authorities, he found the Earl as obdurate as ever. "Why should I reason with you, seeing that we hold not one principle?" Essex demanded of him rudely. Then, after his chaplain warned him that he ran the risk of hellfire if he died impenitent, Essex suffered a sudden nervous collapse. In great torment of mind he called to the Tower Egerton, Buckhurst, Nottingham and Secretary Cecil, and made a much fuller confession than heretofore. Not once, however, did he ask that his sentence might be remitted; on the contrary, indeed, he cried out that his crime was a leprosy, and that the Queen could not be safe while he lived. His only request was that he might be executed in private, so that he should not be sinfully "hoven up" by the acclamations of the people.[60]

A few weeks after this, the Queen told the French ambassador that, if she could have granted Essex his life without endangering the security of the realm, she would willingly have done so, but "he himself had recognized that he was unworthy of it". Her conviction that Essex had left her with no alternative but to proceed with his execution led her to behave with uncharacteristic promptitude and, on 20 February, the very day after his trial, she signed his death warrant. It was only delivered to the Lieutenant of the Tower three days later, but even this might not signify any hesitation on Elizabeth's part, for Robert Cecil said that Essex's execution would have taken place earlier if it had not been for the fact that the Council wanted to give him time to reveal more about his conspiracy.[61]

Despite the fact that Essex had recently shown himself so contrite, there was still concern that he would try and justify his treason to the select audience of peers and royal officials who had been chosen to see him die within the Tower precincts. The Constable of the Tower was given explicit instructions that if Essex should "fall into any ... such speeches, both you and the divines must utterly divert him". In the event, however, there was no need for these precautions, for when Essex mounted the scaffold, just before eight in the morning of 25 February, he was full of remorse. "My sins are more in number than the hairs of my head", he sombrely acknowledged. " ... I have bestowed my youth in pride, lust, uncleanness, vainglory and divers other sins". For these failings he craved pardon of the Almighty, and "especially for this my last sin, this great, this bloody, this crying and this infectious sin, whereby so many for love of me have ventured ... to offend their sovereign". Having hailed the axeman as "the minister of true justice", he knelt down to pray, and then laid his head on the block. At the suggestion of one of the officiating divines, he began to recite out loud the fifty-first psalm, but after completing the second verse he cried out, "Executioner, strike home". Even as he resumed commending his soul to God, he was silenced in mid-sentence as the axe came crashing down.[62]

Few others paid with their lives for Essex's disobedience. Sir Christopher Blount and Sir Charles Danvers were beheaded on 17 March, and Essex's steward and secretary were both hanged at Tyburn. Southampton's sentence was never carried out, although he remained in the Tower for the remainder of the reign. The other leading protagonists were given punitive fines, but the amounts were subsequently reduced, and on the whole they did not even have to pay these lesser sums. Reflecting on the Queen's clemency to the conspirators, Cecil's brother commented, "A thing the like was never read in any chronicle". As for Lord Mountjoy, he was not even summoned over from Ireland for questioning, although the confessions of several of the rebels left no doubt that he had flirted with treason. As the Queen put it on one occasion to James VI, although she did not shrink from severity when necessary, "I am not so unskilful of kingly rule that I would wink at no fault".[63] She accepted that Mountjoy's earlier disloyalty had been no more than a temporary aberration, and thought it better for all concerned that he should be left to carry on his work in Ireland.

In June 1601 Robert Cecil confidently informed a colleague, "Our state here was never quieter, thanks be to God ... The tree into which so many branches were incorporated being fallen, all men that loveth him repenteth their errors". As Cecil well knew, however, it was far from true that Essex had gone unmourned, despite the fact that the Government had sought to use the propaganda machinery at its disposal to discredit his memory. On the Sunday following Essex's execution, one of the Queen's most gifted chaplains, Dr Barlow, was ordered to preach at St Paul's on the subject of

Essex's disobedience. Cecil briefed him as to what to say, urging Barlow to stress "how perilous a thing it was, to have put a lady, a queen, in that fright she must have been in" if Essex had succeeded in forcing his way into her presence. Barlow was told to remind his listeners that Essex could not have entered the palace without encountering resistance, and "blood once drawn, more would have followed, which would have been no small horror to the Queen". Barlow duly made his sermon, but though he tried to avoid antagonizing his audience by paying generous tribute to Essex's virtues, as well as castigating his faults, his address was very ill received. Whereas before, he had been highly regarded as a preacher, he now became very unpopular, and even eighteen months after Essex's death he remained "very greatly maligned by the seditious crew".[64]

On the scaffold, Essex's confederate Christopher Blount had admitted that, though the conspirators "never resolved of doing hurt to her Majesty's person ... yet I know and must confess if we had failed of our ends, we should (rather than have been disappointed) even have drawn blood from herself". Yet even this acknowledgement failed to tarnish the aura of martyrdom that clung to Essex. Writing in the reign of Elizabeth's successor, the historian William Camden remarked of Essex's rebellion, "To this day there are but few that thought it a capital crime". As the man whom the public held responsible for the Earl's downfall, Cecil was widely vilified, and there were several occasions when official rebukes had to be administered to offenders such as Robert Everett of Bath, who was overheard wishing "a pox upon Sir Robert Cecil", and declaring that the Secretary should have been "hanged seven years agone". However much the Government tried to shape public opinion, nothing could shake the belief of the people that Essex had been wrongfully condemned to death. The service he had rendered the Queen in the past was magnified out of all proportion, and even his failures did not diminish him in the public's eyes, for it gave them satisfaction that these had been on a grand scale. There was no one remaining in Elizabeth's circle who could capture their imaginations in the way that Essex had done, for the "goose quilled gentlemen" who now monopolized power were not sufficiently colourful or aristocratic to fulfil their perverse yet exacting standards.[65]

To a certain extent the criticisms levelled against Cecil were symptomatic of a broader malaise. One London gentleman had observed in 1600, "The world here runs crabwise, sidelong driving every man out of his bias, so that if eight men sit at table you shall hear seven of them complain of this corrupt time, and such as have lands wish money in their purses for it. This city is growing to great misery, both with the artificer and merchant groaning under the burden of exactions." An anonymous rhyme that was thrust into the Lord Mayor of London's house said that people now talked of nothing else but "axes and taxes", and this complaint was echoed elsewhere.[66]

Much of the general discontent was economic in origin, for the war with Spain, combined with the expense of military operations in Ireland, was swallowing up resources at a terrifying rate. Between 1599 and 1600, the Queen had sold £212,614 worth of Crown lands, but this did not even pay for the army Essex had taken to Ireland, which in six months had cost her almost £300,000. To raise a little extra cash, she even considered divesting herself of her surplus jewellery. She was not the only person driven to such measures, for during these years there were persistent rumours that poorer taxpayers were having to pawn their pots and pans to meet their fiscal obligations. Undoubtedly the burden of taxation weighed heavier on these individuals than on the more prosperous classes for, as Sir Walter Ralegh observed, for tax purposes it was usually possible for the rich to undervalue their wealth, whereas the estates of those who were less well-off tended to be assessed at much nearer their true worth. It disturbed the Queen to think that her people must "groan under the burden of continual levies and impositions", but there could be no question of her alleviating it while she had to supply the needs of a wartime economy. Cecil told one confidant, "I speak it with grief (whatsoever you think, that there are subsidies and prizes and such perquisites which do accrue her Majesty), that all the receipts are so short of the issue as my hair stands upright to think of it".[67]

In the circumstances the Queen was driven to economize, and during the later years of the reign, attempts to cut down on Court expenditure led to a tightening up in the distribution of patronage. One request for money met with the response from Cecil, "Her Majesty's mind is not so apt to give as before her wars, they having made her sift all corners to maintain them ... The time is not as before, that when a Lord Treasurer had given her his advice upon her gifts it was half won, for now all gifts pass censure". When one Hughes of Newcastle applied to Cecil in 1596 in hopes of obtaining a reversion of the manor of Newcastle under Lyme, he learnt to his sorrow that "Her Majesty in these times is not well disposed to hearken unto like suits". "What little gain is gotten in this time!" sighed one courtier in 1594, scandalized that the Crown could resort to such money-saving devices as keeping Court positions that fell vacant, unfilled. This policy meant that whenever a place did become available, the competition to obtain it was more intense than ever. In November 1593, for example, a position in Ireland worth £300 a year had fallen vacant, and immediately an eager scrum of placehunters had materialized, intent on securing this prize. Sir Francis Allen was among those jostling for preferment, but a friend of his reported, "There are so many that desire the same, and offer in the Chamber and elsewhere such round sums for it, and withal my Lord Treasurer, according to his laudable custom, having an eye to her Majesty's profit, procureth to extinguish the same in such sort as the gentlemen ... do find great difficulties".[68]

The financial squeeze at Court was greeted with shrill cries by those on the upper reaches of society who saw it as the primary duty of the Crown to provide them with a comfortable livelihood. Some years after the Queen's death, the Jacobean Bishop Godfrey Goodman censured her for having grown "very covetous in her old days". He reminisced, "Suits were very hardly gotten, and in effect more spent in expectation and attendance than the suit could any way countervail ... The Court was very much neglected and in effect the people were very generally weary of an old woman's government". Even the fortunate few who had offices at court found it difficult to keep pace with the rising cost of living. In the last years of the reign, only the Lord Treasurer, Lord Keeper, Lord Admiral and Master of the Court of Wards thrived financially, and many of the other great officers of state found themselves running into debt. It began to be whispered that if the Queen were succeeded by James VI of Scotland (who enjoyed a reputation for generosity almost unique among his countrymen), the situation could only improve, and a few individuals started secretly to cultivate the King, in hopes they would be able to capitalize on their connections with him when he ascended the throne. Among these was the Earl of Northumberland, and in one of his confidential letters to King James he painted a graphic picture of an aristocracy chafing at the unaccustomed restraints on their spending power. He told James, "The nobility are unsatisfied that places of honour are not given them ... that offices of trust are not laid in their hands to manage as they were wont; that her Majesty is parsimonious and slow to relieve their wants which from their own prodigalities they have burdened themselves withal".[69]

Inevitably the skimping and retrenchment that characterized the final years of the reign contributed to the atmosphere of disenchantment at court, and even diminished the Queen in some men's eyes. Over the years she had sat ensconced in a web of poetry and romance, but money had always been the substance that had welded together the delicate structure. Now that the supply of this bonding agent was drying up, the gauzy layers were starting to disintegrate, leaving her exposed to harsh scrutiny and uncharitable comment. At its most extreme level, financial embarrassment could even provoke outright disloyalty in her subjects, and prove a spur to treason. Essex was the most obvious example of this, but it was significant that his most prominent adherents had all been almost as penurious as the Earl. As the historian William Camden remarked, "Poverty of all other things is that which plungeth the English into rebellion".[70]

As pickings at Court grew scantier and more elusive, the climate there became more corrupt, for desperation drove suitors to offer ever larger sums to those influential enough to secure them what they wanted. Bribery was of course by no means an entirely novel phenomenon at Elizabeth's Court. One observer stated, "Certain it is that some persons attending near about her would now and then abuse her favours and make sale of it by taking bribes for such suits as she bestowed freely". For obvious reasons, our knowledge of such transactions is shadowy, but it is clear that from quite early in the reign bribes were sometimes offered, although it is often difficult to tell if they were accepted. In April 1566, for example, Sir Anthony Browne offered to pay the Earl of Leicester "£200 and all your charges" if he could obtain for him a valuable wardship, though he specified that Leicester must "get it at the Queen's hands as cheap as you can". Three years later some Genoese merchants tried to bribe William Cecil and Leicester into using their influence to put an end to the trade embargo between England and the Netherlands and, when approached by them, Cecil apparently indicated that he would be willing to help if paid £3,000. In 1573, the Spanish merchant, Antonio de Guaras, told Burghley that if he helped to bring about an accord between England and Spain, he would be given a "gratification" by Philip II. The Lord Treasurer rejected this on the grounds that if his "companions knew that he had a pension from his Majesty it would be his downfall", but de Guaras then suggested that Burghley's "wife would not refuse" if offered a lump sum to help pay for the marriage of their daughter. Burghley "replied by conceding and laughing", and whenever Lady Burghley ran into de Guaras on subsequent occasions she did not fail to remind him that she was waiting for her present.[71]

Nevertheless, although from the start the Queen's advisers may not have been free of all taint of corruption, it seems to have been universally acknowledged that towards the end of the reign, bribery became more widespread. The view is upheld by what statistics are available, for a recent examination of petitions submitted to the Cecils, father and son, throughout the reign, reveals that it was only in the 1590s that it became commonplace to offer them bribes. Indeed it was regarded as so normal that when Sir Thomas Shirley offered to pay Burghley £500 if he could secure for him the position of Comptroller of the Household (an inducement which Burghley, to be fair, appears to have declined, for the appointment was not made), he defended himself for having stooped to this on the grounds that "those who do not offer themselves in this world are seldom advanced". By 1601, corruption was regarded as so integral a part of court life that Fulke Greville could casually remark to Robert Cecil, "The world sayeth all courtiers more naturally love bribes in this age than the former". Cecil himself was indisputably open to bribery, but perhaps he was less rapacious than some of his colleagues, for Greville paid him the somewhat lukewarm tribute that "The world sayeth you are a passing good gentleman, and one that will, after the old manner, do common courtesies to men who are never like to requite you". Even Greville, however, thought it prudent to secure Cecil's goodwill by sending him a present of a fine falcon, and other presents he received were worth considerably more. Cecil himself seems to have been a trifle uneasy when he received the gift of a coach and four horses from the Earl of Northumberland, and he felt impelled to write the donor a pompous letter explaining that he could only accept the articles on the understanding "that this was given me out of the vastness of your kindness", and not because Northumberland hoped to suborn him.[72]

In 1601 the Queen herself alluded to the decline in standards of probity when she remarked to the archivist William Lambarde, "Now the wit of the fox is everywhere on foot, so as hardly a faithful or virtuous man may be found". It was the view of some people, however, that Elizabeth only had herself to blame, and that it was her failure to give legitimate recompense to her servants that drove them to take whatever they could from others. In 1595, for example, the Queen was held indirectly responsible when her lady-in-waiting, Lady Edmondes, indicated to a suitor, who wanted a troublesome Chancery case to be dropped, that she would expect to be paid considerably more than £100 before she would bring her influence to bear on the matter. The intermediary who was conducting negotiations with her commented in disgust, "This ruffianry of causes I am daily more and more acquainted with, and see the manner of dealing which groweth by the Queen's straitness to give these women, whereby they presume thus to grange and huck causes". Yet it was hardly fair to heap all the blame on Elizabeth in this way. It was true that salaries at Court were small, but those in the royal household were well placed to secure other lucrative privileges from the Queen, and Lady Edmondes in particular seems to have done well in this respect.[73]

One way that the Queen could enrich courtiers at no expense to herself was through the grant of a monopoly, which gave its holder the sole right to manufacture or market a commodity. Obviously the price of such articles rose as a result, and the system of monopolies was naturally heartily disliked by all those who were not direct beneficiaries. In the Parliament of 1598, there had been complaints about the excessive number of monopolies, and the agitation had only subsided because the Queen had given orders to her Councillors to scrutinize existing grants. Some monopolies were subsequently repealed, but all the time new ones were being granted, and in August 1601 Lord Treasurer Buckhurst had to admit that they had become so numerous that the situation was in urgent need of review.[74]

In the circumstances it was virtually inevitable that the question of monopolies would be raised when Parliament met again, at the end of October 1601. The matter was a sensitive one, however, for it was an undoubted privilege of the Crown to grant monopolies, and if an act was passed outlawing them, this would amount to a statutory limitation of the

Queen's royal prerogative. So anxious was Cecil to prevent this that he did his best to stifle debate on monopolies, on one occasion whispering in the Speaker's ear to prevent the latter allowing a member to read a bill against them. Nevertheless resentment of this grievance proved too strong to be contained and, despite Cecil's efforts, the Commons refused to proceed with the subsidy bill until they had considered the report of a parliamentary committee that had been formed to enquire into monopolies. It seemed a foregone conclusion that their next step would be to frame a bill against monopolies, and the Queen was so desperate to prevent such a precedent being set that she decided she must beat a hasty retreat. She sent Parliament a message that she would at once alleviate the evil of monopolies, for since, as she put it, "her kingly prerogative . . . was tender", she thought it better to pre-empt unwelcome legislation than to permit her authority to be mauled by Parliament.[75]

On 28 November, a proclamation was issued, repealing all injurious monopolies. In jubilation, the Commons obtained the Queen's permission to send an official delegation to see her at the palace, so that they could thank her for showing them such care. On the afternoon of 30 November, the Queen received about a hundred and fifty gentlemen in the Council Chamber at Whitehall, and having heard the Speaker express the Commons' gratitude for the recent proclamation, she spoke in her turn. Her speech made no reference to the fact that the concession had effectively been extorted from her, and instead she begged them not to blame her if monopolies which she had authorized in good faith had been used to oppress the subject without her knowledge. "That my grants should be grievous to my people, and oppressions privileged under colour of our patents, our kingly dignity shall not suffer it. Yea, when I heard it, I could give no rest unto my thoughts until I had reformed it", she gravely informed her listeners. She was being far from disingenuous, however, when she took this opportunity to reaffirm her unshakeable devotion to her people. "I do assure you", she declared solemnly, "there is no prince that loves his subjects better, or whose love can countervail our love. There is no jewel, be it of never so rich a price, which I set before this jewel: I mean your love. For I do esteem it more than any treasure or riches; for that we know how to prize, but love and thanks I count invaluable. And though God hath raised me high, yet this I count the glory of my crown, that I have reigned with your loves".[76]

In later centuries, this came to be known as the Queen's "Golden Speech", and was cited with nostalgia at times when it was felt that her successors were failing to show a comparable solicitude for their people's welfare. Certainly it was an incomparably graceful surrender, for by her eloquence the Queen had transformed what was, in effect, an involuntary abdication of power into a moving avowal of her love. At the time, the

Commons showed their appreciation in their response to a request from the Crown for a quadruple subsidy, a demand that broke all previous records. When it was put to a final vote on 5 December, "All cried, 'Aye, aye, aye!' and not one 'No'".[77]

Such performances demonstrated that Elizabeth had not lost her touch, but only a superhuman could have possessed the inspirational powers to bring about true national regeneration. Knowing herself to be surrounded by carping and corruption, it was understandable that from time to time the Queen succumbed to bouts of depression. Essex's treachery had left her profoundly disillusioned: in July 1602 she wrote dourly to James VI, "Who longest draws the thread of life, and views the strange accidents that time makes, does not find out a rarer gift than thankfulness is, that is most precious and seldomest found". Soon after Essex's revolt she had bitterly commented to the French ambassador that this betrayal should teach Henry IV "never to trust his subjects or to elevate any of them too much", and certainly no subject of hers was ever permitted to be on so close a footing with her as Essex had been in his heyday. There were attempts to commend to her the good-looking Earl of Clanrikarde, who bore a close resemblance to the executed Earl, but Elizabeth showed no interest, saying that it would only bring her pain to be reminded of her late favourite. Cecil struggled to prevent her life seeming too humdrum by injecting some spice of gallantry into his daily dealings with her. In the autumn of 1602, for example, he sent her a ruby and topaz ornament which he said would match well "the life of her eyes and the colour of her lips", but the polished phrases squared uneasily with his stunted and ill-favoured frame.[78]

There was no denying that Essex's death had left a sad void in Elizabeth's life. In the summer of 1601 she told the French ambassador, "She was tired of life, for nothing now contented her spirit, or gave her any enjoyment", and she referred to Essex "with sighs and almost with tears". But if she grieved at having lost him, she never doubted that she had had no option but to proceed with his execution. In the summer of 1602, when the French Court was being shaken by the discovery of traitors within its midst, she told another French ambassador that the situation called for energetic repression, and she reminded him that she had been firm in similar circumstances, and that she saw no reason to regret this.[79]

Not only was the Queen sometimes prey to melancholia, but as she grew older, her temper grew progressively shorter. One courtier subsequently recalled, "Towards her last, she grew somewhat hard to please", and it was her maids of honour and ladies-in-waiting who had to bear the brunt of her peevish humours. In 1597, when Elizabeth was sixty-four years old, John Harington had noted that she "doth not now bear with such composed spirit as she was wont; but . . . seemeth more forward than commonly she used to bear herself toward her women; nor doth she hold them in discourse with such familiar matter, but often chides for small neglects; in such wise as to make these fair maids often cry and bewail in piteous sort".[80]

Yet although it was acknowledged that the Queen's fits of ill-humour were now more frequent than in the past, on the whole it was fair to say that she had aged extremely well. Occasionally she showed signs of fatigue – as in September 1600, when she visited the Sidneys at Penshurst, and appeared "much wearied in walking about the house" – but in general her level of energy remained remarkable. She still derived immense pleasure from going on progress, much to the regret of her courtiers, who had hoped that with the onset of old age, she would become less keen to go traipsing about the country. In the summer of 1600 she was somewhat put out when some of her nobles appeared reluctant to accompany her when she embarked on a long progress towards Lord Hertford's, but she refused to let this deter her. She remarked scornfully that she had no objection if the old elected to "stay behind, and the young and able to go with her", and though in consequence she was more slenderly attended than was customary, she still enjoyed herself enormously. She concluded her progress with a visit to her hunting box at Oatlands, and once there she engaged in the chase with as much gusto as ever. Her "daily music" was "the sweet cry of excellent hounds", and she remained in the saddle till late in the day.[81]

The next summer, Cecil tried to persuade her to remain nearer London so that she could keep abreast of the latest developments in the Netherlands and Ireland, but the Queen would not hear of it. She found the change of routine as invigorating as ever: Cecil, who had managed to avoid going on progress himself, was informed by his secretary, "Her Majesty, God be praised, liketh her journey, the air of this soil, and the pleasures showed her in the way, marvellous well". To the last, she remained unstoppable, for in the summer of 1602 she was on the road again, deriving as much pleasure as ever from hunting and hawking. She had intended to stay away for longer than she did, but to the great relief of her courtiers, appalling weather and an epidemic of smallpox in the countryside sufficed to convince her that she must curtail her travels.[82]

Regular exercise helped to keep her fit, and she remained vigorous and agile to the end. In 1597, the French ambassador thought it "a strange thing to see how lively she is in body and mind, and nimble in every thing she does". One foreign visitor to court in the autumn of 1602 saw her go for a stroll at Oatlands, "walking as freely as if she had been only eighteen years old". By this time she danced comparatively rarely, but there were still occasions when she could be lured on to the floor, as in February 1600, when a cousin of the Queen of France was in England for a visit. The Queen took great trouble to entertain him, "and to shew that she is not so old as some would have her, danced both measures and galliards in his presence". Two years later, she partnered the French Duke of Nevers when he came to England on a diplomatic mission, though Cecil confided that she had not much enjoyed the experience and had only done it "to observe points of courtesy in which to strangers she is no prince's second". For her part, the Queen took great pride in having remained so well preserved. In 1596 it was her proud boast that "neither her stomach, nor strength, nor her voice for singing, nor fingering for instruments, nor lastly her sight was anywhit decayed", and these faculties never became seriously impaired. Small wonder, then, that in his more gloomy moments, James VI thought it likely that Elizabeth would "endure as long as the sun and moon".[83]

Nor had her wit deserted her, for she retained her love of teasing and, if anything, in the last decade of her life her sense of humour became more robust and unpredictable. In 1600, the Dutch ambassador was nonplussed by her reply when he came to protest that she had allowed an English envoy to visit the Spanish Netherlands, which the Dutch feared would be the prelude to formal peace negotiations. The ambassador's account of how her envoy was being fêted wherever he went only seemed to amuse the Queen. She acknowledged cheerfully, "I hear from others that they are ringing the church bells wherever he goes, and that they have carried him through a great many more places than was necessary", but she refused to treat the matter seriously, and unexpectedly ventured, "I suppose that they think him a monster, and they are carrying him about to exhibit him!" Although she could still be dignified and solemn if the occasion required it, she frequently chose not to stand on any ceremony, and invididuals who were presented to her for the first time found themselves greeted with a spontaneity and lack of pomp that took them by surprise. In 1597 the French ambassador was amused to witness her reception of an Englishman who had resided abroad for some years, and to whom she had never previously been introduced. As the gentleman knelt before her in homage, she had dispelled the reverent atmosphere when she took "him by the hair, and made him rise, and pretended to give him a box on the ears".[84]

One reason why the Queen refused to slacken her pace of life was that she knew that any sign of weakness would be commented on and give rise to rumours that she was in ill health. She had always been stubborn about this: in 1577, she had expressed an interest in taking the waters at Buxton spa, which might help clear up the leg ulcer that had bothered her for some time, but when Burghley had sent her a flask of it, she had angrily refused to touch it, for "somebody told her there was some bruit of it about, as though her Majesty had had some sore leg". Now, however, her efforts to conceal even the most minor indispositions bordered on the comical. In 1597 Robert Cecil confided to a friend, "The Queen hath a desperate ache in her right thumb, but will not be known of it, nor the gout it *cannot* be, nor *dare* not be". Similarly, in August 1602, she briefly felt unwell while on progress, "but would not be known of it, for the next day she walked abroad in the park, lest any should take notice of it".[85]

In the same way she did not relish insensitive allusions to her age. In 1596 she had taken it personally when the Bishop of St David's had preached a sermon before her in which he had made a pointed reference to the time of life "wherein men begin to carry a calendar in their bones, the sense begins to fail, the strength to diminish, yea all the powers of the body daily to decay". Opening the window of the private closet that she occupied during services in her chapel, Elizabeth called out that "he should have kept his arithmetic for himself", and for the next few days she ordered the Bishop to remain confined to his quarters. Nevertheless, if others were well advised to stay off the subject of age, she herself often brought it up, if only to disconcert her interlocutors, and to prompt them into assuring her that she struck them as extremely youthful. In 1597 the French ambassador de Maisse described how in conversation with him, "She often called herself foolish and old, saying she was sorry ... that after having seen so many wise men and great princes, I should at length come to see a poor woman and a foolish". As so often, however, she had no intention of being taken seriously, and was clearly "well contented" when de Maisse politely demurred. On another occasion she was talking to de Maisse in much the same vein, sighing that "she was on the edge of the grave, and ought to bethink herself of death", when "suddenly she checked herself, saying 'I think not to die so soon, Master Ambassador, and am not so old as they think'".[86]

The ambassador did not question that her mind remained extraordinarily acute. In conversation she would frequently stray from the subject and then apologize – "See what it is to have to do with old women such as I am!" – but de Maisse realized that she was deliberately digressing to give herself more time to think about whatever it was they were meant to be discussing. After a few encounters with her, his admiration for her intellect was unqualified. "One can say nothing to her on which she will not make some apt comment ... She is a very great princess who knows everything", was his considered verdict on her.[87]

The Queen prided herself on being "well advertised of everything that happened in the world", and did not take kindly to suggestions that she had been misinformed. When in August 1601 Sir William Browne had arrived at Court bearing despatches from the Netherlands, Elizabeth had taken him aside and "discoursed of many things" relating to the situation there. During this talk, she had complained that the Dutch commander was besieging a town in the north of the Netherlands, when she had been given an undertaking that he would campaign in Flanders that summer. Sir William said he thought the Dutch general had had no choice, but

"Tush, Browne!" she interjected, "I know more than thou dost". She was not often caught out in points of detail, and had as good a recall for points of minor importance as she did for the central issues of the day. At the end of 1601 she was not in the least confused when Cecil surprised her by taking to her bedchamber at seven in the morning a young officer named Boyle, who brought news of a great victory in Ireland. She was clear-headed even at this unaccustomedly early hour, and Boyle happily recounted, "Her Majesty ... remembered me, calling me by name and giving me her hand to kiss ... And after her Majesty had interrogated with me upon sundry questions very punctually, and that therein I give her full satisfaction in every particular, she gave me again her hand to kiss".[88]

In many ways, the Queen seemed unaffected by the passage of time, but though physically vigorous and mentally alert, her appearance was that of an old woman. Admittedly in 1599 one foreign visitor at court found her "very youthful still in appearance, seeming no more than twenty years of age", but three years later the most charitable thing that another foreign traveller could say of her was that "she did not look ugly when seen from a distance". In 1597 de Maisse described her at length and reported, "As for her face, it is and appears to be very aged. It is long and thin and her teeth are yellow ... Many of them are missing so that one cannot understand her easily when she speaks quickly". Even so, he stressed that "save for her face, which looks old, and her teeth, it is not possible to see a woman of so fine and vigorous disposition, both in mind and body".[89]

Wizened and semi-toothless perhaps, but in external magnificence Elizabeth amply made up for this, for she still dressed with an exhibitionism and splendour that was calculated to take the breath away. In 1599 she was observed coming from chapel "most lavishly attired in a gown of pure white satin, gold embroidered, with a whole bird of paradise for panache set forward on her head, studded with costly jewels". This admittedly was her Sunday best, but if at other times her attire was less formal, simplicity was never the keynote. The first time that de Maisse saw her, she was just getting over a slight illness, and therefore she received him in a very grand dressing gown, made of silver gauze with "slashed sleeves lined with red taffeta and ... girt about with other little sleeves that hung down to the ground, which she was for ever twisting and untwisting". She wore a head-dress of matching material, and beneath it "a great reddish coloured wig", with two huge ringlets hanging down on either side. Pearls and rubies were at her throat, and also studded the lining of the high-collared gown. The Queen apologized to de Maisse for receiving him while so underdressed: "What will these gentlemen say, to see me so attired?" she asked roguishly, gesturing at the ambassador's suite. Certainly de Maisse did think her costume eccentric, and he was even more surprised that "she kept the front of her dress open, and one could see the whole of her bosom, and passing low, and often she would open the front of this robe with her hands, as if she was too hot". Nevertheless, though disconcerted, he found the effect intriguing, and he did not think Elizabeth in the least grotesque. On the contrary, he commended her "natural form and proportion", and noted she was "graceful in whatever she does".[90]

If in some respects the nation was in decline during the Queen's last years, news from Ireland at least gave just cause for celebration. Lord Mountjoy, who had gone to Ireland in February 1600, soon proved himself an immensely gifted commander. On his arrival he had found the troops so demoralized by Essex's leadership that for a time he had avoided any major actions against the enemy, but after six months of "being a nurse to this army, as well as general", he felt ready to go on the offensive. His plan was to interfere with Tyrone's communications, and to prevent him from liaising with his allies by establishing forts in strategic places, and these measures were so successful that by August 1601 he was telling Cecil, "I see a fair way to make Ulster one of the most quiet, assured and profitable provinces of Ireland".[91]

The following month, however, his calculations were upset when a force of 5,000 Spaniards landed at Kinsale, on the south coast of Ireland. The Queen promptly despatched 5,000 reinforcements to Ireland, telling Mountjoy she was sure he would make Ireland "serve as a sepulchre to these new conquerors", and by October Kinsale was under siege. Within two months, however, Mountjoy was in difficulties, for Tyrone was on his way from Ulster to relieve the Spaniards, and sickness and the freezing weather conditions were carrying off the English in droves. Fortunately, on Christmas Eve 1601, Tyrone was pressured by his allies into mounting a supposedly surprise attack. Mountjoy was forewarned, and Tyrone had to withdraw in confusion when he found his enemy waiting for him. Mountjoy ordered his men to give chase, and at last was able to confront his opponents on open ground. Delighted to have an opportunity to do battle on their own terms, the English won a great victory, claiming 1,200 Irish lives. Tyrone escaped, but his army disintegrated on the journey back to Ulster, and having been abandoned by their allies, the Spaniards in Kinsale had no alternative but to sue for peace.

On 2 January 1602 they surrendered, after securing an agreement from Mountjoy that they could return to Spain unmolested. The Spanish commander was only too pleased to see the last of a country which he told Mountjoy was fit for none but the devil himself, and Mountjoy commented with satisfaction, "It will be a difficult thing hereafter for the Irish to procure aid out of Spain". The Queen was naturally delighted by the fall of Kinsale, accounting it "one of the most acceptable accidents that hath befallen us". Her only regret was that the Spaniards had escaped with their lives, for she would have preferred it if the town had been taken by storm and its defenders put to the sword.[92]

Indeed, where Ireland was concerned, the Queen generally showed herself more rigorous than her advisers. By July 1602 Tyrone was living as a fugitive in the wilds of Ulster and, since it would be well-nigh impossible to run him to ground, Cecil was in favour of permitting him to make a formal submission. The Queen would not hear of it, utterly refusing "to hold any other way with him than the plain way of perdition". As she explained to Mountjoy, it bit too deeply into her soul, "when we consider how much the world will impute to us of weakness, to shew favour to him now, as if without that we could not give an end to this rebellion". In contrast, all the Council and Mountjoy himself advocated extending mercy to Tyrone, for the war in Ireland was costing £300,000 a year, and as Cecil remarked, "In short time the sword cannot end the war, and long time the state of England cannot well endure it". Elizabeth would not budge: Cecil told Mountjoy wearily, "In these great causes she is pleased to proceed more absolutely than ever, according as she pleaseth ... by the rules of her own princely judgment".[93] It was ironic that the Queen, who in the past had so often been accused of husbanding her treasure to the detriment of national security, should now find herself at odds with her ministers because her relentless attachment to principle was proving so expensive.

Because of his difficulties with the Queen on the Irish question, Cecil occasionally resorted to subterfuge to see that events in Ireland turned out as he desired. He once sent a message to Mountjoy that as Elizabeth was "apter to approve *facta* than *facienda*", he should not refer back to the Queen for permission to carry out measures that he believed to be necessary, but rather "do it in the respects beforehand and ... I will stand his warrant for the well acceptation thereof when it is done". On another occasion he reminded Mountjoy that in his next despatch from Ireland, he should "write that which is fit to be showed to her Majesty, and that which is fit for me to know (*a parte*) in which kinds all honest servants must strain a little when they will serve princes".[94] Cecil was still too much in awe of his mistress to risk openly flouting her wishes, and she would certainly have noticed if he had gone behind her back too often or incautiously, but however much she liked to think that she retained as tight a grip as ever on all threads of policy, some of the strands were in fact starting to slip through her fingers.

On 17 February 1603, Cecil's persistent cajolery prevailed, and Elizabeth agreed that to avoid further bloodshed, Mountjoy might, after all, accept Tyrone's offer of submission, and accord the rebel life, liberty and pardon. On 27 March, Mountjoy was expecting Tyrone to come in and prostrate himself before him, when he received private information that the Queen was dead. Technically, Mountjoy's authority as Lord Deputy had automatically terminated with the Queen's life, but there had been no official notification of her demise, and Mountjoy decided to press on as though he had heard nothing. On 30 March Tyrone made his submission, binding himself to serve the Crown as a loyal subject thereafter. Only on 5 April was it officially announced in Ireland that the Queen had died almost a fortnight before. When Tyrone heard the news, he burst out weeping, and though he claimed that "Tender sorrow for the loss of his sovereign mistress caused this passion in him", at least one observer concluded that his tears were caused by his regret that he had so abjectly surrendered to an opponent who had lost all power to harm him.[95]

As Elizabeth grew older, there were few men in England who had not devoted some anxious thought to the question of what would happen on her death, but one of the Queen's more remarkable achievements was the way she had prevented her subjects from voicing their worries on this score. "Succession!" exclaimed one gentleman who was privately sounded about his views on the matter, "What is he that dare meddle with it?" In 1600, the author of a political treatise identified those who were in the running to succeed the Queen, but declined to elaborate further, commenting, "To determine thereof is to all English capitally forbidden, and therefore so I leave it". Even Sir Robert Cecil claimed he had to be equally circumspect, for "the subject itself is so perilous to touch amongst us as it setteth a mark upon his head for ever that hatcheth such a bird".[96]

Such caution was understandable in view of the severe penalties meted out to any man unwary enough to break the taboo. No one needed to be reminded of the fate of Peter Wentworth, the Member of Parliament for Northampton who had written a tract urging Elizabeth to instruct Parliament to examine the titles of the various claimants to the throne, so it could pronounce, once and for all, who was her rightful heir. He warned the Queen that if she died while the succession was unsettled, she would "leave behind ... a name of infamy throughout the whole world", and in 1591 he had started making arrangements to have this work presented to her. The Council had learnt of his plans, and had promptly imprisoned Wentworth for four months, but this experience left him unchastened. The next meeting of Parliament took place in February 1593, and Wentworth had every intention of addressing the House of Commons on the subject of the succession. To prepare the ground, he had had secret meetings with a few MPs at a house in Lincoln's Inn Fields, and he had asked them to assure him of their support. In doing so, however, he laid himself open to the rigour of the law, for parliamentary business could not be discussed outside the Palace of Westminster. Word of his activities reached the Council, and on 22 February he was sent to the Tower, where he remained until his death in 1597.

Wentworth's punishment obviously served as a deterrent, but it was not only fear of royal retribution that accounted for the universal reticence on the subject of the succession. It was significant that one gentleman whom Wentworth had approached in hopes that he would endorse his campaign was frankly disapproving, objecting that "If we should enter into dealing with titles of the Crown, we had need, I think, of a Parliament a whole year long".[97] There were at least ten possible claimants to the throne, and it was widely recognized that a public debate on the relative merits of each contender could only be highly divisive. It was also obvious that if a successor was named, those claimants who were thereby excluded might resort to arms in defence of their titles. To the Queen, these arguments had always seemed conclusive, and despite the universal dread that her death would be followed by the horrors of a contested succession, it was undeniable that there were compelling reasons for keeping the matter in suspense.

The principal Catholic claimants to the throne were foreigners who were descended from John of Gaunt's daughters by his second wife, Constance of Castile. These included Philip II's daughter, the Infanta Isabel Clara Eugenia, the Portuguese Duke of Braganza, and the eldest son of the late Duke of Parma. None of these could count on a significant degree of support for their claim within England itself: when one political analyst drew up a list of all the claimants to the throne, he marked down the Infanta as "the least to be reckoned of, and furthest off". Nevertheless, if the Spaniards had been prepared to invade England on the death of the Queen, the Infanta could possibly have been imposed on the country by force, but by the beginning of the seventeenth century the Spain of Philip III was too debilitated and lethargic to undertake so massive a venture. In 1600 the Spanish Council of State recommended that the King should draw up plans which could be put into effect the instant the Queen died, but Philip's only response was that the affair was very grave and needed serious consideration.[98] Nothing further was done, not least because France indicated that if the Spaniards sought to put the Infanta on the English throne, Henry IV would regard it as a *casus belli*. Apart from this, the Infanta herself was not interested, for she and her husband, the Archduke Albert, were now acting as regents of the Spanish Netherlands, and they had no wish to take on further responsibilities.

The various English claimants were a far from distinguished bunch. As one nobleman put it, "Either in their worth are they contemptible, or not liked for their sexes", for according to this source, his countrymen wished "no more Queens, fearing we shall never enjoy another like this".[99] The most notable among them were probably the Earl of Hertford's son by Katherine Grey (who was technically a bastard), and Lord Darnley's niece, Arbella Stuart, but as soon as either of these had shown any signs of harbouring ambitions to succeed her the Queen had been quick to stamp on their pretensions. It was true that after the death of Katherine Grey, Hertford had been welcomed back at Court. Nevertheless, when in October 1595 the Queen learnt that he had sought legal advice as to whether it was possible to have his marriage to Katherine validated, thus legitimizing his children, she at once put him under arrest. After a short spell in confinement he was released and restored to favour, but his period in detention had served as a salutary reminder of the Queen's disciplinary powers and deterred him from similar intrigues in future.

Arbella Stuart was the product of a union between Lord Darnley's younger brother, Charles Stuart, and the Earl of Shrewsbury's step-daughter, Elizabeth Cavendish. The match had been arranged behind the Queen's back in 1574 by the young couple's respective mothers, for the Earl of Shrewsbury's termagant of a Countess (better known as Bess of Hardwick) saw in it a means of having a grandchild who might one day sit on the English throne. Elizabeth had been incensed when she had learnt of the marriage, and the bridegroom's mother, the hapless Countess of Lennox, was sent to the Tower for a short time, just as had happened when Lord Darnley had married Mary Queen of Scots. The marriage could not be dissolved, however, and in 1575 the couple's only child, Arbella, had been born. Arbella had been orphaned young and had been brought up by her maternal grandmother, who doted on her "jewel", envisioning in her the future Queen of England. Elizabeth, however, had not conferred any recognition on the child, and had ignored Bess's pointed requests that Arbella should be granted a sizeable pension, so that she could be educated "as is fit for her calling". In 1587, when Arbella was twelve, the Queen had invited her to come to Court, but it would seem that the girl angered her by her arrogance and was shortly afterwards sent back to live with her grandmother.[100]

Cooped up for years on end with Bess, Arbella developed into a tiresome and neurotic spinster, prone to romantic fancies. She had come to loathe her formidable grandmother, who no longer petted her as before, but often abused her "in despiteful and disgraceful words ... which she could not endure". At the end of 1602, Arbella made a desperate bid for freedom by secretly contacting the Earl of Hertford and suggesting that she should marry his grandson. Hertford knew better than to become embroiled in this mad scheme, and at once informed the Council. Elizabeth took the matter seriously, for the proposed match would have fused together two of the existing claims to the throne, and was therefore precisely the sort of union she most abhorred. An official was at once sent to interview Arbella, and much to the fury of her grandmother (who "with much ado refrained her hands" when she learnt what Arbella had been up to), she tearfully confessed all. Enraged at Arbella's folly, Bess wrote to the Queen that she

had been "altogether ignorant of her vain doings", and begged Elizabeth
to remove the girl from her charge, as "I cannot now assure myself of her
as I have done". The Queen nevertheless was of the opinion that old Lady
Shrewsbury was quite capable of keeping Arbella under control, and in
consequence the girl stayed where she was.[101] In March 1603 there was
further trouble when Arbella made an unsuccessful attempt to escape from
her grandmother's house, but by this time Elizabeth was already on her
deathbed, and it was therefore left to her successor to deal with Arbella's
vagaries.

By keeping in check the rival claimants to the throne, Elizabeth can be
said to have tacitly endorsed the title of James VI of Scotland to succeed
her, but she would never officially acknowledge it. Among the Queen's
subjects, James was widely regarded as the most likely person to succeed
her. "I do assure myself the King of Scotland will carry it", was the
comment of one knowledgeable observer, and towards the end of the reign,
the Earl of Northumberland sent James a letter containing the cheering
information that "for matter of your claim after her Majesty, I hear almost
none call it in question". If one may believe Elizabeth's godson Sir John
Harington, she herself had been known to declare in private that "They
were great fools that did not know that the line of Scotland must needs be
next heirs", but she would not dream of saying as much in public. When
she had made an alliance with James in 1586, she had given him a sealed
document in which she promised that she would do nothing prejudicial to
his claim unless he provoked her into doing so, but further than this she
would not go.[102]

To James, this scarcely seemed sufficient, particularly since the Queen
was erratic in her payment of the allowance which he had understood had
been promised to him when he had signed the pact of 1586. Having no
security that in due course he would be bequeathed her crown, his diplomacy with other countries was aimed at making foreign monarchs look
favourably on his candidacy, but when this led him into contacts with
Catholic powers who were hostile to Elizabeth, this in its turn heightened
her mistrust of him. She taxed James with reports that came to her ears
that he was having dealings with the Pope, or that he had offered to send
his eldest son to be educated in Rome, and though James vehemently
denied that such things were true, the Queen had no way of telling if he
was being sincere. Thus, throughout the 1590s, she and James were engaged
in a tense game of Grandmother's Footsteps, with the King not daring to
make any overtly unfriendly moves, but at the same time fearing to remain
immobile in case he found himself outpaced by his competitors.

The Queen's suspicions of James were intensified by his indulgent
treatment of the aristocratic Catholic faction within Scotland. On several
occasions she provided him with evidence that its leaders were plotting

secretly with Spain, but James thought it inadvisable to take action against them. In view of his domestic difficulties, it was understandable that he was so cautious about tackling this problem, but the Queen was withering in her criticism. Loftily she told him he was "well worthy of such traitors" if he did not deal firmly with the Catholic Lords' indiscipline, adding contemptuously, "Good Lord! who but yourself would have left such people to be able to do you wrong!" She invariably adopted this condescending tone in her dealings with James, treating him very much as a novice who had scarcely mastered the rudiments of statecraft. Even when the King acted in a manner calculated to please her, she was not a whit less patronizing. For example, when James finally moved against the Catholic Lords in the autumn of 1594, his only reward from Elizabeth was the supercilious plaudit, "At the first your career was not the best, yet I hope your stop will crown all". Far from showing her approval by cultivating warmer relations with her neighbour, for the next nine months she did not even deign to write to James.[103]

In her admonitory letters to James, Elizabeth explained that he should attribute her forthright manner to her affection for him, and she urged him to "bear with overplain imputation since it springs of so good a root". Understandably, however, James frequently found himself bridling at the way she treated him. Even while he was still in his teens an ambassador had noted of him, "He does not estimate correctly his poverty and insignificance, but is over-confident of his strength and scornful of other princes", and at times he was almost goaded beyond endurance by the fact that Elizabeth made no effort to conceal her disdain for him. In the final analysis, however, James knew that there was little he could do in retaliation. He might flirt with the prospect of forging closer relations with Catholic princes and bringing pressure to bear on the Queen in that way, but the risks inherent in such a course always made him draw back. On the rare occasions when he did try to defy her, he invariably regretted it, for it usually ended with him offering the Queen a grovelling submission. At the end of 1597 he attempted to browbeat Elizabeth by blustering in the Scots Parliament that it was intolerable that having wronged him by murdering his mother, she should now insult him further by failing to pay him his pension or recognize him as her heir. With an imperious jerk, the Queen at once brought him to heel, writing to warn him that she would not have accepted such provocation from "a far mightier and potenter prince" than he. "Look ye not [therefore] that without large amends I may or will slupper up such indignities", she told him with chilling scorn. Suitably chastened, James hastened to atone for his outburst, humbling himself before the Queen in a cringing missive. "It becomes me not to strive with a lady", he remarked meekly. " ... I take not unkindly your passionate letter ... because I perceive sparks of love to shine through the midst of the thickest clouds of passion that are there set down".[104]

Of course, if in February 1601 Essex had succeed in making himself the Queen's master, she would no longer have been in a position to be so dictatorial to James. This was why the King had agreed to Essex's request to provide him with diplomatic support during his rebellion, but by the time James's envoys reached London in mid-March, Essex was already dead. James was described as being "in dumps" when he heard of the collapse of the rebellion, and certainly from his point of view the outlook was gloomy. It seemed probable that Elizabeth would uncover his connections with the conspirators, and James assumed that Cecil and others would use this to persuade her that he was unworthy to be her heir. Anxious to know exactly where he stood, James told his ambassadors to ask the Queen to give him some sign of her goodwill, such as increasing his yearly pension. If, as the King fully expected, this request was turned down, the ambassadors were not to threaten Elizabeth, but they were to warn Cecil and his fellow Councillors that James held them responsible for "all the Queen's hard usage". James wished to remind them that they could not be certain of keeping him off the throne, and as he put it, "The day may come when I will crave accompt of them of their presumption, when there will be no bar betwixt me and them". However, so convinced was the King that Cecil and his colleagues were set in their hostility to him that he had little hope that these threats would change their attitude. He felt sure that, on the Queen's death, he would have to contest his claim by force, and therefore he told his ambassadors that if their voyage was not to prove "utterly unprofitable", they should do their best to build up some sort of party for him in England. In this way, he might at least have a chance of meeting with some support if the Queen died, and if he invaded England in defence of his hereditary rights.[105]

The ambassadors put James's demands to the Queen, but as the King had predicted, she indignantly rejected them. The examinations of Essex's fellow conspirators had left her fully apprised of James's role in the plot, and although she had resolved to turn a blind eye to the King's involvement, she thought it extraordinarily impertinent of him to choose this moment to ask fresh favours of her. From Sir Robert Cecil, however, the ambassadors had an altogether more encouraging response, for the truth was that Essex had grossly wronged the Secretary in claiming that he had dedicated himself to setting the Infanta on the throne. During Essex's lifetime, Cecil had had no hope of overcoming James's prejudice against him, but now that the Earl was dead, Sir Robert believed he could have a fruitful relationship with the King.

Already, at Essex's trial, Sir Robert had done his best to clear himself of the slur that he was pro-Spanish, for when Essex had claimed in court that he had evidence to that effect, Cecil had stepped forward and challenged him to produce it. Essex had asserted that Sir William Knollys would support his contention, but when this independent witness was summoned, he had declined to corroborate the charge against Cecil. As the Secretary had pointed out to Essex, "In this court I stand as an upright man, and your Lordship as a delinquent", and now he could justly regard himself as fully vindicated. Triumphantly he had declared, "As to my affection to advance the Spanish title to England, I am so far from it that my mind is astonished to think of it".[106]

Having prepared the ground in this way, Cecil felt ready to do business with King James, and at a meeting with the Scots ambassadors he proposed that he and James should start to correspond in cipher. He stressed that all knowledge of their communications must be kept from the Queen, because "that language, which would be tunable in other prince's ears, would jar in hers, whose creature I am". Nevertheless, although he could not deny that Elizabeth would have disapproved of this secret intercourse, he felt able to justify it on patriotic grounds. As he smoothly put it, "I know it holdeth ... even with strictest loyalty and soundest reason for faithful ministers to conceal sometime both thoughts and actions from princes when they are persuaded it is for their own greater service". He argued that, if he had continued to hold silence with James, the King might have interpreted this as proof that he was to be excluded from the succession, and this might have driven him to mount an invasion of England, which could only be disastrous for all concerned. As it was, if James would "so vouchsafe me in this to be your oracle, that when that day (so grievous to us) shall happen which is the tribute of all mortal creatures, your ships shall be steered into the right harbour without cross of wave or tide that shall be able to turn over a cockboat".[107] There was of course another reason why Cecil thought it prudent to enter into communications with the King, which the Secretary demurely left unspoken. Sir Robert did not intend his own career to be jeopardized by the Queen's death, and in making these approaches to James he was safeguarding his own position in the state.

The King was delighted to find himself dealing with the English Secretary of State, for it was his opinion that Cecil was "king there in effect". He eagerly accepted all Cecil's advice: when the Secretary told him he should not pester the Queen with "needless expostulations" and demands that she recognize him as her heir, James at once assured him that he had no intention of annoying her with "my too busy behaviour". He even permitted Cecil to draft any correspondence he had with Elizabeth, so that he could be sure of striking exactly the right note. As a result, his relations with the Queen became infinitely more harmonious. By January 1602 he was telling her that he was delighted that she had come to understand the depth of his affection for her, "all the clouds of mistaking being now most happily cleared". It was Cecil who was responsible for this change, and the King assured him of his eternal gratitude for having "so easily settled me in the only right course for my good, so happily preserved the Queen's mind from the poison of jealous prejudice".[108]

That the Queen had no inkling of what was going on is most unlikely. She had always been mournfully aware of mankind's tendency to worship the rising rather than the setting sun, and while it cannot have been a pleasant sensation for her to know that her servants were surreptitiously preparing for the time when she was no longer with them, the development would not have surprised her in the least. She trusted Cecil to see that the transfer of power went smoothly, and to the last she believed that this informal arrangement would suit everyone better than an official acknowledgement that James was her heir.

The Queen once mischievously remarked to James VI that she knew well enough that everything was in readiness for her funeral, but at the beginning of 1603 it appeared that the undertakers would be kept waiting for quite a time. She had spent Christmas at Whitehall, and the festivities that year had been particularly jolly. Unlike the previous Christmas, when attendance at Court had been so thin that the guards "were not troubled to keep the doors at plays and pastimes", an observer reported that this time, "The Court hath flourished more than ordinary. Besides much dancing, bear baiting and many plays, there hath been great golden play" for high stakes among the courtiers. As well as celebrating at Court, Elizabeth had been feasted by the Earl of Nottingham and Sir Robert Cecil at their London houses, and had appeared "marvellous well contented" with their hospitality. On 21 January she moved to Richmond "in very foul and wet weather", and once she was there, a severe frost set in, but Richmond was the warmest of her palaces, and the cold spell did not seem to have affected her. In early February she looked magnificent when she gave an audience to the Venetian ambassador, wearing a taffeta dress of silver and white, trimmed with gold, and "a vast quantity of gems and pearls". The Queen impressed the ambassador with her "lively wit", and she not only struck him as being "in excellent health ... and in perfect possession of all her senses", but he even saw in her the remnants of a "never quite lost beauty".[109]

At the end of February, however, a great change came over her. She was deeply distressed by the death of her cousin, the Countess of Nottingham, who had been in her service since the beginning of the reign, and it seemed that nothing could shake off her depression. She refused to venture out of her private apartments, and when Lady Nottingham's nephew, Robert Carey, was sent in to try and cheer her, he found her in a very bad way. Brightly he told her that he was pleased to see her in good health, but she took his hand, wrung it, and said with great emphasis, "No Robin, I am not well". Throughout the Court, there was anxious speculation as to what could have plunged her into this acute melancholia. Various theories were put forward, and it was conjectured that she was worried by Arbella Stuart's behaviour, or conscience-stricken at having executed Essex, or upset at having agreed to pardon Tyrone. However, when the Queen herself was asked what it was that was afflicting her, she said simply, "She knew nothing in the world worthy to trouble her".[110] Despite this, she remained sunk in terminal gloom.

As the days went by without any improvement, it became apparent that she had entered into a fatal decline. She began to be affected by a variety of symptoms, none of them serious in themselves, but worrying when taken in conjunction: insomnia, loss of appetite, incessant thirst, and, for a time, swollen glands, though these later subsided. It has been suggested that she was suffering from a combination of tonsilitis and flu,[111] but the real problem was that she had lost the will to live. She absolutely refused to take any of the remedies prescribed by the physicians who had been called in to attend her and this was taken as a sure sign that she did not want to get better.

To the consternation of all about her, she also refused to undress or take to her bed. For hours on end she sat motionless and silent on cushions strewn about her chamber, staring at the floor with her finger in her mouth. To try and bring her out of her torpor, Cecil and Whitgift went down on their knees and implored her to look after herself better, but at this she showed a touch of her old asperity, snapping that "She knew her health better than they, and she was not in such danger as they thought". However, having delivered herself of this rebuke, she sank back into her former passivity. The Earl of Nottingham was called in to try and coax her into bed, and by 22 March, "what by fair means, what by force", he had managed it. By this time, however, there was no question of her recovery: she lay quietly on her side, listening to prayers that were read aloud to her, and on 23 March she lost the power of speech. Nevertheless, she did not become altogether insensible, and when the Archbishop of Canterbury came to pray at the dying woman's bedside, the onlookers could see that she derived much comfort from his presence. She appeared to have no dread of death, showing little interest when Whitgift talked of longer life, but "when he prayed, or spake of Heaven and those joys, she would hug his hand". Having knelt beside her till his knees were weary, Whitgift eventually made to rise, but the Queen gestured to him to remain. Obediently he prayed for another half hour, but even then Elizabeth appeared reluctant to let him leave, and he was obliged to resume his orisons. Imperious to the last, the Queen kept the old man on his knees for a further thirty minutes, and it was only as she gradually drifted into unconsciousness that the Archbishop was able to stagger to his feet and creep away.[112]

The Queen died between two and three in the morning of 24 March 1603. She had never made a will, but by this time there could be no doubt as to who would succeed her. It was even given out that during her final illness, she had cleared up all uncertainty on this question, and that when asked whom she wished to be her heir, she had answered, "I will have no rascal to succeed me; and who should succeed me but a King?" Among educated circles there was some scepticism about this story, which was suspected to have been circulated by the Council as an additional way of ensuring that the legitimacy of James's claim was not questioned. The historian John Clapham, who wrote an account of Elizabeth's death shortly after James's accession, commented, "These reports, whether they were true indeed, or given out of purpose by such as would have them so to be believed, it is hard to say. Sure I am they did no hurt".[113]

In Scotland, meanwhile, King James, who for so long had struggled to control his "wild, unruly colt" of a country, was looking forward with growing excitement to the moment when he could mount St George's "towardly riding horse". When it had become clear that Elizabeth's condition would not improve, Cecil had drawn up the proclamation that would be read on her death, announcing James's accession. He had sent a copy to James, and the King had perused it with the deepest satisfaction. James's only concern was that, instead of dying quickly, Elizabeth would linger on "insensible and stupid ... (as is usual in such maladies), unfit to rule and govern a kingdom". He sought assurances that in these circumstances he would be nominated Regent, but fortunately the situation did not arise. On the evening of 26 March, James had retired for the night when Robert Carey was ushered into his bedchamber. After Elizabeth had fallen ill, Carey had taken the precaution of setting a chain of post horses along the main route to Scotland so he could be sure of delivering the news of her death to the King before anyone else, and now, dusty and dishevelled but still triumphant, he saluted James by his title of King of England, Scotland, France and Ireland.[114]

At ten in the morning of 24 March, James had been proclaimed King in London. The reaction was subdued: one witness commented, "I think the sorrow for her Majesty's departure was so deep in many hearts, they could not so suddenly show any great joy". Nevertheless, that evening there were bonfires and bell-ringing to celebrate the accession of the new King, and a certain excitement began to manifest itself at the dawn of a new era. The Queen's Master of Requests noted in his journal, "The people, both in city and counties, finding the just fear of forty years, for want of a known successor, dissolved in a minute, did so rejoice as few wished the gracious Queen alive again". "Ambitious persons and flatterers of all kinds" made hasty preparations to ride north so that they could greet the King as he journeyed from Scotland, while those who remained in the South busied themselves procuring silks and velvets to wear at the coronation. "All men are well satisfied", was one report, " ... and great hope of a flourishing time".[115]

Meanwhile, for the first few days after her death, the Queen lay at Richmond, virtually forgotten. As she had wished, her body was wrapped up in cere cloth rather than being embalmed, but it was done in a "very ill" fashion, "through the covetousness of them that defrauded her of the allowance of cloth was given them for that purpose". The story was confirmed by Clapham, who recorded, "The Queen's body left in a manner alone a day or two after her death, and mean persons had access to it".[116]

The Queen's remains did not long have to suffer this scandalous neglect. Shortly afterwards, her body was conveyed at night downriver to Whitehall, on a torchlit barge draped in black velvet. At Whitehall she lay in state, watched over by her ladies. On 28 April she was given a magnificent funeral. The procession was headed by two hundred and forty poor women, followed by the serried ranks of royal servants and household officers, ranging from the Children of the Woodyard to the Archbishop of Canterbury. Then came the Queen's leaden coffin on its bier, an open chariot drawn by four horses, "trapped with black velvet beset with the arms of England and France". The Master of the Horse, the Lord Admiral, and the Lord Treasurer came next, followed by the wives and daughters of the nobility. The Yeomen of the Guard brought up the rear, with their halberds trailing downwards as a mark of respect.[117]

It was an impressive spectacle, and there were tears from some of the crowd, above all from the women. By no means all the spectators were so sentimental: as the cortege wound its way through the streets to Westminster Abbey, where the Queen was to be interred in the crypt beside her grandfather, Henry VII, there was some muttering against her. Some took the line "They could not lightly be in worse state than they were, considering that the people generally were much impoverished by continual subsidies and taxes ... that little or no equality was used in those impositions, the meaner sort commonly sustaining the greater burden, and the wealthier no more than themselves listed to bear ... that many privileges had passed under name for the benefit of some particular men, to the detriment of the Commonwealth". Others reproved these detractors, reminding them of the Queen's "clemency and other virtues", but by no means everyone was prepared to give her credit for this.[118]

It took the perspective of history to set Elizabeth's real virtues in focus, and after perhaps two decades of Stuart rule, her people were more ready to appreciate the way she had exercised her power. A leading Jacobean churchman recalled, "Then was her memory much magnified – such ringing of bells, such public joy and sermons in commemoration of her, the picture of her tomb painted in many churches". Elizabeth had never anticipated that she would attain immortality of this sort. As one who held that a foremost characteristic of her subjects was their tendency to fix their eyes on the coming generation of rulers, she had doubted even her ability to retain her hold on their affections during her lifetime, and had little hope of being fondly remembered after it. She had declared to Parliament in 1593 that no prince who came after her would "ever be found to exceed myself, in love, I say towards you, or care over you", but she did not expect to be given posthumous recognition for this. She had assumed that on her death, those who survived her would thankfully consign her to the past, but she was wrong in believing that they would let her memory fade. Although in most ways she was an unerring judge of the way her people thought, she had underestimated them in this, for she had awoken in them a capacity for nostalgia that she was unaware they possessed. As a young queen Elizabeth had once declared that she had a great longing to make her fame spread abroad in her lifetime, "and after occasion memorial for ever".[119] Without doubt her wish had been granted.

When Elizabeth ascended the throne, her kingdom was weak, demoralized and impoverished. A member of Parliament subsequently recalled how at her accession, England was "in war with foreign nations, subject to ignorant hypocrisy and unsound doctrine, the best sort under great persecution, some imprisoned, some driven to exile for their conscience, the treasure ... corrupt". Under Elizabeth, the nation regained its self-confidence and sense of direction. At a time when the authority of the majority of her fellow monarchs was under threat or in decline, she upheld the interests of the Crown while not encroaching on those of her subjects, restored the coinage, and created a Church which, for all its failings, came close to being truly national. While many European countries were being rent by civil war, insurrection and appalling acts of bloodshed, she presided over a realm which (with the exception of her Irish dominions) was fundamentally stable and united. She herself was proud of the contrast between the condition of her own kingdom and that of others. In an undated prayer that she composed for her private use, she offered up her thanks to God that at a time "when wars and seditions with grievous persecutions have vexed almost all kings and countries round about me, my reign hath been peaceable, and my realm a receptacle to thy afflicted Church. The love of my people hath appeared firm, and the devices of my enemies frustrate". Besides this, Elizabeth was responsible for raising England's international standing, defying the most powerful nation in Christendom, and frustrating Philip II's attempts to overrun both England and France. It was a feat which moved Pope Sixtus V to remark in involuntary admiration, "She is only a woman, only mistress of half an island, and yet she makes herself feared by Spain, by France, by the Empire, by all".[120]

Undoubtedly, luck played a part in her success. Above all, she was fortunate in her longevity, for unlike Mary Tudor she was granted the time she needed to solve the problems that faced her in her own way. Elizabeth also benefited from the misfortunes that beset her neighbours, as for years potentially hostile foreign powers were too absorbed by their domestic difficulties to pose a serious threat to her. In 1570, Walsingham indeed declared that he looked on "the continuance of others' troubles as the only occasion of our quiet". It would be absurd, however, to believe that Elizabeth's achievements were wholly fortuitous. Henry III of France was nearer the mark when he acknowledged that she had always been "aided ... by marvellous good fortune", while nevertheless paying tribute to the "valour, spirit and prudence" which had enabled Elizabeth to take advantage of this.[121]

It in no way belittles Elizabeth to concede that she was consistently well-served by her advisers. On the contrary, as she herself was responsible for their appointments, it proves she merited her reputation of being (in the words of Francis Bacon) "one of the most judicious princes in discerning of spirits that ever governed", and "a proficient in the reading of men as well as books". Perhaps she herself was inclined to minimize the contribution of her councillors, for if things went well she liked to reserve the credit for herself, and it was only when she suffered a reverse that she would try to shift the blame for it elsewhere.[122] It is a tendency of hers that one must bear in mind when assessing who was responsible for the great triumphs of the reign, but it would be misguided to seek to correct it by exaggerating the role that her advisers played.

Certainly Elizabeth's approach to the question of her marriage owed nothing whatever to her councillors, for her handling of this matter was wholly idiosyncratic. Above all, she was unusual in being prepared to defy the conventional wisdom that stated that it would be madness to embark on marriage negotiations with foreign powers unless she was sincere in wishing to bring them to a successful conclusion. Instead, for as long as she was nubile she insisted on regarding her availability as one of her main assets in the conduct of foreign affairs, ignoring the anguished warnings of her advisers that she would only harm herself by engaging in such dubious practices. Walsingham was actually of the opinion "that no one thing hath procured her so much hatred abroad as these wooing matters, for that it is conceived she dallieth therein", and when Elizabeth was protracting the Alençon marriage negotiations in 1581 he told her directly, "If you mean it not, then assure yourself it is one of the worst remedies your Highness can use, howsoever you conceive that it serveth your turn". But though the Queen's courtships came to nothing, their consequences were not in the least malign. For years she mesmerized the most eligible men in Europe, persuading them that she was attainable and yet never permitting herself to be pinned down in a way that would have deprived her foreign policy of the flexibility that was its hallmark. She displayed real virtuosity, not only in deluding her would-be husbands that doomed marriage negotiations were full of promise, but also in the skilful way she disengaged herself at the optimum moment, rebuffing her suitors without causing undue offence. The Duke of Parma likened the way she dealt with the issue to "the weaving of Penelope, undoing every night what was done before and then reweaving it anew the next, advancing ... neither more nor less than has been done and undone countless times without reaching a conclusion one way or another". Thus, in this devious and clever fashion, she remained to the end "so great a lady that there could be no hold taken of her".[123]

At her accession, Elizabeth's sex was looked on as a grievous disability, but she succeeded in turning even that to her advantage. Although she was sufficiently assertive to prevent her male advisers from contesting her authority, in other ways she flaunted her femininity, using it to appeal to the chivalrous instincts of the men who surrounded her, and investing her dominion over them with an aura of idealism and romance. Furthermore, Elizabeth knew that, precisely because she was a woman, her ministers were ready to make allowances for her when she behaved in a fashion that would have been deemed intolerable in a king. "That which is natural to her sex hindereth resolution", shrugged Burghley resignedly on one occasion,[124] and Elizabeth exploited this indulgent attitude to stave off unwelcome decisions and to avoid being hustled into commitments against her will.

Walsingham accused Elizabeth of hoarding her money in preference to spending it to enhance national security, but the Queen was surely right to fear that she would be brought close to bankruptcy if she pursued the sort of interventionist policy that he advocated. Experience proved that involvement in overseas adventures invariably cost more than had been anticipated, and yielded results which were far from conclusive. On one occasion Elizabeth remarked bitterly, "We were ever won to expense by little and little, and by the representations of our great resolutions in generalities, till they came to particular execution". Much as Walsingham might deplore it, she could not shape her foreign policy without taking financial considerations into account, for as she once observed, "Owning neither the East nor the West Indies, we are unable to supply the constant demands upon us; and although we have the reputation of being a good housewife, it does not follow that we can be a housewife for all the world".[125]

Criticized on some sides for not doing enough to help foreign Protestants, Elizabeth also had to defend herself from the entirely contrary charge that when it suited her she was prepared secretly to collude with rebels and to promote internal dissension in nearby realms. Her aim in doing so, however, was purely defensive, for she wished merely to make it more difficult for the monarchs of those countries to devote their energies to overthrowing her. In 1579 Burghley made this point when he justified Elizabeth's support of disobedient subjects of the Kings of France and Spain on the grounds that "Her Majesty professeth no enmity against any of those Kings, as to the deprivation of them from their crowns, as they do by their profession of their obedience to Rome". At one time or another during her reign, the sovereigns of Scotland, France and Spain coveted her kingdom, but Elizabeth had no such expansionist tendencies, provided that one excludes her desire to repossess Calais, which she looked on as her rightful property. After Elizabeth had turned down an offer of the sovereignty of the Netherlands in 1582 Leicester had commented, "Her Majesty's goodness was such as she would not possess what appertains to another. Few princes have so good conscience." The year before, after an altercation with Mendoza, Elizabeth had been overheard muttering, "Would to God that each one had his own and was at peace". Walsingham was surely right when he commented of his mistress, "I would all princes were affected like her Majesty, and then we should have as general a peace effected throughout the world as in Augustus his time".[126]

Ultimately, of course, it proved impossible for Elizabeth to remain at peace with Philip II. As a war leader Elizabeth had her limitations, but she was not to blame for her kingdom's failure to reach overall victory over the enemy. Nor was it her fault that the revenues of the Crown were inadequate to sustain the struggle with Spain over a fifteen-year period, and as a result, by the time she died taxation was starting to weigh more heavily on the less prosperous sectors of society, economies at Court were provoking discontent there, and she bequeathed a debt to her successor of £365,254. Given the constraints she laboured under, it is impossible to see how she could have avoided these difficulties, for her innate conservatism prevented her from adopting radical solutions to solve the Crown's financial problems. Indeed, when the introduction of a form of wealth tax was proposed in the Parliament of 1593, the Queen's Vice-chamberlain, Sir Thomas Heneage, spoke against this on the grounds that Elizabeth "loved not such fineness of device and novel inventions, but liked rather to have the ancient usages offered". As for the imposition of a poll tax, which had been mooted in the reign of Edward VI and on several occasions thereafter, "she would not suffer [it] to be so much as once named".[127]

Elizabeth's success as a ruler was very much a personal triumph, for much of the devotion and loyalty she inspired was attributable not solely to her authority, but to her glamour, magnetism and charm. As her godson, Sir John Harington, recalled, "Her speech was such as none could refuse to take delight in ... When she smiled it was pure sunshine that everyone did choose to bask in if they could". She combined remarkable talents as an orator with the surest of touches in dealing with individuals, and when she was out to please, she was well-nigh irresistible. In 1599 one of those present when Elizabeth informed Lord and Lady Norris that their son was responsible for a great victory in Ireland described how the Queen "addressed so many good and gracious words to them in particular as were able to revive them if they were in a swoon or half-dead". A few years before this, the Earl of Shrewsbury declared to Elizabeth that his "vital spirits" had been "renewed and quickened" by an affectionate message she had sent him on his sickbed, and he affirmed emotionally, "No application or ministration of physic would have wrought that cure in so short a time as your Majesty's gracious speeches".[128]

It was true that there was an obverse side to the Queen's character, for her temper was far from even, and she suffered from the fault of being "too apt to wrath by the murmurs of backbiters". Burghley commented wryly that all the Queen's servants "must sometimes bear with a cast of cross words, as I myself have had long experience, sometime when I deserve, in my opinion, best, and look least for such mishaps". Yet though it was naturally upsetting for her employees to be censured without good cause, they knew that if Elizabeth was in the wrong, she generally recognized the fact before too long, and proved anxious to make amends. When Elizabeth had humiliated Burghley in 1580 by subjecting him to a public rating, Walsingham consoled the Lord Treasurer with the reflection, "I nothing doubt but in time, her Majesty, who of her own nature is inclined to deal graciously with everybody, will see her error". Burghley knew this to be true, for after an earlier wounding outburst from the Queen he had commented philosophically, "We must all dutifully bear with her Majesty's offence for the time, not despairing but however she misliketh matters at one time, yet at another time she will alter her sharpness, specially when she is persuaded that we all mean truly for her and her surety, though she sometimes will not so understand". As Leicester said of Elizabeth, "God be thanked, her blasts be not the storms of other princes, though they be very sharp sometimes, to those she loves the best".[129]

A courtier cautioning an acquaintance against doing anything to incur the Queen's displeasure described Elizabeth as "slow to revenge and ready to forgive. And yet ... she is right King Henry her father." But though all quailed in the face of her wrath (in 1593 the French ambassador confided, "When I see her enraged against any person whatever, I wish myself in Calcutta, fearing her anger like death itself"), no one feared receiving the sort of treatment that had been meted out in Henry VIII's day, when men who had believed themselves secure in the King's favour were suddenly hustled to the Tower and put on trial for their lives. In 1593 Elizabeth made a speech to Parliament in which she alluded to her father, describing him as one "whom in the duty of a child I must regard, and to whom I must acknowledge myself far shallow", but she was aware of the difference in their methods of ruling, and believed hers to be preferable. In a letter that she sent the Irish Privy Council in 1573, she deliberately contrasted herself with Henry, and it was obvious that she thought the comparison was advantageous to her. Rebuking the Irish Council for having reprieved a murderer without applying to her before-hand, she stated, "If this had been in our father's time ... you may soon conceive how it would have been taken. Our moderate reign and government can be contented to bear this, so you will take this for a warning."[130]

In 1593 Elizabeth stated in Parliament, "The great expense of my time, the labour of my studies and the travail of my thoughts chiefly tendeth to ... the government of you to live in a flourishing and happy condition", and certainly her dedication to her people was beyond question. Towards the end of her life her reputation suffered as a number of her subjects gave rein to "discontentments in their private opinions, though perhaps none in truth", but nothing she had done merited this decline in her popularity. On her death a contemporary remarked, "Amongst her manifold and rare virtues of nature and art, this was the only detraction: that she had not power to give where it was merited", and this was an apt epitaph. She cannot have failed to have been saddened by the fact that her hold over her subjects' affections had proved less absolute than in the past, for she had often stated that it was the goodwill of her people that mattered to her above all else, and she had said that if she ever forfeited it, "Well might I live, but never think I breathed". To the last, however, she had the satisfaction of knowing that for much of her long reign, the love she had lavished on her subjects had been reciprocated in full measure, and there is no reason to doubt the sincerity of her statement that it was this which made a "heavy burden light, and a kingdom's care but easy carriage to me".[131]

Notes

Abbreviations used

BM   The British Library Manuscript room in the British Museum.

Cal. Border.   Calendar of State Papers relating to border affairs.

Cal. Dom.   Calendar of State Papers, Domestic Series.

Cal. For.   Calendar of State Papers, Foreign Series.

Cal. Irish.   Calendar of State Papers, Ireland.

Cal. Rome.   Calendar of State Papers relating to English affairs, preserved in Rome.

Cal. Scot.   Calendar of State Papers relating to Scotland and Mary Queen of Scots.

Cal. Span.   Calendar of State Papers in archives of Simancas, Elizabeth. ed. M. A. S. Hume.

Cal. Ven.   Calendar of State Papers in archives of Venice.

DNB   *Dictionary of National Biography.*

EHR   *English Historical Review.*

HMC   Historical Manuscript Commission.

HMC Sals.   Calendar of Manuscripts of Marquis of Salisbury at Hatfield House.

K. de L.   J.M.B.C. Kervyn de Lettenhove, *Relations politiques des Pays Bas et de l'Angleterre sous le règne de Philippe II.*

L. & P.   Letters and papers of the Reign of Henry VIII.

PRO   Public Record Office.

SP   State Papers in the Public Record Office.

Span. Cal.   Calendar of Letters and State Papers preserved in Archives of Simancas, ed. Pascual de Gayangos et al.

CHAPTER 1
"As towards a child ... as ever I knew any"

1. Span. Cal. IV, ii, 629
2. Span. Cal. IV, ii, 635–42
3. Span. Cal. IV, ii, 788; Mumby, 2
4. Hall, 242–44
5. Mumby, 6; Span. Cal. IV, ii, 887, 881; L. & P. VI, 500; Span. Cal. IV, ii, 894; ibid. V, 95
6. Span. Cal. V. ii, 19
7. Span. Cal. V, i, 114; L. & P. VIII, 58; ibid. 297, 151
8. Ives, *Boleyn*, 238–39; Span. Cal. V, ii, 59
9. Span, Cal. V, i, 234; ibid. V, ii, 84–85
10. Wriothsley, 35n; ibid. 37–38; L. & P. XII, i, 361
11. Ives, *Boleyn*, 390; ibid. 55; ibid. 277–82; Naunton, 78–79; E. Jenkins, 15
12. Haynes, I, 98; Wiesener, II, 284

13. Span. Cal. V, ii, 121; *Statutes at Large*, IV, 422
14. L. & P. VIII, 172–73; ibid. X, 383; Mumby, 16–18
15. L. & P. Xii, i, 318
16. L. & P. XIII, ii, 544; L. & P. XII, i, 361
17. Watson, 177; M. Dowling, *Humanism in the Age of Henry VIII*, 17
18. Hodges & Fox, 23
19. Mumby, 58; Hearne's Sylloge, 150–51
20. Strype, *Cheke*, 5; Cal. For. I, xiv; Strype, *Cheke*, 9; Marples, 19; Mumby, 70; Ascham, *English Works*, 219; K. de L. VII, 346; Cal Span. II, 491
21. Neale, *Parliaments*, II, 128; ibid. I, 149; Ascham, *English Works*, 176; *Queen Elizabeth's Englishings*, xii; Clapham, 89
22. L. & P. XVI, 636
23. L. & P. XIX, i, 477; Mumby, 22–23; *Hearne's Sylloge*, 161–62
24. Margaret H. Swain, "A New Year's Gift from the Princess Elizabeth" in *The Connoisseur*, Vol. 183, no. 738, August 1973
25. *Statutes at Large*, V, 193
26. *Rymer's Foedera*, XV, 116; Heywood, 309; *Rymer's Foedera*, XV, 114
27. Mumby, 29
28. Cal Ven. VI, 1058

CHAPTER 2

"The noblest man unmarried in this land"

1. S. Haynes, 101; PRO SP 10/6/fo. 57
2. *Hearne's Sylloge*, 210
3. *Nugae Antiquae*, I, 65; S. Haynes, 100
4. S. Haynes, 102; ibid. 99
5. S. Haynes, 99
6. PRO SP 10/6 fo. 58v; S. Haynes, 99
7. S. Haynes, 97; ibid. 99–100
8. Mumby, 35–36; *Hearne's Sylloge*, 221–22
9. Giles, lv–lvi
10. Strype, *Cheke*, 8; Mumby, 27–28; Ascham, *English Works*, 245; Mumby, 69–72

11. Ascham, *English Works*, 216; ibid. 190; Stangford, 40; de Maisse, 95
12. Giles, lxxii; *Nugae Antiquae*, I, 96; Camden, 121
13. PRO SP 10/6/fo. 51–51v
14. PRO SP 10/6/fo. 51; ibid. 57v; S. Haynes, 102; PRO SP 10/6/fo. 58
15. PRO SP 10/6/fo. 51–51v
16. S. Haynes, 95, 89
17. S. Haynes, 95; PRO SP 10/6/fo. 58
18. S. Haynes, 96
19. Tytler, *England Under the Reigns of Edward VI and Mary*, I, 140; Dasent, II, 253–54; Haynes, 104–5
20. BM Harleian Mss 523 fo. 80
21. S. Haynes, 70; Cal. For. I, xxxv; S. Haynes, 108; ibid. 70
22. S. Haynes, 71
23. S. Haynes, 88–89
24. Cal. For. I, v
25. PRO SP 10/6/fo. 58; S. Haynes, 94
26. S. Haynes, 94; ibid. 101; ibid. 102
27. S. Haynes, 107–8; Mumby, 55
28. S. Haynes, 108; Mumby, 58; PRO SP 10/6/fo. 58v
29. Mumby, 116 (PRO SP 11/4/2)
30. Foxe, VIII, 603; Mumby, 63; Span. Cal. IX, 489
31. Stangford, passim; Cal. Patent Rolls, Edward VI, III, 239–42; ibid. 415
32. Tytler, *England Under the Reigns of Edward VI and Mary*, I, 249–50; Span. Cal. X, 215
33. Span. Cal. XI, 38; *Chronicle of Queen Jane*, 93
34. *Chronicle of Queen Jane*, 101; Wriothsley II, 88; Camden, 6
35. *Chronicle of Queen Jane*, 12

CHAPTER 3

"The second person in the realm"

1. See Madden; Cal. Ven. V, 538; ibid. VI, ii, 1054–55; Span. Cal. X, 127; Span. Cal. XI, 151
2. Span. Cal. XI, 393; Clifford, 80; Cal. Ven. VI, ii, 1058–59
3. Span. Cal. XI, 169; ibid. 228; ibid. 169
4. Vertot, II, 146; Span. Cal. XI, 220

5. Span. Cal. XI, 221; PRO 31/3/20 fo. 248; Span. Cal. XI, 252–53
6. Vertot II, 234; ibid. 273
7. *Chronicle of Queen Jane*, 93
8. Cal. Ven. V, 539; Span. Cal. XI, 334–35; ibid. 393
9. Span. Cal. XI, 292; ibid. 454
10. Vertot, II, 273–74; Span. Cal. XI, 401, 418
11. Span. Cal. XI, 418; ibid. 440
12. Span. Cal. XI, 314; PRO 31/3/21 fo. 144–45; Neale, *Parliaments*, I, 148
13. Harbison, 127; MacNalty, 230
14. Strype, *Ecclesiastical memorials*, III, i, 126
15. See Harbison, 337–39 for discussion of subject
16. Tytler, *England Under the Reigns of Edward VI and Mary*, II, 426–27; Span. Cal. XII, 125, 106
17. Tytler, *England Under the Reigns of Edward VI and Mary*, II, 313; Foxe VIII, 611; *Chronicle of Queen Jane*, 69, 65; Foxe, VIII, 607; Span. Cal. XII, 140
18. Span. Cal. XI, 335; ibid. XII, 200, 153, 166–67
19. PRO SP 11/4/2 (facsimile in Mumby)
20. Foxe, VIII, 609–10
21. Foxe, VIII, 610
22. Foxe, VIII, 610; Span. Cal. XII, 221; *Chronicle of Queen Jane*, 73–74
23. Foxe, VIII, 613; Span. Cal. XII, 230; ibid. 220
24. Foxe, VIII, 613–14
25. Span. Cal. XII, 261; Vertot, III, 237–38; Bedingfield Papers, 149, 151
26. Bedingfield Papers, 154, 158, 159, 164
27. Ibid. 161, 168–69
28. Ibid. 148, 160–61; 213, 165, 175–76
29. Span. Cal. XII, 286; Bedingfield Papers, 182–83
30. Bedingfield Papers, 193
31. Ibid. 191, 221–22
32. Ibid. 195–96; 209, 214, 208, 217
33. Span. Cal. XIII, 26
34. Bedingfield Papers, 206; Foxe, VIII, 619–21
35. Foxe, VIII, 619–21

36. Vertot, V, 126–27; Cal. Ven. VI, ii, 1060
37. PRO 31/3/22 fo. 118v–119; PRO SP 11/8/fo. 132; PRO SP 11/8/fo. 92
38. PRO 31/3/22/ fo. 118v; ibid. fo. 125; Cal. Ven. VI, i, 484
39. Strype, *Ecclesiastical memorials*, III, i, 547
40. Cal. Ven. VI, i, 423; Span. Cal. XI, 426
41. Cal. Ven. VI, ii, 836, 887
42. PRO 31/3/22 fo. 233v, 241v
43. Cal. Ven. VI, ii, 1015; PRO 31/3/22 fo. 154; Vertot, III, 2; PRO 31/3/22 fo. 221v, 175
44. Cal. Ven. VI, iii, 1538; Prescott, 378
45. Span. Cal. XIII, 372–73
46. Span. Cal. XIII, 372; K. de L. I, 311–12; Span. Cal. XIII, 387, 400
47. Neale, "The Accession of Queen Elizabeth I", in *The Age of Catherine de Medici*, 135
48. Ferria's Despatch, 329–31; Gonzalez, 39–40
49. Naunton, 7

CHAPTER 4
"God hath raised me high"

1. W. Camden, 14
2. Neale, *Parliaments*, I, 365; Hayward, 3
3. Froude, VI, 15–16
4. C. Camden, 28; Knox, *Works*, IV, 374; Henderson and McManus, 51, 54
5. Neale, *Parliaments*, I, 107; PRO SP 78/23 fo. 165; Motley, II, 199; Hodges & Fox, 19; Neale, *Parliaments*, I, 107; Cal. Ven. IX, 533
6. Feria, 331; Cal. Span. I, 7; Klarwill, 37; Cal. For. I, 176–78; Neale, *Parliaments*, I, 49; Hayward, 7
7. Hartley I, 132; Feria, 331; J. E. Neale, "Sir Nicholas Throckmorton's Advice to Queen Elizabeth", EHR, LXV, 1950; Cal. Span. I, 377
8. Read, *Cecil*, 102
9. Feria, 332; *Nugae Antiquae*, I, 66–67
10. A. G. R. Smith, *The Government of Elizabethan England*, 48
11. Peck, 15

12. Peck, 171
13. Peck, 46; HMC Sals. II, 145
14. Strype, Annals, I, i, 15; Hayward, 6–7
15. Cal. Ven. VII, 2, 11; Haigh, 64
16. Hartley, I, 136
17. Froude, VI, 16; Cal. Ven. VII, 1; Feria, 329
18. Gee, *The Elizabethan Prayer Book*, 198; Feria, 342 n; Mumby, 98
19. Cal. Span. II, 364; Feria, 332
20. Froude, VI, 16; de Maisse, 80; Fénelon, V, 158; Wernham, *The Making of Elizabethan Foreign Policy*, 11; for examples of Elizabeth ignoring her Council see Cal. For. V, 93 Cal. Scot. III, 136; Cal. Scot. V, 112
21. Klarwill, 161; *Leicester Correspondence*, 236; SP 12/139/3
22. Wright, II, 74–75
23. Wright, II, 93
24. Cal. Ven. VII, 3
25. Hayward, 15; Neville Williams, "The Coronation of Queen Elizabeth I, *Quarterly Review*, Vol. 291 (July 1953)
26. Osborn, 38, 54; Hayward, 17
27. *Chronicle of Queen Jane*, 14; Osborn, 27, 44; Hayward, 15; Osborn, 28–29
28. Janet Arnold "The Coronation Portrait of Queen Elizabeth I", *Burlington Magazine*, CXX, November 1978
29. Neale, *Parliaments*, I, 149; de Maisse, 58
30. Cal. Span. I, 401; Camden, 17
31. Cal. Span. I, 61–62; Cal. For. XII, 715
32. Hughes & Larkin, II, 102–3
33. Elton, *Parliament of England*, 153–54; Hartley, 34, 37
34. Cross, *The Royal Supremacy in the Elizabethan Church*, 24
35. Neale, *The Elizabethan House of Commons*, 288
36. Pollen, *Queen Mary's letter to the Duke of Guise*, 39
37. For the Religious Settlement of 1559 see Norman Jones, *Faith by Statute* (1982); Winthrop S. Hudson, *The Cambridge Connection and the Elizabethan Settlement of 1559* (1980)
38. Gee, *The Elizabethan Prayer Book*, 197
39. Hartley, 51
40. W. Camden, 28; Cal. Span. I, 86
41. *Zurich Letters*, I, 29; V. J. K. Brook, *Archbishop Parker*, 95; Strype, Annals, I, i, 212
42. A. Dures *English Catholicism, 1558–1642* (1983), 89; Scarisbrick, *The Reformation and the English People* (1986), 137; Susan E. Taylor, *The Crown and the North of England*, University of Manchester D, Phil. thesis (1981), 43
43. *Parker Correspondence*, 50
44. *Parker Correspondence*, 51, 58
45. Haugaard, 49–50; Ridley, *John Knox*, 213
46. *Zurich Letters*, I, 266; V. J. K. Brook, *Parker*, 87
47. *Parker Correspondence*, 157
48. A. G. Dickens, 337; *Parker Correspondence*, 65, 148
49. Heal, 262
50. F. O. White, 61; Haigh, 214; Collinson, *The Religion of Protestants*, 106; Cal. Span. I, 4
51. Heal, 206, 223
52. Rowse, *The England of Elizabeth*, 413n; Haugaard, 158
53. HMC Sals. V. 50
54. Cross, *The Royal Supremacy*, 79; Hill, *Economic Problems of the Church*, 31
55. F. O. White, 283; Heal, 242; DNB Hutton; Heal, 211
56. Feria, 333; Cal. For. I, 386; Cal Span. I, 43
57. Cal. Span. I, 3; ibid. 409; Klarwill, 94
58. Cal. For. I, 331; Span. Cal. XI, 289; Greaves, 226; Murdin, 338
59. BM Harleian Mss 444, fo. 29–29v; Neale, *Parliaments*, I, 48–49
60. Scarisbrick, *Reformation*, 485, 480–81; Cal. Span. I, 70
61. *Zurich Letters*, 2nd Series, II, 68; Cal. Ven. VII, 19; Neale, *Parliaments*, I, 47–49
62. Cal. Span. I, 9
63. Stone, *The Family, Sex and Marriage*, 197–98; C. Camden, 103–4

64. *Statutes at Large* (1891) II, 332–34
65. Melville, 94; Teulet, II, 217
66. Neale, *Parliaments*, I, 127; ibid. I, 366; Klarwill, 80, 193
67. PRO 31/3/26 fo. 134; Cal. Span. I, 73; Neale, *Parliaments*, I, 48; Cal. For. I, 299
68. Epton, 98; Greaves, 265; Pollen, *Mary's letter to the Duke of Guise*, 41
69. For a more detailed examination of this, see L. J. Smither, "Elizabeth I: a Psychological Profile", *Sixteenth Century Journal*, XV, 1984, 47–72
70. Teulet, II, 217; Cal. Span. III, 252
71. Neale, *Parliaments*, I, 112; Melville, 131; Cal. Scot. II, 292
72. Pollen, *Mary's letter to the Duke of Guise*, 41; Neale, *Parliaments*, I, 49
73. Lodge, II, 419; *Sidney Papers*, II, 217
74. Cal. Span. I, 63; ibid. 180
75. W. Camden, 83; Harington, *Tract on the Succession*, 40; Oatterson, 30; Murdin, 559
76. PRO 31/3/26 fo. 156
77. Klarwill, 193; Pollen, *Mary's letter to the Duke of Guise*, 41
78. Cal. Span. I, 463, 468
79. Murdin, 203–4; Cal. Dom. II, 12; Cal. Dom. V, 136–37
80. Cal. Scot. IV, 396; Murdin, 559–60; Fraser, 466
81. Klarwill, 114; Cal. Span. III, 274; Cal. Span. I, 387
82. Klarwill, 231; Cal. For. IX, 419; for further examples see Klarwill, 113, 156–57; Fénélon, IV, 11; Harington, *Tract on the Succession*, 40
83. *All's Well that Ends Well*, I, i, 161–64; E. Partridge, *Shakespeare's Bawdy* (1969), 220; Greaves, 119; Knappen, 452; Neale, *Parliaments*, I, 366
84. Cal. For. I, 443; Cal. For. II, 2; Cal. Span. I, 45
85. Levine, 11
86. Hardwicke Papers, I, 187
87. Hartley, 64, 60, 137–38
88. K. de L. X, 744; Goodman, I, 4; Cal. Span. I, 22–23; Parker & Martin, 281n

89. Cal. Span. I, 2; S. Haynes, 444; Feria, 329–334
90. Cal. Span. I, 37
91. S. Haynes, 212
92. Cal. For. I, 299; Klarwill, 78
93. Cal. Span. I, 18; Feria, 331; Machyn, 206; Klarwill, 113
94. Cal. Ven. VII, 361; Cal. Span. I, 73
95. Cal. For. IV, 222
96. D. A. Wilson, 45, 93
97. Cal. Ven. VII, 81; Cal. Span. I, 58; Klarwill, 113
98. Klarwill, 114–15
99. *Leicester's Commonwealth* (1641), 11; Cal. For. IV, 158
100. Wotton, 175
101. Cal. For. XXI, iii, 90
102. *Leicester's Commonwealth*, 28; Adlard, 57; A. Haynes, *The White Bear*, 151; Cal. Dom. II, 248
103. S. Haynes, 444; D. A. Wilson, 88
104. Naunton, 41–42; Cal. Span. I, 75; see R. C. McCoy, "From the Tower to the Tiltyard", *Historical Journal*, 27 (1984), 425–35; Teulet, I, 370
105. Cal. For. II, 13; Cal. Span. I, 127; Read, *Cecil*, 199; Black, *Reign of Elizabeth*, 235
106. D. A. Wilson, 17; French, 33
107. See D. A. Wilson; Eleanor Rosenberg, *Leicester, Patron of Letters* (New York 1955); Acts of the Privy Council, VII, 134; Roy Strong in *Journal of Warburg and Courtauld Institute*, 1959, XXII, 359–60
108. *Leicester Correspondence*, 176; *Nugae Antiquae*, I, 166; Winwood, I, 167; Read, *Walsingham*, I, 437; Melville, 98
109. Cal. Span. I, 208
110. Klarwill, 114–15; PRO 31/3/26 fo. 95
111. Klarwill, 95–96; Cal. Span. I, 63
112. Cal. For. II, 5; *Zurich Letters*, I, 46
113. Cal. Span. I, 108–9; Cal. For. II, 401
114. Sadler Papers, II, 43; Cal. For. II, 4; Cal. Span. I, 70
115. Klarwill, 153; ibid. 156–58
116. Cal. Span. I, 117
117. S. Haynes, 212

118. W. Tyndale, *Doctrinal Treatises etc.*, ed. H. Walter, Parker Soc. XXXII (1848), 172; J. W. Allen, 129–30
119. Knox, *Works*, IV, 373
120. Forbes, I, 130; Sadler Papers, II, 70
121. Read, *Walsingham*, I, 69; Forbes, I, 388; Sadler Papers, I, 378; Cal. For. I, 370; Murdin, 749
122. Teulet, I, 340, 356
123. Sadler Papers, II, 60
124. Sadlers Papers, II, 114
125. Teulet, I, 383; Cal. For. II, 201
126. Cal. For. II, 223–24
127. Wright, I, 7; Cal. For. II, 220–24; S. Haynes, 230
128. Wright, I, 24–25
129. S. Haynes, 253
130. S. Haynes, 260; Forbes, I, 395
131. Cal. For. III, 72; PRO SP 70/14/17 fo. 28–28v
132. Forbes, I, 454–56; S. Haynes, 305
133. S. Haynes, 349
134. Cal. For. III, 184–85; PRO SP 70/17/209 fo. 40v; PRO SP 70/17/240, fo. 100, 103

CHAPTER 5
"So great a lady that there could be no hold taken of her"

1. Hardwicke, I, 145
2. Read, *Cecil*, 219; ibid. 199
3. Read, *Cecil*, 185
4. Cal. Span. I, 175
5. Cal. Span. I, 58; Ian Aird, "The Death of Amy Robsart", EHR, LXXI, Jan. 1956; Cal. Span. I, 179
6. Adlard, 32–33
7. HMC Sals. I, 253; Haynes, 365
8. Cal. For. III, 347–48; Hardwicke, I, 164; ibid. 123
9. Hardwicke, I, 165–67
10. Cal. For. III, 498
11. Hardwicke, I, 168
12. Collinson, *Letters of Thomas Wood*, 13, i
13. Cal. Span. I, 182
14. Cal. For. IV, 103
15. K. de L. II, 567–68; Collinson, *Letters of Thomas Wood*, 13
16. Cal. For. IV, 158; ibid. 455; Fénelon, II, 121
17. Cal. For. IV, 158; PRO 31/3/26 fo. 95
18. Naunton, 8–9
19. D. Wilson, 132–3; Stone, *Aristocracy*, 426
20. Strype, *Annals*, III, ii, 387; Collinson, *Letters of Thomas Wood*, xxxv; Strype, *Annals*, III, ii, 207–8
21. W. Camden, 58
22. Haynes, 396; W. Camden, 58–59; Ellis, 2nd Series, II, 273; also see Hester Chapman, *Two Tudor Portraits* (1963)
23. J. W. Burgon, *Life of Sir Thomas Gresham* (1839), I, 485
24. See Read, *Cecil*, 194–97; Read, "Profits on Recoinage 1560–61", EHR, VI, 1935–36; A. E. Feaveryear, *The Pound Sterling*, 2nd edn, revised by E. Victor Morgan (1963), 77–84; Nichols, *Progresses*, I, 91
25. Cal. For. III, 247
26. Cal. Scot. I, 498
27. Fraser, 145; Keith, II, 602
28. Cal. Scot. I, 520
29. PRO SP 70/23/687, fo. 615 (Cal. For. III, 573)
30. Keith, II, 45, 51
31. Cal. For. IV, 278 (PRO SP 52/6/61); Cal. Scot. I, 565; S. Haynes, 372; Cal. For. IV, 278
32. Knox, II, 275–76
33. Knox, II, 294; Cal. Scot. I, 543; Cal. For. VI, 399; Cal. Scot. I, 555
34. Wright, I, 62; Pollen, *Mary's letter to the Duke of Guise*, xiv–xv; Cal. For. IV, 237
35. For Maitland's interview, see J. H. Pollen, *Mary's letter to the Duke of Guise*, 38–43
36. Ibid. 43
37. Cal. Scot. I, 638; ibid. 580
38. Cal. Scot. I, 591; ibid. 594; Cal. For. IV, 538
39. Cal. For. IV, 608; PRO SP 70/36/758 fo. 74
40. Klarwill, 215

41. Cal. For. V, 93; ibid. 105; ibid. 157
42. Cal. For. V, 21; ibid. 268
43. K. de L. III, 85; Cal. Span. I, 259
44. Hayward, 100–101; Forbes, II, 61
45. Cal. Fir. V, 458; ibid. 444
46. Cal. Span. I, 263
47. Ibid.
48. Cal. Scot. I, 666; Labanoff, I, 262
49. Cal. For. VI, 370; Forbes, II, 155
50. Forbes, II, 310
51. Cal. For. VI, 351
52. Neale, *Parliaments*, I, 94, 107–8
53. Elton, *Parliament of England*, 178–81;
    Parker Correspondence, 174
54. Neale, *Parliaments*, I, 126–27
55. Nicolas, 157; Clapham, 88–89
56. Harrison, 44; Cal. For. VI, 425 (PRO
    SP 70/59/846 fo. 48v); Forbes, II, 458
57. PRO SP 70/52/406 fo. 132; Cal. For.
    VI, 306

CHAPTER 6
"Contrarily threatenings and chidings"

1. Cal. For. VI, 617, 637
2. Harrison, 46; Hardwicke, I, 174
3. Cal. Span. I, 313
4. Cal. Scot. II, 80; Melville, 91
5. Keith, II, 206; Cal. Scot. II, 19–20
6. Cal. Scot. II, 43–44
7. Cal. Scot. II, 56–57
8. Cal. For. V, 27; Parker, *Philip II*, 88
9. Cal. Span. I, 338; Keith, II, 206
10. For Melville's visit, see Melville, 89–
    99
11. Cal. Scot. II, 95; Keith, II, 251–52;
    Wright, I, 187
12. Hardwicke, I, 173; Melville, 101
13. Cal. Scot. II, 233; Labanaff, I, 296
14. Cal. For. V, 15; *Zurich Letters*, I, 102;
    Strickland, *Scots Queens*, II, 375–76
15. See: Cal. Span. I, 176; Cal. For. V, 12–
    15; Agnes Strickland, *Lives of the
    Queens of Scotland* (1851), II, 375–76
16. Cal. For. VII, 292
17. Cal. Scot. II, 136; Murdin, 758; Keith,
    II, 329
18. Keith, II, 276; ibid. 329; Cal. Scot. II,
    146
19. Cal. Scot. II, 159; Cal. For. II, 423;
    ibid. 475
20. Cal. Scot. II, 168; Keith, II, 292; Cal.
    Scot. II, 171; Keith, II, 283
21. Keith, II, 337
22. Cal. Scot. II, 168; Melville, 103; Cal.
    Scot. II, 171
23. Cal. Scot. II, 181; ibid. 192; Teulet,
    II, 221
24. Teulet, II, 225; Cal. For. VII, 510;
    Cal. Scot. II, 228
25. Wright, I, 219–20
26. Keith, II, 404–6
27. Tytler, *Scotland*, VII, 23; Cal. Scot.
    II, 259, 264–5
28. PRO SP 52/12/fo. 538
29. Keith, II, 478–79; Murdin, 762;
    Labanoff, I, 390
30. HMC Sals. I, 286, 285; Klarwill, 206
31. PRO 31/3/25 159; ibid. 138
32. PRO SP 70/77/915 fo. 128v–29
33. Cal. For. VII, 321; Wright, I, 198;
    PRO 31/3/26 fo. 1; Klarwill, 224
34. PRO 31/3/25/ fo. 200–201
35. Klarwill, 218; ibid. 249; Wright, I, 207
36. Hasler, II, 290; Cal. Span. I, 472;
    Wright, I, 206; Cal. Span. I, 484; PRO
    31/3/26 11 Oct. 1565
37. Cal. Scot. II, 140
38. See Susan Doran, *The Political Career
    of Thomas Radcliffe, Earl of Sussex*,
    London University D. Phil. thesis,
    1977; Cal. Dom. I, 253; Wright, I, 209
39. Strype, Annals, II, ii, 387; PRO
    31/3/26 fo. 102; Cal. Span. I, 511
40. Cal. Span. I, 518; ibid. 527; PRO
    31/3/26 fo. 110
41. Cal. Span. I, 513; Cal. For. VII, 551;
    Klarwill, 258
42. Cal. For. VIII, 99
43. PRO SP 70/85/491 fo. 64; S. Haynes,
    444; HMC Sals. I, 337
44. Elton, *Parliament of England*, 162–63
45. Neale, *Parliaments*, I, 136
46. D'Ewes, 124; Hartley, I, 143; Neale,
    Parliaments, I, 140
47. Levine, 176
48. Cal. Span. I, 591–92
49. Neale, *Parliaments*, I, 147–150

50. Neale, *Parliaments*, I, 155
51. Elton, *Parliament of England*, 331–32
52. Elton, *Parliament of England*, 164; Neale, *Parliaments*, I, 163
53. Neale, *Parliaments*, I, 174–76; Hartley, I, 172–73
54. Hartley, I, 166; Haynes, 444; Hartley, I, 142

CHAPTER 7
"The general cause now of Christendom"

1. Wernham, *Before the Armada*, 272
2. Fraser, 262
3. Harrison, 49; Cal. For. VIII, 198
4. Pro SP 59/12/fo. 693
5. Cal For. VI, 58; ibid. VIII, 202; PRO SP 52/13/39 fo. 139–139v
6. Tytler, *Scotland*, VII, 115
7. Cal. For. VIII, 232; SP 59/13/fo. 238
8. SP 12/43/fo. 23
9. Cal. For. VIII, 256
10. Keith, II, 673
11. Keith, II, 668–69; Read, *Cecil*, 380
12. PRO SP 52/14/189 fo. 716
13. Wright, I, 264
14. Read, *Cecil*, 385; Cal. For. VIII, 311; Keith, II, 703–4
15. PRO SP 52/14/fo. 112; Read, *Cecil*, 385
16. Cal. For. VIII, 360; Pro SP 70/94 fo. 175v
17. Wright, I, 265
18. SP 70/95 fo. 161
19. PRO SP 70/95 fo. 356–37; HMC Bath, II, 17–18
20. Cal. For. VII, 390; PRO SP 70/94 fo. 274–274v
21. Cal. For. VIII, 421, 434; Ferrière-Percy, 208; Teulet, II, 364–67; HMC Sals. I, 353
22. Teulet, II, 369; HMC Sals. XIII, 91–92; Teulet, II, 370
23. S. Haynes, 446; ibid. 448; Cal. For. VIII, 87
24. Cal. Scot. II, 419; Read, *Cecil*, 407
25. Anderson, IV, 33, 54–55
26. Cal. Scot. II, 431
27. Anderson, IV, 38–39; ibid. 107–8
28. Anderson, IV, 74
29. Anderson, IV, 87–88
30. Harrison, 53; Labanoff, II, 434; Cal. Scot. II, 441
31. Anderson, IV, 109–10
32. Cal Scot. II, 441; ibid. 509
33. Cal. Scot. II, 511; ibid. 520–21
34. Anderson, IV, 62; Cal. Scot. II, 587
35. Murdin, 164; Cal. Scot. II, 533–34; Melville, 175–77
36. Fénelon, I, 17–18
37. Cal. Scot. II, 555; ibid. 559; ibid. 564–65
38. Cal. Scot. II, 581–82; ibid. 590
39. Neale, *Parliaments*, I, 126; ibid. 365
40. Cal. Scot. II, 475; Anderson, IV, 54; Cal. For. VIII, 550; Cal. Scot. II, 609
41. Anderson, IV, 57; Wright, I, 311
42. Cal. Scot. II, 688; Fénelon, IV, 391
43. Froude, VIII, 460n; Cal. Span. II, 19; Cal. For. VIII, 547; see also G. M. Bell, "John Man, the Last Elizabethan Ambassador Resident in Spain", *Sixteenth Century Journal*, VII, 1976
44. Elliott, 169
45. Cal. Span. I, 610; ibid. II, 7
46. PRO SP 70/102 fo. 30v
47. Read, *Cecil*, 424; K. de L. V, vii
48. G. D. Ramsay, *The Queen's Merchants and the Revolt of the Netherlands*, 92
49. See: C. Wilson; G. D. Ramsay, *The Queen's Merchants*; C. Read, "Queen Elizabeth's Seizure of the Duke of Alva's Payships", *Journal of Modern History*, V, 1933
50. Froude, VIII, 231; ibid. IX, 193
51. Labanoff, II, 184–86
52. Froude, IX, 264; Cal. Span. II, 72; ibid. 109
53. Cal. Span. II, 132–33
54. Cal. For. IX, 159
55. Sharp, 193; Cal. Span. II, 90
56. Cal. For. I, 26; Wright, I, 180; Camden, 82; Cal. Scot. II, 595
57. Melville, 177; State Trials, I, 985
58. Wright, I, 209; Fénelon, I, 78–79
59. Cal. Span. II, 91; ibid. 136–37, Fénelon, I, 330; Cal. Span. II, 91; Fénelon, I, 234–35

60. Fénelon, I, 235–36
61. Fénelon, I, 259; ibid. 236–37
62. Camden, 122; Cal. Span. II, 166
63. Fénelon, I, 322
64. Murdin, 180
65. Cal. Span. II, 97; Labanoff, II, 363; Murdin, 50
66. Cal. Span. II, 167; Murdin, 30–31; Sharp, 193
67. Murdin, 44
68. Cal. Scot. IV, 35–37
69. Fénelon, II, 169
70. Fénelon, II, 219; K. de L. V, 458; Read, *Cecil*, 451; Cal. Scot. IV, 38
71. Cal. Scot. IV, 38
72. Reid, 189
73. Sharp, 194–95, 196
74. Cal. Scot. II, 684; Fénelon, II, 302; S. Haynes, 571
75. Cal. Scot. II, 674; Cal. Dom. VII, 87; ibid. 74–75, 82
76. Sadler Papers, II, 338; Cal. Scot. II, 674; Cal. Dom. VII, 90; Sharp 196; Cal. Dom. VII, 89, 90
77. Sharp, 21; Cal. Dom. VII, 105; Wright, I, 332–33
78. Sharp, x; R. R. Reid, *Rebellion of Earls*, 179; Froude, VIII, 60
79. Reid, *King's Council in the North*, 195; Cal. For. IV, 191; Aveling, *Northern Catholics*, 11–12; Cal. Dom. VII, 64–65; Sadler Papers, II, 325; Menmuir, 4
80. *Depositions concerning the Rebellion of 1569* (Surtees Soc. XXI, 1834), 158, 161, 173, 170, 167, 191–92; Cal. Dom. VII, 112; S. Haynes, 555; Cal. Span, II, 157
81. Sharp, 28; Cal. Dom. VII, 108
82. Fénelon, II, 371; S. Haynes, 557; Sadler Papers, II, 325; Sharp, 76
83. Cal. Dom. VII, 127–29
84. S. E. Taylor, 251–53, 259; HMC Sals. I, 448–49
85. Sharp, 77
86. Cal. Dom. VII, 119–20; ibid. 128
87. Sharp, 105
88. Cal. Scot. III, 236; Sharp, 144; ibid. 122

89. Sharp, 121–22; Fénelon, II, 21; Sharp, 153; H. B. McCall, "The Rising in the North", *Yorks. Archaeological Journal*, XVIII, 1904–5, 85, 87; Cal. Dom. VII, 186; McCall, 78, 83
90. Sharp, 143; Cal. Dom. VII, 188
91. Sharp, 228–29; Cal. Dom. VII, 272
92. Loades, *Mary Tudor*, 215; J. W. Allen, 132; Cal. Span. II, 53
93. Dietz, 25, 28; Sharp, 131
94. Cal. Dom. VII, 359; Wright, I, 349
95. Cal. Span. II, 167; Cal. Dom. VII, 204
96. Sharp, 219–20; ibid. 222–23n; Cal. Dom. VII, 246
97. S. Haynes, 562, 564; Tytler, *Scotland*, VII, 463; Cal. Scot. III, 54–55; ibid. 58
98. Cal. Span. II, 217; K. de L. V, 603; Cal. Span. II, 217–18; Cal. Dom. VII, 286

CHAPTER 8
"The rarest creature that was in Europe these five hundred years"

1. Lodge, I, 499–500; Cal. Dom. VII, 194
2. Fénelon, III, 54
3. Cal. Scot. III, 136–37
4. Fénelon, III, 187–88
5. Fénelon, III, 258
6. Cross, 152–53
7. Read, *Cecil*, 264
8. S. Haynes, 591–2; Fénelon, III, 177; ibid. III, 226–7
9. Cal. Scot. III, 312; Read, *Burghley*, 27
10. Fénelon, III, 335
11. Cal. Scot. III, 287
12. S. Haynes, 623
13. Fénelon, IV, 20
14. Labanoff, III, 175
15. Hardwicke, I, 190
16. S. Haynes,, 597–8; Murdin, 42
17. Strickland, *Mary's Letters*, I, 126; State Trials, I, 1043, 1011, 1013, 1046; Froude, X, 330n
18. Cal. Rom. I, 394–6; Cal. Span. II, 300
19. Teulet, V. 76; Gachard, 194; Teulet, V, 77
20. Cal. Rome I, 437, 414; K. de L. VI, v; Gachard, 199

21. Fénelon, III, 77
22. Fénelon, III, 438
23. Fénelon, VII, 144, 179
24. Cal. For. IX, 383
25. Cal. For. IX, 384; Digges, 65; Digges, 70; Cal. Scot. IV, 105
26. Digges, 101; Cal. For. IX, 493; Fénelon, IV, 80, 94
27. Fénelon, IV, 167, 187; Fénelon, III, 468
28. Cal. For. IX, 520
29. Cal. Scot. III, 528; Murdin, 10
30. Cal. Scot. III, 570–71; ibid. 652
31. Murdin, 157, 161, 104, 102
32. Murdin, 157; ibid. 18; Cal. Scot. III, 338–39
33. Murdin, 56–57
34. State Trials, I, 1009; ibid. 1013; ibid. 971, 1026
35. Digges, 164; Cal. Scot. IV, 113; Digges, 165–66
36. Cal. Scot. IV, 25, 50; ibid. 90, 105, 107; ibid. 93
37. Cal. For. X, 32
38. Hartley, I, 324; Neale, *Parliaments*, I, 263–4; Hartley, I, 354
39. Hartley, I, 324; Neale, *Parliaments*, I, 263–34
40. Neale, *Parliaments*, I, 277; Hartley, I, 300
41. Cal. Dom. VII, 396
42. Hartley, I, 418
43. Digges, 219
44. PRO SP 70/13/506 fo. 211v (Cal. For. II, 581); S. Haynes, 368; Froude, X, 255–56; Grindal, 332–33
45. Read, *Burghley*, 63
46. Cal. For. X, 3
47. Cal. For. X, 12, ibid. 9–10
48. Cal. For. X, 29
49. Cal. For. X, 12; SP 70/122/18 fo. 49; Cal. For. XVII, 453
50. Cal. Scot. IV, 209; ibid. 238
51. SP 70/123 fo. 146
52. K. de L. VI, 225
53. Teulet, IV, 84; Read, *Walsingham*, II, 16; ibid. I, 316–17
54. SP 70/118/1222; Cal. For. IX, 415, 429; Read, *Walsingham*, I, 149

55. Murdin, 185
56. Digges, 129
57. Digges, 189
58. K. de L. VI, 485; ibid. 425
59. Cal. For. XVII, 453; Digges, 343; ibid. 127
60. Digges, 226
61. Lodge, I, 547; Read, *Walsingham*, I, 239; Lodge, I, 547

CHAPTER 9

"The weaving of Penelope"

1. Nichols, I, 315–20; Cal. Span. II, 410, 417
2. Digges, 257–58
3. Fénelon, V, 127–28; ibid. 142; Digges, 297–98; ibid. 250
4. Read, *Walsingham*, I, 264; Cal. For. X, 248
5. K. de L. IX, 521
6. K. de L. VIII, 268; Nicolas, *Hatton*, 189; ibid. 67; Cal. Scot. V, 115
7. Wright, I, 448–49
8. Cal. Scot. IV, 431
9. Cal. For. III, 104; Murdin, 231
10. Read, *Burghley*, 85
11. Wright, II, 1; K. de L. IX, 69n
12. K. de L. X, 153
13. Murdin, 321; W. R. Scott, III, 493–99
14. Read, *Walsingham*, I, 302; Susan Doran, 351
15. Murdin, 327; Cal. For. XII, 591; K. de L. X, 127
16. Digges, 297–98
17. Fénelon, VI, 117–18
18. Cal. Scot. IV, 668; ibid. V, 3
19. Fénelon, VI, 335
20. Cal. For. XII, 62–63, 73–74; ibid. 81; ibid. 294; Kervyn de Lettenhove, *Les Huguenots et les Gueux*, III, 634
21. Lodge, I, 548; Fénelon, VI, 157; Murdin, 225
22. Cal. Scot, IV, 580
23. Read, *Walsingham*, II, 124; PRO SP 52/26/13 fo. 147; Cal. Scot. V, 153
24. K. de L. X, 660; Nicolas, *Hatton*, 67
25. Gachard, V, 314; ibid. II, 340, 334; Kervyn de Lettenhove, *Les Huguenots et les Gueux*, III, 157

26. K. de L. VI, 773; ibid. VII, 489–90
27. K. de L. VIII, 280
28. Cal. For. XII, 392; Murdin, 298; K. de L. XI, 39; Cal. Span, III, 281
29. Cal. Span. II, 515
30. K. de L. VIII, 289
31. K. de L. VIII, xiii
32. Gachard, V, 205
33. K. de L. IX, 130n
34. Neale, *Parliaments*, II, 70; Hill, *Economic Problems of the Church*, 225
35. Neale, *Parliaments*, II, 99; O'Day, 133; Hill, *Economic Problems of the Church*, 140; Hill, *Society and Puritanism*, 60; O'Day, 74
36. O'Day, 135; Collinson, *Godly People*, 305; Heal & O'Day, 88
37. Hill, *Economic Problems of the Church*, 205; Neale, *Parliaments*, II, 71
38. Collinson, *Elizabethan Puritan Movement*, 27; Hill, *Society and Puritanism*, 14
39. *Puritan Manifestoes*, 17
40. Dawley, 143
41. Murdin, 262; Hill, *Society and Puritanism*, 237
42. Neale, *Parliaments*, II, 100; Elizabeth/James, 63–64; PRO 31/3/27 fo. 404
43. McGrath, 92–93; Collinson, *Letters of Thomas Wood*, 16; Collinson, *Elizabethan Puritan Movement*, 95, 73
44. Collinson, *Elizabethan Puritan Movement*, 27
45. *Parker Correspondence*, 224
46. Collinson, *Elizabethan Puritan Movement*, 101; Dawley, 81–82
47. Ibid. 199, 202
48. Collinson, *Elizabethan Puritan Movement*, 119; *Puritan Manifestoes*, 31
49. Strype, *Whitgift*, III, 33; Collinson, *Elizabethan Puritan Movement*, 33; *Zurich Letters*, I, 425
50. Grindal, 467
51. Grindal, 376–90
52. Collinson, *Grindal*, 251–52
53. K. de L. IX, 240; ibid. 329
54. Cal. For. XII, 371, 391; K. de L. IX, 404
55. K. de L. X, 27
56. K. de L. X, 163; Cal For. XII, 405
57. Cal. For. XII, 485
58. Cal. For. XII, 485; Cal. Span. II, 552–53
59. K. de L. X, 283
60. K. de L. X, 319, 321; ibid. 318
61. Cal. Span. II, 586; Cal. For. XII, 625
62. K. de L. X, 489
63. K. de L. X, 662; ibid. 678–79
64. K. de L. XI, 22; ibid. X, 665
65. K. de L. X, 680; Wright, II, 93; K. de L. X, 742; ibid. 613
66. K. de L. X, 710
67. K. de L. X, 823
68. Cal. For. XIII, 283
69. Cal. For. XIII, 401; K. de L. XI, 304
70. Wright, II, 94; W. Camden, 227; PRO 31/3/27 fo. 277; Lodge, II, 141; HMC Sals. II, 323; ibid. 311
71. W. Camden, 232; PRO 31/3/27 fo. 271v; ibid. 282v; ibid. 277; Cal. For. XIII, 487
72. Cal. Span. II, 674
73. Nicolas, *Hatton*, 107–9; HMC Sals. II, 292
74. PRO 31/3/27 fo. 366–67; Cal. Span. II, 692–93
75. HMC Sals. II, 265
76. Cal. Span, II, 627; PRO 31/3/27 fo. 378
77. Read, *Burghley*, 210
78. B. M. Willmott Dobbie, "An attempt to estimate the true rate of maternal mortality, from the sixteenth to eighteenth centuries", in *Medical History* XXVI, 1982; Eccles, 125, 100, 90–91, 121, 87–88; HMC Sals. II, 240; Read, *Walsingham*, II, 16
79. Cal. Span, II, 658–59; Stubbs, vi
80. Stubbs, 91, 71, 92
81. Stubbs, 147–48; Nicolas, *Hatton*, 133–34
82. PRO 31/3/27 fo. 410v–411
83. W. Camden, 270; *Nugae Antiquae*, I, 158
84. HMC Sals. II, 272; Murdin, 336

85. Murdin, 336–37
86. SP 12/139/3; Cal. Span. II, 704
87. Cal. Span. II, 706; Lodge, II, 161
88. *Leicester's Commonwealth*, 31; Lodge, II, 17
89. C. Read, "Letter from Robert Earl of Leicester to a Lady", *Huntingdon Library Bulletin*, IX, 1936, 24–25
90. Cal. Span. II, 511; Naunton, 41; Harrison, 126
91. George F. Warner (ed.), *The Voyage of Robert Dudley to the West Indies*, Hakluyt Society, 1899, xlv
92. Wright, II, 103–4
93. Wright, II, 104; PRO 31/3/28 fo. 9v; ibid. fo. 82v; SP 12/138/36; HMC Bath, V, 44
94. Cal. Span. II, 704; HMC Sals. II, 275–76
95. Murdin, 338
96. PRO 31/3/28 fo. 8; PRO 31/3/27 fo. 408
97. Wright, II, 107; Cal. Span. III, 45
98. HMC Sals. XIII, 180
99. Thomson, 136
100. Corbett, *Drake*, I, 70; Thomson, 135; Corbett, *Drake*, I, 277
101. Corbett, *Drake*, I, 178
102. Hampden, 237, 230; *Leicester Correspondence*, 173; K. R. Andrews, "The Aims of Drake's Expedition 1577–80", *American Hist. Rev.*, LXXIII, Feb. 1968; Thrower, 4
103. Cal. Span. III, 10
104. Cal. Dom. I, 682; H.R. Wagner, *Drake's Voyage Around the World* (1926), 204; Wright, II, 135; Cal. Span. III, 74–75
105. Cal. Span. II, 666n; C. Petrie "The Hispano-Papal Landing at Smerwick" in *The Irish Sword*, IX, 1969; J.H. Pollen, "The Irish Expedition of 1579" in *The Month*, CI, Jan.–June 1903; J. Pope-Hennessy, *Sir Walter Ralegh in Ireland* (1883), 212–13
106. Wagner, *Drake's Voyage*, 205, 201; Lewis Gibbs, *The Silver Circle* (1963), 117–18, 120; Wagner, 204

107. PRO 31/3/28 fo. 266–67; Cal. Span. III, 93
108. Corbett, I, 313–14
109. Cal. Span. III, 93; PRO 31/3/28 fo. 292–95; 307, 315; Cal. For. XV, 142–43, 172
110. Cal. For. XV, 210; Digges, 361
111. Cal. Span. III, 217; ibid. 226
112. Cal. Span. III, 226
113. W. Camden, 268; Cal. For. XV, 388; ibid. 410; W. Camden, 268
114. Read, *Walsingham*, II, 98; Cal. Span. III, 243; ibid. 251
115. Lodge, II, 203–4; Cal. Span. III, 281, 299
116. A. M. F. Robinson, "Queen Elizabeth and the Valois Princes", *English Historical Review*, II, 1887, 77; Cal. For. XIV, 541

CHAPTER 10
The Phoenix and her nest

1. Lodge, II, 193; HMC Sals. V, 510; Carey, 52–53
2. Stone, *Crisis of the Aristocracy*, 97; Sidney Papers, II, 87
3. Cal. For. X, 101; Naunton, 101n
4. Doran, 419; Stone, *Family and Fortune*, 12–13
5. Boas, 164; MacCaffrey in Bindoff, Hurstfield & Williams, 114, 121
6. A. G. R. Smith, *Servant of the Cecils*, 117
7. A. G. R. Smith, *Government of Elizabethan England*, 63; Hurstfield, *The Queen's Wards*, 342–44
8. Stone, *Crisis of the Aristocracy*, 423–24; Doran, 419; Cross, *Puritan Earl*, 81
9. Nicolas, *Hatton*, 25–26
10. Naunton, 92–93; K. de L. VIII, 266
11. Brooks, 160; Wright, II, 99
12. Brooks, 337; Camden, 401
13. John Aubrey, *Brief Lives* (Penguin, 1978), 417; Naunton, 109–10; Winton, 46; Oakeshott, 151
14. Klarwill, 339
15. Clapham, 93; Handover, 280; Winton, 11; Cecil/James, 66; Winton, 35

16. Murdin, 340; Strype, III, ii, 383
17. K. de L. X, 399; Read, *Walsingham*, III, 169
18. Lodge, I, 501; Doran, 419
19. Cal. Dom. IV, 262; Cal. Dom. I, 309
20. *Nugae Antiquae*, I, 167; Gawdy, 90–91; Pollen, *Babington Plot*, 87–88
21. *Nugae Antiquae*, I, 169, 175; Cal. For. XIX, 19–20; Rowse, *Expansion of Elizabethan England*, 341
22. Clapham, 86; Strype, *Annals*, III, ii, 382–83
23. Chambers, *Elizabethan Stage*, I, 97; Clulee, 196
24. Harington, *Tract on the Succession*, 90; Sargent, 131
25. Lodge, II, 377; HMC Sals. VI, 393
26. Spedding, I, 359; St Claire Byrne, 12; *Nugae Antiquae*, I, 170; HMC Sals. I, 477; Cal. Span. III, 473
27. MacCaffrey in Bindoff, Hurstfield & Williams, 108
28. Loades, *Tudor Court*, 3–4; Braddock, 36–37; Cal. Dom. IV, 254
29. Neale, "The Elizabethan Political Scene", in *Essays*, 151; Hurstfield, *The Queen's Wards*, 208
30. Stone, *Office under Queen Elizabeth*, 282; MacCaffrey in Bindoff, Hurstfield & Williams, 114, 120
31. *Sidney Papers*, II, 87; P. Williams, *Court and Polity*, 270; Birch, I, 136; HMC Rutland, I, 232; *Sidney Papers*, II, 37–38
32. BM Lansdowne MS 3/192; Loades, *Tudor Court*, 58; Arnold, 98–100
33. Cal. Ven. VII, 101; Percival & Percival, 48, 50; *Sidney Papers*, II, 155; de Maisse, 95
34. HMC Sals. II, 107; Wright, I, 308–9; Fénelon, I, 124
35. *Nugae Antiquae*, I, 233, 359
36. C. C. Stopes, *Henry, Third Earl of Southampton* (1922), 124; DNB Southampton; Pulman, 245–46
37. Chambers, *Sir Henry Lee*, 161; PRO SP 12/156/30
38. Cal. For. XXI, i, 86; Cal. For. IV, 338; HMC Rutland, I, 321–22; HMC Sals. X, 121
39. Cal. Span. I, 21; HMC Sals. X, 125; *Sidney Papers*, II, 122; Digges, 300, 302
40. MacCaffrey in Hurstfield, Bindoff & Williams, 114; Nichols II, 9–27; Woodworth, 62, 65, 73
41. Woodworth, 12, 14–15
42. Wilbraham, 58; Woodworth, 12–13; BM Lansdowne Mss 21/67 fo. 41; Braddock, 45
43. Woodworth, 8; Lodge, II, 202; Woodworth, 14; Dietz, 410
44. Loades, *The Tudor Court*, 209; BM Lansdowne Mss 21/67 fo. 41
45. Nichols, I, xlv–xlvi
46. Colvin, IV, 227; Spenser, *Faerie Queene*, II, x, 4; Nichols, I, 430, 490, 495
47. Yates, 78
48. Yates, 63
49. Oakeshott, 148, 81; Strong, *Gloriana*, 125; Nichols, II, 498–99; Young, 150
50. Yates, 115; Strong, *Gloriana*, 101
51. Strong, *Portraits of Queen Elizabeth I*, 25, 10, 6
52. Rodriguez-Salgado et al., 82; Strong, *The English Renaissance Miniature*, 55, 68; Strong, *Portraits of Queen Elizabeth I*, 32
53. Strong, *English Renaissance Miniature*, 118; Strong, *Portraits of Queen Elizabeth I*, 5
54. Arnold, 4–5; *Nugae Antiquae*, I, 170–71
55. See Arnold, 262–311
56. Cheyney, II, 16; Cunnington, 112–13
57. Cal. Ven. VII, 92; Arnold, 195–96
58. Cal. Span. II, 634; Arnold, 195
59. Nichols, I, 109, 113, 116; ibid. II, 251, 263
60. Arnold, 95
61. K. de L. X, 456; de Maisse, 83; Hotson, 198–99
62. Nichols, I, 323–34
63. Arnold, 332, 72, 328
64. Nichols, I, 380
65. Dent, 93; Colvin, IV, 190; Dent, 135; Lodge, II, 168; *Sidney Papers*, II, 120

66. Von Wedel, 25; Bulow & Powell, 235; Hentzner, 22

67. Hentzner, 47; Rye, 18–19; Colvin, IV, 132, 105; ibid. 36–37

68. Colvin, IV, 111; ibid. 316; ibid. 243; ibid. III, 323; ibid. IV, 108

69. Colvin, IV, 27; John Harington, *Metamotphosis of Ajax*, ed. Elizabeth Story (1962), 160; Colvin, IV, 131

70. Nichols, II, 110; Cal. Dom. I, 612; Rowse, *Elizabethan Renaissance*, I, 43; Colvin, IV, 141; Rowse, *Elizabethan Renaissance*, II, 262–63

71. Colvin, IV, 27; Rowse, *Elizabethan Renaissance*, II, 262–63; Nichols, I, 380, II, 255; Arnold, 232–33

72. Yates, 99–100; R. Strong, "The Popular Celebration of the Accession Day of Queen Elizabeth", *Journal of Warburg and Courtauld Institutes*, XXI, 1958

73. Carey, 33; Von Wedel, 258

74. Collinson, *Elizabethan Puritan Movement*, 75; Nichols, II, 263; McClure, I, 180; Nichols, II, 241; Patterson, 30

75. Nichols, I, 439–40; Dasent, XXII, 324

76. Chambers, *Elizabethan Stage*, I, 214; Bradbrook, 67; Chambers, *Elizabethan Stage*, II, 34–35; Gair, 4–6

77. J. F. Andrews, 110; Chambers, *Elizabethan Stage*, IV, 296

78. DNB Tarlton; Cal. Dom. II, 541

79. DNB Shakespeare; Hotson, *First Night of Twelfth Night*, 180

80. Collinson, *Elizabethan Puritan Movement*, 65; Lehmberg in Guth & McKenna, 61; Loades, *Tudor Court*, 172–73

81. Rye, 15–16; Rowse, *Elizabethan Renaissance*, II, 85; Greaves, 464

82. W. L. Woodfill, *Musicians in English Society from Elizabeth to Charles I* (Princeton, 1953); Hentzner, 33

83. Nichols, I, 267; Melville, 96; Fénelon, V, 96; PRO 31/3/28 fo. 205; Rye, 12

84. PRO 31/3/27 fo. 262; Grindal, 379–80; Naunton, 18

85. Cal. Span. II, 50; Nichols, I, 539

86. Nichols, I, 532; ibid. 146

87. Nichols, II, 159; ibid. I, 315; ibid. I, 338–39

88. Nichols, I, 385

89. Lodge, II, 367–68; HMC de l'Isle, II, 477; Dewar, 176; Cal. For. XIII, 159

90. Cal. Span. II, 351; Wright, II, 61

91. Woodworth, 13; ibid. 70; BM Lansdowne Mss XVI/52 fo. 107; ibid. XXI/67 fo. 141v

92. Lodge, II, 75; Woodworth, 13; BM Lansdowne Mss XXI/67 fo. 141v

93. Nichols, I, 426; Cal. Dom. II, 58

94. Strype, *Annals*, III, ii, 381; Nichols, II, 56n; Brennecke, 35–36; Nichols, III, 101

95. *Egerton Papers*, 342, 347; Nichols, II, 236–37; ibid. I, 456; Jean Wilson, 24

96. Nichols, I, 378; Leslie Hotson, *Queen Elizabeth's Entertainment at Mitcham* (1953), 11

97. Wright, II, 482–83; McClure, 177–78; *Sidney Papers*, I, 376; Hotson, *Queen Elizabeth's Entertainment at Mitcham*, 8–9

98. HMC Sals. V, 290; Nicolas, *Hatton*, 270; SP 12/161/15

99. HMC Sals. XI, 174–75; Chambers, *Sir Henry Lee*, 180

100. Chambers, *Elizabethan Stage*, I, 108–9; Haynes, 598; Nicolas, *Hatton*, 223

101. HMC Sals. XI, 184–85, 189, 211

102. SP 12/161/15; Nichols, II, 60–61

103. Nichols, I, 83; *Nugae Antiquae*, I, 314–15; Nichols, III, 119–21

104. A. G. R. Smith, *Servant of the Cecils*, 108; BM Lansdowne Mss 108, fo. 86

105. Nichols, II, 436

106. Nichols, I, 319–20; ibid. 435; N. Williams, *All the Queen's Men*, 160

107. Nichols, I, 514–15

108. Jean Wilson, 122; Chambers, *Sir Henry Lee*, 89

109. McClure, 177–78; Strong, *Cult of Elizabeth*, 71; Nichols, III, 132–34

110. Nichols, III, 110–15

111. Hotson, 199; Naunton, 74; Hurstfield & Smith, 163; HMC Rutland, I, 107; *Nugae Antiquae*, I, 170; BM Add. Mss 41499 B, fo. 13–14

CHAPTER XI
"The blood even of her own kinswoman"

1. Wright, II, 102; Read, *Walsingham*, II, 280; Pollen, *English Catholics in the Reign of Queen Elizabeth*, 261
2. See C. Haigh, "The Continuity of Catholicism in the English Reformation", *Past and Present*, 93, 1981; P. McGrath & J. Rowe, "Marian Priests under Elizabeth I", *Recusant History*, XVII, 1984
3. Pollen, *English Catholics in the Reign of Elizabeth*, 257; Douai Diaries, xiii
4. Anstruthers, 224–25
5. Cal. Span. II, 707
6. Waugh, 127
7. Wright, II, 153
8. See C. Haigh, "From Monopoly to Minority", *Transactions Royal Historical Society*, 5th Series, XXXI, 1981; also P. McGrath, "Elizabethan Catholicism. A Reconsideration", *Journal of Ecclesiastical History*, XXXV, 1984
9. Haigh, "From Monopoly to Minority", loc. cit.; Dures, 23
10. Neale, *Parliaments*, I, 383
11. See Elton, *Parliament of England*, 186–87; Neale, *Parliaments*, I, 388
12. Cal. Dom. II, 69; Cal. Scot. IV, 272; HMC Sals. VIII, 41
13. Waugh, 126, 140
14. A. O. Meyer, 138
15. Bossy, *English Catholic Community*, 37; HMC, Various Collections 37–43; Knox, *Allen Memorials*, 300; P. Holmes, *Resistance and Compromise* (1982), 178
16. Knox, *Allen Memorials*, ix; Kingdom, 121–22; G. Mattingly, "William Allen and Catholic Propaganda", in *Travaux d'humanisme et renaissance*, XXVIII, 1957

17. See Marion Colthorpe, "Edmund Campion's Alleged Interview with Queen Elizabeth", in *Recusant History*, XVII, 1985; E. E. Reynolds, 182
18. *Memoirs of Father Robert Parsons*, Catholic Record Society, Miscellany IV (1907), 43–45
19. Anstruther, 164?
20. Pollen, *Unpublished Documents*, 336; Challoner, 10, 53, 148; Pollen, *Unpublished Documents*, 186
21. See J. H. Langbein, *Torture and the Law of Proof* (1977), 73, 100–119; Robert Southwell, *An humble supplication to her Majesty*, ed. R. C. Bald (1953), 34; John Gerard, *The Autobiography of an Elizabethan*, trans. Phillip Caraman (1951), 72
22. Pollen, *Unpublished Documents*, 207; Challoner, 177; Pollen, *Unpublished Documents*, 210
23. HMC Sals. XI, 519; Strype, IV, 185–86
24. E. E. Reynolds, 147; Kingdom, 47; Bernard Basset, *The English Jesuits* (1967), 119
25. McGrath, 198–200; Aveling, *Northern Catholics*, 122; McGrath, 198–200
26. Aveling, *Handle and the Axe*, 67; Cal. Dom. IV, 356
27. HMC Sals. XIII, 188–89
28. Lodge, II, 2; ibid. 42; Labanoff, IV, 236; ibid. 314
29. Cal. Span. II, 581
30. Cal. For. XII, 506; Sadler Papers, 195; Lodge, II, 255; Cal. Scot. VII, 410; Cal. For. XII, 506
31. Lodge, II, 52; Nicolas, *Hatton*, 197
32. Cal.Scot. VI, 26; Wright, II, 254
33. Cal. Border, I, 82
34. Cal. Span. III, 207–8
35. Cal. Span. III, 336, 333
36. Cal. Scot. VI, 56; ibid. 116–18
37. Cal. Scot. VI, 498
38. Cal. Span. III, 510; Read, *Walsingham*, II, 382–83
39. Harleian Miscellany (1809 ed.), III, 193–200; Bardon Papers, 53–54; HMC Sals. XIII, 273–74

40. Cal. Span. III, 516–17
41. PRO SP 53/13/fo. 69v
42. Cal. Scot. VI, 79
43. Cal. Scot. VI, 421; Sadler Papers, II, 218
44. Labanoff, VI, 125, 133–40
45. A.O. Meyer, 271; Knox, *Allen Memorials*, xlviii
46. Read, *Walsingham*, II, 370–71; Strickland, *Mary's Letters*, II, 28–29
47. Cal. Dom. II, 126; ibid. 210
48. Motley, *United Netherlands*, I, 327–28; *Leicester Correspondence*, 236
49. Neale, *Parliaments*, II, 119; Cal Scot. IX, 15; Cal. For. XXI, ii, 140–41
50. Strickland, II, 30; Neale, *Parliaments*, II, 50
51. State Trials, I, 1161–62; Cressy in Guth & McKenna, 221–24
52. Harington, *A Tract on the Succession to the Crown*, 37; Neale, *Parliaments*, II, 120
53. Sadler Papers, II, 36
55. Neale, *Parliaments*, II, 36
55. State Trials, I, 1163–64
56. Motley, *United Netherlands*, I, 320–21; Cal. For. XIX, 618
57. HMC Bath, V, 45; Motley, I, 298; Wilson, 83
58. *Leicester Correspondence*, 5; Cal. For. XX, 8; SP 12/181/42; *Leicester Correspondence*, 7–8
59. Read, *Walsingham*, III, 123; Cal. For. XX, 202
60. *Leicester Correspondence*, 102–3; *Somers Tracts*, ed. Walter Scott (1809), I, 417
61. *Leicester Correspondence*, 12–13
62. Strong & Van Dorsen, 32; *Leicester Correspondence*, 466; Strong & Van Dorsen, 46, 60
63. *Leicester Correspondence*, 30–31; ibid. 63; Cal. For. XX, 320
64. *Leicester Correspondence*, 110
65. *Leicester Correspondence*, 114, 118, 112, 151
66. Cal. For. XX, 452; *Leicester Correspondence*, 197; Cal. For. XX, 500; *Leicester Correspondence*, 193

67. *Leicester Correspondence*, 268
68. *Leicester Correspondence*, 279; ibid. 237; Cal. For. XX, xlvii; Motley, I, 462n; *Leicester Correspondence*, 243
69. Motley, I, 499
70. Cal. For. XXI, ii, 80
71. J.E. Neale, "Queen Elizabeth and the Netherlands", EHR XLV, 1930, 385, 375–76
72. Cruickshank, 23, 4; Cal. For. XX, 446–47
73. Neale, EHR XLV, 1930, 386; *Leicester Correspondence*, 199
74. Neale, EHR XLV, 1930, 377–78; Cal. For. XXI, ii, 172; ibid. XX, 309
75. *Leicester Correspondence*, 325; Cruickshank, 143, 54–55
76. *Leicester Correspondence*, 13; Neale, EHR XLV, 1930, 388–89; D. Wilson, 80; *Leicester Correspondence*, 324; Cal. For. XXI, ii, 94
77. Cal. For. XXI, ii, 94; ibid. XXI, iii, 396; Neale, EHR XLV, 1930 394
78. SP 12/190/10
79. Dietz, II, 55; *Leicester Correspondence*, 344
80. Cal. For. XXI, II, 106; *Leicester Correspondence*, 312
81. *Leicester Correspondence*, 341; Cal. For. XXI, ii, 94
82. *Leicester Correspondence*, 345; ibid. 438; Cal. For. XX, 126; ibid. 451
83. Cal. For. XXI, ii, 193; ibid. 197
84. *Leicester Correspondence*, 449; Motley, II, 189
85. Cal. Scot. VIII, 566; ibid. 522; Morris, 11; ibid. 40
86. Morris, 49, 51, 126
87. Morris, 258
88. Cal. Span. III, 579; Murdin, 517; State Trials, I, 1213; Pollen, *Babington Plot*, 62
89. Pollen, *Babington Plot*, 21–22
90. Cal. Scot, VIII, 665; ibid. 521; Morris, 224
91. Pollen, *Babington Plot*, 41
92. Morris, 234–35
93. Cal. Scot. IX, 15; Pollen, *Babington Plot*, clxxi

94. Cal. Scot. VIII, 687; W. Camden, 343
95. *Bardon Papers*, 45
96. W. Camden, 344–45
97. Morris, 267–68; ibid. 286
98. Cal. Scot. IX, 52; State Trials, I, 1169
99. Cal. Span. III, 597; State trials, I, 1133; Cal. Scot. IX, 102
100. State Trials, I, 1212
101. Neale, *Parliaments*, II, 110–11
102. Ibid. II, 106; Cal. Scot. IX, 154
103. Neale, *Parliaments*, II, 126–29
104. Morris, 307
105. Labanoff, VI, 475–80; Morris, 338–39; *Leicester Correspondence*, 481; Morris, 346–47
106. Rait & Cameron, 25; ibid. 60–61
107. HMC Sals. III, 196
108. Rait & Cameron, 60–61, 69
109. Rait & Cameron, 80
110. Rait & Cameron, 148–49
111. Von Raumer, 368; Harrison, 183; Cal. Scot. IX, 247; Rait & Cameron, 171
112. Cal. Scot. IX, 119; ibid. 252; Cal. Dom. II, 361
113. Cal. Scot. IX, 287, 288; ibid. 297
114. Cal. Scot. IX, 291, 294
115. Cal. Scot. IX, 291, 292
116. Ibid. 292, 299–300
117. Strickland, *Mary's Letters*, II, 158, 162, 164
118. Cal. Scot. IX, 293; Wright, II, 332; HMC Sals. III, 22021; Cal. Scot. IX, 286; Strype, *Annals*, III, ii, 407
119. Neale, *Parliaments*, II, 141–42
120. Cal. For. XXI, i, 236; ibid. 242
121. Cal. Scot. IX, 300; ibid. 285
122. HMC Sals. III, 234, 230
123. See B. M. Ward, "Queen Elizabeth and William Davidson", EHR XLIV, 1929; R. B. Wernham, "The disgrace of William Davidson, EHR XLVI, 1931
124. Read, *Burghley*, 374; SP 12/200/20; Read, *Burghley*, 378
125. Cal. Scot. IX, 443–44; Strickland, *Mary's Letters*, II, 226; Teulet, IV, 197

CHAPTER 12

"I myself will take up arms"

1. Read, *Walsingham*, III, 240–41; Cal. For. XXI, ii, 377; Motley, II, 248–49
2. Wright, II, 338; Cal. Dom. II, 404; Read, *Walsingham*, III, 241
3. Naval Miscellany, IV, 8; ibid. 3–4; Van der Essen, V, 159; Parker & Martin, 110; Cal. Span. III, 343; ibid. 527–28
4. Van der Essen, V, 161; G. Parker in *History Today*, XXXVIII, May, 1988; Parker & Martin, 114; Duro, I, 252, 274
5. Parker & Martin, 117
6. Ibid. 344; L. V. Pastor, *History of the Popes* (1932), ed. R. F. Kerr, XXII, 34, 51
7. Corbett, *Spanish War*, I, 100; Parker, *History Today*, May 1988
8. Corbett, *Spanish War*, 106–7; ibid. 101; Cal. Dom. II, 403
9. Corbett, *Spanish War*, 108
10. Cal. For. XXI, iii, 341–42; ibid. 49; ibid. 18; Dasent, XV, 176–77
11. Cal. For. XXI, iii, 227
12. Cal. For. XXI, iii, 28, 54; Cal. For. XXI, iv, 485–86
13. Cal. For. XXI, iii, 122; ibid. 408; Wright, II, 354–55
14. Naval Miscellany, IV, 9
15. Motley, II, 310
16. Cal. For. XXI, i, 638
17. John Harvey, *A discoursive problem concerning prophecies* (1588), 89, 115; Mattingly, 167; Cal. Span, IV, 252
18. Harvey, 123
19. W. Allen, *Admonition to the nobility and people of England & Ireland, AD 1588* (reprinted 1842), 54, 19, 28
20. Read, *Burghley*, 407; Motley, II, 407
21. Read, *Burghley*, 405
22. Waters & Naish, 3–4; Parker & Martin, 51
23. Laughton, I, 201
24. Cruickshank, 24; Read, *Burghley*, 415; SP 12/198/63
25. Cal. Dom. II, 387; SP 12/198/64
26. Cal. For. XXI, iv, 312; Dasent XV, xiii; Cal. Span, IV, 241; Wright, II, 358–59; Cal. Dom. II, 471

27. Dasent, XVI, 282, 316, 95; Laughton, I, 156–57

28. Laughton, I, 148, 133, 170

29. R. W. Kenny, *Elizabeth's Admiral* (1970); Corbett, *Drake*, II, 186; Naval Miscellany, IV, 53; Laughton, I, 201

30. Cal. Span. IV, 296; Laughton, I, 201; ibid. 193

31. Laughton, I, 204

32. Cal. Span, IV, 187–88; Fernandez-Armesto, 93; Lewis, *Armada Guns*, 177, 180; Laughton, I, 359

33. Fernandez-Armesto, 6; Cal. Span. IV, 207; ibid. 317–18

34. W. Camden, 411

35. Laughton, II, 63; ibid. 12; ibid. 361

36. Cal. Span. IV, 396

37. Cal. Span. IV, 183; Naval Miscellany, IV, 23; Parker & Martin, 185

38. W. Camden, 415

39. Parker & Martin, 201–2; Cal. Span. IV, 445; Laughton, II, 11; Cal. Span. IV, 444, 446

40. Laughton, II, 40

41. Cal. Scot. IX, 588; H. G. Stafford, 23; Cal. Scot. IX, 533; HMC Sals. III, 322; Naval Miscellany, IV, 23

42. Miller Christy, 45, 47

43. Cal. Span, IV, 301; Laughton, I, 211; Felix Barker, *History Today*, XXXVIII (May 1988); HMC Foljambe (15th Report, Appendix, part v, 1897), 29–30

44. Van der Essen, V, 204; Cal. Span, IV, 262; HMC Foljambe, 49, 53–54, 56, 58

45. Cal. Span, IV, 251–52

46. Christy, 47–48

47. Cabala (1691), 343; Neale, "The Sayings of Queen Elizabeth", in *The Age of Catherine de Medici*, 190; Christy, 52; Felix Barker, *History Today*, XXXVIII, May 1988

48. Christy, 55; Wright, II, 391; Laughton, II, 82–83; "The Progress of Queen Elizabeth to the Camp at Tilbury", *British Museum Quarterly*, X (1936), 166

49. Laughton, II, 65; ibid. I, lxv; G. B. Harrison, 193–94

50. Laughton, II, 59; HMC Foljambe, 59, Read, *Burghley*, 431

51. Dietz, 55; Read, *Burghley*, 424–25; Read, *Walsingham*, III, 312

52. Laughton, II, 140; Naval Miscellany, IV, 75; W. Camden, 417; Laughton, II, 138–39

53. Cal. Span. IV, 432

54. Howarth, 210; Parker & Martin 258; Howarth, 243

55. Parker, *Philip II*, 4, 55; Parker & Martin, 258, 263; Cal. Ven. VIII, 409

56. Tenison, VII, 387; HMC Bath, V, 217

57. Cal. Span. IV, 421; Cal. Dom. II, 489; Christy, 45

58. W. Camden, 419; Cal. Span. IV, 421; BM Cotton Mss, Caligula DI, fo. 333; HMC Bath, V, 94; Cal. Span, IV, 481

CHAPTER 13
"The only wonder of time's begetting"

1. Devereux, I, 207

2. Devereux, I, 172

3. Ibid. I, 186

4. HMC Bath, V, 218

5. HMC De l'Isle, II, 540

6. Wotton, 173–74; ibid. 170; Devereux, I, 292

7. Strong, *Cult of Elizabeth*, 56–83

8. Lodge, II, 418; Young, 70, 72; *Sidney Papers*, I, 362

9. Devereux, I, 497

10. Collinson, *Letters of Thomas Wood*, 15; Spedding, II, 248; Cal. Dom. V, 539–40; Miller McClure, *The Paul's Cross Sermons* (1958), 84

11. Birch, I, 130; Wotton, 175; Devereux, I, 446; Naunton, 110

12. Wotton, 162; Carey, 17–18

13. Birch, I, 167; ibid. 172; Wotton, 166; Cal. Dom. V, 88–89; HMC Sals. XIII, 549–50

14. Devereux, I, 187

15. Naunton, 120; Cal. Dom. II, 566

16. De Maisse, 90; Naunton, 8; *Sidney Papers*, II, 8

17. Wernham, *After the Armada*, 76–77; ibid. 94

18. Lodge, II, 334–35
19. Cheyney, I, 168; Corbett, II, 331; Wernham, *After the Armada*, 104
20. Cal. Dom. II, 600–601; Wernham, *After the Armada*, 114
21. Cal. Dom. II, 608; Cheyney, I, 183; Wernham, *After the Armada*, 130
22. Cal. Span. IV, 89
23. *List and Analysis*, I, 290; Lodge, II, 372–73; Harrison, 209
24. *List and Analysis*, I, 326
25. Wotton, 165; Harrison, 209
26. Unton Correspondence, 55; Harrison 210–211; Unton Correspondence, 73
27. J. B. Black, *Elizabeth and Henry IV*, 45; HMC Sals., IV, 142
28. J. B. Black, *Elizabeth and Henry IV*, 50
29. *List and Analysis*, IV, 398
30. *List and Analysis*, IV, 319; Harrison, 225; Wright, II, 456
31. R. B. Outhwaite in P. Clark, 25; Read, *Burghley*, 562n; Wernham, *After the Armada*, 415
32. Cal. Dom. IV, 313; Outhwaite in P. Clark, 25; Cal. Dom. III, 38
33. Neale, *Parliaments*, II, 201; Wernham, *After the Armada*, 80; R. B. Outhwaite in P. Clark, 26
34. Read, *Burghley*, 439, 458; Wernham *After the Armada*, 416; Chamberlain, I, 59
35. Read, *Burghley*, 439; Wernham, *After the Armada*, 80; Dietz, 63; Outhwaite in P. Clark, 26; Outhwaite, *Inflation in Tudor and Stuart England* (1969); Read, *Burghley*, 473
36. K. R. Andrews, *Elizabethan Privateering* (1964), 73; Stone, *An Elizabethan: Sir Horatio Palavicino* (1956), 218
37. Cal. Dom. IV, 275; Unton Correspondence, 376; Wernham, *After the Armada*, 417; Cal. Dom. III, 342
38. Cheyney, II, 9; P. Clark, 54; Cal. Dom. IV, 317
39. Collinson, *Elizabethan Puritan Movement*, 218–19, 225
40. Collinson, *Elizabethan Puritan Movement*, 206
41. Knappen, 275; Cross, 200, 204
42. Neale, *Parliaments*, II, 26
43. Ibid. 65–66
44. Ibid. 73
45. Ibid. 74–75
46. Collinson, *Elizabethan Puritan Movement*, 280
47. Neale, *Parliaments*, II, 149; Collinson, *Elizabethan Puritan Movement*, 307
48. Neale, *Parliaments*, II, 145
49. *Marprelate Tracts*, ed. William Pierce (1911), 25, 24, 79, 286, 118
50. William Pierce, *An Historical Introduction to the Marprelate Tracts* (1908), 197
51. Unton Correspondence, 372; Cal. Dom. III, 65; ibid. 74
52. *List and Analysis*, II, 115; Murdin, 664
53. Murdin, 657; Cal. Dom. III, 273; Edwards, II, 51
54. Nicolas, *Hattan*, 497
55. Naunton, 138; Neale, *House of Commons*, 244; Handover, 43
56. Wright, II, 367
57. Cal. Dom. III, 65
58. *Sidney Papers*, I, 231; Birch, I, 165; de Maisse, 4
59. Lodge, II, 433; *Sidney Papers*, I, 326; Cal. Dom. II, 97; *Sidney Papers*, I, 357; Cal. Dom. II, 97
60. Devereux, I, 282–83; Strype, III, ii, 307
61. Unton Correspondence, 317; Birch, I, 125–26; ibid. 146
62. Birch, I, 153
63. Cal. For. XXI, i, 276
64. Birch, I, 149
65. Cal. Dom. III, 445–46, 448
66. Birch, I, 152; Cal. Dom. III, 444; see Arthur Dimock "The Conspiracy of Dr Lopez", EHR IX, 1894; M. A. S. Hume, "The so-called conspiracy of Dr Lopez", *Transactions of the Jewish Historical Society of England*, VI, 1908–10
67. Birch, I, 166

68. Birch, I, 149; ibid. 130; ibid. 271;
HMC Sals. V, 188–89
69. Corbett, II, 429; Dietz, 77
70. HMC Sals. VI, 169
71. HMC Sals. VI, 171
72. Harrison, 245; HMC Sals. VI. 195
73. Cal. Dom. IV, 272
74. Birch, II, 49; HMC Sals. VI, 329–30;
Birch, II, 96
75. Cheyney, II, 90; HMC Sals. VI, 329;
Devereux, I, 375
76. *List and Analysis*, III, 328; Stone,
Crisis of the Aristocracy, 71; Cal. Dom.
III, 118
77. Birch, II, 61; ibid. I, 481
78. Birch, II, 153; ibid. 61
79. *Sidney Papers*, II, 26
80. *Sidney Papers*, II, 26
81. HMC Sals. IX, 11
82. *Sidney Papers*, II, 42, 54; ibid. 24, 55
83. Devereux, I, 419; Harrison, 249
84. HMC Sals. VII, 306
85. HMC Sals. VII, 433; Harrison, 254
86. Devereux, I, 461; W. Camden, 534
87. Edwards, I, 245; K. R. Andrews,
Trade, Plunder and Settlement, 238
88. Cal. Dom. II, 600–601; Cal. For. IV,
237
89. *Sidney Papers*, II, 75; W. Camden, 536
90. Devereux, I, 462–63; Cal. Dom. IV,
529
91. *Sidney Papers*, II, 77; de Maisse, 71
92. Cal. Dom. V, 30
93. De Maisse, 107
94. Chamberlain, I, 38
95. Motley, II, 488, 490
96. HMC Sals. VIII, 269; ibid. 441
97. Motley, II, 497
98. W. Camden, 555–56
99. Birch, II, 385–86; ibid. 387
100. Read, *Burghley*, 531
101. Wright, II, 488; Birch, II, 390
102. Chamberlain, I, 43
103. Chamberlain, I, 43; Cal. Dom. V, 88–
89
104. Birch, II, 390–91
105. HMC Sals. IX, 302
106. HMC Sals. IX, 4; Chamberlain, I, 69,
71; Devereux, II, 23

CHAPTER 14
"The tribute of all mortal creatures"

1. Cal. Dom. VI, 198; BM Cotton Mss,
Caligula C.IV, fo. 321; Wright, II,
149; Rowse, *Expansion of Elizabethan
England*, 126; Wright, II, 107; Canny,
30
2. Spenser, 53
3. W. Camden, 63
4. Quinn, 67; Bagwell, II, 449
5. Canny, 19
6. Bagwell, III, 128; Canny, 1
7. Quinn, 127–28
8. Spenser, 104
9. Canny, 134–35; Wright, I, 485; Canny,
121; Bagwell, II, 289
10. Bagwell, III, 286; Devereux, II, 28
11. Bagwell, III, 38; Quinn, 135; Bagwell,
III, 147
12. Canny, 155; Dietz, 59; Bagwell, II, 97;
ibid. III, 136
13. Rowse, *Expansion of Elizabethan
England*, 139; Canny, 139
14. Bagwell, III, 199
15. Falls, 224
16. Spenser, 88–89
17. Bagwell, III, 463–64
18. Cal. Dom. V, 350; Wright, I, 485; Cal.
Irish. VIII, 115; Bagwell, III, 264;
Wright, I, 387
19. Falls, 222
20. Spedding, II, 182; Falls, 232; Cal.
Irish. VIII, 30–31, 65; Cal. Dom. V,
348; Falls, 228
21. Cal. Irish, VIII, 5; Devereux, II, 18–
19
22. Cal. Irish. VIII, 106
23. Devereux, II, 20; ibid. 24
24. Cal. Irish. VIII, 42
25. Cal. Irish. VIII, 123; Chamberlain, I,
74
26. Devereux, II, 51; ibid. 40–41
27. Devereux, II, 43–45
28. Cal. Irish. VIII, 98–100
29. Devereux, II, 63
30. Cecil/James, 107–109
31. Cal. Irish, VIII, 136
32. *Nugae Antiquae*, I, 305–6

33. *Sidney Papers*, II, 127
34. Cal. Irish. VIII, 1
35. Winwood, I, 118–19; Bagwell, III, 348–49
36. *Sidney Papers*, II, 134–35, 141
37. Spedding, II, 249
38. HMC Sals. X, 183; Cal. Dom. V, 347–48; HMC De l'Isle and Dudley, II, 402
39. Spedding, II, 177
40. Spedding, II, 177; Cal. Dom. V, 393–94
41. *Sidney Papers*, II, 169
42. HMC Sals. X, 199
43. Devereux, II, 127; ibid. 125–26; Spedding, III, 135–36
44. Devereux, II, 120
45. Cecil/James, 101, 96
46. Cecil/James, 104
47. Murdin, 639, 641; Birch, II, 183
48. Cal. Scot. XIII, xv; Cecil/James, 9, 82–83
49. Stafford, 222–23
50. Birch, II, 478; Cal. Dom. V, 577–78; Cecil/James, 90
51. *Nugae Antiquae*, I, 179
52. W. Camden, 603
53. For descriptions of Essex's rebellion, see Cal. Dom. V, 550–51; ibid. 586–87; HMC Sals. VI, 46–47; ibid. 67–68; Spedding, II, 266–71
54. Jardine, 347
55. A. Wall, "An Account of the Essex Revolt", in *Bulletin of Institute of Historical Research*, 54, 1981; Cecil/Carew, 69
56. Winwood, I, 301; Chamberlain, I, 119
57. Laffleur de Kermaingant, *Boissise*, I, 477
58. Jardine, 314, 350, 360
59. Ibid. 363
60. Jardine, 367; Devereux, II, 172, 185
61. Laffleur de Kermaingant, *Boissise*, I, 502–3; Essex's death warrant is on display in the King's Library in the British Museum; Cal. Dom. V, 591–92
62. Cal. Dom. V, 591; ibid. 592–94
63. HMC Sals. XI, 295; Elizabeth/James, 76–77

64. Cal. Dom. V. 598–99; Miller Maclure, *The Paul's Cross Sermons* (1958), 83–84; HMC Sals. XII, 201
65. Spedding, II, 318; W. Camden, 612; HMC Sals. XI, 285; ibid. 586
66. HMC Sals. X, 382; PRO 31/3/32 fo. 45
67. Dietz, *Parliaments*, 87, 93; Cal. Dom. V. 476; Neale, II, 413–14; Wilbraham's Journal, 49; Cal. Irish. VIII, 98; Cecil/Carew, 147–48
68. HMC Sals. XIV, 232; ibid. VI, 845; A. G. R. Smith, *Servant of the Cecils*, 67; Birch, I, 130
69. Goodman, I, 96–97; Stone, *Crisis of the Aristocracy*, 158, 490; Cecil/James, 59
70. Stone, *Crisis of the Aristocracy*, 483–85; W. Camden, 609
71. Clapham, 87; Cal. Dom. VII, 6; G. D. Ramsay, *The Queen's Merchants and the Revolt of the Netherlands*, 158; K. de L. VI, 722–23, 749
72. Stone, *Crisis of the Aristocracy*, 490; Cal. Dom. II, 688; Neale, "The Elizabethan Political Scene", passim, in *The Age of Catherine de Medici and Essays in Elizabethan History*; HMC Sals. XI, 433–34; ibid. X. 347
73. Nichols, *Progresses*, III, 553; Birch, I, 354–55; Hurstfield, *The Queen's Wards*, 346; Neale, *The Elizabethan Political Scene*, 151
74. HMC Sals. XI, 324
75. Neale, *Parliaments*, II, 350, 379, 385
76. Ibid. 389–91
77. Ibid. 416
78. Cal. Scot. XIII, ii, 1013; Laffleur de Kermaingant, *Boissise*, I, 477; Cal. Dom. VI, 260
79. J. B. Black, *The Reign of Elizabeth*, 494; Laffleur de Kermaingant, *Beaumont*, I, 39
80. Naunton, 14; *Nugae Antiquae*, I, 235
81. *Nugae Antiquae*, I, 315; *Sidney Papers*, II, 210; HMC De l'Isle and Dudley, I, 481; *Sidney Papers*, II, 214
82. HMC Sals. XI, 354; ibid. 362; Chamberlain, I, 160

83. De Maisse, 60–61; Bulow & Powell, 51; Chamberlain, I, 115; Cal. Scot. XIII, 974; *Nugae Antiquae*, II, 218; Birch, II, 512

84. Motley, III, 595–96; de Maisse, 60–61

85. HMC Sals. II, 159; Cal. Dom. IV, 487; ibid. VI, 232

86. HMC Sals. VI, 139; *Nugae Antiquae*, II, 217; de Maisse, 37–38; ibid. 82

87. De Maisse, 58–59, 61

88. *Sidney Papers*, II, 229–231; Bagwell, III, 415

89. Platter, 192; Stettin, 51; de Maisse, 25, 82

90. Platter, 192; de Maisse, 25, 39, 26

91. Falls, *Mountjoy*, 123; Moryson, II, 424

92. Winwood, I, 378; Rowse, *Expansion of Elizabethan England*, 435; Moryson, III, 129

93. Moryson, III, 131; ibid. 230–31; ibid. 174; ibid. 189–90

94. Cecil/Carew, 143; Harrison, 301

95. Moryson, III, 303–4

96. Neale, *Parliaments*, II, 259; T. Wilson, 5; Cecil/James, 13

97. Neale, *Parliaments*, II, 259

98. T. Wilson, 5; Cal. Span. IV, 663–65

99. Cecil/James, 55

100. Bradley, I, 52; Cal. Ven. IX, 541

101. Bradley, I, 101; HMC Sals. XII, 596, 593

102. T. Wilson, 5; Cecil/James, 54; Harington, *Tract on the Succession*, 46

103. Elizabeth/James, 58; ibid. 109; ibid. 111

104. Ibid. 58; D. H. Willson, 53; Cal. Scot. XIII, 149; Elizabeth/James, 124

105. Birch, II, 512–13

106. Jardine, 353, 356

107. Cecil/James, 5; ibid. 22–23

108. Birch, II, 512; Cecil/James, 7, 10; Cal. Scot. XIII, 935; Cecil/James, 15

109. Cal. Ven. IX, 529, 565

110. Carey, 71; Clapham, 98

111. MacNalty, 242

112. PRO 31/3/35, De Beaumont–Henry IV, 18/28 March 1603; ibid. 14 March; Manningham, 146; Carey, 74

113. Nichols, III, 608; Clapham, 99

114. Cecil/James, 31–32; ibid. 46; Carey, 78

115. Manningham, 147; Wilbraham, 54; Wright, II, 495

116. Manningham, 159; Clapham, 110

117. Clapham, 112; Henry Chettle, *The order and proceedings at the funeral of Elizabeth* in Somers Tracts, ed. Walter Scott (1809–15), I, 248–50

118. Clapham, 113

119. Goodman, I, 98; Neale, *Parliaments*, II, 322; SP 70/17/209 fo. 40v

120. Neale, *Parliaments*, I, 244; Hodges, 19; Cal. Ven. VIII, 345

121. PRO SP 12/45/fo. 30; Cal. Span. IV, 470

122. Devereux, II, 5; Naunton, 96; *Nugae Antiquae*, I, 357

123. Nicolas, *Hatton*, 94; ibid. 195; C. Wilson, 75; Cal. For. XV, 640

124. Cal. Dom. II, 253

125. Devereux, II, 62; Motley, III, 135

126. Murdin, 326; Lodge, II, 207–8; Cal. Span. III, 190; HMC Rutland, I, 141

127. Guy, 384; Neale, *Parliaments*, II, 309; W. Camden, 440–41

128. *Nugae Antiquae*, I, 180, 358; McClure I, 74; HMC Bath, V, 85

129. Murdin, 281; PRO SP 12/138/26; K. de L. X, 593–94; Strype, *Annals*, III, ii, 123

130. HMC Sals. II, 121; Motley, II, 254; Neale, *Parliaments*, II, 321; Nicolas, *Hatton*, 33

131. Neale, *Parliaments*, II, 321; Wilbraham, 55; Stone, *Crisis*, 489; Cal. Scot. XIII, ii, 1013; Neale, *Parliaments*, II, 117; ibid. I. 175

Bibliography

Note: unless otherwise stated, London is the place of publication.

Adams, Simon, "Faction, Clientage and Party, 1550–1603", *History Today*, XXXII, 1982.

Adams, Simon, *The Protestant Cause. Religious alliance with the West European Calvinist Communities as a political issue in England, 1585–1630*, Oxford University D. Phil. thesis, 1972.

Adlard, George, *Amye Robsart and the Earl of Leicester*, 1870.

Allen, J.W., *A History of Political Thought in the Sixteenth Century*, 1928.

Alsop, J.D., "The Theory and Practice of Tudor Taxation", *English Historical Review*, XCVII, 1982.

Anderson, James, *Collections relating to the history of Mary of Scotland*, 1728.

Andrews, John F. (ed.), *William Shakespeare. His World, His Work, His Influence*, New York, 1985.

Andrews, K.R., *Drake's Voyages. A Reassessment of their Place in Elizabethan Maritime Expansion*, 1967.

Andrews, K.R., *Elizabethan Privateering*, Cambridge, 1964.

Andrews, K.R., *Trade, Plunder and Settlement*, Cambridge, 1984.

Anstruther, Godfrey, *The Seminary Priests*, 1968.

Arnold, Janet, *Queen Elizabeth's Wardrobe Unlock'd*, 1988.

Ascham, Roger, *English Works*, ed. William Aldis Wright, Cambridge, 1904.

Auerbach, Erna, *Tudor Artists*, 1954.

Aveling, J.C.H., *Northern Catholics*, 1966.

Aveling, J.C.H., *The Handle and the Axe*, 1976.

Bagwell, Richard, *Ireland Under the Tudors*, 1885.

Bardon Papers, ed. Conyers Read, Camden Society, 3rd Series, XVII, 1909.

Barnett, Richard C., *Place, Profit and Power. A study of the Servants of William Cecil*, North Carolina, 1969.

Basset, Bernard, *The English Jesuits*, 1967.

Bayne, C.G., "The Coronation of Queen Elizabeth", *English Historical Review*, XII, 1907.

Beckinsale, B.W., *Burghley, Tudor Statesman*, 1967.

Beckinsale, B.W., *Elizabeth I*, 1963.

Bedingfield Papers, "State Papers relating to the custody of the princess Elizabeth at Woodstock in 1554", ed. C.R. Manning, *Norfolk Archaeology*, Vol. IV, Norwich, 1855.

Bindoff, S.T., Hurstfield, J., Williams, C.H. (eds.), *Elizabethan Government and Society*, 1961.

Bingham, Caroline, *The Making of a King*, 1968.

Birch, Thomas, *Memoirs of the Reign of Queen Elizabeth*, 1754.

Black, J.B., *The Reign of Elizabeth*, Oxford, 1936.

Black, J.B., *Elizabeth and Henry IV*, Oxford, 1914.

Boas, F.S., *Sir Philip Sidney*, 1955.

Bossy, John, "The Character of English Catholicism", *Past & Present*, XXI, 1962.

Bossy, John, *The English Catholic Community, 1570–1850*, 1975.

Boynton, Lindsay, *The Elizabethan Militia*, 1967.

Bradbrook, Muriel, *Drama as Offering. The Princely Pleasures at Kenilworth*, Rice Institute Pamphlet, XLVI, 1960.

Bradbrook, Muriel, *Shakespeare. The Poet in his World*, 1978.

Braddock, R.C., "The Rewards of Office Holding in Tudor England", *Journal of British Studies*, XIV, 1975.

Bradley, E.T., *Life of the Lady Arabella Stuart*, 1869.

Bradner, Leicester (ed.), *The Poems of Queen Elizabeth I*, Providence, Rhode Island, 1964.

Brennecke, Ernest, "The Entertainment at Elvetham, 1591", in John H. Long (ed.), *Music in English Renaissance Drama*, Lexington, Kentucky, 1968.

Brook, V.J.K., *A Life of Archbishop Parker*, Oxford, 1962.

Brook, V.J.K., *Whitgift and the English Church*, 1957.

Bülow, Gottfried von, and Powell, Walter (eds.), "Diary of Philip Julius Duke of Stettin Pomerania through England in 1602", *Transactions of the Royal Historical Society*, 2nd Series, VI, 1892.

Buxton, John, *Elizabethan Taste*, 1966.

Calendar of Letters, Despatches and State Papers relating to Negotiations between England and Spain preserved in the Archives at Simancas and elsewhere, ed. Pascual de Gayangos et al., 1862–1954.

Calendar of Letters and State Papers relating to English affairs, preserved principally in the Archives of Simancas, Elizabeth, ed. M.A.S. Hume et al., 1892–99.

Calendar of State Papers relating to Border Affairs, ed. Joseph Bain, Edinburgh, 1894–96.

Calendar of State Papers, Domestic Series, ed. Robert Lemon & M.A.E. Green, 1856–72.

Calendar of State Papers, Foreign Series, ed. Joseph Stevenson et al., 1863–1950.

Calendar of State Papers relating to Ireland, ed. H.C. Hamilton et al., 1860–1905.

Calendar of State Papers Relating to Scotland and Mary Queen of Scots, ed. Joseph Bain et al., Edinburgh, 1898–1952.

Calendar of State Papers relating to English Affairs, preserved principally at Rome in the Vatican Archives and Library, ed. J.M. Rigg, 1916–26.

Calendar of State Papers and Manuscripts existing in the Archives and Collections of Venice, ed. Rawdon Brown et al., 1864–98.

Camden, Carroll, *The Elizabethan Woman*, 1952.

Camden, William, *History of the Most Renowned and Victorious Princess Elizabeth*, 1675.

Canny, Nicholas P., *The Elizabethan Conquest of Ireland: a pattern established, 1565–6*, 1976.

Carey, Robert, *Memoirs of Robert Carey*, ed. G.H. Powell, 1905.

Cecil/Carew, *Letters from Sir Robert Cecil to Sir George Carew*, ed. John Maclean, Camden Society, LXXXVIII, 1864.

Cecil/James, *Correspondence of King James VI of Scotland with Sir Robert Cecil and others in England during the Reign of Queen Elizabeth*, ed. John Bruce, Camden Society, LXXVIII, 1861.

Challoner, Richard, *Memoirs of the Missionary Priests*, ed. J.H. Pollen, 1924.

Chambers, E.K., *The Elizabethan Stage*, Oxford, 1923.

Chambers, E.K., *Sir Henry Lee*, Oxford, 1936.

Cheyney, E.P., *A History of England from the Defeat of the Armada to the Death of Elizabeth*, 1914.

Christy, Miller, "Queen Elizabeth's Visit to Tilbury in 1588", *English Historical Review*, xxxiv, 1919.

Chronicle of the Greyfriars of London, ed. J.G. Nichols, Camden Society, LIII, 1852.

Chronicle of Queen Jane and two years of Queen Mary, ed. J.G. Nichols, Camden Society, XLVIII, 1850.

Clapham, John, *Elizabeth of England*, ed. E.P. Read and Conyers Read, Oxford, 1951.

Clark, Peter (ed.), *The European Crisis of the 1590s*, 1985.

Clifford, Henry, *Life of Jane Dormer, Duchess of Feria*, 1881.

Clulee, Nicholas H., *John Dee's Natural Philosophy*, 1988.

Collinson, Patrick, *The Elizabethan Puritan Movement*, 1967.

Collinson, Patrick, *The Religion of Protestants*, Oxford, 1982.

Collinson, Patrick, *Archbishop Grindal*, 1979.

Collinson, Patrick, *Godly People*, 1983.

Collinson, Patrick, *Letters of Thomas Wood, Puritan*, 1960.

Colvin, H.M. (ed.), *History of the King's Works*, Vols III and IV, 1975, 1982.

Corbett, Julian S., *Drake and the Tudor Navy*, 1899.

Corbett, Julian S., *Papers relating to the Navy during the Spanish War, 1585–87*, Navy Records Society, 1898.

Cowan, Samuel, *The Last Days of Mary Stuart*, 1907.

Cross, Claire, *The Royal Supremacy in the Elizabethan Church*, 1969.

Cross, Claire, *The Puritan Earl: The Life of Henry Hastings third Earl of Huntingdon*, 1966.

Cruickshank, C.G., *Elizabeth's Army*, Oxford, 1966.

Cunnington, C.W., and P., *Handbook of English Costume in the Sixteenth Century*, 1954.

Dasent, J.R. (ed.), *Acts of the Privy Council*, 1895–1907.

Dawley, P.M., *John Whitgift and the English Reformation*, 1955.

De Maisse, André Hurault, *A Journal of all that was accomplished by Monsieur de Maisse, ambassador in England from King Henri IV to Queen Elizabeth, 1597*, trans. and ed. by G.B. Harrison and R.A. Jones, 1931.

Dent, John, *The Quest for Nonsuch*, 1962.

Devereux, Walter Bouchier, *Lives and Letters of the Devereux Earls of Essex*, 1853.

Dewar, Mary, *Sir Thomas Smith. A Tudor intellectual in Office*, 1964.

D'Ewes, Simonds (ed.), *The Journals of all the Parliaments during the reign of Queen Elizabeth*, revised and published by Paul Bowes, 1682.

Dickens, A.G., *The English Reformation*, 1967.

Dietz, F.C., *English Public Finance 1558–1641*, New York & London, 1932.

Digges, Dudley (ed.), *The Compleat Ambassador*, 1655.

Donaldson, Gordon, *All the Queen's Men. Power and Politics in Mary Stuart's Scotland*, 1983.

Donaldson, Gordon, *The Edinburgh History of Scotland*, Edinburgh, 1971.

Donaldson, Gordon, *The First Trial of Mary Queen of Scots*, 1969.

Doran, Susan, *The Political Career of Thomas Radcliffe, Earl of Sussex*, London University D. Phil. thesis, 1977.

Douai Diaries, *The First and Second Diaries of the English College, Douai*, ed. T.F. Knox, 1878.

Dunlop, Ian, *Palaces and Progresses of Elizabeth I*, 1962.

Dures, Alan, *English Catholicism 1558–1642*, 1983.

Duro, Cesareo Fernandez, *La Armada Invencible*, Madrid, 1884.

Eccles, Audrey, *Obstetrics and Gynaecology in Tudor and Stuart England*, 1982.

Edwards, Edward, *The life of Sir Walter Ralegh together with his letters*, 1868.

Egerton Papers, ed. J. Payne Collier, Camden Society, XII, 1840.

Elizabeth, James, *Letters of Queen Elizabeth and James VI of Scotland*, ed. John Bruce, Camden Society, XLVI, 1849.

Elliott, J.H., *Europe Divided*, 1968.

Ellis, Henry (ed.), *Original Letters Illustrative of English History*, Series 1, 2 & 3, 1824, 1827, 1846

Elton, G.R., *The Parliament of England, 1559–1581*, Cambridge, 1986.

Elton, G.R., *The Tudor Constitution*, Cambridge, 1960.

Elton, G.R., "Tudor Government: Points of Contact: III: The Court", *Transactions of the Royal Historical Society*, 5th Series, XXVI, 1976

Epton, Nina, *Love and the English*, 1960.

Erickson, Carolly, *The First Elizabeth*, 1983.

Falls, Cyril, *Elizabeth's Irish Wars*, 1970.

Falls, Cyril, *Mountjoy, Elizabethan General*, 1955.

Fénelon, Bertrand de Salignac de la Mothe, *Correspondance diplomatique*, Paris, 1838.

Feria, Count, "The Count of Feria's Despatch of 14 November 1558", J. Rodriquez Salgado and S. Adams, in *Camden Miscellany*, XXVII, 1984.

Fernandez-Armesto, Felipe, *The Spanish Armada. The Experience of War in 1588*, Oxford, 1988.

Ferrière Percy, Hector de la, *Le XVIième siècle et les Valois*, Paris, 1879.

Fleming, David Hay, *Mary Queen of Scots: from her birth to her flight into England*, 1898.

Forbes, P., *A full view of the Public transactions in the reign of Queen Elizabeth*, 1740.

Foxe, John, *Acts and Monuments*, 4th Edition, Revised and Corrected by the Rev. Josiah Pratt, 1877.

Fraser, Antonia, *Mary Queen of Scots*, 1969.

French, Peter J., *John Dee. The World of an Elizabethan Magus*, 1972.

Friedmann, Paul, *Anne Boleyn*, 1884.

Froude, James Anthony, *History of England*, 1893.

Gachard, M., *Correspondance de Philippe II sur les affaires des Pays Bas*, Brussels, 1851.

Gair, Reavley, *The Children of Paul's*, Cambridge, 1982.

Gamzue, B.B., "Elizabeth and Literary Patronage", in *Publications of Modern Language Association of America*, XLIX, 1934.

Gawdy, Philip, *Letters of Philip Gawdy*, ed. I.H. Jeayes, Roxburghe Club, 1906.

Gee, Henry, *The Elizabethan Prayer Book and Ornaments*, 1902.

Gee, Henry, *The Elizabethan Clergy and the Settlement of Religion*, Oxford, 1898.

Giles, T.A. (ed.), *The Whole Works of Roger Ascham*, 1865.

Girouard, Mark, *Robert Smythson and the Architecture of the Elizabethan Era*, 1966.

Gonzalez, Tomas, *Documents from Simancas relating to the Reign of Elizabeth*, trans. and ed. Spencer Hall, 1865.

Goodman, Godfrey, *The Court of James I*, ed. J.S. Brewer, 1839.

Graves, Michael A.R., *Elizabethan Parliaments*, 1987.

Graves, Michael A.R., *The Tudor Parliaments*, 1985.

Greaves, Richard L., *Society and Religion in Elizabethan England*, Minneapolis, 1981.

Grindal, Edmund, *Remains of Edmund Grindal*, ed. William Nicholson, Parker Society, VIII, Cambridge, 1843.

Guth, D.J. and McKenna, J.W. (eds.), *Tudor Rule and Revolution. Essays for G.R. Elton by his American Friends*, Cambridge, 1982.

Guy, John, *Tudor England*, Oxford, 1990.

Haigh, Christopher, *Elizabeth I*, 1988.

Haigh, Christopher (ed.), *The Reign of Elizabeth I*, 1984.

Hall, Edward. *Henry VIII*, ed. Charles Whibley, 1904.

Hampden, John (ed.), *Francis Drake, Privateer*. 1972.

Handover, P.M., *The Second Cecil*, 1958.

Harbison, E.H., *Rival Ambassadors at the Court of Queen Mary*, Princeton University Press, 1940.

Hardwicke Papers. ed. Philip Yorke, Earl of Hardwicke, 1775.

Harington, John, *A Tract on the Succession to the Crown*, Roxburghe Club, 1880.

Harington, John, *A New Discourse of a Stale Subject called the Metamorphosis of Ajax*, ed. Elizabeth Story, 1962.

Harrison, G.B. (ed.), *The Letters of Queen Elizabeth*, 1935.

Hartley, T.E., *Proceedings in the Parliaments of Elizabeth I*, Leicester University Press, 1981.

Hasler, P.W., *The House of Commons 1558–1603*, History of Parliament Trust, 1983.

Haugaard, William P., *Elizabeth and the English Reformation*, Cambridge, 1968.

Haynes, Alan, *The White Bear*, 1987.

Haynes, Alan, *Robert Cecil, Earl of Salisbury*, 1989.

Haynes, Alan, "The Islands Voyage", in *History Today*, XXV, 1975.

Haynes, Alan, "Supplying the Elizabethan Court", in *History Today*, XXVIII, 1978.

Haynes, Samuel (ed.), *A collection of State Papers relating to affairs from the years 1542–1570 left by William Cecil Lord Burghley*, 1740.

Hayward, Sir John, *Life and Reign of King Edward VI*, 1636.

Hayward, Sir John, *Annals of the First four years of the Reign of Queen Elizabeth*, ed. John Bruce, Camden Society, VII, 1840.

Headlam Wells, Robin, *Spenser's Faerie Queen and the Cult of Elizabeth*, 1983.

Heal, Felicity, *Of Prelates and Princes*, Cambridge, 1980.

Heal, Felicity, and O'Day, Rosemary, *Church and Society in England from Henry VIII to James I*, 1977.

Hearne's Sylloge, *Sylloge Epistolarum*, ed. Thomas Hearne. In *Vita Henrici Quinti*, Oxford, 1716.

Heisch, Allison, "Queen Elizabeth I and the Persistence of Patriarchy", in *Feminist Review*, IV, 1980.

Henderson, Katherine Usher, and McManus, Barbara F., *Half Humankind. Contexts and Texts of the Controversy about Women in England 1540–1640*, Chicago, 1985.

Henderson, T.F., *Mary Queen of Scots*, 1905.

Henry, L.W.,"The Earl of Essex and Ireland", in *Bulletin of the Institute of Historical Research*, XXXII, May 1959.

Hentzner, Paulus, *A Journey into England in 1598*, Edinburgh, 1881–82.

Heywood, Thomas, *England's Elizabeth*. In *Harleian Miscellany*, X, 1813.

Hibbert, Christopher, *The Virgin Queen*, 1990.

Hill, Christopher, *Economic Problems of the Church*, Oxford, 1956.

Hill, Christopher, *Society and Puritanism in Pre-Revolutionary England*, 1964.

Historical Manuscripts Commission, *Calendar of Manuscripts of Marquis of Bath at Longleat*, 1904–80.

Historical Manuscripts Commission, *Calendar of Manuscripts of Marquis of Salisbury Preserved at Hatfield House*, 1883–1923.

Historical Manuscripts Commission, *Foljambe Papers*, 15th Report, Appendix, Part V, 1897.

Historical Manuscripts Commission, *Report on the De l'Isle and Dudley Mss. at Penshurst*, 1934–46.

Historical Manuscripts Commission, *Mss. of the Duke of Rutland at Belvoir Castle*, 12th Report, Appendix, Part IV, 1888.

Hodges, J.P., and Fox, Adam (eds.), *A Book of Devotions composed by Her Majesty Elizabeth R.*, Gerrards Cross, 1977.

Holinshed, Raphael, *Chronicles of England, Scotland and Ireland*, 1807–8.

Hotson, Leslie, *The First Night of Twelfth Night*, 1954.

Hotson, Leslie, *Queen Elizabeth's Entertainment at Mitcham*, Yale, 1953.

Howarth, David, *The Voyage of the Armada*, 1981.

Hudson, Winthrop S., *The Cambridge Connection and the Elizabethan*

Settlement of 1559, Durham, North Carolina, 1980.
Hughes, P.L., and Larkin, J., *Tudor Royal Proclamations*, Yale, 1969.
Hughes, Philip, *The Reformation in England*, 1954.
Hurstfield, Joel, *Freedom, Corruption and Government in Elizabethan England*, 1973.
Hurstfield, Joel, *The Queen's Wards*, 1958.
Hurstfield, Joel, and Smith, A.G.R. (eds.), *Elizabethan People. State and Society*, 1972.

Ives, E.W., *Anne Boleyn*, Oxford, 1986.
Ives, E.W., *Faction in Tudor England*, Historical Association, 1979.

Jardine, David, *Criminal Trials*, 1832.
Jenkins, Elizabeth, *Elizabeth the Great*, 1958.
Jenkins, Elizabeth, *Elizabeth and Leicester*, 1961.
Jensen, de Lamar, *Diplomacy and Dogmatism. Bernardino de Mendoza and the French Catholic League*, Cambridge, Massachusetts, 1964.
Johnson, Paul, *Elizabeth I. A Study in Power and Intellect*, 1974.
Jones, Norman L., *Faith by Statute*, 1982.
Jordan, W.K., *Edward VI: The Young King*, 1968.
Jordan, W.K., *Edward VI: The Threshold of Power*, 1970.

Keith, Robert, *History of the affairs of church and state in Scotland from the beginning of the Reformation to 1568*, Edinburgh, 1844.
Kendall, Alan, *Robert Dudley, Earl of Leicester*, 1980.
Kenny, Robert W., *Elizabeth's Admiral*, Baltimore, 1970.
Kervyn de Lettenhove, M. le baron J.M.B.C., *Les Huguenots et les Gueux*, Bruges, 1883.
Kervyn de Lettenhove, M. le baron J.M.B.C., *Relations Politiques des Pays Bas et de l'Angleterre sous le règne de Philippe II*, Brussels, 1882.
Kingdom, R.L. (ed.), *The execution of Justice in England* by William Cecil, and *A True, sincere and Modest defence of English Catholics*, by William Allen, Ithaca, New York, 1965.
Klarwill, Victor von, *Queen Elizabeth and Some Foreigners*, 1928.
Knappen, M.M., *Tudor Puritanism*, Gloucester, Massachusetts, 1963.
Knox, John, *Works*, ed. David Laing, Edinburgh, 1848.
Knox, T.F. (ed.), *Letters and Memorials of William, Cardinal Allen*, 1882.
Kouri, E.I., *England and the Attempts to form a Protestant alliance in the late 1560s*, Helsinki, 1981.
Kouri, E.I., and Scott, Tom, *Politics and Society in Reformation Europe*, 1987.

Labanoff, A., *Lettres, instructions et mémoires de Marie Stuart*, 1844.
Lacey, Robert, *Robert Earl of Essex. An Elizabethan Icarus*, 1971.

Lacey, Robert, *Sir Walter Ralegh*, 1973.

Laffleur de Kermaingant, P., *Mission de Jean de Thumery, Sieur de Boissise, 1598–1602*, Paris, 1886.

Laffleur de Kermaingant, P., *L'ambassade de France en Angleterre sous Henry IV. Mission de Christophe de Harlay, Comte de Beaumont*, Paris, 1895.

Latham, Agnes (ed.), *The Poems of Sir Walter Ralegh*, 1929.

Laughton, J.K. (ed.), *State Papers relating to the defeat of the Spanish Armada*, Navy Records Society, 1894.

Law, T.G., "English Jesuits and Scottish Intrigues", in *Collected Essays*, ed. P.H. Brown, Edinburgh, 1904.

Leader, J.R., *Mary Queen of Scots in Captivity*, 1880.

Lee, Maurice, *James Stewart, Earl of Moray*, New York, 1953.

Lehmberg, Stanford E., *Sir Walter Mildmay and Tudor Government*, Austin, Texas, 1964.

Leicester Correspondence. Correspondence of Robert Dudley, Earl of Leicester during his Government of the Low Countries, ed. John Bruce, Camden Society, XXVII, 1844.

Letters and Papers of the Reign of Henry VIII, ed. J.S. Brewer et al., 1862–1910.

Levine, Mortimer, *The Early Elizabethan Succession Question*, Stanford, California, 1966.

Lewis, Michael, *Armada Guns*, 1961.

Lewis, Michael, *The Spanish Armada*, 1960.

List and Analysis of State Papers, Foreign Series, ed. R.B. Wernham, 1964.

Lloyd, Howell A., *The Rouen Campaign 1590–92*, Oxford, 1973.

Loades, D.M., *The Reign of Mary Tudor*, 1979.

Loades, D.M., *The Tudor Court*, 1986.

Loades, D.M., *Two Tudor Conspiracies*, Cambridge, 1965.

Loades, D.M., *Mary Tudor*, Oxford, 1989.

Lodge, Edmund, *Illustrations of British History, Biography and Manners*, 1838.

Loke, William, "An Account of Materials furnished for the use of Queen Anne Boleyn and the Princess Elizabeth", in *Miscellanies of the Philobiblon Society*, 1863.

MacCaffrey, Wallace, *The Shaping of the Elizabethan Regime*, 1969.

MacCaffrey, Wallace, *Queen Elizabeth and the Making of Policy 1570–1588*, Princeton, New Jersey, 1981.

MacCaffrey, Wallace, "The Anjou Match and the Making of Elizabethan Foreign Policy", in *The English Commonwealth 1547–1640*, ed. Peter Clark, A.G.R. Smith & Nicholas Tyacke, Leicester, 1979.

McCall, H.B., "The Rising in the North", *Yorkshire Archaeological Journal*, XVIII, 1904–5.

McClure, N.E., *The Letters of John Chamberlain*, Philadephia, 1939.

McGrath, Patrick, *Papists and Puritans Under Elizabeth I*, 1967.

MacNalty, Sir Arthur Salusbury, *Elizabeth Tudor: The Lonely Queen*, 1954.

Machyn, Henry, *Diary of Henry Machyn*, ed. J.G. Nicholas, Camden Society, XLII, 1848.

Madden, F., *Privy Purse Expenses of the Princess Mary*, 1831.

Manningham, John, *Diary of John Manningham*, Camden Society, XC, 1868.

Mattingly, Garrett, *The Defeat of the Spanish Armada*, 1959.

Marples, Morris, *Princes in the Making*, 1965.

Martienssen, Anthony, *Queen Katherine Parr*, 1973.

Melville, Sir James, *Memoirs of Sir James Melville of Halhill*, ed. A. Francis Steuart, 1929.

Menmuir, Charles, *The Rising of the North*, Newcastle, 1907.

Meyer, A.O., *England and the Catholic Church Under Queen Elizabeth*, 1916.

Meyer, C.S., *Elizabeth I and the Religious Settlement of 1559*, St Louis, 1960.

Miller, Amos C., *Sir Henry Killigrew*, Leicester, 1963.

Miller, H., "Subsidy Assessments of the Peerage in the Sixteenth Century", in *Bulletin of the Institute of Historical Research*, XXVIII, 1955.

Mirror of the Sinful Soul, prose translation from the French of a poem by Queen Marguerite of Navarre, made in 1544 by Princess Elizabeth, ed. Percy W. Ames, 1897.

Moody, T.W., Martin, F.X., and Byrne, F.J. (eds.), *A New History of Ireland*, Vol. III, Oxford, 1976.

Morris, Christopher, *Political Thought in England: Tyndale to Hooker*, Westport, Connecticut, 1980.

Morris, John (ed.), *The Letter Books of Sir Amias Paulet*, 1874.

Moryson, Fynes, *An Itinerary containing his ten years travel*, Glasgow, 1807–9.

Motley, J.L., *History of the United Netherlands*, 1860.

Mumby, Frank A., *The Girlhood of Queen Elizabeth*, 1909.

Murdin, William, *A collection of state papers relating to affairs in the reign of Queen Elizabeth, 1571–96*, 1759.

Naunton, Robert, *Fragmenta Regalia*, 1824.

Naval Miscellany, Vol. IV, ed. Christopher Lloyd, Naval Records Society, 1952.

Neale, J.E., *The Age of Catherine de Medici and Essays in Elizabethan History*, 1965.

Neale, J.E., *Elizabeth I and her Parliaments*, 1953.

Neale, J.E., *The Elizabethan House of Commons*, 1949.

Neale, J.E., *Queen Elizabeth I*, 1934.

Nichols, John, *The Progresses and Public Processions of Queen Elizabeth*, 1823.

Nicolas, Nicholas Harris, *Memoirs of the Life and Times of Sir Christopher Hatton*, 1848.

Notestein, Wallace, "The English Woman, 1580–1650", in J.H. Plumb (ed.), *Studies in Social History. A tribute to G.M. Trevelyan*, 1955.

Nugae Antiquae by John Harington, ed. Henry Harington, 1804.

Nuttall, Zelia, *New Light on Drake*, 1914.

Oakeshott, Walter, *The Queen and the Poet*, 1960.

O'Connell, J.R., "Richard Topcliffe, Priest Hunter and Torturer", in *Dublin Review*, CXCV, 1934.

O'Day, Rosemary, *The English Clergy, 1558–1642*, Leicester, 1979.

Oppenheim, M., *A History of the Administration of the Royal Navy*, 1896.

Osborn, James, *The Queen's Majesty's passage through the City of London to Westminster the day before her coronation*, ed. J.E. Neale, New Haven, 1960.

Outhwaite, R.B., *Inflation in Tudor and Stuart England*, 1969.

Outhwaite, R.B., "Royal Borrowing in the Reign of Elizabeth I. The aftermath of Antwerp", in *English Historical Review*, LXXXVI, 1971.

Palliser, David Michael, *The Age of Elizabeth*, 1983.

Parker Correspondence. Correspondence of Matthew Parker, ed. John Bruce and T.T. Perowne, Parker Society, Cambridge, 1853.

Parker, Geoffrey, *The Dutch Revolt*, 1975.

Parker, Geoffrey, *Philip II*, 1979.

Parker, Geoffrey, & Martin, Colin, *The Spanish Armada*, 1988.

Patterson, R.F. (ed.), *Ben Jonson's Conversations with William Drummond of Hawthornden*, 1923.

Peck, Francis, *Desiderata Curiosa*, 1779.

Percival, Rachel and Allen, *The Court of Elizabeth I*, 1976.

Perry, Maria, *The Word of a Prince. A Life of Elizabeth I*, 1990.

Platter, Thomas, *Thomas Platter's Travels in England*, ed. Clare Williams, 1937.

Plowden, Alison, *The Young Elizabeth*, 1971.

Plowden, Alison, *Two Queens in One Isle*, 1984.

Pollard, A.F., *The History of England 1547–1603*, 1910.

Pollen, J.H. (ed.), *Queen Mary's letter to the Duke of Guise*, Publications of Scottish History Society, XLIII, 1904 .

Pollen, J.H., *Mary Queen of Scots and the Babington Plot*, Scottish History Society, 3rd Series, III, 1922.

Pollen, J.H., *The English Catholics in the Reign of Queen Elizabeth*, 1920.

Pollen, J.H., "The Politics of English Catholics during the Reign of Queen Elizabeth", in *The Month*, January–December 1902.

Pollen, J.H., "The Question of Elizabeth's Successor", and "The Accession of James", in *The Month*, CI, 1903.

Pollen, J.H. (ed.), *Unpublished Documents Relating to the English Martyrs*, Catholic Record Society, V, 1908.

Pope-Hennessy, John, *Sir Walter Ralegh in Ireland*, 1883.

Prescott, H.F.M., *Mary Tudor*, 1952.

Prior, Mary (ed.), *Women in English Society 1500–1800*, 1985.

Procter, Francis, and Frere, W.H., *A New History of the Book of Common Prayer*, 1925.

Pulman, Michael Barraclough, *The Elizabethan Privy Council in the 1570s*, Berkeley and Los Angeles, 1971.

Puritan Manifestoes, ed. W.H. Frere and C.E. Douglas, 1907.

Queen Elizabeth's Englishings, ed. Caroline Pemberton, Early English Text Society, CXIII, 1899.

Quinn, D.B., *The Elizabethans and the Irish*, New York, 1966.

Rait, R.S., and Cameron, A.I., *King James's Secret*, 1927.

Ramsay, G.D., *The City of London in International Politics at the Accession of Elizabeth Tudor*, Manchester, 1975.

Ramsay, G.D., *The Queen's Merchants and the Revolt of the Netherlands*, Manchester, 1986.

Raumer, Frederick von, *Queen Elizabeth and Mary Queen of Scots*, 1836.

Read, Conyers, *Mr Secretary Cecil and Queen Elizabeth*, 1962.

Read, Conyers, *Lord Burghley and Queen Elizabeth*, 1960.

Read, Conyers, *Mr Secretary Walsingham and the Policy of Queen Elizabeth*, 1967.

Reid, Rachel R., *The King's Council in the North*, 1921.

Reid, Rachel R., "The Rebellion of the Earls, 1569", in *Transactions of the Royal Historical Society*, 2nd Series, XX, 1906.

Reid, Rachel R., "The Political Influence of the North Parts under the Later Tudors", in *Tudor Studies*, ed. R.W. Seton Watson, 1924.

Retamal Favereau, Julio, *Anglo-Spanish Relations, 1566–70. The mission of Guerau de Spes*, Oxford University D. Phil. thesis, 1972.

Reynolds, E.E., *Campion and Parsons. The Jesuit mission of 1580–81*, 1980.

Ridley, Jasper, *Henry VIII*, 1984.

Ridley, Jasper, *Elizabeth I*, 1987.

Ridley, Jasper, *John Knox*, Oxford, 1968.

Robertson, William, *The History of Scotland during the Reigns of Queen Mary and King James*, 1802.

Robinson, Agnes M.F., "Queen Elizabeth and the Valois Princes", in *English Historical Review*, II, 1887.

Rodriguez-Salgado, M.J., and the Staff of the National Maritime Museum, *Armada, 1588–1988*, 1988.

Rowse, A.L., *The Elizabethan Renaissance, I: The Life of the Society*, 1971.

Rowse, A.L., *The Elizabethan Renaissance, II: The Cultural Achievement*, 1972.

Rowse, A.L., *The England of Elizabeth*, 1981.

Rowse, A.L., *The Expansion of Elizabethan England*, 1955.

Rowse, A.L., *Ralegh and the Throckmortons*, 1962.

Rowse, A.L., *Eminent Elizabethans*, 1983.

Rowse, A.L., *William Shakespeare*, 1963.

Russell, E., *Maitland of Lethington*, 1912.

Ryan, Lawrence V., *Roger Ascham*, 1963.

Rye, W.B., *England as seen by Foreigners in the Days of Elizabeth and James I*, 1865.

Rye, Walter, *The Murder of Amy Robsart*, 1885.

Rymer, Thomas, *Foedera*, The Hague, 1739–45.

Sadler Papers. *State papers and letters of Sir Ralph Sadler*, ed. Arthur Clifford, Edinburgh, 1809.

St Clare Byrne, Muriel, *Elizabethan Life in Town and Country*, 1925.

St John Brooks, Eric, *Sir Christopher Hatton*, 1946.

Sargent, Ralph M., *At the Court of Queen Elizabeth. Life and Lyrics of Sir Edward Dyer*, Oxford, 1935.

Scarisbrick, J.J., *Henry VIII*, 1974.

Scott, William Robert, *The Constitution and Finance of English, Scottish and Irish Joint Stock Companies to 1720*, Cambridge, 1911.

Scott Pearson, A.F., *Thomas Cartwright and Elizabethan Puritanism*, Cambridge, 1925.

Sharp, Cuthbert, *Memorials of the Rebellion of 1569*, 1841.

Sidney Papers, ed. A. Collins, 1746.

Simpson, Richard, *Edmund Campion*, 1867.

Smith, A.G.R., *The Government of Elizabethan England*, 1967.

Smith, A.G.R., *Servant of the Cecils. The Life of Sir Michael Hickes*, 1977.

Smith, Edward O., "Crown and Commonwealth. A study in the official Elizabethan doctrine of the Prince", *Transactions of the American Philosophical Society*, New Series, LXVI, 1976.

Smith, Lacey Baldwin, *Elizabeth Tudor. Portrait of a Queen*, 1976.

Smith, Lacey Baldwin, *The Elizabethan Epic*, 1966.

Spedding, James, *Letters and Life of Francis Bacon*, 1890.

Spenser, Edmund, *A View of the Present State of Ireland*, ed. W.L. Renwick, Oxford, 1970.

Stafford, Helen Georgia, *James VI of Scotland and the Throne of England*, New York, 1940.

Stangford, Viscount, *Household Expenses of the Princess Elizabeth during her residence at Hatfield*, Camden Miscellany, 2. Camden Society, LV, 1853.

Starkey, David (ed.), *The English Court from the Wars of the Roses to the Civil War*, 1987.

State Trials, *A Complete Collection of State Trials*, ed. William Cobbett, 1809.

Statutes at Large, Cambridge, 1763.

Stone, Lawrence, *An Elizabethan. Sir Horatio Palavicino*, Oxford, 1956.

Stone, Lawrence, *The Crisis of the Aristocracy*, Oxford, 1965.

Stone, Lawrence, *Family and Fortune*, Oxford, 1973.

Stone, Lawrence, *The Family, Sex and Marriage*, 1977.

Stone, Lawrence, "Office Under Queen Elizabeth", in *Historical Journal*, X, 1967.

Stone, Lawrence, "Elizabethan Overseas Trade", in *Econonomic History Review*, 2nd Series, II, 1949.

Stopes, C.C., "Elizabethan's Fools and Dwarfs", in *Shakespeare's Environment*, 1918.

Strickland, Agnes (ed.), *Letters of Mary Queen of Scots*, 1842.

Strickland, Agnes, *Lives of the Queens of England*, 1866.

Strickland, Agnes, *Lives of the Tudor Princesses*, 1868.

Strong, Roy C., *The Cult of Elizabeth*, 1977.

Strong, Roy C., *Portraits of Queen Elizabeth I*, Oxford, 1963.

Strong, Roy C., *Gloriana. The Portraits of Queen Elizabeth I*, 1987.

Strong, Roy C., *The English Renaissance Miniature*, 1983.

Strong, Roy C., & Van Dorsen, J.A., *Leicester's Triumph*, Oxford, 1964.

Strype, John, *Annals of the Reformation*, Oxford, 1824.

Strype, John, *Ecclesiastical Memorials*, Oxford, 1822.

Strype, John, *Life of the Learned John Cheke*, Oxford, 1821.

Strype, John, *Life of Archbishop Whitgift*, Oxford, 1822.

Stubbs, John, *John Stubb's Gaping Gulf with letters and other relevant documents*, ed. Lloyd E. Berry, Charlottesville, 1968.

Sugden, John, *Sir Francis Drake*, 1990.

Sutherland, Nicola, "The Sea Beggars and the Capture of Brill", in *Princes, Politics and Religion*, 1984.

Taylor, E.G.R., *Tudor Geography*, 1930.

Taylor, Susan E., *The Crown and the North of England, 1569–70. A study of the Rebellion of the Northern Earls and its causes*, Manchester University D. Phil. thesis, 1981.

Tenison, E.M., *Elizabethan England*, 1933.

Teulet, Alexandre, *Relations politiques de la France et de l'Espagne avec l'Ecosse au XVIième siècle*, Paris, 1862.

Thompson, J.V.P., *Supreme Governor*, 1940.

Thompson, J.W.T., *The Wars of Religion in France*, 1909.

Thomson, George Malcolm, *Sir Francis Drake*, 1972.

Thrower, N.J.W. (ed.), *Sir Francis Drake and the Famous Voyage of 1577–80*, California, 1984.

Tittler, Robert, *Nicholas Bacon. The Making of a Tudor Statesman*, 1976.

Torne, P.O. de, *Don Juan d'Autriche et les Projets de conquête de l'Angleterre*, 1915.

Trimble, W.R., *The Catholic Laity in Elizabethan England*, Cambridge, Massachusetts, 1964.

Tytler, P.F., *England Under the Reigns of Edward VI and Queen Mary*, 1839.

Tytler, P.F., *History of Scotland*, 1870.

Unton Correspondence. *Correspondence of Sir Henry Unton*, ed. Joseph Stevenson, Roxburghe Club, 1848.

Usher, R.G. (ed.), *The Presbyterian Movement in the Reign of Queen Elizabeth as illustrated by the minute Book of the Dedham Classis*, Camden Society, 3rd Series, VIII, 1905.

Van der Essen, Leon, *Alexandre Farnese, Prince de Parme, Gouverneur Général des Pays-Bas*, Brussels, 1937.

Vertot, René, *Ambassades des Messieurs de Noailles en Angleterre*, Leyden, 1763.

Ward, B.M., *The Seventeenth Earl of Oxford*, 1928.

Warnicke, Retha M., *The Rise and Fall of Anne Boleyn*, Cambridge, 1989.

Waters, D.W., and Naish, G.P.B. (eds.), *The Elizabethan Navy and the Armada of Spain*, Greenwich National Maritime Museum, Maritime Monographs and Reports no. 17, 1975.

Watson, Foster (ed.), *Vives and the Renaissance Education of Women*, 1912.

Waugh, Evelyn, *Edmund Campion*, 1935.

Wedel, Leopold von, *Journey Through England and Scotland*, ed. Gottfried von Bülow in *Transactions of the Royal Historical Society*, New Series, IX, 1895.

Wernham, R.B., *Before the Armada*, 1966.

Wernham, R.B., *After the Armada*, Oxford, 1984.

Wernham, R.B., *The Making of Elizabethan Foreign Policy*, California, 1980.

White, F.O., *Lives of the Elizabethan Bishops*, 1898.

Wiesener, Louis, *La Jeunesse d'Elisabeth d'Angleterre*, Paris, 1878.

Wilbraham, Roger, *Journal of Roger Wilbraham*, ed. H.S. Scott, *Camden Miscellany*, X, 1902.

Williams, Neville, *Elizabeth I, Queen of England*, 1967.

Williams, Neville, *All the Queen's Men*, 1974.

Williams, Penry, *The Tudor Regime*, Oxford, 1979.

Williams, Penry, "Court and Polity under Elizabeth I", in *Bulletin John Rylands Library*, LXV, 1983.

Williamson, J.A., *The Age of Drake*, 1938.

Williamson, J.A., *Hawkins of Plymouth*, 1969.

Willson, D. Harris, *King James VI and I*, 1956.

Wilson, Charles Henry, *Queen Elizabeth and the Revolt of the Netherlands*, 1970.

Wilson, Derek, *Sweet Robin*, 1981.

Wilson, Elkin Calhoun, *England's Eliza*, Cambridge, Massachusetts, 1939.

Wilson, Jean, *Entertainments for Elizabeth I*, 1980.

Wilson, Jean, "The Harefield Entertainment and the Cult of Elizabeth I", in *Antiquaries Journal*, LXVI, 1986.

Wilson, Thomas, *The State of England 1600*, in *Camden Miscellany*, XVI, 3rd Series, LII, 1936.

Winwood, Ralph, *Memorials of Affairs of State*, 1725.

Woodworth, Allegra, "Purveyance for the Royal Household in the Reign of Queen Elizabeth", in *Transactions of the American Philosophical Society, Philadephia*, New Series, XXXV, part i, December 1945.

Wormald, Jenny, *Mary Queen of Scots. A study in failure*, 1988.

Wotton, Sir Henry, *Reliquiae Wottoniae*, 1685.

Wright, Thomas (ed.), *Queen Elizabeth and Her Times*, 1838.

Wriothsley, Charles, *A Chronicle of England during the Reign of the Tudors*, ed. William Douglas Hamilton, Camden Society, 1875–77.

Yates, Francis A., *Astraea. The Imperial Theme in the Sixteenth Century*, 1975.

Young, Alan, *Tudor and Jacobean Tournaments*, 1987.

Zurich Letters. Comprising the Correspondence of Several English Bishops and others with some of the Helvetian Reformers, ed. H. Robinson, Parker Society, Cambridge, 1842.

Zurich Letters, Second Series. Parker Society, XVIII, Cambridge, 1845.

Index

Index by Douglas Matthews